BTEC NATIONAL IN
SPORT
and EXERCISE
SCIENCE

Jennifer-Stafford Brown
Simon Rea
John Chance

Hodder & Stoughton

A MEMBER OF THE HODDER HEADLINE GROUP

Orders: please contact Bookpoint Ltd, 130 Milton Park, Abingdon, Oxon OX14 4SB. Telephone: (44) 01235 827720. Fax: (44) 01235 400454. Lines are open from 9.00–6.00, Monday to Saturday, with a 24 hour message answering service. You can also order through our website www.hodderheadline.com.

British Library Cataloguing in Publication Data
A catalogue record for this title is available from the British Library

ISBN 0 340 871768

First Published 2003

Impression number   10 9 8 7 6 5 4 3 2
Year   2007 2006 2005 2004 2003

Copyright © 2003 Jennifer Stafford-Brown, Simon Rea and John Chance

Photographs in the text appear courtesy of the following:
Fig 1.2 (a) (b) (c) Life File Photo Library; Fig 1.4, 3.9A, 6.1, 8.9, 10.7, 11.1, 12.4, 12.5, 17.1, 17.2, 18.1, 18.2, 19.3, 19.6 Action Plus; Fig 12.3, 14.1, 14.2, 16.12 Science Photo Library; Fig 10.7 Popperfoto; 19.1, 19.5 EMPICS

Cover photo from CORBIS

Papers used in this book are natural, renewable and recyclable products. They are made from wood grown in sustainable forests. The logging and manufacturing processes conform to the environmental regulations of the country of origin.

Typeset by Pantek Arts Ltd, Maidstone, Kent
Printed in Great Britain for Hodder & Stoughton Educational, a division of Hodder Headline, 338 Euston Road, London NW1 3BH by Arrowsmiths

CONTENTS

CONTENTS

ACKNOWLEDGEMENTS

I enjoyed writing this book, but it did take time and effort and I am grateful to my family and friends for their help throughout this period. In particular I would like to thank my wonderful husband, Matt, for his encouragement and keen interest in my work and for always being there for me. I would also like to thank my parents, Ann and Brian, for their tremendous support and for giving me the opportunity to pursue my interest in Sports Science. Finally, my thanks go out to my friend Julie for being so incredibly reliable in looking after Eleanor my gorgeous baby daughter and thereby giving me the time to work on this book.

Jennifer Stafford-Brown

Thanks to my wife, Jacqui, for putting up with all the lost hours during writing and to my parents, Tony and Pam for all of their continued support. Also to the various people who helped me find information for the book, particularly to Simon Rhodes-Chamberlin, and Lee Janaway.

Simon Rea

I would like to thank the many people that have helped and motivated me during my career in Sports Science and enabled me to gain the knowledge to write this book. However, special thanks go to three people: my mother and father for their endless support and to Anna, my daughter, for helping me keep things in perspective.

John Chance

SCIENTIFIC PRINCIPLES OF SPORT AND EXERCISE

The aim of this chapter is to introduce basic scientific principles that underpin the study of sport and exercise sciences. It contains basic chemical, physical and biological information that relates to other disciplines within sport and exercise science. It has been divided into four areas. Biological chemicals are discussed, specifically the three major nutrients (carbohydrates, fats and proteins) and water. The second area is the science of materials, the structures, properties and functions of which are examined. Next is the mechanics of motion, which is the study of movement, describing and explaining how movement occurs at a physical level. The final area is energy, which is investigated both physically and chemically.

By the end of this chapter students should be able to:

✪   review the structure and functions of the major biological chemicals

✪   evaluate the use of materials

✪   describe the mechanics of motion

✪   describe energy and energy transfer.

BIOLOGICAL CHEMICALS

Carbohydrates

Carbohydrates are a group of **organic** compounds, vital for life, that are found in the body. They are more commonly known as sugars and starches. Sugars refer to the type of carbohydrates in confectionary, fruit and energy drinks, for example. Starches are found in bread, pasta, rice and potatoes. The main function of carbohydrates is to provide energy for essential functions (respiration, digestion, etc.) and for physical activity (sport, exercise, work). Carbohydrates also act as a fuel reserve, a store of energy for when readily available energy is not obtainable. Some carbohydrates can be converted into proteins or fats, which can then be used as energy reserves or building blocks to be used for growth and repair.

Carbohydrates are made up of carbon, hydrogen and oxygen, hence the name. *Carbo* relates to carbon, and *hydrate* means to gain water, which consists of hydrogen and oxygen. In fact, carbohydrates contain hydrogen and oxygen in exactly the same ratio as water. The ratio is always two hydrogen **atoms** to one oxygen atom. An example is a glucose **molecule**, which comprises six carbon atoms, twelve hydrogen atoms and six oxygen atoms. This can be represented in a formula as $C_6H_{12}O_6$. There are three major groups of carbohydrates: monosaccharides, disaccharides and polysaccharides.

Monosaccharides are also known as simple sugars. Their structure consists of a single chain or ring, with between three and seven carbon atoms. Blood sugar (glucose), the major source of energy in the body, is a monosaccharide. Fructose is another example of a monosaccharide; it has the same molecular formula as glucose (i.e. $C_6H_{12}O_6$), but the atoms are arranged in a different order. A chemical compound that has the same number of atoms as another compound, but in a different arrangement, is called an **isomer**. Fructose is an isomer of glucose.

Two monosaccharides can join together to form a disaccharide (**di** meaning two). The process or chemical reaction of them joining together is termed **dehydration synthesis**. This name is derived from the fact that a water molecule is lost from the two chemicals that join together. The reverse of this process is **hydrolysis**. Probably the most common disaccharide is sucrose, or cane sugar. This is the type of sugar you buy from the supermarket, where it is called granulated or table sugar. Another disaccharide is lactose, which is the type of sugar found in milk.

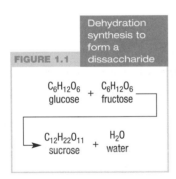

FIGURE 1.1 Dehydration synthesis to form a dissaccharide

$C_6H_{12}O_6$ glucose + $C_6H_{12}O_6$ fructose

$C_{12}H_{22}O_{11}$ sucrose + H_2O water

Dehydration synthesis also results in the formation of **polysaccharides**. These are long chains made up of three or more monosaccharides. The prefix **poly** means many, and polysaccharides are examples of polymers, a **polymer** being a chainlike molecule made up of sub-units or smaller molecules. Polysaccharides are different from mono- and disaccharides in that they are not normally soluble in water and they lack that characteristic sweetness. Two of the most important polysaccharides are starch and glycogen. These are both derived from glucose. **Glycogen** is the primary store of carbohydrate in the body. It is found principally in skeletal muscle, however, it is also stored in the liver. During exercise or times of energy need, glycogen can be broken down into glucose, which can supply energy. As with disaccharides, the process is performed via hydrolysis reactions. In the case of breaking down glycogen, the specific hydrolysis reaction is called glycogenolysis. **Starch** is a carbohydrate produced by plants. When it is eaten it is broken down (digested) into glucose molecules.

Proteins

Proteins are another group of vital organic compounds. Their structure is somewhat more complex than carbohydrates'. Like carbohydrates they always contain carbon, hydrogen and oxygen, but they also contain nitrogen. In addition, some proteins contain sulphur and phosphorous. Proteins have many functions in the body, and most are involved in helping the body perform physical activity. There are structural proteins, which actually form various parts of the body such as skin and hair. Skeletal muscles are largely made up of actin and myosin, which are contractile proteins – they allow muscles to contract, which in turn produces movement. **Haemoglobin** is an example of a transport protein. It is used to transport carbon dioxide and oxygen in the blood. Proteins that function as hormones are called regulatory proteins. Insulin is an example. If blood sugar (glucose) rises too high, insulin is released by the body in order to regulate it. Other functions of proteins include acting as **enzymes** (which control chemical reactions) and protecting the body in the form of antibodies. Proteins can also be used as a source of energy, however, in practice very little is used for this. The body's preferred sources of energy are carbohydrates and fats.

In a similar way to carbohydrates being made up of monosaccharides, proteins are made up of **amino acids**. There are 20 familiar amino acids. When amino acids are joined together, such as in a protein, the join or bond is called a peptide bond, and the process is another example of dehydration synthesis. A compound consisting of two amino acids joined together is called a dipeptide. A tripeptide is made up of three amino acids. A peptide of more than ten amino acids is called a polypeptide.

Proteins are sometimes described by their structure. A primary structure protein is one that consists of a linear chain of amino acids. If these chains are twisted together, this is called a secondary structure. When a secondary structure becomes folded, a more complex molecule is formed, which is known as a tertiary structure.

Lipids/fats

Another essential group of organic compounds that is found in the body are lipids. Lipids provide energy for the human body. For the same weight, lipids contain more energy than carbohydrates. There are many different types of lipids. Similar to carbohydrates, they are made up of carbon, hydrogen and oxygen. They are large compounds and the majority do not dissolve in water. Phospholipids are one type of lipid, of which lecithin is an example. Lecithin is found in blood and is also a component of cell membranes.

Fat is another type of lipid. Fats offer protection and insulation to the human body, in addition to being a source of energy. A fat molecule is made up of glycerol and fatty acids. It consists of one glycerol molecule combined with three fatty acid molecules, hence fats are called **triglycerides**. The formation of triglycerides from fatty acids and glycerol takes place via dehydration synthesis. The reverse, as with carbohydrates, is hydrolysis.

Fats can be divided into three types: saturated, unsaturated and polyunsaturated. Saturated fats are so called because each carbon atom is attached to as many hydrogen atoms as possible, that is, they are saturated with hydrogen. Examples of saturated fats are those contained in animal foods such as meat, butter, eggs and milk. Not all saturated fats are found in animal products – coconut oil is a plant-based saturated fat. Unsaturated fats have fewer hydrogen atoms connected to each carbon atom; they are not completely saturated with hydrogen. Monounsaturated fats have one double bond between carbon atoms, polyunsaturated fats have several. Olive oil is a monounsaturated fat. Corn oil is a polyunsaturated fat.

⭐ STUDENT ACTIVITY

Food labels

Obtain food labels from different foods (e.g. drinks bottles, packets, boxes, cans etc.). Analyse the content of each food or drink to find the answers to the following questions.

1 How much carbohydrate does each item contain?
2 How much of that is sugar?
3 What is the protein content?
4 How much fat is in the product?
5 What amount of fat is saturated fat?
6 Work out values, in grams, of the nutrient per 100 g of the food stuff (or 100 ml if a liquid).
7 Produce a variety of tables showing foods that contain the most of a certain nutrient (e.g. fat, sugar, protein, carbohydrate).
8 Based on the contents of each product, what would be the use of such food in training or competition?

REVISION QUESTIONS

1) Outline the structure of carbohydrates.
2) Give some of the functions of protein.
3) What is the difference between saturated and unsaturated fats?
4) What properties of water make it useful to the human body?

Water

Pure water is practically colourless and it has no taste or smell. The chemical representation of water is H_2O. There is one atom of oxygen attached to two atoms of hydrogen. The two hydrogen atoms are bound to one side of the oxygen atom. This results in the water molecule having a positive charge on one side, the side where the hydrogen atoms are. The other side of the oxygen atom is negatively charged. Since opposed electrical charges attract each other, water molecules also have a tendency to attract each other, which is why water forms drops.

Scientifically, water is of interest for many reasons. It is the only natural substance that is found in all three states: liquid, solid and gas (water, ice and steam).

Water is also unusual in that in a solid state it is less dense than in a liquid state. This means ice is less dense than water, which is why ice floats. The freezing point of water ($0°C$) is the zero point or baseline on the Celsius scale which is used to measure temperature.

Water is the most common substance in the human body. It makes up over two-thirds of most living cells. Water is an excellent solvent, which means

FIGURE 1.2   The three states of water

things dissolve in it readily. Salt, for example, dissolves in water to form a solution (salt water). Due to its solvent properties, water is a good means of transport in the body. Blood plasma is made up almost entirely of water (92%). Water has a high specific heat index, which means that it can absorb a lot of heat. Therefore, it provides an excellent means of **thermoregulation**. In addition, water has a high surface tension. Since surface tension causes capillary action, water can move through small blood vessels.

MATERIALS

Metals

Metals can be broadly divided into two types, **pure metals** and **metal alloys**. Pure metals are single **elements** from the Periodic Table. Examples of pure metals include copper and iron. Metal alloys contain more than one metallic element (e.g. stainless steel, which is an alloy of iron, nickel and chromium). Their properties can be changed by changing the elements present in the alloy.

All metals fall into the category of crystalline structures. Metal structures use space as efficiently as possible, that is, each metal atom forms bonds with the largest number of neighbouring metal atoms. The structure of individual metals explains their characteristic physical properties.

Properties of metals

Metals have various properties. They generally have good electrical and thermal **conductivity** (the property that enables a metal to carry heat or electricity). Metals vary in their capacity to conduct heat. Copper, for instance, has a relatively high heat conductivity and is a good electrical conductor.

Many metals have high strength and stiffness. Some metals, such as iron, are magnetic. Many metals and alloys have high densities and are useful when a high mass (see pages 17 and 395) but a small volume is necessary. Some metal alloys, such as those based on aluminium, have low densities and are used when the reduction of mass is essential, for example to improve fuel economy. Many metal alloys also have high fracture toughness, which means they can withstand impact and are durable.

Hardness is the ability of a metal to resist abrasion, cutting or permanent distortion. Hardness may be increased by heat-treating the metal, as is the case with steel. Hardness and strength are closely related properties of metals. **Brittleness** is the property of a metal that allows little yielding or bend without shattering. In other words, a brittle metal is likely to break or crack without a great change of shape. Cast iron and hard steel are brittle metals. A metal that can be hammered or pressed into various shapes without breaking is said to be **malleable**. Copper is an example of a malleable metal. **Ductility** is the property of a metal that permits it to be permanently bent or twisted into various shapes without breaking. This property is essential for metals used in making wire, for example. Ductility and malleability are similar properties. **Elasticity** is the property that enables a metal to return to its original shape after experiencing a force. This property is extremely valuable in metals, because it is undesirable to have an object permanently distorted after a load has been removed. Each metal has a point known as the elastic limit, beyond which the metal cannot be loaded without causing permanent distortion. A metal that has been permanently distorted is referred to as strained. Stress is the internal resistance of any metal to distortion.

Ceramics

A ceramic could be defined as any inorganic, non-metallic material. Examples can range from table salt (NaCl) to clay (a complex silicate). By this definition, ceramic materials would also include glasses; however, many material scientists add the stipulation that ceramics must also be crystalline. A glass is an inorganic, non-metallic material that does not have a crystalline structure. Such materials are said to be **amorphous**. Examples of glass range from the soda-lime silicate glass in bottles to the high-purity silica glass in optical fibres.

Some of the useful properties of ceramics and glasses include high melting temperature, low density, high strength, stiffness, hardness, wear resistance and corrosion resistance. Many ceramics are good electrical and thermal insulators. Some ceramics have special properties: some ceramics are magnetic, some are **piezoelectric**, and a few are **superconductors** at very low temperatures. Ceramics and glasses have one major drawback, which is that they are brittle. The recent demand for microelectronics and structural composite components has created a high demand for ceramics. Silicon, a semiconductor but also a ceramic material, has made computers possible. Ceramic fibres with their extremely high stiffness have led to the production of fibre-reinforced composites. (See opposite for an explanation of composites.)

Glasses have normally been used for low technology applications such as bottles and windows. However, glasses, like ceramics, have recently been used in developing the microelectronics industry, where silica is used as an insulator in transistors and where high-purity silica glass is used in producing fibre optic cables used for advanced telecommunications. As a result of their unique properties, ceramics and glasses are materials which will be used extensively in areas such as microelectronics and telecommunications.

Polymers

Polymer means many units, and a polymer has a repeating structure which results in large chain-like molecules. Polymers are useful because they are lightweight, resistant to corrosion and are generally inexpensive to produce. The important characteristics of polymers include their size (or molecular weight), softening and melting points and structure. The mechanical properties of polymers include low strength and high toughness. Their strength is often improved using reinforced composite structures. The softening point (**glass transition temperature**) and the melting point of a polymer will determine which applications it will be suitable for. These temperatures usually determine the upper limit at which a polymer can be used. For example, many industrially important polymers have glass transition temperatures near the boiling point of water (100°C), and they are most useful for room-temperature applications. Some specially manufactured polymers can withstand very high temperatures.

Polymers can be crystalline or amorphous, but they usually have a combination of crystalline and amorphous structures (**semi-crystalline**). The polymer chains can be free to slide past one another (thermoplastic) or they can be connected (thermoset or elastomer). Thermoplastics can be reformed and recycled, while thermosets and elastomers cannot. Polymers are used widely in many industries. About 85% of the world's plastics consumption is from four polymers that can be produced in high volumes at a low cost. They are all thermoplastics: Polyethylene (PE) used in flexible tubing and bottles; Polypropylene (PP) used in ropes and thermal clothing; Polystyrene (PS) used in packaging foams and as the core of windsurfing boards; Polyvinyl Chloride (PVC) used in bottles, waterproof clothing, pipes, electrical wire insulation, toys, raincoats, etc.

Composites

Composites are formed from two or more types of materials. Examples include polymer/ceramic and metal/ceramic composites. Composites are used because they contain the properties of the individual components. For example, polymer/ceramic composites have a greater **modulus** than the polymer component, but are not as brittle as ceramics. Composites are also found in nature. Wood, a natural composite containing cellulose fibres, is one of the main materials used in the construction industry.

Composites fall into two categories: fibre-reinforced composites and particle-reinforced composites. **Fibre-reinforced** composites can be made of metals, ceramics, glasses or polymers. Fibres increase the modulus of the material. Fibres are difficult to process into composites, making fibre-reinforced composites relatively expensive. Fibre-reinforced composites are used in the development of sports equipment (e.g. carbon fibre in racing bikes), however, due to its cost these materials are found at the top end of the market.

Particles used in **particle-reinforced** composites include ceramics, glasses and metal particles such as aluminium. Particles are used to increase the modulus and to decrease the ductility of the material. Particles are also used to produce inexpensive composites. Making particle-reinforced composites is much easier and less costly than making fibre-reinforced composites.

The use of advanced material in sport

Consider the use of various materials in cycling. Mountain bikes must be strong to withstand the damage resulting from riding off-road, and are commonly made of cromoly, a steel alloy designed to be hard and durable.

Cromoly is cheaper and more able to withstand blows than other frame materials such as aluminium or carbon fibre composites. A disadvantage of using cromoly is the overall weight of the bike. Road cyclists need lighter bikes, which are stable, strong and durable. Some bikes are built from titanium, a

STUDENT ACTIVITY

Different materials

1 Take each type of material (i.e. metal, ceramic, polymer and composite) and give examples of how they are used to increase performance in sport.

2 For each type of material, try and find examples of how they are used to decrease the risk of injury in sport.

metal which is extremely light and strong, but more expensive than the traditional metals used for frame building (steel and aluminium). Carbon fibre reinforced composites are also used to build frames. These composites can be more easily processed into different shapes than metals. This helps with the aerodynamic design of the bike. The drawback of carbon fibre is that it is less ductile and may break if hit with a hard object. To reduce the overall weight of a bike, titanium, aluminium or carbon fibre components are used.

Another area that relies heavily on material science is motor racing. Different materials are used to build each part of a race car. The nose cone of the car could be made of lightweight glass fibre-reinforced composites, which contribute to fuel economy. The frame is made of high-strength cromoly. The area between the cockpit and the engine compartment is made of a carbon fibre-reinforced composite which has a high strength to weight ratio. The engine would be made of an aluminium alloy that is lightweight for performance and fuel economy. The wheels are also made of aluminium. The tyres are made of a rubber polymer and are reinforced with small particles to reduce wear.

Ski equipment and clothing uses technologically advanced materials. Ski clothing is made from a polymer microfibre fabric designed to be breathable and waterproof. This fabric keeps the skier dry while allowing sweat to evaporate from the skier's body. Skis are made from many materials: the outer surface is normally a fibre-reinforced composite. This makes skis strong and light. Metal alloy edges are attached to the skis for added strength where they experience repeated impacts. Ski poles are also made of stiff fibre-reinforced composites or aluminium metal alloy, again for strength and reduced weight.

Windsurfing is another sport that uses various materials to improve performance. Boards are made of polystyrene foam, which is very lightweight. The outer surface of the board and the mast are made of a carbon fibre material. Again, this is lightweight, but it is also more impact resistant. The sail is made of waterproof polymer fabric.

Golf clubs are made of materials that enable players to hit the ball further and more accurately. The club head of a modern driver is a hollow shell made of a titanium alloy. The titanium alloy has a higher modulus than steel. Unlike old wooden club heads that absorb moisture, those made of metal are not affected by humidity. The use of titanium allows the club head to be bigger, so that players can hit more accurate shots. The shaft of the driver is made of a carbon fibre reinforced composite. Compared with a steel shaft, carbon fibre composites are lighter so that players can produce greater club speed in order to hit the ball further.

Specialist materials can be used to prevent injury as well as to improve performance. Helmets consist of polycarbonate polymer shells that are highly impact resistant. They contain polymer foam linings that absorb energy from impacts. Some sports helmets have polycarbonate polymer face shields or steel alloy cages to cover the face, which also serve to resist high impacts. Pads and gloves need to allow for greater movement, so they contain energy absorbing padding made from a polymer foam.

REVISION
QUESTIONS

1) List the characteristics of different metals.
2) For what are ceramics commonly used?
3) What are the major polymers manufactured in industry?
4) Why might composites be superior to other materials?

MECHANICS OF MOTION

Linear motion

Motion is simply the change in position of an object over time. If you look at an object in one location and, when you look at it later, it is in a different position, you can say that it has moved. Linear motion is motion in which all parts of an object or body move the same distance, in the same direction, in the same time. You can see an object in motion. You can also feel motion when you are moving. All motion is relative to another object. If you are sitting in a moving car, objects outside look like they are moving with respect to you. Usually, we consider motion with respect to the ground or the earth.

In describing linear motion, the first principal encountered is position. An object's position is its location in space. For example, imagine you were just about to run a 100 m race. Your position could be described as at the start or at 0 m. This would be your location. (See also page 394.)

Distance

The most basic method of describing motion is to record change in position. If an object changes position, the length of path followed by that object is termed distance. The standard unit of measurement is a metre (m). In the example of the 100 m race, the distance travelled would be 100 m.

Displacement

A similar concept to distance is displacement, also measured in metres. While distance is the length of path a body follows, displacement is change in position from initial position. It is the straight-line distance between the start and end of a movement. In the 100 m example, distance and displacement would be the same. However, consider a 400 m race. The distance of the race is obviously 400 m, yet displacement is not. The start and end of the race occur at the same place, so the end position is the same as the initial position, meaning that displacement is zero.

Displacement is an example of a vector quantity. A **vector** is something that is represented by magnitude and direction.

Speed

Distance and displacement measure motion by examining how far something has moved. Speed looks at how quickly this movement or change in position takes place. It is the rate of change of distance. Speed can be calculated from distance travelled divided by the time it took to travel that distance, and is measured in metres per second (ms^{-1}). Two types of speed are referred to: average speed and instantaneous speed. **Average speed** is just that, the speed averaged out for the entire race or event you are measuring. Average speed is calculated as follows:

$$s = \frac{l}{t} \text{ where } s = \text{average speed}$$
$$l = \text{distance}$$
$$t = \text{time taken}$$

STUDENT ACTIVITY

1 Research the world record times for either male or female:
   a) 100 m sprint
   b) 400 m sprint
   c) marathon.
2 Work out the following for each athlete:
   a) distance covered
   b) displacement
   c) speed.

For example, if a cyclist travels 40 miles in 2 hours, their average speed would be the distance of 40 miles divided by the time of 2 hours, equalling 20 miles per hour (mph). If it takes a runner 8 minutes to travel 1 mile, their speed is 1 mile divided by 8 minutes, which equals $\frac{1}{8}$ mile per minute, or 7.5 mph. **Instantaneous speed** is speed at any given point. It is the distance travelled in a very small time interval. Instantaneous speed is that which you would see on a computer on a bike or the speedometer in a car. If it was reading 22 mph it would not necessarily mean you had travelled 22 miles in the last hour, but that is your rate of motion at that moment.

Velocity

The terms speed and velocity are similar, but they mean something slightly different. Speed is how fast something is going and is derived from distance. Velocity indicates the speed of an object in a direction of motion and is derived from displacement. Velocity is the rate of change of displacement with time and has the same units as speed. For example, if you say a car is going at 30 mph, you are talking about its speed. If you say it is going at 30 mph in a northerly direction, you are talking about its velocity. As with displacement, velocity is a vector. It can be reported as an average or instantaneous value. Average velocity is:

$$v = \frac{d}{t}$$ where v = average velocity
$$\qquad\qquad d = \text{displacement}$$
$$\qquad\qquad t = \text{time taken}$$

Acceleration

Acceleration is the change in velocity over a period of time. If velocity goes down it is called **deceleration**. When you start running, you accelerate (increase your velocity) until you reach a constant speed. Mathematically, acceleration is the change in velocity divided by the time for the change. Average acceleration is given by:

$$a = \frac{(v_f - v_i)}{t}$$ where a = average acceleration
$$\qquad\qquad v_f = \text{final velocity}$$
$$\qquad\qquad v_i = \text{initial velocity}$$
$$\qquad\qquad t = \text{time taken}$$

For example, if a car speeds up from a velocity of 40 mph to 60 mph in a time period of 10 seconds, the acceleration is calculated as follows $\frac{(60-40)}{10} = 2$ miles /per second/ per second. The standard unit of measurement for acceleration is metres per second per second (ms^{-2}).

There is a simple set of relationships between position, velocity and acceleration of an object. The velocity is the rate of change of position. The acceleration is the rate of change of velocity. In more mathematical terms, the velocity is the derivative of the position with respect to time, and the acceleration is the derivative of the velocity with respect to time.

STUDENT PRACTICAL

Linear motion

Aim

The aim of this investigation is to measure and explain the displacement and velocity of an athlete.

Equipment

running track

cones

video camera with a playback facility

monitor

Method

1   Place markers at each 10 m interval of the running track.

2   Video tape your athlete running your chosen distance.

3   When timing from the video, remember that one frame takes 0.04 s (there are twenty-five frames in a second).

(Rather than recording information directly, you could use previously shot footage or use existing information).

4   Play back the recording and analyse the results

Results

Produce a table containing information for position and time. The first column will have the position values which should each be 10 m (i.e. 0 m, 10 m, 20 m and so on), and the second column will have the time values (the time taken to reach each point). From this table, plot a position/time graph.

Position (m)	Time (s)
0	
10	
20	
30	
40	

From the position time/graph produce a new table with time, displacement and velocity information. The first column is time and goes up in increments of one second (i.e. 0 s, 1 s, 2 s, 3 s and so on). The second column is position information taken from the graph and is the position at each one-second interval. The third column is displacement and is the difference between two successive position values.

For example, if the position at 1 s is 6 m and the position at 0 s was 0 m, the displacement in the first second is 6 m. Equally, if the position at 2 s is 13 m, the displacement between one and two seconds is 7 m (13 − 6). The final column is velocity and these values will be the same as the displacement column.

Take the second example above: if you travel 7 m (displacement) in one second (time) then your average velocity must be 7 ms^{-1} (velocity is displacement divided by time taken, which in this example is 7 divided by 1). Since the time increment in the first column is always one second, time taken is always one, hence displacement and velocity are the same. From this table plot a velocity/time graph.

Time (s)	Position (m)	Displacement (m)	Velocity (ms^{-1})
0	0		
1	6	6	
2	13	7	

Conclusion

In your conclusion you should be able to answer the following questions:

1   When is maximum speed reached and why?

2   What is the value of maximum speed?

3   What might this depend upon?

4   What is the duration of maximum speed?

5   Does deceleration occur? If so, how much velocity is lost and why?

Newton's laws

Newton's first law of motion is sometimes referred to as the law of inertia. The law states: 'an object at rest tends to stay at rest and an object in motion tends to stay in motion with the same speed and in the same direction unless acted upon by an unbalanced force'. There are two parts to this statement, one that looks at the behaviour of stationary objects and the other which refers to the behaviour of moving objects.

All objects tend to keep on doing what they are doing (unless acted upon by an unbalanced force). If at rest, they will continue in this same state of rest. If in motion with a leftward velocity of $2\,\text{ms}^{-1}$, they will continue in this same state of motion ($2\,\text{ms}^{-1}$, left). All objects resist changes in their state of motion; they tend to keep on doing what they are doing. Consider being in a car. The sensation you experience in a car while it is braking, is your body resisting a change in motion (inertia). You continue in motion, hence the need of a seat belt to provide a force to stop your motion.

Newton's first law of motion predicts that if the forces acting upon an object are balanced, then the acceleration of that object will be zero. Objects in **equilibrium** (the condition in which all forces are in balance) will not accelerate. According to Newton, the presence of an unbalanced force will accelerate an object, changing its speed, its direction, or both.

Newton's second law of motion examines objects for which all existing forces are not balanced. Newton suggests that acceleration of an object is dependent upon the **net force** (the sum of all the forces) acting upon the object and the mass of the object. As the net force increases, so will the object's acceleration. However, the greater the mass of the object, the more its acceleration will decrease. Newton's second law of motion states: 'the acceleration of an object as produced by a net force is directly proportional to the magnitude of the net force, in the same direction as the net force, and inversely proportional to the mass of the object'.

In terms of an equation, the net force is equal to the product of the object's mass and its acceleration:

$$F = m \times a \quad \text{where } F = \text{force}$$
$$m = \text{mass}$$
$$a = \text{acceleration}$$

The acceleration is directly proportional to the net force. If all the individual forces acting upon an object are known, then the net force can be determined. The above equation indicates that force is equal to mass multiplied by acceleration. By substituting standard units for force, mass and acceleration into the above equation, the following is observed: 1 newton (N) is equal to $1\,\text{kg ms}^{-2}$. The definition of the standard metric unit of force is given by the above equation. One newton is defined as the amount of force required to give a 1 kg mass an acceleration of $1\,\text{ms}^{-2}$.

Whatever change is made to the net force, the same change will occur in the acceleration. Double, triple or quadruple the net force, and the acceleration will do the same. On the other hand, whatever change is made to the mass, the opposite or inverse change will occur in the acceleration. Double, triple or quadruple the mass, and the acceleration will be a half, a third or a fourth of its original value.

In conclusion, Newton's second law explains the behaviour of objects upon which unbalanced forces are acting. The law states that unbalanced forces cause objects to accelerate proportional to the force applied to the object and inversely proportional to the mass of the object.

A force is a push or a pull upon an object. Some forces result from contact (e.g. frictional force, applied forces), while other forces can exist with no contact (e.g. gravity, magnetic forces). According to Newton, whenever objects interact with each other, they exert forces upon each other. When you walk, your body exerts a downward force on the floor and the floor exerts an upward force on your body. These two forces are called **action** and **reaction** forces and are the subject of Newton's third law of motion: 'for every action, there is an equal and opposite reaction'. When two objects interact, they experience forces. The size of the force on the first object equals the size of the force on the second object. The direction of the force on the first object is opposite to the direction of the force on the second object.

Imagine a triathlete in a race. When they are in the water swimming, they push the water backwards with their hands and feet. In turn, the water reacts by pushing the triathlete forward, propelling them through the water.

The same is true on a bike. The bike has wheels, which push backward on the road when the triathlete spins the pedals. The road reacts by pushing the wheels forward. In the final part of the race, the run, the triathlete is pushing directly against the ground (down and back). The ground reacts by pushing upward and forward on the triathlete. The size of the force on the road or in the water equals the size of the force on the triathlete, and the direction of the force on the road or in the water is opposite to the direction of the force on the triathlete.

Friction

Friction is a force that is created whenever two surfaces move or try to move across each other. Friction always opposes the motion or attempted motion of one surface across another surface. It is dependant on the texture of both surfaces, and on the amount of contact force pushing the two surfaces together (normal force). There are two different kinds of contact friction. **Static friction** is the force of friction present when there is no relative motion (no sliding) between the two surfaces in contact. **Kinetic friction** is the force of friction present when there is relative motion (sliding) between the two surfaces in contact. Friction will act to slow down a moving object. Imagine the friction between a cyclist's tyres and the road. The greater the friction, the harder it is to cycle, hence road-racing tyres have a high pressure and are thin.

Weight, mass and gravity

Weight and mass are often confused. Mass is a measure of inertia, an object's resistance to movement. Weight is the force an object feels due to gravitational attraction and depends on location. The mass of an object remains constant in any location. For example, near the surface of the earth the weight of an object is a due to its mass and the gravitational force of the earth. The acceleration caused by gravity is equal to 9.8 ms^{-2} and is directed toward the centre of the earth. If an astronought were standing on the moon, their weight would be a product of their mass and the gravitational force of the moon. Acceleration due to gravity on the moon is 1.6 ms^{-2} and is directed towards the centre of the moon

For convenience, when examining the motion of objects the total weight of a body is said to be concentrated at its centre of gravity. Every body or object has a centre of gravity. It is not necessarily within the body – it may be situated in space outside the body. For example, the centre of gravity of a ring is in the space in the centre of the ring.

The centre of gravity of a rectangular object is at the point of intersection of its diagonals, while for a circle the centre of gravity is at its centre.

In linear motion, each point on a body undergoes the same displacement as any other point. The motion of a body can be described as the motion of its centre of gravity. The term centre of mass is often confused with the centre of gravity. The two terms are so similar that they can be used interchangeably. The centre of gravity of an object coincides with its centre of mass if the object is in a completely uniform gravitational field. If the body is not located in a uniform gravitational field, its centre of mass and centre of gravity will be at two different locations.

Stability and equilibrium

A structure has high stability if, when it experiences a force, it returns to or remains in the same position. The more quickly it returns, the more stable it is. The amount of stability depends on the base, the height and the weight of the structure. The weight of an object is due to the force of gravity pulling down on the mass of the object. If the position of the centre of gravity is low and lies inside a large base area, the object is very stable. An example of this is a Formula One racing car.

If the centre of gravity lies to one side of the base area, the object is much less stable. If the centre of gravity is outside the base area, the object is very unstable. A tall object tends to be unstable because the centre of gravity is very high. It can be easily moved outside the base area by the application of external forces. Shorter, heavier people are more stable than taller, lighter people. This is why short, heavy people are successful in sports that require stability (e.g. judo, front row forward in rugby).

Equilibrium is a condition characterized by a balance of forces. A body is said to be in equilibrium if it is at rest or moving with uniform velocity. If the combined effect of all the forces acting on a body is zero, and the body is in a state of rest, then its equilibrium is termed **static equilibrium**. Therefore, in a static equilibrium, forces compensate each other so that the system is motionless. In a **dynamic equilibrium**, the system is moving and forces complement each other so that the system's behaviour is predictable. That is, a body is in a state of uniform motion and the resultant of all forces acting upon it is zero. Jumping with a parachute is an example. If the linear and angular acceleration of a body are zero, the body is said to be in **equilibrium**. When two or more forces act on a body such that their resultant or combining effect on the body is zero and the body remains at rest or in uniform motion, then the body is said to be in equilibrium.

Moments

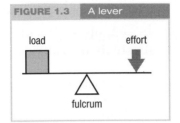

FIGURE 1.3 A lever

load   effort

fulcrum

The **torque** or moment of force can be defined as the tendency of a force to produce rotation in a body about an axis. The turning effect of a force depends upon two factors: the magnitude of force (F) and moment arm (r). The moment arm is the product of force and moment arm gives the torque about any axis:

$$T = F \times r \text{ where } T = \text{torque}$$
$$F = \text{force}$$
$$r = \text{moment arm}$$

If a body rotates about its axis in an anticlockwise direction, then the torque is taken as a positive. If the body rotates in a clockwise direction, then the torque is taken as a negative.

A lever produces a moment. Levers comprise a lever arm, a pivot point (fulcrum), a load force (the thing to be moved) and an effort force (the thing that does the moving). The effort force creates a turning effect (moment) around the pivot.

The size of this turning effect is dependent on the size of the force and its distance from the pivot. Changing the distance from the pivot to the load force changes the amount of load force magnification. There are three main types of levers: first class, second class and third class. The location of the pivot point in relation to the load and the effort determines the lever class. This is discussed in more detail in Chapter 15 (see page 387).

The effort arm is the part of the lever between the fulcrum and the effort force. The resistance arm is the part of the lever between the fulcrum and the load. There is a direct relationship between the length of the lever arm and the force acting on that arm. The relationship is: the length of the effort arm is the same number of times greater than the length of the resistance arm as the resistance to be overcome is greater than the effort you must apply. Writing these words as a mathematical equation, we have:

$$\frac{l_e}{l_r} = \frac{R}{E} \text{ where } l_e = \text{length of effort arm}$$
$$l_r = \text{length of resistance arm}$$
$$R = \text{resistance weight or force}$$
$$E = \text{effort force}$$

Remember that all distances must be in the same units (metres), and that all forces must be in the same units (newtons).

REVISION QUESTIONS

1) What is the difference between distance and displacement?
2) Explain speed and velocity.
3) How is acceleration calculated?
4) Outlines Newton's three laws of motion.
5) Explain the difference between weight and mass.

ENERGY AND ENERGY TRANSFER

Energy transfer

Energy exists in numerous forms. **Chemical energy** is the energy stored in bonds of chemical substances, for example it is stored in food. **Mechanical energy** is the energy involved in movement. Physical activity requires mechanical energy. Other forms of energy include heat energy, light energy and electrical energy

Energy is essential for human life. It is needed for all functions of the body, including growth, repair and physical activity. Humans obtain energy from food. During exercise, humans need to convert chemical energy stored in the body into mechanical energy that allows muscles to contract. In this process, some heat energy is also produced from chemical energy. In fact, up to 70% of the energy produced from chemical energy during physical activity is heat energy. This makes the human body relatively inefficient.

Energy is constantly being transferred from one form to another. Energy cannot be created or destroyed, it is just converted between different forms. In science, this is called the first law of thermodynamics.

In sport and exercise, it is important to measure energy, particularly the amount of energy intake (via food) and expenditure (in the form of exercise). There are a number of different units that can be used when measuring energy. The international standard is the **joule** (J). A joule is defined as the energy required to apply a force of 1 N over a distance of 1 m. Although the joule is the international standard for energy measurement, a unit still common in nutrition is the 'diet calorie' or kilocalorie. A kilocalorie is the amount of energy required to heat 1 kg of water by 1°C.

Mechanical energy

Mechanical energy is the energy of motion needed for physical activity. There are two different types of mechanical energy: **potential energy** (stored energy) and **kinetic energy** (energy of motion).

Potential energy

Potential energy is stored energy and comes in two forms: gravitational potential energy and elastic potential energy. **Gravitational potential energy** is the energy stored in an object as the result of its vertical position. The energy results from the gravitational attraction of the earth. The gravitational potential energy of a pole-vaulter in midair is dependent on two things: the mass of the athlete and the height to which they have vaulted.

There is a direct relation between gravitational potential energy and the mass of an object: more massive objects have greater gravitational potential energy. There is also a direct relationship between gravitational potential energy and the height of an object: the higher an object, the greater the gravitational potential energy. These relationships are expressed by the following equation:

$$\text{potential energy} = m \times g \times h \text{ where } m = \text{mass}$$
$$g = \text{acceleration due to gravity}$$
$$h = \text{height}$$

Since mass is measured in kilograms (kg), acceleration in metres per second per second (ms^{-2}) and height in metres (m), the unit of energy derived from the equation above is $kg\,ms^{-2}{\cdot}m$. We know that a $kg\,ms^{-2}$ is the same as a newton (see Newton's second law), therefore the unit for potential energy could be displayed as Nm, which is the same as a joule.

The second form of potential energy is **elastic potential energy**. This is the energy stored in elastic materials as the consequence of their stretching or compressing. Elastic potential energy can be stored in trampolines or bent pole vaults, for example. The amount of elastic potential energy stored in such a piece of equipment is related to the quantity of stretch or compression of the equipment.

Kinetic energy

Kinetic energy is the energy of motion. An object that has motion, whatever the direction (e.g. vertical or horizontal), has kinetic energy. The amount of kinetic energy an object has depends on the mass of the object and the speed of the object. The following equation is used to represent the kinetic energy of an object:

$$\text{kinetic energy} = \frac{1}{2} \times m \times v^2 \text{ where } m = \text{mass of object}$$
$$v = \text{speed of object}$$

Units for kinetic energy derived from this equation would be kilograms (kg) multiplied by metres per second (ms^{-1}), multiplied by metres per second again (since velocity is squared). The units would be $kg\,ms^{-1}\,ms^{-1}$ or $kg\,m^2\,s^{-2}$. As with potential energy, $1\,kg\,ms^{-2}$ is the same as 1 N, hence we have Nm or joule. The equation above reveals that the kinetic energy of an object is directly proportional to the square of its speed. This means that for a twofold increase in speed, the kinetic energy will increase by a factor of four; for a threefold increase in speed, the kinetic energy will increase by a factor of nine; and for a fourfold increase in speed, the kinetic energy will increase by a factor of sixteen. The kinetic energy is dependent upon the square of the speed.

The mechanical energy of an object is due to its motion (kinetic energy) and/or its stored energy of position (potential energy). The total amount of mechanical energy is the sum of the potential and kinetic energy. This sum is simply referred to as the total mechanical energy (TME).

An object that possesses mechanical energy is able to do work. In fact, mechanical energy is often defined as the ability to do work. That is, mechanical energy enables an object to apply a force to another object in order to cause it to be displaced. The mechanical energy of a cricket ball gives the ball the ability to apply a force to a batsman's bat. The ball has mechanical energy (kinetic energy), so is able to do work.

Work and power

Work is defined as a force acting upon an object to cause a displacement. In order for a force to qualify as having done work on an object, there must be a displacement and the force must cause the displacement. An example is a weightlifter lifting a barbell above his head. Mathematically, work can be expressed by the following equation:

$$W = F \times d \text{ where } W = \text{work}$$
$$F = \text{force}$$
$$d = \text{displacement}$$

Work has nothing to do with the amount of time that a force acts to cause displacement. Power is the rate at which work is done. Mathematically, it is computed using the following equation:

$$P = \frac{W}{t} \text{ where } P = \text{power}$$
$$W = \text{work}$$
$$t = \text{time}$$

The standard metric unit of power is the watt (W). As is implied by the equation for power, a unit of power is equivalent to a unit of work divided by a unit of time. Thus, a watt is equivalent to a joule per second. For historical reasons, horsepower is occasionally used to describe the power delivered by a machine. One horsepower is equivalent to approximately 750 W. A person is a machine, which could have a power rating. Some people are more powerful than others; that is, they are capable of doing the same amount of work in less time or more work in the same amount of time.

The expression for power is work divided by time. Since the expression for work is force multiplied by displacement, the expression for power can be rewritten as force multiplied by displacement all divided by time. Yet, displacement divided by time is velocity, so the expression for power can be rewritten once more as force multiplied by velocity. This is shown below:

$$P = \frac{W}{t} = F \times \frac{d}{t} = F \times v \text{ where } P = \text{power}$$
$$W = \text{work}$$
$$t = \text{time}$$
$$F = \text{force}$$
$$d = \text{displacement}$$
$$v = \text{velocity}$$

This new expression for power reveals that a powerful machine needs a high force (strength) and a high velocity (speed). The stronger and faster you are, the more power you can produce.

★ STUDENT PRACTICAL

Power

Undertake the following practical on power and produce a report.

Aim

Power gives us a measure of the intensity of exercise. It is defined as the rate of doing work. That is, the amount of work done in a certain time. The aim of this experiment is to measure power and understand the implications for sport.

Equipment

tape measure
stopwatch
scales.

Method

1. Record the subject's weight.
2. Subject runs up (as fast as possible) a set of stairs.
3. Measure the time it takes to complete the climb and the total vertical distance of the climb.
4. Record the time as *t* and the height as *h*.
5. Calculate power for each subject using the following equation and enter each subject's data into a table:

$$P = \frac{(w \times h)}{t}$$ where P = power
W = weight
h = height
t = time

Results

Name	Height (m)	Time (s)	Work (J)	Power (W)

Conclusion

The following points should be discussed in your conclusions.

1. Who produces the largest power value and why?
2. In which sport does power play an important part? Why?
3. Calculate the horsepower produced by your subjects.

Metabolism

Metabolism refers to the countless chemical processes going on continuously inside the body that allow life and normal functioning. These processes require energy from food. The number of kilojoules (kJ) your body burns at any given time is regulated by your metabolism. Metabolism involves two complementary processes: catabolism and anabolism. **Catabolism** is the breakdown of food components (such as carbohydrates, proteins and fats) into their simpler forms, which can then be used to provide energy. **Anabolism** is the combination of chemicals to create new substances (e.g. building and repairing muscle tissue). Metabolism is governed by hormones (chemical messages secreted by the glands of the endocrine system). The rates of catabolism and anabolism are monitored to ensure they stay in balance.

The amount of metabolism carried out in a person's body is called the metabolic rate. The body's metabolic rate is divided into two states: the number of kilojoules burned at rest (basal) and the number of kilojoules burned during physical activity. The basal metabolic rate (BMR) refers to the amount of energy the body requires to maintain itself. This accounts for between 50% and 75% of total energy expenditure of the average person. An average male may have a basal metabolic rate of around 7000 kJ per day, while an average female may have a basal metabolic rate of around 6000 kJ per day. Regularly active people have higher basal metabolic rates than less active individuals. Since basal metabolic rate can account for as much as two-thirds of total daily energy expenditure, this is a significant amount.

A person's metabolic rate is influenced by a number of factors. Metabolism slows with age, mainly due to a loss in muscle tissue. Strength and resistance training can reduce or prevent the decline in muscle mass that is generally observed with ageing. The amount of lean muscle tissue is an important factor since it is muscles that utilise energy. If the environmental temperature is low the body has to work harder to maintain its normal body temperature, so this increases the basal metabolic rate. Infection or illness increases basal metabolic rate because the body has to work harder to build new tissues and to create an immune response. Certain drugs (e.g. caffeine) can increase basal metabolic rate.

During heavy physical exertion, a 70 kg man running at 7 mph may use in excess of 3000 kJ per hour. The amount of energy expended for different activities varies with the intensity and type of exercise. The energy cost of many activities has been determined, usually by monitoring the oxygen consumption during the activity to determine an average oxygen uptake per unit of time. The average daily energy expenditure for female and male cross-country skiers when they are training is 14 500 kJ per day for women and 21 000 kJ per day for men. Nowadays, energy values are given in kJ not kilocalories (kcal). To obtain values in kcal, divide the kJ by 4.2.

Energy systems

Where does energy come from during exercise? All energy that causes movement comes from adenosine triphosphate (ATP), a complex chemical compound formed with the energy released from food and stored in all cells, particularly muscles. Only with the energy released by the breakdown of this compound can the cells perform work. The breakdown of ATP produces energy, phosphate and adenosine diphosphate. The muscle stores enough ATP for two seconds of maximal contraction. In strength/power events (e.g. power lifting, shot putting) energy comes from ATP. What if we need energy for longer duration exercise? We make more (re-synthesise) ATP. This can be done in two ways.

1   Adenosine diphosphate can be joined with creatine phosphate (a high-energy substance stored in the muscle) to form ATP. This process does not require oxygen (it is **anaerobic**). Creatine phosphate (CP) is in short supply. The muscles store enough for less than ten seconds of maximal activity, so this source of energy would be useful in, for example, the long jump (short, high-intensity effort).

2   Adenosine diphosphate and phosphate can be joined together to re-form ATP with the help of certain fuel reserves (carbohydrates, fats and proteins). This can be done with or without oxygen (aerobically or anaerobically).

In longer duration activity, alternative energy supplies would be needed. Carbohydrate is the main source of energy in most types of physical activity. Carbohydrate is stored in the muscle and liver as glycogen. It is transported in the blood stream as glucose. Carbohydrate can be used to produce ATP aerobically or anaerobically. The breakdown of glycogen (carbohydrate) without oxygen to produce ATP is called **anaerobic glycolysis**. This breakdown is rapid and results in the production of lactic acid. The 400 m race is a good example of when this process is predominately used. After around 60–90 seconds, the build-up of lactic acid inhibits muscle contraction and hence limits the use of this process any further. This energy system does not produce large amounts of ATP. The combined actions of the ATP/CP and anaerobic glycolysis systems allow the muscles to generate force even when the oxygen supply is limited. These two systems predominate during the early minutes of high-intensity exercise.

If oxygen is present in large supply, glycogen can be broken down to form ATP without the production of lactic acid. This process is complex and time consuming; hence, if energy is needed quickly it may not be possible to obtain sufficient oxygen to utilise this system. **Aerobic glycolysis** produces carbon dioxide as a byproduct. This is not as big a problem as lactic acid because it can be breathed out. This process can continue until supplies of glucose or glycogen become limited. This is in excess of an hour under normal conditions (healthy human, average diet, etc.).

Another source of aerobic energy is fat. Fat is stored as intra-muscular triglyceride (in the muscle) or as adipose tissue (the fat under the skin). Fat is broken down into **fatty acids**, and it is these fatty acids that undergo **beta oxidation** to form ATP. This is done aerobically. Again, this is a complex process that requires time. The average human stores enough fat for several days of continuous moderate-intensity exercise.

FIGURE 1.4

Long-distance cycling is an aerobic activity

Protein can also be used to produce ATP. Proteins are stored as amino acids. The body consists of a lot of protein (e.g. as vital organs, muscles), most of which we need for bodily functions. The breakdown of amino acids to form ATP is an aerobic process. Under normal conditions (not in extreme cases like starvation), only about 10% of total energy comes from protein, even in very long-duration activities. Exercises that rely on mainly aerobic energy sources are long-duration exercises (e.g. swimming, walking, running, cycling).

There are, therefore, three methods of generating energy (ATP) for physical activity. The ATP/CP system, also called the phosphogen system; anaerobic glycolysis or the lactic acid system, and the aerobic energy systems. Although all energy systems are constantly working, the recruitment of an alternative system to become the major supplier of energy occurs when the current energy system is almost depleted.

In sport, both the aerobic and anaerobic energy systems work together to provide energy. As exertion time increases, the utilisation of anaerobic energy decreases. For example, for the first minute of a marathon the runner may use 70% anaerobic energy, while at one hour the runner uses only 2% anaerobic energy (that means almost all the energy at this point is aerobic). However, energy production is both time and intensity related. Running at a very high intensity, as in sprinting, means that an athlete can operate effectively for only a very short period of time. Running at a low intensity, as in gentle jogging, means that an athlete can sustain activity for a long period of time.

REVISION QUESTIONS

1) What is basal metabolic rate?
2) Explain the distinction between kinetic and potential energy.
3) Give different ways of calculating power.
4) Outline the major energy systems in the body.

STUDENT ACTIVITY

Energy requirements

1 Select a number of different types of sport and try to establish the contribution from each of the energy systems during an entire match or race.
2 Estimate percentage overall contributions and consider the involvements of the various energy systems at different times within the activity.

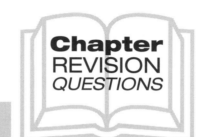

Chapter REVISION QUESTIONS

1) What are the functions of carbohydrate, fat, protein and water in the human body?
2) How might each of these substances be of benefit to an athlete?
3) What are the general characteristics of metals, ceramics, polymers and composites?
4) Give examples of how each of these are used to improve performance in sport.
5) Explain the following concepts: distance, displacement, speed, velocity and acceleration.
6) Give examples of Newton's laws of motion in sport.
7) What effects do gravity and friction have on the sports performer?
8) How can creatine phosphate be used for muscle contraction?
9) What is anaerobic glycolysis?
10) What are the differences in the three aerobic sources of energy?

FURTHER READING

Marieb, E. N. (1998) *Human Anatomy and Physiology*, 4th edition. Menlo Park, California: Benjamin Cummings

Williams, C. A. and James, D. V. B. (2001) *Science for Exercise and Sport*. London: E & F N Spon.

SCIENTIFIC PROJECTS FOR SPORT AND EXERCISE

Research is about finding solutions to problems, obtaining facts and determining what is the truth. A research project allows you to bring different areas of study together. You can use your knowledge of sport and exercise science to investigate a particular topic or question you have an interest in. It could be related to a certain sport (e.g. fitness in football referees), general issues in sport and exercise (e.g. the amount of physical activity undertaken by school children), or it may arise from one of the disciplines within sport and exercise (e.g. sports injuries). Whatever topic you choose, you will have to spend a large amount of time working independently. This will include reading literature, collecting and analysing data and writing up the whole project.

By the end of this chapter you should be able to:

✪   plan a sport and exercise science project

✪   implement the sport and exercise science project

✪   interpret the outcomes of the sport and exercise science project

✪   report the sport and exercise science project.

PLANNING A PROJECT

Getting started (action plan)

The hardest part of the project is getting started. Thinking of a good idea or subject matter takes time and effort. It is useful to have several topics or questions you wish to address, then if one idea proves impractical or too difficult to test, you have an alternative to fall back on. Before arriving at a question to investigate, it is worth considering what makes a good research question. First, it should be a question, something which you can answer (i.e. yes, there is a difference or no, the two things are not related). It also needs to be something you can test, so you need to consider what time, equipment, resources and access to subjects you have. Importantly, it needs to be of practical value, so at the end of your research you can draw implications. How will your research help an athlete, coach, official, teacher, administrator or manager? The final thing to remember is that your research should be of interest. Others have to find it interesting so that they will read it, but more vitally you need to be interested in it to maintain your motivation. As mentioned, research is time consuming – your project might take in the region of six to eight months – so self-motivation is essential.

Unless you already have a specific topic in mind, you need some method of arriving at a research question. One way to begin is to narrow your research to one sport or form of exercise. If, for example, you are a keen cyclist, you may then wish to do a project on some aspect of cycling. Another way to narrow the area is to do it by a discipline within sport and exercise science. For example, you may decide to do a project involving biomechanics. You could even combine the two areas to arrive at the biomechanics of cycling.

A good research project requires a good action plan. The plan is crucial to set out clearly what is to be done and why it is necessary. By writing the plan, a lot of the problems that you may otherwise have encountered can be avoided. You should also devise a timetable for the implementation of the project. Include deadlines for researching information, carrying out testing, analysing results and when the individual sections of the research will be written up.

The aim or objective of the research is vital – without a clear aim the research has no guidance. This is an area that people undertaking research projects regularly have difficulty with. They often have a general idea for a project (e.g. fitness in football players), but not a specific objective. Using this example (fitness in footballers), what would you test? Who would you test? The topic is too general; it needs to be focused on one particular aspect of fitness in football players. Contrast this with the following topic: the anaerobic fitness levels of college male first-team and second-team football players. This project is far clearer. What is to be measured is specific (i.e. anaerobic fitness), however, you would still need to decide how to measure it and justify your chosen method. The people you are going to investigate are clearly stated. The objective is now unambiguous, so you can devise a **hypothesis** – something which you can test. You might hypothesise that first-team players will have a higher level of anaerobic fitness than second-team players. This would be easy to test by measuring it in both sets of players and then comparing the values. Stating a hypothesis helps make the research clear. It helps the researcher to think about how data will be collected and analysed.

The action plan will need an **introduction**, which should be the background to the research. This will consist of how you arrived at the idea, previous knowledge in the area and the usefulness of any conclusions you may draw. This last point should not be overlooked. There would be little benefit in asking a group of people to follow a six-month training programme involving cycling, running and walking and then hypothesising that their aerobic fitness levels would increase. The results of such an investigation could be predicted in advance. It would be better to compare different training methods, intensities or durations.

The introduction will be followed by information about how you intend to collect your evidence, including research design, resources, experimental procedures and methods of data collection. The **research design** is largely determined by what you hope to conclude about your results. If you aim to examine the effectiveness of a training programme on a certain measure (e.g. flexibility), you would need to determine the value of this measure before and after the training programme. This would allow you to gauge any changes in what you are measuring. This is referred to as a pre-test post-test research design, measuring something before and after a treatment (training programme) to see if it has had an effect. The actual parameter you intend to measure (the **dependent variable**) should be clearly stated. It is called this because it depends on something. In the above example, flexibility is the dependant variable – it depends on the training your subjects have done. Wherever there is a dependent variable there will be an **independent variable**; this is what you manipulate or change. In the flexibility example, the independent variable could be the type, amount or length of training undertaken. You can have more than one dependant variable and more than one independent variable.

Resources and equipment will be determined by what you are measuring. The key concern here is availability of equipment and having the necessary skills to use such equipment. Adequate planning should prevent these factors becoming a problem.

Besides how to measure variables, careful thought needs to be given to the **recording of data**. It could be that you have to devise a score sheet or record sheet on which to write data. You may be intending to use a computer-based system to store the results directly. Is there enough space on the system? Do you need portable storage? What about backing up the data?

Although at the planning stage you do not know what results you will get, you can outline how you intend to present them. If there are any calculations on your data, what will they be and why are they necessary? What tables and graphs do you hope to produce? How are you going to analyse your results? Which **statistical tests** could you use on your data?

Sources of information

Once the topic of research has been decided, the next consideration is obtaining information about the topic. The first part of any research project will consist of reporting what is already known about the subject area (this will form the literature review). The evidence gathered will either be from a primary source or a secondary source. **Primary data** or information is that which is reported directly by the author who measured or observed it. **Secondary data** is reported from the original primary source by another author. If you include information from a secondary source you are trusting that the information has been recorded and analysed correctly.

Libraries

The majority of information for a research project will be obtained using some form of library information system. All libraries have a method of cataloguing their information, and contain a vast array of resources and referenced information, from books, journals and conference reports to newspapers, videos and CD-ROMs. All this information needs to be made easy to access by a researcher, hence the use of the library information system. The system will be computerised (in most cases) and will record all sources of information (books, journals, etc.) using a standard reference. The most common method of cataloguing information is by the authors that wrote or recorded it. If have a particular author in mind, you enter their name (or names) into the system and it will report all books by these authors in the library. These systems usually have more than one way of reporting each item, so as well as being listed by author, items would be listed by title. 'Author/title' is another method used. This is useful if you already know what you are looking for and just want to locate it in the library. 'Author/keyword' can be useful if you want to limit the search to a certain area by a particular author. To widen the search to include any author you could do a 'keyword' search (e.g. injuries). To widen the search still further the system may have a 'subject' search, which will include all works in a subject area (sports therapy, for example). In addition, all items in a library are given a classification number to identify them from any other work. The classification number is based on the subject area (and the lead author in some cases). Books, journals, etc. are located on shelves in a library based on their classification number, so all books with a similar number will be located together.

There are searchable databases that have been created that contain information in different areas. These can also be accessed via some libraries. 'SPORTSDiscus' is an example. It is an international database of documentation in the area of sport and exercise science dating from 1949. It can be accessed via the internet, although subscription is required.

The internet

A more recent source of information is the internet. Information contained on the internet should be used with caution. Books, journals and other sources of published information have been reviewed to ensure that the information is reliable and accurate; this is not always the case with the internet. Information can be posted on a website by anybody who wants to do so. It is not reviewed or checked in any way. However, the internet does contain some useful and interesting sites and websites are starting to appear that do have peer-reviewed papers on them. One good use of the internet is obtaining information that would otherwise have to be sent for by post. For example, you might want to obtain some information from the American College of Sport Medicine (ACSM) and rather than having to write to them or send off for some information, it may be found on their website. Similarly, you might need the medal table from the Barcelona Olympics, or possibly the mission statement of Sport England. For this type of information, the internet is ideal.

Whatever the source of the information, it is important that it is reliable and valid. Reliable information is information that can be backed up. It is evidence that is reproducible. If it is valid, it is an accurate and true account of something. In sport and exercise science, it is essential that any information, evidence or research that can be reproduced is accurate.

STUDENT ACTIVITY

Internet sites
Use the internet to investigate selected topics. The following internet sites are good starting points for general information.

www.sportscoachuk.org – Sports Coach UK (Formerly NCF).

www.aafla.org – Amateur Athletic Federation of Los Angeles. Includes publications, research reports and sports library.

www.culture.gov.uk/sport – Government site including policy documents and research information on sport and media.

Ethical and legal issues

When reporting information or research, be it your own or from another author, confidentiality is vital. Individuals should not be referred to directly. Initials or numbers can be used to identify people if necessary. Researchers should adhere to the 1998 Data Protection Act.

Special consideration is also needed in sport and exercise because research often involves humans as subjects. Care needs to be taken when designing experiments so that any treatments administered are ethical. For example, asking people to undergo training or a diet that may have negative effects could be unethical. A great deal of thought therefore needs to go into designing a research project. Even when research has been approved, the health and safety of subjects is paramount. The American College of Sport Medicine suggested that researchers should adhere to the Declaration of Helsinki, which gives code of practice for measurements in humans.

Research design

Type of design

The idea of research is to find out something that has not previously been known; to investigate something. This is often done by comparing things, such as different training programmes, different diets, different schools or different types of exercise. The training, the diet, or whatever, is termed the treatment (or the experimental condition). Data or evidence can be collected either quantitatively or qualitatively. Quantitative data is recorded using numbers, such as weight, energy expenditure and heart rate. Qualitative data is someone's opinion or what they can remember, usually obtained by asking questions (via an interview or questionnaire).

In **quantitative** research, the most common research design is a pre-test post-test design. In a pre-test post-test design something is measured (e.g. body mass), then the subject undergoes a treatment (e.g. a weight-training programme) and then the subject is re-measured (e.g. body mass is recorded again). Any difference in the pre-test and post-test results is said to be due to the treatment. Often a control group (a group that has no treatment) is used to ensure that any changes in the post-test result are due to the treatment and not any other factors (differences over time, diet, other training subjects might be doing).

Qualitative research can also involve the pre-test post-test design. It could measure, for example, the attitudes to exercise of a group of people before and after taking part in an exercise programme. This could easily be done using a questionnaire. Another method of investigation used in qualitative research is the comparative study. This involves obtaining some information (e.g. amount of exercise undertaken by college students) and comparing it with something else (e.g. amount of exercise undertaken by non-students of the same age).

Whichever type of research design you decide upon, assuming the research involves people, you will need a group (or groups) of people to test. The group you choose is called the sample. The sample will be part of the population you

are investigating. In the case of the amount of exercise undertaken by college students, it would not be practical to question all the students, so you just examine a sample. The sample you use should not be biased in any way (e.g. not all the same age, or all from one course, unless you specifically state 18-year-old college students, for example). Realistically, your sample will be made up of volunteers or those who are available at the time; however, bias should be eliminated where possible. If the sample is biased, this will limit the conclusions you can draw from your results.

Data collection method

Having determined the type of research design, it is then necessary to establish the method of data collection. In some cases this will be governed by the actual investigation you are doing. You may be using specialist apparatus (e.g. a heart rate monitor, a sphygmomanometer) or simple equipment (e.g. a stopwatch, a ruler) to record data in the form of numbers. Your major consideration will be the truthfulness or exactness of the data. **Accuracy** and **precision** are two measurement issues, and with appropriate equipment and skilled technique, data should be accurate and precise. The data can only be as precise as the measuring system allows. If a set of weighing scales only has kilogram increments, you can only record mass in whole units (i.e. 75 kg, not 75.5 kg). The accuracy of the data relates to how close your measurement is to what you actually intend to measure. For example, if somebody's mass is 68.4 kg and a set of weighing scales records 68 kg, these would be accurate. However, if a second set of scales records 65 kg, they would be less accurate. Checking that equipment is calibrated correctly will help ensure accuracy.

Having recorded the data, it will be necessary to comment on its validity and reliability. **Validity** is a measure of whether the actual test measures precisely what you set out to quantify. Imagine you wish to compare the strength of a group of people who have taken part in a number of different weight-training programmes. One of the main problems you have to address is how to measure strength. You could choose to measure it via a one repetition lift of a certain exercise (e.g. bench press), but you would then have to establish this exercise as a valid measure of strength. A maximal bench press measures how much you can lift (via the bench press) in one go, it does not measure strength; however, you might wish to infer strength from it.

The second issue, having measured the correct value, is whether you could do the same again. **Reproducible data** is said to be reliable, and it is essential that your data is **reliable**. Research has to be repeatable so that you (and others) can say that your findings were not just due to luck or chance, or caused by some extraneous factors (the weather, the time of day, etc.). Reliability is relatively easy to account for when designing research as you can make repeat measurements. You could even use different people to record the same thing (as in judging boxing and gymnastics) – this is called objectivity as opposed to reliability.

Not all research involves collecting and analysing numbers. Some research requires information on a person's behaviour or attitude towards something. This is common in qualitative research. Questionnaires, interviews and observations are used to gather evidence and, although the data or information is in a different format to quantitative research, the question of truthfulness or exactness is just as important. Is the information you obtain valid? If you set out to measure anxiety levels and do so using a questionnaire, are the answers you receive accurate? Does your questionnaire actually measure anxiety? Do people tell the truth? All these issues need addressing. What about reliability? If you repeated your questionnaire in similar situations, would you obtain similar results? The design of the questionnaire, the type of questions and the way they are worded are all things that can affect the validity and reliability of your results.

REVISION *QUESTIONS*

1) What is a hypothesis?
2) What limits the information you can obtain from the internet?
3) Outline the ethical issues in using humans as subjects.

STUDENT ACTIVITY

Action plan

Devise an action plan for a project. Make sure the plan has a clearly testable objective (something you can measure). As well as a brief introduction, you should also include the resources you will need and your research design (how you aim to test your objective). Outline how you will record and analyse data. Give a realistic timetable for your plan.

Present the plan to your peers, justifying your research methods, and defend it from questioning.

IMPLEMEN-TING THE PROJECT

Pilot test

Research can be time consuming, testing can take several months and if things go wrong you could be left with little time in which to repeat or change things. This is why a pilot test or **pilot study** is a good idea. Carry out tests on a couple of people first, not the same ones you are going to use in your main project. This should help highlight potential problems. If you are asking subjects to fill in a questionnaire, trying it out on a few people first will allow you to modify it and make improvements. The time spent doing a pilot test could save hours of wasted testing at a later date. The pilot study may highlight minor changes that need to be made to your testing, or skills or procedures that have to be practised to make measurement more reliably.

Recording results

A clear data sheet can save both time and confusion when recording results. Imagine you have designed a questionnaire to investigate at the amount of sport and exercise undertaken by college students. Once all the completed questionnaires have been returned, you need to record all the results in a clear and effective format. Putting them in one table will allow you to see all the results together and will be better for subsequent analysis. In the example below (Figure 2.1) each row represents one question from the questionnaire. Columns

FIGURE 2.1 Data sheet used to record information obtained via a questionnaire

Question	Value entered			
	subject 1	subject 2	subject 3	subject 4
GENDER	m	f	f	m
AGE	19	21	18	18
COURSE	sport	science	language	IT
WORK	no	yes	yes	yes
EXERCISE	run	swim	run	cycle
AMOUNT (E)	10	3	5	8
SPORT	volleyball	none	tennis	rugby
AMOUNT (S)	3	0	2	2

are used to record each subject's response. The first couple of questions are obvious, asking the subject's gender and age. After that the questions might have been, what course they are on, whether they have a part time job, what their main form of exercise is, how many hours a week they take part in it, and so on.

Displaying data

When you are clear on the type and amount of data you will have, you can think about how best to display it. Large amounts of **raw data** are not needed. Too much information can be difficult to view. Therefore, data is best summarised in tables or graphical form. The key to working out what to put in is to think what it shows. If a table or graph shows a trend, a difference, or noteworthy values then include it. If it merely replicates other data, consider leaving it out.

Tables and figures

Tables and figures are excellent methods of presenting information in a clear, concise and orderly manner. The following rules apply to the preparation and presentation of tables and figures.

- ✪ Graphs and illustrations (which include photographs, diagrams, and drawings) are referred to collectively as figures and are labelled as such.

- ✪ Tables and figures should be placed in the body of the text near the material referring to them.

- ✪ Every table and figure should have some reference in the text. Tables and figures are numbered consecutively (e.g. 1, 2, 3 or 1.1, 1.2). See table below.

- ✪ The table number and title are written above the table (see Table 2.1). The figure number and title can be written above or below the figure (see Figure 2.1).

Table 2.1 Anthropometric data

Subject	Height (cm)	Body Mass (kg)	BMI
1	168.0	65.0	23.0
2	168.0	48.0	17.0
3	165.5	55.0	20.8
4	163.0	75.0	20.2
5	165.0	51.9	19.1
6	168.0	51.0	18.1
7	156.0	57.0	23.4
Mean	164.8	57.6	20.2

Titles of tables and figures should be brief and accurately descriptive. To make reading easy, figures and tables should be placed so that they can be viewed without turning the page. When placed in an appendix, tables and figures should be able to stand alone (i.e. not need supporting text).

Tables should be concise and easy to read. Do not include too much material in one table. Two or three short tables can be used if necessary. Do not leave blanks in a table as this indicates that data has been left out. If no measurement was taken or recorded, use a dash. Units are placed under or besides the variables name and are enclosed in brackets. If columns are long they can be broken into smaller groups.

Graphs

The following information applies to the preparation and presentation of graphs.

✪ The graph should appear so that it is read in the same manner as a page of text.

✪ It does not have to take up the whole page. A key can be placed inside the limits of the graph itself, for example, if more than one line appears on the same graph.

✪ Label axes with appropriate quantity measured and include units.

✪ Choose easy-to-read units, for example multiples of 1, 2, 5 or 10. Too many units clutter the graph.

✪ Small tick marks can be used on the axis to help identify where the scale divisions occur.

✪ If units do not start at zero, an interrupted axis may be used.

✪ When labelling scale divisions, numbers less than one always have a zero to the left of the decimal point.

✪ Be realistic with the use of numbers (too many decimal places are meaningless).

✪ Use symbols to indicate data point. Symbols should not be used for calculated or predicted data; the use of a symbol suggests that the data was actually measured.

✪ Provide a legend (key) for symbols if more than one is used on a graph.

In addition to tables and figures, it maybe necessary to include an equation in the main text. Centre equations in the middle of the text and number them consecutively with the number enclosed in brackets flush to the right-hand margin:

$$E = mc^2$$

(1)

REVISION
QUESTIONS

1) What are the important considerations when displaying tables?

2) How should graphs be presented?

INTERPRETING THE OUTCOMES

Describing results

Statistics are used to help explain numbers. At the simplest level, statistics can be used to describe data. With a large group of numbers (the height of twenty people, for example) one number can be used to represent all the values. This number is the **average**. Rather than talk about all the values, you can just discuss the average height. The average is a measure of what is termed the central tendency, the middle (or majority) value that the numbers group around. The mean (the sum of the values divided by the number of values) is one type of average.

Central tendency is only one type of statistic that is regularly used to describe results. **Dispersion** is another common descriptive statistic. It can be seen as the opposite of central tendency – rather than reporting the middle or most frequent values, it is a measure of how spread out the scores are, or the difference in the scores. One measure of dispersion is the range, which is the difference between the highest and lowest values in a group. Using the height example, if the tallest person was 1.98 m and the shortest 1.54 m, the range would be 0.44 m.

A further descriptive measure that is used in statistics is the **distribution** of the data. This is determined by looking at the frequency of all the values. Normally, you would expect to find most of the values in the middle of the data. For example, most people are about average height. There are fewer values towards the extremes. The higher and lower values occur less frequently. Data that follows this pattern is termed normally distributed data. If displayed in a frequency graph (e.g. a histogram) the data will look bell shaped, peaking in the middle.

Analysing results

Besides describing results, statistics can be used to analyse results to allow conclusions to be drawn. These are called inferential statistics. They allow you to make factual statements about your results. Consider an investigation to see if a given training programme lowered the resting heart rate of a group of individuals. Your results might show that the average resting heart rate of the training group is 58 bpm (beats per minute), while that of a control group (a group of subjects who did no training) is 61 bpm. There is a difference of 3 bpm, but is this meaningful or is the difference just due to chance? A statistical difference test (e.g. t-test – see Chapter 9) would be able to establish if the difference in the values was significant, i.e. large enough to mean something.

Drawing conclusions

The final part of a research project is to draw the whole process together. When discussing the results, you should attempt to cover three main areas. Initially, in conjunction with the statistical analysis, **evaluate** the results. What happens to the values you are measuring? Do they go up, down, stay the same or fluctuate? Are there any differences, similarities or relationships? Are your values in line with what you would expect, based on previous evidence? After the analysis, **be critical** of your results. Are your results valid? Do they display reliability and objectivity? What errors did your investigation contain and how did this affect your results? What may limit any conclusions you aim to make? Finally, what are the **implications** of your results? What have you found out and what does it mean? To recap, be analytical, be critical and make clear conclusions.

REPORTING THE PROJECT

Layout

The project will be reported in writing. The general structure of a written project is given below.

1	Abstract	**6**	Results
2	Preliminary pages	**7**	Discussion
3	Introduction	**8**	Conclusion
4	Literature review	**9**	References
5	Method	**10**	Appendix

1   The **abstract** is so called because it is abstracted from all sections of the report. It is a summary of the entire project. The abstract must be understandable independently of the main body of the report. Normally in the region of 250 words, it will comprise information on the aims, research design, results and overall conclusions. This summary of the research appears as the first page of the report; however, it is usually written last.

2   **Preliminary pages** will contain acknowledgements. This is the part of the project where you can write something personal. Extend thanks to whomever may have helped you during the project. It should certainly include thanks to the supervisor for support and guidance, but there might be others who deserve a mention. These pages will also include a contents page, and possibly a list of figures and a list of tables. The contents page should include the titles of the chapters and of the main sections within the chapters, together with the number of the page on which each begins.

3   The function of the **introduction** is to outline the area of research. It should address the question of why you are doing the project. The introduction prepares the reader to receive what the writer intends to present. Reports attempt to make information and ideas clear and convincing. The introduction should make clear the precise subject to be considered. It needs to be interesting, to make the reader want to find out more. The end of the introduction should be the aim of the research.

4   The **literature review** (or review of literature) is a comprehensive analysis of the area of research. It should contain information on all aspects of the project. Any key terms should be defined. It is important to be critical of previous research and explain why your research is needed and the benefits it will provide for athletes, coaches and physical educators. Show how your research builds on prior knowledge by presenting and evaluating what is already known about your research problem. The reader should understand why the problem was researched and why the study represents a contribution to existing knowledge. The end of the review should be the hypotheses that you aim to test.

5   The **method** should be simple to write, as it explains what you did. It is often divided into subsections. The first part details the number of subjects and if and how they were placed in groups. The average age, height, weight, etc. of the subjects is also frequently reported. This gives a good general description of the groups you are investigating. This section can be followed by the research design (i.e. what you intend to do). Next would be the apparatus or equipment needed to perform the project. Finally, you would report the procedures you undertook. A precise record of the procedures used is vital in establishing the validity of the results. Give enough information for your readers to be able to reproduce the experiments.

6   The **results** will consist of the data collected for the project. They should be presented as concisely and clearly as possible, and should provide the summary details about what you found, rather than an exhaustive listing of every possible analysis and every data point. Results will be summarised using descriptive statistics (raw data can go in the appendix). Trends in the data ought to be reported (e.g. heart rate increases with time). Tables and graphs are the most appropriate method of presenting the results, but these should be supported with text to describe and explain them. Do not repeat in words what is already apparent from examination of the tables and figures. Statistical analysis (inferential statistics) is also recorded here. Where calculations are performed in analysing data, a sample calculation is helpful to explain the analysis. This can be included in the main text or in an appendix. Although you are familiar with the work, others are not. Avoid taking too much for granted. Since many symbols have different meanings in various fields of science, define all symbols used in a report, including those in figures and tables. No symbol may be used for more than one concept, and usage of symbols and units must be consistent throughout the text, appendixes, tables and figures. Define acronyms, abbreviations and symbols at their first occurrence in the main text (e.g. American College of Sports Medicine (ACSM)).

In any report concerned with numerical values, the accuracy, precision and reproducibility of the data presented must be clearly stated. Discrepancies within the data should be explained. **Accuracy** usually denotes the absolute correctness of the information; **precision** generally denotes the extent to which a result is free from random accidental errors. A result can be very precise (i.e. all measurements agree), but also inaccurate because of inherent errors in the measurements. **Reproducibility** denotes the agreement between values. Poor reproducibility may be the result of either the precision or the accuracy.

7   The **discussion of results** is one of the most important parts of a research report. The discussion is a critical analysis of the results. But discuss the results; do not merely recapitulate them. First, the discussion should summarise your findings in words. This should then be related back to the aim of you project (Were your hypotheses correct or not?). Next, refer your results back to previous research. Then consider the limitations of your project, what went wrong and why. Include a discussion of possible

errors involved in measurements. Explain how the project could be improved. After this, discuss the implications of your findings (Of what use is the information you have found?). Finally, give suggestions for future research. This is an important part of the research process, to evaluate what you have done at the end of the project. End the discussion with a short summary explaining the significance of your work.

8 The **conclusion**, sometimes contained at the end of the discussion section, is a clear statement of your main findings. These should relate directly to your aims and hypotheses. The conclusion should not use tables, figures, references and appendixes. It simply restates the major findings of the investigation. All of the material presented must have appeared in the main body of the report. If more than one conclusion is drawn, present them in the order of importance.

9 The **reference section** is a list of the references used in the main body of the text. Referencing is the process of acknowledging other people whose ideas and findings you have used in your work. This involves inserting citations in your text to indicate others' work and then including appropriate details at the end of the report. It is important that all work and ideas that are not your own, including direct quotations, are correctly referenced. The Harvard system of referencing is commonly used in sport and exercise science academic work.

In the Harvard System, you report the reference by including in brackets after the reference the author who is the source of the idea, followed by the year of publication. The full title of the work is then given in the reference section. If work is transferred into your own words, this is termed paraphrasing and quotation marks are not used. If a direct quote is used, then single quotation marks are used to indicate this. Quotations should be kept to a minimum.

In the text, the reference would appear as follows: 'Recovery for athletes is essential (Child, 1999)'. If you are referencing more than one piece of work, you can refer to them all: 'The stresses imposed by training can be harmful (Child, 1999; Wallace, 1989; Watt, 2001)'. If more than one author was involved in the work you would reference them all: (Ball, Brees, Chance and Stokes 1988). Subsequently you can refer to the first author followed by *et al*. This is only the case if there are more than two people involved, for example, 'Ball *et al*. (1989) have shown that...'. If you encounter authors with the same surname, use initials to distinguish them: 'A report (Jones, N., 1986) has indicated...'. If you need to reference more than one piece of work for the same year use letters to indicate different references: 'Thomas (1996a, 1996b) showed that...'.

Sometimes it may be necessary to refer to letters, e-mails or conversations; these are called personal communications. They would be referenced as follows: 'In a telephone conversation on 10th August 2001, Mr J. A. Gilbert pointed out that...' or 'Mr D. Goodchild's letter dated 1st May 1998 claimed that...'.

You may need to refer to work with no author's name, for example:

'A recent report by the American College of Sports Medicine (2001) states...' or 'the *Teesside Times* (31st August 2002, p.4) reported that…'.

There are guidelines for entries in the list of references, depending on what you are referring to. Books are referenced:

Thomas, J. R. and Nelson, J. K. (2001) *Research Methods in Physical Activity*. 4th edition. Illinois: Human Kinetics

Hardy, L., Jones, G. and Gould, D. (1996) *Understanding Psychological Preparation for Sport: Theory and Practice of Elite Performers*. Chichester: John Wiley & Sons Ltd.

Journals and periodicals are referenced:

Morris, T. (2000) Psychological characteristics and talent identification in soccer. *Journal of Sports Sciences*, **18**, pp. 715–26.

Online (electronic) material is a little different, as it has not been published in the traditional way. Sometimes the date it was posted on the internet is given. Whether it is or not, the date you accessed it should be given. Therefore, an online reference would appear as follows:

Sugarman, K. (1998). Peak performance [Online]. http://www.psywww.com/sports/peak.htm [accessed August 31st 2002].

10 After the reference section is the **appendix**. This is where you can include any information that does not fit into the rest of the project. Commonly it contains such things as raw data (which would just fill up the results section), technical specifications of equipment and data collection sheets. Each appendix should be referred to at some point in the main body of the report. Appendixes should be labelled using capital letters (example: Appendix A). If you were to refer to the appendix in the body of your report you would do so as follows: 'Appendix A shows that…'. If you are not referring to the appendix in the sentence, but would like to support a claim using an appendix, use parentheses (round brackets) around the appendix you are referring to. For example, 'Crowd attendances are on the increase (see Appendix A)'.

Presentation

When writing the project, there are several guidelines that you should adhere to.

✪ The project should be **written in the third person** – avoid using 'I' and 'we'; for example, 'heart rate was recorded every 30 seconds' is better than 'I recorded heart rate every 30 seconds'.

✪ Use the past tense. That is, record what was done (e.g. heart rate was measured), the results that were found (e.g. average heart rate was 167 bpm) rather than 'will be' and 'is'.

✪ The style of writing should be scientific, so the report will be factual and subjective comments should be avoided. Simple, clear and unambiguous language should be used. Remember, keep it simple. Long-winded sentences should be avoided. Jargon and technical terms should be explained where they first occur (if necessary an index of special terms can be included in the report as an appendix).

- ✪ Make sure you **write in sentences** and **check for spelling errors** (these are unsatisfactory and produce a bad impression).

- ✪ Proof-read the whole thing before you hand it in to be marked. Better still, get somebody else to proof-read it. Remember, the marker will scrutinise it in some detail, so it is important that you have done so and made corrections.

- ✪ There is no optimal length for a paragraph, but it should contain related material. For this reason **paragraphs** might be quite long or very short. In general, a mixture of paragraph lengths produces a pleasing appearance. Note that paragraphs usually consist of at least two sentences.

- ✪ **Headings** serve two purposes: they act as a guide to readers to assist them to find their way around the report, and they act as a framework within which the author can construct the report. However, readers often ignore headings, so in general they should not be made part of the text but as far as possible be treated as separate entities.

- ✪ If source material is included in the main text in the form of **quotations** it should be placed in quotation marks (if short) or indented from the left margin (if long). Note that the actual words used must be exactly reproduced even down to grammatical errors. Quotations from published material must not be too long. Plagiarism is passing off the ideas of others as your own. You must not do it. Any significant ideas which are not your own must be attributed.

- ✪ **Numbering** of the pages of the report should be of two types. Beginning with the first page of the introduction each page should be numbered in the bottom margin using Arabic numerals (1, 2, 3, 4). Any numbering of preliminary pages should use Roman numerals (i, ii, iii, iv), again in the bottom margin. However, the title page is never numbered.

- ✪ If there is any doubt about the meaning of an abbreviation, it should be spelt out at the point where it is first used. Do not assume that your audience is familiar with all the abbreviations even within the specialised area of your project. As a general rule, capital letters in abbreviations are not followed by a full stop. Thus, use BASES for the British Association of Sport and Exercise Sciences. Be careful in the use of i.e. and e.g. – both abbreviations come from Latin; i.e. is short for *id est*, which means 'that is', whereas e.g. is short for *exempli gratia*, which translates as 'for the sake of example'. Do not use an apostrophe to indicate missing letters, for example, *don't* should be written *do not* and *it's* as *it is*.

Often you will be asked to make a short **presentation** of your research. Your presentation may include a slide show, posters, video, illustrations and handouts. For this to be successful, preparation is vital. You will not have time to talk about the entire project, so it is important that you pick out the most relevant parts. Begin with an introduction, including your topic and the names of the presenters. Next, state what it is you tested, what the research question was. You can then give a brief outline of the area, remembering to define any key terms. This introduction should include why you chose the project, why and to whom it will be beneficial and what is already known in this area. Next, you can give a summary of the method. After this, present the results, which will consist mainly of graphs and tables. Visually, graphs are far easier to analyse so, if possible, use them in preference to a table. Your data and resulting discussion of it will be the major part of the presentation. In discussing the results, talk about what you found and why; examine the limitations of your study and its implications. Finish the presentation with an overall conclusion relating back to your original aims. It is a good idea to allow time at the end of your presentation to answer questions on your research.

When giving a visual presentation, remember that each slide should contain main points, not the entire text of your presentation. You should use the points for elaboration and not clutter each slide. Font size should be large and the style should be consistent throughout the slide show. Font colour should contrast with the background colour. Use correct grammar, spelling, punctuation, and capitalization. Include a reference slide. Rehearse your seminar; it is very easy to misjudge timing unless you have had a full-scale rehearsal. Avoid simply reading out information. You may well rely on a script, but remember, one task is to maintain the interest of the audience. Your own experience will tell you that listening to someone reading is not very exciting. Diagrams tend to hold interest better than text. Avoid speaking too quickly and maintain eye contact with people in all parts of the room.

REVISION QUESTIONS

1) What sections should a research report contain?
2) Outline what each of these sections should contain.
3) Explain the Harvard system of referencing.

STUDENT ACTIVITY

Presentation

Present some research to the rest of the class. Concentrate on two main areas: the reason for the research, and the results and how they were obtained.

SUGGESTED FURTHER READING

Thomas, J. R. and Nelson, J. K. (2001) *Research Methods in Physical Activity*. 4th edition. Illinois: Human Kinetics

Williams, C. A. and James, D. V. B. (2001) *Science for Exercise and Sport*. London: E & FN Spon

SPORT AND EXERCISE PSYCHOLOGY

Historically, sport science has focussed on how to improve the physical performances of sportspeople. Exercise physiology and biomechanics have developed a wealth of information in this area and it continues to include new, exciting research. New, improved training techniques have helped to push back the sporting barriers.

At the highest level, individuals will have similar physiological traits and fitness levels. Thus, they need to gain something extra to ensure that they will reach the very top, or win the gold medal rather than just reach the final.

Psychology (or study of (ology) the human mind (psyche)) can give athletes the mental edge over their rivals. Mental preparation by 'mental coaches' has become as crucial in modern sport as physical preparation. The recent work of John Syer in football, Stephen Bull with the England cricket team, Richard Cox with British bobsleigh teams and Dave Collins with British international weightlifters has shown the value of psychologically preparing athletes.

Many athletes and coaches will use psychological means to give their team an advantage or to minimise their disadvantage. In our own way we are all 'amateur' psychologists, as we discuss why we won or lost, and why people behave on the sports field in a certain manner. We rarely discuss the fitness or physical shape of players – usually we ask whether the team is motivated enough, or will be able to hold their nerve to win.

This chapter examines:

✪   the key factors of an individual's personality and motivation, and the effect these have on performance

✪   how the environments in which sport takes place will affect the performance of the team or individual

✪   the role of psychologists and the skills they use to influence performance.

PERSONALITY

Research in sport psychology has attempted to ask the following questions:

- ✪ Can sporting excellence be predicted by assessing personality?

- ✪ Are certain personality types attracted to certain sports?

- ✪ Does sport change a performer's personality?

From a non-scientific viewpoint the answer to all of these questions would appear to be 'yes'. However, before addressing these issues, we need to examine what is meant by the term 'personality', how personality can be tested and the different viewpoints psychologists take on personality and its development.

Credulous versus sceptical

Psychologists researching personality and its relationship to sporting performance fall into two categories: first, the credulous group, who believe that personality can be assessed and results can be used to make predictions about an individual's chances of success. Secondly, the sceptical group, who believe that personality research is limited in predicting the chances of sporting success.

Definitions

Personality

There are a range of definitions of **personality**, each with their merits and drawbacks. Kluckhorn and Murray (1949) say: '*each individual is like all other men, like some other men, like no other men*'.

This is a good starting point as it suggests we all have traits and behaviours that we share with other people, but we also have some particular to ourselves. However, it does lack depth of information; as does Cattell's (1965) attempt to define personality: '*that which tells what a man will do when placed in a given situation*'.

This suggests that if we know an individual's personality, we can predict behaviour. However, human beings tend to be less than predictable and can act out of character, depending upon the situation. Their behaviours may also be affected by their mood, fatigue or emotions.

Hans Eysenck (1960) sought to address these limitations with his definition:

the more or less stable and enduring organisation of an individual's character, temperament, intellect and physique which determines their unique adjustment to the environment.

Eysenck's statement that personality is more or less stable allows the human element to enter the equation and explain the unpredictable. He also makes the important point that personality is 'unique'. We may have behaviours in common with other people, but, ultimately every person has a set of characteristics unique to themselves.

STUDENT ACTIVITY

Choose one of the following groups of sports people and discuss in pairs what personality characteristics each person has, based on your observations of their behaviours and interviews with them.

✪ Are there personality characteristics they have in common?
✪ Are these characteristics important in their sport?
✪ Can these characteristics explain their success?

Football
Roy Keane
Sol Campbell
Michael Owen
Rio Ferdinand
Ryan Giggs

Golf
Colin Montgomery
Tiger Woods
Sergio Garcia
David Duval
Darren Clarke

Athletics
Paula Radcliffe
Iwan Thomas
Denise Lewis
Ashia Hansen
Johnathon Edwards

Tennis
Andre Agassi
Tim Henman
Venus Williams
Pete Sampras
Martina Hingis

Rugby Union
Jason Robinson
Keith Wood
Martin Johnson
Robert Howley
Jonny Wilkinson

By giving labels to a person's character and behaviour in the activity, you have started to assess personality. By observing sports people we are using a **behavioural** approach, i.e. assessing what they are like by assessing their responses to various situations. In reality, our observations may be unreliable because we only see sports people in one environment, and although we see them interviewed as well, we do not know what they are truly like. A **cognitive** psychologist believes we need to understand an individual's thoughts and emotions as well as watching their behaviour. This we cannot do without the use of a questionnaire or an interview.

THEORIES OF PER-SONALITY

Hollander's view of personality

Hollander addresses the issues discussed previously and shows how personality can only be understood by combining behaviourist and cognitive methods of assessment.

Hollander sees personality as being structured at three levels, as shown in Figure 3.1.

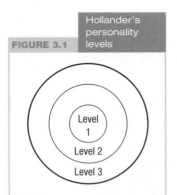

Hollander's personality levels

FIGURE 3.1

⭐ **Level 1 – The psychological core** is the deepest component of personality and is at its centre. It includes an individual's beliefs, attitudes, values and feelings of self-worth. It is 'the real you' and, as a result, it is relatively permanent and seen by few people. You can only assess a person's psychological core by seeing them in a wide range of situations, and understanding their thoughts and emotions. Some people are very good at hiding their psychological core, while others are happy to reveal it.

⭐ **Level 2 – Typical responses** are how we usually respond to situations and adapt to our environment. It is seen as the relatively consistent way we behave. If we have to describe our own or another's personality we would usually give labels to their typical responses. For example:

▶ Tiger Woods – calm, laid back, even tempered
▶ Roy Keane – aggressive, competitive, volatile
▶ Paul Gascoigne – extroverted, happy-go-lucky, sociable.

Our typical responses are good indicators of our psychological core, but, they can be affected by the social environment. A person who is very outgoing and sociable with his rugby-playing friends may become more reserved at a party with people he does not know.

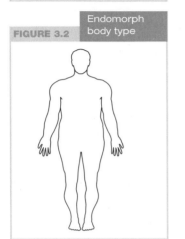

Endomorph body type

FIGURE 3.2

⭐ **Level 3 – Role related behaviours** are the shallowest level of our personality, and this level shows how we change our behaviours to adapt to the situation we are in. For example, throughout the day we may play the roles of sports person, student, employee, friend, son/daughter, coach, etc. In order to survive we need to adapt our personalities, as it would not be appropriate to behave on the sports field in the same manner as when studying in class. We need to modify our personalities to suit the situation. Some people play roles to hide their psychological core, while others are more open and let us see their true feelings. To illustrate this, observe the difference between Goran Ivanisevic's reaction to winning Wimbledon in 2001, compared with the more muted celebrations of Pete Sampras in recent years.

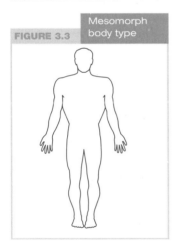

Mesomorph body type

FIGURE 3.3

Sheldon's (1942) constitutional theory

One of the first attempts at a theory of personality was Sheldon's constitutional or body-type theory. He tried to relate personality to **somatotypes** (Figure 3.2–3.4 and Table 3.1).

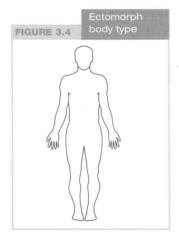

Ectomorph body type

FIGURE 3.4

Table 3.1 Body types and personality

Body type	Description	Personality type
Endomorph	Predominantly fat or pear shaped	Sociable, friendly, fun loving
Mesomorph	Predominantly muscular	Outgoing, confident, risk taking, adventure loving
Ectomorph	Predominantly lean or linear	Tense, shy, introverted, socially inhibited

This theory has gathered some 'folklore' validity in that we use first impressions to make assumptions about people's personalities. We use physique, clothing, hairstyles, piercing/tattoos and other visual information to assess what a person will be like and how they will behave.

In sport we see certain body types attracted to certain sports, and to be successful in these sports they need to exhibit certain behaviours, and thus we make generalisations about the personalities of these sports people.

For example, we have long-distance runners or cyclists who are predominantly ectomorphic, and we see them as being introverted and shy (traits needed because many hours of training are spent alone). We have rugby players and footballers who are predominantly mesomorphic and tend to be extroverted and group centred (traits needed in order to work together with team mates).

Even within a sport we can see individual differences. In track and field athletics the sprinters tend to be mesomorphs, and the middle to long-distance runners tend to be ectomorphs. It is easy to see personality differences between Maurice Green, Dennis Mitchell, Linford Christie and Haile Gabreselassie, Paula Radcliffe and Liz McColgan.

Physique may play a part in personality and behaviour, but people should not be **sterotyped**. It should not be assumed that people of certain statures will behave in certain ways, and physique cannot be used to assess success in sport. Above all it cannot be used to assess individual differences between people, and ignores the uniqueness of each person.

Trait theory

Trait or factor theory is based on the belief that personality is the sum of several traits that cause an individual to behave in a certain manner. Traits can be seen as being **enduring** and consistent behaviours across a range of situations. They could be compared to the 'typical behaviours' described in Hollander's theory. Trait theorists such as Cattell and Eysenck believed that traits could be assessed through the use of questionnaires, and these traits could then be used to predict how a person would behave in any given situation.

Eysenck's Personality Inventory (1965)

Hans Eysenck used the following questionnaire to assess personality through two dimensions: introversion/extroversion and stable/unstable. He called these 'types', and then showed the traits each type would exhibit.

STUDENT ACTIVITY

These questions relate to how you behave, feel and act. Answer each one yes or no. The answer should reflect how you would usually act or feel, and they should be answered quickly to reflect your first reaction. Be sure to answer all questions.

	Yes	No
1 Do you often long for excitement?		
2 Do you often need understanding friends to cheer you up?		
3 Do you stop and think things over before doing anything?		
4 If you say you will do something, do you always keep your promise, no matter how inconvenient it may be to do so?		
5 Do your moods go up and down?		
6 Would you do almost anything for a dare?		
7 Do you suddenly feel shy when you want to talk to an attractive stranger?		
8 Once in a while do you lose your temper and become angry?		
9 Generally, you prefer reading to meeting people?		
10 Are your feelings rather easily hurt?		
11 Do you occasionally have thoughts and ideas that you would not like other people to know about?		
12 Do you prefer to have a few but special friends?		
13 Do you daydream a lot?		
14 Are all your habits good and desirable ones?		
15 Can you usually let yourself go and enjoy yourself at a lively party?		
16 Would you call yourself tense or highly strung?		
17 Are you mostly quiet when you are with other people?		

	Yes	No
18 Do you sometimes gossip?		
19 Do ideas run through your head so that you cannot sleep?		
20 Do you like the kind of work that you need to pay close attention to?		
21 Do you get attacks of shaking or trembling?		
22 Would you always declare everything at customs, even if you knew you would never be found out?		
23 Do you like doing things in which you have to act quickly?		
24 Do you worry about awful things that may happen?		
25 Have you ever been late for an appointment or work?		
26 Do you like talking to people so much that you never miss an opportunity of talking to a stranger?		
27 Are you troubled by aches or pains?		
28 Of all the people you know, are there some whom you definitely don't like?		
29 Would you say you were fairly self-confident?		
30 Are you easily hurt when people find fault with you or your work?		
31 Can you easily get some life into a dull party?		
32 Do you sometimes talk about things you know nothing about?		
33 Do you worry about your health?		

continues overleaf

continued

Scoring

1. E score

Question number	Response
1	Yes
3	No
6	Yes
9	No
12	No
15	Yes
17	No
20	No
23	Yes
26	Yes
29	Yes
31	Yes

For each answer you have that corresponds to the above responses give yourself one point. You will get a score out of 12 and this is your E score.

2. N score

Question number	Response
2	Yes
5	Yes
7	Yes
10	Yes
13	Yes
16	Yes
19	Yes
21	Yes
24	Yes
27	Yes
30	Yes
33	Yes

Again give yourself one mark for each answer you have that corresponds to the above responses. This will give you a score out of 12 for your N score.

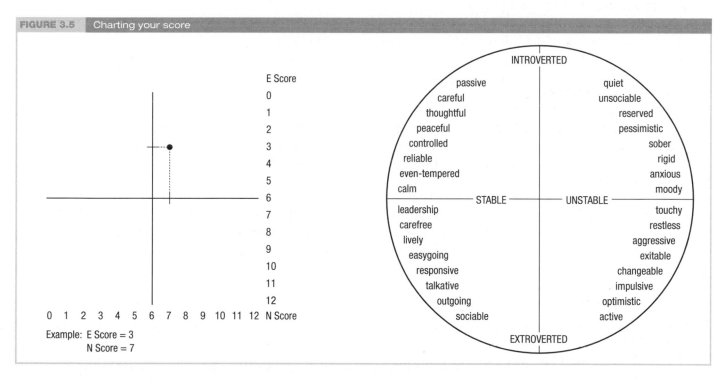

FIGURE 3.5   Charting your score

The E score describes to what extent you are introverted or extroverted; 1 being very introverted and 12 very extroverted.

The N score describes whether you are stable or unstable in your thoughts and emotions and the extent to which you worry about things. A score of 1 is very stable, while a score of 12 is very unstable or **neurotic**.

Research using Eysenck's Personality Inventory in sports

Morgan and Costill (1972) found that long-distance runners were mainly introverted, and Eysenck *et al.* (1982) found that extroverts were well represented in sports such as football, where the action is fast paced and gives them the excitement they need. They also found, that as a group, athletes are towards the unstable or neurotic end of the scale when compared with the general population. Perhaps this worry about performances gives them the stimulus to train hard and prepare properly.

Cattell's 16PF

Cattell's 16 Personality Factors test expanded on Eysenck's questionnaire to develop a test using 187 statements, such as:

3. I would rather have a house
    a. in a sociable suburb
    b. in between
    c. alone in the deep woods

6. I hold back from criticising people and their ideas
    a. yes
    b. sometimes
    c. no

11. It would be more interesting to be
    a. a construction engineer
    b. uncertain
    c. a writer of plays

The questionnaires are scored and the subject is given a standardised score for each or the 16 dimensions or traits. These are plotted to reveal a profile. The personality factors are shown in Figure 3.6.

This theory is attractive because, using the questionnaire, we can conduct research by comparing different groups of athletes. For example, tennis players versus swimmers; international athletes versus county-standard athletes, athletes versus non-athletes, and assess where the differences are and what traits are needed for success.

Findings of research

The majority of research using trait theory was done in the 1970s and 1980s. In 1977 Schurr, Ashley and Joy conducted a large comparative study of over 2000 athletes. Their findings included the following when comparing athletes with non-athletes:

✪ athletes who played team sports were:
  ▶ more outgoing and warm (A)
  ▶ less intelligent (B)
  ▶ more group dependent (Q2)
  ▶ less emotionally stable and affected by feelings (C)

FIGURE 3.6 Cattell's 16 Personality Factors

FACTOR	Raw Score			Standard Score	LOW SCORE DESCRIPTION	STANDARD TEN SCORE (STEN) Average	HIGH SCORE DESCRIPTION
	Form A	Form B	Total			1 2 3 4 5 6 7 8 9 10	
A					RESERVED, DETACHED, CRITICAL, ALOOF (Sizothymia)	• • • • •A• • • • •	OUTGOING, WARMHEARTED, EASY-GOING, PARTICIPATING (Affectothymia, formerly cyclothymia)
B					LESS INTELLIGENT, CONCRETE-THINKING (Lower scholastic mental capacity)	• • • • •B• • • • •	MORE INTELLIGENT, ABSTRACT-THINKING, BRIGHT (Higher scholastic mental capacity)
C					AFFECTED BY FEELINGS, EMOTIONALLY LESS STABLE, EASILY UPSET (Lower ego strength)	• • • • •C• • • • •	EMOTIONALLY STABLE, FACES REALITY, CALM, MATURE (Higher ego strength)
E					HUMBLE, MILD, ACCOMMODATING, CONFORMING (Submissiveness)	• • • • •E• • • • •	ASSERTIVE, AGGRESSIVE, STUBBORN, COMPETITIVE (Dominance)
F					SOBER, PRUDENT, SERIOUS, TACITURN (Desurgency)	• • • • •F• • • • •	HAPPY-GO-LUCKY, IMPULSIVELY LIVELY, GAY, ENTHUSIASTIC (Surgency)
G					EXPEDIENT, DISREGARDS RULES, FEELS FEW OBLIGATIONS (Weaker superego strength)	• • • • •G• • • • •	CONSCIENTIOUS, PERSEVERING, STAID, MORALISTIC (Stronger superego strength)
H					SHY, RESTRAINED, TIMID, THREAT-SENSITIVE (Threctia)	• • • • •H• • • • •	VENTURESOME, SOCIALLY BOLD, UNINHIBITED, SPONTANEOUS (Parmia)
I					TOUGH-MINDED, SELF-RELIANT, REALISTIC, NO-NONSENSE (Harria)	• • • • •I• • • • •	TENDER-MINDED, CLINGING, OVER-PROTECTED, SENSITIVE (Premsia)
L					TRUSTING, ADAPTABLE, FREE OF JEALOUSY, EASY TO GET ALONG WITH (Alaxia)	• • • • •L• • • • •	SUSPICIOUS, SELF-OPINIONATED, HARD TO FOOL (Protension)
M					PRACTICAL, CAREFUL, CONVENTIONAL REGULATED BY EXTERNAL REALITIES, PROPER (Praxeeria)	• • • • •M• • • • •	IMAGINATIVE, WRAPPED UP IN INNER URGENCIES, CARELESS OF PRATICAL MATTERS, BOHEMIAN (Autia)
N					FORTHRIGHT, NATURAL, ARTLESS, UNPRETENTIOUS (Artlessness)	• • • • •N• • • • •	SHREWD, CALCULATING, WORLDLY, PENETRATING (Shrewdness)
O					SELF-ASSURED, CONFIDENT, SERENE (Untroubled adequacy)	• • • • •O• • • • •	APPREHENSIVE, SELF-REPROACHING WORRYING, TROUBLED (Guilt proneness)
Q₁					CONSERVATIVE, RESPECTING ESTABLISHED IDEAS, TOLERANT OF TRADITIONAL DIFFICULTIES (Conservatism)	• • • • •Q₁• • • • •	EXPERIMENTING, LIBERAL, ANALYTICAL, FREE-THINKING (Radicalism)
Q₂					GROUP-DEPENDANT, A 'JOINER' AND SOUND FOLLOWER (Group adherence)	• • • • •Q₂• • • • •	SELF-SUFFICIENT, PREFERS OWN DECISIONS, RESOURCEFUL (Self-sufficiency)
Q₃					UNDISCIPLINED SELF-CONFLICT, FOLLOWS OWN URGES, CARELESS OF PROTOCOL (Low integration)	• • • • •Q₃• • • • •	CONTROLLED, SOCIALLY PRECISE, FOLLOWING SELF-IMAGE (High self-concept control)
Q₄					RELAXED, TRANQUIL, UNFRUSTRATED (Low ergic tension)	• • • • •Q₄• • • • •	TENSE, FRUSTRATED, DRIVEN, OVERWROUGHT (High ergic tension)

4.6   6.4

A sten of   1   2   3   4   5   6   7   8   9   10   is obtained
by about   2.3% 4.4% 9.2% 15.0% 19.1% 19.1% 15.0% 9.2% 4.4% 2.3%   of adults

✪   athletes who played individual sports were:

▶   more group dependent (Q2)
▶   less anxious (Q4)
▶   less intelligent (B)

Williams (1980) compared female athletes with female non-athletes and found that the athletes were:

✪   more independent (Q2)

✪   more aggressive and dominant (E)

✪   more emotionally stable (C)

The research proved fairly inconclusive and the theory is seen to have several flaws.

✪   The answers given to the questionnaire are influenced by mood and motivation.

✪   The situation and how it affects personality is not taken into account.

✪   Human beings are, by nature, unpredictable in their responses and their personalities cannot be labelled.

✪   Personality will change and develop over time.

✪   Trait approach may explain why people choose certain sports, but not how successful they will be.

Social learning theory

Social learning theory, or the situational approach, takes the view that personality is determined by the environment and the experiences a person has as they grow up. Other theories (e.g. trait) take the nature or biological approach to personality in that they see it as being largely genetic or inherited; the social learning theory sees personality as the result of nurture or upbringing.

Richard Cox (1985) outlines the two mechanisms of learning: modelling and social reinforcement.

1   **Modelling** – We observe and imitate the behaviour of significant others in our lives. At first, this is our parents and siblings, then our friends, teachers, sports stars and anyone we regard as a role model. We often hear sports people, such as Michael Owen and David Beckham, being praised for being good role models to young people; this means their conduct is good to observe and imitate.

2   **Social reinforcement** – This means that when a behaviour is rewarded positively it is more likely that it will be repeated; conversely, a behaviour negatively rewarded is less likely to be repeated. At an early age our parents teach us right and wrong by positively or negatively rewarding behaviour.

In sport there is a system of negative reinforcement to discourage negative behaviours on the sports field. Thus, rugby players get sent to the sin bin, cricketers get fined part of their match fee and footballers get yellow and red cards as a means of social reinforcement.

Young people will copy the behaviour of sports stars, as can be seen by the imitation of David Beckham and Freddie Ljungberg's haircuts. Another good example is in the England versus Mexico game of 1994, when the Mexican goalkeeper, Rene Higuitta, produced a scorpion kick to save a goal, and immediately young goalkeepers started to imitate. Eventually, the Football Association banned the move because they felt it was dangerous.

The situational approach is difficult to use to predict behaviour and analyse why some people are more successful than others. However, it can help us understand why people behave in certain ways, such as aggressively, due to past experiences and observations.

The interactional approach

The interactional approach considers the person's psychological traits and the situation they are in as equal predictors of behaviour.

$$\text{behaviour} = f\,(\text{personality, environment})$$

Thus, we can understand an individual's behaviour by assessing their personality traits and the specific situation they find themselves in. Bowers (1973) says the interaction between a person and their situation could give us twice as much information as traits or the situational approach alone.

An interactional psychologist would use a trait–state approach to assess an individual's personality traits and then assess how these traits affect their behaviour in a situation (state). For example, an athlete who exhibited high anxiety levels as a personality trait would then have an exaggerated response to a specific situation.

Other personality measurements

Profile of mood states (POMS)

POMS was developed by McNair, Lorr and Droppelmann (1971) to show how moods changed in certain situations. The mood states assessed were tension, depression, anger, vigour, fatigue, confusion

Morgan's (1979) research using POMS developed the positive mental health model to predict athletic performance and success. He showed that if an athlete can exhibit the trait of vigour above population norms and all other traits below the population norm then their chances of success are greatly enhanced. He called this the 'Iceberg profile' as plotted in Figure 3.7. The figure also shows the profiles of less successful athletes.

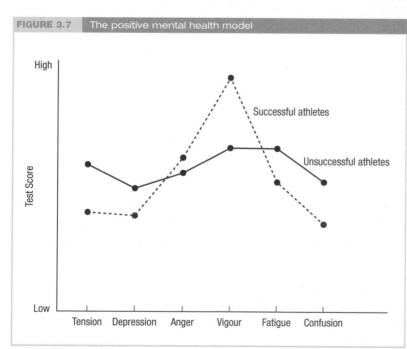

FIGURE 3.7 The positive mental health model

Type A and type B personalities

This questionnaire was initially developed to identify people who were prone to stress and stress-related illnesses. However, it has some application to sport and exercise. The following questionnaire can be used to identify which personality type you fit into.

Statement		Score	Statement
1	Don't mind leaving things temporarily unfinished	1 2 3 4 5 6 7	Must get things finished once started
2	Calm and unhurried about appointments	1 2 3 4 5 6 7	Never late for appointments
3	Not competitive	1 2 3 4 5 6 7	Highly competitive
4	Listen well, let others finish speaking first	1 2 3 4 5 6 7	Anticipate others in conversation by interrupting
5	Never in a hurry even when pressured	1 2 3 4 5 6 7	Always in a hurry
6	Able to wait calmly	1 2 3 4 5 6 7	Uneasy when waiting
7	Easy going	1 2 3 4 5 6 7	Always going at full speed
8	Take one thing at a time	1 2 3 4 5 6 7	Try to do more than one thing at a time
9	Slow and deliberate in speech	1 2 3 4 5 6 7	Vigorous and forceful in speech, using gestures
10	Concerned with satisfying self, not others	1 2 3 4 5 6 7	Want recognition from others for a job well done
11	Slow at doing things	1 2 3 4 5 6 7	Fast at doing things
12	Relaxed	1 2 3 4 5 6 7	Hard driving
13	Express feelings openly	1 2 3 4 5 6 7	Hold feelings in
14	Have a large number of interests	1 2 3 4 5 6 7	Have few interests
15	Satisfied with life	1 2 3 4 5 6 7	Ambitious
16	Never set own deadlines	1 2 3 4 5 6 7	Always set own deadlines
17	Feel limited responsibility	1 2 3 4 5 6 7	Always feel responsible
18	Never judge things in terms of quantity, just quality	1 2 3 4 5 6 7	Quantity is more important than quality
19	Casual about work	1 2 3 4 5 6 7	Take work very seriously
20	Not very precise	1 2 3 4 5 6 7	Very precise and careful about detail

Total your score _____

What does your score mean?

Between 0 and 29: a type B personality; you are usually relaxed and cope well with stressful situations.

Between 30 and 59: a type B personality; you are generally relaxed and cope adequately with stress.

Between 60 and 79: you have a mixed personality and show traits of both types. You should be aware when you exhibit type A behaviours.

Between 80 and 109: a type A personality; you do not cope well with stress and may be prone to stress-related illnesses.

Between 110 and 140: a type A personality; you are in a high-risk group, especially if you exhibit other factors which may contribute to heart disease.

Type A behaviour:

❂   highly competitive

❂   achievement oriented

❂   eat fast, walk fast, talk fast

❂   aggressive, restless and impatient

❂   find it difficult to delegate or not be in control

❂   experience high levels of stress

Type B behaviour:

❂   less competitive

❂   more relaxed

❂   delegate work easily

❂   take time to complete their tasks

❂   calm, laid back and patient

❂   experience low levels of stress

Type B's will exhibit the opposite types of behaviour to type As.

In sport we see both personality types being equally successful. However, with people exercising recreationally, we see higher levels of retention on their exercise programmes. Type As would benefit from exercise as it promotes type B-related behaviours.

ISSUES IN PERSONALITY TESTING

There are problems with personality testing, as can be seen by the difficulty in defining personality. We have no universally agreed definition of personality, so if we cannot decide what it is, how can we test it? This brings into question the **validity** of personality testing, i.e. are we testing what we say we are testing?

Secondly, we have covered five theories of personality and there are many more; so if we cannot decide which theory is correct, again we will struggle to understand and test it.

The way that people answer questions or may modify behaviour can create problems for the researcher. We all want to be seen in the best light, so may be untruthful in some of our responses to make ourselves look good. The way we answer questions will also depend upon our mood. For example, we will give different responses to a post-match questionnaire based on how we performed and the result! This brings into question the **reliability** of the testing.

Thirdly, there are ethical issues regarding testing, as results could be misused and a coach could use the results as a basis for his team selection. If he can predict how people will respond to a stressful situation, then he can use this to choose his team.

REVISION QUESTIONS

1) Choose one definition of personality and discuss its good points and bad points.
2) Discuss the three levels of personality as outlined by Hollander.
3) How does Sheldon (1942) see physique as influencing personality?
4) Explain the trait theorists' view of personality.
5) Outline the two ways that social learning theorists say we learn our behaviours.

6) What other factor does the interactional approach take into account that trait theory does not, and why is this important?
7) Explain what is meant by the 'iceberg profile'.
8) How do type A and type B personality types differ?
9) Discuss three problems regarding personality research in sport.

STRESS, AROUSAL AND ANXIETY

Stress is usually talked about in negative terms. People complain that they have too much stress or are stressed out; sports people claim the stress of competition is too much for them. However, we should not see stress as an entirely negative thing because it provides us with mental and physical energy to motivate us into doing things and doing them well.

If we did not have any stress in our lives, we might not bother to do anything all day. We need stressors to give us the energy and direction – without any stress we would become bored and psychologically stale. This type of positive stress is called **eustress** (good stress), however, if we have too much stress is can become damaging and we call this **distress** (bad stress).

eustress _____ distress

Stress

'...any influence which disturbs the natural equilibrium of the body' (Wingate, 1982).

Too much stress in our lives over a long period of time can seriously damage our health, causing things like coronary heart disease, high blood pressure, ulcers, impotence, substance addiction, mental health problems and suicidal tendencies.

Sport is a source of stress for some sports people. As the importance of a game rises and the rewards for winning increase, so the symptoms of stress start to appear. The effect of this stress can be mixed, as sometimes it will bring out best performances and sometimes worst.

The classic definition of stress sees the body as having a natural equilibrium or balance, when the heart rate is at its resting level, the breathing rate at its resting level, and blood pressure at normal levels. Anything that changes these natural levels is a stressor. Theoretically, we could say we become stressed as soon as we get out of bed, as our heart rate, breathing rate and blood pressure all rise. Indeed, to some people the alarm going off is a real source of stress!

However, our bodies can cope with the stresses that it is subjected to on a daily basis and remain unaffected. We can compare it with the chair that you sit on everyday: as you put your weight on the chair it becomes stressed, but it is designed to deal with this stress and can cope for about twenty years without any problems. If you were to go away for a while and double your body weight, then sit on the chair, it may well break because it is not able to take the stress you have put upon it. Our bodies are similar to this: they can cope with normal levels of stress, but if too much stress is placed on us, or stress is put on us over a long period of time, then our bodies will start to suffer physical and mental breakdown.

Causes of stress

Chinese proverb:

> *That the birds of stress and worry fly above your head, this you cannot change; but that they build nests in your hair, this you can prevent.*

The causes of stress are many and varied, but crucially they are specific to an individual. For example, you can have two people in the same event, each with a different stress response.

The sources of stress can generally be divided into four categories.

1 **Internal** – Things we think about such as past memories and experiences, past injuries, our own feelings of self worth, and so on.

2 **External** – Things in our surroundings and our environment, such as competition, our opponents, the weather, spiders and snakes, transport problems.

3 **Personal factors** – People we share our lives with such as friends, family, partners; and life factors such as money and health.

4 **Occupational factors** – The job we do, the people we work with (the boss) and our working conditions. In sport it could include our relationships with team mates and coaches/managers.

Stress levels also depend upon personality. Those people who have a predominantly type A personality will find more situations stressful, as will people who have a high N score using Eysenck's personality inventory.

The physiology of stress

When we perceive ourselves to be in a situation which is dangerous, our stress response is activated. This has been developed as a means of ensuring our survival by making us respond to danger. For example, if we walking home at night through dark woods and we hear noises behind us our body will instigate physiological changes, called the 'fight or flight' response, as the body is preparing to turn and fight the danger or run away as fast as it can.

The response varies depending upon how serious we perceive the threat to be. The changes take place in our involuntary nervous system which consists of two major branches:

- ✪ the sympathetic nervous system
- ✪ the parasympathetic nervous system.

The **sympathetic nervous system** produces the stress response, and its aim is to provide the body with as much energy as it can to confront the threat or run away from it. The circulatory system also takes blood away from less important areas, such as the skin and stomach, and diverts it to the working muscles to provide more oxygen. The sympathetic system produces the following effects:

- ✪ increased adrenaline production
- ✪ increase in heart rate
- ✪ increase in breathing rate
- ✪ increased metabolism
- ✪ increased heat production
- ✪ muscle tension
- ✪ dry mouth
- ✪ dilated pupils
- ✪ hairs on the skin stand on end (to make us look bigger)
- ✪ digestive system slows down.

The **parasympathetic nervous system** produces the relaxation response, its aim being to conserve energy. It is activated once the stress has passed. The parasympathetic system produces the following responses:

- ✪ slowed heart rate
- ✪ slower breathing rate
- ✪ smaller pupils
- ✪ dry skin

- muscle relaxation
- slower metabolism
- lower body temperature
- saliva produced
- digestion speeded up.

It is not healthy for the body to be in a constant state of stress because of the activation of the sympathetic nervous system. The excess production of adrenaline is dangerous because the body requires more cholesterol to synthesise adrenaline. This excess cholesterol production raises blood cholesterol levels and is a risk factor for coronary heart disease (CHD).

Arousal and anxiety

Arousal and anxiety are terms related to stress. **Arousal** is seen as being a **positive** aspect of stress and shows how motivated we are by a situation. The more aroused we are, the more interested and excited we are by a situation. We can see this when we watch a football match involving a team we support: we are so aroused that we are engrossed in the action to the point of where we don't hear noises around us and time seems to go very quickly. During a match that does not arouse us to the same extent, we find that our attention drifts in and out as we are distracted by things happening around us.

Anxiety can be seen as a **negative** aspect of stress, and it may accompany high levels of arousal. It is not pleasant to be anxious and is characterised by feelings of nervousness and worry. Again, the stress and anxiety responses are unique to each individual.

Arousal and performance

Arousal levels will have an influence on performance, but it is not always clear-cut what this relationship is. The following theories help to explain the relationship.

Drive theory

This theory, initially the work of Hull (1943), states that as arousal levels rise, so do performance levels. This happens in linear fashion and can be described as a straight line (see Figure 3.8).

The actual performance also depends on the arousal level and the skill level of the performer. Arousal will exaggerate the individual's dominant response, meaning that if they have learnt the skill well their dominant response will be exaggerated positively, but if they are a novice, their skill level will drop to produce a worse performance.

This theory is too simplistic as it does not take into account the type of task performed. It might work for a strength-related task such as weight lifting or performing press ups, but for more complex tasks, such as playing snooker or throwing darts, it may not apply as the arousal levels may damage performance.

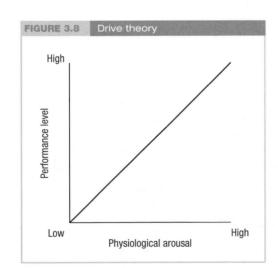

FIGURE 3.8 Drive theory

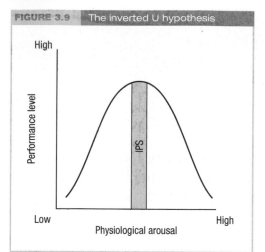

FIGURE 3.9   The inverted U hypothesis

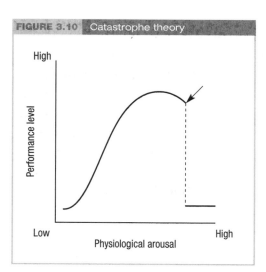

FIGURE 3.10   Catastrophe theory

The inverted U hypothesis

This theory is based on the Yerkes and Dodson Law (1908) and seeks to address some of the criticisms of the Drive Theory. This theory agrees that arousal does improve performance, but only up to a point, and once arousal goes beyond this point performance starts to decline. Figure 3.9 shows the curve looking like an upside down U.

This theory's main point is that there is an optimum level of arousal before performance starts to diminish. This is also called the ideal performing state (IPS) and is often referred to as 'the Zone'. At this point the arousal level meets the demands of the task, and everything feels good and is going well.

This theory has been taken a step further by Hardy and Fazey (1988), who agree with the inverted U hypothesis, but say that once arousal level has passed, the IPS will drop off drastically, rather than in steadily (see Figure 3.10). The point where performance drops is called the point of catastrophe. The Americans refer to this phenomenon, when performance drops, as 'choking', and the history of sport is littered with examples of when people or teams have thrown away seemingly unassailable positions.

A classic example was in the British Open Golf Championships of 1999, when Jean van der Velde went to the 72nd hole of the tournament with a three-shot lead. All he had to do was hit the ball straight on to the fairway and then he would have five shots to get the ball down. However, Jean went for glory and sliced his drive into the rough, then chipped into the brook and had to take his shoes off to play the next shot. He eventually got down for a seven, which lead to a three-way play off and this he lost to Paul Lawrie.

Whole teams have also been known to choke collectively, such as the Brazilian football team in the World Cup final of 1998, when they were clear favourites but failed to perform in the final, losing 3–0 to France.

The effect of stress on performance depends upon a range of factors:

✪ personality of performer

✪ skill level of performer

✪ type of skill performed.

Oxendine (1970) focused on the skill level of sport when he developed his taxonomy of sport (Table 3.2). He showed that high levels of arousal would improve the performance of gross skills in sports, such as weight lifting; however, they would inhibit the performance of fine skills involving high levels of co-ordinated movement, such as golf or cricket.

Table 3.2 Oxeninde's taxonomy of sport

Arousal level	Sports
5	weight lifting; gym exercises; tackling in rugby; 200/400 metre racing
4	wrestling/judo; long jump; shot putt; long-distance running
3	soccer; basketball; high jump; gymnastics; boxing
2	tennis; baseball; fencing; diving
1	golf; archery; bowling; snooker; darts

Stress management

One of the key roles of the sport psychologist is to help performers to try to control their stress levels and maintain a level of arousal appropriate to the task they are performing. This is not an easy role as the individual personalities have to be taken into account, as do the differing skills of the sport. For example, a hooker in rugby is required to perform some gross skills, such as pushing in the scrum, tackling, rucking and carrying the ball forward; however, they then have to perform the fine skill of throwing the ball into the lineout, which requires low levels of arousal. A footballer also performs gross skills of tackling and blocking, then fine skills of passing, shooting and dribbling. In order to do this, the performers need to recognise when they have low and high levels of arousal, and when each is appropriate.

The aim of the sport psychologist is to get their athletes to be familiar with their optimum level of arousal, and then to teach them how to achieve and sustain that level of arousal.

The main methods of stress management are:

✪   progressive muscular relaxation

✪   mind-to-muscle relaxation

✪   biofeedback

✪   meditation/centering

✪   systematic desensitisation.

Progressive muscular relaxation (PMR)

This technique involves an athlete tensing and relaxing their muscle groups individually and sequentially in order to relax their whole body and their mind. It is also called muscle-to-mind relaxation, as muscles are tensed and relaxed in order to induce complete relaxation.

Each muscle is tensed and relaxed in order to teach the athlete the difference between a tense muscle and a relaxed muscle. After a muscle is tensed, the relaxation effect is deepened, which also has an effect on the involuntary muscles. The technique is practised using a series of taped instructions, or with the psychologist giving the instructions, and usually starts at the hands by making a tight fist and then relaxing. The tensing and relaxing carries on up the arms into the shoulders, the face and neck, then down to the stomach and through the hips and legs.

An example of an PMR training session follows:

> *Make a tight fist with both hands and hold for five seconds, feeling the tension in the hand and the forearm. Now relax and, as the muscles relax, feel the tension replaced by relaxation spreading through the muscle groups. Remember this sensation and feel how pleasant it can be. Now shrug your shoulders and feel the tension in your shoulders. Hold for five seconds, then relax and feel the relaxation spreading through your shoulders.*

These sessions last between 20 and 30 minutes, but they need to be practised about five times to gain the maximum effect. Each time they are practised they have an increased effect and an athlete can relax more quickly and more deeply, the aim being that when they need to use the relaxation technique quickly they can induce relaxation using a trigger, such as tensing the hand or the shoulders.

Mind-to-muscle relaxation

This technique is also called imagery and involves the use of a mental room or a mental place. This is a place where an athlete can quickly picture themselves in order to produce feelings of relaxation when they need to relax.

Again, it involves the athlete using a taped script or a psychologist giving instructions. Usually the psychologist asks an athlete to build a mental picture of a room; this is a room where they can feel relaxed and where there is somewhere to sit or lie down; it should be decorated in a pleasing manner. Alternatively, an athlete may imagine a relaxing place, such as somewhere they went on their holidays or a beach or quiet place where they feel calm and relaxed. The athlete is taught to vividly imagine this place and feel the sensations associated with being there. They do this about five times, so that eventually they can go there when they need to and are able to relax more quickly and deeply.

As the athlete relaxes their mind, they feel the sensations transferring to their muscle groups and they can achieve overall body relaxation. It tends to work best for individuals who have good skills of imagery; other individuals may feel that PMR is more effective for them.

Biofeedback

This method relies upon us being aware of what happens to our bodies when we become aroused and anxious. For example, we will experience changes in our heart rate, skin temperature and blood pressure. These can be monitored by various devices such as heart rate monitors and blood pressure monitors, or a biodot which monitors our skin temperature. As we learn to relax we will see falls in skin temperature and heart rate. The athlete starts to learn what relaxation feels like and can attempt to reproduce this feeling when they need it.

Centring/meditation

These techniques involve the athlete focusing on one thing, such as their breathing (centring) or a mantra (meditation), and by focusing their attention they become more and more relaxed. Again, these feelings of relaxation can eventually be produced when needed.

Systematic desensitisation

This technique was initially developed by psychologists to deal with people who had developed phobias. It involves a person being put in situations of increasing stress to slowly desensitise them to whatever they fear. For example, if a person had a fear of snakes they may take the following steps.

1   The person is shown a snakeskin.

2   The person is shown a picture of the snake.

3   The person is put in a room with the snake, but they cannot see it.

4   The person is put in the room with the snake in a glass cage.

5   The person is shown the snake by someone holding it.

6   The person attempts to touch the snake.

7   The person is able finally to hold the snake.

This technique can be applied to sport where athletes find themselves going into a situation more stressful than they are used to. The coach will seek to desensitise them by putting them in situations which simulate the stress and allow them to get used to it. For example, non-league football teams have used taped crowd noise during training sessions to prepare their players for the noise of a Premiership crowd; or they visit their opponent's ground before the match to get them used to the situation and limit their stress levels.

Cognitive control strategies

Cognitive control strategies are used to prepare an individual for their forthcoming performance and aspects within their performance. For example, if we observe Jonny Wilkinson, the English rugby union fly half, before he takes a kick for goal he takes a series of very deliberate steps to prepare himself (Figure 3.11). We see him putting down the ball and taking several steps backwards, then he turns sideways and stares at the ball, he then stares at the goal posts. Then he mentally rehearses his kick – he closes his eyes and we see him making small jerking movements; at this point he runs up and kicks the ball.

This is a personal performance routine and we see it with golfers, high jumpers, long jumpers and many other sports people. They have a set routine they follow every time they perform and it may include some of the following psychological techniques:

✪   attention control

✪   concentration

FIGURE 3.11 Jonny Wilkinson preparing to take a penalty

- ✪ relaxation
- ✪ imagery
- ✪ mental rehearsal
- ✪ self-talk.

Concentration is a vital aspect of any sports performance, as one lapse in concentration can mean the difference between success and failure. This was aptly demonstrated in the World Cup final by the German goalkeeper, Oliver Kahn, who had been outstanding in six games, but one fumble in the final presented a scoring chance to Ronaldo, who happily took it.

Concentration involves two important factors.

1. **Relevant environmental cues** – Information present in the game which is relevant to the athlete's performance; for example, the information that is relevant to a cricketer playing a stroke includes the ball, the movement of the bowler's hand, the flight and bounce of the ball and the position of the fielders. Irrelevant information includes noises from the crowd, the remarks of the fielders, the umpires and the weather. The batsman must focus on relevant cues to successfully play the delivery.

2. **Maintaining attentional focus** – Concentrating on the relevant cues and not being distracted by any outside distractions. Stephen Hendry is the most successful snooker player of all time, although some may argue not the most talented. However, on top of his talent he has the ability to stay focused throughout a match and not be distracted by the actions of other players, his own bad shots and the noise of the crowd.

Concentrating on information relevant to your sport is called an **associative attentional strategy**; however, some sports performers such as marathon runners, swimmers or long-distance cyclists find they compete better using a **dissociative attentional strategy**. This means that in order to take their mind off the pain and boredom they think about other things or imagine themselves elsewhere. The problem with this is that they may not be aware of the movements of their competitors or what is happening to their own energy levels and performance.

STUDENT ACTIVITY

Take the following situations and work out what environmental information is relevant to the athlete's performance and what information is not relevant:

- ✪ a footballer taking a corner kick
- ✪ a sprinter preparing for a race
- ✪ a tennis player receiving a serve.

Self-talk is when you think about yourself and talk to yourself during a performance. For example, during a competition you may say 'that was a great shot' or 'what are you doing?' and this can affect your confidence levels. Positive self-talk helps you focus on the performance and stay in the present; it also helps you maintain concentration levels. Negative self-talk can distract from your performance and create negative emotions and self-doubts.

? REVISION QUESTIONS

1) Explain why stress can be a positive force in our lives.

2) Discuss why stress is a problem for sports people and in general life.

3) Why are stressors specific to the individual?

4) What happens to the body whenever we become stressed?

5) Explain the terms 'arousal' and 'anxiety'.

6) Discuss three theories of arousal and performance.

7) What does Oxendine's taxonomy of sport explain?

8) Outline three methods of controlling stress.

9) Briefly describe how a psychologist can help an athlete prepare for a competition.

AGGRESSION

Aggression in sport seems to be becoming more and more commonplace, but in reality, aggressive acts in sport are becoming rarer. Witness some of the famous footballers of the 1970s and 1980s such as Tommy Smith, Ron 'Chopper' Harris, Norman 'bite yer legs' Hunter and Graeme Souness to see what aggressive play is really about. However, the media tend to sensationalise aggressive acts and give them plenty of coverage.

Psychologists have studied aggression over several years and asked the following questions:

✪   What do we mean by aggression?

✪   Why do sports people commit acts of aggression?

✪   What effect do these acts have on the outcome of the game?

✪   What can be done to prevent aggressive acts occurring?

STUDENT ACTIVITY

1 Describe two occasions when you behaved aggressively on the sports field.

2 What caused you to be aggressive in this situation? Were you provoked? Was it to gain an advantage, or could you just not help it?

3 What effect did it have on the outcome of the game? Did it improve your chances of victory, have no effect, or decrease your chances of victory?

If you have never behaved aggressively, think of two occasions when you witnessed aggressive acts.

Discuss your answers with a partner and them contribute them to a class discussion.

Definitions

Aggression

In general life we refer to a range of behaviours where a person is being over zealous as being aggressive. Often these actions are mis-labelled.

Baron (1977) defined aggression as: '*any form of behaviour directed towards the goal of harming or injuring another person who is motivated to avoid such treatment.*'

In sport psychology aggression has a specific meaning: aiming to harm or injure an opponent to gain an advantage, rather than playing in a hard manner. Gill (1986) gives us four criteria which must all be met to allow us to label an action as aggressive.

1 There must be a physical or verbal behaviour.

2 It must involve causing harm or injury, whether it be physical or psychological.

3 It must be directed towards another living thing.

4 There must be the intention to cause harm or injury.

STUDENT ACTIVITY

Look at the following examples and decide whether they are aggressive or not.

1 A footballer who has been hurt in a tackle kicks their opponent.

2 A runner elbows a competitor during an 800 m race in order to get in front of them.

3 A boxer lands a punch which knocks their opponent to the ground.

4 A rugby player tackles an opponent and lands on top of them, causing their ribs to be bruised.

5 A hockey player smashes their stick into an opponent's nose by mistake.

6 A bowler hits the batsman on the helmet with a bouncing delivery.

7 A rugby player tramples on an opponent's head in a ruck.

8 In going for a cross, two players collide causing a blood wound to each other's heads.

9 An ice hockey player swears at an opponent who makes an illegal challenge.

10 A tennis player kicks a ball away in a moment of rage.

Having looked at the situations in the activity we start to realise that aggression is a grey area. We cannot tell whether it is aggression unless we know the motives of the person who produces the action. Plenty of sports people get injured, but not necessarily through acts of aggression. In order to be more specific about this area we need to split aggressive acts into three distinct categories.

1 **Assertive acts** – When a person plays with high energy and emotion but within the rules of the game; for example, a footballer puts in hard, uncompromising tackles, or a tennis player is playing in a very tough and upbeat manner but always within the rules. This is assertive play because it is not intended to do any harm or cause any injury to their opponent, and uses force that is legitimate and within the rules.

2 **Instrumental aggression** – When acts of aggression are used to achieve a non-aggressive goal, such as improving a team's chances of victory, they are not usually accompanied by feelings of anger. For example, if you target the opposition's star player for rough treatment by one of your team, but you are willing to accept the punishment, then you are committing instrumental aggression. This also explains the sport of boxing, where the aim is to hurt your opponent to win the fight, rather than because you do not like your opponent. Also, in a rugby scrum, ruck or maul players use a legitimate amount of force, but this may actually harm or injure an opponent.

3 **Hostile aggression** – An act where the primary goal is to inflict harm or injury on an opponent purely for the sake of it, usually accompanied by feelings of anger. It often occurs when an individual is continually blocked from achieving a goal and their frustration and anger build up. For example, if a player is continually fouled or verbally abused they may eventually respond aggressively as a result.

STUDENT ACTIVITY

Go back to the previous activity and, based on the above information, categorise each action as assertive, instrumental or hostile aggression.

Theories of aggression

1. Instinct theory

This theory says that all people have an instinctive, inborn need or tendency to be aggressive. This theory is based on the work of Sigmund Freud in the early twentieth century. He said that man has two basic needs: the need to be aggressive and the need to have sex. He saw aggression as an innate instinct to ensure survival of human beings. It can be directed towards another person or it can be displaced. This release of aggression is called **catharsis**. People will say they play rugby or football at the weekend to get rid of the tension and aggression that builds up during the week. Other people will go swimming or running to achieve the same release of aggressive tendencies in a socially acceptable manner. This theory has also been used to explain why people fight at football matches as an outlet for their aggression, albeit it in a less socially acceptable manner.

There is little research to support this theory, and it cannot explain why some people are more aggressive than others. Indeed, you may know some people who never show aggressive behaviours. It also differs across cultures and this suggests there must be external influences which make the chances of aggression more likely.

2. Frustration–aggression theory

This theory states that aggression is the direct result of frustration that has built up due to goal blockage or failure. This theory was first proposed by Dollard *et al.* (1939), who claimed frustration would always produce aggression. However, in 1993 Berkowitz refined this theory by saying that frustration will lead to anger rather than aggression, particularly if we feel we have been unfairly treated, but we will not always produce an aggressive action. He went on to say that an aggressive action is more likely if aggressive cues are present (things related to aggression), but a person may be able to control their anger.

Social learning theory

This theory says that aggression is learnt through modelling and imitative behaviour, rather than being an inborn instinct. Albert Bandura (1973) conducted research involving groups of children watching groups of adults playing with a doll. The children who watched the adults punching and beating up the doll produced this reaction more than the group who watched the adults playing passively with the doll. This aggressive behaviour was increased when the children were positively rewarded for their actions.

Ice hockey has attracted a lot of research due to the regularity of fighting and fouling in the sport. Smith (1988) found that the violence in the game is the result of young amateur players modelling the professionals' behaviour.

It is easy to see how a young footballer may learn to be aggressive; at a football match he sees a player making hard tackles, some of which are illegal and dangerous, and being cheered on by the crowd and his coach. The harder the player tackles the more praise he gets and he develops a following by the fans who like this type of player. The young footballer learns that this is a positive way to behave and mimics the play in his own matches.

Research has shown that aggressive acts are more likely to be imitated if produced by a person of the same sex and if they are witnessed live rather than on television or in cartoon form.

Social learning theory is a very convincing theory, and we can see how the levels of aggression in sport are accompanied by rises in the level of violence in society, particularly on television and in films. However, it fails to explain how people can witness the same events and yet the majority of them will not produce an aggressive response, while a minority will mimic the behaviour. For example, a boxing match will have a cathartic effect on some supporters and will cause an aggressive response in others. It comes back to personality type and brings in the instinct theory.

Aggression–performance relationship

The research on the aggression–performance relationship is mixed. Widmeyer (1984) found aggressive behaviour improved performance, while Gill (1986) found it had no effect. Research in Belgian football by Lefebre and Passer (1974) into 240 games found that losing teams received more yellow cards for fouls than winning teams; Underwood and Whitwood (1980) showed no difference in fouls committed by winning and losing teams in the English First Division. Studies into ice hockey have shown that defending players commit more fouls than attacking players. Young (1993) found that violence in contact sports has increased recently as a results of the increasing rewards on offer and increasing

professionalism in sport. While the relationship is unclear, we can predict that aggression is more likely to occur in certain situations than in others. For example, Leith (1991) and Cox (1998) say that aggressive acts are more likely to occur if a team is losing, their opponents are aggressive, the crowd is hostile and emotions are running high. Volkamer's (1972) research into football found the lower a team was in the league, and if they were playing away from home, then the more aggression they showed. Russell and Drury (1976) found the highest levels of aggression in the teams just behind the leaders.

Ultimately, the relationship between aggression and performance is unclear. It seems that some aggressive acts pay off while others do not. To summarise the research we can make the following points:

✪ aggression can increase levels of arousal which may be good or may be bad, depending on how high the arousal was initially

✪ aggression can improve team cohesion, as the team may become supportive of the aggressor or the opposition may become intimidated

✪ aggressive acts may receive negative reinforcement (sendings off, suspensions) which may have a detrimental effect on performance

✪ aggression can cause distractions from the game and therefore affect performance negatively.

Preventing aggression in young athletes

As a coach or a player it is possible to influence the number of aggressive acts players or team-mates commit. These approaches can be used to prevent aggressive play by young athletes or to re-educate those athletes who display aggressive behaviours.

1 Present non-aggressive role models for players to live up to. The perfect role model was Gary Lineker who was never riled and never retaliated no matter what punishment defenders gave him.

2 Punish severely acts of aggression. The various governing bodies are now taking aggressive acts very seriously and imposing long bans. The Rugby Football Union has taken steps to cite players who behave aggressively after a match and then punish them if they deem it necessary.

3 Punish coaches or teams as a whole who encourage aggressive play. This is done through fines or suspended fines.

4 Practice emotional control by teaching athletes how to manage their tempers, such as counting to ten before saying or doing anything. Relaxation techniques can also help here.

5 Limit external stimuli which are capable of provoking aggressive acts. If you know an athlete is vulnerable in certain situations or against certain teams, then consider whether you can prevent them going into that situation. For example, local derby matches are particularly heated affairs and often result in either player or crowd aggression.

BTEC NATIONAL IN SPORT AND EXERCISE SCIENCE

STUDENT ACTIVITY

In the role of a sport psychologist, draw up a contract between yourself and a player you know. You must state which behaviours you want to eliminate, what you will do to help, the punishment for breaking the contract and the rewards for fulfilling the contract.

6 Contracting. A sport psychologist may attempt to minimise their athlete's aggressive behaviour by using a contract stating which behaviours the athlete is trying to minimise. In return, the psychologist will suggest a course of action they can offer to help. Also the sanctions for breaking the contract and reward for adhering to the contract will be stated The contract is agreed and signed by both parties.

REVISION QUESTIONS

1) Explain what is meant by the term 'aggression'.
2) Explain the four criteria used by Gill to label an act as 'aggressive'.
3) Using examples, explain the difference between assertive behaviour, instrumental aggression and hostile aggression.
4) Briefly explain the three theories of aggression.
5) Explain which theory works best for you and why.

6) Do you think sport is a socially acceptable way for people to release their aggression?
7) Explain the relationship between aggression and performance.
8) Are there certain situations when aggression is more likely to occur than others?
9) What can be done to minimise the number of aggressive acts committed by children in contact sports?

MOTIVATION

If a sport psychologist were asked why athletes of similar talents achieve different levels of performance, they would consider several factors, such as personality and ability to cope with stress. However, if one subject could be said to influence everything in sport psychology it would be motivation – the reasons why we do what we do and behave and respond in the manner particular to us.

Psychologists would say that there is a reason for everything we do in life, and some of these motives are conscious and some are subconscious; as a result it can be difficult to assess our own motivating factors, let alone anyone else's.

Motivation is important to coaches and managers as they seek to get the best performances out their athletes. Kevin Keegan and Alex Ferguson are two managers who are also seen as being great motivators of people.

Motivation can be a difficult subject to pin down and deal with, because it is not steady and constant and depends on many factors. Most people will experience fluctuations in motivation in that some days they are fully prepared for the competition mentally, and on other days they just cannot seem to get themselves in the right frame of mind. This applies to all things we may do in a day, as sometimes it takes all our powers of motivation just to get out of bed!

Definitions

Motivation

Here are a number of definitions of motivation as put forward by various psychologists: '*Motive – the desire to fulfil a need*' (Cox, 1998).

Cox sees motivation as our behaviour being influenced by our needs and meeting these needs. Sage (1977) gives a more detailed definition: '*The internal mechanisms and external stimuli which arouse and direct behaviour*'.

This definition considers that motivation is produced by factors inside our bodies (or brains) and factors external to ourselves. However, these stimuli cause our arousal levels to rise and this influences our behaviour in certain ways.

Miller's (1967) definition expands on these internal and external factors: '*The study of motivation is the study of all those pushes and prods – biological, social or psychological that defeat our laziness and move us, either eagerly or reluctantly to action.*'

This definition takes a slightly pessimistic view of human beings: that we are essentially lazy and without pushes and prods would be inclined to do nothing. However, it makes the important point that rather than being motivated by one big thing, we are usually motivated by many small things which push and prod us into action.

STUDENT ACTIVITY

Consider each of the following statements made by athletes as to why they are motivated and decide whether it is an intrinsic or extrinsic motivating factor.

I want to win medals.

I want to earn an England cap.

I want to reach my full potential.

I want to make money.

I want to play in a good team.

I want to play in front of large crowds.

I want to give the public enjoyment.

I want to feel good about my performance.

I want to be recognised by the public for my ability.

I want to feel mastery in my own ability.

I want to feel the joy of winning.

Intrinsic and extrinsic motivation

To expand on Sage's definition, we can see motivation as coming from internal mechanisms or sources inside the body. We can call these **intrinsic factors**, or rewards coming from the activity itself. These include motives such as fun, pleasure, enjoyment, feelings of self-worth, excitement and self-mastery. They are the reasons why we do a sport and keep doing it.

The external stimuli can also be called the **extrinsic rewards** and they come from sources outside the activity. This would include the recognition and praise we get from other people, such as our coach, friends and family. It could also be the approval we get from the crowd who support us. For example, footballer Matthew Le Tissier said he is motivated by seeing the fans going away happy at the end of the match. Extrinsic motivating factors would also include trophies, medals, prizes, records and any money derived from success.

Initially, most people are motivated by intrinsic factors such as fun and enjoyment, however, their motivation can be changed and enhanced by the addition of extrinsic factors. Even professional footballers who gain huge extrinsic rewards from their sport will have started for the love of the game, but would they still play the game if you took their extrinsic rewards (their pay cheques) away from them?

STUDENT ACTIVITY

Consider the following story to further understand the complex relationship between intrinsic and extrinsic rewards.

> Every evening two young lads play tennis against the walls of a block of flats for two hours. Inside, Mrs Jones is trying to watch her favourite television programmes and is disturbed by the constant bouncing of the ball against her wall. So she hatches a plan to stop the boys playing. She tells the boys that because she likes to hear them playing tennis she will pay them £1 a day to play tennis against her wall. However, after a week she says she is running out of money and can only afford 50p a day. The boys are unconcerned and keep playing and collecting their money. After another week Mrs Jones says she can now only afford 20p a day. At this the boys become angry and tell Mrs Jones that it was not worth their effort to play for 20p a day, so they will not be coming back. Now Mrs Jones can watch her programmes in peace.

How can you explain this story in terms of intrinsic and extrinsic motivation? Can you relate this to professional sports people?

Achievement motivation

'I do not play to win, I play to fight against the idea of losing' (Eric Cantona, Manchester United, 1997).

Achievement motivation is seen as a personality factor and describes our persistence to keep striving for success, irrespective of the bad experiences and obstacles that are put in our way. It can be seen as our level of 'competitiveness' or desire for success. To watch the progress of long-distance athlete, Paula Radcliffe, is to see a person driven by a deep desire to be successful. She has a gruelling training schedule to make up for any shortcomings she is perceived to have, and finally she found the success her efforts deserve, winning the 2002 London Marathon.

Achievement motivation is not that simple, as the quote from Eric Cantona shows. Some people are driven to success and have no fear of failure, while other people are driven to succeed because they have a deep-rooted fear of failure. This paradox was addressed by McClelland and Atkinson in their theory of need achievement.

When in a certain sporting situation, we may have conflicting feelings: on one hand, we want to take part and achieve success, on the other hand, we are motivated to avoid the situation by our need to avoid failure. The relative strength of these emotions influences our achievement motivation:

$$\text{achievement motivation} =$$
$$\text{need to achieve (nACH)} - \text{need to avoid failure (naF)}$$

If our nACH outweighs our naF, then we are said to be high in achievement motivation; if our naF outweighs our nACH, we are said to be low in achievement motivation. This will influence our behaviour in sport and the types of challenges we seek.

A sports person with a high need to achieve will choose competitive situations and opponents close to their skill level who will challenge them. A person with a high fear of failure will choose opponents of much higher skill or much lower skill because these are less threatening to them; they will also tend to avoid situations involving personal challenges.

The situation will also affect achievement motivation. If the probability of success is high, it tends to weaken the need to achieve because the reward for success is low; on the other hand, if the probability of success is low and failure is likely, it tends to weaken the need to avoid failure. We can see this in the FA Cup, where non-league football teams play Premiership teams, and the outcome is often closer than it should be. For example, Dagenham and Redbridge nearly beat Charlton Athletic in 2001. This is because there is no real motive for success for the big team and thus no real reward because success is expected; for the smaller team, failure is expected so the value of success is massive. In terms of achievement motivation, the Premiership team is motivated to avoid failure, while the non-league team is motivated to achieve.

Weiner's attribution theory

STUDENT ACTIVITY

Think of the following situations:
- You play well, but lose to an opponent who is better than you.
- You play well and beat a tough opponent.
- You play badly, and still manage to win against a weak opponent.
- You play badly and lose to an opponent you know you can beat.
1   Number the situations from 1 to 4 starting with the one which you find most satisfying (1), and ending with the one which you find least satisfying (4).
2   Take the situation ranked first, and explain why it is most satisfying. Why may this result have occurred?
3   Take the situation ranked fourth, and explain why it is least satisfying. Why may this result have occurred?

The reasons we give for an outcome are called attributions. We are attributing that outcome to a certain factor. We all make attributions about our own performances as well as those of other people. It is important for us to make attributions because:

❂ they affect our motivation levels

❂ we need to understand the outcome so that we can learn from our experiences

❂ they will affect our future expectations of success and failure.

Attributions fall into four categories:

1 **Ability or skill** – A performer's capability in performing skills.

2 **Effort** – The amount of physical or mental effort put into a task.

3 **Task difficulty** – The problems posed by the task, e.g. strength of the opposition or difficulty of a move.

4 **Luck** – Factors attributed to chance, such as the effect of the weather, the referee or the run of the ball.

As shown in Table 3.2, these can be classified as internal (inside an individual); external (outside the individual); stable (not subject to change); unstable (continually changing).

Table 3.2 Locus of control		
	internal	external
stable	ability	task difficulty
unstable	effort	luck

STUDENT ACTIVITY

Look at the following statements and decide which of the four attributions' categories each one fits into.

Reasons for success

'I played well today, the training is paying off'

'I think I've got a natural talent for running – it comes easily to me'

'I tried like mad in the final set – that's what pulled me through'

'I was lucky to get away with that one'

Reasons for failure

'I played like an idiot! I deserved to lose'

'I can't play this game – it's impossible'

'I was really lazy today'

'I didn't get the rub of the green today'

Now that you know what attributions are, do a piece of your own research. Look through the newspapers on Monday morning and try to find the reasons sports people and coaches give for their success or failures. Also, think why they are choosing to make these particular attributions.

Research findings

Research shows that winners tend to give internal attributions and take responsibility for their successes. They will usually say 'I won because I tried hard' or, 'I am more talented'. Losers, on the other hand, tend to give external attributions and distance themselves from their failures. For example, they will say 'the task was too difficult' or 'the referee was against me'. These attributions can be seen as ego enhancing and ego protective respectively. Winners give internal attributions to make themselves feel even better about themselves and losers give external attributions so they don't feel so bad.

FIGURE 3.12 Attributions and self confidence model

From S.5 Bull, (1991)

Attributions and self-confidence

If we make a more stable attribution, i.e. to ability or task difficulty, it is more realistic and gives a clearer indication of future expectations and confidence. However, attribution to unstable factors can act to protect the ego and reduce loss of self-confidence.

This is important because confidence levels will influence motivation – the more confidence we have the more motivation we will have for a task.

STUDENT ACTIVITY

How can attribution theory prevent learned helplessness?

Learned helplessness

In the 1960s, experiments were done on animals to test the phenomenon of learned helplessness. Animals were put in a maze and given an electric shock to make them move. They tried to find their way out, but there was no exit. When they were put into a second maze they did not bother to find the way out. They had learnt to be helpless: learned helplessness.

This happens in sport: when a first experience is negative, the athlete will continue to expect the experience to be negative, thinking, for example 'I am rubbish at Badminton and never will be any good', 'What's the point, it won't work'.

There are problems if athletes attribute an outcome incorrectly, as it affects future expectations of success. For example, if a team has beaten a better team due to the amount of effort they have expended and they attribute this correctly, then they will continue to play energetically in the next game. However, if they incorrectly attribute it to ability, then in the next game they may lose the ingredient that made them successful. We can see this happen in football when teams in the lower half of the league go on a winning streak of four or five matches that suddenly comes to an end. This is because they have started to believe that they are actually a team high in ability, rather than a team of average ability who are trying very hard. Once the effort goes, they start to lose again.

Participation motivation

Many people in Britain have been persuaded to start exercising as they are aware of the benefits of exercise. People are also persuaded by impressive facilities and the atmosphere of these centres.

However, after six months, 55% of people who start an exercise programme have given up, but if a person carries on beyond nine months they are 90% likely to keep exercising long term. This is a question of motivation – once the motivation is lost then people drop out of their fitness programmes. We call the ability of people to stick to their programmes 'exercise adherence'.

Strategies to prevent dropout and promote adherence to exercise programmes

1 **Setting goals and targets** – In order to direct an individual's efforts and to give them something to work for we can set them goals. However, this has to be done with great care so as not to negatively affect motivation. To help us do this we can use the acronym SMART:

> **S**pecific goals – related to a particular aspect of fitness
> **M**easurable – the goal must be quantifiable
> **A**chievable – the goal must not be set too high
> **R**ealistic – the goal must be realistically achievable
> **T**ime constrained – there must be a time frame

Goals can be set in the long term and the short term. A long-term goal may be achived over the course of a year, and can be broken down into shorter-term goals, such as one-month, three-month or six-month goals. We can use **outcome goals** which are related to the final result and **process goals** which are goals we can meet to help us achieve the outcome goal. For example, if a person's outcome goal is to lose 3% body fat over a three-month period, their process goal may be to exercise three times a week for the first month.

2 **Using a decision balance sheet** – An individual writes down all the gains they will make by exercising and all the things they may lose through taking up exercise. Hopefully the gains will outweigh the losses and this list will help to motivate them at difficult times.

3 **Prompts** – An individual puts up posters or reminders around the house which will keep giving them reminders to exercise. This could also be done with little coloured dots on mirrors or other places where they regularly look.

4 **Rewards for attendance/completing goals** – The individual is provided with an extrinsic reward for completing the goal or attending the gym regularly. This may be something to pamper themselves, such as a free massage, and should not be something that conflict with the goal – such a slap-up meal!

5 **Social support approaches** – You can help people exercise regularly by developing a social support group of like-minded people with similar fitness goals, so that they can arrange to meet at the gym at certain times. This makes it more difficult for people to miss their exercise session. Also, try to gain the backing of people they live with to support them rather than tease or criticise them.

REVISION
QUESTIONS

1) Define the term 'motivation'.

2) Explain the difference between intrinsic and extrinsic motivation.

3) Is it possible for a person's motivation to change? Why might this happen?

4) Explain how achievement motivation can influence the types of challenge a person may choose.

5) Why is it important to make attributions?

6) What is meant by the locus of control dimension in attribution theory?

7) What is meant by the stability dimension in attribution theory?

8) Do winners and losers make different types of attribution?

9) What is leaned helplessness?

10) What is meant by the term 'adherence'?

11) How can a psychologist help people adhere to their exercise programmes?

GROUP DYNAMICS

Group processes

Throughout our sporting and social lives we are involved in working in groups, such as our families, our school groups, our friendship groups and the sports teams we play in. Sports teams have different characteristics; for example, an athletics team will have different teamwork demands to a rugby team or a cricket team. However, all groups rely on the fundamental characteristic of teamwork.

Defining a group is not easy, however, the minimum number required for a group is two people. A group can be seen as two or more like-minded people interacting to produce an outcome they could not achieve on their own. Groups involve interaction or working with other people in order to influence the behaviour of other people and in turn be influenced by them.

Definitions

Group

To define a group we can use the distinguishing characteristics of groups as devised by Weinberg and Gould (1995). A group should have

✪ a collective identity

✪ a sense of shared purpose or objectives

✪ structured modes of communication

✪ personal and/or task interdependence

✪ interpersonal attraction.

Opinion is divided on whether groups are really more effective than individuals. Look at the following contradictory sayings:

Two heads are better than one	vs.	Too many cooks spoil the broth
The more the merrier	vs.	Three is a crowd
If you want a job done well do it yourself	vs.	A jack of all trades is the master of none
There is strength in numbers	vs.	A chain is as strong as its weakest link

(from A. V. Carron, 1988)

So why is the outcome of the group not always equal to the sum of its parts? For example, we can see in football that the teams with the best players do not always get the results they should. Chelsea have often been criticised as underachieving, as they have had some of the best European talent and yet not managed to challenge for the Premiership trophy. In the season 1996–97, Middlesborough had outstanding players such as Juninho, Fabrizio Ravanelli and Emerson and yet they ended the season being relegated. At the 1996 Olympic Games, the brilliant sprinters of the USA were beaten in the 4×100 m relay by the unfancied Canadian team. Groups do not always achieve what they should due to the following:

- ✪ communication difficulties

- ✪ co-ordination of the group

- ✪ lack of motivation

- ✪ laziness or reduced effort.

Stages of group development

A group of people coming together does not form a team. Becoming a team demands a process of development. Tuckman (1965) proposed a four-stage model of group development:

- ✪ forming

- ✪ storming

- ✪ norming

- ✪ performing.

Each group will go through the four stages; however, the length of time they spend in each stage is variable.

Forming

The group comes together, with individuals meeting and familiarising themselves with the other members of the group. The structure and relationships within the group are formed and tested. If it is a team, the coach may develop strategies or games to 'break the ice' between the group members.

Storming

A period of conflict will follow the forming stage as individuals seek their roles and status within the group. This may involve conflict between individual members, rebellion against the leader or resistance to the way the team is being developed or managed or the tactics they are adopting. This is also a period of intense inter-group competition, as group members compete for their positions within the team.

Norming

Once the hostility and fighting has been overcome, either by athletes leaving the group or accepting the common goals and values of the group, a period of norming occurs. Here, the group starts to cooperate and work together to reach common goals. The group pulls together and the roles are established and become stable.

Performing

In the final stage, the group members work together to achieve their mutual goals. The relationships within the group have become well established, as have issues of leadership and strategies for play. It is unrealistic to see the group as being stable and performing in a steady way. The relationships within the group will change and develop with time, sometimes for the good of the group and sometimes to its detriment. As new members join the group there will be a new period of storming and norming, as this person is either accepted or rejected. This re-evaluation of the group is often beneficial, and stops the group becoming stale. Successful teams seem to be settled and assimilate two or three new players a year to keep them fresh. Bringing in too many new players can disrupt the group and change the nature of the group completely.

It is interesting to see how Manchester United developed through the 1990s. They had a large influx of new players who had come up through the youth and reserve sides into the first team, and because they were already familiar with the group norms and expectations they became successful fairly quickly. Each year they bought in two or three new players to keep things fresh and keep the group developing. Their least successful season in 2001–02 was blamed on the introduction of Juan Sebastien Veron, who was seen to disrupt group dynamics and reduce the team's effectiveness.

Group effectiveness

The aim of a group is to be effective by using the strengths of each person to better the effectiveness of the group. However, the outcome is often not equal to the sum of its parts.

Steiner (1972) proposes a model of group effectiveness:

$$\text{Actual productivity} = \text{Potential productivity} - \text{Process losses}$$

Where: actual productivity = the actual performance achieved
potential productivity = the best possible performance achievable by that group based on its resources (ability, knowledge, skills)
process losses = losses due to working as part of a group (co-ordination losses, communication problems, losses in motivation)

For example, in a tug of war team each member can pull 100 kg on their own; as a team of four they pull 360 kg in total. Why do you think this would happen?

Social loafing

One of the problems of working in groups is that it tends to affect motivation. People do not seem to work as hard in groups when compared with working on their own. Research shows that rowers in larger teams give less effort than smaller teams:

> 1 person = 100% effort
> 2 people = 90% effort
> 4 people = 80% effort
> 8 people = 65% effort

This phenomenon is called the **Ringelman effect** or **social loafing** and is defined as the tendency of individuals to lessen their effort when part of a group.

Research done into social loafing

1   Relationship between group size and rope-pulling performance.

Table 3.3	1	2	3	4	5	6	7	8
Ringelmann	100	93	85			49		
Ingham (1974a)	100	91	82	78	78	78		
Ingham (1974b)	100	90	85	86	84	85		

2   Latane, Williams and Harkins (1980) used a hand-clapping task:

> 1 person clapping – 100%
> 2 people clapping – 71%
> 4 people clapping – 51%
> 6 people clapping – 40%

3   Latane and Hardy (1988) found that cheerleaders produced 94% as much noise when in pairs as when performing alone.

Why does social loafing occur?

1   Being part of a group reduces identifiability and accountability. The individuals may not feel that their efforts can be identified and thus that people will not know how hard they worked.

2   Athletes may feel working hard in a group does not bring recognition. We all like to gain recognition for our hard work and therefore, if there is no chance of this, we may not be so concerned about being successful.

3   Athletes may feel they do not need to work hard as team-mates will take up the slack. We realise that if people do not know how little or how much effort we are putting in there are always other people who will do the work for us. This often happens when a team contains a 'star' player;

we think we can let them do the work or, if we give them the ball, they will win the match for us.

Cohesion

Cohesion is concerned with the extent to which a team is willing to stick together and work together.

The forces mentioned in the definition will tend to cover two areas:

- ✪ the attractiveness of the group to individual members

- ✪ the extent to which members are willing to work together to achieve group goals.

To be successful in its goals, a group has to be cohesive. The extent to which cohesion is important depends upon the sport and the level of interaction needed.

How can social loafing be minimised?

1 Give examples from your own experience of social loafing.
2 How does social loafing occur in the following sports and what strategies can be used to prevent social loafing occurring?
   a) 4 × 100 m or 4 × 400 m relay
   b) eight-person rowing race
   c) rugby scrummage
   d) doubles in tennis
   e) football.

Hint: think about how performances can be quantified (put into figures) or how individual performance can be identified.

Student activity

Place the following ten team sports in order depending upon the level of interaction and thus cohesion needed to be successful.

Rowing eights	Tennis doubles	4 × 100 m relay
Golf team	Bobsleigh four	Cricket team
Volleyball team	Cycling team	Curling team
Synchronised swimming team		

Types of cohesion

There seem to be two definite types of cohesion within a group.

- ✪ **Task cohesion** – The willingness of a team to work together to achieve their goals.

- ✪ **Social cohesion** – The willingness of the team to socialise together.

It would appear that task cohesion comes first as this is why the team has formed in the first place. If the group is lucky they will find that they develop social cohesion as well, and this usually has a beneficial effect on performance. This is because if you feel good about your team-mates you are more likely to want success for each other as well as yourself.

However, history has shown many examples where individuals or groups which have no interpersonal attraction can still be successful. For example, Andy Cole and Teddy Sheringham formed an excellent striking partnership for

 **Definitions**

Cohesion is defined by Festinger *et al.* (1950) as *'the total field of forces which act on members to remain in the group.'*

Manchester United while never being on speaking terms. There is the famous example of the East German rowing eight who won the Olympic gold medal in 1968 despite the fact that they could not stand each other's company; also the relationship between Steven Redgrave and Andrew Pinsent had been so tested by the time they won the Olympic gold medal in 1996 that they had decided the only way to carry on was to move up to a four-man crew, which meant that more relationships had to be developed.

In summary, the research says that cohesion is important in successful teams, but that task cohesion is more important than social cohesion. It does depend upon the sport being played, as groups that need high levels of interaction need higher levels of cohesion.

Research also suggests that success will produce increased cohesion rather than cohesion coming before performance. Being successful helps to develop feelings of group attraction, and this will help to develop more success, and so on. This can be seen by the cycle of success, in that once a team has been successful once they tend to continue being successful, i.e. success breeds success.

LEADERSHIP

STUDENT ACTIVITY

Before reading the section on leadership, take time to answer the following questions.

1   How would you define 'leadership'?
2   Make a list of eight people you consider to be effective leaders. Choose four from sport and four from other areas.
3   List eight personality qualities or traits that you think are needed to make an effective leader.
4   Are the leadership qualities needed to lead in sport the same as in all leadership situations?
5   Do you think an effective leader will be effective in all situations? Why?

Definitions

Leadership
Leadership can be defined in the following manner: '*The behavioural process of influencing individuals and groups towards goals*' (Barron, 1977)

Leadership in sport

The choice of a manager, coach or captain is often the most important decision a club's members have to make. They see it as crucial in influencing the club's chances of success. Great leaders in sport are held in the highest regard, irrespective of their talent on the pitch. Sports people such as Sven Goran Eriksson, Kevin Keegan, Martin Johnson, Nasser Hussain and Linford Christie are all regarded as 'great' leaders.

Leadership behaviour covers a variety of activities, hence we call it multidimensional, it includes:

- ✪ decision-making processes
- ✪ motivational techniques
- ✪ giving feedback
- ✪ establishing interpersonal relationships
- ✪ confidently directing the group.

Leaders are different from managers: managers plan, organise, budget, schedule, recruit; leaders determine how a task is completed.

People become leaders in different ways; not all are appointed. **Prescribed leaders** are appointed by a person in authority, e.g. a chairman appoints a manager, a manager appoints a coach, a principal appoints a teacher. **Emergent leaders** emerge from a group and take over responsibility. e.g. David Beckham emerged to become the leader of the England football team. Emergent leaders are often more effective as they have the respect of their group members.

Theories of leadership

Sport psychologists have sought to explain leadership effectiveness for many years and they have used the following theories to help understand effective leadership behaviour.

Trait approach

In the 1920s researchers tried to show that characteristics or personality traits were stable and common to all leaders. Thus, to be a good leader you needed to have intelligence, assertiveness, independence and self-confidence. Therefore, a person who is a good leader in one situation will be a good leader in all situations.

Behavioural approach

The trait approach says that leaders are 'born', but the behavioural approach says that anyone can become a good leader by learning the behaviour of effective leaders. Thus, this approach supports the view that leadership skills can be developed through experience and training.

Interactional approach

Trait and personal approaches look at personality traits. The interactional approach looks at the interaction between the person and the situation. It stresses the following points.

1   Effective leaders cannot be predicted solely on personality.

2   Effective leadership fits specific situations, as some leaders function better in certain circumstances than others.

3   Leadership style needs to change to match the demands of the situation.

BTEC NATIONAL IN SPORT AND EXERCISE SCIENCE

STUDENT ACTIVITY

What type of leadership (task-oriented or relationship-oriented) would be relevant in the following situations:

- ✪ A PE teacher
- ✪ A Premiership team captain
- ✪ A Member of Parliament
- ✪ Captain of over 50s badminton team
- ✪ A student leading a group in a presentation
- ✪ An aerobics teacher.

If you feel a mixture of the two styles would be appropriate, state what percentage of each would be needed.

For example, relationship-oriented leaders develop interpersonal relationships, provide good communication and ensure everyone is feeling good within the group. However, task-oriented leaders are concerned with getting the work done and meeting objectives.

The multidimensional model of sport leadership

The three models previously discussed were adapted from non-sporting examples. Although they help us understand leadership behaviour, each model has its shortcomings. In 1980, P. Chelladurai presented a sport-specific model. He proposed the view that effective leadership will vary depending on the characteristics of the athletes, the leader and the situation.

What does Figure 3.13 mean?

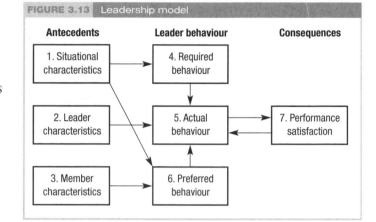

FIGURE 3.13 Leadership model

1   **Situational characteristics** – The characteristics such as size, type of sport, winning or losing, of the situation the group is in.

2   **Leader characteristics** – The personal qualities of the leader. Some of the qualities needed are confidence, intelligence, assertiveness and self-motivation.

3   **Member characteristics** – The different personality types of different groups of athletes, these characteristics include age, gender, ability level and experience.

4   **Required behaviour** – The type of behaviour required of a leader in a particular situation. For example, if a team is losing with five minutes to go, it is best for the leader to make a decision themselves rather than discuss it with their team-mates.

5   **Actual behaviour** – The behaviours the leader actually displays.

6   **Preferred behaviour** – The preferred leadership of the group, depending on their characteristics.

7   **Performance satisfaction** – The extent to which the group members are satisfied with the leader's behaviour and with the outcome of the competition.

The model says that if a leader behaves appropriately for the particular situation and these behaviours match the preferences of the group members, then they will achieve their best performance and feel satisfied.

The leadership scale for sport

The leadership scale for sport was developed by Chelladurai to assess the five main behaviours of coaches in their positions of leadership, and to evaluate how often they use each.

1 **Training and instruction** – Information is provided by the coach, aimed at improving the performance of the athlete in terms of technique and strategy.

2 **Democratic behaviour** – The athlete is involved in reaching decisions regarding group goals and group strategy.

3 **Autocratic behaviour** – The coach acts independently, forcing decisions on the group.

4 **Social support behaviour** – This is aimed at improving the wellbeing and welfare of the athletes and developing group relationships.

5 **Positive feedback behaviour** – This rewards individual and group actions through acknowledging athletes' efforts and performance.

Leadership in sport is a complex subject as it involves the process of influencing people towards achieving their personal goals and the goals of the group. Individuals will respond to different types of leader and different types of leadership behaviour. Different leaders have different strengths and ways of leading, and may find that what was successful in one situation is not so effective in another.

Social facilitation

Social facilitation is the change in performance that occurs due to the presence of others; whether the presence is an audience or fellow competitors.

There is no doubt that our performances change as the result of the presence of other people. Think about how you feel when your parents or friends come to watch you, or when you start to perform in front of an audience.

Zajonc (1965) defined the different types of people present, separating them into those people who are competing against you and those people who are merely present and not competing (Figure 3.14).

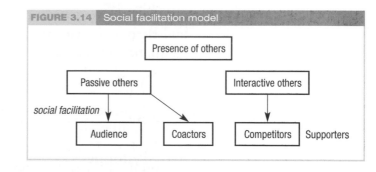

FIGURE 3.14   Social facilitation model

Coactors are people involved in the same activity, but not competing directly. Triplett (1898) did some of the earliest experiments in sport psychology. He examined coaction in the following three conditions, using cyclists: 1. unpaced; 2. paced (coactor on another bike); 3. paced competitive (coactors pacing and competing). His findings were that cyclists in condition 2 were 34 seconds per mile faster than cyclists in condition 1, while cyclists in condition 3 were 39 seconds per mile faster than cyclists in condition 1.

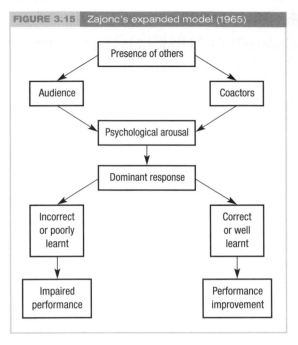

FIGURE 3.15 Zajonc's expanded model (1965)

The reasons for social faciliation are not always clear; however, Triplett concluded that in his experiment it was due to the physical effects, such as suctioning and sheltering resulting from travelling behind another rider, and psychological effects such as encouragement, anxiety, pressure and competitiveness which are felt as the result of cycling with someone else. Triplett concluded that it did not matter if the cyclists were competing; what was important was that the: 'bodily presence of another rider is stimulus to a rider in arousing the competitive instinct'.

Zajonc's expanded model showed that whether the audience or coactors have a positive or negative effect on performance depends upon how well the skill has been learnt. A poorly learnt skill will become worse, while a well-learnt skill will be improved (Figure 3.15). This links in well with the effect of stress on performance, and it can be seen that the presence of others would cause more stress.

Zajonc also looked at the relationship between the audience effect and the standard of the performer. His results are shown in Figure 3.16.

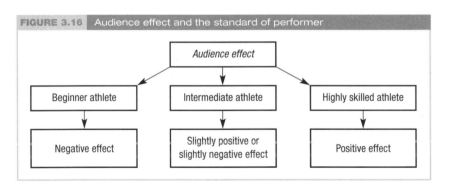

FIGURE 3.16 Audience effect and the standard of performer

The effect also depends upon the nature of the task, i.e. whether it is strength or skill related. Strength tasks will usually be enhanced by the presence of others. However, skilled tasks (especially poorly learnt skills) may suffer. Social facilitation effects tend to disappear as the individual gets used to it.

Cottrell (1968) said that it is not the mere presence of an audience which creates arousal, but that the type of audience is also very important. For example, a blindfolded audience had no facilitation effect. The following factors will affect social facilitation.

1   **Audience expertise** – An expert audience will increase arousal level.

2   **Type of audience** – A **pro-winning** audience will have more of a facilitation effect than a **pro-enjoyment** audience.

3   **Performer's evaluation of the audience** – The performer decides what they think the audience wants and is aroused accordingly.

4   **Size** – A larger audience will have more of a facilitation effect.

Home advantage

Home advantage is the view that the team playing at home has a disproportionately high chance of winning in relation to the team playing away from home. This phenomenon was apparent in the World Cup of 2002 where the joint hosts South Korea and Japan both did far better than they had ever previously done, particularly South Korea, who progressed to the semi-finals.

Why is there a home advantage?

There are many reasons why home teams are more successful; some of these are physical and some are psychological:

- ✪ familiarity with the surroundings and the surfaces
- ✪ a supportive home crowd who give positive approval
- ✪ less intimidation by opposing supporters
- ✪ the territory is theirs and claimed by display of their playing colours
- ✪ there is less travel involved in getting to the match
- ✪ travel can cause boredom and staleness
- ✪ players do not have to stay in unfamiliar surroundings and eat unfamiliar food
- ✪ home teams are more likely to play offensively
- ✪ away teams may not be treated well by their opponents
- ✪ referees and officials may unconsciously favour the home team to seek the crowd's approval.

Home advantage may be seen as being as a disadvantage to the away team rather than an advantage to the home team. It is the job of the coach and psychologist to find ways of minimising this away disadvantage.

STUDENT ACTIVITY

To see whether a home advantage does exist, take the sports supplement from a paper on Sunday or Monday and examine the results from three or four sports, such as football, rugby, hockey or cricket. Work out the following percentages:

- ✪ teams winning at home
- ✪ teams drawing at home
- ✪ teams losing at home.

1. Do your results support the theory of home advantage?
2. Would there be a home advantage in individual sports such as athletics, tennis or golf?

REVISION QUESTIONS

1) Explain what is meant by the term 'group'.
2) Outline the four stages of group development.
3) Explain Steiner's model of group effectiveness
4) What is meant by the term 'social loafing'?
5) How can social loafing be minimised?
6) What is cohesion? Describe the two types.
7) How important is cohesion in group performance?
8) Explain the three theories of leadership.
9) Discuss the multidimensional model of leadership and how it explains group success.
10) What is social facilitation and why does it exist?
11) Why do home teams seem to have an advantage due to playing at home?

Chapter REVISION *QUESTIONS*

1) Explain the relationship between personality and sports performance.

2) Discuss the view that people are motivated predominantly by material rewards.

3) Choose two different sports skills and explain how performance is affected by stressful situations.

4) Discuss the view that there is no such thing as an non-cohesive group.

FURTHER READING

There is a wealth of excellent texts available, either completely devoted to sport psychology or where sport psychology constitutes a large part. The following are recommended.

Beashel, P. and Taylor, J. (1996) *Advanced Studies in Physical Education and Sport*. Nelson

Davis, R. J., Bull, C. R., Roscoe, J. V., Roscoe, D.A. (2000) *Physical Education and the Study of Sport*. London: Mosby

Jarvis, Matt (2000) *Sport Psychology*. London: Routledge

Weinberg, Robert S. and Gould, Daniel (1995) *Foundations of Sport and Exercise Psychology*. Illinois: Human Kinetics

Wesson, K., Wiggins, N., Thompson, G., Hartigan, S. (2000) *Sport and P.E.: A Complete Guide to Advanced Level Study*. London: Hodder and Stoughton

Woods Barbara (1998) *Applying Psychology to Sport*. London: Hodder and Stoughton

REFERENCES

Bandura, A. (1977a) *Social Learning Theory*. Eaglewood Cliffs, NJ: Pentice-Hall.

Bandura, A. Self-efficacy: Toward a unifying theory of behavioural change. *Psychological Review*, 84, 191–215.

Beashel, P. and Taylor, J. (1996) *Advanced Studies in Physical Education and Sport*. Nelson.

Berkowicz, L. (1969) Roots of Aggression. Atherton Press.

Cattell, R. B. (1965) *The Scientific Analysis of Personality*. London: Penguin

Chelladurai, P. and Carron, A.V. (1978) Leadership. *Sociology of Sport Monograph Series*.

Cox, R. (1994) *Sports Psychology: Concepts and Applications*. 3rd Edition. Wm C. Brown Communications.

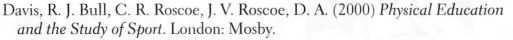

Davis, R. J. Bull, C. R. Roscoe, J. V. Roscoe, D. A. (2000) *Physical Education and the Study of Sport.* London: Mosby.

Dollard, J. Doob, J. Miller, N. Mowrer, O. and Sears, R. (1939) *Frustration and Aggression.* New Haven, Conneticut: Yale University Press.

Eysenck, H. J. and Eysenck, S. B. G. (1964) *Manual of Eysenck Personality Inventory.* University of London Press.

Fazey, J. and Hardy, L. (1988) The inverted U hypothesis: a catastrophe for sport psychology? *British Association of Sports Sciences Monograph*, no.1. NCF.

Hollander, E. P. (1971) *Principles and methods of Social psychology*, 2nd edition. Oxford University Press.

Jarvis, Matt (2000) *Sport Psychology.* London: Routledge.

Latane, B. Harkins, S. G. and Williams, K. D. (1980) *Many Hands make Light Work: Social Loafing as a Social Disease.* Unpublished manuscript. Columbus: Ohio State University.

Oxendine, C. B. (1970) Emotional Arousal and Motor Performance. *Quest*, 13, 23–30.

Triplett, N. (1898) The dynamogenic factors in pacemaking and competition. *American Journal of psychology*, 9, 507–533.

Weinberg, Robert S. and Gould, Daniel (1995) *Foundations of Sport and Exercise Psychology.* Illinois: Human Kinetics.

Wesson, K. Wiggins, N. Thompson, G. Hartigan S. (2000) *Sport and P.E.: A complete Guide to Advanced Level Study.* London: Hodder and Stoughton.

Zajonc, R. B. (1965) Social Facilitation. *Science*, 149, 269–274.

Woods, Barbara (1998) *Applying Psychology to Sport.* London: Hodder and Stoughton.

CHAPTER 4

EXERCISE PHYSIOLOGY

This chapter covers the cardiovascular system and its role in delivery and removal of respiratory gases and waste products at rest and during exercise. The different energy systems and their production of adenosine triphosphate (ATP) are explored, together with their recovery from exercise. Mechanisms of fatigue and exercise adaptation to the cardiovascular, respiratory and neuromuscular systems are also examined.

By the end of this chapter students should be able to:

✪ understand how the cardiovascular system delivers and removes respiratory gases and metabolites to the body at rest and during exercise

✪ comprehend when and how the different energy systems produce ATP

✪ describe how the body recovers from fatigue

✪ understand how the cardiovascular, respiratory and neuromuscular systems adapt to chronic training.

CARDIO-VASCULAR SYSTEM

The **cardiovascular system** consists of the heart and the blood vessels through which the heart pumps blood around the body. During exercise, a number of changes take place to the cardiovascular system to ensure that the muscles receive the required amounts of oxygen and nutrients. The structure of the cardiovascular system is discussed in more detail in Chapter 7.

Cardiac cycle

The **cardiac cycle** is all of the events that occur in one heartbeat. As it is a cycle there is no beginning or end – the end of the cycle only occurs when you die! One heartbeat takes 0.8 seconds and consists of two phases.

1 **Systole**, when the heart contracts, lasts 0.3 seconds. The ventricles contract and blood flows into the aorta.

2 **Diastole**, when the heart relaxes, takes 0.5 seconds. When the heart relaxes blood flows from the atria and into the ventricles.

Nervous control of the heart

The heart is **myogenic** which means it can contract without receiving nervous stimulation from the central nervous system (CNS). There are four main neural sites which work together in order to ensure that the four chambers of the heart beat regularly. These sites are:

✪ the sino-atrial node (SAN)

✪ the atrioventricular node (AVN)

✪ the Bundle of His

✪ the Purkinje fibres

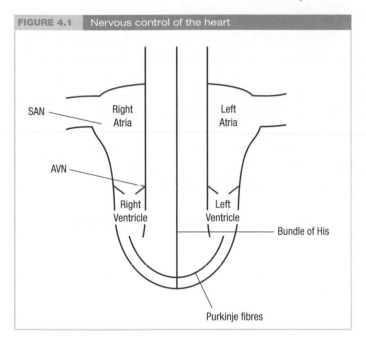

FIGURE 4.1 Nervous control of the heart

The sino-atrial node (SAN) is also known as the pacemaker, as it sets the pace at which the heat beats. It is located at the top right-hand side of the heart in the right atrium. It sends a nervous impulse which travels across the two atria and makes them contract at the same time.

This nervous impulse then reaches the atrioventricular node (AVN), which is located at the bottom of the right atrium, and travels down to the two ventricles via the bundle of His. The impulse lastly travels up the Purkinje fibres, which are located at the bottom of the two ventricles and make them contract simultaneously.

Although the SAN sets the pace of the heart, the heart rate can also be made to increase or decrease through the **sympathetic** and **parasympathetic** nervous systems of the CNS, which is controlled by the medulla. The sympathetic nervous system acts to increase the heart rate through the release of **adrenaline**; the parasympathetic nervous system acts to decrease the heart rate through the release of **acteylcholine**.

Effects of exercise on the cardiac cycle

During exercise the heart rate needs to be increased in order to ensure that the working muscles receive adequate amounts of nutrients and oxygen, and that waste products are removed. Before you even start exercising there is an increase in your heart rate, called the **anticipatory rise**, which occurs because the sympathetic nervous system releases adrenaline. Once exercise has started, there is an increase in carbon dioxide and lactic acid in the body which is detected by **chemoreceptors**. The chemoreceptors trigger the sympathetic nervous system to increase the release of adrenaline, which further increases heart rate. As exercise continues, the body becomes warmer, which will also help to increase the heart rate because it increases the speed of the conduction of nerve impulses across the heart.

STUDENT PRACTICAL

Heart rate and exercise

Aim

The aim of this practical is to examine what happens to heart rate during exercise.

Equipment

stopwatch or heart rate monitor

sports clothes

pen and paper

bench

skipping rope

Method

1   If you have a heart rate monitor, place it around your chest. If not, find your pulse point either on your neck or at your wrist.

2   Sit quietly for five minutes, then take your resting heart rate. If you have a heart rate monitor, write down the heart rate that appears on the monitor. If not, feel for your pulse point, then count your heart rate for 30 seconds. Double this figure and write it down.

3   Think about what exercise you are about to perform.

4   Record your heart rate after having thought about your exercise.

5   Perform step ups onto a bench for five minutes or skip for three minutes with a skipping rope.

6   Immediately after you have finished your exercise, record your heart rate.

Results

Resting heart rate (bpm)	Pre-exercise heart rate (bpm)	Post-exercise heart rate (bpm)

Copy and complete the results table above.

Conclusion

In your conclusion try to answer the following questions:

1   What happened to your heart rate immediately before you started exercising?

2   What caused this change in your heart rate and why is it necessary?

3   Try to explain why there is a difference between your resting heart rate and your post-exercise heart rate.

Electrocardiogram (ECG)

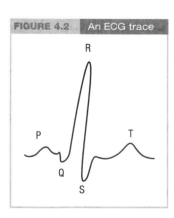

FIGURE 4.2   An ECG trace

An ECG is a test that measures the electrical activity of the heart. The information obtained from an ECG can be used to discover different types of heart disease. In the case of athletes, it can also demonstrate thickening of the heart muscle (left ventricular hypertrophy). An ECG gives a trace like the one shown in Figure 4.2. Each section of the trace is given a letter to identify it, which corresponds to the electrical activity of the heart:

✪   **P wave** – this occurs just before the atria contract

✪   **QRS complex** – this occurs just before the ventricles contract

✪   **T wave** – this occurs just before the ventrices relax.

Cardiac output

Cardiac output is the amount of blood pumped from the heart every minute and is the product of heart rate and stroke volume.

$$\text{cardiac output (litres per minute)} =$$
$$\text{heart rate (bpm)} \times \text{stroke volume (litres)}$$

The shorthand for this equation is: $Q = HR \times SV$.

The stroke volume is around 70 to 90 millilitres, however, it varies depending on a variety of factors. Generally, the fitter you are, the larger your stroke volume is and males tend to have larger stroke volumes than females. At rest a person's cardiac output is approximately 5 litres per minute, while during exercise it can increase to as much as 30 litres per minute.

STUDENT ACTIVITY

Calculate your stroke volume

1 Take your resting heart rate by finding a pulse point and recording your heart rate for 30 seconds. Double this figure to give you beats per minute.

2 The average cardiac output for a person is 5 litres per minute. By rearranging the equation we can estimate a person's SV:

$$Q = SV \times HR$$

$$SV = \frac{Q}{HR}$$

e.g. If your heart rate was 70 bpm:

$$SV = \frac{5}{70}$$

$$SV = 0.071 \text{ litre} = 71 \text{ ml}$$

3 Note down the rest of the class's stroke volumes and then take an average.

4 Separate your class stoke volumes into males and females and then calculate an average stroke volume for the males and another for the females. Is there a difference between the two? If so, try to explain why.

5 What conclusions can you draw about the fitness of your class?

Rate of blood flow

As stated previously, the average cardiac output is around 5 litres per minute. When this blood is circulated around the body, some organs receive more than others. However, during exercise, the working muscles need a greater proportion of blood in order to supply them with energy. The body is able to redirect blood flow by constricting the blood vessels leading to organs that do not require such a large blood flow, and dilating the blood vessels feeding the muscles that do. As you can see from Table 4.1 (overleaf), the liver and gut take 25% of the blood flow at rest. This is to help to digest the food you have eaten. During exercise, the liver and gut only receive 1.5% of the blood flow, which means that less food can be digested. This can help to explain why people are prone to stomach upsets if they eat too soon before exercising.

Table 4.1 Blood flow at rest and during exercise

Organ	Blood flow at rest (%)	Blood flow during maximal exercise (%)
Skeletal muscle	15	85
Brain	15	2.5
Kidneys	25	1
Liver and gut	25	1.5
Skin	5	2.5
Heart	5	4
Other	10	3.5

Blood pressure

Blood pressure is necessary in order for blood to flow around the body. The pressure is a result of the heart contracting and forcing blood into the blood vessels. Two values are given when a person has their blood pressure taken, and a typical blood pressure is $\frac{120}{80}$ for the average adult male. The two values correspond to the systolic value (when the heart is contracting) and the diastolic value (when the heart is relaxing). The higher value is the systolic value and the lower is the diastolic value. Blood pressure is measured in milligrams of mercury, **mmHg**.

The value for a person's blood pressure is determined by the cardiac output (Q), which is a product of stroke volume and heart rate, and the resistance the blood encounters as it flows. This can be put into an equation:

$$\text{blood pressure} = Q \times R$$
$$\text{where } Q = \text{cardiac output (stroke volume} \times \text{heart rate)}$$
$$R = \text{resistance to flow}$$

Resistance to blood flow is caused both by the size of the blood vessels through which it travels (the smaller the blood vessel, the greater the resistance) and by the thickness of the blood (the thicker the blood the greater the resistance).

Changing the resistance to blood flow can alter blood pressure. This is done by involuntary smooth muscles in the arterioles relaxing or contracting in order to alter the diameter of the arterioles. As the smooth muscle contracts, the diameter of the blood vessel gets smaller, so blood pressure is increased; as the smooth muscle relaxes, the diameter of the blood vessel is increased, which decreases the pressure of the blood flowing through it. The same principle can be applied to altering the diameter of water flow through a hose. If you place your finger over part of the opening of the hose, making the diameter smaller, the water will flow out quite forcibly because it is under higher pressure. However, if the water is left to flow unhindered through the end of the hose it is under lower pressure, and will therefore not 'spurt' so far because there is less resistance.

A reduction in blood pressure is detected by **baroreceptors** in the aorta and the carotid artery. This detection is passed to the CNS, which then sends a nervous impulse signal to the arterioles to constrict. This increases the pressure of the blood and also has the effect of increasing the heart rate.

When blood pressure is increased, the baroreceptors detect this and signal the CNS, which makes the arterioles dilate, and reduces blood pressure.

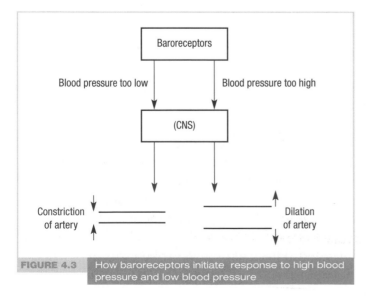

FIGURE 4.3 How baroreceptors initiate response to high blood pressure and low blood pressure

Changes to blood pressure during exercise

During exercise there is an increase in heart rate, which will result in an increased cardiac output. As previously stated, cardiac output = heart rate × stroke volume, therefore, as heart rate increases, cardiac output will also increase.

Dilatation of the blood vessels feeding the working muscle acts to reduce blood pressure, but this is counteracted by the increase in blood pressure caused by increased cardiac output.

Exercise raises systolic pressure, but there is only a slight change in diastolic pressure. Immediately after exercise there is a fall in systolic pressure as the skeletal muscular pump is no longer pumping blood from the muscles to the heart. This can lead to blood pooling in the muscles and cause the athlete to faint as not enough blood is being pumped to the brain.

STUDENT PRACTICAL

Blood pressure and exercise

Aim

The aim of this practical is to try to determine what happens to blood pressure during and after different types of exercise.

Equipment

electrical sphygmomanometer

pen and paper

sports clothes

treadmill or cycle ergometer

free or fixed weights

Method

1 Decide on two types of exercise; one must be an aerobic exercise which lasts a minimum of 10 minutes (a treadmill or cycle ergometer) and the other should be an explosive exercise such as lifting weights.

2 Attach the sphygmomanometer to your subject and record their resting blood pressure.

3 Your subject should perform 10 minutes of aerobic exercise. After about 9 minutes of exercise take their blood pressure (ensure that your subject continues to exercise throughout).

4 After a break of at least 15 minutes, record your subject's blood pressure.

5 Your subject should then perform some weight lifting. Try to record your subject's blood pressure while they are lifting a heavy weight with either their legs or their arms.

Results

Activity	Blood pressure
Resting	
Aerobic exercise	
Resting	
Explosive exercise	

Copy and complete the table above.

Conclusion

In your conclusion, try to answer the following questions:

1 What happened to the blood pressure during each type of exercise?

2 Which reading was affected the most during the different types of exercise?

3 Why do you think the blood pressure changed during each type of activity?

Transport of respiratory gases

Oxygen

Only 1.5% of oxygen is carried in the blood plasma; the majority of oxygen is transported in blood by **haemoglobin**. Oxygen reacts with haemoglobin to make **oxyhaemoglobin**. The reaction of oxygen with haemoglobin is temporary and completely reversible, which means that oxygen can be unloaded from haemoglobin. The binding of oxygen to haemoglobin is dependent on the **partial pressure** of oxygen. Oxygen combines with haemoglobin in oxygen-rich situations, such as in the lungs.

Oxygen is released by haemoglobin in places where there is little oxygen, such as in exercising muscle.

Myoglobin is a haemoglobin-like, pigment found in muscle fibres, which binds only less oxygen to it compared to haemoglobin. It takes up oxygen from the haemoglobin in the blood and stores oxygen within the muscle itself.

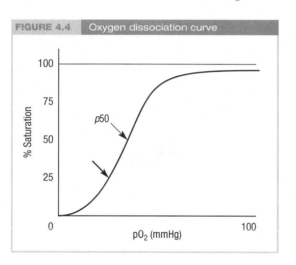

FIGURE 4.4 Oxygen dissociation curve

Oxygen dissociation curve

This is an S shaped curve (see Figure 4.4) that represents the ease with which haemoglobin will release oxygen when it is exposed to tissues of different concentrations of oxygen. The curve starts with a steep rise because haemoglobin has a high **affinity** for oxygen. This means that when there is a small rise in the partial pressure of oxygen, haemoglobin will pick up and bind oxygen to it easily. Thus, in the lungs the blood is rapidly saturated with oxygen. However, only a small drop in the partial pressure of oxygen will result in a large drop in the percentage saturation of haemoglobin. Thus, in exercising muscles, where there is a low partial pressure of oxygen, the haemoglobin will readily unload the oxygen for use by the tissues.

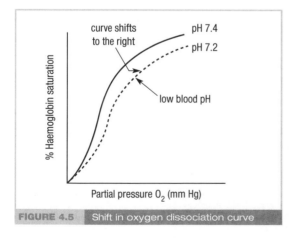

FIGURE 4.5 Shift in oxygen dissociation curve

Effects of pH and temperature on the oxygen dissociation curve

Changes in blood carbon dioxide level and hydrogen ion concentration (pH) cause shifts in the oxygen dissociation curve. These shifts enhance oxygen release in tissues and increase oxygen uptake in the lungs. This is know as the **Bohr effect**, named after the Danish physiologist Christian Bohr who discovered it. During exercise, the blood becomes more acidic because of the increased production of carbon dioxide.

This increase in carbon dioxide and decrease in pH shifts the dissociation curve to the right for a given partial pressure of oxygen, releasing more oxygen to the tissues (see Figure 4.5).

In the lungs there is a low partial pressure of carbon dioxide and low hydrogen ion concentration which shifts the dissociation curve to the left for a given partial pressure of oxygen, and therefore enhances oxygen uptake.

As muscles exercise, they also increase in temperature. This has the effect of shifting the curve to the right, which means oxygen is released much more readily. Conversely, a decreased temperature will shift the curve to the left, which increases oxygen uptake.

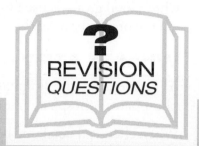

REVISION QUESTIONS

1) Describe how the heart initiates its own nervous impulse to beat.

2) Explain what the cardiac cycle is.

3) Draw a diagram that illustrates the nervous control of the heart.

4) How does the heart rate increase in response to exercise?

5) Why is it necessary for the heart rate to increase during exercise?

6) What is the equation to work out a cardiac output?

7) What factors influence a person's blood pressure?

8) What is the normal reading of a healthy adult's blood pressure?

9) Why would atherosclerosis (narrowing of the arteries) increase a person's blood pressure?

10) What happens to a person's blood pressure during exercise and why?

11) Why is it not a good idea to eat a heavy meal prior to taking part in exercise?

12) How is oxygen transported around the body?

13) With regard to the Bohr effect, explain why and how oxygen transfers from the blood to working muscles.

ENERGY SYSTEMS

In order for our muscles to contract they require energy in the form of adenosine triphoshate (ATP). The food we eat is broken down and used in one of three energy systems in order to produce ATP. In some ways ATP can be likened to petrol or diesel. In order for our cars to work they need energy in the form of petrol or diesel. Petrol or diesel is made from dead animals and vegetation that has been left for thousands of years and eventually turns into the said fuels. Therefore, you could not pick up a dead branch from the side of the road and shove it in your petrol tank – it needs to be turned into petrol first. In the same way, the food we eat needs to be turned into ATP before our muscles can use the energy. Thus, if you were to directly 'feed' your muscles a chocolate bar, they would not be able to use the energy from it. Instead, the energy from the chocolate bar needs to be fed into an energy system which will then produce ATP.

Sources of fuel

We gain fuel from the food we eat. There are many different types of food available, but these can all be placed into one of the following food groups: carbohydrates, fats and proteins. The type of exercise done will determine which food group is used to produce ATP. Food groups and their effects on energy production can be explored further in Chapter 8.

What is ATP?

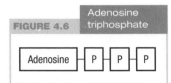

FIGURE 4.6 — Adenosine triphosphate

ATP (adenosine triphosphate) is basically a protein (adenosine) with three (tri) phosphates (phosphate) attached to it (see Figure 4.6).

When chemical bonds are broken, energy is released. Therefore, when a phosphate is broken off the ATP to make ADP (adenosine diphosphate (di = two)) energy is released which is used to make the muscles contract (see Figure 4.7).

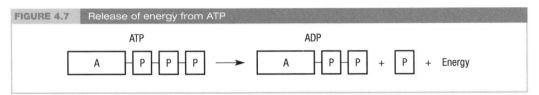

FIGURE 4.7 | Release of energy from ATP

However, ATP is not stored in large amounts in skeletal muscle and therefore has to be continually made from ADP in order for our muscles to continue contracting. In order to make ATP there are a three main energy systems, which differ in the rate at which they make ATP. If we are taking part in a running sprint, then we will want ATP supplied very quickly. However, if we are on a long walk we don't need such a fast production of ATP, so the body uses a different energy system to make it.

The energy systems

The energy system that supplies ATP most quickly is the phosphocreatine system; second fastest is the lactic acid system, and the slowest system is the aerobic energy system. Usually all three energy systems are working at the same time, but one system is responsible for making the majority of ATP at any one time.

Anaerobic energy systems

The first two energy systems produce ATP in the absence of oxygen, hence the name **anaerobic**.

Phosphocreatine (PCr) – This energy system is also known as the **creatine phosphate (CP)** system. Phosphocreatine is made up of a phosphate and a creatine molecule. When the bond between the phosphate and the creatine is broken, energy is released which is then used to make the bond between ADP and a phosphate (see Figure 4.8).

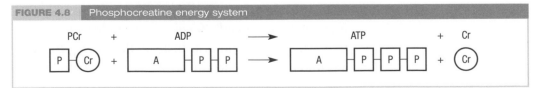

FIGURE 4.8 | Phosphocreatine energy system

PCr stores are used for rapid, high-intensity contractions, such as in sprinting or jumping; however, these stores only last for about ten seconds.

Lactic acid system – This is also known as **anaerobic glycolysis**, which literally means the breakdown of glucose in the absence of oxygen. When glucose is broken down it is converted into a substance called pyruvate. When there is no oxygen present, the pyruvate is converted into **lactic acid**. This system produces ATP very quickly, but not as quickly as the PCr system.

The lactic acid energy system is the one that is producing the majority of the ATP during high intensity exercise lasting between thirty seconds and three minutes, such as an 800 m race.

Aerobic energy system

This is also known as **aerobic glycolysis** as it occurs when oxygen is available to break down glucose. As in the anaerobic energy system, glucose is broken down into pyruvate, however, because oxygen is present, pyruvate is not turned into lactic acid, but continues to be broken down through a series of chemical reactions.

The reactions of aerobic energy system supply ATP quite slowly and produce the majority of our energy while our bodies are at rest or taking part in low-intensity exercise such as walking.

The glucose can come from four different places:

- glycogen supplies in the muscles

- breakdown of the liver's glycogen into glucose

- absorption of glucose from food in the intestine

- fatty acids from fat reserves.

In extreme cases, such as starvation, proteins can also be broken down and used to make ATP. Aerobic respiration would use carbohydrates first, then fats and finally proteins, if necessary. The aerobic energy system produces ATP at the slowest rate of the three systems.

Although all energy systems basically turn on at the same time, the recruitment of an alternative system occurs when the current energy system is almost depleted. So, as exercise commences the energy system that dominates ATP production follows the general guidelines given below.

1   The muscle cells burn off the ATP they have stored in about three seconds.

2   The PCr system supplies energy for eight to ten seconds.

3   If exercise continues for longer, then the lactic acid system produces the majority of the ATP.

4   As exercise continues, the aerobic energy system takes over as the main producer of ATP.

Table 4.2 gives an approximate percentage contribution of the energy pathways in certain sports.

Table 4.2 Percentage contribution of energy pathways

Sport	PCr (%)	Lactic acid (%)	Aerobic (%)
Distance running	10	20	70
Sprinting	90	10	0
Football	50	20	30
Tennis	70	20	10

Training energy systems

Elite athletes can maintain a maximum sprinting speed of around 22 miles per hour for approximately 200 m. However, the average speed for elite athletes running a marathon is around 13 miles per hour. For the two races, different energy systems have been trained and adapted in order to produce ATP as quickly and efficiently as possible.

The PCr energy system

To develop this energy system, sessions of four to seven seconds of high-intensity work at near peak speed are required. For example, a training session might consist of:

- 60 m runs performed 15 times with a 60-second recovery period
- 20 m shuttle runs repeated 20 times with 45 seconds recovery.

By following this type of training, the body will produce more enzymes that make ATP via the PCr energy system and may even be able to store more PCr in the muscles.

Lactic acid system

Sessions that will help to train this energy system are:

- 300 m runs repeated eight times with a 45-second recovery period
- 150 m intervals with 20 seconds recovery until pace significantly slows
- 300 m repeated eight times with three minutes recovery.

By performing this training, the body will be able to withstand higher levels of lactic acid and produce more enzymes that will help in the production of ATP via the lactic acid system.

Aerobic energy system

Aerobic endurance can be trained through the use of continuous and interval training.

Continuous long-duration training will improve maximal oxygen uptake and increase the capacity for storing liver and muscle glycogen. The exercise session should last at least one hour. By performing this type of training, the body adapts by producing more **mitochondria** in the working muscles, which will help to increase the production of ATP through the aerobic energy system. There is also an increase in the number of capillaries (capillarisation) around the working muscles which will help to increase the amount of blood and therefore oxygen that the working muscles receive which again will help to increase the amount of ATP produced by the aerobic energy system.

REVISION QUESTIONS

1) What is ATP?
2) What is the main method of ATP production during the following sporting activities?
a) sprinting
b) 800 m running
c) long-distance cycling
3) What limits production of ATP from the lactic acid system?

4) What does glycolysis mean?
5) How would you train the PCr system?
6) Where does the glucose come from that supplies the aerobic energy system?
7) How does the body adapt to aerobic training?

MECHAN-ISMS OF FATIGUE

We cannot continue to exercise indefinitely because of neuromuscular fatigue, which occurs as a result of a number of systems which will be explored later on in this chapter:

✪   reduced quantities of phosphocreatine

✪   reduced quantities of glucose and glycogen

✪   increased production of lactic acid

✪   increased production of carbon dioxide

✪   reduced levels of oxygen in haemoglobin and myoglobin.

As a result, it is necessary to rest in order to recover and return the body to its pre-exercise state.

Effects of metabolic by-products

Lactic acid is the main by-product of anaerobic glycolysis. Blood always contains a small amount of lactic acid; however, during high-intensity exercise this increases greatly. The increased production of lactic acid results in the pH of the blood decreasing. A blood pH of 6.4 or lower affects muscle and neural function.

Onset blood lactate accumulation (OBLA)

OBLA is also known as the **anaerobic threshold**. OBLA is the point at which lactic acid begins to accumulate in the muscles. OBLA is considered to occur somewhere between 85% and 90% of your maximum heart rate.

Recovery process

The oxygen debt

Oxygen debt occurs when the exercise performed is totally or partially anaerobic. When this happens, PCr stores are depleted and lactic acid builds up within the muscle. Oxygen is then required to break down the lactic acid and convert it back to pyruvic acid. Therefore, the heart rate and respiratory rate should remain elevated for a period of time after the main exercise has been completed in order to allow for the pay-back of the oxygen debt.

After a bout of vigorous exercise, five events must happen before the muscle can operate again:

1 ATP must be replaced

2 PCr stores must be replenished

3 lactic acid must be removed

4 myoglobin must be replenished with oxygen

5 glycogen stores must be replenished.

The replacement of ATP and PCr, and the removal of lactic acid take place within 20 minutes of stopping exercise, but the oxygen replenishment of myoglobin and refilling the glycogen stores take between 24 and 48 hours. If the exercise bout was of a very high intensity then it will take longer to recover; however, the fitter you are the faster you will recover. The faster the debt can be repaid, the more quickly the performer can exercise again.

The oxygen debt consists of two separate components: the alactacid debt and the lactacid debt.

Alactacid oxygen debt is the process of recovery that does not involve lactic acid. The aerobic energy system is used to produce the ATP required to replenish the PCr stores and ATP stores in the body:

$$ADP + P + oxygen \rightarrow ATP$$
$$ATP + Cr + P \rightarrow PCr + ADP$$

Around 50% of the replenishment occurs during the first 30 seconds, while full recovery occurs at about three minutes.

The alactacid oxygen debt ranges between 2 to 3.5 litres of oxygen. The fitter you are, the greater the debt because training increases the PCr content within the muscle cells. However, the recovery time of a fitter person is reduced because they have enhanced methods of oxygen delivery, such as increased capilliarisation and an improved cardio-respiratory system, which will increase the rate of ATP production from the aerobic energy system.

The **lactacid** oxygen debt takes much longer to complete and can last for minutes or hours, depending on the severity of the exercise. The process involves oxygen, which is required to break down the lactic acid produced during anaerobic glycolysis into pyruvate. Pyruvate can then enter the aerobic energy system and eventually be broken down into carbon dioxide and water.

$$lactic\ acid + oxygen = pyruvate$$

Lactic acid can also be converted in the liver to glycogen and stored either in the liver or in muscle tissue. Research has shown that an active recovery increases the rate of removal of lactic acid, so walking or slow jogging after a bout of exercise will help to decrease the time it takes to rid the body of lactic acid. An active recovery keeps the heart rate and breathing rate up, which has the effect of increasing the rate of delivery of oxygen to the working muscles, which will then help to rid the body of the lactic acid. Therefore, a cool down is very important after any form of activity in order to maximise recovery. Failure to cool down adequately means that the levels of lactic acid will remain elevated. It is thought that this acidity level effects the pain receptors and contributes to muscle soreness which people may feel some time after having exercise. This muscle soreness, termed 'delayed onset of muscle soreness' (DOMS), is at its most uncomfortable 36 to 48 hours after exercise has ceased.

Muscle glycogen stores must also be restored. This is attained through a high carbohydrate diet and rest, and can take several days to recover, depending on the intensity of the exercise.

Excess post-exercise oxygen consumption (EPOC)

Oxygen debt is sometimes called EPOC. EPOC refers to the total oxygen consumed after exercise in excess of a pre-exercise baseline level. EPOC occurs when a person exercises at a high intensity, when oxygen cannot be supplied to muscle fibres fast enough. As a result, energy is supplied by the anaerobic energy systems, which results in lactic acid production. When the person stops exercising, extra oxygen is breathed in order to break down lactic acid to carbon dioxide and water, to replenish ATP, phosphocreatine and glycogen, and to pay back any oxygen that has been borrowed from haemoglobin and myoglobin.

STUDENT PRACTICAL

Recovery from exercise
Aim
The aim of this practical is to see what happens to heart rate after exercise.

Equipment
stopwatch
running track/gym
sports clothes

continues overleaf

continued

Method

1 Copy the table drawn in the results section.
2 Take your resting pulse rate and make a note of it in the results table.
3 Take part in some form of high intensity exercise that lasts at least 1 minute.
4 Find your pulse, then record your pulse for a 10-second count every minute after the exercise until your heart rate returns to its original level.
5 Convert your heart rate into beats per minute by multiplying by 6.

Results

Activity	Heart rate (bpm)
Rest	
1 minute after exercise	
2 minutes after exercise	
3 minutes after exercise	
4 minutes after exercise	
5 minutes after exercise	
6 minutes after exercise	

Plot a line graph of the above results.

Conclusion

In your conclusion, try to explain what has happened to your heart rate after exercise. Comment on any sharp changes in your heart rate (you can see this on your graph) and why it takes this pattern of recovery.

Training and fatigue

Training has the effect of increasing the body's ability to exercise for longer without tiring. However, it is necessary to carry out specific training in order to ensure the body adapts to the type of exercise an athlete is competing in, i.e. a marathon runner would have to run continuously for long distances in order to adapt their body to increase the aerobic production of ATP. A sprinter, however, would have to train anaerobically in order to increase their tolerance to lactic acid and increase their PCr stores.

REVISION *QUESTIONS*

1) What does fatigue mean?
2) What does OBLA stand for and when does it occur?
3) How long does it take to replenish the body's PCr stores?

4) Explain what oxygen debt is and why it occurs.
5) Explain what an active cool down is and why it is the best way help the body recover from exercise.

CARDIO-VASCULAR, RESPIRAT-ORY AND NEURO-MUSCULAR ADAPT-ATIONS TO EXERCISE

Cardiovascular adaptations to endurance/aerobic training

The main adaptations that occur to the cardiovascular system through endurance training are concerned with increasing the delivery of oxygen to the working musles. If you were to dissect the heart of a top endurance athlete, you would find that the size of the walls of the left ventricle are markedly thicker than those of a person who did not perform endurance exercise. This adaptation is called **cardiac hypertrophy**. It occurs in the same way that we increase the size of our skeletal muscles – the more we exercise our muscles the larger or more toned they become. In the same way, the more we exercise our heart through training for long periods of time, the larger it will become. This will then have the affect of increasing the stroke volume, which is the amount of blood that the heart can pump out per beat. The heart, as a result, can pump more blood per beat as the thicker wall can contract more forcibly. As the stroke volume is increased, the heart no longer needs to beat as often to get the same amount of blood around the body. This results in a decrease in heart rate which is known as **bradycardia**. An average male adult's heart rate is 70 bpm, however, Miguel Indurain, who was a Tour de France cyclist, had a resting heart rate of 30 bpm! As stroke volume increases, cardiac output also increases, so an endurance athlete's heart can pump more blood per minute than a non-trained person's. However, resting values of cardiac output do not change.

An endurance athlete's capillaries become bigger, allowing more blood to travel through them, and new ones develop which aids in the extraction of oxygen.

Increase in haemoglobin and in the number of red blood cells (which contain the haemoglobin) further aid the transport of oxygen.

Though haemoglobin content rises, the increase in blood plasma is greater and consequently the blood **haematocrit** (ratio of red blood cell volume to total blood volume) is reduced, which lowers **viscosity** (thickness) and enables the blood to flow more easily.

Respiratory adaptations to endurance/aerobic training

The respiratory system deals with the receipt of oxygen and deals with waste products associated with muscle metabolism. Training reduces the resting respiratory rate and the breathing rate during sub-maximal exercise. Endurance training can also provide a small increase in lung volumes: **vital capacity** increases slightly, as does **tidal volume** during maximal exercise. The increased strength of the respiratory muscles is partly responsible for this as it aids lung inflation.

Endurance training also increases the capillarisation around the **alveoli** in the lungs. This will help to increase the rate of gas exchange in the lungs and, therefore, increase the amount of oxygen entering the blood and the amount of carbon dioxide leaving the blood.

Neuromuscular adaptations to endurance/aerobic training

Endurance training results in an increase in the muscular stores of muscle glycogen. There is increased delivery of oxygen to the muscles through an increase in the concentration of myoglobin and increased capillary density through the muscle. The ability of skeletal muscle to consume oxygen is increased as a direct result of an increase in the number and size of the mitochondria and an increase in the activity and concentration of enzymes involved in the aerobic processes that take place in the mitochondria. As a result, there is a greater scope to use glycogen and fat as fuels. **Slow twitch fibres** can enlarge by up to 22%, which gives greater potential for aerobic energy production. Hypertrophy of slow twitch fibres means that there is a corresponding increase in the stores of glycogen and triglycerides. This ensures a continuous supply of energy, enabling exercise to be performed for longer.

These adaptations result in an increased maximal oxygen consumption (VO_2 max see page 314) being obtained before the anaerobic threshold is reached and fatigue begins. However, research suggests that a person's VO_2 max is largely genetic and training can only result in a 10–20% improvement.

Cardiovascular and respiratory adaptations to strength/anaerobic training

Strength training produces very few adaptations to the cardiovascular and respiratory systems.

Neuromuscular adaptations to strength/anaerobic training

High-intensity training results in hypertrophy of **fast twitch fibres**. There are increased levels of ATP and PCr in the muscle and an increased capacity to generate ATP by the PCr energy system. This is partly due to the increased activity of the enzymes which break down PCr. ATP production by anaerobic glycolysis is increased as a result of enhanced activity of the glycolytic enzymes. There is also an increased ability to break down glycogen in the absence of oxygen.

As lactic acid accumalates it decreases the pH levels of the blood, making it more acidic. This increased level of hydrogen ions will eventually prevent the glycolytic enzyme functioning. However, anaerobic training increases the **buffering** capacity of the body and enables the body to work for longer in periods of high acidity.

Reversibility of training

If a person stops training then, over a period of time, the body reverts back to its pre-training state. This is also known as **detraining**. Detraining affects everyone from the elite athlete to the amateur. A study was carried out in which endurance-trained athletes underwent complete bed rest. After this, they were fitness tested and shown to have the following:

✪ a decrease in maximum oxygen uptake

✪ loss of muscle mass

✪ an increase in heart rate during exercise

✪ a decrease in stroke volume

✪ a decrease in cardiac output

✪ an increase in blood lactate during exercise

✪ reduced oxygen transportation through capillaries

✪ weakened muscles, tendons, ligaments and bones.

Therefore, in order to ensure the beneficial effects of training are not lost, it is necessary to maintain training frequency and intensity. Hence, athletes who are injured may take quite some time to return to their pre-injury fitness level unless they are able to continue to take part in some form of exercise that is relevant to their sport.

REVISION
QUESTIONS

1) How does the cardiovascular system adapt to endurance training?

2) How does the respiratory system adapt to endurance training?

3) How does the neuromuscular system adapt to endurance training?

4) Why do you think strength training produces very little adaptation in the cardiovascular and respiratory systems?

5) How does strength training affect the neuromuscular system?

6) What happens to a person if they don't train for a period of time?

7) Give four different reasons why an athlete might not train for a period of longer than two weeks.

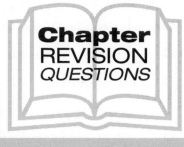

Chapter REVISION QUESTIONS

1) Explain how the cardiovascular system responds to
a) acute endurance training
b) chronic endurance training.
2) Why does the body fatigue?
3) Explain the processes and the time frame involved for a person's body to completely recover after a marathon run.

4) How does:
a) strength training
b) endurance training
increase a person's ability to produce energy and recover from activity?

FURTHER READING

Beashel, P. (1995) *Advanced Studies in Physical Education and Sport.* Nelson
Clegg, C. (1995) *Exercise Physiology.* Feltham Press
Crisfield, P. (1996) *Coaching Sessions: A guide to Planning and Goal-Setting.* National Coaching Foundation
Davis, R. J., Bull, C. R., Roscoe, J. V., Roscoe, D. A. (2000) *Physical Education and the Study of Sport.* London: Mosby
Dick, F, (1997) *Sports Training Principles.* A & C Black
Foss, M., Keteyian, S. (1998) *Fox's Physiological Basis for Exercise and Sport.* McGraw-Hill
Honeybourne, J., Hill, M., Moors, H., (2000) *Advanced physical education and sport: for A-level.* Stanley Thornes
McArdle, W., Katch, F., Katch, V. (2001) *Exercise Physiology: Energy, Nutrition and Human Performance.* WMS & Wilkins
Sharkey, B. (1990) *Physiology of Fitness.* Illinois: Human Kinetics
Wesson, K., Wiggans, N., Thompson, G., Hartigan, S. (2000) *Sport and PE – A Complete Guide to Advanced Level Study*, London: Hodder & Stoughton

SKILL ACQUISITION

This chapter looks at how performers learn skills and then store this information. The following information will be covered:

✪ the nature of skilled performance

✪ classification of skills

✪ the difference between skills and abilities

✪ models of information processing and how these explain skill learning

✪ the different theories of how we learn skills

✪ how skills can be taught to facilitate learning.

THE NATURE OF SKILLED PERFORMANCE

It is a wonderful thing to observe the skill of the best athletes; whether it is the pace, balance and control of Michael Owen, the power, precision and touch of Tiger Woods, or the controlled speed generation of 100 m world record holder, Tim Montgomery. As we admire these skills, we start to wonder why these athletes are so skilled and how they came to be this way. We understand that physiology and biomechanics are important factors in this performance, but psychology also has a hugely important role to play. We have already examined mental preparation and the effects of personality on performance. There is more to psychology than these aspects and this is covered under the title 'skill acquisition'.

How skilled performance is produced

All movement originates in the brain. Messages are sent from the brain in the form of electrical impulses to the muscles. Muscles are attached to the nerves to form motor units. The messages leave the brain through the brain stem and then pass into the spinal cord. The spinal cord has many branches attached to it, and these service all the different areas of the body. These branches are called peripheral nerves. In order to learn a skill, you have to establish a nervous pathway between the brain and the muscles.

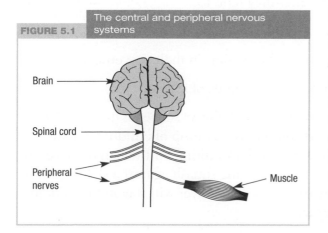

FIGURE 5.1 The central and peripheral nervous systems

Brain

Spinal cord

Peripheral nerves

Muscle

What is skill?

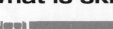 **Definitions**

Skill

As you may have found during your discussions, it can be difficult to explain what a skill is and who is more skilled than others. It is important to say that skills are things we learn, and that we improve our skills through practice. As we learn skills we start to change the way we behave or play our sport. Barbara Knapp (1964) gave a classic definition of skill as being:

> *The learned ability to bring about pre-determined results with maximum certainty, often with minimum outlay of time and energy.*

There are several important points made here. First, that skill is learned rather than something which occurs naturally. Secondly, that to be recognised as a skill the movement you create produces a result that you intended to occur. There will be times that we are able to produce an outstanding golf shot or a brilliant backhand shot as a result of fluke rather than something truly intended. The third point about skill is that it will look effortless in that the effort expended is exactly the amount the task requires and not more. For example, if we watch Rio Ferdinand defending, he appears do it with a minimum of effort and he never seems to expend excess energy.

The difference between a skilled performer and a novice

If you were to watch a tennis match being played by a novice against an experienced performer, you would notice the following differences in play due to the differing skill levels.

1 The novice may produce some good skills, but, these may be flukes. A truly skilled performer can perform the same skill time and again.

2 The skilled performer plays with 'a maximum certainty'. They perform as they intend to perform, meaning that before the skill is produced the outcome is clear.

3 If you observe a skilled performer they tend to:

a) use economic, efficient movements

b) show good co-ordination and precision in their movements

c) fit the energy required to the demands of the task.

A novice player will use a lot of energy and not always succeed; this is called 'the headless chicken syndrome'. If you observe a group of children playing football, they will all follow the ball rather than waiting for the ball or player to come to their area of the pitch. A novice playing squash against a skilled player will do all the running around, while the skilled player will stay in the middle and only move when truly necessary.

Types of skills present in sport

Would you say that the following are skills:

- a goalkeeper tracking the swerve of a free kick
- a batsman working out the spin of a bowl
- a chess player working out how to checkmate his opponent
- a high jumper mentally rehearsing a skill
- a darts player working out how many points he needs to win?

These are probably different from examples previously discussed, however, we would have to agree that they are still very important factors in sporting performance. There are at least three different types of skills.

Categories of skill

1 **Cognitive skills** – Stated simply, these are skills where we use the brain. **Cognitive** means involving thoughts and mental processes. Success in sport involves being able to think about developing and applying tactics, making decisions quickly when faced with many choices, and planning how to play. The use of verbal skills to motivate and lead a team will also rely considerably on cognitive skills.

2 **Perceptual skills** – Perceptual skill is the process of interpreting the information which comes into our brain through our senses. We then process this information and pick out the relevant detail from this vast amount of received information.

3 **Motor skills** – These are skills involved in the movement of the body. When you see the term 'motor' it always refers to movement. There are two types of motor skill:

   a) gross motor skills involve large muscular movements and a low level of expertise, for example, if you were to perform a set of press ups it involves large muscle groups and a low level of co-ordination

   b) fine motor skills involve more delicate, highly controlled movements. One of the finest motor skills we use daily is writing. It involves very precise movements and we see that our handwriting improves over about twenty years, so we can assume fine motor skills take longer than gross motor skills to perfect.

To perform skills effectively and successfully we need to utilise cognitive, perceptual and motor skills at the same time. For example, a hockey player taking a corner flick will use perceptual skills to pick out where their players are and where the opposition are placed, then they will use cognitive skills to decide how hard to hit the ball and in which direction, and finally they use their motor skills to translate their plan into action. Their skilled performance relies on all aspects of skill and, as a result, it is not enough just to practice skills physically, we need to practice the skills in a game situation and learn to

STUDENT ACTIVITY

Take one sport and give two motor, two perceptual and two cognitive skills which are used to produce an effective performance.

understand and predict the game. This is often referred to as 'reading the game', and players who are good at reading the game could be said to have well-developed cognitive skills.

A CLASSIFICATION OF SKILLS

In order to understand skills further, we have found ways to classify them. This will help when we come to look at methods of teaching and presenting new skills. To help us classify skills we use a continuum, which is a method of presenting information in the form of a line, which gives us the opportunity to show that there are many variations in between the two poles.

Open and closed skills

This classification is based on the extent that environmental conditions will affect the performance of a skill. A **closed skill** is one where the environment is stable, and an **open skill** is one where the environment is constantly subject to change. For example, a trampolinist completing a somersault knows that their environment will never change and they will not have to alter their skill to match the environmental needs. However, a rugby player receiving a pass will know that the situation they find themselves in will always be different in terms of where they are on the pitch, where their opponents are positioned and where their team-mates are positioned.

A closed skill is one which could be performed identically each time, as there is no change in the environment or situation. However, we do find that some skills are closed but the situation is open. For example, a footballer taking a penalty is performing what is essentially a closed skill in an activity which is predominantly open.

Open skills:

✪ environment is constantly changing

▶ skill needs constant modification

▶ needs practice in a range of conditions

▶ e.g. dribbling in basketball, tackling in football, passing in netball.

Closed skills:

✪ environment is stable

▶ skill is predictable

▶ a movement pattern can be established

▶ e.g. gymnastics, routine throwing darts, weightlifting.

The idea of a continuum can be used to show that some skills are more open or more closed than others. For example, take a four-person bobsleigh team whose members know the run they are about to perform. Because the actual route is always the same, the skill is predominantly closed. However, because the ice gets warmer or cooler, there is an open element, which is increased by the effect of the wind and the weight of the crew. Snooker is regarded as an open sport. During the break, the balls will always be in the same places, but after that the environment will always be different as the balls will sit in slightly different places, except when all the balls are on their spots. However, snooker has some closed elements, therefore the skills it requires are halfway between the open end and the middle of the continuum.

Self-paced and externally paced skills

The self-paced/externally paced skill continuum assesses the degree of control a performer has over the timing of the skill. Self-paced skills are when the performer has control over the timing of the skill. Externally paced skills are when the performer is reliant on the actions of other players and the situation to time the skill. For example, a batsman facing a bowler is dependant upon external factors such as when the bowler delivers the ball, the speed of the ball and the effect of the pitch on the ball. This makes it an externally paced skill. However, a high jumper has complete control over when they start to perform the skill, making it self-paced.

Self-paced:

- ✪ performer controls the timing of the start of the skill
- ✪ performer controls the speed at which the skill is performed
- ✪ usually involves closed skills
- ✪ e.g. vaulting horse, javelin, bowling.

Externally paced:

- ✪ performer has no control over when the skill is started
- ✪ performer has to react to the environment
- ✪ usually involves open skills
- ✪ e.g. passing in hockey, drop kick in rugby.

Continuous, serial and discrete skills

This classification relates to how clearly defined are the start and completion of the movement. A continuous skill is one which has no clear beginning and end. The end of one cycle is the start of the next. Therefore, continuous skills tend to be regular and rhythmical in nature, such as running or cycling. A discrete skill is one with a clear beginning and ending. They are performed in one single exertion and would include skills such as a tennis serve, a shot in basketball or a tackle in football. A serial skill is one composed of several discrete skills rapidly following each other to become one movement. These would all be different types of skill, and serial skills would include a gymnastics floor routine, an ice dance display and the triple jump.

Continuous:

- ✪ no clear start or end
- ✪ end of one skill is the start of the next
- ✪ usually lasts a long time
- ✪ e.g. swimming.

Serial:

- ✪ several discrete skills put together to make a sequence
- ✪ order the skills follow is important
- ✪ e.g. pole vault, dribbling in football.

Discrete:

- ✪ clear start and end
- ✪ to repeat a skill you have to go back to the start of the skill
- ✪ usually last a short time
- ✪ e.g. snooker shot, board diving.

★ STUDENT ACTIVITY

Put the following skills into their continuous, discrete or serial category:

- ✪ long jump
- ✪ rowing
- ✪ 400 m hurdle race
- ✪ putting in golf
- ✪ throw in
- ✪ downhill skiing
- ✪ cross-country skiing.

ABILITY

The terms **skill** and **ability** are often used interchangeably. However, in reality they are very different. We have seen how skills are learnt, but abilities are largely inherited from our parents. They can be said to be innate or a natural level of skill. Abilities are needed to produce skilled performance. We can improve our abilities, but the start point is fixed and can be used to predict how well we will develop skill. Often we note at school that some people are 'good at sport', meaning that whatever they try they seem to be successful in, while other people have a natural ability for mathematics, singing or acting. This natural ability is the starting point from which skills can develop.

Abilities in sport would include the following:

- ✪ co-ordination
- ✪ balance
- ✪ speed
- ✪ strength
- ✪ suppleness
- ✪ stamina
- ✪ agility.

Fleishman (1964) helped us to understand abilities by categorising them further into **motor** abilities and **psychomotor** abilities. Motor abilities are related to bodily movement and would include the seven abilities previously

STUDENT ACTIVITY

What abilities are needed to be successful at the following skills? Think about motor, psychomotor and affective abilities:

✪ an attacking header in football

✪ a rugby full back catching a high ball under pressure from the opposition

✪ 100 m hurdle race

✪ pole vault

✪ a hockey goalkeeper trying to save a shot from a short corner.

mentioned. Psychomotor abilities would involve the skill of perception as well as movement. For example, the ability to pick out detail and aim at a target. Depth perception is our ability to place objects in relation to each other and is important in delivering a long pass. Reaction time is a psychomotor ability in that it involves the brain picking out information and responding to it. Thus, some people are naturally quicker than others at reacting.

There is one more type of ability we could highlight – **affective** abilities, or abilities related to our emotions. For example, aspects of sport such as courage, confidence and emotional control under pressure are all affective abilities.

Relationship between skills and abilities

All skills will require us to apply our abilities. For example, the main abilities a good gymnast will need are:

✪ good balance

✪ suppleness at the shoulder and hips

✪ upper-body and leg strength

✪ speed of movement

✪ courage and bravery.

REVISION *QUESTIONS*

1) Skills can be categorised into three types: cognitive, perceptual and motor. Explain each type of skill and give a sporting example for each.

2) Differentiate between fine motor skills and gross motor skills, using examples to help explain your answer.

3) How does Barbara Knapp (1964) define skill?

4) Differentiate between skill and ability.

5) Give five abilities needed to perform well at football, and five skills present in the game.

6) You are watching two students playing squash. One is a skilled performer and one is a novice. How would the skilled player's performance differ from that of the novice?

7) Explain why the tennis serve may be classified as a closed skill.

8) Using another example from sport, explain what is meant by an open skill.

9) Here is a list of activities drawn from a variety of sports: triple jump; tennis serve; cycling; shot putt; dribbling a hockey ball and running.

a) Classify each of these according to whether they are discrete, continuous or serial skills.

b) Justify your decision in the case of the first two activities.

10) Skills can be classified using a pacing continuum.

a) Explain what is meant by a 'self-paced skill'. Illustrate your answer using an example from sport.

b) Explain what is meant by 'externally paced skills'. Illustrate your answer using an example from sport.

INFORMATION PROCESSING MODELS

Information processing is the system by which we take information from our surrounding environment, use it to make a decision and then produce a response. We are processing information all the time; for example, as we walk down a street we are looking at where we are going to avoid other pedestrians and lamp-posts and to stop ourselves falling off the pavement; we are listening out for movements on the pavement and cars on the roads we cross. As we walk we make very subtle adjustments to our position and our speed in order to avoid coming to any harm.

This process also happens as we play sport. For example, the tennis player returning a serve is looking out for the ball as it is thrown in the air, the movement of their opponent's racket, the noise of the ball as it is struck by the racket and then the trajectory of the ball as it comes towards them and increases in size. The player must quickly process this information and produce a response.

We are subconsciously processing information in the same way a computer processes information that is fed into it. This process is vital when we analyse how skilled performance is produced and how people learn new skills.

There are two models which can be used to illustrate information processing: Whiting's (1969) model and Welford's (1976) information processing model.

Whiting's (1969) model

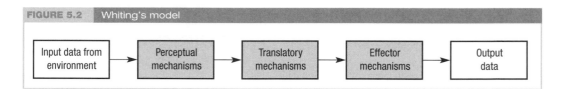

FIGURE 5.2 Whiting's model

- **Input data** refers to information coming in from the performer's environment.

- **Perceptual mechanisms** record information as it comes, for example, the retina will record an image of the ball on the retina.

- **Translatory mechanisms** make sense of the information coming in and decide what is and is not relevant. Once the information has been organised a decision is made. For example, the direction and speed of the tennis ball has been recorded and the performer decides to produce a backhand reply.

- **Effector mechanisms** perform the movement. The system of brain, nervous system and muscles will be co-ordinated to produce the response. The tennis ball is returned in the appropriate direction with the right amount of force.

- **Output** refers to the actual response produced.

Welford's model

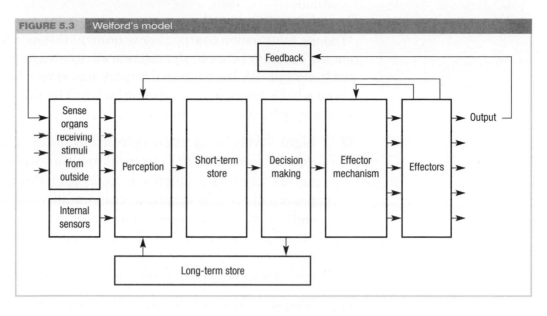

FIGURE 5.3 Welford's model

A summary of the stages

1 **Sensory input** – In sport we tend to use three senses: sight, sound and touch. Smell and taste have little relevance in sport.

2 We also have **internal sense receptors** – These are called proprioceptors, and they are a subconscious sense that tells us about the position of our limbs. We have sensory receptors in our muscles, ligaments and tendons which tell the brain whether our joints are straight or flexed and whether our muscles are tensed or relaxed.

3 **Perception** – This enables us to decide what information is relevant and what information is irrelevant.

4 **Short-term memory (STM)** – Relevant information is stored in our short-term memories.

5 **Decision making** – A decision is made based on the information in our short-term memories.

6 **Long-term memory (LTM)** – We store information based on our previous experiences and the decisions we have made previously, and their outcome.

7 **Effector control** is the system of brain, spinal cord and nerves that starts the movement and sends messages to the working muscles.

8 **Effectors** are the muscles which actually produce the movement.

9 **Output** is the performance of the skill specified by a motor programme.

10 **Feedback** is information about the performance.

Expansion of Welford's model

1.   Sensory input

We take information from our environment through our sense organs, which are the medium between the external environment and the internal environment. We have internal sensory receptors which give us information about what is happening inside our bodies. The three senses predominantly used are sight, sound and touch.

- ✪   **Sight** – As light waves are detected by the eyes, images land on the retina that are converted into electrical impulses and delivered to the brain via nerves. The brain is then able to interpret this information through a process of visual perception. Vision is the most important of the senses, with up to 90% of sensory input being delivered to the brain through the eyes. Thus, we are able to detect the presence of objects relevant to the sport, track balls and the movements of our opponents and have an appreciation of our own position on the pitch.

- ✪   **Sound** – The ears will detect sound waves and convert these into electrical impulses to be delivered to the brain. The brain uses a process of auditory perception to make sense of this information. Hearing is an important sense in sport because we use it to time our own skills. For example, in tennis we will hear the ball strike the strings of the racket before we actually see the ball come towards us. The sound made will also tell us about the quality of the contact between the ball and the object being struck. If we play cricket there is a big difference in sound between the ball coming off the middle of the bat and the ball being edged or coming off the toe of the bat. The sound of the ball being edged will alert the wicketkeeper and slips before they see the ball coming towards them.

- ✪   **Touch** – The sensory receptors around our body enable us to the send information to the brain via the nervous system, mainly about pressure. For example, the feel of the football on our feet as we kick it will tell us how well we have struck the ball; if we hit a golf ball well we almost do not feel it on the club, but if the golf ball is mishit the feeling of the vibrations up the shaft will tell us it was a bad shot before we see the result.

2.   Internal sense receptors

While sight, sound and touch will deliver information from our external environment to the brain, we also receive a lot of information about what is happening internally. This is called **proprioception** and includes information about how our body is moving in space, where our limbs are positioned, whether our muscles are contracted or relaxed and whether our joints are flexed or extended. We have a system of nerves and sensory receptors in our muscles, joints and connective tissue which relay information back to the brain. Proprioception has three components.

- ✪   **Touch** – Although touch picks up information from outside the body it will also tell us about internal information. For example, pain and pressure are picked up by our tactile sense.

Proprioception

Proprioception has been defined by Dickinson (1967) as being:

an appreciation of movement and position of the body and its parts based on information from other than visual, auditory or superficial cutaneous sources.

STUDENT ACTIVITY

When we play sport we will receive huge amounts of information every second. Some of this information is relevant and some of it is irrelevant. Consider the following examples and decide what information is relevant and what is irrelevant to the performer:

- ✪ a goalkeeper facing a penalty
- ✪ a batsman facing a spin bowler
- ✪ an athlete running a 3000 m steeplechase race.

✪ **Balance** – Our sense of balance and correction of balance is the result of the work of the vestibular apparatus in the inner ear. This is important in virtually every sport as we are reliant on balance and changes in our centre of gravity to perform skills well and stop ourselves from falling over. This is of obvious importance to gymnasts and trampolinists.

✪ **Kinaesthesis** – This is the sense which tells the brain about the state of contraction of the muscles and the position of joints. Kinaesthesis will also tell our brain how well we have executed a skill by the feeling the movement produces; we can tell how well we have done a skill by how it felt. Our kinaesthetic sense helps to prevent us becoming injured. For example, if we go over on our ankle we quickly sense this and correct it. After an injury to a muscle or a joint our kinaesthetic sense is weakened due to the nerve damage and we need to develop it to ensure we protect against a repeat injury. For example, a wobble board helps to mobilise the ankle after injury, but it also improves the effectiveness of the nervous system and the kinaesthetic sense.

It is vitally important that we receive the right information via our senses so that we can make the right decisions and produce the correct responses.

3. Perception

The brain is bombarded with a huge amount of information every second, and perception is the process by which the brain interprets and organises this information. For example, at this moment you are probably sitting in a classroom trying to read this book. On top of the information you are taking in from the book, you will have visual information such as the sights of your teacher and classmates, information on the board and posters around the room. There may be auditory information such as the noise made by your classmates talking or coughing, and noises from outside such as a road or people walking about. There may be smells such as your neighbour's feet or the smell from the canteen. There is a plethora of information coming into your senses, which you have to filter and process. The process of perception involves the brain doing the following:

✪ detecting the presence of a stimulus or information

✪ deciding what information is relevant

✪ deciding what information goes into the short-term memory

✪ deciding what information is irrelevant and should be discarded.

The input is filtered, leaving only the relevant information. Imagine this as a sieve that you use to drain your pasta. The sieve retains what is relevant (the pasta) and discards what is irrelevant (the water).

The brain has help in deciding whether information gets through to the short-term memory. This depends upon the following features of the stimulus.

✪ **Size** – We are more likely to detect something large than something small.

✪ **Colour** – Certain colours, such as white, red and yellow are easier to detect than dark colours such as black or brown.

✪ **Brightness** – We are more likely to detect bright objects than dark objects, for example the tennis balls at Wimbledon are bright yellow to help players see the ball more quickly.

✪ **Speed** – We find it easier to detect an object moving slowly than one moving fast. For example, cricketers facing a fast bowler for the first time may not actually see the ball until they hear it fly past them.

✪ **Loudness** – We will always hear something very loud, but we may miss a quiet sound.

✪ **Familiarity** – We will detect and process something which is familiar to us. As we become more experienced we become better players because the stimuli we are presented with are ones we have dealt with previously.

4. Short-term memory

Once the information has been filtered, the relevant information goes forward into the short-term memory store. This information will be used to make a decision, but it is stored in the short-term memory for 15 to 30 seconds to allow it to be processed. The short-term memory can be seen as the 'work space' or conscious part of our brain.

It is generally agreed that the capacity of our short-term memory is seven plus or minus two pieces of information. Therefore, you should have been able to recall the first two numbers and possibly the third, but not the fourth. However, the capacity of the short-term memory can be enhanced if you develop a technique. The technique used for numbers five and six is called 'chunking', where groups of numbers are chunked together to form discrete patterns. The seventh set of numbers can easily be recalled if you notice the pattern of the numbers as being 1 squared, 2 squared, etc.

We are aware that our short-term memory is limited, but we cannot attend to all the information in our short-term memory store. We tend to focus on one piece of information at any one time, and this is called **selective attention**. Consider yourself relaxing at home; you have the television on, the radio on for the football commentary and your mum talking to you. Is it possible to attend to all these three things at once? Immediately we might say, yes, you can be aware of what is happening in each situation. However, if we were questioned in detail on each of the three sources of information we would find gaps. What happens is that while we are conscious of all three we very quickly switch our attention between them, rather than processing all three at once. So while it looks like we are dealing with all three stimuli, in reality we are not. It generally is not possible to do more than one thing at any one time, unless one task is a motor task and the other one a mental task.

5. Decision making

Once the brain has received information (sensory input), made sense of and organised the information (perception), a decision can be made. This decision will initiate a plan of action, and it is crucial that we make this decision as quickly as possible. The space between a stimulus being presented and the performer's response to it is called **reaction time**.

STUDENT ACTIVITY

Practical tests to assess the capacity of our short-term memory.
Look at each of these numbers for five seconds and then cover them up and try to write them down from memory.
85032
3965297
573625841
83492870264
493-7265
538-075-192
14916253649

STUDENT ACTIVITY

Think of five examples of sports situations which require fast reactions.

Response time is also important.

response time = reaction time + movement time

✪ Reaction time – the time between the first presentation of a stimulus and the performer's first reaction.

✪ Movement time – the time between the first reaction to the stimulus and the completion of the movement.

✪ Response time – the time from the presentation of the stimulus to the completion of the movement.

For example, if we have a sprinter on their blocks at the start of a 100 m race, the reaction time is the time from the gun going off to the first pressure exerted by their feet on the blocks. Movement time is the time from that first pressure to both feet leaving the blocks. Response time is the time from the gun going off to both feet leaving the blocks.

So, while it is important to react very quickly to a stimulus, it is also important to complete the movement or response as quickly as possible.

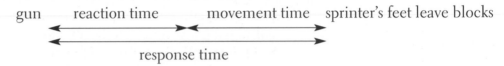

Reaction time is an ability and varies between individuals. It is also influenced by the nature of the stimulus, such as its intensity, the probability of the stimulus occurring, the sense being used and whether any warning signals are given prior to the stimulus being presented.

The reaction time will also be influenced by the number of possible variations there may be to the stimulus. If the performer is waiting for one stimulus (**simple reaction time**) their response time may be quicker than if a variety of stimuli are presented (**choice reaction time**).

STUDENT ACTIVITY

Try the following experiment involving the task of catching tennis balls.

Go to either a sports hall or a playing field and choose one person to be a subject. Record out of 20 attempts how many times the subject successfully catch the tennis ball.

Condition 1 – there is one person throwing the tennis ball to the catcher.

Condition 2 – there are two throwers who randomly throw the ball to the catcher.

Condition 3 – there are four throwers who randomly throw the ball to the catcher.

Condition 4 – there are eight throwers who randomly throw the ball to the catcher.

Throwers should be about a metre apart and about ten metres from the subject, and the time gap between each ball being thrown should be varied.

Repeat the experiment with four or five catchers and write the results up on the board.

What did you find, what did you observe and why did you find this?

You should find that response time increases as the number of possible choices of stimuli increases. This relationship is called Hick's Law (1952) which states that: 'Reaction time will increase logarithmically as the number of stimulus response choices increases.'

This has huge implications for sport because if, as a performer, you keep performing the same skill then your opponent will be able to predict what stimulus is coming. For example, a good bowler in cricket will be able to vary their deliveries to the batsman; a good tennis player will have a range of serves; and a good penalty taker will be able to vary where they place the ball and how hard they hit it.

It is in your interests as a performer to respond as quickly as possible, therefore you need to develop strategies to speed up your response time.

1   **Practice** – The more often you practise a response the faster you will become and the more familiar you will become with the possible stimuli presented.

2   **Predicting a stimulus** – The more familiar you become with a sport, the better you will become at predicting what stimuli will follow from certain cues or signals. For example, as a defender in football playing against a skilful winger you need to be able to predict what skills will be produced by observing the movement of your opponent's body; as they drop their left shoulder you know they are feinting to go to the left but will really go to the right. As you play sport you build up experience and this helps you to predict stimuli.

3   **Anticipation** – This means responding to a stimulus before it has been presented, and is closely linked to predicting a stimulus. However, in this case the response is even earlier. It is a dangerous tactic as you may be caught out. For example, if you are playing tennis against a fast server then the only way to return their serve is to anticipate what serve they will produce and move accordingly. If you anticipate correctly it gives you an advantage, but you may be made to look very stupid by going the wrong way! Anticipation has also been used in sprinting to guess when the gun will go off. Again, this is very effective if it comes off successfully, but you may be disqualified if it does not.

The second way of giving yourself an advantage is to delay your opponent's response time. This can be done in several ways.

1   **Hide or disguise relevant information** – Your opponent can gain information from watching your hands, feet or the ball which will tell them what may occur. For example, the batsman in cricket can tell from the seam position of the ball and how it is held what type of delivery can be expected. Therefore, the bowler will try to hide the ball for as long as possible. A similar ploy is used by table tennis players, who hide their bat hand behind their other hand while they serve.

2   **Present non-relevant information** – This is like using a decoy, as you will present other information to your opponent and thus give them more

information to process. We can see this when goalkeepers use tactics to put off penalty takers, and it usually involves flapping arms or excess movement.

3   **Faking or selling a dummy** – This is seen as utilising the psychological refractory period (PRP). If we can make our opponent respond to a stimulus they will have to complete that movement before they can respond to a second stimulus. So what we do is present a stimulus to our opponent and while they deal with this information we present a second stimulus, different to the first stimulus, and this gives us the advantage of a split second of time to enable us to beat our opponent. For example, a tennis player is playing a volley at the net and they swing the racket back to make it look they are going to smash the ball to the back of the court. They wait for their opponent to move backwards and then they slow down their swing and play a stop volley which just lands over the net. Their opponent has to complete their first movement before trying to make their way to the front of the court to play the stop volley. As a result their response time has been lengthened and it is very unlikely they will be able to reach the ball in time. This delay in response is called the **psychological refractory period** and is represented in Figure 5.4.

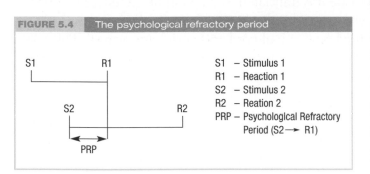

FIGURE 5.4   The psychological refractory period

S1 – Stimulus 1
R1 – Reaction 1
S2 – Stimulus 2
R2 – Reation 2
PRP – Psychological Refractory Period (S2 → R1)

Key

S1 represents the presentation of the first stimulus (the smash)

R1 represents the opponent's first response

S2 represents the presentation of the second stimulus (the stop volley)

R2 represents the opponents second response

PRP represents the time period that elapses, after the second stimulus has been presented, during which the opponent is still responding to the first stimulus. It is the increase in response time that has been created and is in effect 'dead time'.

We can see the same phenomenon working when a player hits the top of the net with their return shot. Their opponent has already initiated their response to the shot and as the ball strikes the net they then have to complete their first response and produce a second response. The psychological refractory period can often make a player look stupid and this is why we call it 'selling a dummy'.

★

STUDENT ACTIVITY

Think up three sporting situations where you could use the psychological refractory period to your advantage.

6.   Long-term memory

We can use our long-term memory to help us to make an appropriate decision. While we know that the capacity of our short-term memory is severely limited, our long-term memory is able to store a limitless amount of information over an indefinite period. Our long-term memories store cognitive, perceptual and motor skills as well as vast amounts of information and memories of events and emotions. We can use this memory store to recover information regarding past events and use it to make a decision.

This uses a process of detection, comparison and recognition (DCR). For example, as we walk through our shopping centre we pass hundreds of people and we detect each of their faces (detection), we subconsciously compare them to the store of faces we have in our long-term memory (comparison) and if we cannot make a match we quickly discard the information. However, if we can find a match for that person we can put a name to them and recognise them (recognition). If we have not seen this person for a while then recognition may not happen immediately.

In sport, as we watch our opponent making responses we use our long-term memory to compare and recognise the responses produced. If we can make a match we use this information to help us to make a response and thus we predict the outcome of the opponent's actions. For example, a goalkeeper will watch penalty takers to see how they usually take their penalties and build up a long-term memory; therefore, when they are actually facing a penalty they can predict what response they need to produce. Also, if you play against the same opponent regularly you will become better at facing them as you build up a store of how they play and how they usually respond. This can be seen as building up experience and it means we are expanding our long-term memory store.

7 and 8.   Effector control and effectors

Once a decision has been made it is translated into action by the effector control and the effectors. The effector control is the system that actually initiates the movement and consists of the brain, spinal cord and peripheral nerves. The effectors are what actually produce the movement, and can be seen as being the muscle groups which have been initiated by the nervous system to produce a set pattern of movement. The effector control and effectors follow a very specific set of commands to produce the appropriate response. This set of commands is called a **motor programme** and can be defined as a set of muscle movements occurring in a specific sequence to produce a pre-planned response.

9.   Output and motor programmes

The motor programme specifies what movements the skill is composed of and the order in which these movements occur. For example, a rugby player taking a penalty kick will follow a specific set of movements. Once the player has set the ball on the ground they will:

- ✪ position feet and body
- ✪ run up to the ball
- ✪ plant balancing foot beside the ball
- ✪ swing kicking leg back
- ✪ swing kicking leg forward
- ✪ strike the ball
- ✪ follow through.

These stages are called subroutines and they make up the skill, which is called the executive programme. A motor programme comprises an executive programme and its subroutines.

STUDENT ACTIVITY

Identify the subroutines which make up the following executive programmes:
- ✪ a penalty flick in hockey
- ✪ a javelin throw
- ✪ a golf drive.

STUDENT ACTIVITY

List all the ways that information can be received intrinsically and extrinsically.

Motor programmes for open skills need to be adaptable to be able to cope with the changing situations in the game. For a closed skill, the motor programme can be learnt and need not be modified.

10. Feedback

Feedback is any information about your performance and it can be received in a variety of ways. There are two main types of feedback.

- ✪ **Intrinsic** – Information received from inside the body as a result of the movement, for example, how a ball felt when striking a racket. It is received by the internal sense organs.

- ✪ **Extrinsic** – Information received from an outside source, such as your coach's comments, or information gained from watching a video recording.

There are two specific types of extrinsic feedback.

1 **Knowledge of results** is information regarding the outcome of your actions and whether you have been successful or not, for example, whether you scored a goal, whether you won the point, what time you achieved or how far you jumped. This information can be seen as being **quantitative** in nature.

2 **Knowledge of performance** is information about how well you performed the skills, for example, how technically correct the skill was or how smooth it looked. It is possible to be successful without being technically correct and vice versa. This information is **qualitative** in nature and is of more use to an advanced performer who knows they can perform the skill, but needs more information about their technical proficiency. A novice may be satisfied initially with knowledge of results.

Feedback is the single most important factor in learning as it allows the performer to determine how successful they have been. Without any feedback only a limited amount of learning will occur.

Feedback affects learning in three ways.

1 **A reinforcement of learning** – Success will strengthen the bond between the stimulus and the response.

2 **Motivation** – The encouragement given to a performer by the coach, teacher or friends will act as a reward and an incentive to continue learning.

3 **Adaptation of performance** – Feedback will allow any errors to be detected and changes to be made to techniques and movements.

Other types of feedback include the following.

1 **Concurrent** and **terminal** feedback relate to the point at which the feedback is produced. Concurrent feedback is generated while the skill is being produced and terminal feedback is generated once the skill has

been completed. For example, as you run the 100m race you get an idea of how fast you have run by how good you feel and how much speed you feel you generated – this is the concurrent feedback. However, you do not know the important issue of time until after the race – this type of feedback is terminal.

2   **Immediate** and **delayed** feedback relate to the timing of providing the information to the participant. Immediate feedback is given as soon as the participant has finished. This is seen as being the most effective time to give feedback as the memory of the skills is still clear in their mind. However, it is important to remember that this may be an emotional time for the participant as they may experience feelings of success or failure and your comments may not be appreciated. We could see this happen when Paula Radcliffe's coach and husband, Gary Lough, chose to criticise her performance in the 10,000m final at the World Championships in 2001 immediately after she had finished. Paula, who was disappointed enough after finishing fourth, was seen to argue and become even more upset. We can also see how emotional football managers become in post-match interviews and say things that they later regret. So it is important to be sensitive about when you choose to give feedback.

REVISION QUESTIONS

1) What does an information processing model explain?

2) Give the four main sources of sensory input.

3) What does the process of perception involve, according to Welford?

4) What is the capacity of the short-term memory store?

5) Explain the relationship between short-term and long-term memory.

6) Give three ways in which memory can be improved.

7) Give three sporting situations where fast reactions are required.

8) Define the following terms:

a) reaction time

b) movement time

c) response time.

9) How can a player receiving a tennis serve cut down on their response time?

10) Explain what you understand by Hick's Law.

11) Explain, using an example, the psychological refractory period.

12) The brain stores sports skills as motor programmes. Choose a skill and show how it can be broken down into subroutines.

13) What does the DCR process of memory stand for?

14) Explain the different types of feedback that may occur.

THEORIES OF LEARNING

Introduction to learning theories

We have looked at different types of skills and made an attempt to classify them. We then examined how we process information from our environment to enable us to produce skills. This section looks at the different theories that have been proposed to explain how we actually learn skills and knowledge.

Behaviourist theories

Behaviourist theories are involved in looking at the behaviour of individuals, and they see learning as producing changes in behaviour.

Clark Hull's (1943) drive reduction theory

Hull's theory is based on the importance of motivation in relation to behaviour. He says that for an individual to learn, they must have a need or an initial drive. The drive is seen as being the stimulus to learning and is essential for appropriate responses to occur. For example, as an individual becomes involved in a sport, the need to learn the skills associated with competence in that sport arise.

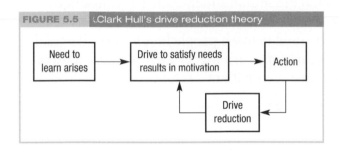

FIGURE 5.5 Clark Hull's drive reduction theory

As the individual learns the skill they will experience a reduction in drive, until they have mastered the skill when their drive will disappear because their need has been satisfied.

However, like other learning theories, reinforcement is the primary factor that produces learning and it must be considered in conjunction with motivation. Initially the learner may not be successful, but as they become successful they start to be rewarded for their competence. This reward acts as the reinforcement they need and thus learning occurs and behaviour is changed.

The implications of this theory for coaches and teachers of sports are that they can only teach if their learners are motivated and have a need for learning to occur. The fact that motivation will be reduced as learning occurs means that once a skill has been learnt they must teach something else, but all the motivation has gone. There is no point going over the same thing once it has been learnt because their learners will become bored and lose interest.

The main points of Hull's theory of drive reduction are:

✪   drive is essential for learning to occur

✪   as learning occurs this drive to learn is reduced

✪   reinforcement of learning is needed for changes in behaviour to occur.

Pavlov's classical conditioning

Pavlov was a notable Russian physiologist who won the Nobel Prize in 1904 for his physiology research into digestion in animals. He studied the sequence of digestion that starts with the secretion of saliva before eating, and then the process of the breakdown and absorption of food. He applied this process to the process of learning.

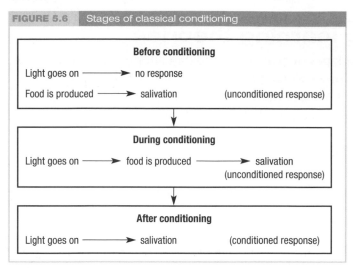

FIGURE 5.6 Stages of classical conditioning

Pavlov noticed that his dog salivated when he saw the bowl that his dog food was going to be served. The dog had been conditioned to associate the sight of his bowl with food. Pavlov decided to see whether he could condition the dog to associate a different stimulus with food, so before he produced the dog's bowl he made a point of turning on the light in the larder. Eventually the dog started to salivate when the light was turned on, as he had learnt to associate this with food. This is called a **conditioned** response, as it is one which has been taught; the original response, which had not been taught, is called an **unconditioned** response.

This theory can be applied to sport by examining how athletes' behaviour can be conditioned by a coach. The coach can teach an athlete to produce a certain response on the presentation of a certain stimulus. For example, if a tennis coach wants to teach their player when to play a volley at the net, they will set up a situation so the stimulus to the volley is consistently presented. Through practice the learner discovers when to produce their conditioned response. It can also be used to teach people how to relax. The skill of relaxation is usually taught as the response to a trigger such as a tensed fist or a specific command, which will produce a conditioned response to relax.

The main points of Pavlov's theory of classical conditioning are:

✪ existing behaviour is known as an unconditioned response

✪ behaviour can be conditioned by teaching a response to a specific stimulus.

Operant conditioning

This theory, proposed by B F Skinner, is based upon the idea that learning will be the result of the effect of our voluntary actions. If the outcomes are pleasant then we are more likely to repeat them, and if they are unpleasant we are less likely to repeat them. Rather than behaviour being the outcome of a response to the stimulus, Skinner sees behaviour as being the result of the action and its consequences. He said that: 'behaviour is shaped and maintained by its consequences.'

Reinforcement is the key element to Skinner's theory. He described a reinforcer as anything that strengthens the desired response. This may be verbal praise, a good mark or grade, or positive feelings of satisfaction or enjoyment. Reinforcement can be positive or negative.

✪ **Positive reinforcement** is any event that increases the likelihood of the same response being produced in the future.

✪ **Negative reinforcement** is any event that decreases the likelihood of the same response being produced in the future.

Skinner proposed that positively reinforced responses will be strengthened and will dominate in the future, while negatively reinforced responses will eventually disappear.

Skinner also proposed that skills should be built up through 'behaviour shaping'. If you were coaching a novice to shoot in football, you would teach them the skills and then allow them to practise. As they practise, you would positively reinforce the aspects of the skill they were performing correctly and ignore the aspects that were incorrect. Hopefully, the positive aspects would predominate over the negative aspects, and the negative aspects would eventually disappear. It does rely on the hope that eventually they will produce each of the aspects correctly at some point to give the coach a chance to positively reinforce them.

The main points of Skinner's operant conditioning are:

- learning is not the result of an association between a stimulus and response, rather the result of an action and its outcome.

- behaviour that is reinforced positively will reoccur

- behaviour which is not positively reinforced will eventually disappear

- learning can be produced through shaping an individual's behaviour.

Thorndike's laws of learning

Thorndike's (1931) theory is the original stimulus response theory. He said that learning is the result of an association being formed between a stimulus and its response. As the association becomes strengthened a habit is developed, so that when a stimulus is presented it will automatically produce a learned response from the performer. This habit can be seen as conditioning an individual to behave in certain ways.

Thorndike's theory is based on three primary laws.

1   **The law of effect** – Responses to a situation which are positively rewarded will be strengthened and become a habitual response to that situation. Thus, the development of the stimulus–response bond is dependent upon the consequences the behaviour has on the learner.

2   **The law of readiness** – If a learner achieves their intended outcome they will experience feelings of satisfaction. However, if the intended outcome is not achieved the learner will experience frustration or annoyance. The learner must also be physically and psychologically strong enough to perform the action.

3   **The law of exercise** – The connection between stimulus and response will become strengthened through practice and weakened when practice is discontinued.

The main points of Thorndike's theory are:

- learning is caused through a bond between a stimulus and the response it produces

- learning is based on the laws of effect, readiness and exercise.

Gestalt theory

Gestalt psychology takes a different view to explaining behaviour and learning. It originated in Germany in the early part of the twentieth century and it contended that learning can be explained better if we look at the parts which make up the whole, rather than looking at the parts separately outside the whole experience. The outcome or feedback received from learning only make up a small part of the experience of learning and you also have to look at how individuals experience learning differently. Each individual will bring a different set of experiences to the learning situation and this will influence how they learn and the meaning they give to the learning experiences. The term **perception** is commonly used by Gestaltists and means how we see and interpret an experience. Two people can experience the same thing and give it different meaning. For example, a goal in football could be experienced in different ways, depending upon your perception or interpretation: it may be skill on behalf of the striker, poor defensive skills on behalf of the defenders or poor positioning by the goalkeeper.

Principles of learning according to Gestalt theory

1.　Perception

The behaviourist theories believe that we take in information, organise it and use it to make a decision. Gestaltists do not believe it is that simple – they believe we take information to the brain, and the brain will then actively transform this information and use it to create useful meaning or understanding. In effect, the received information is tweaked or altered to fit what we need or can understand. This tweaking is based on past experiences we have had and how we have learnt to interpret information. We try to place all experience into a context that gives it meaning and helps us to understand it. If we cannot understand it, we will discard the information and not be able to learn from it.

2.　The law of closure

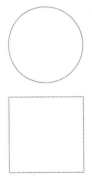

In order to completely understand an event we often need to add or assume information which is not necessarily present. For example, if we saw a circle made up of a series of dots, or a circle with a segment missing, we would add in the missing pieces and interpret the shape as a circle in order to give it meaning as something we understand and can relate to. We can still identify the shapes on the left by applying closure, even though they are incomplete.

This can be applied to our own experiences because, if we are asked to recall an experience which was less than perfect, we will add or take away parts to make it complete or perfect. If we learn a skill but are not too sure of certain parts of it, we will add in our ideas to ensure closure or completeness. This is the law of closure, or the law of Pragnanz.

3.　Insightful learning

This theory suggests that we do not learn slowly and bit by bit, but that learning is insightful. This means that when we practise we will be

unsuccessful initially and then it will come suddenly together and we find we have learnt. This is called the 'Aha experience', because once learning has occurred we say 'aha' as it has fitted into place. Either we have learnt the skill or we have not, we know the information or we do not, and once we have learnt it there is no more to do or say. This theory is based on the work of Kohler, a Gestaltist psychologist, who studied primates in the Canary Islands while serving there during the First World War from 1913 to 1917. By providing tools and boxes, Kohler created situations where primates were given the opportunity to acquire food. In one situation the primates had to stack the boxes on top of each other to get to the food, and in another they had to join two sticks together and then reach food outside the cage. Of course, once the primates had learnt they were able to repeat the steps to continually acquire the food. Kohler said insightful learning has two aspects: first, we have to understand the situation or the essence of the situation and secondly, learning is not a step-by-step process but occurs partially by subconscious processes.

Insightful learning can be seen in sport where you have a person learning the triple jump. They understand what needs to be done and they can perform the three stages, but they cannot put them together. Suddenly, they will perform the jump in perfect sequence as the parts have all come together and the relationship between the parts has been established. It is usually a sudden discovery rather than a bit-by-bit process. This contradicts the behaviourists, as they see learning as happening slowly and steadily, for example the drive reduction theory sees motivation gradually decreasing as learning occurs.

4.   Transposition

Transposition is the tendency of individuals to apply the solution of one problem to another similar problem. For example, the English cricket batsmen discovered how to play against the Australian leg spinner, Shane Warne, so they applied this solution to playing against the Sri Lankan leg spinner, Muttiah Muralitharan. Unfortunately, it did not work because, although the situation is the same, the sum of the parts is different. We all use transposition because we cannot learn every single situation, but this example shows that we have to adapt our learning to the specific situation. Max Wertheimer, who is considered to be the founder of Gestalt theory, showed the difference between meaningful and arbitrary learning. He said that **meaningful learning** will create understanding and give meaning. This understanding can be applied to solve problems and is more useful in general life. **Arbitrary learning** is being able to remember and recall information without necessarily applying it, for example, knowing which players play for which Premiership teams and in what positions. This information is arbitrary and it will not make us any more intelligent as it cannot be applied. Learning should improve understanding, and we become more intelligent because we can think productively and apply our information to solve problems and give meaning to situations, rather than by learning through memorisation. We could learn information for an exam and use it to answer a question, however, without understanding the information it is useless and will be a fairly pointless and hollow experience.

The main points of Gestalt theory are as follows.

✪ 'The whole is greater than the sum of its parts', meaning we should experience the whole skill and understand how each of the parts of the skill contributes to the whole skill.

✪ Learning needs to consider how the individual will experience events differently depending upon their past experiences.

✪ Learning is often insightful in that it will suddenly all come together rather than happen slowly and steadily.

✪ Learning needs to create understanding and give meaning to situations so that the concepts can be applied to new situations. Using transposition learning is dangerous and misguided.

✪ Meaningful learning promotes clear understanding and will leave the strongest influences on our behaviour. Learning is only useful if it changes or influences our behaviour.

Open- and closed-loop theories of learning

The open- and closed-loop theories relate to the importance of feedback in learning. Open-loop control refers to the absence of feedback in the learning process, while closed-loop control refers to the presence of feedback in the learning process.

Open-loop control

This theory shows that in certain actions no feedback is provided (see Figure 5.7).

The loop is incomplete and is not a long one. Some movements will be produced and will occur too quickly for feedback to be recorded or to be of any benefit. This is very important in sport-related skills, however, it can also be seen in skills such as typing, where you produce such quick movements that you will be unaware of any mistakes you may have made.

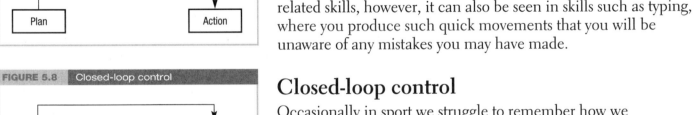

FIGURE 5.7 Open-loop control

Plan → Action

FIGURE 5.8 Closed-loop control

Plan → Action → Feedback → Plan

Closed-loop control

Occasionally in sport we struggle to remember how we performed a skill, such as a long dribble in football, but if we make a mistake we usually are provided with feedback on how we made the mistake. Closed-loop control is much more common in sport (see Figure 5.8).

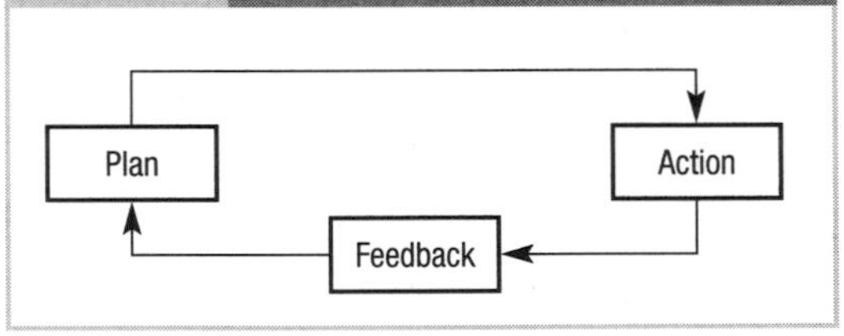

Closed-loop control stresses the importance of feedback and how we use feedback to produce learning. The loop is completed by feedback from intrinsic and extrinsic sources.

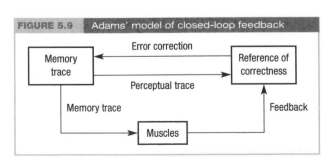

FIGURE 5.9 Adams' model of closed-loop feedback

Error correction

Memory trace → Reference of correctness

Perceptual trace

Memory trace → Muscles → Feedback → Reference of correctness

Adams' closed-loop theory

Adams (1971) produced a theory based on his experiments with animals, which he applied to humans.

His theory had two main elements: the perceptual trace and the memory trace. He produced a model of closed-loop feedback (see Figure 5.9).

Definitions

Definitions of terms used in the model

Feedback – information provided on performance.

Control centre – system of brain and nerves that controls movement. The brain also stores patterns of movement.

Memory trace – produces the movement. It provides the link between the brain and the muscles.

Perceptual trace – laid down with practice. It is the feeling of doing a movement correctly. If the movement is continually practised it will produce a reference of correctness.

Reference of correctness – the store of the correct movement in the brain.

Motor programme – specifies what movements the skill is composed of and the order of these movements. Motor programmes are stored in the long-term memory and are used to produce the memory trace.

Below is an explanation of Adams' closed-loop theory.

1   The movement (motor programme) is stored in the memory in the control centre (brain).

2   The movement is produced by the memory trace and results in muscle contraction.

3   While the movement is taking place, and when completed, feedback is provided about its success.

   a)   Intrinsic feedback provides information about the feeling of the movement.

   b)   Extrinsic feedback provides knowledge of results (KR) which is whether the skill resulted in success or failure. Knowledge of performance (KP) is information about whether the skill looked correct.

4   This feedback is compared with the reference of correctness, i.e. the memory of how the movement should feel.

5   This reference of correctness (ROC) is provided by the perceptual trace.

6   If the reference of correctness is identical to the feedback given, there will be no change or amendment to future performance. However, if the reference of correctness does not equate to the feedback received, then the error will be corrected by comparison with the reference of correctness.

The implications for learning are:

✪   practice is used to produce a correct perceptual trace

✪   only perfect practice will produce a perfect perceptual trace

✪ feedback is essential to learning

✪ we only learn if we know the outcome of our learning.

Schmidt's schema theory (1975)

Schmidt's schema theory is based around the importance of variability in practice. It suggests that to learn an open skill effectively we need to continually vary the conditions in which we practise the skill. The schema theory says that we learn skills by learning the rules of how our bodies function, developing an understanding of how our muscles are activated, what movements the muscles will produce, how these movements feel and then memorising this information. This information is generated through experience, so a schema is another term for the memory of the relationships between how our muscles produce movement and how this movement feels.

The main points of the theory are as follows.

✪ There are very few skills that are 100% closed, as most skills have some open aspect.

✪ As most skills are open we cannot store knowledge of these skills as a motor programme.

✪ We store skills as a schema or a 'generalised set of movements'.

✪ The schema is a motor programme which can be modified slightly to meet the differing demands of a task. For example, a rugby pass needs to be varied in terms of strength and direction because the position the passers find themselves in will always differ slightly, as will the situation in which they are producing the pass.

Recall schema/recognition schema

Schmidt suggests that when a movement takes place, four items of information are stored.

1 **Knowledge of initial conditions** – This includes the state of contraction experienced by the muscles and the situation of the environment before the movement started.

2 **Knowledge of movements required to produce the skill** – This is the sequence of contractions and relaxation of the muscles.

3 **Knowledge of the outcome and its results** – Schmidt proposed that knowing the outcome is the most important aspect because it helps to develop the strength of the schema.

4 **Sensory consequences of the movement** – This would include information about how the movement looked and how it sounded.

Recall schema is the scheme responsible for producing the movements. It comprises the first two pieces of information produced.

Definitions

A schema is '*a rule, concept or relationship formed on the basis of experience*' (Beashel and Taylor, 1996).

Thus, we learn through experience and practising skills.

Recognition schema is the scheme responsible for evaluating the response. It comprises the third and fourth pieces of information produced.

The implications for learning are:

✪ training must be varied, so we practise a range of movements within one skill, thus a strong schema is stored

✪ the further towards the open end of the continuum the skill can be placed, the greater the need to vary practice and create variety.

Fitts and Posner's (1967) stages of motor learning

These American psychologists set out the changes and phases that learners pass through in order to acquire a skill. They proposed that there are three stages to learning a new skill.

1. The cognitive stage

At this point the learner is attempting to understand what they have to do and how they do it. It relies heavily on mental or cognitive processes. Often, the learner gives labels to the movement and talks themselves through the movements. For example, a person learning a golf swing will go through the following routine:

a) position the feet correctly

b) make sure the ball is in the right position

c) position right hand

d) interlock with the left hand

e) place the club beside the ball

f) bend the knees, look at the target

g) point the club at the target

h) relax

i) breathe steadily

j) swing back

k) swing forward

l) lead with the hips

m) contact

n) follow through

o) hold the head down

p) hold the club in the finish position

q) look for the ball.

The focus is fixed on the movement and how it feels. As a result, little attention is paid to the surrounding environment. The learner may experience many errors and the errors tend to be gross in nature. For example, the golfer may miss the ball completely, or a person dribbling a basketball may lose control of the ball and run into it by mistake.

The teacher needs to work hard with beginners by offering them lots of feedback and guidance, which may include visual demonstrations, verbal instructions or physically guiding the learner through the movement. The learner needs to learn and feel the requirements of the movement.

2. The associative phase

Once the basic understanding and techniques of the skill have been acquired, the learner will enter a period of extended practice. The learner will be mastering the new skill and trying to eliminate or minimise mistakes. There will be fewer and less gross errors, such as not timing the skill correctly, applying too much or too little force or taking up slightly incorrect positions. Tactics will start to be developed as the basics of the skill are present and the learner can start to apply these to real situations. The learner will also learn to analyse their own performance and to detect and correct their own errors.

This may be a long stage and the learner may never reach the third stage, in particular if the skill is not practised regularly.

3. The autonomous stage

The autonomous stage is reached when the performer is able to produce the skill automatically, without conscious control of the production of the movement. The performer is able to perform without thinking about it and is able to concentrate on what is happening in their environment. Thus, they are able to think about tactics and their own movements, as well as the movement of team-mates and opponents. The performer will perform consistently and produce few if any errors; the errors themselves will be minor mistakes of judgement with regard to position and the amount of force they put into their movements. They have such high control over their skills that they are able to analyse their own performances and correct any faults they may produce.

When a person learns to drive they can clearly see themselves pass through the three stages. At the beginning they learn by placing the movements into a sequence which they follow. This sequence will be given labels and, to ensure they perform correctly, the learner will think and talk themselves through the sequence of movements. They will have to concentrate intensely to come to terms with the amount of information they are required to process.

However, once the learner has passed their test they enter a period of consolidating their new skills. Although they still have to think quite hard about what they are doing, they will begin to relax and, because they know the movements, will be able to concentrate more on what is going on around them.

About six months after passing their test they will realise that they can get into the car and drive off without even thinking about what they are doing. This is because they have entered the third stage, where the skill has become automatic because it is so well learnt.

Transfer of learning

The transfer of learning is so basic to learning that we almost assume it occurs. It is based on the theory that certain aspects of a skill learnt in one situation can influence performance in another skill. For example, if you can kick a football it is likely you can kick a rugby ball.

Singer (1982) refers to this as: 'relating the then with now'.

STUDENT ACTIVITY

Consider a hockey player who is a novice to the game. Explain what you would observe as they went through the three stages of learning. Your answer should include how they perform the skills, what errors they may make and sources of feedback.

'the effect of the learning and performance of one skill on the learning and performance of another' (Davis *et al.*, 2000).

STUDENT ACTIVITY

Give examples of positive and negative transfer between the following sports.

1   You have knowledge of tennis and try to learn badminton.

2   You have knowledge of squash and try to learn tennis.

3   You have knowledge of hockey and try to learn cricket.

4   You have knowledge of high jump and try to learn pole vault.

5   You have knowledge of netball and try to learn basketball.

After our early years we rarely have to learn a skill from new, as we transfer knowledge from one skill to the learning of another. This is called the transfer of learning.

However, not all transfer of learning will enhance the learning of a new skill.

Positive transfer is produced when the learning of a skill is facilitated by the knowledge of another skill. For example, a tennis player may find the learning of squash is made easier because they already have well-developed hand–eye co-ordination and understand the importance of timing and producing a smooth swing of the racket.

Negative transfer occurs when learning of a skill is made harder by the knowledge of another. For example, a squash player who learns to play tennis may find that they keep hitting the ball into the net because squash demands that the ball is kept low, while in tennis is important to give the ball some upward trajectory.

Stallings (1982) categorised the different types of transfer that can occur.

1   **Skill to skill** – As explained previously, this occurs between two similar skills.

2   **Practice to performance** – For any skill to be of use it must be transferred from the practice situation to the real game situation. We will hear of athletes who are good in practice but cannot transfer their skill from the training ground to the sports pitch.

3   **Abilities to skills** – The performance of skills is based on the abilities which underpin the skills. To be effective in performing a skill we have to transfer our relevant abilities to the skill.

4   **Bilateral transfer** – Transfer of learning occurs between limbs. This may be from hand to hand or leg to leg. Transfer will usually occur between the dominant and non-dominant limb. For example, we are all able to write with our non-dominant hand even though we have never specifically practised writing with that limb.

5   **Stage to stage** – The development of motor skills is dependent on building new skills on those learned previously.

6   **Principles to skills** – When we learn skills we also learn principles of skills. For example, we appreciate the importance of timing and body shape, and relaxing under pressure to produce a flowing movement. These principles can be applied to the learning of all skills.

Practical examples of the transfer of learning

Many sports have been developed for young children – games which are miniature versions of the major games. The aim of these is that the children learn the movements and principles behind the major games through trying out the minor games (e.g. kwik cricket, short tennis, mini rugby and athletics using foam javelins and shot putts). The development of skills is based on positive transfer between the minor and major games and their ability to adapt their newly developed skills to the new game.

REVISION QUESTIONS

1) Explain the theory of Pavlov's classical conditioning and what use it would be to a to a teacher delivering new skills.

2) Skinner's theory of operant conditioning (1938) is concerned mainly with responses rather than stimuli. A key factor of this type of conditioning is reinforcement.

a) What is meant by the term 'reinforcement'? Give an example from a physical activity.

b) Explain how you would teach a sports skill using the operant method).

3) What is the difference between open-loop and closed-loop control?

4) Draw the diagram of Adam's theory of closed-loop feedback, and explain the diagram with reference to a skill you have learnt during practical sessions.

5) Schmidt's schema theory advocates that practice conditions should be varied.

a) What do you understand by the term 'variability of practice'?

b) What are the main features of Schmidt's theory?

6) Fitts and Posner (1967) say that learning can be divided into three phases. What are these phases and what happens in each phase?

7) Explain what is meant by the term 'transfer of learning' and give examples of positive and negative transfer.

8) How is transfer used to promote the process of learning?

THE IDEAL LEARNING ENVIRON-MENT

Teaching or coaching sports is a complex process because we first have to understand how people learn new skills and information, then ensure that we have sufficient knowledge and skills to teach people, and finally consider what the best way would be to deliver our information and skills. There are four stages to actually presenting a new skill to the group of learners.

Stage 1 – Introduce the skill and explain why it is important that the learner learns the skill.

Stage 2 – Present the skill through demonstration and explanation of the points of technique.

Stage 3 – Practice: learners will go through a period of practising the skill.

Stage 4 – Feedback: information will be provided to the learners and errors corrected.

This section will focus on stages 2 and 3, where the coach or teacher is presenting new skills to the learners and they are then practising the skills. There is a range of methods the coach/teacher can employ and these will now be discussed.

The presentation of skills

Whole versus part learning

Whole learning means that the skill is taught and learnt in its entirety, and ideally a skill should be learnt this way. Part learning means a skill is broken down into smaller parts which are learnt separately before being joined together as the whole skill. This method is useful if a skill is complex, and thus difficult to learn. When deciding which method to use, ask yourself the following questions:

✪   How many parts are there in the task?

✪   How much information do I need to convey to the learners?

✪   How mentally challenging is the task?

✪   How difficult are the techniques involved?

This information will give you an idea of the complexity of the task. You then need to ask two final questions:

✪   How easily can the activity be broken down into parts?

✪   Will these smaller parts still be meaningful?

For example, shooting in football would become too disjointed and meaningless if it were broken down into practising the parts of placement of foot, backlift, strike and follow through. On the other hand, a complex trampoline routine may comprise front drop, seat drop, pike, back drop and front somersault. The individual components could be learnt separately and then joined together.

1   Learn the front drop.

2   Learn the seat drop.

3   Learn the pike.

4   Learn the back drop.

5   Learn the front somersault.

6   Learn the routine of front drop, seat drop, pike, back drop, front somersault.

Alternatively, the components could be joined together as each one is learnt.

1   Learn the front drop.

2   Learn the seat drop.

★

STUDENT ACTIVITY

Look at the following skills and decide whether they would be taught most effectively by using the whole, part or whole-part-whole method of presentation. Choose two skills and show how they could be broken down into parts for teaching.

High jump
High board dive
Tennis serve
Breast stroke
Volleyball lay up
Dance sequence
A bench press
Bowling in cricket
Passing in rugby

3 Learn front drop, followed by seat drop.

4 Learn the pike.

5 Learn front drop, followed by seat drop, followed by pike.

6 Learn the back drop.

7 Learn front drop, followed by seat drop, followed by pike, followed by back drop.

8 Learn the front somersault.

9 Learn front drop, followed by seat drop, followed by pike, followed by back drop, followed by the somersault.

Whole-part-whole learning

This method involves the skill being presented in its whole form, then broken down into its parts, and then back in its full form. For example, a cover drive in cricket could be presented using this method.

1 Skill is demonstrated as 'whole'.

2 Forward movement of the foot is presented.

3 Back swing of the bat is presented.

4 Forward swing and follow through is presented.

5 Skill is demonstrated as 'whole' again.

This method is probably the most preferable because it gives the learner the chance to feel the whole movement, then to practise each component and to pay attention to the more difficult parts. Finally, the parts are put back together as a whole, with the learner achieving a greater understanding of the demands of the skill. This skill relies on the transfer of learning between the individual components and the whole skill.

Practice conditions

Massed versus distributed practice

Practice can be organised under different conditions, with reference to the amount of time allocated to rest periods. This is referred to as **massed** or **distributed practice** (see Table 5.1).

Massed practice occurs when there is no time allocation for rest, while distributed practice occurs when there are rest periods between practice within a practice session, or between practice sessions.

Research suggests that distributed practice is more effective because periods of rest enhance concentration and motivation levels, which can be difficult to maintain for long periods of time. Also after a period of learning the learning will diminish and the learner skill level may decrease and they may experience negative learning.

Table 5.1 Massed versus distributed practice

Massed	Distributed
• Best for simple skills	• Best for complex skills.
• Good for skilled, fit and motivated learners	• Good for younger and less fit learners
• Time efficient	• Can waste time
• Little time for reflection on performance	• Breaks can be used for mental rehearsal

Fixed versus variable practice

Fixed practice is when the same skills are practised in the same conditions or situation. **Variable practice** is when skills are practised in an ever-changing environment or situation.

These techniques can be applied to closed and open skills. Closed skills will be most effectively practised through fixed practice, because this replicates the game situation. Open skills need variable conditions of practice and the greater the variety, the more beneficial the practice.

Styles of teaching

Teaching involves the delivery of skills and knowledge to people, and this can be achieved in different ways (styles). Each style will be effective in different situations. It is the responsibility of the teacher to keep their learners interested, enthused, motivated and, above all, to create a situation where learning can occur. Different types of learners will learn in different ways, and the teacher needs to take into account factors such as the number of learners, their age, experience level, ability and motivation to learn. Once this has been done the teacher can adopt an appropriate teaching style.

Teaching style refers to the respective roles of the teacher and the learner in the learning process, and the extent to which the teacher involves the learners. This was examined by Mosston and Ashworth (1986), who developed a spectrum to illustrate the descision-making balance between teacher and learners regarding what is taught and learnt. It also shows the extent to which each party has responsibility for the learning.

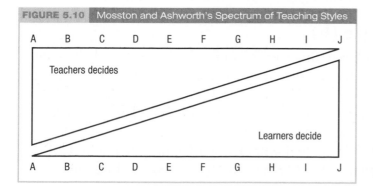

FIGURE 5.10 Mosston and Ashworth's Spectrum of Teaching Styles

The two extremes would be where either the teacher or the learners made decisions about what was learnt and how it should be learnt. Teaching style A is called the command style, while teaching style J is called the discovery style.

Command style (A)

This could also be called 'the dictator' or 'the authoritarian' style. Here, the teacher makes all the decisions and the learners are expected to do what the teacher tells them. There is no feedback between the teacher and the learners, and the learners have no interaction or influence over what is delivered. The role of the learner is to listen, digest information and learn.

The command style is appropriate where the teacher has a large group, such as in a university lecture where they may be teaching to over one hundred students and they may have a large amount of information to convey. This method of teaching is usually backed up by more personal seminars or group tutorials. It is often used where the teacher is in a position of responsibility and the learners are subordinate to the teacher, for example, when the drill sergeant is teaching soldiers how to do drill properly. It can also be used where there are very young or inexperienced learners such as a group of primary school pupils, or an outdoor pursuits instructor teaching a potentially dangerous activity like canoeing, as it is important to maintain control. The command style is inappropriate for more mature or experienced learners who want active involvement in the learning process. The lack of feedback makes it difficult for the teacher to assess whether learning is taking place, and does not allow the learners to develop independent thought or discuss opinions. It is also difficult for learners to maintain concentration over a long period of time when the information is all one way, and it is suggested that little learning will take place after the first 20 minutes.

Reciprocal style (C)

This style is also called 'paired learning' and enables learners to become more involved in the learning process. Once the teacher has explained what is going to be taught and given a demonstration or introduction, the learners will work in pairs. In turn they will assume the role of teacher and learner. The teacher will observe and analyse the learner's performance and attempt to give them feedback and correct their errors. The role of the actual teacher is to supervise the session and help the learners teach each other. This is still fairly demanding on the teacher as their responsibility is to ensure that effective learning occurs.

This type of teaching starts to actively involve the learners and will maintain their interest levels, particularly if they are well motivated. It also gives the learners more personal attention and enables them to receive feedback quickly. On the negative side, the teacher is relying heavily on the learners to help each other learn, which involves a fair amount of trust. A group of less motivated and less responsible learners may not benefit from this method. The teacher will have to work hard to monitor each group and facilitate the learning process.

Problem-solving style (F)

This style involves the teacher setting a problem for the learners and allowing them to use their own resources to solve it. This gives the learners a free rein to use their creative talents in developing solutions. It may take the form of a sports teacher asking a group to develop tactics at a corner kick or free kick situation. In the classroom, the teacher may present a problem or subject the students have to research by going to the library or an appropriate source of information. This is nicknamed the FOFO, which is fly off and find out!

This method is excellent for learners who want to take responsibility for their learning and have the necessary skills and experience to do so effectively. It will benefit motivated learners and, in turn, create more motivation and enjoyment. Because the focus is on the learner, their understanding of the subject or problem will be enhanced, particularly if they are expected to report to the rest of the group or contribute to a discussion. The drawbacks are that the teacher may not be able to establish whether learning has taken place. If the learners are unsuccessful in finding a solution or information it could be seen as a waste of time and a lost opportunity. Also, because there may be more than one solution to the problem, it requires the teacher to have a deep knowledge of the subject, and they have to evaluate the learners' outcomes.

Laissez-faire style (J)

This is an extreme style which is rarely used. It involves the learners making decisions about what to learn and how to learn it. The teacher gives full responsibility to the learners and gives up all their own authority. This style could be utilised by learners at home, for example when they prepare revision for an exam or study independently. In the classroom it may occur if the teacher is absent or late and the learners decide to run the session themselves. Also, a young sports person may work at their game on their own as they attempt to perfect a certain skill or to reach the standard of selection for a certain team.

The role of the teacher is redundant in this situation and, as a result, they may not be keen to use this style. However, for the learners this style allows them to assume full responsibility for their learning and, particularly for more experienced learners, this may hold some appeal.

Forms of guidance

The teacher will help learners to learn by providing demonstrations, explanations and then allowing the learners to experience the skills for themselves. However, while learners practise, the teacher can provide additional assistance by using forms of guidance. Guidance takes three forms:

✪ visual

✪ verbal

✪ manual.

Each of these is aimed at utilising different senses, which is particularly important because different people learn in different ways. Some people respond best through hearing (auditory learners), other people learn best through seeing (visual learners) and the final group learn through experiencing a movement (kinaesthetic learners).

Visual guidance

Visual guidance comes in the form of visual aids and is particularly useful for establishing a model for learners to copy in the first stages of learning. This may take the form of the teacher providing a demonstration, or using a video recording of a performer perfectly completing the movement. The learners will become aware of what they aspire to when they learn, and can copy the role-model provided. It is important that the teacher does not talk during the demonstration because the learner may find it harder to concentrate on information through two sensory channels.

The teacher may also use other visual aids such as charts, models, diagrams on overhead transparencies or pictures. Visual guidance can also mean the teacher making markings on the environment to give the learners an idea of where they should be aiming. For example, they may mark a box on a tennis court to give the server a target to aim for, or they may teach a bowler in cricket about line and length by marking a target on the wicket where they want the ball to pitch.

Verbal guidance

The majority of teaching will be delivered verbally and received through the auditory channel. This will be used to explain the skill and then to give feedback during practice to help learners modify their performance. It is important that the teacher considers how they are delivering their verbal guidance because the learners may not understand the instructions or be able to translate the instructions into action. Any guidance given verbally should be clear, concise and easily understood.

Manual guidance

This provides physical guidance and occurs when a teacher uses physical contact to take a student through a skill or a movement. It helps the learner understand what the movement feels like and then to build a memory of the feeling to provide a reference of correctness. This reference of correctness is the feeling of doing the skill perfectly, and if it is strong then the learner can compare their actual performance with how it should feel.

The first type of manual guidance is called a **forced response**, which is when a teacher will physically guide the learner through the movement. For example, if they were teaching a forehand shot in tennis, they would hold the racket with the learner and take them through the shot. The second type is called **physical restriction** and occurs when a person or piece of equipment supports the body to restrict the learner's movement. For example, a trampoline coach can use 'the rig' to guide the learner through the movement. This will give the learner a sense of safety and enable them to build up their confidence without the fear of becoming injured. It will also serve to give them the correct feeling of the movement.

REVISION *QUESTIONS*

1) Define whole and part learning and give an example of how a skill could be taught by each method.

2) What are the benefits of distributed practice over massed practice?

3) What does Mosston and Ashworth's spectrum of learning styles show?

4) What type of learners would benefit from the command style of teaching?

5) Why is the discovery style beneficial to learners?

6) Explain why a teacher needs to provide guidance to their learners.

7) Why is it important to give visual, verbal and manual guidance to learners?

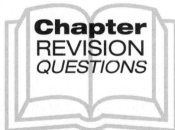

Chapter REVISION *QUESTIONS*

1) Explain why skills need to be classified and the different ways they can be classified.

2) How do information processing models help us to understand the production of sports skills?

3) Using some of the theories of learning, explain your view as to how learning occurs.

4) Discuss ways that teachers can enhance the learning of sports skills.

FURTHER READING

There many texts available either completely devoted to skill acquisition or where skill acquisition constitutes a large part. The following are recommended:

Beashel, P. and Taylor, J. (1996) *Advanced Studies in Physical Education and Sport.* Nelson

Davis, R. J., Bull, C. R., Roscoe, J. V., Roscoe, D. A. (2000) *Physical Education and the Study of Sport.* London: Mosby

Schmidt, R. A. (1999) *Motor Learning and Performance.* Ilinois: Human Kinetics

Wesson, K., Wiggins, N., Thompson, G., Hartigan, S. (2000) *Sport and P.E.: a complete guide to Advanced Level Study.* London: Hodder and Stoughton

Woods, Barbara (1998) *Applying Psychology to Sport.* London: Hodder and Stoughton

REFERENCES

Adams, J. A. Closed-loop theory of motor learning, *Journal of Motor Behaviour,* **3**, 111–150

Beashel, P. and Taylor, J. (1996) *Advanced Studies in Physical Education and Sport.* Nelson

Davis, R. J., Bull, C. R., Roscoe, J. V., Roscoe, D. A. (2000) *Physical Education and the Study of Sport.* London: Mosby

Fitts, P. M. and Posner, M. I. *Human Performance.* Belmont, CA: Brooks and Cole

Hick, W. E. On the rate of gain of information, *Quarterly Journal of Experimental psychology,* **4**, 11–26

Hull, C. L. *Essentials of Behaviour.* New Haven, Conneticut: Yale University Press

Matt Jarvis (2000) *Sport Psychology.* London: Routledge.

Mosston, M. and Ashworth, S. *Teaching Physical Education.* Colombus, Ohio: Merrill Publishing Co.

Schmidt, R. A. (1975) A schema theory of discrete motor skill learning, *Psychological Review,* **82**, 225–260

Skinner, B. F. (1938) *The Behaviour of Organisms.* New York: Appleton-Century-Crofts.

Thorndike, C. L. (1931) *Human Learning.* New York: Appleton-Century-Crofts.

Welford, A. T. (1952) The psychological refractory period. *British Journal of Psychology,* **43**, 2–19.

PRACTICAL SPORTS COACHING

During your time studying sport science you will be involved in a huge number of sports and will experience a variety of coaches and coaching sessions. You will have numerous opportunities to coach sessions and will need to be prepared.

The aims of this chapter are:

- ✪ to help you understand the coaching process and the issues involved in coaching
- ✪ to highlight issues that need consideration when coaching
- ✪ to identify some of the skills, techniques and components of a successful coach
- ✪ to assist you in delivering your coaching sessions
- ✪ to help you analyse your own coaching skills.

THE COACHING PROCESS

Sport is currently benefiting from an explosion of coverage by the media. Television schedules are frequently upset by major sports events such as the Commonwealth Games or the football World Cup; indeed there are numerous satellite television channels given over entirely to sport. There also appear to be more and more people playing sport, thus the opportunities for becoming involved in sport are rapidly increasing. This involvement can be as a participant, a spectator or a coach (see Figure 6.1).

Coaching offers a wealth of new experiences to people. We may dream of sharing the successes of our athletes and gaining plaudits for masterminding their successes. However, coaches are often held responsible for the failures of their athletes and bear the brunt of the criticisms.

The coach has a range of roles to perform. They must be able to educate their athletes and teach them the correct skills and techniques of their sport. They must be able to help athletes gain the physical fitness levels necessary to succeed, and they must be able to plan their training schedules. They will also

FIGURE 6.1   A coach working with athletes

need many personal skills to attend to their athlete's psychological needs and help them cope with the highs and lows of success and failure.

What is the purpose of coaching?

Coaching is helping to develop a person through the improvement of their athletic performance. It involves the physical and psychological development of the person to take them beyond their present level.

Physical development involves the following:

- ✪ working to improve an individual's physical skills and techniques
- ✪ working to improve speed, strength, flexibility and endurance
- ✪ developing techniques and strength to minimise the risks of injury.

Psychological development will involve the following:

- ✪ developing good habits and a routine of training
- ✪ developing mental toughness and a positive mental attitude
- ✪ learning to control emotions and cope with success and failure
- ✪ learning teamwork and interaction in a competitive environment.

The coach must always bear in mind that sport is an area of life that people enter into in order to have fun and enjoy themselves. The coach must prepare teams and individuals to maximise their chances of winning, but they must not lose sight of the pleasure that sport can bring.

This development of skills must always be practised in a safe environment and ensure the safety of participants and the coach.

ISSUES TO CONSIDER WHEN COACHING

Before we examine the skills of coaching it is important to look at the risks involved. You will be placed in a position of great responsibility, either by the athletes you are coaching or by the parents of the children you are asked to coach. You need to understand what this responsibility involves.

You need to remember that you owe a 'duty of care' to anyone that you coach. This means it is your responsibility to make sure you are not putting their safety or welfare at risk. If you are in any way negligent you could face the risk of being sued. So, it is important that every session you run is carefully prepared and that you have made the relevant safety checks beforehand.

You owe it to your athletes to fulfil the following 10 legal duties.

1 Plan out the activity thoroughly beforehand.

2 Ensure that the coaching you provide is safe and correct.

3 Ensure that the environment you are working within is safe and free from hazards.

4 Provide equipment that is up to date and properly maintained.

5   Check all equipment before use.

6   Always check your athletes for injuries and illnesses.

7   Ensure that your athletes are adequately prepared for the activity in terms of rest and nutrition, and that they are properly warmed up before commencing.

8   Warn the athletes of any risks present in an activity and how to minimise these risks.

9   Once the coaching session is underway make sure you pay close attention to your athletes and supervise the activity properly.

10 Be prepared for an emergency situation and provide emergency assistance when necessary.

If you are appropriately qualified and have planned the session carefully you should be able to offer the 'duty of care' necessary. As a result, you should not be negligent. If this is not the case, you could leave yourself open to being sued. It is also important that you keep records of your coaching sessions and any actions you had to take in response to an incident.

Insurance

We live in an increasingly litigious society and in order to protect ourselves from being sued we need to understand insurance. Insurance is essential and we must never coach a session without the relevant insurance. It is our responsibility to find out whether we are insured or if we need to have our own insurance. If you are coaching on behalf of someone else, such as a large organisation or company, you may be covered by their insurance. It is important to check beforehand. If you are self-employed you need to organise your own insurance. This can be done through contacting the national governing body of the sport and asking their advice about insurance. Most bodies will be able to advise you on what insurance you need and where you can obtain it.

Insurance is a complex area and just having insurance is not enough: you need to know and understand what it covers. You will need to be able to answer the following questions about your insurance.

❂   What activities are covered?

❂   Where am I covered to coach?

❂   What events are covered?

❂   How much loss am I insured for?

❂   What equipment and property are covered?

❂   What losses are covered?

❂   How long does the cover last?

❂   Am I covered to transport athletes?

✪   Are there any special conditions that are excluded?

✪   What should I do in the event of a claim?

You should expect to pay around £100 per year for insurance, although this amount varies drastically between sports. It should cover you for loss of at least £2 million and any costs associated with a claim.

Child protection

Coaching children throws up some specific issues with regard to child protection and abuse. Sports organisations are becoming aware that some unscrupulous people will use sport as a means to gain access to children with the aim of abusing them. It is also fair to say that young people can suffer abuse through inappropriate coaching or an excessive emphasis on competition and success. Agencies who hold responsibility for coaching activities have a duty of care to remove or minimise risks to children.

Sport England completed an audit of national governing bodies of sport in December 2000 to discover their child protection policies and procedures. Their published findings showed that:

✪   only 35 national governing bodies had a child protection policy in operation

✪   17 of these national governing bodies had allegations or suspicions of child abuse within their sport.

Several positive steps have been taken to prevent children being abused in sport; they take their lead from the 1989 Children's Act.

1   In January 2001, a Child Protection in Sport Unit (CPSU) was established. This is based at the national training centre of the NSPCC and is co-funded by the NSPCC and Sport England.

2   New legislation covering cultural and leisure services, including sporting organisations, recommends that organisations have child protection procedures in place and that this is supported by training. The aim is to establish working practices and codes of conduct that minimise the chances of child abuse occurring.

3   The new Criminal Records Bureau has been established to provide information about the suitability of an individual to work with children.

4   Sport England's active sports programmes require evidence that child protection procedures are in place before any activities can commence.

5   Ninety-eight per cent of the national governing bodies of sport that receive public funding have child protection policies.

In summary, each national governing body of sport has been required to draw up and put in place a child protection policy. It is your responsibility as a sports coach to get hold of the document and implement its recommendations. It is likely that when you train to be a coach by undertaking coaching awards, these documents will be brought to your attention.

STUDENT ACTIVITY

Before reading this section, think of two coaches that you admire. One should be a person who has coached you in the past and one should be well known in top-level sport. Make a list of the personality characteristics that you think make them an effective coach.

Personal skills of a coach

Research seems to show that there is room for lots of different personalities and different styles in coaching. However, effective coaches will all have at least five factors in common.

1   **A professional approach** – They pay great attention to detail and conduct themselves in an appropriate manner.

2   **They are positive role models** – The coach behaves in the way that they would want their athletes to behave. This means that the way they accept success and failure or good and bad performances is the way they would expect their athletes to accept them. They should also set an example in terms of punctuality and good personal habits.

3   **Knowledge of the sport** they are coaching – It is imperative that a coach has a sound knowledge of the rules, techniques and tactical requirements of the sport. This will immediately establish them as a role model and gain them the respect of the athletes. It also means they understand the skills and are able to teach and evaluate them correctly.

4   **Motivational skills** – They must be able to keep players interested and working to the best of their abilities. The history of sport is littered with talented individuals who did not achieve their potential due to loss of motivation.

5   **Communication skills** – This involves verbal and non-verbal communication. Verbal communication is what we say and how we say it; non-verbal communication involves the gestures and body language we use to accompany our verbal communication. In sport it will also include demonstrations of skills and techniques.

There are other skills a coach may need, such as patience, approachability, responsibility, objectivity and organisational skills. Often, successful coaches have an X-factor, in that they are inspirational but we cannot say quite why.

Coaching qualifications

To become qualified as a coach it is necessary to undertake coaching awards with the national governing body of the sport you want to coach. Unfortunately each national governing body has a slightly different system, so you need to make yourself familiar with which awards you need relevant to the level of coaching you wish to undertake.

As you advance through the awards you will be able to progress from coaching young children up to adults and performers of higher standards and abilities. An example of a coaching course structure is given below.

The FA Coaching Course Structure

Level	FA Course	UEFA Award
5	FA Coaching Diploma	UEFA 'Pro' Coaching Award
4	FA Advanced Coaching Licence	UEFA 'A' Coaching Award
3	FA Coaching Licence	UEFA 'B' Coaching Award
2	FA Coaching Certificate	
1	FA Junior Team Manager's award	
	FA Teaching Certificate	

Components of an effective coaching session

✪ **Planning and organisation** – This is essential to help you get the best from your session. The session must be clearly planned out, showing progression, and planning should also show consideration for athletes, equipment and facilities.

FIGURE 6.2 The components of an effective coaching session

✪ **Communication** – This should be relevant to the group of athletes and take into consideration their age, experience and ability level.

✪ **Monitoring and evaluating** – Performance level should be continually monitored and evaluated so that progress can be assessed and recorded.

✪ **Analysing and problem solving** – The coach needs to analyse performance in terms of strengths and weaknesses, and to address any problem areas.

✪ **Tactics** – As the athletes become more skilful they need to understand how best to use these skills in a match situation and thus develop their tactics. Coaching should increase an athlete's understanding of tactics.

✪ **Sports science** – Effective coaching will involve the practical application of many sport science disciplines. This may include physiology, sport psychology, biomechanics, skill acquisition, nutrition and sports injury.

✪ **Health and safety** – As always we must ensure the safety of our athletes and prevent them from becoming injured.

Benefits of effective coaching

These benefits can be broken down into benefits for the athletes and benefits for the coach.

Benefits for the athlete

The athlete will benefit from effective coaching because they will stand the best chance of achieving the aims and objectives that they have set for themselves. If they get the right coaching to complement their own abilities they will develop their sports skills and go on to win their competitions and enjoy competing in the sport. This mixture of fun and success will keep them motivated to succeed and should mean that they continue in the sport and continue to be successful. This success in sport will contribute to their own personal development and complement their development in other areas of life, offering them great personal satisfaction.

Success as part of a team will produce additional benefits. The positive feelings of shared success will increase social bonds and make an athlete feel that they belong to a group with all the social benefits this offers.

Benefits for the coach

The coach will not benefit from the feelings created by first-hand success, but will share in the success of their athletes and team, which will bring much satisfaction and enjoyment. The coach will also derive satisfaction from observing the physical, psychological and social development of their athletes. There may also be a feeling of reciprocation for a coach, in that when they were competing they received coaching and guidance and now they are putting their expertise back into the sport. As a result, they help to maintain and raise the standards of a sport they care about. The coach will also earn the recognition and respect of the athletes and, possibly, the general public for their skills; this may lead to their earning a good reputation. A major benefit for some coaches is that if they are successful they can earn a living through their skills and they may gain promotion into more responsible positions.

Styles of coaching

There are three basic styles of coaching that can be illustrated on a continuum showing the extent to which the coach or athletes make the decisions.

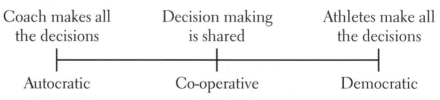

Coach makes all the decisions	Decision making is shared	Athletes make all the decisions
Autocratic	Co-operative	Democratic

Autocratic style

This is also called the **command style** or the **dictator style**, and involves the coach making the decisions and imposing these on the group. Autocratic means 'the power of one', giving the athletes no say in their coaching. The coach tells the participants what to do and how to do it, using phrases such as 'I want…', 'You will do this…', etc.

Democratic style

This is also called the **submissive style** or the **babysitter**. It involves the coach throwing the session open to the participants and letting them decide what to do and how to do it. The coach will provide few instructions and let the participants control and organise the session, only intervening when safety is compromised or discipline is out of control.

Democratic means power (*cratic*) of the people (*demo*) and it gives athletes the chance to develop themselves and be responsible for their own actions.

Co-operative style

This is also called **liberal style** or the **teacher** and it involves shared decision making between the coach and the athletes. Coaches using this style recognise that they need to provide a lead and direct their athletes, but they also recognise the value of letting athletes make decisions and be responsible for the decisions they make.

In reality most coaches will use the co-operative style, as the autocratic and democratic styles are theoretical extremes. However, different coaches will use different amounts of each style. For example, a coach who mainly makes the decision themselves would be regarded as autocratic, while a coach who usually consults their athletes will be regarded as democratic.

There will also be times when a coach adapts their style to suit the situation in which they find themselves. For example, coaching very young athletes demands that coaches make the decisions and keep a tight control of the athletes. Whereas, coaching a group of knowledgeable athletes means the coach can effectively use a more democratic style – failure to do so may result in resentment from the athletes. However, if the group of experienced, mature athletes were losing their final with five minutes to go, then this would be a time for the coach to become more autocratic and impose decisions on the team.

STUDENT ACTIVITY

Consider each of the coaching styles discussed and draw up a list of advantages and disadvantages of each style.

REVISION QUESTIONS

1) Define 'coaching' and explain the role of the coach.

2) How can a coach help athletes?

3) How can a coach prevent themselves from being negligent?

4) How can a coach make certain that they are properly insured?

5) How can you find out about the child protection procedures in the sport you coach?

6) What personal qualities would you expect a coach to possess?

7) Why can coaching be beneficial to athletes?

8) Summarise the three styles of coaching.

PLAN AND DELIVER EFFECTIVE COACHING SESSIONS

Athlete's needs

Before you start to plan your coaching session you need to consider who your athletes are and what needs they have. Once you have established this you have to decide how to meet these needs and what adaptations you need to make to your session.

Factors to consider are shown in Figure 6.3.

1. **Individual or group** – Do you have enough equipment and space? How can you allocate your time equally to each person? What style of coaching will you use? What type of tasks can you set?

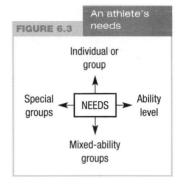

FIGURE 6.3 An athlete's needs

2. **Ability level** – The coaching you do needs to meet the ability level of the athletes and seek to improve this ability level.

3. **Mixed-ability groups** – It can be quite challenging to coach mixed-ability groups. You need to set tasks and goals to keep all ability levels happy or you will start to lose the interest of your athletes. You may find that you can use the athletes of higher ability to help the athletes of lower ability.

4. **Special groups** – you may find that you become involved in coaching disabled athletes and you will need to amend your coaching sessions accordingly. You may be coaching athletes who have illnesses such as asthma and diabetes, and you need to understand these medical conditions and make any additional safety arrangements.

Planning

There are many areas a coach needs to look at when preparing a coaching session. Successful coaching sessions come from good planning and organisation. **Proper planning prevents poor performance**.

Planning needs to be split into two sections:

✪   a plan for the season

✪   a plan for each session.

Planning can be a time-consuming process, however, it will make your coaching more effective in the short and long terms. It will ensure that you are able to cover all aspects of skills, techniques, tactics and physical fitness during each stage of the season. It will also enable you to evaluate your performance and the team's performance at the end of the season, working out where you went right and where you went wrong.

Season plan

When planning for a season, break the planning down into various stages.

1   Establish the long-term goals for the season.

2   Break the coaching year down into three stages or periods: preparation for competition, competition, and transition from competition to the next season.

3   Establish short-term goals for each of these stages.

4   Select what information and skills need to be delivered to achieve each goal.

5   Plan individual sessions.

Before you plan your programme for the year, you must consider all the factors that will affect your planning. You need to know answers to the following questions.

❂   How many sessions have we got a week?

❂   How much time have we got for each session?

❂   When do the competitions start?

❂   How many competitions do we have a year?

❂   How many athletes are in the squad?

❂   How much assistance will I get with coaching?

❂   What are the current skill and ability levels of the athletes?

❂   What ages are the athletes?

❂   What facilities have we got?

❂   What equipment and other resources have we got?

❂   What factors will cause a disruption to the programme?

1.   Long-term goals for the season

The long-term goals can be listed as a series of outcomes for the season and will summarise what you are trying to achieve. For example, the long-term goals for a college hockey or football team may be some of the following:

❂   to gain promotion into the league above their current level

❂   to reach the semifinal of the college cup

❂   to increase the number of goals scored by 30% on last season

❂   to decrease the number of goals conceded by 20% on last season

❂   to concede 25% fewer fouls.

2.   The coaching year

The coaching year will differ depending upon the sport being coached. However, it will fall into three stages or periods.

1   **Preparation period** – This is the period prior to the start of competition and involves the development of physical fitness and work on sports techniques. For example, a footballer's preparation phase will run from July to mid-August and will involve very hard physical conditioning work before some sport-specific skills work and then the introduction of pre-season friendly matches. A track and field athlete will have a much longer preparation phase running from October to May. During this phase the types of training will change significantly. Up to Christmas the training will involve general conditioning work; after Christmas it will become more specific and increase in quality and decrease in quantity. The athletes may prepare for the competition phase with some indoor competitions or warm-up meetings.

2   **Competition period** – This period will involve the athletes maintaining their fitness levels and preparing for competition. For the footballer this period lasts for around nine months, while the track and field athlete will have a season of around five months. Training will start to ease down and the athletes will aim to 'peak' at certain times in relation to their most important competitions.

3   **Transition phase** – This period, between the end of the competitive phase and the start of the preparation phase, will involve a period of complete rest or active rest. The athlete will take part in gentle exercise different to their specialist sport. For example, a runner may do some gentle swimming or cycling.

3.   Short-term goals for each stage

The short-term goals for a team and the coach will fall into one of five categories.

1   **Techniques** – Goals related to learning and producing skills needed for performance.

2   **Tactics** – Goals related to learning when to implement these techniques.

3   **Fitness** – Goals relating to physical preparation for competition.

4   **Psychological** – Goals related to mental preparation for competition.

5   **Conduct** – Goals related to behaviour on the pitch towards officials and opponents.

These goals can be described as being performance goals, since the outcome or long-term goals will be dependent on these performance goals being achieved.

Each of the stages of the training year needs a series of short-term goals devised to help achieve the long-term goals. The content will depend upon the needs of the team, but may include some from the following example of a college football team. These goals should be specific and measurable, but, for these purposes we will just state what the goals are.

1   **Techniques** – Improvements in the major skills of the game: passing, shooting, heading, dribbling and control.

2 Tactical – Appreciation of different styles of play in relation to attacking and defensive play.

3 Fitness – Improvements in the components of fitness: speed, strength, flexibility and stamina.

4 Psychological – Improvements in key skills such as arousal control and mental rehearsal.

5 Conduct – Improvements in eliminating foul play and behaviour towards opponents and officials.

These goals need to be separated into each stage of coaching, so you decide what is important at which stage.

4. Select information and skills needed to achieve each short-term goal

Having decided upon your goals it is necessary to look at the content required to achieve each goal. For example, the technical skill of shooting requires the following detail:

- ✪ correct body position
- ✪ backswing
- ✪ contact with the boot – laces, inside or outside of the foot
- ✪ follow through.

The goal of achieving stamina requires the following detail:

- ✪ steady state runs
- ✪ hill running
- ✪ interval training
- ✪ fartlek running.

5. Plan individual sessions

Now we know what has to be taught and when it has to be taught, we can look at the session plans for each of the coaching sessions.

Session plan

The main factors a coach has to consider when planning a coaching session are:

- ✪ aims and objectives of the session
- ✪ how they fit in with long- and short-term goals
- ✪ how the session fits in with previously taught skills
- ✪ the environment
- ✪ equipment needed
- ✪ participants
- ✪ safety of participants
- ✪ progression of the session.

A coaching session will have various stages which will alter depending upon the sport coached and the stage in the training year. Typical stages will include the following.

1. **Warm up** – This is very important and will include raising the pulse, mobilising joints and possibly stretching muscles appropriate to the sport. This will help prevent injuries and prepare athletes mentally and physically for the coaching to come.

2. **Skills practice** – This may be a continuation of the warm up, but this time you will include elements of the sport. For example, sprinters will do drills, whilst rugby players may incorporate passing work into their running.

3. **Tactical skill work** – It is important to spend time on tactical and specific skill development. This may involve a team or individual situation. For example, in coaching football this may include working on specific skills such as taking corners, crossing or long passing.

4. **Fitness work** – Components of fitness relevant to the period of the year are worked on here. For the rugby player this may be fartlek training or speed work. For track and field athletes this would comprise the bulk of the session.

5. **Tactical work** – Usually this will involve simulation of game play, allowing the coach to work on putting the techniques and skills learnt into real situations.

6. **Cool down** – This will involve the athletes lowering their pulses and then performing some maintenance and developmental stretches. It is vital for speeding up the removal of waste products produced by the exercise and reducing soreness and stiffness.

Session planning paperwork

It is easiest to devise a template for yourself that you can complete prior to each session. This session plan will ensure that the session is well organised and that you achieve all your aims and objectives. A sample session plan is provided opposite.

These individual plans should be kept together in a file as a record of coaching sessions or as a coaching logbook. The logbook should include all your coaching materials, such as your long-term and short-term goals and your planning for the season. You may also keep your evaluation of coaching forms here, along with insurance and health and safety documents.

SESSION PLAN

Date: .... Time: ....

Duration: .... Stage of season: ....

Aims and objectives: .... Facilities: ....

Participants: Number: .... Equipment required: ....

    Age: ....

    Ability: ....

Safety checks required: ....

How the session fits in with previous sessions: ....

How the session will progress: ....

Time	Content
	Warm up
	Skills practice
	Fitness work
	Tactical work
	Cool down

Safety considerations

Obviously the health and safety of your athletes and yourself is of paramount importance and therefore must be an issue during every session. It is important to complete some simple checks before each session.

Safety of facilities

Before your coaching session, walk around the playing area to check for areas of damage, holes in the surface, discarded glass or cans, damp areas and any other hazards. If the facility is inside, check the walls, lights, wall plugs, windows and inspect the roof. Report any problems to the facility manager.

Safety of participants

Check the clothing of your participants to see if it is appropriate and does not cause any hazards, such as loose laces or dangling clothing. Check that they have taken off jewellery and watches, that their hair is secured and that they are not chewing gum. Finally, check that they are free from injury and have not suffered illness or injury since your last meeting.

Safety of coaching

Check that the coaching session you have designed is relevant to the needs of the participants and will not cause them any damage.

Emergency procedures

Check that all participants are aware of fire exits and assembly points in case of fire, that they know where the first aid kit and nearest telephone are kept and who is the nominated first aider.

If there is an accident or injury you will need to complete an accident report form, so you must be aware of where they are kept.

REVISION QUESTIONS

1) What are the five steps to developing a coaching plan for the season?

2) Explain the three stages of the coaching year.

3) What six stages will there be in a typical coaching session?

4) What checks do you need to make prior to a coaching session to ensure it will be safe?

EVALUATING AND ADAPTING COACHING SESSIONS

Evaluating strengths and weaknesses

Once you have completed your coaching session it is important to evaluate your performances so that you can:

- ✪ adapt the session the next time you coach
- ✪ adapt your coaching style to suit the athlete's needs
- ✪ correct any errors you made
- ✪ improve your performance and effectiveness
- ✪ make the sessions more enjoyable.

Time spent planning sessions is very important, but only if you reflect upon and evaluate your performance will you actually start to improve as a coach. Evaluation can be done by answering questions under several headings, as shown in the sample evaluation form opposite. Positive and negative comments should be included, and strengths and weaknesses mentioned.

EVALUATION FORM

Date: .... Facility: ....

Aims and objectives: ....

Brief summary of coaching session: ....

....

1. Did I achieve all my aims and objectives?
2. Did the session progress effectively?
3. How safe was the session?
4. What feedback did I receive from the athletes?
5. How enjoyable was the session?
6. What changes will I make in the future?

STUDENT ACTIVITY

Think how you could adapt your coaching session to cover the following unforeseen circumstances:

- ✪ you are short of the equipment you need
- ✪ the sports hall roof is leaking
- ✪ a beginner has come to join your coaching group of intermediate athletes
- ✪ the athletics track has puddles due to heavy rain.

Adapting sessions

In order to help your athletes to improve you need to observe them and then adapt their techniques. You must identify whether the errors are performance errors or technical errors. A **performance error** occurs when you know an athlete can perform a skill, but for some reason they are not performing it as well as they can. A **technical error** will occur whenever they have not learnt the skill or technique properly.

In order to identify these errors you must have a knowledge and understanding of the skill, or you will become frustrated, as you know something is wrong but you do not know what it is or how to correct it!

Using videotapes is a very useful method to evaluate performance as it gives you a chance to repeatedly view a skill and analyse where the problem lies. Videotapes of techniques can also be analysed using computer packages so that minute details can be picked up. A knowledge of biomechanics and access to a sport science lab are needed for this level of analysis.

Once errors have been identified it is necessary to give feedback to the athlete. There are some simple pieces of advice to consider when giving feedback.

1 Give feedback as soon after performance as you can, or the athlete will have forgotten their own performance.

2 Give simple, straightforward information about the performance.

3 Focus on correcting one error at a time; it is necessary to decide which error is the most damaging.

4 Try and give positive feedback as well as negative, so that the athlete does not become disheartened. This is particularly important for beginners.

5 Encourage athletes to help you in the feedback process.

Contingency plans

Every good coach needs to be prepared for situations that do not go to plan. For example, athletes do not enjoy training in the rain, and wet surfaces can pose a health and safety risk.

REVISION *QUESTIONS*

1) Why does a coach need to evaluate their coaching sessions?
2) What is the difference between performance errors and technical errors?

Techniques used to analyse performance

During your practical sports sessions you will be taught how to coach sessions and develop skills in a range of sports. Now it is your chance to deliver coaching sessions and improve the performances of the athletes in your group. There are various techniques you can use to analyse the performance of an athlete:

- ✪ formally test the skills of an athlete
- ✪ observe the athletes informally while they are involved in the activity
- ✪ talk to the athletes to hear their views and feelings
- ✪ ask athletes to evaluate each other's performance
- ✪ use a video recorder to tape their performance
- ✪ use results and records of competitions
- ✪ use computer packages specifically designed to analyse performance
- ✪ use specialist equipment.

Once you have analysed the performance of an athlete you will then need to feed back to them by identifying their strengths and weaknesses. This will also enable you to suggest areas for improvement.

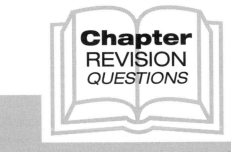

Chapter REVISION *QUESTIONS*

1) As a coach in a sport of your choice, explain what skills and you require to be an effective coach.
2) Prepare a plan for a coaching session that you intend to deliver to a group of fellow students or a group of young athletes.
3) Why is evaluation of your performance important? Suggest methods to carry this out.

REFERENCES AND FURTHER READING

Gervis, M. and Brierley, J. (1999) *Effective Coaching for Children*. Crowood Press Ltd.
Martens, R. (1997) *Successful Coaching*. Illinois: Human Kinetics
Wesson, K., Wiggins, N., Thompson, G., Hartigan, S. (2000) *Sport and P.E. – A Complete Guide to Advanced Level Study*. London: Hodder and Stoughton

Websites
Sports Coach UK: www.sportscoachuk.org
Sport England: www.sportengland.org

ANATOMY FOR SPORT AND EXERCISE

This chapter introduces the biological principles of how the body moves, and includes a detailed exploration of the skeleton and neuromuscular systems. The anatomy and physiology of the cardiovascular and respiratory systems are also discussed.

By the end of this chapter students should be able to:

✪ understand the structure of the skeleton

✪ be aware of the different types of joint and the movements they permit

✪ have an understanding of the different types of muscle and how skeletal muscle contracts

✪ explain how the skeletal and neuromuscular systems act on the skeleton to produce movement

✪ have an understanding of the structure and function of the cardiovascular and respiratory systems.

THE SKELETON

At birth, the human skeleton is made up of 275 different bones. As the skeleton matures, some bones **fuse** together, leaving the average adult with a skeleton consisting of 206 bones.

The function of the skeleton is five-fold.

1. **Movement** – The skeleton plays an important part in movement by providing a series of movable **levers** to which muscles are attached. The muscles can then pull on these levers to move different parts of the body.

2. **Protection** – The skeleton protects important internal organs. For example, the cranium protects the brain. What do the ribs and sternum protect?

3. **Shape** – The skeleton provides the human with the basic framework that gives the body its particular form.

4. **Red and white blood cell production** – Red and white blood cells are produced from the skeletal bone marrow of certain bones.

5. **Mineral storage** – The bones store calcium and phospherus which can be used by the body when the diet does not supply adequate amounts.

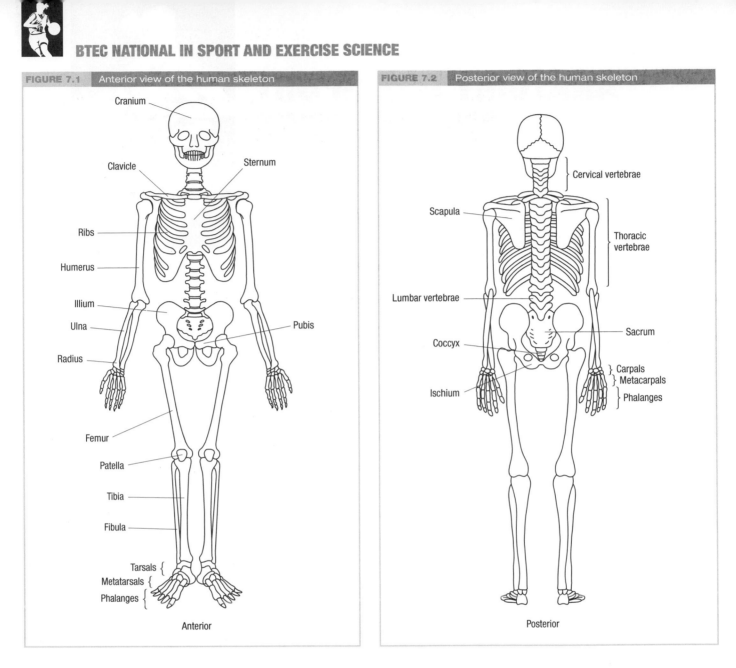

FIGURE 7.1   Anterior view of the human skeleton

FIGURE 7.2   Posterior view of the human skeleton

- **Skull** – This is the bony framework of the head and is made up of eight **cranial** bones (the cranium) and fourteen **facial** bones.

- **The chest** – This is made up of the **sternum** and the **ribs** and protects the heart and lungs. The sternum is a flat, dagger-shaped bone situated in the middle of the chest. The ribs are thin, flat, curved bones. There are 24 ribs in total, arranged in 12 pairs. The first seven pairs are connected to the spine at the back of the body and directly to sternum by cartilage at the front of the body. The next three pairs of are attached to the spine at the back of the body and to the rib above at the front of the body. The last two pairs are called floating ribs. They are attached to the spine but are not connected to anything at the front of the body.

- **Vertebral column** – The vertebral column is also known as the **spine**, the **backbone** or the **spinal column**. It consists of 33 vertebrae which are divided into five categories, depending on where they are located in the column. At the top of the vertebral column there are seven **cervical** vertebrae. The first is called the **atlas** and the second is called the **axis**. The next twelve vertebrae are called the **thoracic** vertebrae. They are larger than cervical vertebrae and increase in size from top to bottom. The next five bones are called the **lumbar** vertebrae and are the largest vertebrae in the spinal column. They support the majority of the body's weight. The **sacrum** is located just below the lumbar vertebrae and consists of five fused bones. The bottom of the spinal column is called the **coccyx** or tailbone. It consists of four bones that are fused together.

✪ **Arm** – This consists of the **humerus**, **radius** and **ulna**. The humerus is in the upper arm and its head fits into the scapula in the shoulder. The lower arm consists of the radius and ulna. The radius is located on the side away from the body (lateral side) and the ulna is located on the side towards the body (medial side) when standing in the anatomical position. To help you remember this, the radius is in line with the thumb.

  The elbow is occasionally referred to as the funny bone. This is due to the tingling and often quite unpleasant and painful sensation caused by a blow to the ulnar nerve, which is located alongside the humerus bone. However, the feeling that results is usually not very humerous!

✪ **Hand** – The hand comprises three parts: the **wrist** the **palm** and **five fingers**, totalling 27 bones. The wrist is made up of eight small bones called the **carpal bones**. The palm consists of five **metacarpal bones**, one aligned with each of the fingers. The fingers are made up of 14 bones called **phalanges**.

✪ **Leg** – The thigh is composed of a single bone called the **femur**, which is the longest, largest, and strongest bone in the body. The lower leg consists of the **fibula** and the **tibia**. The tibia is also known as the shin-bone. The fibula is located on the lateral side of the body, and the tibia on the medial side. The tibia is larger than the fibula because it bears most of the weight. The **patella**, more commonly called the **kneecap** is a large, triangular bone located within a tendon between the femur and the tibia. It protects the knee joint and strengthens the tendon that forms the knee. The bones of the lower extremities are the heaviest, largest, and strongest bones in the body because they must bear the entire weight of the body when a person is standing in the upright position.

✪ **Foot** – This contains 26 bones and includes the **ankle**, the **instep** and **five toes**. The ankle is made up of seven **tarsal** bones. The **metatarsal** and **phalanges** bones of the foot are similar in number and position to the metacarpal and phalanges bones of the hand.

✪ **Shoulder girdle** – This is also known as the **pectoral girdle**. It is composed of four bones: two clavicles and two scapulae. The **clavicle**, more commonly called the **collarbone**, connects the humerus to the trunk of the body. One end of the clavicle is connected to the sternum and one end is connected to the scapula. The **scapula** is also called the **shoulder blade**. It is a large, triangular, flat bone located on the back of the rib cage. The head of the humerus fits into its shallow depression called the glenoid cavity. The primary function of the pectoral girdle is to provide an attachment point for the numerous muscles that allow the shoulder and elbow joints to move.

STUDENT ACTIVITY

1   Look at the labelled diagram of the skeleton on page 164, then draw up a list of **all** the bones in:
a)   the axial skeleton
b)   the appendicular skeleton.
2   Shade the bones of the axial skeleton with one colour and all the bones of the appendicular skeleton with a different colour.

✪   **Pelvic girdle** – Also called the **hip girdle**, this part of the skeleton is made up of two **coxal** (hip) bones. The coxal bone consists of three separate parts: the **ilium**, the **ischium** and the **pubis**. The two coxal bones are connected at the front of the body by the pubic symphysis. At the back of the body they meet at either side of the sacrum. The pelvic girdle supports the weight of the body from the vertebral column and offers protection for the bladder, the reproductive organs, and the developing foetus in a pregnant woman.

The axial and appendicular skeleton

The skeleton is split into two different parts: the axial skeleton and the appendicular skeleton.

The axial skeleton consists of 80 bones and includes the cranium, ribs, sternum and vertebral column. The primary function of the axial skeleton is to protect the major organs in the body: the brain, heart, lungs and spinal cord.

The appendicular skeleton has 126 bones and is made up of the shoulder girdle, hip girdle, arms, hands, legs and feet. There are 64 bones in the shoulders and upper limbs and 62 in the pelvis and lower limbs. The main purpose of the appendicular skeleton is to work in conjunction with the muscular system to provide movement.

There are very few differences between the skeletons of the male and the female. Male bones are usually larger and heavier than the corresponding female bones. The female's pelvic cavity is wider than the male's in order to accommodate childbirth. Due to the biblical story of Adam and Eve, some people believe that males and females have a different number of ribs, but this is not true; both males and females have 24 ribs.

Bone

Bone is a living tissue that is continually being broken down and remade. Approximately every seven years your body will have replaced the equivalent of the whole of your skeleton!

Classification of bones

The bones of the body fall into five general categories based on their shape.

1   **Long bones** are longer than they are wide and work as levers. The bones of the arms are of this type.

2   **Short bones** are short, cube-shaped, and found in the wrists and ankles.

3   **Flat bones** are not totally flat, but have broad smooth surfaces. Their function is primarily to protect organs and to attach muscles. Examples of these bones are the ribs, cranial bones and the scapulae.

4   **Sesamoid bones** are bones located within a tendon. An example is the patella. The person who named this type of bone gave it this name because they thought it looked like a sesame seed!

5   **Irregular bones** are all the bones that do not fall into the previous categories. They have varied shapes, sizes and surface features. This type of bone can be found in the vertebral column.

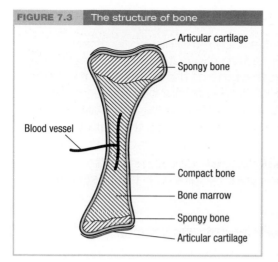

FIGURE 7.3 The structure of bone

- Articular cartilage
- Spongy bone
- Blood vessel
- Compact bone
- Bone marrow
- Spongy bone
- Articular cartilage

Structure of bone

Bones are composed of tissue that may take one of two forms: compact or spongy/cancellous. Most bones contain both types of tissue. **Compact** bone is dense, hard, and forms the protective external portion of all the bones. **Spongy** bone is inside the compact bone and is full of tiny holes filled with bone marrow. The spongy bone is usually found at the ends of the long bones.

Bone formation

The technical term for bone formation is **osteogenesis**. The process involves three main steps:

1 the production of an extracellular organic matrix

2 mineralization of the matrix to form bone

3 bone remodelling by resorption and reformation.

Osteoblasts, osteocytes, and **osteoclasts** are cells involved in the formation of bone. **Osteoblasts** start the process of bone formation by making collagen, which is the precursor of the extracellular matrix. Osteoblasts are also involved in laying down minerals in the matrix, supplied by the food a person eats. The minerals make the bone hard and able to withstand external forces. If a person has a diet lacking in calcium, they may suffer from a condition called osteoporosis, where the bones are weak and are more likely to break. As the process of bone formation progresses, the osteoblasts come to settle in the tiny spaces within the mineralized extracellular matrix of bone. Once the osteoblasts are positioned in the bone matrix, they are then called **osteocytes**.

Bone continually undergoes a process called **remodelling**. This involves bone reabsorption, where the bone is broken down by **osteoclasts** and then rebuilt by osteoblasts. This process allows us to grow, to repair broken bones and to build bigger, stronger bones in response to **weight bearing** exercise. Sunlight and/or Vitamin D are also necessary in order to ensure bone remodelling produces strong bones, as they help the process of laying down minerals in the bone.

STUDENT PRACTICAL

Bone measurements

Aim

The aim of this activity is to try to determine how the length of a person's bones contributes to their overall height and sporting potential.

Equipment

tape measure

pen and paper to record results

Method

Working in groups of three or four carry out the activity on the next page.

continues overleaf

continued

1 Draw up a table with the following columns: name, height, sport, humerus, radius and ulna, femur, tibia and fibula.

2 Write the names of the members of your group in the name column.

3 Record the height (in cm) of each member of your group.

4 Identify and write in the table the favourite sport of each member of your group.

5 With a tape measure, record in cm the length of the humerus of each person. Place the tape measure right at the top of the shoulder then measure down to the bony protrusions of the elbow. Write the length in the table.

6 Now measure the distance from the elbow down to the bony protrusions of the wrist. Record this distance in the radius and ulna column.

7 Feel for the top of the hip bone, then measure down the outside of the leg to the bony protrusions of the outside of the knee. Record this in the femur column.

8 From the knee joint, measure down to the outside of the lower leg to the bony protrusions of the ankle. Record this in the tibia and tibula column.

9 Compare your results with the rest of the group.

Conclusion

Try to answer the following questions.

1 What do you notice about the height of a person and the length of their limbs?

2 Is there a bone that is consistently the longest in each person? Which one is it?

3 Is there a relationship between a person's height and the type of sport they take part/compete in? Try to explain this relationship

STUDENT ACTIVITY

Bony features

Aim

The aim of this activity is to try to feel the bony features of the skeleton.

Equipment

Skeleton and selection of bones

Method

Students should work in pairs.

1 Run your fingers along different types of long, short, flat and irregular bones. Feel for bumps and dents on the surface of these bones. These bony features are called **protrusions** and **depressions** respectively.

2 Identify the following types of depressions.

a) A **fossa** – this is a rounded depression, e.g. the acetabular fossa located on the pelvis.

b) A **groove** – an elongated depression, e.g. the deep bicipital groove near to the head of the humerus which is occupied by one of the tendons of the biceps muscle.

c) A **notch** – a v-like depression, e.g. the sciatic notch on the pelvis.

3 Identify the following types of protrusions.

a) A **tuberosity** – this is a broad, rough, raised bump for muscle attachment, e.g. the tibial tuberosity.

b) A **tubercle** – this is a smaller version of the tuberosisty, e.g. the tubercle of the illiac crest.

c) A **spine** – this is a sharp pointed feature for muscle attachment, e.g. the iliac spine.

d) A **ridge**, **crest** or **line** – this is a moderately raised ridge along the shaft of a bone, e.g the tibial crest.

4 Protrusions that form part of a joint are called **condyles** and **epicondyles**.

a) Identify a **condyle** this is a rounded bump that usually fits into a fossa of another bone, thus making a joint.

b) Identify **epicondyle** this is a bump near a condyle and often gives the appearance of a bump on a bump.

![star] **STUDENT ACTIVITY**

Bone size

Aim

The aim of this activity is to try to determine if there is a difference in bone density and size between the different sexes, and between people from different ethnic origins.

Equipment

tape measure

paper

pen

Method

On a partner, measure the circumference of the bones at the wrist, elbow, ankle and knee. Ensure that you have measured the bony area of each body part.

Results

Make a results table with the headings shown:

Name	Wrist (cm)	Elbow (cm)	Ankle (cm)	Knee (cm)

Compare the class measurements.

Conclusion

In your conclusion try to answer the following questions.

1 Is there a difference between the measurements of the males and the females?

2 Is there an age-related difference in the measurements?

3 Try to explain the differences in circumference measurements.

4 Can you determine if there is a difference in bone density from these measurements?

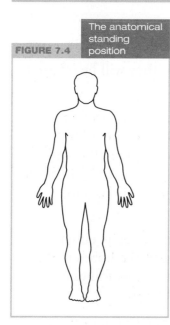

FIGURE 7.4 The anatomical standing position

Anatomical language

Various terms are used to describe the body in anatomical positions and the position of structures related to each other. Correct anatomical terms must be used to express oneself clearly. All terms are related to the anatomical standing position of the human body, which is where the person stands with their feet hip

![star] **STUDENT ACTIVITY**

Terms of relationship

Copy out the list of names below and give an example of a body part that fits the description.

Anterior (ventral) – nearer the front of body, **e.g.** *the nose is on the* anterior *side of the body*

continues overleaf

continued

Posterior (dorsal) – nearer the back surface of body, **e.g.**
Superior – towards the head or upper part of the body **e.g.**
Inferior – towards the feet or lower part of the body, **e.g.**
Medial – towards the midline or median plane of the body, **e.g.**
Lateral – away from the median plane of the body, **e.g.**
Terms of comparison
Proximal – nearest the trunk, **e.g.** *the humerus is proximal to the radius and ulna*
Distal – farthest from the trunk, **e.g.**
Superficial – nearer to the skin surface, **e.g.**
Deep – further from the skin surface, **e.g.**
Ipsilateral – on the same side of the body, **e.g.**
Contralateral – on the opposite side of the body, **e.g.**

JOINTS

distance apart, arms by the sides of their body and their palms facing forwards.

A joint is the place at which two or more bones meet, and can also be referred to as an **articulation**. The shape of a joint will determine how the bones can move in relation to each other. Some joints allow a lot of movement, while others allow no movement.

Types of joint

There are three classifications of joint which are based on the amount of movement they allow:

✪ **immoveable**, also know as **fibrous** joints

✪ **semi-moveable**, also known as **cartilaginous**

✪ **moveable**, more commonly called **synovial joints** (they will be referred to as such for the remainder of this chapter).

Immovable joints have no joint cavity and the bones are joined together by strong fibrous connective tissue. They can be found in the **sutures** of the cranium in the skull. At birth the skull has some 'soft spots' where the skull has not fused together. As a person grows, the skull sections grow in order to cover these soft spots. Where these skull sections join, immovable joints are formed.

Semi-moveable joints have no joint cavity either, however, there is cartilage between the bones in the joint. An example of where they can be found is between the clavical and the sternum.

Synovial joints allow the greatest range of movement because they contain synovial fluid and have a joint cavity (see Figure 7.5).

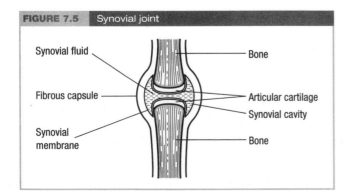

FIGURE 7.5 Synovial joint

Synovial fluid
Fibrous capsule
Synovial membrane
Bone
Articular cartilage
Synovial cavity
Bone

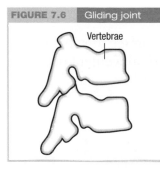
FIGURE 7.6 Gliding joint
Vertebrae

Synovial joints

There are six types of synovial joint. The shape of the joint will determine how much movement is allowed – some synovial joints have a very wide range of movement, whereas others allow comparatively little.

Gliding

This type of joint allows one bone to slide over another (see Figure 7.6). This type of joint is present between the vertebrae. The movement between the two surfaces is extremely small. The joints between the carpals and tarsals are also gliding joints.

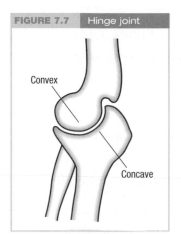
FIGURE 7.7 Hinge joint
Convex
Concave

Hinge

This joint is so named because it allows movement like that of a hinge (see Figure 7.7). It has one **convex** surface, which fits into another **concave** surface. It allows movement in one plane about a single axis, just like the hinge of a door. The types of movement it allows are called flexion and extension. The elbow joint is an example of this type of joint.

Ball and socket

This type of joint allows the greatest range of movement of all the synovial joints as it has the capacity to move in three planes, about three axes (see Figure 7.8). The actions of flexion, extension, inward and outward rotation, abduction, adduction and circumduction are all possible with this type of joint. The hip and shoulder joints are examples of a ball and socket joint.

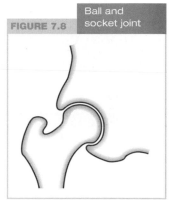
FIGURE 7.8 Ball and socket joint

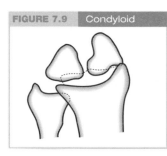
FIGURE 7.9 Condyloid

Condyloid

This joint is also known as an **ellipsoidal** joint (see Figure 7.9). It is similar to the ball and socket joint, except that movement can occur in only two planes, forward and backward (flexion and extension), and from side to side (abduction and adduction). The wrist is an example of this type of joint.

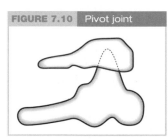
FIGURE 7.10 Pivot joint

Pivot

This joint allows rotation, which is a movement in one plane about one axis (see Figure 7.10). An example of this joint can be found between the atlas and the axis of the neck.

Saddle

This joint allows movement principally in one plane, about one axis (see Figure 7.11). A limited amount of rotation and sliding can also occur. The thumb is an example of a saddle joint.

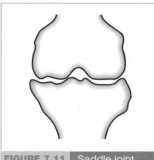
FIGURE 7.11 Saddle joint

Types of movement

Ways in which joints move have technical names which will be described. Remember, when you are describing a type of movement, always refer to the joint that is moving. For example, when a person is kicking a ball you would say that the knee joint was flexing rather than the leg was flexing, because the leg consists of three joints – the hip, the knee and the ankle.

Joint movements are generally divided into four types: gliding, angular, rotation and circumduction.

Gliding

Gliding is the simplest type of motion. It is basically one surface moving over another without any rotary or angular motion. This type of movement occurs between two adjacent surfaces.

Angular

Angular motion decreases or increases the angle between two adjoining bones. The more common types of angular motion are as follows. (See also pages 388–89.)

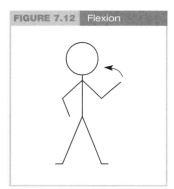

FIGURE 7.12 Flexion

- ✪ **Flexion** – This means decreasing the angle of the joint, therefore the joint is bending, for example flexing the elbow (see Figure 7.12).

- ✪ **Extension** – This means increasing the angle of the joint, therefore the joint is straightening, for example straightening the elbow (see Figure 7.13).

- ✪ **Hyper extension** – This means extension beyond 180° (see Figure 7.14).

- ✪ **Abduction** – This means movement away from the midline of the body (see Figure 7.15).

- ✪ **Adduction** – This means movement towards the midline of the body (see Figure 7.16).

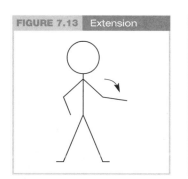

FIGURE 7.13 Extension

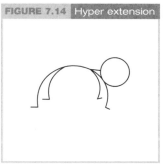

FIGURE 7.14 Hyper extension

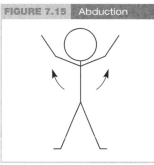

FIGURE 7.15 Abduction

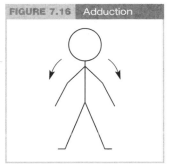

FIGURE 7.16 Adduction

Rotation

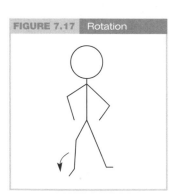

FIGURE 7.17 Rotation

Rotation is a movement in which the bone moves around a central point without being displaced, such as turning the head from side to side. Both internal and external rotation can occur. At the hip, when the leg is straight and turned so that the foot turns in to the body, internal rotation is occurring; when the leg is turned outwards, external rotation is occurring (see Figure 7.17).

Circumduction

Circumduction involves a combination of flexion, extension, abduction and adduction. This type of action can only occur at ball and socket joints at the shoulder and the hip (see Figure 7.18).

FIGURE 7.18 Circumduction

Other types of movement

Other types of movement generally used to indicate movement at specific anatomical positions include the following. (See also page 389.)

- **Supination** – Turning upwards, as in turning the palm of the hand upwards.

- **Pronation** – Turning downwards, as in turning the palm of the hand downwards.

- **Eversion** – Turning outwards, as in turning the sole of the foot to the outside.

- **Inversion** – Turning inwards, as in turning the sole of the foot inwards.

- **Plantar flexion** – This only occurs at the ankle joint, and involves pointing the foot downwards.

- **Dorsi flexion** – This only occurs at the ankle joint, and involves bringing the foot up towards the shin.

- **Elevation** – Moving the shoulders upwards.

- **Depression** – Moving the shoulders downwards.

STUDENT ACTIVITY

Devise an aerobic/dance routine that includes the following movements in their correct order. You decide which joint carries out the movement. Write down the routine as you go and make a note of each joint you will be moving. You may repeat each movement as many times as you wish and must also be prepared to repeat your whole routine at least three times. You could use music to accompany your routine if the equipment is available.

1   Circumduction
2   Flexion
3   Extention
4   Plantar flexion
5   Dorsi flexion
6   Hyperextension
7   Abduction
8   Adduction

REVISION QUESTIONS

1) What are the functions of the skeleton?
2) The skeleton is split into two main sections, the axial and the appendicular. Name the bones of each.
3) Where would you find spongy bone?
4) Explain how bone is formed.

5) What are the different classifications of bone? Give an example of each type.
6) Draw a diagram of a synovial joint.
7) How many different types of joint are there? Give an example of where you would find each in the body.

MUSCLE

Humans use muscles in order to produce movement. Muscles produce this movement by converting the chemical energy of ATP into mechanical work. Three different kinds of muscles are found in humans:

- cardiac muscle

- smooth muscle

- skeletal muscle.

Both **cardiac** and **smooth** muscle are also known as **involuntary** muscle, which means we do not have to think about moving them. **Skeletal** muscles are also known as **voluntary** muscles as they are under our conscious control – in order to move them we have to think about moving them. This means that we can think, 'I want to throw this ball', and our skeletal muscles move in order for us to carry out this movement.

Cardiac muscle

Cardiac muscle, as its name implies, is only found in the heart. It makes up the wall of the heart. It has a striped appearance under the microscope.

Throughout life, the heart is constantly contracting and then briefly relaxing. If the heart stops contracting the person dies. An adult's heart beats around 70 times per minute and pumps about 5 litres of blood each minute. Cardiac muscle has a number of unique features:

✪ it does not **fatigue**

✪ all parts of the cardiac muscle contract in a synchronous wave because the cells are interconnected

✪ cardiac muscle can generate its own nervous impulses; this is known as being **myogenic**.

Smooth muscle

This is found in the walls of all the hollow organs of the body (except the heart). It contracts in order to reduce the size of these organs. Examples of where it is found and what it does are as follows:

✪ regulates the flow of blood in the arteries

✪ moves food through the **gastrointestinal tract**

✪ expels urine from the bladder

✪ regulates the flow of air through the lungs.

Smooth muscle is made of single, spindle-shaped cells. It gets its name because no striations (stripes) are visible in them.

Smooth muscle is entirely dependent on aerobic respiration, and therefore has many **mitochondria**. Smooth muscles do not contract as rapidly as skeletal muscle, but the contraction can be for a much longer time than contractions of skeletal muscles.

Skeletal muscle

As the name implies, skeletal muscle is attached to the skeleton. It is also called **striated muscle** because of its striated (striped) appearance under the microscope.

The primary function of skeletal muscle is locomotion and posture. The skeletal muscles are the longest of the three types and are controlled voluntarily. Skeletal muscle is called voluntary muscle because it is the only type that can be consciously controlled. Skeletal muscle fibres are **multi-nucleate**, meaning that each muscle cell has many nuclei. Also, because of their tremendous demand for energy, muscle cells have a high concentration of enzymes and mitochondria which are necessary for the production of energy (ATP).

Skeletal muscles can contract rapidly and can exert tremendous amounts of force, but they tire quickly and have to rest after periods of activity.

Structure of skeletal muscle

Attachment to the skeleton

Muscles are attached to the skeleton in two places by tendons. The **origin** of the muscle is where the muscle is attached to a large area of bone – this is the part of the muscle that tends not to move during muscle contraction. At its other end is the **insertion**. Taking the triceps as an example, the origin is at the humerus and the insertion is on the ulna (see Figure 7.19).

As the triceps contracts, the insertion is pulled toward the origin and the arm is straightened or extended at the elbow.

Gross muscle structure

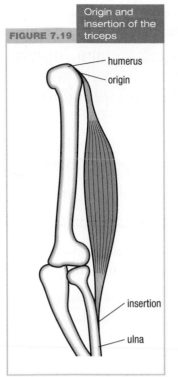

FIGURE 7.19 Origin and insertion of the triceps

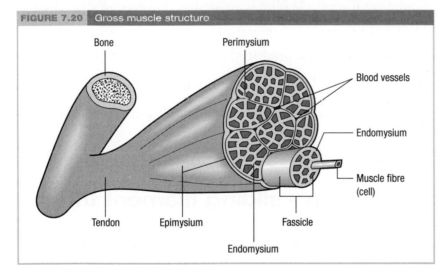

FIGURE 7.20 Gross muscle structure

- ✪ **Tendons** – These are made up of collagen and attach muscle to bone.

- ✪ **Epimysium** – This is the outer layer of the muscle, which is made up of dense connective tissue.

- ✪ **Fassicle** – A fassicle is a collection of muscle fibres that lies under the epimysium. Inside each fassicle there are many muscle fibres.

- ✪ **Perimysium** – The perimysium is a fibrous tissue that covers each fassicle and is made up of collagen fibres.

- ✪ **Muscle fibres** – Inside each fassicle, there are many muscle fibres. The muscle fibre is the place where contraction occurs. The separate muscle fibres are held together by endomysium. Each muscle fibre consists of many contractile units called myofibrils.

- ✪ **Endomysium** – Each muscle fibre is surrounded by endomysium, which holds the fibres together.

Cellular structure of muscle fibres
The muscle fibre is composed of smaller microscopic elements (see Figure 7.21).

- ✪ **Sarcolemma** – The sarcolemma is the correct term for the cell membrane of the muscle cell. Its functions are exactly the same as the functions of a typical cell membrane.

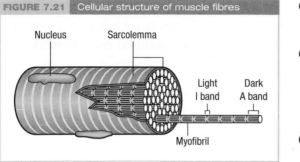

FIGURE 7.21 Cellular structure of muscle fibres

Nucleus Sarcolemma

Light I band Dark A band

Myofibril

✪ **Myofibrils** – The myofibrils contain the small, contracting units of the muscle called the sarcomeres.

✪ **Sarcoplasm** – The sarcoplasm is essentially the same as the **cytoplasm** of a normal cell. It contains all of the usual cell organelles and some that are specific to the muscle cells.

✪ **Sarcoplasmic reticulum** – This is essentially the same as **endoplasmic reticulum**, which is present in all cells.

✪ **Sarcomere** – This is the smallest functional part of the skeletal muscle.

✪ **Actin** – This is the thin filament involved in muscle contraction.

✪ **Myosin** – This is the thick filament involved in muscle contraction. It is called thick because it has 'heads' that attach it to the actin filament.

✪ **Troponin and tropomyosin** – These are proteins that bind to the myosin filament and prevent it from attaching to the actin filament when the muscles are at rest.

The anatomy of a sarcomere

The striated appearance of the muscle fibre is created by a pattern of alternating bands of material (see Figure 7.22).

FIGURE 7.22 Bands of muscle fibre

Dark A band Light I band

H zone Z line

✪ **A band** is dark in colour and is produced by the thick and thin filaments

✪ **I band** is light in colour and is made up of the thin filaments

✪ **H zone** is the portion of the A band where the thick and thin filaments do not overlap

✪ **Z line** separates sarcomeres.

Muscle contraction – sliding filament theory

Muscle contraction requires energy. We get tired after exercising because our muscles run out of energy. Energy production is discussed in Chapter 4 Exercise Physiology.

So how does energy enable our muscles to contract? The contraction process occurs in four steps.

1 At rest, troponin and tropomyosin cover the actin and myosin filaments and prevent myosin from binding to actin. When we give the signal for our muscles to contract, calcium is released into the sarcoplasm. Calcium binds to troponin and takes it away from the myosin binding site. As it moves away, it moves the tropomyosin molecule with it. Therefore, as the troponin and tropomyosin bind to calcium, the myosin binding site is exposed.

2 The mysoin heads bind to the actin filament and slide it across the myosin filament, which results in the sarcomere getting shorter.

3   Energy is used to break the attachment of the actin and myosin filaments. The myosin heads then re-attach at a site further up the actin filament which results in further shortening of the sarcomere.

4   When the stimulus to the muscle ends, calcium ions are released from the troponin and are pumped out of the sarcoplsam. This causes the troponin and tropomyosin to bind to the myosin heads once again, which means they cannot bind to the actin molecule, and contraction cannot occur.

The entire process is extremely fast and only takes a fraction of a second. The cycle then repeats itself until the muscle relaxes.

Why dead people are called 'stiffs'

When a person dies, their body becomes very rigid and stiff. This process is called rigor mortis. The muscles begin to stiffen three to four hours after the time of death and the stiffness will usually last 48 to 60 hours. Studying rigor mortis can help to determine the time of death in murder cases.

The reason rigor mortis occurs is because there is a high level of calcium ions inside the muscle, which enables the actin and myosin filaments to bind together. As there is no longer any energy production to break the bond between the actin and myosin filaments, the myosin heads cannot release from the actin fibres, so the muscle remains contracted and stiff.

Muscle fibre types

Not all skeletal muscle fibres are alike in structure or function: they vary in colour, contract with different velocities, fatigue at different rates and vary with respect to the metabolic processes they use to generate ATP. Therefore, based on the various structural and functional characteristics, skeletal muscle fibres are classified into three types (see Table 7.1, overleaf).

1   **Type I fibres** – These fibres, also called **slow twitch** or **slow oxidative** fibres, and are a red colour because they contain large amounts of **myoglobin**. They also contain many mitochondria and many blood capillaries. As they split ATP at a slow rate, they have a slow contraction speed. They are very resistant to fatigue and have a high capacity to generate ATP by oxidative metabolic processes. Such fibres are found in large numbers in the legs of world-class endurance runners.

2   **Type II A fibres** – These fibres are also called **fast twitch** or **fast oxidative** fibres. They are very similar to type 1 fibres as they are also red in colour, contain very large amounts of myoglobin, many mitochondria and many blood capillaries. They also have a very high capacity for generating ATP by oxidative metabolic processes and are resistant to fatigue. However, these fibres differ from type I fibres because they split ATP at a very rapid rate and have a fast contraction speed.

3   **Type II B fibres** – These fibres are also called **fast twitch** or **fast glycolytic** fibres. They are white in colour because they contain a low content of myoglobin, relatively few mitochondria, few blood capillaries

and large amounts glycogen. They generate ATP by anaerobic metabolic processes, fatigue easily, split ATP at a fast rate and have a fast contraction speed. Such fibres are found in large numbers in the leg muscles of world-class sprinters.

STUDENT ACTIVITY

From the list of sports people below, state which fibre type dominates in their arms and legs. Explain your decisions.

Steve Redgrave
David Beckham
Denise Lewis
Paula Radcliff
Lennox Lewis
Ian Thorpe
Tiger Woods
Venus Williams

Table 7.1 Characteristics of muscle fibre types

Characteristic	Type 1 fibres	Type II A fibres	Type II B fibres
Contraction speed	Slow	Fast	Very fast
Colour	Red	Red	White
Resistance to fatigue	High	Intermediate	Low
Force production	Low	High	Very high
Capillary density	High	Intermediate	Low
Mitochondria	Lots	Lots	Few
Energy system	Aerobic	Aerobic and anaerobic	Anaerobic

Most skeletal muscle is a mixture of all three types of skeletal muscle fibres. However, the proportion of the muscle fibres in each muscle varies in relation to the usual action of the muscle. For example, postural muscles of the neck, back and leg have a higher proportion of type I fibres as they are almost constantly being used.

Effects of exercise on muscle fibre type

Research to date suggests that it is not possible to change the proportion of muscle fibre types within your muscle tissue. Therefore, the proportion of the different types of muscle fibre you have in your body is determined by your parents' genes. So, if a child has two parents who are world-class sprinters, it would be assumed that they have a very high proportion of fast twitch muscles in their legs. Their child would then inherit these fast twitch muscles in their legs and therefore also have the potential to be a very good sprinter.

However, despite the fact that it appears you are born with a certain proportion of fast and slow twitch muscles in your body, which cannot be altered, it is possible to change the **characteristics** of some muscle fibre types. Endurance exercises, such as running long distances or swimming long distances, can gradually transform type II B fibres into type II A fibres. Prolonged endurance training has been shown to increase the diameter of type II B fibres, increase the number of mitochondria in the muscle fibres and increase the number of blood capillaries surrounding the muscle fibre. All these changes enable the muscle fibre to use the aerobic energy system more efficiently because there is an increased supply of oxygen to the muscle tissue. Strength training has an effect on the type II B fibres by increasing the size of the fibres. The number of muscle fibres will remain the same, but because the size of the muscle fibres is increased, the athlete will have a greater muscle mass which will make them stronger.

REVISION QUESTIONS

1) What are the differences between the different types of muscle tissue?

2) Give examples in the body where you would find each of the different types of muscle tissue.

3) What does myogenic mean?

4) Draw and label a diagram of skeletal muscle. Include in your drawing the following structures:

- ✪ epimysium
- ✪ perimysium
- ✪ fassicle
- ✪ endomysium

- ✪ muscle fibres
- ✪ sarcomere.

5) Explain the processes involved in a muscle contraction.

6) Name the different muscle fibre types and give the characteristics of each.

7) Explain how endurance training affects muscle fibre types.

8) Why is it said that you have to be 'born a sprinter' rather than becoming one through training?

9) How does weight training increase a person's strength?

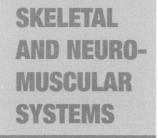

SKELETAL AND NEURO-MUSCULAR SYSTEMS

Muscle

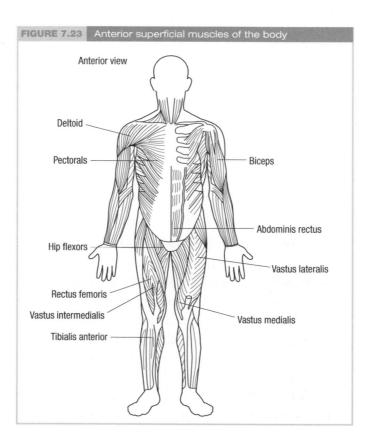

FIGURE 7.23 Anterior superficial muscles of the body

Anterior view

Deltoid

Pectorals

Biceps

Abdominis rectus

Hip flexors

Vastus lateralis

Rectus femoris

Vastus intermedialis

Vastus medialis

Tibialis anterior

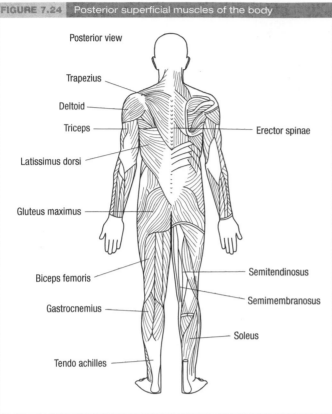

FIGURE 7.24   Posterior superficial muscles of the body

Posterior view

Trapezius
Deltoid
Triceps
Latissimus dorsi
Erector spinae
Gluteus maximus
Biceps femoris
Semitendinosus
Semimembranosus
Gastrocnemius
Soleus
Tendo achilles

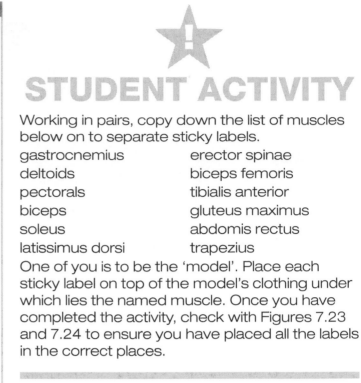

STUDENT ACTIVITY

Working in pairs, copy down the list of muscles below on to separate sticky labels.

gastrocnemius	erector spinae
deltoids	biceps femoris
pectorals	tibialis anterior
biceps	gluteus maximus
soleus	abdomis rectus
latissimus dorsi	trapezius

One of you is to be the 'model'. Place each sticky label on top of the model's clothing under which lies the named muscle. Once you have completed the activity, check with Figures 7.23 and 7.24 to ensure you have placed all the labels in the correct places.

Types of contraction

There are four main types of muscle contraction. (See also page 387–88.)

1   **Concentric** – This is the most common type of muscle contraction. It takes place when the ends of the muscle come closer together so the muscle is getting shorter. An example of this is the hamstrings (semimembranosus, semitendinosus and biceps femoris) contracting and flexing the knee.

2   **Eccentric** – An eccentric contraction occurs when the muscle is exerting a force but the ends of the muscle are moving further away from each other. This type of contraction usually occurs when a muscle is exerting a braking type of force in order to control a body part. An example of this is the biceps working eccentrically during the lowering phase of a biceps curl.

3   **Isometric** – An isometric contraction is where the muscle is exerting a force but there is no movement of the body part and no change in length of the muscle. If you push down hard on to your desk with your hand, you are still creating tension in your arm muscles but no movement is taking place (unless the desk breaks, that is!). A sporting example of this would be a tug of war when there is no movement of the rope.

4   **Isokinetic** – An isokinetic contraction occurs when the muscle is producing a tension but is working at a constant speed. This type of contraction can only occur if specialised weight-training equipment is used.

★ STUDENT ACTIVITY

Muscle contractions

Wearing appropriate clothing and with appropriate equipment if available, carry out the following activities:

✪ a press up
✪ a sit up
✪ an arm wrestle
✪ a ski squat.

For each exercise, analyse one muscle and complete and extend the table below for each exercise.

Activity	Phase	Muscle	Type of contraction
Press up	Downwards phase	Triceps	
Press up	Upwards phase	Triceps	

Function of muscles

Muscles work in pairs; as one muscle contracts the other relaxes. Muscles that work together are called **antagonistic pairs** (see also pages 389–90). Muscles have to work in pairs because a muscle can only pull on a bone, it cannot push the bone back to its original position – the other muscle is responsible for this. A good example of this pairing is the biceps and triceps (see Figure 7.25). As the biceps contract, the triceps relax and the elbow joint is flexed. To straighten the arm, the biceps relax and the triceps contract.

Prime movers (agonists) – The muscle that is mainly responsible for producing a movement is called the prime mover or agonist. Therefore, in the upwards phase of a biceps curl the biceps are the prime mover.

Antagonist – These muscles pull in the opposite to the direction to that of the agonist. When the movement by the prime mover is completed, the antagonist contracts and returns the part moved to its original position. An example of this is the triceps during the downwards phase of a biceps curl.

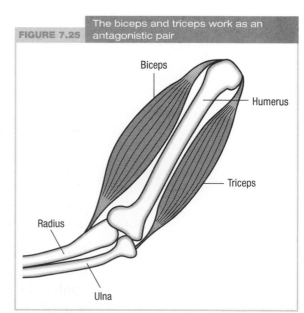

FIGURE 7.25 The biceps and triceps work as an antagonistic pair

★ STUDENT ACTIVITY

Work out which muscles are paired with the muscles below.
hamstrings
gastrocnemius
latissimus dorsi
abdominals
pectorals
deltoids
gluteals
abductors

Synergist – A synergist acts to 'help' the prime mover. It produces an additional force in the same general direction as the prime mover.

Stabilizer – A stabilizer muscle ensures that the joint being moved is properly maintained.

Fixator – A fixator acts to keep the other joints of the body still when one joint is being moved.

Table 7.2 Muscle groups and their actions

Muscle group	Origin	Insertion	Joint	Action
Biceps	Shoulder and scapula	Radius	Elbow	Flexion
Triceps	Humerus and scapula	Ulna	Elbow	Extension
Deltoids	Scapula and clavicle	Humerus	Shoulder	Abduction
Latissimus Dorsi	Spine	Scapula	Shoulder	Adduction
Abdominals	Pubis	Ribs	Spine	Flexion
Erector Spinae	Ribs and illium	Spine and ribs	Spine	Extension
Gastrocnemius	Femur	Calcaneous (heel)	Ankle	Plantar flexion
Tibialis anterior	Tibia	Ankle	Ankle	Dorsi flexion
Hip flexors	Spine and hips	Femur	Hip	Hip flexion
Gluteals	Illium and sacrum	Femur	Hip	Hip extension
Quadriceps	Illium	Patella and tibia	Knee	Extension
Hamstrings	Ischium	Tibia	Knee	Flexion
Abductors	Illium	Femur	Hip	Abduction
Adductors	Pubic bone	Femur	Hip	Adduction
Pectorals	Clavicle and sternum	Top of humerus	Shoulder	Rotation and shoulder

Production of movement

As previously stated, the muscles work in pairs to produce movement. Now we know which muscles produce what sort of movements, and the technical term for each movement, we can analyse sporting performance.

★ STUDENT ACTIVITY

A biceps curl

Study these drawings.

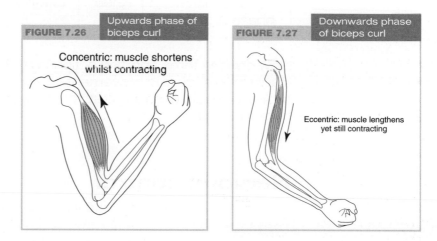

FIGURE 7.26 — Upwards phase of biceps curl

Concentric: muscle shortens whilst contracting

FIGURE 7.27 — Downwards phase of biceps curl

Eccentric: muscle lengthens yet still contracting

Now study the table below.

Sport movement	Joint	Type of movement	Agonist	Antagonist
Biceps curl – upwards phase	Elbow	Flexion	Biceps	Triceps
Biceps curl – Downwards phase	Elbow	Extension	Triceps	Biceps

A football kick

Study these drawings.

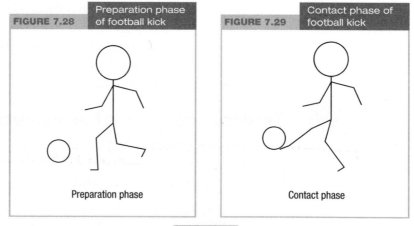

FIGURE 7.28 — Preparation phase of football kick

Preparation phase

FIGURE 7.29 — Contact phase of football kick

Contact phase

continues overleaf

continued

Now copy and complete the table below.

Sport movement	Joint	Type of movement	Agonist	Antagonist
Football kick – phase 1	Knee Hip	Flexion	Gluteals	Quadriceps
Football kick – phase 2	Knee Hip	Extension	Hip flexors	Hamstrings

Now choose three sporting actions with two phases. Draw a stick man diagram to show the movement you are going to analyse, then complete tables for each, ensuring that you analyse at least two joints in each type of movement.

Nervous control

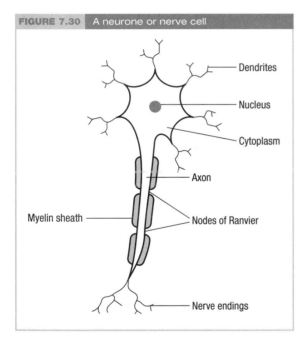

FIGURE 7.30 A neurone or nerve cell

- Dendrites
- Nucleus
- Cytoplasm
- Axon
- Myelin sheath
- Nodes of Ranvier
- Nerve endings

Muscle contracts in response to stimulation from nerves. The central nervous system (CNS) includes the brain and spinal cord and is responsible for stimulating the nervous system to carry an electrical impulse to the required muscle in order to produce movement. The nervous impulse is carried through **neurones** or nerve cells (see Figure 7.30). Some neurones stretch all the way from the CNS to the muscle, whereas others are shorter and connect to other neurones in order to transmit the stimulation to the correct muscle group. The connection between two neurones is called a **synapse**.

The nervous impulse travels down the axon, which is covered in a myelin sheath. The thicker the myelin sheath, the faster the nerve impulse will travel. The myelin sheath has gaps in it which are called 'Nodes of Ranvier'. The nervous impulse actually jumps from one Node of Ranvier to the next, which means that the speed of the impulse is increased. When the impulse reaches the axon terminal the electrical signal is converted to a chemical signal, as a chemical nerve transmitter called acetylecholine is released at the **neuromuscular junction**.

Transmission of a nervous impulse

FIGURE 7.31 An axon at resting potential

The transmission of a nervous impulse is quite a complicated procedure, but it basically involves changing the inside of a nerve cell's axon from being negatively charged to being positively charged.

1 At rest, the inside of the nerve axon is negatively charged and the outside is positively charged (see Figure 7.31). This is called the **resting potential**.

FIGURE 7.32 An axon at action potential

FIGURE 7.33 Repolarisation of an axon

2 When the CNS stimulates a nerve, the inside of the axon becomes positively charged and the outside becomes negatively charged (see Figure 7.32). This change is called the **action potential**.

3 When the CNS stops stimulating the nerve, the axon returns to its resting state, where the inside of the axon is negatively charged and the outside is positively charged (see Figure 7.33). This process is called **repolarisation**.

Reflex

Reflexes are used to protect the body without having to think about what is happening, e.g. if a person puts their hand on a hot stove they will immediately remove their hand without having to think about it.

The knee jerk is a well-known reflex. It is called a **monosynaptic** reflex, which means there is only one synapse in the circuit. The movement it produces takes place very quickly because there is only one synapse. The reflex works by tapping just below the knee, which makes the quadriceps muscle stretch. This information travels to the spinal cord. There, after one synapse in the spinal cord, the information is sent back out to the muscle, which makes it contract, and the knee extends.

STUDENT ACTIVITY

Reflex tests

There are a range of other reflexes that can be demonstrated by carrying out the following activities. Work in pairs for these activities.

1) One person should sit on a chair with their legs crossed. The other person should then tap the first person's top leg just below the knee.

2) For this activity, make sure you are in a well-lit room. Close your eyes and place your hand over your eyes for one minute. Your partner should then observe the size of your pupils when you open your eyes, and see what happens to them over the following few seconds.

3) Gently stroke the outer edges of the soles of your partner's feet with the blunt end of a pen or ruler. Check to see if their big toe extends out as a result. This is called the Babinski reflex.

4) Carry out some research to find an example of another reflex.

The muscle spindle

The knee jerk reflex works because of muscle spindles located within the muscles. The purpose of muscle spindles is to record the change in length of a muscle and transmit this information to the spine (see Figure 7.30).

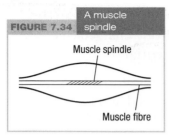

FIGURE 7.34 A muscle spindle

This will then make the muscle attempt to resist this change in length by contracting the stretched muscle. The quicker the change in muscle length, the stronger the muscle contractions will be.

Therefore, the muscle spindle helps to maintain muscle tone and helps to protect the body from injury. Flexibility training is based on training the muscle spindle to become used to an increased length of muscle. Therefore, stretches should be held for a period of time so that the muscle spindles will eventually allow greater lengthening of the muscles.

THE CARDIO-VASCULAR SYSTEM

Close your hand into a fist and look at it. Your fist is approximately the same size as your heart, around 12 cm long, 9 cm wide and 6 cm thick. It is located behind the sternum and tilted to the left. The heart is made up mainly of cardiac muscle, which is also known as **myocardium**.

Anatomy of the heart

The heart is divided into right- and the left-hand sides by the **septum** (see Figure 7.35). It is further divided into four chambers. The upper two chambers are called **atria**. The atria receive blood returning to the heart via the veins. The lower two chambers are called **ventricles**, and these act as pumps to squeeze blood out of the heart into the arteries.

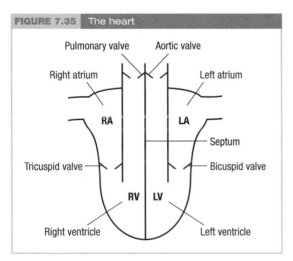

FIGURE 7.35 The heart

- ✪ **Right atrium (RA)** – This receives deoxygenated blood from the organs of the body.

- ✪ **Right ventricle (RV)** – This pumps deoxygenated blood to the lungs.

- ✪ **Left atrium (LA)** – This receives oxygenated blood from the lungs.

- ✪ **Left ventricle (LV)** – This pumps oxygenated blood to all organs of the body. It is larger and therefore stronger than the right ventricle as it has to pump the blood through the body.

- ✪ **Valves** – There are four one-way valves in the heart, that open or close in response to pressure of blood flow:

  ▶ bicuspid valve – separates the left atrium from the left ventricle

  ▶ tricuspid valve – separates the right atrium from the right ventricle

  ▶ aortic valve – separates the left ventricle from the aorta

  ▶ pulmonary valve – separates the right ventricle from the pulmonary artery.

All these valves ensure that blood flows in one direction and prevent the back flow of blood into the ventricles.

The blood vessels leading to and from the heart are as follows.

- ✪ The **aorta** carries oxygenated blood out of the left ventricle to the body.

- ✪ The superior **vena cava** returns deoxygenated blood to the right atrium from the head and upper body; the inferior vena cava returns deoxygenated blood to the right atrium from the lower body.

- ✪ The **pulmonary vein** carries freshly oxygenated blood from the lungs to the left atrium.

- ✪ The **pulmonary artery** carries deoxygenated blood from the body to the lungs.

Blood flow through the heart

Pulmonary circulation

The right ventricle pumps blood through the pulmonary artery to the lungs (see Figure 7.36). Here, the blood 'picks up' oxygen and carbon dioxide is released into the lungs. From the lungs, the oxygenated blood is carried to the left atrium. This short loop is called the **pulmonary circulation**.

Systemic circulation

From the left atrium the blood flows down to the left ventricle. The left ventricle pumps oxygenated blood through the Aorta to all tissues of the body (see Figure 7.36). Oxygen and nutrients are released from the blood to nourish cells, and carbon dioxide and other waste products are carried back to the heart via the two venae cavae. The blood enters the right atrium. Carbon dioxide is carried to the lungs and removed from the body.

FIGURE 7.36	Blood flow through the heart

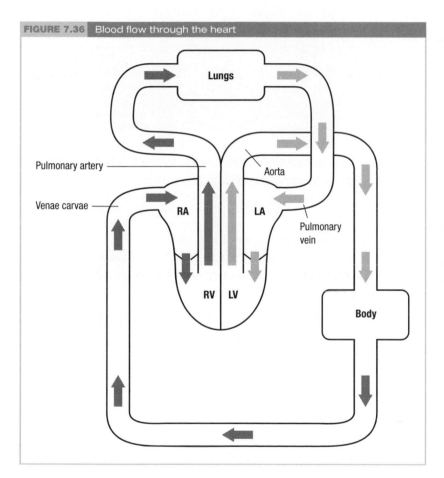

STUDENT PRACTICAL

Heart dissection

Aim

The aim of this practical is to examine the structure of a mammalian heart.

Equipment

sheep or pig hearts	dissection boards
tweezers	scalpels
scissors	lab coats
latex gloves	disinfectant
disposal bag/bin for	worksheets
hearts and used gloves	

Method

Working in groups of three or four put on lab coats, goggles and latex gloves then complete the following activities.

1 Examine the outside of the heart and make a note of its texture and appearance.

2 Try to determine the orientation of the heart in the body.

3 The valves inside the heart should still be intact and can be shown to still work. Go to a sink and pass running water into the left and right atria; it should be possible to see the valves close.

4 Place the heart back on the dissection board, dome side up, and make an incision with the scalpel or with the scissors from the right atrium right down to the right ventricle. This should expose the whole of the inside of the right-hand side of the heart. Make a note of the appearance and texture of the inside of the heart.

5 The tendons that hold the valves in place can be seen clearly. Use the tweezers to pull on these, and make a note of their strength.

6 Dissect the left-hand side of the heart, from the left atrium down towards the left ventricle. Compare the thickness of the right- and left-hand side ventricle walls.

7 Try to ascertain which blood vessel is which by pushing your finger down the blood vessels into the heart. Where your finger appears should give you enough of a clue to work out which blood vessel is which.

Conclusion

In your conclusion look, back at the comments you have made throughout the dissection, then write down what you have found out about the heart's anatomy and try to explain why it has these anatomical features.

STUDENT ACTIVITY

Structure of the heart

Fill in the blanks

The heart is split into _____ sides and has _____ chambers. The top two chambers are called ____ and the bottom two chambers are called _____. The heart is split into two separate sides by the _____.

There are ____ valves that allow the blood to pass through the heart in one direction.

The valve between the atrium and ventricle on the right side of the heart is called the _____ valve. The valve on the left side of the heart between the atrium and the ventricle, is called the _____ valve. The valve between the pulmonary artery and right ventricle is called the _____ valve. The valve between the left ventricle and the aorta is called the _____ valve.

Types of blood vessels

Blood travels through a series of vessels, each varies in structure because of its function. There are five categories of blood vessel:

- ✪ artery
- ✪ arteriole
- ✪ capillary
- ✪ venuole
- ✪ vein.

The blood travels through these vessels in the above order.

Structure of arteries and arterioles

An artery carries blood under high pressure away from the heart. An arteriole has basically the same structure as an artery, except an artery is bigger. They both have a strong outer layer, a thick middle layer made of smooth muscle and a thin linining or inner layer made of endothelium (see Figure 7.37).

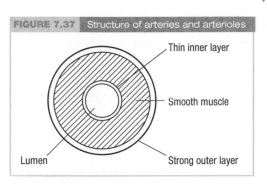

FIGURE 7.37   Structure of arteries and arterioles

Thin inner layer

Smooth muscle

Lumen

Strong outer layer

As the arteries get smaller and become arterioles, the greater the amount of smooth muscle they contain. This increase in smooth muscle allows the blood vessels to dilate (vasodilation) or constrict (vasoconsriction) depending on whether areas of the body require more or less blood.

Capillaries

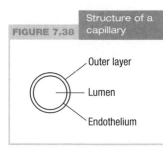

FIGURE 7.38   Structure of a capillary

Outer layer

Lumen

Endothelium

Capillaries are the smallest blood vessels in the body. It is in the capillaries that the gases and nutrients leave and/or enter the bloodstream. As this is where the 'action' occurs, the capillaries will only allow blood through them one red blood cell at a time. Capillaires are not only very narrow, but they also have very thin walls which allow for easier diffusion of gases and nutrients through them (see Figure 7.38).

Veins and venuoles

Veins and venuoles return blood under low pressure back to the heart. They have a very similar structure to arteries and arterioles except that they have a much thinner layer of smooth muscle in their walls. Veins also contain one-way valves to help ensure blood flows in one direction back to the heart.

Blood

An average adult male has 5 litres of blood in his body, which accounts for approximately 8% of his total body weight. Blood is made up of four main things:

- ✪ plasma
- ✪ red blood cells (erythrocytes)
- ✪ white blood cells (leucocytes)
- ✪ platelets.

Plasma makes up 55% of the blood volume. It is yellow in colour and conisists mainly of water. However, dissolved in plasma you will also find the following substances:

- oxygen and carbon dioxide
- salts
- glucose
- fatty acids
- waste products.

Red blood cells are responsible for making blood its red colour. Their main function is to transport oxygen around the body. They contain a protein called **haemoglobin** which picks up oxygen and carries it to where it is needed. A red blood cell is a biconcave disc shape and contains no nucleus (see Figure 7.39).

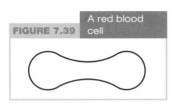

FIGURE 7.39 A red blood cell

White blood cells are responsible for protecting the body from infection.

Platelets aid in clotting blood, which is necessary if we cut ourselves.

Distribution of blood

At rest, cardiac output is about 5 litres per minute. Most of the blood from the heart goes to six major organs:

- brain   0.75 l
- heart   0.25 l
- kidneys   1.25 l
- skeletal muscle   1.00 l
- gastrointestinal (GI) tract   1.25 l
- skin   0.50 l

After a meal, more blood goes to the GI tract in order to aid digestion. During physical activity, more blood goes to the muscles to supply the necessary nutrients and oxygen and take away the waste produces. The amount of blood to the brain, however, is constant at all times.

The lungs

Structure of the lungs

Pulmonary ventilation is the term used to describe the process of bringing the surrounding air into the body and exchanging it with the air in the lungs. The average lung has a volume of 4–6 l and weighs approximately 1 kg. Lungs have a very large surface area, which means that if you were to dissect a person's lungs and spread them out on the ground they would cover 60–80 m^2, which is the equivalent of half a tennis court!

The lungs are enclosed by a set of membranes known as the **pleura**, which are arranged like a double-skinned bag. The visceral pleura are found on the outer

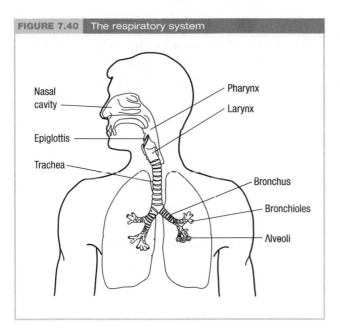

FIGURE 7.40 The respiratory system

Nasal cavity

Pharynx

Larynx

Epiglottis

Trachea

Bronchus

Bronchioles

Alveoli

surface of lungs and the parietal pleura line the chest cavity. In between these two pleura there is a lubricating fluid called **pleural fluid**, which helps the two pleura to glide over each other as the lungs continually expand and contract.

The lungs consist of lots of different tubes through which the air flows (see Figure 7.40). Air enters the body through the **nose and mouth**. The air is warmed and filtered in the nose, and then passes into the **pharynx** (throat) and then into the **larynx** (voice box). The **epiglottis** is a flap of cartilage which prevents food from entering the trachea (windpipe). The air then passes into the **trachea**, which is a tubular passageway approximately 12 cm long and 2.5 cm wide. It has horse-shoe shaped rings of cartilage (hyaline cartilage) that keep the airway open. In between the rings of cartilage lies smooth muscle. From the trachea the air passes into the right and left **bronchi**, which are large tubes passing into the lungs. Each bronchus further divides into smaller tubes called **bronchioles**, which are made of smooth muscle. Eventually these tubes connect to the **alveoli**, which are like micro-sized bundles of grapes at the end of the respiratory tract.

The alveoli provide a huge surface area for **gaseous exchange** (swapping of oxygen and carbon dioxide) to take place. They are surrounded by a dense network of capillaries and gases are able to **diffuse** easily through the very thin semi-permeable walls of the alveoli and the blood vessels. Oxygen diffuses from the alveoli into the blood, and carbon dioxide diffuses from the blood to the alveoli. **Gaseous exchange** takes less than a second to occur. Breathing alters the composition of air by changing the proportions of the gases it contains (see Table 7.3).

Table 7.3 Effect of gaseous exchange on air

Gas	Air breathed in	Air breathed out
Oxygen	21%	16%
Carbon dioxide	0.04%	4%
Nitrogen	78%	78%

Mechanics of breathing

The muscles involved in breathing are the **diaphragm** and the external and internal **intercostals**. The intercostal muscles are between the ribs. The internal intercostal muscles contract to pull the ribs downwards and so help with breathing out. The external intercostal muslces pull the ribs upwards and therefore assist with breathing in. The diaphragm is a large, dome-shaped muscle located beneath the lungs; it is responsible for approximately 75% of the breathing mechanism.

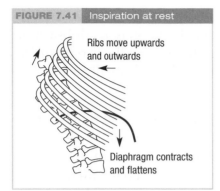

FIGURE 7.41 Inspiration at rest

Ribs move upwards and outwards

Diaphragm contracts and flattens

Inspiration at rest

During **inspiration** (breathing in) the diaphragm contracts and moves downwards, and the external intercostal muscles contract, moving the ribs and sternum upwards and outwards (see Figure 7.41). As a consequence of this the chest cavity enlarges. This increase in space reduces the pressure in the lungs in relation to atmospheric pressure. This change in pressure inside the lungs results in the air being drawn into the lungs from the atmosphere, inflating the lungs until the pressure in the lungs is equal to the atmospheric pressure.

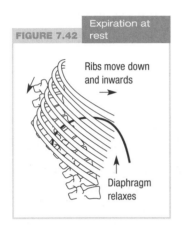

FIGURE 7.42 Expiration at rest

Ribs move down and inwards

Diaphragm relaxes

Expiration at rest

Expiration (breathing out) does not require any muscle contraction and is called a passive activity. The lungs that have been stretched recoil and the diaphragm relaxes. The sternum and ribs move downwards as the diaphragm moves upwards (see Figure 7.42). This decreases the space in the chest cavity and squeezes the air out of the lungs and out through the nose and mouth.

Lung volumes and capacities

A number of different names are given to the various amounts of air we breath in and out in different circumstances. Some of these volumes can be measured using a spirometer.

1   **Tidal volume (TV 500 ml)** – This is the volume of air moved with each breath. Breathe in and out normally; the amount of air you have breathed in and out is your tidal volume. This volume will change depending on whether you are at rest or exercising. Exercise usually results in an increase in the tidal volume.

2   **Residual volume (RV 1200 ml)** – Breath out as hard as possible. The amount of air that remains in the lungs after full expiration is your residual volume and is necessary in order to prevent your lungs collapsing.

3   **Vital capacity (VC 5000 ml)** – The VC is the amount of air that can be expired after maximum inspiration.

4   **Forced expiratory volume (FEV)** – This is the volume of air forcibly exhaled in the first second after maximal inhalation. It should be around 80% of vital capacity, values less than this indicate asthma or bronchial problems.

5   **Inspiratory Reserve Volume (IRV 3,000 ml)** – This is the maximal volume of air inspired after the end of inspiration.

6   **Expiratory Reserve Volume (ERV normal 1200 ml)** – This is the maximal volume of air breathed out at the end of the normal inspiration.

7   **Total Lung capacity (TLC 6000 ml)** – This is the sum of all lung volumes.

8   **Minute ventilation (VE 7500 ml)** – This is the volume of air breathed in and out per minute.

These values will all depend on a variety of factors, including:

- size of lungs/ribcage, which is genetically determined

- strength of respiratory muscles

- resistance to airflow in bronchioles and alveoli as a result of lung disorders, colds and smoking.

REVISION QUESTIONS

1) What is the function of the heart?

2) Why is the heart some times called a 'double pump'?

3) Which heart chamber contains the thickest myocardium? Why do you think this is?

4) Why are valves necessary inside the heart?

5) List the blood vessels leading to and from the heart through which the blood flows.

6) Give a brief account of how the structure of arteries, arterioles, capillaries, venuoles and veins is related to their function.

7) What is blood made up of?

8) Describe which structures air flows through on its way from the mouth to the alveoli.

9) Explain the mechanics of breathing in and out.

10) What happens to tidal volume during exercise? Explain why this occurs.

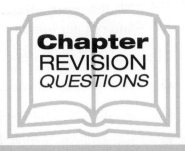

Chapter REVISION QUESTIONS

1) Explain how the muscles work with the skeleton in order to produce movement.

2) Give examples of how a sports person produces different types of muscle contraction during a game of rugby.

3) How do the respiratory system and cardiovascular system supply oxygen to the working muscles?

4) What are the different types of muscle tissue and where could you find them?

5) What happens to blood flow to the various organs during exericse and how is it controlled?

FURTHER READING

Blakey, P. (2000) *The Muscle Book*. Himalayan Institute Press

Kingston, B. (2000) *Understanding Joints*. Stanley Thornes.

Kingston, B. (1998) *Understanding Muscles*. Stanley Thornes

Seeley, R. R., Stephens, T. D., Tate, P. (2000) *Anatomy and Physiology*. McGraw Hill

Stone, R. J., Stone, J. A., (1999) *Atlas of Skeletal Muscles*. McGraw Hill

NUTRITION FOR SPORT AND EXERCISE

Nutrition plays a major role in the sporting success of all athletes. This chapter explores the role and function of carbohydrates, fats, proteins, vitamins, fibre and water in the diet, and how much of these should be included in a person's daily food intake. Methods of assessment of dietary intake and energy expenditure will be discussed. Lastly, diet plans, fluid intake and supplementation for different athletes will be examined.

By the end of this chapter students should be able to:

✪ explain the function and source of nutrients

✪ know what a healthy diet consists of

✪ investigate dietary intake and energy expenditure

✪ understand different types of nutritional strategies.

NUTRIENTS AND HEALTHY DIET

Definitions

✪ **Nutrients** are chemical substances obtained from food and used in the body to provide energy, structural materials, and regulating agents to support growth, maintenance and repair of the body's tissues.

✪ **Energy** is measured in kilocalories or kilojoules. A calorie is a small unit of heat. In nutrition a calorie is the same as one kilocalorie (1 kcal).
One kilocalorie or 1000 calories is the amount of energy required to raise the temperature of 1 kg of water by 1°C.
One joule is the amount energy required to lift 100 g, with a strength of 1 N, 1 m high. One kilojoule in 1000 joules.
$1 J = 0.239$ cal, 1 kcal $= 4.186$ kJ.

✪ **Metabolism** is the total of body processes that store or use energy. Everybody has a different metabolic rate, which refers to the amount of energy used at any given moment. An individual's basal metabolic rate (BMR) is a measure of the number of calories or joules used to keep the person's heart, lungs and muscles working while the body is at rest.

✪ **Digestion** is the process of breaking down food into simpler forms that can be taken in and used by the body.

Nutrients can be divided into two main groups; **macro-** and **micronutrients**. The macronutrient group contains carbohydrates, fats and protein. The micro nutrient group contains vitamins and minerals. This classification is based on the quantities of a nutrient needed in a person's daily diet. Therefore, we must eat larger quantities of carbohydrates, fats and proteins each day than vitamins and minerals.

Carbohydrates

Almost every culture relies on carbohydrates as the major source of nutrients and calories, e.g. rice in Asia, wheat in the Mediterranean, Middle East and North Africa, oats and barley in the British Isles, corn and potato in the Americas.

The name carbohydrate comes from the Latin for hydrated (watered) carbon. Carbohydrates are composed of carbon, hydrogen and oxygen to form compounds. They have the general molecular formula CH_2O, which means for every carbon and oxygen atom there are twice as many hydrogen atoms, e.g. if there are 6 carbon atoms, there will be 6 oxygen atoms and 12 hydrogen atoms: $C_6H_{12}O_6$.

Carbohydrates are made up of sugar molecules. They can be classed into different groups depending on how many sugars the carbohydrate contains. First there are **monosaccharides**, which consist of one sugar, then there are disaccharides, which are made up of two sugars, and lastly there are **polysaccharides**, which are made up of many sugars.

The mono- and disaccharides are sometimes called 'simple carbohydrates' – they taste sweet and will dissolve in water. Simple sugars enter the bloodstream soon after eating. Polysaccharides are sometimes called 'complex carbohydrates' – they do not taste sweet and will not dissolve in water. Polysaccharides are broken down more slowly than simple sugars, so glucose is released from them into the bloodstream at a much slower rate.

Carbohydrates provide the main energy source (4 kcal/g) in most diets, and starches provide the bulk of that (see polysaccharides below).

Monosaccharides

This group consists of three carbohydrates. Although they all share the same molecular formula of $C_6H_{12}O_6$, they are different from each other because of how their atoms are arranged. As these carbohydrates contain six carbon atoms, they are sometimes called **hexose** sugars. They are:

❂ **glucose** – 'blood carbohydrate', the immediate source of energy for energy production (see Figure 8.1)

❂ **galactose** – a carbohydrate in milk (and yogurt) (see Figure 8.2)

❂ **fructose** – a carbohydrate found in honey and fruits (see Figure 8.3).

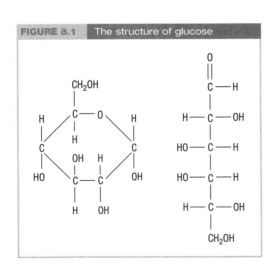

FIGURE 8.1 The structure of glucose

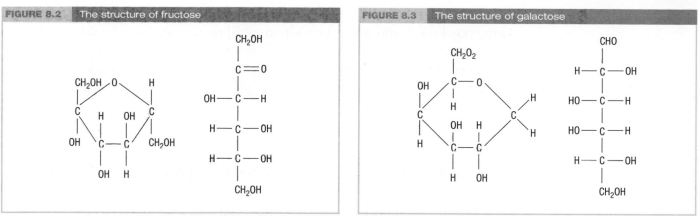

FIGURE 8.2 The structure of fructose

FIGURE 8.3 The structure of galactose

Both galactose and fructose are converted into glucose in the liver. This glucose can then be used by the body for energy production.

Disaccharides

Two monosaccharides can be linked together to form a 'double' carbohydrate or disaccharide. There are three disaccharides:

✪ **sucrose** – common table sugar, this is made from the linking of glucose and fructose

✪ **lactose** – major carbohydrate in milk, made from the linking of glucose and galactose

✪ **maltose** – product of starch digestion, made from the linking of glucose to glucose.

The process (called a **condensation** reaction) of linking the two monosaccharides results in the loss of a molecule of water (H_2O). Thus, the molecular formula of each of these disaccharides is $C_{12}H_{22}O_{11}$.

Polysaccharides

Starches

Starches are made up of lots of glucose molecules joined together. Animals store excess glucose by converting it into **glycogen**. Glycogen is digested back into glucose when energy is needed. The liver and skeletal muscles are major depots of glycogen.

Fibre

Dietary fibre is the part of a plant that is resistant to the body's digestive enzymes. As a result, only a relatively small amount of fibre is digested, with the majority of it moving through the gastrointestinal tract and ending up in the **stool**. You can witness this by eating a large quantity of sweet corn (half a small can, for example) and then investigating the resulting stool (taking care to be as hygienic as possible). You will see the fibrous husk of the sweet corn has not been digested. The main benefit in eating fibre is that it retains water, resulting in softer and bulkier stools that prevent constipation and haemorrhoids.

Research suggests that a high-fibre diet also reduces the risk of colon cancer. All fruits, vegetables, and grains provide some fibre.

STUDENT ACTIVITY

Copy out the table below, then place the foods listed into their correct carbohydrate category.

table sugar   sweet corn   baked potato   strawberry jam
coca cola   orange   pasta   honey
apple   milk-shake   bread   all bran

Monosaccharide	Disaccharide	Starch	Fibre

Role of carbohydrate

The main role of carbohydrate is to provide energy for exercise. Once carbohydrate has been digested, it will either be used as an energy source immediately or turned into glycogen by the liver and stored as glycogen in either the liver or skeletal muscle

Recommended daily intake of carbohydrate

Minimum recommended daily intake is at least 50% of total kilocalories consumed should come from complex carbohydrate sources. The British Nutrition Foundation found that in Britain the average intake of carbohydrate is 272 g for men and 193 g for women, which provides just over 43% of the energy in the diet. Daily recommended fibre intake is 20–35 g.

If a person eats too much food in the form of carbohydrate then the excess is turned into fat and stored in fat stores.

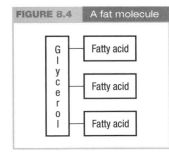

FIGURE 8.4   A fat molecule

Fats

Fats are also called **lipids**. The word lipid comes from the Greek *lipos*, which means fat. Fats are made up of carbon, hydrogen and oxygen molecules, as are carbohydrates; however, fats contain many more oxygen atoms per molecule than carbohydrate molecules.

The building blocks of fat are **fatty acids** and **glycerol** (see Figure 8.4).

Types of fatty acid

Fatty acids can be divided into:

- ✪ saturated fatty acids

- ✪ monounsaturated fatty acids

- ✪ polyunsaturated fatty acids

A fatty acid consists of chains of carbon atoms with an acid group (COOH) at one end and a methyl group (CH_3) at the other. The structure of the chains of fatty acids attached to the glycerol molecule will determine whether the fat is classed as saturated, monounsaturated or polyunsaturated.

If a fatty acid has all the hydrogen atoms it can hold it is said to be saturated (see Figure 8.5). **Saturated** fatty acids are completely loaded with hydrogen, so the molecule has no double bonds between carbon atoms. Saturated fats are solid at room temperature and tend to be from animal sources. The Department of Health recommends a person should have a maximum of 10% of daily kilocalories coming from this type of fat.

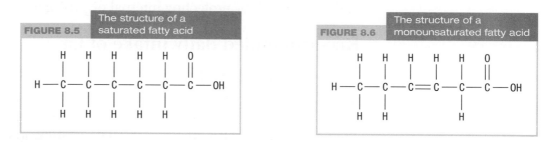

FIGURE 8.5 The structure of a saturated fatty acid

FIGURE 8.6 The structure of a monounsaturated fatty acid

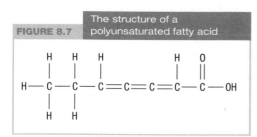

FIGURE 8.7 The structure of a polyunsaturated fatty acid

If some of the hydrogen atoms are missing and have been replaced by a double bond between the carbon atoms, then the fatty acid is said to be **unsaturated**. If there is one double bond, the fatty acid is known as a **monounsaturated** fatty acid (see Figure 8.6). The Department of Health recommends a person should have a maximum of 12% of daily kilocalories coming from this type of fat.

If there is more than one double bond, then the fatty acid is known as a **polyunsaturated** fatty acid (see Figure 8.7). The Department of Health recommends a person should have a maximum of 10% of daily kilocalories coming from this type of fat.

Most unsaturated fats are liquid at room temperature and are usually vegetable fats.

Essential fatty acids

The body can make all the fatty acids it needs except for two, the essential fatty acids (EFAs), which must be supplied in the diet. These fatty acids are **linoleic acid** and **linolenic acid**.

The richest sources of linolenic acid include seed oils, nuts, meat from grass-fed animals and green, leafy vegetables. Linoleic acid is found in fish oils and is also present in the flesh of oily fish such as mackerel, salmon, kippers, herring, trout and sardines. If these fatty acids are not eaten it may result in the person suffering from growth retardation, reproductive failure, skin lesions, kidney and liver disorders, and subtle neurological and vision problems.

Cholesterol

Cholesterol is a particular fat that is an essential part of our bodies; it is found in cell membranes and several hormones. Some cholesterol comes from our diet, but most is made in the liver from saturated fats. Cholesterol levels can be increased if a person is obese, does not take part in exercise or consumes a large amount of saturated fatty acids.

Role and function of fat

Fat provides a concentrated source of energy. One gram of fat provides 37 kJ (9 kcal), more than double that provided by either protein or carbohydrate, which provide 17 kJ/g (4 kcal) and 16 kJ/g (3.75 kcal) respectively. Fat stores fat-soluble vitamins A, D, E and K. Fat is important in the formation of cell membranes, particularly in nerve tissue. It provides an energy reserve and helps to insulate the body against temperature extremes. Fat stores will also help to cushion impacts by protecting internal organs against shock.

Recommended daily intake of fat

Fat intake should make up no more than 30% of total kilocalories. Only 10% of kilocalories should come from saturated fat. Dietary cholesterol should be limited to 300 mg or less per day.

There are many **health** problems related to eating an excess of fat, especially saturated fats. These include obesity, high blood pressure and coronary heart disease.

As fat provides just over twice as much energy per gram as carbohydrate, a diet high in fat can make over-consumption more likely. It is thought that excess dietary fat may be more easily converted to body fat than excess carbohydrate or protein. Research suggests that today, more people are obese than ever before. Obese people are more likely to suffer from a range of illnesses, including coronary heart disease, adult-onset diabetes, gallstones, arthritis, high blood pressure and some types of cancer. However, most of the health problems associated with obesity are removed once the extra weight is lost.

Protein

The amount of protein in food varies, but the main sources include meat, fish, eggs, milk, cheese, cereals, nuts and pulses (peas, beans and lentils). Two-thirds of the average intake is obtained from animal sources, such as meat, fish, eggs and dairy products. Some is also obtained from cereal products, nuts and pulses.

The name protein comes from a Greek word meaning 'of prime importance'. Protein consists of carbon, hydrogen, oxygen and nitrogen (plus sulphur, phosphorus and/or iron). A protein is made up of **amino acids**. Every amino acid contains an amino group (NH_2), an acid group (COOH), a hydrogen atom (H), and a distinctive side group all attached to a central carbon atom.

Essential amino acids (EAA) – There are nine EEA that the body cannot make in sufficient quantities and, therefore, must obtain them from food.

Non-essential amino acids (NEAA) – The body can synthesise these amino acids from nitrogen, carbohydrates and fat.

Roles of proteins in the body

The main role of protein is to act as a building material. Proteins are needed for the manufacture and repair of most body structures. Enzymes are also made of proteins and are needed to facilitate chemical reactions in the body. Some hormones are made up of protein (e.g. insulin). Antibodies that work to inactivate foreign invaders and protect against disease are made of protein. Proteins are also used to help maintain the volume and composition of body fluids; to help maintain the body's pH levels by acting as **buffers**; to help with the transport of lipids, vitamins, minerals and oxygen around the body; and, in cases of starvation, can be used as an energy source to provide a fuel for the body.

Recommended intakes of protein

The average daily intake of protein in the UK is 85 g for men and 62 g for women. The recommended daily amount of protein for healthy adults is 0.8 g per kilogram of body weight, or about 15% of total kilocalories. Protein needs are higher for children, infants and many athletes.

STUDENT ACTIVITY

Draw a table like the one shown below. On a separate piece of paper, write down the last 10 foods you ate. Now place these foods into their correct category in the table.

Simple sugars	Complex carbohydrate	Saturated fat	Unsaturated fat (mono or poly)	Protein

National surveys indicate that the typical diet in the UK derives too little energy from protein and far too much from fat and carbohydrate. The proportion of fat in the diet has increased dramatically since the Second World War, which has had the effect of significantly increasing cases of obesity within the UK.

Vitamins

These are organic substances which the body requires in small amounts. The body is incapable of making vitamins for its overall needs, so they must be supplied regularly by the diet.

Vitamins are not related chemically and differ in their physiological actions. As vitamins were discovered, each was identified by a letter. Many of the vitamins consist of several closely related compounds of similar physiological properties.

Vitamins may be subdivided into:

- water soluble – C and B

- fat soluble – A, D, K and E.

The **water soluble** vitamins cannot be stored in the body, so they must be consumed on a regular basis. If excess quantities of these vitamins are consumed, the body will excrete them in the urine. **Fat soluble** vitamins are stored in the body's fat, so it is not necessary to consume these on such a regular basis. It is also possible to overdose on fat soluble vitamins, which can be detrimental to health.

Varying amounts of each vitamin are required – the amount needed is referred to as the recommended daily intake (RDI).

Vitamin A
- **Function** – The main function of this vitamin is to help maintain good vision, healthy skin, hair and mucous membranes and to serve as an **antioxidant**. It is also needed for proper bone and tooth development.

- **Source** – liver, mackerel, milk products.

- **RDI** – 5000 international units (iu).

Betacarotene
- **Function** – This performs a similar function to vitamin A and is found in plants. When there is a shortage of vitamin A in the diet it will be used in place of vitamin A. However, where vitamin A is a minor antioxidant, betacarotene is a super antioxidant.

- **Source** – sweet potatoes, carrots, cantaloupe, spinach and other dark green leafy vegetables.

- **RDI** – 5 to 15 mg or 10 000 to 25 000 iu.

- **Deficiency** – night blindness, impaired growth and dry skin.

B Vitamins

These vitamins are not chemically related, but often occur in the same foodstuff. Their main function is to aid in metabolism of food.

Vitamin B-1 (thiamine)

✪   **Function** – Helps convert food to energy. Aids the nervous and cardiovascular systems.

✪   **Source** – rice bran, pork, beef, peas, beans, wheat germ, oatmeal and soybeans.

✪   **RDI** – 1.5 mg.

Vitamin B-2 (riboflavin)

✪   **Function** – Aids in growth and reproduction. Helps to metabolise fats, carbohydrates and proteins. Promotes healthy skin and nails.

✪   **Source** – milk, liver, kidneys, yeast, cheese, leafy green vegetables, fish and eggs.

✪   **RDI** – 1.7 mg.

Vitamin B-3 (niacin)

✪   **Function** – Helps to keep the nervous system balanced and is also important for the synthesis of sex hormones, thyroxine, cortisone and insulin.

✪   **Source** – poultry, fish, peanuts, Marmite, rice bran and wheat germ.

✪   **RDI** – 20 mg.

Vitamin B-5 (pantothenic acid)

✪   **Function** – Helps in cell building and maintaining normal growth and development of the central nervous system. Helps form hormones and antibodies. It is also necessary for the conversion of fat and sugar to energy.

✪   **Source** – wheat germ, green vegetables, whole grains, mushrooms, fish, peanuts, Marmite.

✪   **RDI** – 10 mg.

Vitamin B-6 (pyridoxine)

✪   **Function** – Helps in the utilisation of proteins and the metabolism of fats. It is also needed for production of red blood cells and antibodies.

✪   **Source** – chicken, beef, bananas, Marmite, eggs, brown rice, soybeans, oats, whole wheat, peanuts and walnuts.

✪   **RDI** – 2 mg.

✪   **Deficiency** – anemia, digestive disturbances, fatigue, nervousness, dry or rough skin, nervous system disorders and immune system problems.

Vitamin C (ascorbic acid)

✪ **Function** – This vitamin is essential for the formation of **collagen**. It helps to strengthen tissues, acts as an antioxidant, helps in healing, production of red blood cells, fighting bacterial infections and regulating cholesterol. It also helps the body to absorb iron.

✪ **Source** – most fresh fruits and vegetables.

✪ **RDI** – 60 mg.

✪ **Deficiency** – bleeding gums, bruise easily, dental cavities, low infection resistance and slow healing of wounds.

Vitamin D (calciferol)

✪ **Function** – Essential to calcium and phosphorus utilisation. Promotes strong bones and teeth. Our main source of vitamin D is sunlight.

✪ **Source** – sunlight, egg yolk, fish, fish oils, fortified cereals.

✪ **RDI** – 400 iu.

✪ **Deficiency** – brittle and fragile bones, diarrhoea, irregular heartbeat, low blood calcium, rickets and osteoporosis.

Minerals

There are several minerals required to maintain a healthy body.

Folic acid

✪ **Function** – Helps the body form genetic material and red blood cells, and aids in protein metabolism. It also acts as an antioxidant. Research has shown that if folic acid is taken on a daily basis 30 days before conception, the foetus is less likely to suffer from birth defects such as spina bifida.

✪ **Source** – green vegetables, kidney beans, and orange juice.

✪ **RDI** – 400 mg.

✪ **Deficiency** – depression, fatigue, anaemia and birth defects in pregnant women.

Calcium

✪ **Function** – It is needed to build strong bones and teeth, helps to calm nerves and plays a role in muscle contraction, blood clotting and cell membrane upkeep. Correct quantities of calcium consumption have been shown to significantly lower the risk of osteoporosis.

✪ **Source** – milk and milk products, whole grains and unrefined cereals, green vegetables, fish bones.

✪ **RDI** – adults 1000 mg.

✪   **Deficiency** – fragile bones, osteoporosis, rickets, tooth decay; irregular heartbeat and slowed nerve impulse response. Vitamin D is essential for proper calcium absorption and utilisation.

Copper

✪   **Function** – Assists in the formation of haemoglobin and helps to maintain healthy bones, blood vessels and nerves.

✪   **Source** – barley, potatoes, whole grains, mushrooms, cocoa, beans, almonds and most seafoods.

✪   **RDI** – 2 mg.

✪   **Deficiency** – fractures and bone deforminities, anaemia, general weakness, impaired respiration, skin sores.

Iron

✪   **Function** – It is required for the production of haemoglobin.

✪   **Source** – liver, lean meats, eggs, baked potatoes, soybeans, kidney beans, whole grains and cereals, dried fruits.

✪   **RDI** – males 10 mg, females 18 mg.

✪   **Deficiency** – dizziness, iron deficiency anaemia, constipation, sore or inflamed tongue.

Magnesium

✪   **Function** – Aids in the production of proteins and helps regulate body temperature. Helps lower blood pressure and assists with the proper functioning of nerves and muscles.

✪   **Source** – whole grain foods, wheat bran, dark-green leafy vegetables, soybeans, fish, oysters, shrimp, almonds, peanuts.

✪   **RDI** – 400 mg.

✪   **Deficiency** – decreased blood pressure and body temperature, nervousness, interference with the transmission of nerve and muscle impulses.

Phosphorus

✪   **Function** – Essential for metabolism of carbohydrates, fats and proteins. It aids in growth and cell repair and is necessary for proper skeletal growth, tooth development, proper kidney functions and the nervous system.

✪   **Source** – meat, fish, poultry, milk, yoghurt, eggs, seeds, broccoli and nuts.

✪   **RDI** – 1000 mg.

✪   **Deficiency** – bone pain, fatigue, irregular breathing, nervous disorders.

Potassium

- **Function** – In conjunction with sodium, it helps to maintain fluid and **electrolyte balance** within cells. Important for normal nerve and muscle function. Aids in proper maintenance of the blood's mineral balance. It also helps to lower blood pressure.

- **Source** – bananas, dried apricots, yoghurt, whole grains, sunflower seeds, potatoes, sweet potatoes and kidney beans.

- **RDI** – 3500 mg.

- **Deficiency** – decreased blood pressure, dry skin, salt retention, irregular heartbeat.

Sodium

- **Function** – This works in conjunciton with potassium to maintain fluid and elecrolyte balance within cells.

- **Source** – virtually all foods contain sodium: celery, cheese, eggs, meat, milk and milk products, processed foods, salt and seafood.

- **RDI** – 500 mg.

- **Deficiency** – confusion, low blood sugar, dehydration, lethargy, heart palpatations and heart attack.

Selenium

- **Function** – It is a powerful antioxidant and aids in normal body growth and fertility.

- **Source** – seafood, **offal**, bran and wheat germ, broccoli, celery, cucumbers and mushrooms.

- **RDI** – 70 to 200 mg. (no current official RDI).

- **Deficiency** – heart disease, muscular pain and weakness.

Zinc

- **Function** – Necessary for healing and development of new cells; is an antioxidant and plays an important part in helping to build a strong immune system.

- **Source** – beef, lamb, seafood, eggs, yoghurt, Marmite, beans, nuts and seeds.

- **RDI** – 15 mg.

- **Deficiency** – decreased learning ability, delayed sexual maturity, eczema, fatigue, prolonged wound healing, retarded growth, white spots on nails.

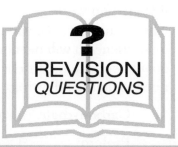

REVISION QUESTIONS

1) Explain what macronutrients and micronutrients are and give examples of where you would find each in the diet.

2) How much of each macronutrient should healthy adults be eating every day?

3) What are the fat-soluble vitamins?

4) What macronutrient may vegetarians be lacking in their diet and why?

5) What are the different types of carbohdyrate?

6) What is an essential amino acid?

7) Why do we need to eat some fat in our diet?

8) Why are plant sources of fat better for us than animal sources of fat?

9) Give an example of five different foods that contain high quantities of vitamins and minerals.

DIETARY INTAKE

Assessing dietary intake

The simplest method of assessing a person's dietary intake is to keep a food diary, in which everything that is drunk or eaten and how much is eaten should be recorded. From this, a person can track how many kilocalories they are consuming and the percentage of each macronutrient. It is then possible to try to lose weight by consuming fewer kilocalories, decreasing the amount of fat consumption, and so on.

Food diary

Food	Quantity	Total kcal	Carbohydrate g	Carbohydrate kcals	Fat g	Fat kcals	Protein g	Protein kcals

Today, most foods have their kilocalorie and macronutrient content written on their wrappings. In these cases, it is easy to record the details in the food diary. Occasionally food tables may need to be used if the foods do not have this information written on the packaging. Most food tables (and occasionally food labels) only have the values for 100 g of food. If you have only eaten 25 g of the food, then you will need to divide the values by four. If you only have the quantity of macronutrient in grams and want to convert it to kilocalories you need to do the following:

Carbohydrate: $4 \times$ quantity in grams = kcals

Protein: $4 \times$ quantity in grams = kcals

Fat: $8 \times$ quantity in grams = kcals

STUDENT ACTIVITY

Food diary

Copy the food diary plan on page 207 and record everything you eat and drink for 24 hours. Try to eat the same things you usually eat and, if possible, weigh any foods you eat that do not come in pre-packed portions. For example, weigh your breakfast cereal. It may be easier to try to eat foods with their nutrition conent written on the labels while carrying out this activity.

Once the food diary is complete, carry out the following:

✪ record the total kilocalories consumed during the day
✪ record the total kilocalories consumed from carbohydrate during the day
✪ record the total kilocalories consumed from fat during the day
✪ record the total kilocalories consumed from protein during the day.

From this information it is possible to work out if you are eating the correct proportion of each macronutrient. You will need to use the following calculations:

✪ $\dfrac{\text{kilocalories consumed from carbohydrate}}{\text{total kilocalorie intake}} \times 100 = $ % kilocalories from carbohydrate consumed

✪ $\dfrac{\text{kilocalories consumed from protein}}{\text{total kilocalorie intake}} \times 100 = $ % kilocalories from protein consumed

✪ $\dfrac{\text{kilocalories consumed from fat}}{\text{total kilocalorie intake}} \times 100 = $ % kilocalories from fat consumed.

From these calculations try to establish whether you are eating the correct amount of macronutrients per day. If not, how can your diet be improved?

Later on in this chapter you will be able to work out how many kilocalories you should consume in order to maintain your weight. From this you can decide if you are eating the correct amount of kilocalories or if you need to increase or decrease your kilocalorie intake in order lose, gain or maintain your body weight.

ENERGY EXPEND-ITURE

When we take part in activities, we use up more kilocalories in order to give us the energy for our muscles to contract. The more strenuous the activity, the more kilocalories we burn in order to provide us with the required energy. Below is a list of various activities people take part in every day. The values given are only approximate values, as larger people will burn more kilocalories because they have larger bodies to move around, and vice versa for smaller people. Also, some people put more or less effort into the activity, so these figures can only be approximate values and act only as a guideline.

Type of exercise	Kilocalories used per hour
Aerobics	450
Aqua aerobics	400
Bicycling	450
Cross-country ski machine	500
Eating	85
Golf, with trolley	180
Hiking	500
Jogging, 5 mph	500
Rowing	550
Running	700
Sitting	85
Skipping with rope	700
Sleeping	55
Spinning	650
Standing	100
Step aerobics	550
Squash	650
Swimming	500
Table tennis	290
Tennis	350
Walking, 3 mph	280

★ STUDENT ACTIVITY

Activity diary

Copy out the table below.

Time	Activity	Kilocalories

Try to make a note of every activity you do in a 24-hour period. Try to carry out this activity on a normal day, when you are feeling well. At the end of the 24-hour period, total the number of kilocalories you have expended during that day.

Basal metabolic rate (BMR)

Basal metabolic rate is the minimal caloric requirement needed to sustain life in a resting individual. This is the amount of energy your body would burn if you slept all day (24 hours). A variety of factors will affect your basal metabolic rate: some will speed it up so you burn more kilocalories per day just to stay alive, whereas other factors will slow your metabolic rate down so that you need to eat fewer kilocalories just to stay alive.

1   **Age** – In youth, the BMR is higher due to the fact that as you get older you start to lose more muscle tissue and replace it with fat tissue. The more muscle tissue a person has, the greater their BMR, and vice versa. Hence, as you get older this increased fat mass will have the effect of slowing down your BMR.

2   **Height** – Tall people have higher BMRs.

3   **Growth** – Children and pregnant women have higher BMRs. In both cases the body is growing and needs more energy.

4   **Body composition** – The more muscle tissue, the higher the BMR; the more fat tissue, the lower the BMR.

5   **Fever** – Fevers can raise the BMR. This is because when a person has a fever, their body temperature is increased, which speeds up the rate of metabolic reactions (which will help to fight off an infection) and will result in an increased BMR.

6   **Stress** – Stress hormones can raise the BMR.

7   **Environmental temperature** – Both heat and cold raise the BMR. When a person is too hot, their body tries to cool it down, which requires energy; when a person is too cold they will shiver, which again is a process that requires energy.

8   **Fasting** – When a person is fasting, as in dieting, hormones are released which act to lower the BMR.

9   **Thyroxin** – The thyroid hormone thyroxin is a key BMR regulator; the more thyroxin produced, the higher the BMR.

⭐ STUDENT ACTIVITY

There are a number of calculations available to try to determine a person's BMR; some are more accurate than others as they take into account a variety of factors such as the age, sex and activity level of a person.

First of all, you need to know your weight in kilogrammes and your height in meters. To convert pounds to kilograms divided by 2.2 (kg = pounds / 2.2). So if you weigh 180 lbs you would carry out the following calculation:
$\frac{180}{2.2}$ = 81.8 kg (remember that there are 14 pounds in a stone).

To convert feet and inches to cm:
    cm = (feet × 12 + inches) × 2.54)

So, if you are 5 ft 4 inches you would carry out the following calculation:
    (5 × 12 + 4) × 2.54 = (60 + 4) × 2.54 =
    64 × 2.54 = 162.56 cm.

Now work out your BMR using the following methods.

Method 1

Men: kg (body weight) × 24 = kcal per day
Women: kg (body weight) × 23 = kcal per day
This calculation does not take physical activity, height or age into consideration.

Method 2

Males: BMR = 66 + (13.7 × wt in kg) +
                    (5 × ht in cm) – (6.8 × age in yrs)

Females: BMR = 65 + (9.6 × wt in kg) +
                    (1.8 × ht in cm) – (4.7 × age in yrs)

Method 3

Males   0–2 yrs (60.9 × wt) – 54
            3–9 yrs (22.7 × wt) + 495
            10–17 yrs (17.5 × wt) + 651
            18–29 yrs (15.3 × wt) + 679
            30–59 yrs (11.6 × wt) + 879
            over 60 yrs (13.5 × wt) + 487

Females 0–2 yrs (61.0 × wt) – 51
            3–9 yrs (22.5 × wt) + 499
            10–17 yrs (12.2 × wt) + 746
            18-29 yrs (14.7 × wt) + 496
            30–59 yrs (8.7 × wt) + 829
            over 60 yrs (10.5 × wt) + 596

Method 4

From the answer you have obtained from method 3, to include exercise, multiply the BMR figure you have by the appropriate activity factor.

Level	Activity factor
1	Very light: cooking, driving, ironing, painting, sewing, standing
	1.3 males **1.3 females**
2	Light: walking 3 mph, electrical trades, sailing, golf, child care, house cleaning
	1.6 males **1.3 females**
3	Moderate: walking 3.5–4.0 mph, weeding, cycling, skiing, tennis, dance
	1.7 males **1.6 females**
4	Heavy: manual digging, basketball, climbing, football,
	2.1 males **1.9 females**
5	Exceptional: training for professional athletic competition
	2.4 males **2.2 females**

For example, if you are an 18-year-old male who weighs 70 kg and takes part in exceptional training for professional athletic competition you would use the following equation:
    (15.3 × 70kg) + 679 × 2.4 =

✪ You should end up with four different estimates for you basal metabolic rate. Which one do you think is the most accurate and why? (If you have completed a food diary and activity diary this may help you to make your decision.)

✪ Repeat the above calculations with the details of a person of the opposite sex who is either older or younger than you, such as a member of your family or an athlete. Ensure that you know the person's age, height and weight.

✪ Comment on what you notice about their BMR compared with your own and try to explain why there is this difference.

REVISION QUESTIONS

1) How would you assess the dietary intake of a sports person?

2) Why is it necessary for sports people to ensure they are taking in enough kilocalories?

3) Give examples of five things that affect a person's BMR.

4) Why would a very low calorie diet decrease a person's BMR?

5) Carry out research to find out how many calories a day on average the following would need to consume in order to maintain their body weight.

- ✪ Cross-country skier
- ✪ Gymnast
- ✪ Footballer
- ✪ Windsurfer
- ✪ Basketball player

NUTRITIONAL STRATEGIES

Diet plans

Weight loss

In order to lose weight it is necessary to consume fewer calories than your body needs. Athletes may not be overweight, but may need to lose excess weight in order to compete in a lower weight category. Excess weight in the form of fat usually acts to hinder a person's performance because a heavier body requires more energy for transport. Therefore, athletes may diet to get rid of any unessential fat. The best type of diet to help the person lose weight but still have enough energy to train seems to be a low-fat diet.

Low-fat diets

A low-fat diet recommends low-fat options whenever possible, plus regular consumption of complex carbohydrates like potatoes and brown bread. Low-fat diets are usually quite filling because they involve eating large amounts of complex carbohydrates, which include fibre. Weight loss is steady at about 1.5 to 2 pounds per week. Most experts agree that faster weight loss is not sustainable as the weight lost is from the glycogen stores and not from the fat stores of the body.

What you eat on a low-fat diet
- ✪ **A typical breakfast**:
  - ▶ glass of freshly squeezed orange
  - ▶ large bowl of cereal with fat-free milk
  - ▶ toast with no margarine, and marmite or jam
  - ▶ tea/coffee.

✪ A typical lunch:
  ► large brown bread sandwich with lean meat and large salad with low-fat dressing
  ► low-fat yogurt.

✪ A typical dinner:
  ► 4oz lean chicken with potatoes (no butter) and two helpings of vegetables
  ► chopped fruit topped with low-fat ice-cream or low-fat fromage frais.

✪ Typical snacks:
  ► fruit
  ► low-fat yogurts
  ► whole-wheat sandwiches
  ► cereal.

What diet is best for athletes?

All athletes need a diet that provides enough energy in the form of carbohydrates and fats, as well as essential protein, vitamins and minerals. Most athletes will aim to eat a diet that consists mainly of carbohydrates – around 55% to 60%, (10% to 15% from sugars and the rest from starches). No more than 30% of kilocalories should come from fat, and 10% to 15% from protein.

Carbohydrates and the athlete

When a person eats carbohydrate, it is broken down into glucose molecules. Glucose is the only form of carbohydrate used directly by muscles for energy. The glucose is carried in the bloodstream to the muscles and used to produce muscle contraction. Any glucose that is not used is stored as glycogen in the liver and muscles. When an athlete takes part in exercise, the glycogen is broken down in the muscles to provide energy. However, the body can only store a limited amount of glycogen, usually enough to provide fuel for 90 to 120 minutes of exercise.

Therefore, for exercise that lasts longer than 90 minutes, the athlete would benefit from consuming carbohydrates during the exercise in order to help maintain their blood glucose levels.

Another method athletes use is carbohydrate/glycogen loading (see the next section), which helps to increase the amount of glycogen stored in the body.

High-protein diets

Studies have shown that exercise increases protein breakdown and, therefore, dietary requirement. The exact amount depends on the following factors:

✪ The type, intensity and frequency of training. The longer a person exercises, the more protein is broken down. If not enough protein is eaten to compensate, or if a person trains too frequently, this net loss of lean tissue will eventually affect performance.

213

- ✪ How long a person has been training. Studies have shown that beginners have higher requirements per kg of body weight than more experienced athletes. However, as the body becomes used to training, it becomes more efficient at recycling proteins.

- ✪ Kilocalorie and carbohydrate intake. If a person does not consume enough kilocalories to meet their needs, protein will be broken down for energy rather than being used for growth and repair.

However, eating more protein in the diet will not increase the size of your muscles! Muscles develop from training and exercise. A certain amount of protein is needed to help build the muscles, but extra servings of protein in foods or protein supplements do not assist in muscle development. Extra protein is not converted into muscle and does not cause further increases in muscle size, strength or stamina. Protein cannot be stored in the body and any excess will be burned for energy or stored as body fat.

What you eat on a high-protein diet
- ✪ **Typical breakfast**: bacon and eggs.

- ✪ **Typical lunch**: small salad and double cheeseburger (no bread).

- ✪ **Typical dinner**: steak or fried chicken, with salad topped with cheese dressing.

Diet before, during and after exercise

Before
Before exercise an athlete should consume some complex carbohydrates such as bananas. The athlete should aim to eat this meal one to four hours prior to exercise participation – the timing of this meal depends on athlete's preference. With intense activities such as sprinting, blood flow is diverted from the stomach to the working muscles. Therefore, the athlete should leave four hours between eating and the event as that is the time needed for a typical meal of around 1200 calories to empty from the stomach. However, a snack of around 300 calories should only take around an hour to digest.

During
During exercise, athletes will usually sweat in order to maintain their internal body temperature. Therefore, it is important to drink plenty of water. If the exercise lasts for over 90 minutes then drinking a sports drink or other beverage with some sugar in it will help maintain blood glucose levels.

After
If the exercise was strenuous and lasted longer than 90 minutes, the body's glycogen stores will need refuelling. Consuming foods and drinks high in carbohydrates right after exercise will help to increase the refuelling of the glycogen stores. Research has found that a high-carbohydrate food or drink should be consumed within two hours after exercise in order to help maximise glycogen resynthesis.

Fluid intake

Healthy adults can survive for many weeks without food, but they can live for only a few days without water.

As we know, exercise generates heat, which must be released to prevent the body overheating, and sweating is the most important body mechanism to control this temperature rise. Therefore, during exercise, the body starts to dehydrate due to loss of fluids from sweating. Losses of as little as 2% of the body weight as fluid can impair physical and mental performance. Further losses of fluid as a percentage of body weight have the following effects:

✪ impaired performance   2%

✪ capacity for muscular work declines   4%

✪ heat exhaustion   5%

✪ **hallucinations**   7%

✪ heat stroke and circulatory collapse   10%

The body responds to dehydration by triggering various mechanisms in order to try to conserve fluid and return itself to normal. First of all a person will feel thirsty; this is followed by a reduced urine output and conservation of sodium by the kidneys; lastly there is a reduced sweat output. However, the reduced sweat output brings about a further rise in core temperature and the demand for more sweat increases. Failure to produce more sweat is followed by another rise in temperature. The blood thickens and the heart rate increases, which will eventually lead to heat stroke and circulatory collapse.

It is very rare that athletes suffer from severe dehydration, however, a number of athletes will regularly become dehydrated during training or competition. One of the main reasons for this is because in humans, thirst is a very poorly developed mechanism – when a person feels thirsty they are already in a state of dehydration. As we know, if an athlete is dehydrated by only 2% of their body weight, it will have a detrimental effect on their performance. Therefore, if the effects of fluid loss can be prevented, an individual will feel better, continue to perform better and recover more quickly. This is one of the reasons why sports drinks have become so popular and why so much time and money has been spent researching which ingredients in a sports drink will accelerate the rehydration process.

Research has shown that plain drinking water is not the best fluid replacement for rapid correction of dehydration as it has the effect of reducing the feeling of thirst before sufficient fluid has been consumed to replace losses. Drinking plain water alone also stimulates urine production, which will again delay rehydration.

FIGURE 8.8

Sports drinks are designed to rehydrate and energize athletes as quickly as possible

Water

Although is it not a nutrient, human beings would be unable to survive without water. It is taken into the body by fluid consumption and foods that contain water. It is not necessary to only drink 'pure' water; although this is a good choice, squash, carbonated drinks, fruit juices and so on will also supply the body with water. Like everything else we consume, selection depends on personal preference and availability. Roughly a third of an adult's daily fluid intake is supplied by what is eaten rather than what is drunk. Fruit and vegetables provide most of this additional fluid, but small amounts also come from bread and dairy products

The body is composed of 50% to 75% of water, depending on age and body fatness. The younger you are and the less fat you have, the more water your body will contain. Water is used for two essential body processes: temperature regulation, and cellular processes. Water is lost by urine excretion, stool excretion, sweat and respiration.

The average man should consume at least 2.9 litres of water per day and the average woman at least 2.2 litres a day for optimal cellular and metabolic processes. This amount will vary depending on the time of year, climatic conditions, diet and how much physical activity a person does.

Another important indicator to use for hydration is the colour of your urine. If urine is a dark yellow colour or very little is excreted, you are probably dehydrated and need more fluids.

Sports drinks

It has been rumored that the first sports drink originated many years ago with the coach of the American Football team the Gators. The story goes that he felt because the athletes lost fluids and other substances in their sweat during a game, it was necessary to replace these losses afterwards in order to maximise their recovery. Hence, he took the athletes socks and clothing after a game, and rung them out so that the sweat was collected in a bucket. He would then add fluid to this fresh sweat and probably some flavourings, then shared this drink out among the players after the game!

Nowadays sports drinks are a huge business. They are specially formulated carbohydrate and electrolyte drinks designed not only to rehydrate athletes, but also to deliver a boost of carbohydrate energy to working muscles. Together these help to maximise performance and endurance.

There are two main factors that affect the speed at which fluid from a drink gets into the body:

✪ the speed at which it is emptied from the stomach

✪ the rate at which it is absorbed through the walls of the small intestine.

Both of these factors are influenced by the composition of the fluid and should be taken into account when a sports drink is designed.

STUDENT ACTIVITY

Sports drinks

Name as many different sports drinks as you can. Look through magazines, the internet or sports shops to help you. Write down the prices of these drinks and any claimed benefits of consuming this drink.

1. Stomach emptying

The higher the carbohydrate level, the slower the rate of stomach emptying. Drinks with a carbohydrate level of between 6% and 8% are emptied from the stomach at a rate similar to water. If the carbohydrate content is higher, the rate of fluid emptying from the stomach is reduced. The volume of fluid in the stomach can also have an effect on the speed of stomach emptying. The greater the volume of fluid, the faster it is emptied from the stomach, so, the more you drink, the quicker the fluid will enter the small intestine.

2. Fluid absorption

Glucose stimulates the absorption of fluid from the intestine. Drinking plain water reduces the drive to drink well before sufficient fluid has been consumed to replace the losses.

Electrolytes in a sports drink, especially sodium and potassium, reduce urine output which will help to promote rehydration.

Types of sports drinks

There is a range of sports drinks available made by a variety of companies. Deciding which sports drink is most appropriate for the athlete depends on the intensity and duration of the exercise undertaken, as well as climatic conditions. This will then help to determine whether the individual's primary requirement is for fluid replacement, carbohydrate energy or both. Taste is also very important when designing a sports drink – if a product does not taste good, then a sports person will be reluctant to consume it.

The optimal sports drink should strike a balance between physiological effectiveness and **palatability**. Taste perception changes between rest, exercise and after exercise. Sweet, strongly flavored beverages are preferred at rest, while exercising individuals tend to prefer cool, moderately sweet, lightly flavored drinks rather than plain water.

Isotonic drinks

Isotonic drinks contain roughly the same number of particles of dissolved substances (including carbohydrates) as blood plasma. As a result, isotonic drinks quickly replace fluids lost through sweat, and supply a useful boost of carbohydrate energy to the working muscles.

Hypotonic drinks

Hypotonic drinks provide fluid, but only very low levels of carbohydrate, and are therefore ideal for those individuals who need fluid without extra calories; for example, jockeys, gymnasts and ballet dancers, who sweat and lose fluid but need to maintain a low body weight.

Hypertonic drinks

Hypertonic drinks, in general, contain more dissolved particles than blood plasma and are used to supplement daily carbohydrate intake after exercise to help top up muscle glycogen stores. For most athletes, hypertonic drinks are not suitable for use during exercise as the fluid takes a long time to empty from the stomach and can cause stomach cramps. The exception is in ultra-endurance events, such as the Tour de France cycle race, where hypertonic drinks are used to provide high levels of energy in conjunction with isotonic sports drinks to help to rehydrate the athlete.

STUDENT PRACTICAL

Designing a sports drink

Aim

The aim of this practical is to make a sports drink. You need to decide which athletes you are making the drink for and when it should be consumed (i.e. if you want to make an isotonic, hypertonic or hypotonic drink).

Equipment

For this experiment, if you are using equipment taken from the science lab, it must have been thoroughly sterilised.

    measuring cylinders
    beakers
    weighing scales
    glucose
    sweeteners
    flavourings – your choice
    colourings – your choice
    tasting cups
    drinking water
    salt

Method

Isotonic drink

1   If you are designing an isotonic drink, you need to ensure that the carbohydrate content of your drink is between 6% and 8%. To do this, for every 100 ml of water, you need to add between 6 to 8 g of glucose.

2   You can then add other flavourings to your drink to make it taste better – however, these flavourings should not contain any carbohydrates, so use things that contain sweetners, such as reduced sugar squash.

Hypertonic drink

1   If you are designing a hypertonic drink, it should contain at least 9% carbohydrates. This means for every 100 ml of water, you need to add at least 9 g of glucose

2   You can then add other flavourings, which can contain carbohydrates.

Hypotonic Drink

1   If you are designing a hypotonic drink, it should contain 5% or less carbohydrates. To do this, to every 100 ml of water add 5 g of glucose or less.

2   You can then add other flavourings, but these should not contain any carbohydrates, so you could use things that contain sweeteners.

Experiment with different flavours and different quantities of flavour. Ensure that, each time, you write out exactly how much of each ingredient you use. When you have made a drink that you think tastes acceptable place it in a beaker.

Results

Go around the class and sample other people's sports drinks. Do this by pouring their drink from the beaker into your tasting cup. Ensure that you rinse the cup out after each tasting. Fill in a table like the one below.

Name	Type of drink	Taste	Colour	Would you you buy it?

Conclusion

In your conclusion, try to answer the following questions.

1   For whom was your drink designed?
2   Did your drink taste acceptable?
3   Would people buy your drink?
4   What could you have done to improve the taste of your drink?
5   Out of the class tasting session, which drinks tasted the best and why?

Supplementation

Vitamin and mineral supplements

The main two reasons that most athletes take vitamin and mineral supplements are:

✪   to compensate for less than optimal diets

✪   to improve performance.

However, a poor diet is not redeemed by supplementation. Supplementation may be appropriate if someone is consuming a low-calorie diet (1200 calories or less), a vegetarian diet, is in a diseased state, or has a lack of food choices or availability. The supplement should not contain more than 100% of the RDA for any vitamin or mineral. The best way to obtain vitamin and mineral requirements is to eat a healthy, well-balanced diet.

With regard to performance, to date there is no evidence that consuming more than 50–100% of the RDA of a vitamin or mineral will increase performance. A supplement will only work if the athlete or individual is deficient in that particular vitamin or mineral. If there is no deficiency, then they are not benefiting in any way.

Protein supplements

Protein supplements often consist of powdered milk and/or egg protein or soya, and claim to increase muscle growth. But they do not in themselves encourage increases in muscle growth, strength or endurance.

Protein requirements should be met adequately from food. One pint of milk, for example provides roughly the same amount of protein as one serving of a standard protein supplement. The only case where supplements may be useful is for people with very high calorie and protein requirements, who would otherwise find it difficult to eat enough food to fulfil these.

The athletes who might consume protein supplements are those who are training to gain muscle mass such as body builders, or sprinters. A high-protein diet would involve eating large quantities of protein in unrestricted amounts, including red meat, fish, shellfish, poultry, eggs and cheese. It also involves limiting carbohydrate-rich foods. The problem with such a diet is that it can encourage over-consumption of saturated fat and cholesterol, which can increase the risk of heart disease. A high-protein diet also puts extra stress on the kidneys, which may lead to kidney damage. With such a low carbohydrate intake, chemicals called ketones are released into the bloodstream and can cause headaches, tiredness, nausea, dehydration, dizziness, constipation and bad breath.

Creatine supplementation

Creatine comes from two sources:

✪   the diet, from meat products

✪   internally manufactured.

What is not present in the diet is easily made by the liver and kidneys from a few amino acids. A 70 kg adult has about 120 g of creatine in the muscles, and the daily turnover is roughly 2 g. About half of this is replaced by the diet and half is made by the body.

Creatine is eliminated from the body by the kidneys, either as creatine, or as creatinine, which is formed from the metabolism of creatine.

Creatine is not a banned substance and is used by athletes for the following reasons:

- ✪ it may increase the Phosphocreitine (PCR) concentration in skeletal muscle, which will increase anaerobic ATP production during maximal exercise

- ✪ it may increase the resynthesis of PCr during recovery periods between short bouts of maximal exercise

- ✪ The PCr energy system is anaerobic and is therefore potentially **ergogenic** (energy-generating) only for activity that has a high anaerobic component, not for endurance activity.

The most common method of supplementation uses a five- or six-day loading period, and consists of approximately 20 g of creatine per day. The side-effects of taking creatine are not clear as it is still a relatively new ergogenic aid. Whether creatine really does increase performance is not clear; some research suggests that it does, while other states that it does not.

Carbohydrate/glycogen loading

This type of supplementation is carried out by endurance athletes who are taking part in exercise that is going to last longer than 90 to 120 minutes, so marathon runners are the type of athletes who would frequently follow this regime.

The diet lasts for seven days and is combined with an exercise program which is initially designed to deplete the body's store of glycogen. This is followed by a loading period which is designed to increase the amount of glycogen the body can store – this is termed super-compensation.

Seven days prior to the event the athlete consumes a low-carbohydrate diet and takes part in strenuous exercise. This is repeated for two more days. For the next three days, the carbohydrate intake is increased and the amount of exercise is tapered off. Eventually, the day before the marathon, the athlete has a complete rest day and consumes a high quantity of carbohydrate – this is why some athletes go to 'pasta parties' the night before the marathon! Most research has shown that the amount of glycogen stored after completing this kind of diet and exercise regime is increased, which will enable the athlete to exercise at a higher intensity for longer. Athletes who 'hit the wall' have depleted their glycogen stores so completely that they have to rely on fat to supply their energy. As fat supplies energy very slowly, the athlete is no longer able to run and, in extreme cases, has to resort to crawling.

REVISION *QUESTIONS*

1) Give examples of diets a person can follow in order to try to lose weight.

2) Which athletes require large amounts of carbohydrate in their diet and why?

3) What are the problems associated with eating a high-protein diet?

4) Which athletes might eat a high-protein diet?

5) Why should a person be properly hydrated when taking part in exercise?

6) Do sports drinks increase a person's sporting performance? Explain your answer.

7) What sports drink would a person competing in the Tour de France consume and why?

8) Should athletes take vitamin supplements? Explain your answer.

9) Why would an athlete carbohydrate load?

10) Which athletes may benefit from creatine supplementation?

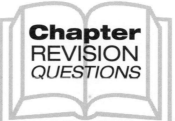

Chapter REVISION *QUESTIONS*

1) Give an example of a day's diet for a sports person of your choice. Ensure that the person is having:

a) the correct amount of macronutrients

b) the correct amount of calories

c) a range of vitamins and minerals

d) enough fluid.

2) Explain the problems a person may encounter if they eat:

a) too much saturated fat

b) not enough vitamin A or C

c) not enough iron

d) too few calories

e) too little protein

f) too much simple carbohydrate.

3 Give examples of diets available today that claim they will help a person:

a) lose weight quickly

b) gain muscle mass

c) lose weight over a period of time

d) increase their energy levels.

Assess each diet and explain the pros and cons of each.

FURTHER READING

Burke, L., Deakin, V. (1994) *Clinical Sports Nutrition.* McGraw Hill

Eisenman, P., *et al.* (1990) *Coaches' Guide to Nutrition and Weight Control.* Leisure Press

Hartigan, S., Thompson, G., Wesson, K., Wiggins, N. (2000) *Sport and PE, A Complete Guide to Advanced Level Study.* London: Hodder and Stoughton

McArdle, W., Katch, F. I. and V. L. (2001) *Exercise Physiology: Energy, Nutrition and Human Performance.* Williams & Wilkins

McArdle, W. D., Katch, F. I. and V. L. (1999) *Sports and Exercise Nutrition.* Williams & Wilkins.

Williams, S. (1997) *Nutrition and Diet Therapy.* London: Mosby

CHAPTER 9

QUANTITATIVE AND QUALITATIVE SPORT AND EXERCISE RESEARCH

This chapter explains methods used in **quantitative** and **qualitative** research by sport and exercise scientists. It will enable you to understand research in all disciplines of sport and exercise science. It should allow you to develop research skills, including collecting data, handling data, mathematical and statistical skills that will be required by you to carry out your own research. Numbers and mathematical concepts put off a lot of students, but the purpose of research methods and statistics is to help you understand and interpret the meaning of sets of numbers. The major difference between quantitative research and qualitative research is that quantitative research is based more on numerical evidence (numbers, e.g. heart rate) while qualitative research places more emphasis on what people do or say (e.g. answers given in an interview).

By the end of this chapter you should be able to:

- ✪ review types of quantitative data

- ✪ review types of qualitative data and issues relating to them

- ✪ collect sport and exercise science quantitative research data

- ✪ plan to collect sport and exercise science qualitative research data

- ✪ interpret quantitative research results

- ✪ collect and interpret qualitative research results

- ✪ present sport and exercise science quantitative research using IT

- ✪ present the sport and exercise science qualitative research using IT.

TYPES AND QUALITY OF DATA

Classification

A group or set of numbers is referred to as data. The resting heart rates of a group of people would be a set of data. Data can include more than one type of measurement, for example, the height and weight of a number people. Each different type of measurement is called a **variable**, because the value of the measurement can vary. In sport and exercise a variable is something that we measure (e.g. blood pressure, anxiety levels, flexibility). If the variable can be recorded using a number it is described as a **numeric variable**. However, not all variables or sets of data have to use numbers. An example of this would be recording the gender of a group of people – instead of numbers, labels would be used (male and female). Variables with letters or words in place of numbers are called **string variables**.

Numbers can be classified according to their level of measurement. The most basic type of numeric measurement uses a nominal scale, where nominal value (a number) is assigned to a category. If gender is to be recorded in a table, males could be denoted by a 2 and females by a 1. These values would be nominal; that is, classification is for identification purposes only. Values are assigned arbitrarily and are nominated by the measurer. The values have no numerical meaning, so 2 is not twice as good as 1. They are just labels to distinguish each category. **Nominal data** is sometimes referred to as **discrete data**, because you can only have discrete values (e.g. male or female, yes or no).

A second type of numeric measurement is ordinal. **Ordinal values** occur when numbers are assigned to categories, and these numbers indicate rank (e.g. Liverpool = 1st, Leeds = 2nd, Man Utd = 3rd). In the example given each number indicates football league position, that is Liverpool is first, Leeds is second and so on. This sort of data provides us with more information than nominal data (e.g. we can now say who is the tallest, quickest or heaviest). It is important to note that the distance between categories is still unknown. In the league position example, the team in first place maybe one point ahead of the team in second, while the team in second could be three points in front of the team in third. This type of data only gives a rank order (i.e. first, second, third) and not an exact value.

A further type of numerical variable is that given by **interval** or **ratio level** data. These are actually two different classifications of data, but due to their many similarities can be referred to as one. An interval scale has equal distances between values and is an accepted unit of physical measurement, for example, the Fahrenheit scale. It is different from a ratio scale in that it has an arbitrary zero point. Ratio scales have a zero point determined by nature (e.g. time, distance, weight) or what is called an absolute zero. Therefore, a distance of 20 km is twice that of 10 km. The same cannot be said for Fahrenheit, that is, 20°F is not twice has hot as 10°F. Interval or ratio data is continuous. Continuous data can have any numeric value with any number of decimal places. The time taken to run the 100 m would be a continuous measure (e.g. a value of 11.43 secs). Interval or ratio data can be converted into ordinal or nominal scales. If you were to measure the precise height of subjects, you could then categorise the subjects into the following groups based on their height: tall = 1, medium height = 2, short = 3. This would be converting ratio data into ordinal data.

STUDENT ACTIVITY

Data classification

Determine the levels of measurement of the following variables and give explanations for why you have chosen each particular classification.

1 blood pressure
2 compliance with an exercise programme:

a) followed programme = 1
b) dropped out = 2

3 finishing time:
a) < 10 secs = 1
b) 10–20 secs = 2
c) >20 secs = 3

4 heart rate
5 distance walked

Primary and secondary data

Why do we need to take measurements in sport and exercise science? Measurement allows us to quantify things (e.g. it is possible to give a value for the number of times a heart beats in a minute). With sufficient measurement, data can be produced, so heart rate over a given time could be displayed. The production of data is important in science as it allows analysis; hence, it would be possible to examine what happens to heart rate during a set time period or in a given situation (e.g. during exercise). Does heart rate increase, decrease, or stay the same during exercise? This analysis in turn allows interpretation to infer meaning. The reason for an increased heart rate could be examined. Why did the heart rate go up? What caused it?

Data that you measure yourself is called **primary data**; somebody else's data that you use is would be secondary data. If you were examining the number of yellow and red cards for the teams competing in the last three football world cups, you would need to collect the data from these world cups. This might involve looking up information on the internet, for example. This would be secondary data, which is originally recorded by somebody other than you.

Quality of data

Accuracy and precision

If you are a sport and exercise scientist testing and assessing athletes, you need to take special care when interpreting results of tests. Because people can only measure something to a certain degree of accuracy, it is important to realise that a measurement always has some level of uncertainty. This depends on the precision of the measuring device. For example, if you weigh two people on a bathroom scale, the bathroom scale may show that both weigh 75 kg. But if you weigh the two on a digital set of scales, the digital scales may show that one weighs 74.88 kg while the other weighs 75.21 kg. Could it be said that these two people have the same mass?

225

Precision is related to the care and refinement of the measuring process. It is assessed via the repeatability of the readings. Precision can be observed by duplicating a measurement (i.e. taking a number of readings of the same thing, e.g. measuring a person's height three times). When the number of repetitions of a measurement, using a specific method, is sufficiently high, a statistical measure of precision can be computed (called standard deviation).

Accuracy determines conformity with the truth or with a gold standard. Are you recording the actual value of something as you intended? If you were measuring heart rate with a heart rate monitor and it was displaying a value of 144 beats per minute (bpm), yet the real heart rate was 150 bpm the monitor would be inaccurate. **Validity** is a measure of accuracy (see below). Accuracy relates to the quality of a result, and is distinguished from precision, which relates to the quality of the operation by which the result is obtained. A measurement can be precise but inaccurate, as well as accurate but imprecise. For example, if a measurement was made with care, using a highly refined piece of equipment, repeated readings of the same quantity would agree closely and thus precision would exist (recording the mass of a person three times with readings of 80.6, 80.3 and 80.4kg is an example). However, if the instrument was calibrated incorrectly the results would be inaccurate (so, let us say the scales are consistently giving results that are 2 kg too high, the true readings would have been 78.6, 78.3 and 78.4kg).

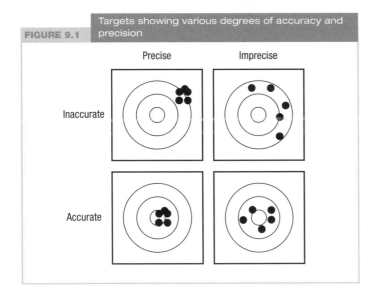

FIGURE 9.1 Targets showing various degrees of accuracy and precision

An easy way to illustrate the difference between accuracy and precision is to use the analogy of a marksman. For the marksman the truth (or the gold standard) is represented by the bull's-eye. Precision relates to the quality of an operation by which a result is obtained, and is distinguished from accuracy, which relates to the quality of the result. In Figure 9.1, the top left target, the marksman has achieved uniformity (good precision), although it is inaccurate. In the bottom right target, the marksman has grouped shots around the bull's-eye, but without great precision. The bottom left target represents both accuracy and precision. It differs from the top left target in that the degree of precision has not changed greatly, but its closeness to the bull's-eye (the truth) has improved.

Error

As can be seen by examining accuracy and precision, measurement is inexact. The amount of this in exactness is called the error. In research, an error is not a mistake; a mistake would be due to carelessness. Error is a part of measurement, and incorporates such things as the precision of the measuring equipment, its calibration and competent use. Errors are unavoidable even for the most carefully trained and determined researcher.

There are two types of errors: systematic and random. **Systematic errors** are predictable, correctable and, as such, avoidable. **Random errors**, however, are unavoidable because of imperfections in measurement systems. Random errors can be controlled and minimised, but not eliminated. Systematic errors are constant and can usually be attributed to instrument maladjustment, lack of calibration, or the environment. If they are discovered, they can be quantified and via calibration they can be corrected. Random errors are so named because they follow random patterns (the laws of chance). Although the magnitude of a random error is unknown, it can be estimated. These errors are caused by human and equipment flaws, as well as the effects of the environment on measurements. Random errors occur naturally, even when the individual is attempting to perform the procedure correctly.

Errors can result from a number of sources.

- **Natural errors** result from measurements that are made in uncontrollable environments. They are affected by such factors as temperature, humidity, atmospheric pressure, heat, wind and gravity. If you were measuring heart rate in a warm room, it would be elevated due to the requirements of thermoregulation; this would have to be taken into consideration when discussing any results.

- A second source of error is **instrumental errors**. Most measurements make use of variety of apparatus; error is always present in the measurements due to imperfections in the equipment.

- **Personal errors** are another area for consideration. Humans are nearly always directly involved with measurements and therefore human errors are inevitable.

- Finally **calculation errors** exist. Round-off errors can occur when sufficient digits are not recorded and carried through all calculations. Significant figures recorded while measuring directly affect the significant figures in calculated results.

Care needs to be taken when recording error, since error scores can be misleading. Imagine you were conducting an experiment that required subjects to move forward to a target, your error scores would have both plus and minus values. A situation could arise whereby a subject is 10 cm short of the target on the first attempt (the error would be recorded as –10 cm) and then 10 cm over on the second attempt (recorded as 10 cm). Overall, if the mean error is calculated the two error values have cancelled each other out, the mean error being 0 cm. This type of error recording is termed **relative error**. A more realistic measure would be **absolute error**. This is the average absolute deviation away from the target, irrespective of direction. Therefore, in the above example (being 10 cm short and then 10 cm over), the absolute error would be 10 cm in both cases giving a mean absolute error of 10 cm, quite a difference from the relative error of 0 cm.

Reliability

This is a measure of how repeatable a set of data is. That is, if you measured the same thing on separate occasions, would you record the same value. Imagine you were coaching a cyclist, and to monitor his training and recovery you recorded his resting heart rate each morning. Assuming your cyclist was not overtraining or suffering from an illness, you would expect the resting heart rate to remain fairly constant over a number of weeks. If you measured similar values each morning this would display good reliability. You would then be assured that your measuring technique was reliable. If the values did change, you could then be sure it was due to something other than your measuring – your athlete may be suffering from a cold, which might have elevated their resting heart rate.

The two biggest causes of unreliability in sport and exercise research are errors and **intra-subject variation**. Error, as previously mentioned, can be caused by poor or inaccurate equipment or the inability of the tester to use the equipment correctly. These can easily be overcome with adequate maintenance and the right training. The second factor affecting reliability, intra-subject variation, is harder to control. Even when measuring physiological variables using accurate equipment it is difficult to record exactly the same value due to variations within each subject. From day to day people eat different amounts, sleep for different lengths of time, undertake different levels of physical activity, have differing mental states and so on. So, resting heart rate will vary from day to day due to these factors. Researchers try and minimise these effects by standardising the testing situation. In the above example you could record heart rate at the same time each morning, before breakfast and before the person has had the opportunity to be affected by what happens that day, both physiologically and psychologically. It is also common for researchers to make repeated observations and report the average value, thus averaging out any errors or variations.

Validity

Validity refers to the meaningfulness of a set of data. Did you measure what you set out to measure? You may have decided, as a cricket coach, to measure the aerobic fitness of your players by getting them to perform the bleep test. Your results may be very reliable, but are they valid (that is, do the results of the bleep test relate to levels of fitness in your players)? This is a difficult question to answer. It is often difficult, especially in a **field setting**, to measure exactly the variable you are looking at. A cricket coach could not practically measure the aerobic capacity (VO_2max) of his players, but he could quite easily measure their performance on the bleep test and relate it back to VO_2max values (see page 314).

Choosing a valid test can be a problem in sport and exercise science research. All too often people use a test to measure certain variables, then make generalisations based on the results, which can lack validity. For example, the sit and reach test is often used to measure flexibility, however, it only incorporates leg and back flexibility. Even then there is debate about its usefulness in measuring this. So, to make statements about an athlete's overall flexibility based on one test (the sit and reach test) would be incorrect; it would not be valid. When making claims regarding measurements it is therefore very important to be specific about such claims or to have a wide range of measurements on which to base any statements.

Objectivity

If a similar measurement is obtained by two different experimenters it is said to be objective. As a measure of the number of times your heart beats, heart rate recorded at the radial artery is an objective measure. Two different people would obtain similar values when measuring somebody's pulse. It is a simple matter of counting the number of beats in a given time, then converting this to beats per minute. Measuring blood pressure (at the brachial artery with a manual sphygmomanometer) would be less objective. For example, the person measuring blood pressure has to decide the value of systolic pressure based on when they can hear a constant tapping sound (the Kortikoff sounds). Similarly, diastolic pressure is recorded on the absence of a rhythmic tapping sound. Both these points will be slightly subjective, that is, different people could record them differently.

In sport and exercise, measuring systems are designed to be objective; however, there are times when this is not always possible. Physiological measures tend to display the greatest objectivity. The most difficult areas in which to gain objectivity are when an opinion is required or when people are expected to judge performance. For example, scoring in gymnastics can be subjective. Detailed scoring systems, involving a number of judges, have been developed to try and overcome this problem.

REVISION QUESTIONS

1) Give two examples of the different types of data.

2) How do accuracy and precision differ? Give a sporting example to illustrate your answer.

3) Explain the difference between absolute and relative error.

★ STUDENT ACTIVITY

Accuracy/precision and validity/reliability

The following is a set of body fat percentage values recorded on a group of people using body fat callipers. Body fat was measured at two different times during the day. Body fat was also recorded via under-water weighing (considered to give a truer value of % body fat).

Subject	1	2	3	4	5	6	7	8
Body fat % (callipers a.m.)	22	15	13	11	26	26	27	13
Body fat % (callipers p.m.)	21	15	14	10	24	25	27	12
Body fat % (under water)	25	17	14	12	28	29	31	16

1 How could you determine the precision of the body fat callipers?
2 How precise are they?
3 How could you establish how accurate they are?
4 How accurate are they?
5 Review the results of the body fat callipers in terms of reliability and validity.
6 How could reliability and validity be assessed?
7 How do reliability and validity relate to accuracy and precision?

COLLECTING DATA

Ethical and legal issues

A lot of testing, measuring and research in sport and exercise science involves working with other people (athletes, clients of a health club, etc.). It is important to respect the rights of other people and ensure they are not negatively affected by your tests or work. This is especially true when working with children. Your subjects should be made aware of their right to withdraw from a test or programme of exercise. The decision to take part in an activity is down to the individual (if they decide to stop the test, then you must comply with their wishes). It is therefore necessary to explain the full procedures and plans of an activity, and inform them of others who maybe involved in the activity. This will enable subjects to be aware of what is happening, and will ensure that an individual's performance on a test is limited only by what is being measured, and not by a lack of understanding in how to perform the test. It is also essential to make clear that any information taken or recorded about a subject will be confidential.

It may be necessary to prove that the above considerations have been adhered to. For example, you may be conducting some research at a local health club, and one of the clients is injured while undergoing a fitness test. The manager of the club will want to know if it was your testing that caused the injury. In such a case it is not only important that you have stuck to certain guidelines while testing, but that you can show this to be the case. This is the reason that informed consent forms are used in research and testing situations. An **informed consent** form is a signed agreement demonstrating that the subject has both been informed of the test (told of what is going to happen) and has given their consent (agreed to undertake the test). A good informed consent form should outline the risks and discomforts associated with the tests, along with any expected benefits from taking part in the testing. The form should also highlight that permission to take part in the test is voluntary and that, having given initial consent to take part, the subject is free to withdraw at any time. The procedures of the test should be clearly explained and should be understandable to the subject. For example, with children or in cases were the test is very detailed or complicated, the procedures should be simplified. The subjects should be told to ask about anything they do not understand, or if they have any concerns regarding the testing. Finally, it is crucial that the subject signs the form to say they have read and understood it and are willing to take part in the testing.

Data protection

As mentioned previously, any information on a subject, athlete or client should be kept confidential. This is in line with the Data Protection Act, which was last updated in 1998. Records (hard copy or computerised) should be kept where only authorised personnel can access them. When reporting information to third parties, personal details should be omitted. For example, if you were reporting back to a group of athletic coaches regarding some research you had done on strength training, you would not include in your report or presentation the names of the subjects you had used. It would be sufficient for you to give general background information, such as age, gender, ability level, years of training and so on.

Treatment, variables

When collecting information or data you will have a research problem or question you are trying to answer. A research problem is a statement that asks what relation exists between two or more variables. For instance, what effect does exercise have on heart rate? Remember, a variable is something measurable, in this case the amount of exercise and the subject's heart rate. The thing that you are trying to affect, and that you are uncertain of, is called the **dependent variable** (in this example, heart rate). It is dependant upon the other variable, that is, your heart rate depends on the amount of exercise you do. The variable you have control over is the **independent variable** (exercise, in this case). The independent variable is termed the **treatment**; you control it to determine what effect it has on the dependant variable.

Research design

There are a number of steps involved in designing a research project.

1   First, you need to develop the problem or arrive at the question(s) you want answers to (e.g. How does exercise affect heart rate?).

2   Step two is to formulate the **hypothesis**. What you think will happen, based on previous evidence that you have researched (e.g. heart rate increases with exercise).

3   The next step would be to gather information or collect the data (e.g. measure heart rate during exercise).

4   Finally you will need to analyse and interpret the results to see if your expectations are correct (e.g. Does heart rate go up and by how much?).

Good research problems should:

❂   be a question

❂   be open to testing

❂   be of interest

❂   be of practical value.

The most common type of research design is to have two groups, one undergoing a treatment and the other being the **control group** (having no treatment). Both groups are measured on a variable(s) pre- and post-treatment. This is termed a pre-test post-test research design. For example, if you wanted to determine if relaxation reduced anxiety before an examination, you could have two groups. Group one would receive relaxation treatment, while group two would have no treatment. It would then be possible to create the hypothesis for this investigation. Rather than just saying relaxation affects anxiety it is usual in research methods to state three hypotheses: the null hypothesis, the alternative hypothesis and the directional hypotheses. In the above example the hypothesis would be expressed as follows:

- ✪ **Null hypothesis**: there will be no difference in pre-examination anxiety between groups one and two.

- ✪ **Alternative hypothesis**: there will be a difference in pre-examination anxiety between the two groups.

- ✪ **Directional hypothesis**: group one (who undergo relaxation) will rate their pre-examination anxiety lower than will group two (the control group).

Not all research uses the pre-test post-test design. Sometimes there may not be a treatment, or not one you impose. You might wish to examine how much sport and physical education children do in schools and the effect it has on the sport they take part in outside of school. In this case the dependent variable (the thing you are measuring) is how much sport is played outside of school. The independent variable (normally the treatment or the thing you change) would be the amount of sport and physical education done in school. Obviously you cannot change this; it is determined by the school, local education authority and the government. What you can do is compare one school with another, one area with another, or even compare countries (e.g. France v England). This is termed a **comparative study** and is more common in the sociological area of sport and exercise.

A similar method is to compare evidence, data or information over time, instead of comparing one region with another. You may wish to see how the amount of physical education in schools has changed over the years. This method works if you have the data or can obtain it, but in some instances for what you hope to measure there may be little or no data. If this is the case, you would have to set up a study to examine things in the future. Let us imagine you wish to see the effect of school sport and physical education on the health of children in your area. However, you have no information on the current state of health of the children. What you would have to do is monitor the sport and physical education participated in by the children, and their level of health. You would have to do this over a period of time to see if their health improved, declined or stayed the same. This type of study is called a **longitudinal study**. It is often used in the study of health and disease. Unfortunately, it requires time for any effects of changes to be seen – some longitudinal research can last for over 30 years. Therefore, this method would not be suitable for a small research project (the sort of project outlined in Chapter 2).

Questionnaire design

A widespread method of obtaining data in both qualitative and quantitative research is the questionnaire. A questionnaire is a survey used in research in which information is obtained by asking subjects to respond to questions. The major limitation with a questionnaire is that the results consist of what people say they do or believe, and this is not always reliable. Therefore, careful planning is needed to ensure valid results. Sometimes researchers use techniques to try and identify whether people are telling the truth. This is difficult, but one way it can be done in a questionnaire is by repeating questions or asking very similar questions. If a person is telling the truth or answering each question properly (and not just skimming through the questions) you would expect the same answer to these repeated or similar questions.

It is important to consider what you wish to obtain from the questionnaire (i.e. what information you hope to collect). Careful consideration also needs to be given to the actual questions asked. For example, there are two general types of questions that could be asked in a questionnaire, closed questions and open questions. A **closed question** is one where you only give a certain number of options and the respondent has to pick from them. An example would be 'How do you rate your fitness?', with the possible answers being; not at all fit, slightly fit, moderately fit, very fit or extremely fit. You know the answer will be from this list. With an open question there is no such list; the question is open-ended (e.g. How could you improve your level of fitness?). In this case the range of possible answers is almost endless. A further concern is the order in which you put the questions. Often questionnaires collect general information first, things like age, gender, job, sport played and so on. This gets people in to the habit of answering the questions. They are more likely then to complete the questionnaire. If the questions become more difficult or detailed it may be necessary to give examples. A major problem with research involving questionnaires is people either not completing the questionnaire sufficiently or not completing it at all.

To obtain the best results from a questionnaire it should be relatively short, as you are more likely to get a response. You also need to think about how you are going to present your results. A lot of open questions may give you lots of information in return, but this will be hard to summarise in a table or graph. Too many open questions are difficult to analyse and are time consuming. Numerical data is easier to analyse, so you should try and code or score the possible answers (e.g. yes = 2, no = 1). There are different ways that questions can be coded. **Scaled questions** use what is called a Likert scale, which is a level of agreement or rating with a given statement. Using the previous example on fitness, the following is a scaled question: How do you rate your fitness?

Not at all fit	Slightly fit	Moderately fit	Very fit	Extremely fit
1	2	3	4	5

With a scaled question you are looking for one answer that best fits the level the respondent feels they are at. It maybe that you are seeking more than one answer, in which case you could use a ranking questions. **Ranking questions** place alternatives in order. An example could be, 'Which sport do you enjoy participating in most?', where 1 is the most preferred and 5 is the least, and where the options are basketball, rugby, cricket, running and cycling. The respondent would then rate each sport from 1 to 5 based on their level of enjoyment of that sport. **Categorical questions** are used when a discreet answer is required, so a choice of categories is offered. For example:

Have you ever been skiing?	Yes	No
	1	2

In this example, only two choices are needed – you have either been skiing or you have not. If necessary, further categories can be used, such as a 'do not know' option.

When designing a questionnaire you are trying to make it as easy as possible to fill in, but also easy for you to report the results accurately and clearly. You should try and avoid **leading questions**, that is, ones where you are suggesting the answer in the question. 'Do you think football players receive too much money?' could be considered a leading question, as it almost implies that footballers are paid too much money. Also to be avoided are unclear terms. If a question begins with 'usually' or 'mostly', how often would you take this to mean? Once a day, once a week, or may be something different? Similarly, try not to use jargon or technical terms. If you ask a member of the public, 'How many times per week do you take part in aerobic exercise?' they may not understand the term aerobic. They may not answer the question or may answer it incorrectly. Not only do the questions need to be made very clear, but how you want them answered. Will there be tick boxes or do respondents circle a number.

Once you have compiled your questionnaire you should examine its usefulness. Try it out on a small group of people first (not the ones you aim to use it on later). Ask yourself some simple questions. Could it cause offence? Check the wording of the questions. Are all alternatives considered? If you ask 'Which sports do you enjoy?' and then proceed to give a list, what if somebody wants to put a sport you have not listed? You could include 'other' in the list or ask 'Which of the following sports do you enjoy?'. Is the response easy? People tend to fill in questionnaires as quickly as they can; they do not want to spend time having to complete the answers. Are there any overlapping categories? Asking how old somebody is and then having answers of 16–20, 20–24, for example, is annoying to a 20 year old. Which category are they in?

STUDENT ACTIVITY

Questionnaire design

1 Design a questionnaire to investigate an area of sport/exercise (e.g. exercise participation).

2 Use the questionnaire to obtain data.

3 Write a report of the results of the questionnaire and provide a brief discussion of these results.

4 Prepare a presentation of the results of your investigation (this can be done individually or as a group). Things to discuss in your presentation are:

a) an explanation of the questionnaire (why you have asked certain questions, why they are in that order)

b) the scoring/coding system; present the data in the most effective format (tables, graphs, etc.)

c) an analysis of your results with constructive criticism (e.g. whether they could be improved, whether they are valid and reliable), and remember to have some implications at the end (what you have found, if you have any recommendations).

Interviews and observations

Questionnaires are used to collect general information from relatively large groups of people. With smaller groups (or with individuals) it is possible to gain more detailed information via an interview. Interviews are a method of information gathering used almost exclusively with qualitative research. An interview is normally a series of open-ended questions asked by the interviewer to the interviewee, and takes place face to face. To aid the interviewer the questions will be written down in advance. Supplementary questions can be asked if needed.

Information is usually recorded via a tape recorder or videotape. A tape recorder is less obtrusive (some people feel nervous faced with a video camera); however, the use of a videotape can give some non-verbal information that may prove beneficial. If a tape recorder or video camera is not available, the interviewer will have to record responses by hand. To become a good interviewer requires both ability and practice. If the answers obtained are to be valid it is essential that the respondent is relaxed and at ease. It is vital that the answers given are genuine and, for this reason, it is important that the interviewer does not influence the response by the nature of their questioning or even by their presence. As with questionnaires, the researcher is relying on what the subject says, which may or may not be the truth. Comparable techniques, as used with questionnaires, can be used to test the validity of a person's answer (i.e. repeated or similar questions can be asked to see if the answers are the same).

A further means of gaining information or data for research is to observe the subject in a given situation. Observations are common in psychology-based research – seeing what a person will do in a certain situation. This method is used because it is less obtrusive then administering a questionnaire or asking questions in an interview. Coaching is another area that relies on observations for obtaining information. In some sports, elaborate systems have been developed to code categories of actions or behaviour. These systems can be used by researchers to analyse coach or player behaviour, in addition to being used by the coach themselves to help players improve performance. A good example of this is in football, where notational analysis systems designed to examine the amount of activity (walking, running, jumping, etc.) undertaken by players of different positions can be used to devise individualised training programmes for players.

Sampling

In sport and exercise, when we take measurements for research purposes we are doing so for a group of people. If it were possible we would measure the entire population. The **population** is the whole group a researcher is interested in; the people the researcher wishes to draw conclusions about. If you measure the entire population and calculate a value like the average height, this is called a **parameter**. However, especially with large populations, it is more practical to examine a sample of the population (a smaller group). A value (the average height for example) which is based on a sample of a population is referred to as a **statistic**.

STUDENT ACTIVITY

Interview

1   Write a list of approximately 20 questions that you would like to ask a sports person of your choice.

2   Take part in a role play exercise where a fellow student pretends to be your chosen sports person. Conduct the interview using whichever method you wish to record the answers to your questions.

3   Write an evaluation of the interview stating what went well and how it could have been improved.

One method of selecting a sample is random sampling. **Random sampling** is a sampling technique where a group of subjects (a sample) is selected for study from a larger group (a population) by chance and all individuals have an equal chance of being included in the sample. With the use of random sampling, the chance of bias is reduced.

Bias refers to how far a statistic lies from the parameter it is estimating, that is, the error which occurs when estimating a value from a sample of a population. In other words, the value you obtain from a sample tends to be incorrect. The difference between the actual value (the parameter) and what you measure (the statistic) is called the **standard error**. The bigger your sample size, the less the standard error will be. This is because the greater your sample, the closer you are getting to measuring the whole population.

Numbers and units

When trying to measure the value or quantity of something, it is necessary to have a standard against which to compare. A unit is a standard by which a measured value can be described. There are two different sets of units used in measurements: British Engineering units (the imperial system) and the metric or SI system (*le Systéme International*). Most countries use the metric system (see Table 9.1), including Britain. In the United States, the British system is often used (for example, in boxing the Americans refer to a fight's weight (mass) in pounds (lbs)). However, for consistency in sport and exercise science research, the metric system is used.

The fundamental units are not always convenient (i.e. expressing the mass of a golf ball in kilograms is ridiculous), so prefixes are used to change the size of the unit (see Table 9.2). For example, 1000 metres (or 10^3 m) can be expressed as 1 km (kilometre).

Another important factor in recording a measurement, besides the unit, is the number of significant figures in the value. Significant figures should not be confused with decimal places. For example, 9.87 seconds is recorded to two decimal places, but has three significant figures. When using significant figures in calculations, the number of significant figures in the result should be the same as the number in the least precise measurement. For example: $4.28 \times 8.3 = 35.524$ before correction; after correction of significant figures, the result should be 36, since the limiting term (8.3) has only two significant figures.

Table 9.1 The SI system of measurement

Variable	Unit	Symbol
mass	kilograms	kg
length	metres	m
volume	litres	l
time	seconds	s
electric current	ampere	A
temperature	kelvin	K

Table 9.2 Common prefixes

Prefix	Symbol	Factor
giga	G	10^9
mega	M	10^6
kilo	k	10^3
centi	c	10^{-2}
milli	m	10^{-3}

Recording and displaying data

For numeric variables, one way to summarise the values is to graph them as a frequency distribution. One type of frequency distribution is a scatter plot, which shows a point for the number of times each value occurs. However, it is more common to show the frequencies as vertical bars rather than points, in which case the figure is called a histogram (see Figure 9.2). The most important consideration when displaying data is the presentation. The data should be summarised and displayed in the most effect format (there is no need to include all the raw data). Tables of data should include units and must have an appropriate title (which, by convention, is always placed above the table). Graphs should also include units and labels and have a title. Any picture, photograph or diagram including graphs and histograms but not tables, is referred to as a figure.

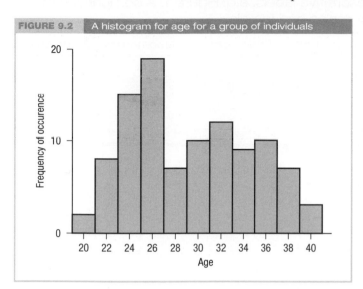

FIGURE 9.2 A histogram for age for a group of individuals

STUDENT ACTIVITY

Displaying data

This activity should enable you to enter data into tables and to produce graphs. Based on the data in the table below, create tables with the following columns (in a spreadsheet, e.g. Excel or SPSS).

For male subjects:

> Subject no | Height | Body mass | BMI | Endomorph | Mesomorph | Ectomorph

For female subjects:

> Subject no | Height | Body Mass | BMI | Endomorph | Mesomorph | Ectomorph

✪ The data should be to one decimal place (e.g. 84.0).

✪ The last row in each table should contain an average of each column.

✪ The headings and averages should stand out clearly.

✪ Each table should be given a title to be placed above the table, e.g. Table 1. Anthropometric data for male subjects.

continues overleaf

continued

Using the graph/chart option in a spreadsheet, produce a pie chart(s) to show average somatotype values (endomorph, mesomorph and ectomorph) for male and female subjects. The chart(s) should contain a title, actual values and descriptive labels. e.g. Figure 1. A comparison of average somatotypes for males and females.

Gender	Height (cm)	Mass (kg)	BMI	Endomorphy	Mesomorphy	Ectomorphy
M	186	80	23.4	2	4	3
M	187	74	21.2	1.5	2	4
M	190	82	22.7	2	4.5	3
M	177	72	23.0	2	4	4.5
M	188	78	22.1	3.5	3	2.5
M	176	97	31.3	5.5	8.5	0.5
M	185	89	26.0	3.5	5.5	2
M	179	66	20.6	1	4.5	4
M	192	84	22.7	3.5	3.5	3.5
M	190	85	23.5	4	5	3.5
F	165	55	20.8	3.5	2.5	3.5
F	163	75	20.2	4	3	1
F	165	51	19.0	2.5	3.5	4
F	168	51	18.7	1.5	2.5	4.5
F	156	57	23.4	4	2.5	1

REVISION QUESTIONS

1) Explain what informed consent is.

2) Write an example of an informed consent form.

3) How does the Data Protection Act relate to research methods?

4) What are null, alternative and directional hypotheses?

5) Give an example of each type of hypothesis.

6) Explain what the benefits are of carrying out research using questionnaires.

7) What are the drawbacks with research that uses interviews to gain data?

STUDENT ACTIVITY

Central tendency

Choose an easily measurable variable, such as shoe size or height, then ask each member of your class to find out what the following class values are for your chosen variable:

mean

mode

median.

With a group of data, rather than displaying all the data, it is possible to use one number to represent all the data. This number is the average or central tendency. The three most commonly used measures of central tendency are the following.

1   **The mean**, which this is the sum of the values divided by the number of values. This is the most common type of average. For example, the mean of the following numbers: 8, 12, 16 and 24, would be calculated as follows:

$$\frac{8 + 12 + 16 + 24}{4} = 15.$$

2   **The median** is the value which divides the values into two equal halves, with half of the values being lower than the median and half higher than the median. If there are an odd number of values, the median is the middle value. With an even number of values, the median is the arithmetic mean (see above) of the two middle values. The median of the following five numbers: 23, 47, 50, 67 and 88, is 50.

3   **The mode** is the most frequently occurring value (or values) in the set. For individuals having the following ages, 17, 18, 19, 20, 20, 20, 23 and 27, the mode is 20.

For nominal data (such as gender), the mode is the only valid measure of central tendency. For ordinal data (such as league position), only the mode and median can be used.

Dispersion

Some statistics give an idea of spread, variation or dispersion of the numbers. When a researcher talks about spread in a set of numbers, they may be referring to the difference in the scores (e.g. weight) across the group. Equally, the set of numbers could represent the weight of a single subject measured many times. The terms 'between-subject variation' and 'within-subject variation' are used to distinguish between these two types of spread. The simplest measure of spread is the **range**, expressed either as the biggest and smallest number in the data (e.g. 67–74), or as the difference between the biggest and smallest (e.g. 7). The range is a bad measure of spread because it is dependent on the size of your sample: the more numbers, the bigger the range is likely to be. It is also affected by outliers (see below). Two measures of spread that avoid these problems are the **standard deviation** (SD) and **percentile ranges**. Standard deviation is a measure of dispersion describing the spread of scores around the mean. The mean and standard deviation are often written as mean ± SD (e.g. 77.2 ± 1.8 kg). It has a complicated definition: take the distance of each number from the mean, square it, average the result, then take the square root. In short, it is the root mean square of the distances (or differences) from mean. The best way to think about the standard deviation is that about two-thirds of the values of a variable are found within one deviation each side of the mean (for normally distributed data, see below). Inter-quartile range is similar to range, but it discounts the top and bottom 25% of the data. The type of dispersion used depends on the measure of central tendency. With mean, the standard deviation is normally used. For the median it is the inter-quartile range, and with the mode it is range.

STUDENT ACTIVITY

Central tendency and dispersion

1 For the following set of data, calculate or determine the mean, median and mode (this can be done easily in a spreadsheet).
2 Comment on why the values are different. It may help to plot a frequency distribution (histogram).
3 In addition, calculate or determine the standard deviation, inter-quartile range and range (use a spreadsheet).

Subject	1	2	3	4	5	6	7	8	9	10	11
Age	22	19	16	21	23	27	24	19	26	19	17

Normal distribution

Normally distributed data looks like that in Figure 9.3, that is, it peaks in the middle. In this example, if we measured IQ for a sample of the population we could say that the majority of people have an average IQ, while a small number have high and low values.

Normally distributed data is typically bell-shaped when graphed (see Figure 9.3). The distribution is theoretical because the height of the curve is defined by a mathematical formula. In a true normal distribution, the mean, median and mode are all the same value. If the distribution is asymmetrical the data is not normally distributed, which can be due to skewness (the peak is more to the left or right) or kurtosis (the curve excessively peaked or flat). A **negative skew** is asymmetry in a distribution in which the scores are bunched to the right side of the centre, while a **positive skew** is asymmetry in a distribution in which the scores are bunched to the left side of the centre. A **latykurtic curve** is when the distribution is flatter than a normal distribution. This is to say that there are more cases in the extremes of the distribution than would normally be the case. The opposite of this is **leptokurtic**: this is when a distribution is more peaked than a normal distribution; there are more cases concentrated close to the mean than in a normal distribution. Whether or not the data is normally distributed determines which measure of central tendency and dispersion to select. The other information that is needed is the level of measurement (i.e. interval, ratio, nominal – see Table 9.3).

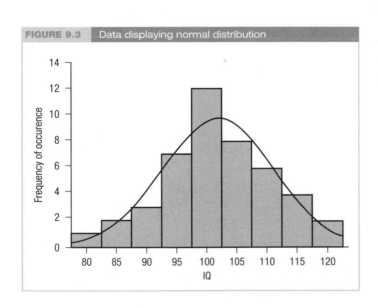

FIGURE 9.3 Data displaying normal distribution

Table 9.3 Which measure of central tendency to select based on the distribution of the data and the level of measurement.

Central tendency	Data
Mean	interval/ratio data and normally distributed
Median	data that is not normally distributed (e.g. skewed)
Mode	nominal data and normally distributed

There is a general rule that applies with a normal or bell-shaped distribution. Starting with the average (the centre of the distribution), if you go left and right one standard deviation, you will include approximately 65% of the cases in the distribution. If you go left and right two standard deviations, you will include approximately 95% of the cases. If you go plus or minus three standard deviations, you will include 99% of the cases.

Outliers

Outliers are unusual data values. They can occur due to data recording or entry errors. Alternatively, they may be caused by some rare event or extreme observation (such as a thermometer left in direct sunlight, or a subject who has an abrupt change in heart rate). The problem with outliers is that some statistics (e.g. the mean) can be distorted, which can lead to faulty conclusions. In such cases the median would be a more dependable measure of central tendency, as it is not affected greatly by outliers. There is a temptation to ignore outliers, but only as a final option should you delete them. This could be done if you find there are genuine errors (results that should not have been recorded) that cannot be corrected. If you have any uncertainty, you can include results both with and without outliers to see how much they differ.

STUDENT PRACTICAL

Normal distribution

Aim

The aims of this activity are to determine if data is normally distributed and to produce an appropriate measure of central tendency.

Method

1 Enter the data from the table into a spreadsheet (e.g. Excel or SPSS), coding where appropriate.

2 Produce a variable to illustrate the difference between resting heart rate and maximum heart rate.

3 Sort your data by the age variable (descending order).

4 For each variable, look at the data and determine the level of measurement (e.g. nominal, ordinal, interval/ratio).

continues overleaf

continued

5   For variables that are at the interval/ratio level, determine whether they are normally distributed. To do this you will need to produce a histogram: if you are using Excel you will have to make a new table from which you can create the histogram; in SPSS you can just select 'histogram'. From this information you can establish the appropriate measure of central tendency and dispersion for each variable.

Age	Sport	Heart rate (rest)	Heart rate (max)
18	Badminton	80	200
19	Football	81	180
19	Hockey	88	182
18	Climbing	72	200
20	Hockey	66	189
29	Football	77	175
25	Hockey	72	200
19	Hockey	69	176
18	Football	72	190
19	Hockey	69	191
19	Hockey	79	192
19	Hockey	62	188
18	Hockey	62	193
19	Football	79	189
19	Badminton	63	193
19	Climbing	87	183
20	Climbing	68	194
19	Golf	49	183
19	Climbing	76	198
20	Badminton	57	194

Statistical tests

Numerical analysis of data is called statistics. **Descriptive statistics** are just that, describing data (i.e. central tendency and dispersion). **Inferential statistics** are more in depth – rather than just describing data they examine relationships and differences in data. They can be used to determine the answer to your research question or your hypothesis. Inferential statistics analyse whether the null hypothesis is true or false (at a given level of significance). Relationships look at how one thing affects another and are analysed via correlations. Differences determine if one group (or set of data) is different from another. There are numerous difference tests that will be explained letter.

Correlations

To measure if two things are related, a correlation can be performed. Correlation means association or relationship. For example, if the question 'Is heart rate related to environmental temperature?' is asked, it can be answered with a test of correlation. The correlation will give an exact quantification of the association between the two factors. This value or number is called the **correlation coefficient** and is commonly symbolised by the letter **r**. If two variables are in perfect association, so that as one increases so does the other (without exception), they have a **perfect positive correlation**. The correlation coefficient (r) to represent this is +1. If there is absolutely no relationship r is 0. However, if the association is inverse, where one goes up as the other goes down, this is described as a **negative correlation**. For this, r is denoted by –1. Thus, r can be any value between +1 and –1 (see Figure 9.4).

FIGURE 9.4 Correlation coefficients

```
  |_____|_____|
  -1                  0                 +1
Inverse              No               Totally
relationship     relationship         related
```

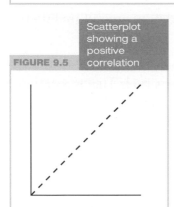

FIGURE 9.5 Scatterplot showing a positive correlation

Visually, the correlation or association can be displayed by a scattergram or scatterplot, as shown in Figure 9.5.

It must be remembered that a high correlation, association or relationship is just that; it does not necessarily mean that one variable causes the other. Association does not mean causation.

Having measured r, how can it be interpreted? What does it mean? When a correlation is performed, besides an r value being reported, a probability or **significance value** is given. This significance value is given as a decimal (e.g. 0.10). This value indicates the probability of what you are testing being true or untrue. For example, if you were testing a relationship, a significance value of 0.10 would mean that 10 times in 100 you would be wrong if you said there was a relationship (it could be due to luck). Which means 90 times in 100 you would be correct. In social science (e.g. sports science, psychology, etc.) the accepted significance value is 0.05 (being wrong 5 times in 100). If the significance value is higher than 0.05 then there is no relationship (or at least, it is not significant). Statistically, the specific significance value of 0.05 is written as $p < .05$, which means the probability must be less than 5 in 100.

A further measure that can be calculated is the **coefficient of determination**. This indicates the amount of influence one variable has over another. The coefficient of determination is equal to r^2 and is often given as a percentage (e.g. .50 is 50%). For a correlation of .70 (r), the coefficient of determination would be .49 (r^2), which means 49% of the variance in a factor is due to the other variable – obviously 51% is due to other things. Returning to the question, 'Is heart rate related to environmental temperature?', a coefficient of determination of 0.49 would suggest that 49% of the variance (change) in heart rate is due to changes in environmental temperature, and 51% of the variance is due to other factors.

Pearson product-moment correlation

A Pearson product-moment correlation is one type of test that can be performed. In order to do this, a number of criteria must be met. The underlying assumptions are as follows.

- **Data** must be from **related pairs**, i.e. it should be collected from the same subject (e.g. height and mass from the same person)

- **Data** should be **interval or ratio** (explained previously).

- Each variable should be normally distributed (**normality**). There are a number of ways to explore this e.g. skewness and kurtosis

✪ The relationship of the two variables must be linear (**linearity**). Linearity is assessed using a scatter plot, and is determined from the shape of the data: if it forms a straight line (roughly), it is said to be linear.

✪ Variability in scores should be roughly the same (**homoscedascity**). Homoscedascity is also assessed using a scatter plot. If the scores cluster uniformly around a straight line through the points, then homoscedascity can be assumed.

If the assumptions for a Pearson product-moment correlation are not met then a Spearman rank-order correlation is performed.

If the relationship is significant, the statistics would be reported as ($r = .844$, $p < .05$). The Pearson product-moment correlation r value is .844. That is a strong positive relationship between the two variables measured. The significance value is less than .05; this means the relationship is statistically significant (it is meaningful).

★ STUDENT ACTIVITY

Correlation

An exercise physiologist is interested to see if there is a relationship between maximum volume of oxygen consumed ($maxVO_2$) as measured in a physiology lab and marathon performance (best time to run a marathon). The results collected are given below.

MaxVO$_2$ (ml per kg per min)	80.56	75.48	69.23	56.12	75.82	63.45	68.04	64.67	69.75	76.91
Marathon performance (mins)	141	138	172	149	154	165	161	155	144	134

1 Identify the null and alternative hypotheses for this inquiry.
2 Determine which test of correlation is appropriate and run the test in EXCEL, SPSS or a similar spreadsheet.
3 From your results explain the value of the correlation coefficient and what it means.
4 Which hypothesis should be accepted and why?
5 What might affect the results?

Difference tests

Difference tests can be divided into two types: parametric and non-parametric statistics. **Parametric** statistics are used when the data is normally distributed and interval/ratio level. **Non-parametric** statistics are often referred to as distribution-free statistics, as they are used when the data may not demonstrate the characteristics of normality (i.e. follow a normal distribution). They are used with nominal data, where the response set can be converted to counts of events, and the measurement scale is ignored. As in all research designs, there are specific assumptions which underlie the selection of the various statistical procedures.

Difference tests are evaluative procedures for studying the effect of a given treatment on a randomly selected group of individuals, for example, how training affects fitness levels. Following the imposition of the experimental condition (treatment), the researcher tests whether the experimental condition was effective by observing the distributions of the responses on a selected dependent measure (fitness). The results of difference tests are reported in a similar way to correlations, but instead of referring to a significant relationship, a significant difference is talked about. For example, there is a significant difference (t =1.352, p < .05) in heart rate between a group that does exercise and a group that does not.

With parametric data the most common difference tests are t-tests. An **independent t-test** is used when investigating differences between groups (the samples are independent, hence the name). The **dependent t-test** is used when the data is from the same group (paired samples) and you are examining a difference within the group.

If the data is not parametric, then t-tests can not be performed, so alternative tests must be used. The Mann-Whitney U test is a non-parametric difference test that can be used with different groups (independent samples). The Wilcoxon matched-pairs test is a non-parametric test that can be used with paired samples (data from one group).

The Chi square test is a further non-parametric test that is used to compare observed frequency in a group with expected group frequency (the frequency due to a chance occurrence). It requires nominal data from independent categories with a large sample size.

STUDENT ACTIVITY

t-test

A fitness instructor runs two different circuit training classes. She thinks that one class may more strenuous than the other. She measures the heart rates of the members of each of the two classes (no one attends both classes). The average heart rate for each person during the session is given below (values are in bpm).

Class 1	123	132	117	143	129	136	118	134	111	127	124	115	128	130	122	112
Class 2	136	128	136	131	115	117	151	147	126	135	128	134	116	129	136	127

1   Identify the null and alternative hypotheses for this inquiry.
2   Determine which t-test is appropriate and run the test in Excel, SPSS or a similar spreadsheet package.
3   From your results, explain what the significance value means.
4   Which hypothesis should be accepted and why?
5   What might affect the results?

REVISION QUESTIONS

1) Distinguish between the mean, median and mode.
2) How do you explain the different types of central tendency?
3) Explain the concept of dispersion.
4) What is a correlation and how is it determined?
5) What are the different measures of correlation?

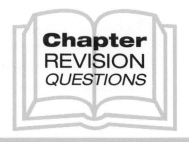

Chapter REVISION QUESTIONS

1) Explain the following terms: reliability, validity and objectivity.
2) What are the ethical issues involved in research in sport?
3) How would you go about designing a questionnaire?
4) What is normally distributed data?
5) Outline the use of a variety of statistical tests.

SUGGESTED FURTHER READING

Clegg, F. (1993) *Simple Statistics: A Course Book for the Social Sciences.* Cambridge University Press

Silverman, D. (2001) *Doing Qualitative Research: A Practical Guide.* Sage Publications

Thomas, J. R. and Nelson, J. K. (2001) *Research Methods in Physical Activity.* 4th Edition. Illinois: Human Kinetics

SOCIAL ASPECTS OF SPORT

This chapter looks to examine sport in its social setting. Sports exist due to the actions of human beings who play, administer and spectate sport. We cannot understand how sports have developed to the stage they have today without examining society and the people who make up this society. This chapter will cover the following:

- ✪ the development of modern sports

- ✪ sociological theories and how they can be applied to sport

- ✪ the influence of the media in sport

- ✪ current issues in sport.

Sports in certain forms have been played as long as humans have walked on the earth. There is no activity more fundamentally simple than kicking or throwing a ball. However, by the twenty-first century the interest and importance of sport has grown beyond all recognition. International sports festivals such as the football World Cup and the Olympic Games draw the attention of the world, and television audiences larger than for any other occasion. Sports have developed over time and we can see that the values of society are reflected in sport. For example, as society has become affluent, so has sport; as society has tackled issues of sexism, racism and illicit drug use, so has sport. Sport and society are inextricably interlinked and by studying the development of society we can see how this has affected sports; likewise sports will mirror the society within which they are played.

THE DEVELOPMENT OF MODERN SPORTS

Sports in their current forms are fairly recent developments. It was mainly the last quarter of the nineteenth century that saw sporting bodies lay down rules and use officials to implement these rules. However, there is a wealth of belief regarding the prominence of sport as a leisure activity in many early societies, although at times the evidence to prove this is scarce or short on detail.

Records from the Egyptians (circa 2100BC) suggest that wrestling was prevalent, and later on the use of chariots for racing and hunting as sport. The Minoan Crete society (circa 2000–1400BC) revealed pictorial evidence of forms of boxing, bullfighting and competitive dancing. The Mycenaean Empire (circa

1600–1200BC) has a lot of written evidence taken primarily from the classic works of Homer, which are *The Odyssey* and *The Iliad*. The sports presented include hunting, chariot racing, spear throwing and archery contests, all activities related to improving men's skills for war.

The Ancient Greeks were the first society to show evidence of organised sports festivals. The Ancient Olympics were held regularly over a period of over one thousand years, from 776BC to 393AD, and had a strong religious element. Although the Games were held over five days, two and a half of these were given over to religious ceremonies. The sports were again of military origin and included foot racing, chariot racing, horse racing, racing in armour, boxing, wrestling and the 'pancration', which was combat in full armour. Needless to say, the boxing, wrestling and pancration featured high levels of violence and were brutal contests of strength.

Around this time, we get the first mention of football as a sport which was being played in China during the Han Dynasty (206BC–25AD). This sport, called tsu-chu, was indeed played by kicking a ball, however, to say it was football is a gross misrepresentation. Soccer, as we know it, emerged in nineteenth-century England and is a sport defined by its specific rules, such as eleven men on each side, the use of hands by the goalkeeper only and the complex offside rule.

The ancient Romans were famed for their sports such as gladiatorial contests and chariot races; there is also evidence that the Roman baths housed facilities for ball games of a type. The gladiators held very powerful positions in Roman society, due to their sports skills, not dissimilar to the position held by top-level footballers in this country who are regarded as role models.

By the Middle Ages, the focus of the history of sport moves to Europe and, in particular, England. Forms of folk football, folk cricket and golf were being played in parts of Britain; in reality they only bear a passing resemblance to the sports we know today. They were excessively violent and rules were usually agreed locally.

This section aims to concentrate on two distinct periods in Britain: sport before the Industrial Revolution and sport after the Industrial Revolution. The Industrial Revolution covers a specific period of time from 1780 to 1850. In 1800 only one in five people lived in towns; however, by 1851, for the first time over 50% of the population lived in urban environments. By the 1880s this had risen to 75% of the population. This was a period of major development in society, because the ways people lived and worked were changing. Rather than being a country where people lived predominantly in the countryside and farmed areas of land, Britain became a society of city dwellers who worked for a wage in factories. This had a profound effect on leisure time and the form that sports took. It led to rapid changes in sports, with sports taking on the features we recognise in these activities today.

Pre-industrialised sports forms

Medieval England

The period from 1066 to 1485 is commonly known as the Middle Ages. At this time Britain's population mainly lived in rural areas, although there were a growing number of townspeople who worked mainly as lawyers, doctors and merchants. Society was split into three specific social groups: the nobility, the bourgeoisie (business people who were gaining wealth) and peasants. It was a period of growing prosperity because trade between merchants was booming due to the lack of conflict between lords and landowners.

Sport in the Middle Ages was split down class lines. The peasants had their folk games, such as football; the bourgeoisie had archery and crossbow tournaments, and the nobility had their tournaments, between medieval knights. Sport did not cross class barriers in terms of participation and spectating.

Tudor and Stuart periods

Henry Tudor's victory at the Battle of Bosworth field is the event that signalled the end of the Middle Ages and started a period known as the Renaissance (1485–1640). Tudor rule ran from 1485 to 1617, when the Stuart's rule commenced. England, during this period was still a rural, agricultural society with London as the only recognised city, with a population of 300 000. Around 10% of people lived in the towns and the main source of income was farming. Society was becoming more commercial as the feudal lords who had become landlords started to see their estates as sources of income.

Sport was still being used to maintain distance between social groups. The upper class had their hunting, predominantly of red deer, boar and hares on their private land. Other popular sports activities were hawking and jousting. All these activities were used to prepare for war and sharpen their combat skills.

The peasants were involved in sport in the role of servicing the sports of the upper classes. They also had their own activities such as mob football and baiting animals. These sports were characterised by high levels of violence which allowed the peasants an avenue to channel their energies.

Hanoverian period

This phase, from 1714 to1790, saw a change in how people earned their livings. The movement from the spacious environment of the countryside to the cramped conditions of urban living was brought on by a decline in farming and a growth in the production of consumer goods. Factories were offering better wages and promising a better standard of living.

CASE STUDY

The development of football

Football has already been mentioned in its folk format. Folk football was popular in England from the Middle Ages but, although it was played with a round ball and involved kicking, it bore little resemblance to what we would call football today.

It went through a long and turbulent period of transition before rules were agreed in 1863.

Up until the agreement of rules in 1863, the term for contact ball sports of all types was football, with no differentiation between the dribbling game, which would become soccer, and the handling game, played at Rugby School amongst others. The development of football is used here because it is a good example of how sports developed in England and also shows us how society was developing.

Eric Dunning and Ken Sheard (1979), in their book *Barbarians, Gentlemen and Players*, show how football passed through four distinct stages of development. At each stage the game became more ordered and less violent.

Stage one lasted from the fourteenth century to the nineteenth century, when football was in its folk stage. At this stage it incorporated a variety of sports that involved a ball and physical contact. Games were played to local rules, which were agreed verbally rather than committed to paper. It was a rough, brutish game, characterised by violence and bloodshed, which was played predominantly in the countryside.

Stage two overlaps with the first stage; however, it was played in its folk form by pupils at public schools from 1750 to 1840. The games varied between schools, depending on the space available, but the aggression and roughness associated with the folk game was common to all schools' play.

Stage three lasted from 1830 to 1860, when public schools underwent reform. Rules for games were set down and the players were expected to adhere to certain modes of behaviour. In particular they were expected to control their emotions and any displays of violence. This was the beginning of the modernisation of the games of football.

Stage four lasted from 1850 to 1900, when an organised, rule-regulated version of football spread to the rest of society, and organisations were set up in order to organise and administrate the sport.

There is evidence that folk football was played in Britain before the Industrial Revolution, and this comes mainly from records showing orders to prohibit the playing of football. These orders, issued by central and local authorities, were to limit the damaging effects of football. Football was seen as a threat to law and order because it was associated with violence and drunkenness; also, if people were playing football it meant they were not working, and they could sustain injuries which prevented them from working. Between 1314 and 1660 there were at least 30 orders of prohibition from all parts of the country.

Although the games were subject to local variations they all had similar aims and characteristics. The ball was usually an inflated pig's bladder and the aim was to transport this ball to the church gates of the team from the opposing village. The church gates acted as the parameters of the goal, and the game was played by the inhabitants of two local villages. These games tended to take place over public holidays and lasted several days. The number of players on each side could be as high as 400 or 500, and the players had often consumed large amounts of alcohol. Each game was characterised by local customs rather than formal stated rules, and this resulted in anarchic, violent struggles. Games were often likened to battle and a high level of physical violence was socially tolerated.

Public schools, which had been set up originally as charitable institutes for the education of poorer people, became fee-paying institutions in the nineteenth century. The Industrial Revolution had started to produce a prosperous middle-class group of people who were able to afford fees to give

continued

their children an education. They joined the sons of aristocratic families at the fee-paying boarding schools. These public schoolboys played forms of folk football in the late eighteenth and early nineteenth centuries. The structure of the game was defined by the type and amount of space available. There may have been some rules, but these were specific to each school and were not written down. There were no officials or restrictions on numbers and, as a result, the games were characterised by the roughness and violence of the folk games.

The educational experience of the public schoolboys at this time was twofold. First, they received a formal education from schoolmasters, usually in classical subjects such as Greek and Latin. Secondly, they received an informal education outside the classroom. The boys were left to a system of self-rule, because the masters tended to be of a lower social standing than the mainly aristocratic boys. As a result, they were unable to assert power over the boys, especially the older boys. This resulted in a system of control in favour of the older, stronger boys called the prefect-fagging system.

The prefects used the younger, physically weaker boys as 'fags', whom they made perform menial tasks, such as cleaning their boots, as an expression of their power. This system was prevalent in football, as one of the duties of the younger boys was to keep goal for the senior boys. Keeping goal meant the younger boys lined up along the baselines to prevent their opponents from scoring a goal. The prefects adopted the glamorous attacking roles and, in reality, the younger boys were there to be roughed up. Physical violence was tolerated, as was any behaviour to win and then keep the ball. The roughness of the game was summed up by the use of 'navvies' by some of the prefects. Navvies were iron-tipped boots with a thick sole, and these were used to inflict injury on the shins of the younger boys.

This form of football carried on in public schools until around the 1830s; however, as industrial society developed so did football.

This was characterised by an increasing 'civilising' of the game and reflected by an increasing clean-up of society and refining of manners. As a result, football became more organised and formal. The main features of this process were:

- formal rules committed to writing
- clearly defined pitch and boundaries
- fixed limits on the duration of the match
- a reduction and standardisation of the numbers of participants
- an introduction of officials and administrative bodies
- a restriction on the level of physical violence tolerated.

These were the first steps in the development from the folk game to modern sports.

The prefect-fagging system was reformed successfully at Rugby School. Thomas Arnold was the influential Headmaster at the school from 1824 to 1842, and he lead the process of reform. The system still allowed an element of self-rule by the boys. However, the major difference was that the prefects were given authority by the Headmaster and they worked for him rather than in their own interests. The role of the prefects was clearly defined by the Headmaster and thus their actions were controlled by the masters.

This reform, in conjunction with a new set of values, changed the experience of public schools for the boys. The new set of values were those of Muscular Christianity. Arnold saw Rugby School as an ideal training ground for 'Christian gentlemen', who could then take these Christian values on to universities and working-class communities. Part of the Christian gentleman's role was to help the poor and needy in society. Arnold was unable to hide his distaste for the aristocracy, whom he felt shirked their responsibility to the less fortunate.

Arnold acted to exclude some of the sons of aristocrats from Rugby School and also to exclude any leisure activities associated with that class. He banned the field sports of hunting and shooting, partly because they were aristocratic and partly because they

continues overleaf

continued

were incompatible with the civilised ideal of the Christian gentlemen. A consequence of these bans was that more boys were available to play the increasingly popular team sports. Team sports were suited to implementing the ideals of 'Muscular Christians', as the participants had to learn the values of fitness, effort, commitment and strength. The values of sport participation helped to prepare the Muscular Christians for the challenges facing them in the world, and brought the benefits of health and enjoyment to the people converted to Christianity.

At this time, different schools played by different rules. For example, the game played at Rugby School was predominantly a handling game, while in 1847 Eton School produced a set of rules which placed a complete ban on the use of hands. This Eton field game is seen as being the first prototype of the Association football.

When these public schoolboys moved on to universities they continued to pursue their sports pursuits. However, the written rules differed between the various public schools from which the students were drawn. Therefore, there were clashes between boys who played the handling game and those who played the dribbling game. These conflicts lead to the construction of common rules, produced at Cambridge between 1837 and 1842, and then in 1846, 1848, 1856 and 1863.

Around the 1850s football diffused into society at large, again due to the influence of ex-public schoolboys who set up football clubs. The first reliable record of a football club being established is that of Sheffield in 1855. According to James Walvin (1994) this was under the influence of Old Harrovians, who taught local villagers to dribble the ball and made them wear white gloves to persuade them not to handle the ball. Other teams grew up under the influence of ex-public schoolboys and university men, but unlike Sheffield, most of these teams were in the South of England. For example, Blackheath (established 1858), Forest Club in Essex (1859) and Richmond (1859). However, the main problem was once again that some clubs played games deriving from the Rugby School rules and some from the Eton School rules.

The conflict between the different types of games had become a national issue, because teams playing each other had to have common regulations, and these could not be agreed. On 26th October 1863 representatives from several London and suburban clubs met for the first of six meetings at the Freemason's Tavern in Lincoln Inn Fields, with the aim of agreeing on a set of rules. The rules would eliminate the carrying of the ball and the practice of hacking, which involved the use of heavy boots to kick the opponents' shins. The game appeared to be losing the characteristics of the Rugby School game. The fourth meeting produced the first signs of controversy over hacking, as a group of people tried to reinstate its use into the rules. The argument for eliminating hacking was that its presence would prevent the spread of the game amongst adults, while those in favour of hacking argued that if it was excluded the aggressive nature of the game would be reduced and serve to make it less masculine.

The conflict over hacking was resolved by the withdrawal of the Blackheath club at the sixth meeting on 8th December 1863. They would go on to help form the game of rugby union under different rules in 1871. The remaining 11 clubs formed the Football Association (FA) rules, or 'laws' as they are known. The sixth meeting represented the splitting of rugby and Association football (soccer), and a conclusion to the various forms of folk football. The two separate codes became two highly structured, rule-regulated sports.

It is a commonly held belief that rugby union gained its distinctive features from the exploits of William Webb Ellis at Rugby School. Indeed, the Rugby Union World Cup Trophy is named the William Webb Ellis Trophy in his honour. A commemorative stone has been placed in the Close at Rugby School, bearing the inscription:

This Stone Commemorates The Exploit Of William Webb Ellis Who With a Fine Disregard For The Rules Of Football, As Played In His Time, First Took The Ball In His Arms and Ran With It, Thus Originating The Distinctive Feature Of The Rugby Game

AD 1823

continued

While this event may have taken place, there is reason to suggest it is a myth. The first claim to this event was made in 1880 in *Meteor*, the Rugby School magazine, by a former pupil, Matthew Bloxam, who had left the school in 1820. He had heard about it by second-hand account and after 60 years. Also, there were no clearly agreed rules of football until 1863, so it would have been impossible to break these rules in 1823. The game did not acquire its distinctive features of H shaped goals and the scoring of tries until the second quarter of the nineteenth century. Undoubtedly Webb Ellis existed, and he may have been an innovator of the game, but he was not the inventor. Rugby School and the actions of Thomas Arnold, his fellow masters and pupils are of paramount importance in the development of rugby. However, sports are never invented, they develop over long periods of time and are never the outcome of one individual's behaviour.

The Industrial Revolution

From around the mid-eighteenth century the English economy underwent a vast transformation. It had been based on agriculture, with particularly busy periods of work for planting and harvesting. However, working hours varied and there were long periods of free time available for workers to enjoy leisure activities. The Industrial Revolution saw the development of factories producing a wide range of consumer goods. Factory owners required their workers to accept longer hours and less free time. Typically, a worker would have a six-day week, working from 7a.m. to 7p.m.; there may also have been a nightshift. This was to maximise the output of factories and reduce their unit costs. Overhead costs were high and could only be reduced if machinery was being worked for as many hours as was possible. The second issue was that there was a shortage of people living in the towns and cities where these factories were based, so they had to attract workers in from their countryside homes. This was done by offering better wages and the lure of consumer goods to raise standards of living.

The reality was a little different from the promise because these workers traded increased wages for longer working hours and less leisure time. Also, the standards of housing were much worse than the countryside where they enjoyed plenty of space. The perceived rise in spending and standard of living never occurred because it was more expensive to live in cities. In the cities families and workers were herded into 'slum' accommodation with as little space as could be provided. Leisure activities became a problem because the violent sports could result in serious injuries, the excessive drinking led to hangovers and absenteeism, and gambling undermined the work ethic. Leisure cost the factory owners money and affected output. Factory owners supported the middle-class efforts to clean up society and impose a new form of morality. Campaigns were mounted against excessive drinking, idleness, sexual promiscuity, gambling, violent sports and the excessive holidays. The aim of the middle classes was to impose a work ethic on the population and make behaviour more polite and respectable.

The agriculture industry also underwent a parallel revolution with the scope and quantity of production increasing. This meant that the population of England became better fed, more healthy and had more energy for work.

The economic forces contributed to changes in traditional sports because the employees had to bow to their employers' demands and, moreover, they had little time or energy to play aggressive contact sports. These demands were supplemented by the efforts of religious reformers, who believed violent sports led to moral corruption, and sport on the Sabbath was eventually banned. The Royal Society for the Protection of Animals (RSPCA) put pressure on the authorities to ban sports involving cruelty to animals. The Industrial Revolution led to a growth in the size of towns and cities and a reduction in the amount of space available for recreation. Folk football, which was played across vast swathes of countryside, was completely inappropriate for the urban setting. The result of all these changes was that sports slowly disappeared.

Why did sports disappear?

1   The effects of the Industrial Revolution led to an increase in working hours and a decline in leisure time.

2   Many activities were banned because they became costly in terms of working hours and productivity being lost.

3   The workers had a low spending power in reality.

4   The urban setting provided an inappropriate environment for playing sports.

It is important to say here that sports for the leisured upper classes and middle classes were still popular and carried on in pre-industrialised forms

The 1830s and 1840s started to see an upturn in fortune for the workers, because the development of the railways led to an increased mobility. The sports of cricket and horse racing benefited from the easier access to the countryside, allowing the workers to go and watch meetings and matches. The 1840s saw a genuine improvement in real wages, meaning an increased spending power, improving diets and standard of living. There was also money available to spend on entrance fees into sports events.

The 1860s saw the development of nationally agreed rules, known as the codification of sport, and a changing attitude of the middle-class factory owners to their employee's sports activities. Two groups promoted the benefits of sport. First, the industrialists, who saw sport as promoting values which would make their workers more productive, such as teamwork and loyalty. Secondly, the Muscular Christians took team sports to working-class communities to teach the bible through sport and promote the value of a healthy mind in a healthy body.

Figures from the time suggest sport was still a minority activity; however, spectatorship was growing, as was professionalism in the sports of football, cricket and horse racing. Social change included the urban population growing from 50.2% in 1851 to 77% in 1900; working-class wages rose by 70% and a half-day holiday was granted on Saturday. This meant sport could be played and watched on Saturday afternoons and is the origin of the three o'clock kick off in football matches.

Post-industrialisation

The end of the period of industrialisation is generally seen as being 1851. Thus, the period after 1851 is known as the post-industrialisation period. This period saw the codification of modern sports. This means that rather than being sports which were played to locally agreed, oral rules involving high levels of violence and low levels of organisation, they became highly structured and rule-regulated activities.

Eric Dunning and Ken Sheard, in their influential book *Barbarians, Gentlemen and Players* (1979), gave us a comparison between the structural properties of folk games, as played pre-Industrial Revolution, and modern sports as played post-Industrial Revolution.

Folk games had the following characteristics:

✪ varied, informal activities

✪ simple, unwritten rules which were verbally agreed

✪ regional variation of rules and specification of equipment

✪ no fixed boundaries for territory or numbers of participants

✪ strong social divisions in activities played

✪ little difference in the roles of players

✪ little distinction between the roles of spectators and players

✪ high tolerance of the use of physical violence and no restraint of emotions

✪ emphasis on physical force as opposed to skill

✪ strong pressure from the community to participate

✪ contests were only meaningful on a local level.

Modern sports have the following characteristics:

✪ highly specific, formalised activities

✪ formal and elaborate rules worked out by appointed bodies

✪ national and international guidelines for the standardisation of rules and equipment

✪ played on pitches with clearly marked boundaries and a specific number of players on each side

✪ less evidence of social differences between players

✪ strict distinction between the roles of playing and spectating

✪ low levels of physical violence tolerated and high restraint of emotion expected

✪ emphasis on skill rather than physical force

✪ activities are freely chosen

✪ contests have local, national and international significance.

(adapted from Eric Dunning and Ken Sheard, *Barbarians, Gentlemen and Players*)

The development of modern sports led to a need to develop rules and implement these rules with officials and administrators. One of the key features of modern sports is the growth of governing bodies of sport to fulfil these and other functions. For example, the Football Association was formed in 1863 to implement and safeguard the rules and football. Later, the Rugby Football Union was formed in 1871 to implement the rules of the handling game of football.

Rational recreation is the term given to the introduction of leisure activities which were seen as being productive and moral. Up until the 1860s and 1870s the workers had relied on their public houses for amusement and entertainment, which were often socially destructive. Rational recreations were brought in by various philanthropic groups, such as the Muscular Christians and other middle-class groups who introduced new alternatives. Thus, societies such as the Mechanics Society, the Boys Brigade and the Young Men's Christian Association developed, and facilities such as libraries, baths and sports grounds offered more purposeful activities.

This is an example of using sport and leisure as a means of social control, whereby people are persuaded to take part in positive, socially acceptable activities to prevent them from participating in socially destructive activities such as drinking, gambling and fighting. The middle-class philanthropists wanted to provide better activities for the working class to improve their standard of living; however, their ulterior motive was to make sure they were healthier, fitter and more productive workers.

Twentieth-century development

We will now look at the four major developments of sport in the twentieth century.

Globalisation of sport

The forms of sport that were established in England in the late nineteenth century quickly spread around the world, particularly through the influence of the British Empire. Officers and soldiers brought the new codified forms of sport to the countries they were stationed in, and the sports in turn were adopted by the natives. By the end of the nineteenth century the Olympic movement, under the influence of the French, was finding its feet and starting to involve more and more nations. The influence of sport by the end of the twentieth century can be seen by the fact that three of the four largest international organisations are sporting organisations: the IAAF (International Amateur Athletic Federation), with 184 member countries; FIFA (Fédération International de Football Association) with 178 members; the IOC (International Olympic Committee) with 171 members – the only non-sporting organisation is the United Nations, with 180 member countries.

Professionalism

The increasing playing demands of the sports of rugby, football and cricket meant that players have had to devote increasing amounts of time and energy to their sports. By the end of the nineteenth century all of these three sports had embraced professionalism, as the standards of the sports rose and payments had to be made to players to compensate for the wages they would otherwise have earned. Professionalism was initially looked down upon because the upper classes thought that sport should be played purely for the enjoyment derived from the activity. A class distinction arose between the upper-class amateurs and the working-class professionals, which remained until the latter part of the twentieth century. By the end of the twentieth century, professionalism was an accepted part of all sports and necessary to uphold the high standards of play demanded by the sophisticated audiences.

The development of sport as a profitable industry

As sports have increasingly embraced professionalism, their expenditure has increased. As a result they have had to increase the amount of money coming into the sport to pay these expenses. Sports and their clubs have increasingly sought sponsorship as a source of income, along with trying to make the sport more attractive and increase the number of spectators coming to matches. As sports have become more popular and widely watched, they have increasingly drawn the attention of the media; this has opened up new sources of revenue to sports and has led to increased profits.

There is also an expanding industry in sport for non-competitive participants, and this has created a variety of opportunities for private companies to invest their money and make profits. It has also resulted in a growing industry with new, exciting employment opportunities.

The development of sport in education

The key element in the expansion of sport in the education system was the 1944 Education Act, which made it policy for local authorities to provide adequate facilities for the teaching of physical education. Sport and physical education became compulsory elements of children's education and are now key features in the National Curriculum. Added to that, there are now many more opportunities to study sport at GCSE, A/AS level, National Diploma and degree level.

REVISION *QUESTIONS*

1) Why is it important to study sport in the societies they are played within?

2) When did sports start to appear in the forms we recognise today?

3) Why did sports have to change? Give three reasons.

4) Briefly outline the four stages in the development of soccer.

5) Explain what happened to society during the Industrial Revolution.

6) Explain the major differences between folk games and modern sports.

7) What is meant by the term 'rational recreation'?

8) Discuss the four main themes in the development of sport in the twentieth century.

SOCIOLOGY AND ITS APPLICA-TION

Sociological theory

Sociology is a science which studies, in a systematic manner, human beings and the societies they form. Historians report observable facts, while sociologists place facts in a theoretical perspective in an attempt to understand human behaviour. Facts as recorded in history cannot speak for themselves; they are open to a range of interpretations. Likewise, there are a range of theories in sociology. There is no broad agreement between sociologists over which perspective is most suitable; sociology is a contested subject. Four of the main perspectives will now be examined in an attempt to provide a sociological perspective for study.

Functionalism

Functionalism was developed in nineteenth-century Europe. Emile Durkheim, a French sociologist, was one of the early proponents of the view. He compared society to the functioning of the human body. The human body is made up of structures such as the heart, lungs, liver, kidneys and skin, all of which play a vital role in maintaining the function, stability and health of the person. If there is illness or dysfunction in any of the structures then the effects are felt by the whole person rather than just in that one organ. In the same way functionalist sociologists see society as a 'whole' unit. Individual relationships combine to form structures (such as family, education, sport) which work together to contribute to the order and stability of a society. Sport is examined in terms of the functions it performs in contributing to this stability.

Functionalism has been criticised because its stresses consensus between groups in society, rather than conflict, and because it struggles to explain society as a process, characterised by change and development. For example, the family's function is to socialise the new members of the society, while the educational system's function is to provide young people with the skills and knowledge they need to perform effectively in the workplace. Sport performs certain key functions, such as providing an acceptable means of venting energies and frustrations which build up. Stephenson and Nixon (1972) see sports institutions performing five functions.

1   They provide an acceptable means of releasing pent up emotions and feelings.

2   They provide a means of socialising new members into a society and showing what behaviour is acceptable.

3   They are a means of integrating people into groups in society.

4   They are a political function to reinforce the society's success and to sanction and reward other societies.

5   They provide a means of mobility between classes for performers.

Symbolic interactionism

Symbolic interactionism focuses on individuals and is based on the small-scale face-to-face interaction which occurs between people. Verbal and non-verbal

symbols are used to communicate and interpret communication – people can build up an image for themselves using these symbols. When examining sporting subcultures, we can see the different symbols that are employed by the subculture's members, and what these symbols are conveying.

Marxism

Marxism is based on the belief that in industrialised societies the minority elite of the population takes advantage of the majority of the population and exploits them. In return, they offer rewards which make the majority consumers. The majority work hard in their meaningless jobs to buy clothes, cars and toys to make them happy, and attend sports events to seek distractions. The Marxist alternative to this exploitative society is that all members are treated equally and that society takes responsibility for its citizens and acts according to that responsibility. This society works to discourage greed, ignorance and the baser natures of its citizens, rather than promoting them. The basis of Marxism is that each person takes from the society according to their needs, and contributes according to their abilities.

Marxist theory is named after its founder, the German philosopher, economist and sociologist, Karl Marx (1818–1883). The theory became popular in the 1970s, when the influence of functionalism started to wane – Marxism offered the answers that functionalism failed to provide. Marxist theory is based on the belief that the key to understanding the social relations of any society is to be found in the economic structure of that society. When examining capitalist societies we see a 'bourgeoisie' that owns the means of production, such as the factories and the machines, and a 'proletariat' or working class, which sells its labour as a means of production in return for a wage. This relationship between the owner and the worker is an exploitative relationship between groups of people of different classes. The exploiting party is the bourgeoisie, who are trying to gain as much output as they can from their workers. The workers, who are the exploited, are fighting to improve their working conditions and their pay, and to limit their exploitation.

Cashmore (1996) writes about sport under capitalism, suggesting that the relationship of exploitation is reproduced in sport, as capitalists use sport as a means of 'social control' to appease the working class. Sporting activities give them diversion for their otherwise dull, routine lives. The bourgeoisie also use sport to prepare workers for the workplace by producing a fitter, more disciplined and more productive workforce. Marxism is criticised because the development of society is said to be reliant on only one factor, the economy, and this singular emphasis tends to be limiting. There are other factors that influence social change, such as gender and race.

Figurational sociology

Figurational sociology focuses on the networks of social relationships that human beings form; humans are social by nature and they exist in a social context, thus they develop relationships. A relationship is intangible and is said to exist when a person or group has an effect on another person or group; thus, relationships are characterised by interdependency. These networks of social relationships, which can be referred to as 'figurations', are constantly changing as individuals interact and react to each other during the processes in which they are involved. These dynamic networks are global in scope and rooted in history; the social world we are a part of is inherited from previous generations and then modified and passed on to future generations.

Power

A feature of all social relationships is power or power balances. The power relationship within a figuration is the outcome of the interplay between conflict and consensus. A better understanding of the relationship between groups is found if the distribution of power and its dynamic nature are examined. Power of a person or a group of people over another person or group of people can be expressed in different ways. If a person or group wants another person or group to behave in a certain way, there are three different strategies available: physical coercion or threats of physical behaviour; explaining the rewards or sanctions of behaving in a certain way; persuasion through strength of argument. Power balances in a relationship tend to be unequal; they also tend to be unstable as they are processes. It must be noted that very important people or groups are rarely all powerful because they rely on the consensus of other people or groups. The attempts of people or groups to express their power are often impeded by the actions of less powerful groups.

To summarise, all relationships and their power balances are processes, in that they are constantly changing. Relationships can be face to face, or they may be with unseen people on a global scale – as long as each party affects the other, the relationship has interdependency.

The civilising process

The second important concept of figurational sociology is the civilising process, as described by Norbert Elias. This focuses on the continual process of change, from the Middle Ages to the present day, that has occurred with regard to personality, behaviour and habits. The process shows how etiquette and manners have become refined, particularly regarding bodily functions and in a decrease in the tolerance thresholds of violence and aggressive behaviour. Pressure was placed on people to exercise more self-control over feelings and behaviour. Elias asserts that this pressure was brought by people in the upper and middle classes, and thus was passed down. Dunning (*Figurational Sociology and the Sociology of Sport*) and Elias explain that the civilising process relies on an effective monopolisation of violence by the state, which in turn pacifies the members of the state. This process is interdependent with the process of economic growth, which in turn increases the income of the state through its tax monopoly. This increasing revenue enables the state to strengthen its monopoly of violence.

Summary of figurational sociology

1   Society is made up of a network of social relationships.

2   A relationship is said to exist when a person or a group has an effect on another person or group. A relationship is like electricity in that we know it exists because, although we cannot see it, we can feel its effects.

3   Relationships are two way (interdependent). They can be relationships of co-operation or conflict.

4   Relationships can be global in scope and are rooted in history. We inherit material things such as buildings, houses, roads and stadiums, and less concrete things such as language, education, culture, music, sporting rules, values and morals.

5   Each generation inherits these things. During their lifespan they modify them, then pass them on to the next generation.

6   All relationships have power or power balances. Power is neither good nor bad, but an aspect of all relationships. It is the extent to which you are able to influence the other person or group, and is usually unequal.

7   If a person wants another person to do something, they have three options:

a)   physical coercion

b)   offering economic rewards or sanctions

c)   verbal persuasion.

8   We are all parts of networks of social relationships. These networks are called 'figurations', hence the name of the theory.

9   Relationships and their power balances are always changing, they are processes. Therefore, if we want to examine why something is the way it is we have to understand what came before – its history. All human action has an outcome or consequence. Some consequences are intended, but other consequences are unintended or unforeseen. For example, the development of the car was intended to improve mobility, but it has also resulted in environmental damage and health problems. All-seater stadium were developed to make watching football safer, but they have also resulted in higher prices (and some financial problems for certain clubs) and the attraction of more female supporters and more middle-class supporters. Even very small-scale action can be examined in this way.

10   Central to figurational sociology is 'the civilising process'.

STUDENT ACTIVITY

Think of all the groups of people with whom you have a relationship that enables you to complete your education at your college. (Use a spider diagram.)

Social influences on sports participation

Levels of participation in sport

How would you define participation in sport? Would a person have to do an activity once or more a week, once or more a year? According to Sport England it is 'participation in at least one activity over a four-week period.'

Sport England (see page 442) estimates that 25 million people play sport or take part in active recreation at least once a month, and they declared in 1996 that the top ten participation sports are:

1   Walking   44.5%

2   Swimming   14.6%

3	Keep fit/yoga	12.3%
4	Snooker/billiards	11.3%
5	Cycling	11%
6	Weight training	5.6%
7	Soccer	4.8%
8	Golf	4.7%
9	Running	4.5%
10	Ten pin bowling	3.4%

(Source: Office of Population Censuses and Surveys, Living in Britain, 1996)

They also published the top ten participation sports for schoolchildren. Participation is defined as at least once in the year of 1994.

1	Swimming	85%
2	Athletics	81%
3	Cycling	79%
4	Football	77%
5	Rounders	75%
6	Gymnastics	69%
7	Tennis	67%
8	Walking/hiking	62%
9	Cricket	59%
10	Cross-country running	51%

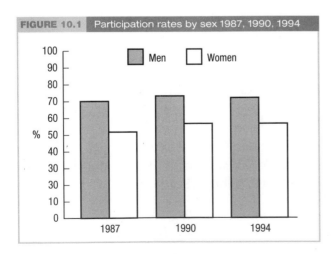

FIGURE 10.1 Participation rates by sex 1987, 1990, 1994

However, these figures do not present the whole picture because there are certain groups that are better represented than others in sport.

Participation in sport has risen steadily since the 1960s for several reasons.

1 Increasing private car ownership:

Year	% households with cars
1990	66%
1980	59%
1970	52%
1960	31%
1950	14%

2   More time is available to people because there is now a shorter working week, longer holidays and people are increasingly taking early retirement, often in their fifties.

3   An increased number of sports facilities. There has been a boom in the provision of facilities since the 1960s. The public sector had a large expansion in the late 1960s and early 1970s while there has been a steady growth in private sector provision since the late 1980s.

4   Increased promotional activities by the Sports Council/Sport England, the government and through the media.

5   There is a growing knowledge and understanding of the relationship between sport and health.

Sport would appear to be an area of relatively free choice, which is formally open to everyone. However, there are many factors that affect participation in sport in terms of:

✪   the amount of time spent playing sport

✪   the choice of sports activity.

Personal factors

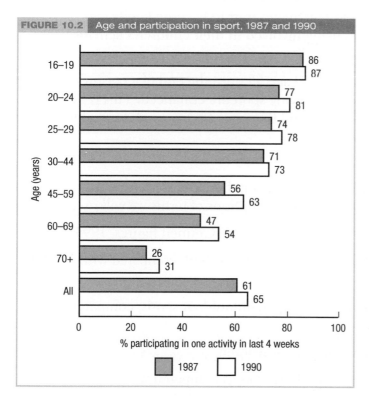

FIGURE 10.2   Age and participation in sport, 1987 and 1990

Age

Sports Council research shows that participation is highest among young people and declines steadily with age. This is common sense, but people are still physically fit for sport into their sixties or seventies. Figures from 1987–1990 show that more men than women take part in sport (see Figure 10.1) and that growth in participation is fastest among middle-aged and elderly age groups (see Figure 10.2).

Many older people enjoy physical activity, especially when they play at their own pace and level. This can be seen in the success of over 35s football leagues, veteran's races and 50+ sessions.

The types of sports played, and the way they are played, also changes with age. Young people are usually involved in highly competitive sports, while older people tend to be more involved in non-competitive sports or recreational activities. The older people become then the more susceptible they become to physical injuries due to a decline in the skeleton and muscular system, so they tend to favour non-contact sports.

Some activities will show no relationship between age and participation levels, such as swimming, which is a sport enjoyed by all age groups.

Stage in the lifecycle

Age is closely aligned to family status and stage in the lifecycle. This is a theory researched by Robert and Rhona Rapoport (1975). The Rapoports saw four stages in the lifecycle:

1 adolescence phase

2 young adulthood phase

3 establishment phase

4 retirement phase.

The adolescence phase occurs from ages 13 to 19 and is a period when young people are trying to find their own identities and have new experiences. They will try out lots of sports activities and decide which ones they like and which ones they do not. It is also a period when they are seeking to become more independent and can make choices for themselves as to what activities they want to do, and they may have a part-time job that gives them some financial independence.

The young adulthood phase is approximately from ages 20 to 30 and represents a period of independence for young adults, where they are employed and usually have little responsibility. They may be in a relationship, and sporting activities may start to include their partner rather than their own sporting interests.

The establishment phase lasts approximately from 30 to 55, where most people will be part of a family and sports activities start to become family centred. The parents often find themselves being involved in their children's activities, rather than playing sport themselves.

The retirement phase is from around age 55 until the end of a person's life and is a period when their chances of playing sport are enhanced. This is because they now have plenty of time spare and they may have a good disposable income if they have invested wisely.

Sex

Before starting a discussion of the relationship between sex and sports participation it is useful to examine the definitions of terms we will use.

Comparison of men's and women's sport (Sports Council figures, 1994).

1 Seventy-two per cent of men participate in sport, compared with 57% of women.

2 Forty-two per cent of men participate in outdoor sports, compared with 24% of women.

3 Twice as many men watch sport as women.

4 There are very few female professionals as compared with men.

5 There are few women in administrative positions in sport.

6 The history and growth of sport is documented mainly in terms of the development of male sport.

7 Sport in the media is dominated by male sport.

 **Definitions**

Sex – the biological and therefore genetic differences between males and females.

Gender – the learned social and cultural differences between males and females, in terms of their habits, personality and behaviour.

STUDENT ACTIVITY

In pairs or threes, discuss what you understand by the quotes opposite, and find the flaws in each person's argument.

Definitions

Sexism

Sexism means different things to different people. The following definition gives us a framework to work within:

'Sexism is a practice based on the ideology that men are superior to women. The ideology is expressed through a system of prejudice and discrimination that seeks to control and dominate women. It is systematically embodied in the structures and organisations of that society.'
(J. Hargreaves, 1994)

The following quotations are taken from people in positions of power, and represent some of the 'older' views people hold of women playing sport.

> *I am personally against the participation of women in public competitions. At the Olympics their primary role should be like in the ancient tournaments – the crowning of the male victors with laurels.*

> *Women should once again be prohibited from sport … they are the true defenders of humanist values which emanate from the household, the values of tenderness, nurture and compassion.*

> *Women should be banned from football because it is not good for their health.*

Sexism is essentially about power; how it is expressed and how it manifests itself to the detriment of women. Britain has a patriarchal society, i.e. one that is organised and run by men for men. This power is expressed through physical and psychological differences. Women have started to break down this patriarchy; however, the majority of positions of power are still held by men.

Sexism and its effects are displayed through structures of society, such as language, behaviour, attitudes, religion and culture. It is childhood that the roots of acquiring and practising sexist attitudes begin, and this continues through life. For example, male babies and female babies will be treated in different ways, with male babies expected to be tougher and female babies being handled more tenderly. Even the simple allocation of pink colours for a girl and blue colours for a boy shows our different attitudes to the sexes. This inevitably leads to people conforming to gender roles that can inhibit an individual's abilities, preferences and aspirations.

The Sports Council states:

> *Sex stereotyping feeds prejudice, which is mainly negative and damaging, it expresses an attitude, feeling or opinion about women individually or collectively.*

Why are women's participation rates lower than men's?

1   **Lack of time** – Women in partnerships with men tend to take on domestic responsibilities and thus any sport is fitted in between responsibilities of childcare, cooking, cleaning, washing and so on. Sport can be time consuming and costly, especially if childcare is needed.

2   **Class inequalities** accentuate gender inequalities. Middle-class women have much higher participation rates than working-class women, as they typically have more money and access to private transport. The fitness boom has mostly benefited middle-class women.

3   The major **biological difference** between men and women is that women can bear children, and this has psychological and social repercussions.

Women are allocated to reproductive, mothering and childcare roles, which limit the time and opportunity women have for sports activities. However, women are waiting longer now before having a family and this has improved their situation; also, gender equality has meant that childcare and nurturing roles are more commonly shared between partners.

4 Every society has a set of **beliefs and values** that dictate what is acceptable behaviour for women (and men) in all spheres of their lives; sport is included in theses values. For example, many people consider that some sporting activities can induce masculine traits in women, especially in competitive sports. Strong opinions are held as to what sports are acceptable or unacceptable for girls or women. Even strong peer pressure may prevent women from considering certain sports.

STUDENT ACTIVITY

Discuss the following with a partner.
1 Which sports are regarded as socially acceptable for females?
2 Which sports are not so socially acceptable for women, and may conflict with the behaviour expected of them?

The conventional image of sport is based on chauvinistic values and male identity formation. Sport is the arena for the celebration of masculinity. To be successful at sport you need to show skill, power, muscularity, competitiveness, aggression, assertiveness and courage. To be successful at sport is to be successful as a man, and to be uninterested or not talented is to be less of a man.

Therefore, to be successful at sport a woman must show masculine traits that so-called contrast with the feminine traits of agility, balance, flexibility, co-ordination and gentleness. Successful sportswomen not only have to be exceptional athletes, they also have to retain their femininity. We can clearly see this in Britain, where the female athletes who receive the most attention are those who manage to achieve the two criteria, such as Denise Lewis, Ashia Hansen, Paula Radcliffe and Denise Marsten-Smith. International tennis shows this phenomenon perfectly, where Anna Kornikova, who is not in the top sixteen in the world, has not won a top-level competition, yet receives more coverage than all the other female tennis players put together.

The amount of coverage sport receives in the media has grown beyond all recognition. The media is important because it helps shape our views and attitudes. The coverage of women's sport in the media accounts for around 3% of all sports coverage (less in the tabloids), which suggests that the editors think we don't want to read about women's sport, or that it is just not important.

The problem is not only the quantity of coverage, but also the quality.

1 The attention is often on the woman's appearance, rather than her performance. Women are portrayed first as a female and secondly as an athlete. Commentators will often refer to their physical features, for example, saying that they are pretty, slim or leggy.

2 Women's performances are often trivialised by irrelevant frames of references to their husbands, boyfriends or children. For example, we know that Paula Radcliffe and Sonia O'Sullivan are married and that O'Sullivan has two children, but do we know or care about the family life of Alan Shearer or Martin Johnson? The media tries to soften women's images to show that while they are tough and competitive, they can also be caring and 'feminine'. This softening rarely happens to men, although

it can be observed in men's tennis, and with an increasingly intrusive media it is becoming more common in other sports.

3   Not all photographs of women in the media are action shots, many are posed or of women wearing casual or smart clothes. Increasingly, we are seeing sportswomen in men's magazines, such as FHM and GQ.

In conclusion, while more and more women are playing sport, and it is becoming more acceptable for women to be involved in what are regarded traditionally as 'masculine' sports, such as rugby and football, some old prejudices still remain. These prejudices and stereotypes are perpetuated by men and women and the attitudes they hold. Sportswomen themselves often reinforce the stereotype by acting to reaffirm their feminine values, showing that they can be successful at sport while retaining their femininity.

Marital status

Marital status is a factor affecting both men and women. In simple terms, it relates to responsibility and independence. A single person has independence and does not have to consider anyone else when making a decision, while a married person has a partner and maybe children to consider. Some sports, such as cricket, which may involve playing all day Saturday and Sunday, do not make for a harmonious relationship unless the other partner is also actively involved!

Fitness level

Our fitness level will also influence the activities in which we participate. Loss of fitness due to injury or laziness acts as a de-motivator for most people. If we are fit and healthy, we will be ready to participate in any activity; however, losses in fitness can lead to embarrassment and a restriction in available activities.

Social factors

Income and type of employment

Income and type of employment can be considered together as one is dependent on the other. They are generally referred to as socio-economic status, which is a categorisation used in general household surveys in preference to social class, which is seen as something static and permanent. Socio-economic status is a ranking based on occupations, and therefore relates to income.

Socio-economic groups

Group	Type of work	Examples
A	professional	doctors, lawyers, bankers
B	managerial	department managers, teachers
C1	clerical/supervisory	shift managers, nurses
C2	skilled manual	electricians, plumbers
D	semi-skilled manual	postal workers, bus drivers
E	unskilled manual	porters, cleaners

These are generalisations, because within most professions (e.g. police officers, teachers and bank workers) there will be a range of levels. Also, footballers, who would be regarded as skilled manual workers, are some of the richest people in our society. However, it is a useful way of identifying groups of people in relation to their professions.

STUDENT ACTIVITY

State which social group you think has the highest participation rates in each of the following activities. Also consider which social groups form the spectators in each sport.

Polo	Rugby league	Coarse fishing
Darts	Skiing	Fly fishing
Football	Archery	Badminton
Hockey	Rowing	Golf
Athletics	Weightlifting	Bowls
Whippet racing	Fox hunting	Cycling
Yacht racing	Aerobics	Swimming
Tennis	Horse racing	Walking
Squash	Greyhound racing	Netball
Rugby union	Boxing	Mountaineering

In summary, the higher the social group a person belongs to, the more of their time they are likely to spend playing sport, and the wider their choice of activities (see Figure 10.3). This is due to several factors.

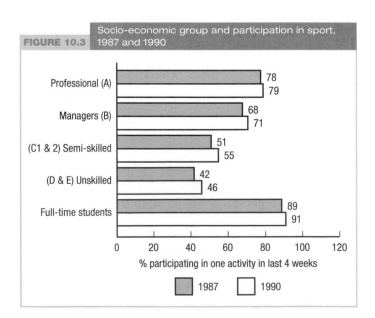

FIGURE 10.3 Socio-economic group and participation in sport, 1987 and 1990

% participating in one activity in last 4 weeks

1987   1990

1. **Historically**, sport has been developed by the upper classes for the upper classes. In the nineteenth century the working class had no time, money or energy to play sport, due to the long hours they had to work. Sport in the twentieth century has become more democratic.

2. **Economically**, the financial cost of certain sports is a major restricting factor. For example, sports such as polo or yachting demand huge financial outlays, and even tennis and golf are expensive to play and the equipment can be costly. This is also the main limiting factor for sports people who aspire to elite sport, as they need financial resources to fund coaching, training and living costs.

3   There are sometimes **barriers to sports participation** due to status exclusivity. In certain sports restrictions to membership are based on social status rather than ability. This exclusivity is retained by charging high membership fees, and membership being based on approval or election by a committee. This is still prevalent in golf and tennis clubs.

4   One of the functions of leisure is to provide a means of **socialising** with other people. Most people will feel at home with people from similar backgrounds and socio-economic status. Certain sporting events (e.g. Royal Ascot and the Henley Regatta) are associated with certain social groups. If you were to visit Lord's to watch cricket, Twickenham to watch rugby or Wembley to watch football, you would observe different social groups behaving in different manners.

5   The amount of **time required** can be prohibitive. Higher social groups have more leisure time to participate in 'non-productive' activities. The group with the least leisure time is working-class women, and they are also the group with the lowest levels of participation in sport. The groups with the most time are those groups with the most power (groups A and B). This is because the more power you have, the more control you may have over your working hours.

Research from other countries (USA, Canada, Australia, Belgium, Poland, Germany) shows broadly the same findings, although with some variations in the sports. However, all research shows that manual workers have lower levels of participation than non-manual workers.

Cultural background

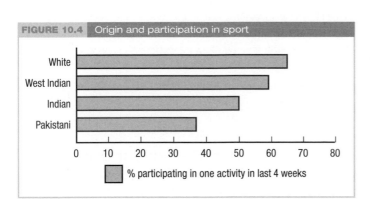

FIGURE 10.4   Origin and participation in sport

% participating in one activity in last 4 weeks

This refers to the environment in which we are brought up. If we look at Britain as a whole, we can see that some sports are more popular in some areas and less popular in other areas. One of the major factors influencing the sports we play is where we are brought up. For example, rugby league is more prevalent in the north of England and rugby union in the south of England and Wales; Scotland has its own sports, such as skiing, curling and its Highland Games, and Ireland has sports such as hurling and gaelic football. However, there are differences in ethnic origin and sports participation (see Figure 10.4).

Britain has developed into a multiracial society. Many members of the population are from Afro-caribbean or various Asian and European backgrounds. Many were initially drawn to Britain by the need for jobs during the 1950s.

Some ethnic groups choose to retain separate cultural identities within British society, but black sports people participate successfully in most sports in Britain. However, racism does still occur in British sport, although it is not usually the overt racism that black footballers suffered in the eighties and early nineties. Racism in British sport occurs in two ways, through racial stereotyping and stacking.

Definitions

Race is the physical characteristics of a person.

Ethnicity is the cultural adherence of a person or group, and is characterised by their customs and habits (e.g. religious beliefs, diet, clothing, leisure activities and lifestyles).

Racism describes the oppression of a person or group by another person or group on the grounds of physical differences.

1   **Stereotyping** – Racial discrimination has excluded black people from achieving in the workplace, so many black people have entered sport as an arena where they can improve their life chances. Thus, many young black people have spent more time improving their sporting ability at the cost of their academic abilities. This has produced two stereotypes:

a)   black people are naturally good at sport

b)   black people are not intelligent.

2   **Stacking** – Black people tend to be guided into certain sports and certain positions within teams. They tend to predominate in sports such as track and field athletics, football, basketball and boxing. These sports tend to be inexpensive, requiring little specialist equipment, and can be practised relatively cheaply. Within these sports black people tend to dominate in certain positions or events, usually those requiring physical rather than intellectual or decision-making qualities, such as wingers in football and rugby rather than positions of centrality.

This stacking comes from a stereotype that black people have a natural, genetic ability to be quick and powerful, but lack high intellectual abilities. This stereotype is perpetuated by teachers and coaches of sports who, when choosing teams, place black people in a position or an event because they believe all black people are fast and powerful.

CASE STUDY

Football

There are now black players in every professional football league club. A survey in 1989/90 showed that one-third of the Professional Football Association's membership was black players; however, the same study showed that black players predominate in certain positions.

Position	Percentage of black players		
	1985/6	1989/90	1995/6
Goalkeeper	0.9% (1)	0% (0)	15%
Full backs	19.8% (22)	15.8% (24)	13%
Centre backs	12.6% (14)	15.2% (23)	28.7%
Midfielders	15.3% (17)	12.5% (19)	21.5%
Forwards	51.3% (57)	56.5% (86)	47.9%

Observations on the figures.

1   The majority of black players are forwards.

2   Few black players have captained Premier League clubs, and none have yet managed one, despite many black players now being in retirement. Paul Ince became the first black player to captain England.

3   Very few black players play in pivotal roles.

4   The 1995/96 FA Premier League survey showed that 98.9% of fans are white, with Asians accounting for 0.5%, Afro-Caribbeans for 0.1%, Chinese for 0.1% and other non-whites 0.5%.

STUDENT ACTIVITY

How does racism through stacking/ stereotyping occur in the following sports in Britain?

Cricket

Tennis

Golf

Athletics

Swimming

Rugby

Racism has been tackled on the terraces under the 1991 Football Offences Act, which makes it illegal to take part in racist chanting. However, an arrest can only be made if there is one or more people chanting and if the chants are causing distress to the person they are aimed against.

The measures to combat racism in British football have been fairly successful and it is now less of an issue. However, there are constant allegations of racism against black players in British teams when they are involved in international competitions.

Influence of friends and family

Initially, the influence of our family will be huge because it is our parents who lead us to try new activities. This may be playing in the back garden or involving us in a local club. Usually, parents will involve us in sports they enjoy. Some parents are accused of living their dreams through their children and pushing them hard in activities they have chosen for their children. This often leads to rebellion in later life. Later on, our friends will influence us to participate in activities which they like, and vice versa. Some people are persuaded to give up sports by their friends who no longer regard them as 'cool' activities to be involved in.

REVISION QUESTIONS

1) Briefly outline how functionalism helps us to understand how societies work.

2) Sport performs certain vital functions in maintaining the stability of society. Explain some of these functions.

3) Marxism sees societies as being in conflict. Who is in conflict and why?

4) Explain the terms 'bourgeoisie' and 'proletariat'.

5) How does Marxist theory explain the role that sport plays in societies?

6) Figurational sociology concerns itself with relationships. What is meant by the term 'relationship' and why are they important?

7) How do figurational sociologists see power being expressed?

8) What is meant by the phrase 'the civilising process'?

9) How does the Sports Council define 'participation in sport'?

10) Outline three reasons why participation in sport has risen since the 1960s.

11) What effect does age have on sports participation?

12) Give three reasons why men have higher sports participation rates than women.

13) Explain the term 'socio-economic status' and explain what effect it has on sports participation.

14) Why does our cultural background affect what sports we play?

15) Explain two ways in which racism can be seen in sport.

THE INFLUENCE OF THE MEDIA IN SPORT

STUDENT ACTIVITY

To understand the importance of sport to the media undertake, the following study.

1   Visit a newsagent and work out the percentage of space taken up by magazines on the topic of sport. Compare it with magazines covering other leisure activities, such as music or cinema.

2   Are any sports more actively covered than others? If so, why is this the case?

Introduction

The media refers to the means of communication that reach large numbers of people. The happenings in sport are reported through a variety of media:

- newspapers
- television
- radio
- internet
- films
- books
- magazines
- teletext services.

It is important to understand that when reporting on sport the media professional will give their view or interpretation of an event, and this may differ from our view or another person's views. Sports events are described as being 'polysemic', meaning they are open to a wide range of interpretations. This process is called 'mediation' and it means that the facts are not always reported – they are an individual's view of the facts. Occasionally you may read a report of a game that you attended, and find that the reporter saw the game completely differently, almost as if you were at different games.

Newspapers

Sport is a major part of all national and local newspapers. The sports news is often the first thing that people turn to after buying their paper, or they decide which paper to buy based on its sports coverage. Often sport will be on the front page to help sell that paper. Sports coverage has expanded over the last 10 years, and now some papers have separate sports sections which may account for around a quarter of the paper's content.

Newspapers can be seen as fitting into three categories.

1   **Popular tabloids** – These include *The Sun*, *The Mirror* and *The Star* and their Sunday equivalents *The News of the World*, *The Sunday People* and *The Sunday Mirror*. They tend to focus on a small number of sports and often use sensational stories to sell their newspapers which are not necessarily related to action on the pitch. They are particularly interested in what is happening at clubs in terms of transfers, and which clubs are interested in which players. These papers are mainly targeted at male readers. *The Sun* and *The Mirror* have the highest circulation figures of any paper, at around four million copies a day.

2   **Tabloids**. These include *The Mail* and *The Daily Express* and their Sunday equivalents *The Mail on Sunday* and *The Sunday Express*. These papers are also intensely interested in sport, and will again focus on a few

sports. On the whole, these tabloids will be broader in the topics they report on and are generally aimed more at women.

3 **Broadsheets**. These are so called because they are printed on broad sheets of paper. They include the *Daily Telegraph, The Guardian, The Independent* and *The Times*. Their Sunday equivalents are *The Sunday Telegraph, The Observer, The Independent on Sunday* and *The Sunday Times*. They will focus on a much broader range of sports coverage and will include many articles relating to sporting issues, and insight into sports. They tend to have more interviews with sports people and have less speculation about sports people.

STUDENT ACTIVITY

For this experiment the teacher needs to buy a selection of newspapers for the same day. The newspapers on a Monday are best because they report all the weekend sport.

Complete a quantitative and qualitative analysis of sport in the British media. A quantitative analysis looks at the amounts of sports represented, and can be represented in figures. A qualitative analysis looks at the quality of the reports in terms of language used and the style of the report.

Choose three newspapers, one of which must be a broadsheet, one a tabloid and one a popular tabloid. Answer the following questions on each paper, and try to draw some conclusions.

Quantitative analysis

1 How many sports are reported? On which sports are there reports? Which sports do you think the paper sees as being most important?

2 How many reports are concerned with male competitors and how many with female competitors? Where is the first mention of a female competitor?

3 Are the photographs of males or females?

4 Are there any reports about minority sports?

5 Are there any reports about what are regarded as ethnic minority sports?

6 Are there any reports on sports for the disabled?

7 What percentage of the back page is headline, what percentage photograph and what percentage writing?

Qualitative analysis

Focus on the report of one sports contest which is reported by all newspapers.

1 What is the headline like? Is it comical, attention grabbing, scandalous, clever, a pun, an alliteration, poetic?

2 Look at the language and style of the report. Are the sentences long or short? Are the words long or short? Are the paragraphs long or short?

3 Does the report focus on one particular incident or player (or other person)?

4 To what extent do you think the report reflects reality?

5 Using the FOG index, establish the reading age of each newspaper.

The FOG index

To calculate the reading age of written materials you need to follow these steps.

1 Select a passage of writing. Count to 100 words, and then count how many sentences these 100 words are contained in (count the last sentence as well, even if it is incomplete).

2 Count the number of words of three or more syllables. Do not include proper names or hyphenated words (e.g. book-keeper).

continues overleaf

continued

3 Divide the number of words by the number of sentences,

e.g. words = 100, sentences = 5, $\frac{100}{5} = 20$

4 Add this figure to the number of words of three or more syllables: 20 + 15 = 35.

5 Multiply this figure by 0.4 and add 5 35 × 0.4 + 5 = 19. This is the reading age for that particular piece.

At the end of the session, report your findings to the rest of the group.

Television

Sport on television has grown rapidly over the last 15 years, and the people who own the broadcasting companies have gained more and more power in sport. We have recently seen the profound effect the collapse of the ITV Digital deal has had on football in the Nationwide leagues. In reality, the growth of sport has occurred through satellite and cable television companies, who now have four channels devoted to covering sport, plus a rolling news network and a pay per view channel. We have also recently seen both Manchester United (MUTV) and Chelsea launch their own television channels on satellite.

Table 10.1 shows the extent of coverage of sport on television in 1998. The figures show the number of minutes of coverage. The research was done by RSL.

Table 10.1 Sports Services from July–August 1998 in minutes of coverage

Sport	BBC1	BBC2	ITV	CH4	Eurosport	Sky	CH5	Percentage of total coverage
Football	4800	650	7475	2930	29725	102765	2815	16.54
General	935	295	215	7705	10610	76106	16610	12.31
Golf	1485	3548	0	60	2160	83900	90	9.98
Motorsport	390	1680	5620	0	26065	31945	645	7.26
Cricket	3042	9327	135	0	0	44970	0	6.29
Tennis	1130	2466	0	0	21035	15955	0	4.44
Motor cycling	175	90	0	0	14880	11310	0	2.89
Racing	2581	1161	60	7655	0	13460	0	2.72
Boxing	95	0	140	0	7845	16260	0	2.66
Rugby League	40	160	0	0	0	22910	0	2.53

Sport is presented on television in a 'mediated' form, meaning that television professionals have made decisions about how the sport is presented. It is usually done to make the sports event more attractive to the floating viewer. They know that the devoted sports fans will watch anyway, they are seeking to attract the attention of viewers who are less committed to the sport, but may enjoy the sense of occasion. As a result, television changes sport to maximise its attractiveness and its number of viewers.

How does television change sport?

1   Through choice of **camera positions**. The number of cameras at sports events has grown to include handheld cameras and cameras in all parts of the ground. This contributes to our enjoyment of the game, as we always receive the best view and we can observe the emotions and expressions of individual players. In the 1970s there were only cameras at one end of the game in the coverage of cricket; as a result, half the time was spent watching the batsman from behind. Today the innovations have included stump cameras and moving cameras.

2   Through the addition of **commentary** to interpret polysemic images. A new breed of commentators explains the action and interprets the events.

3   Through the addition of **expert comment**. This is done by using former and current players to add their views, as people who have been in those positions. These 'pundits' have become celebrities in their own rights.

4   By employing a **narrative technique**. The action is developed as a story to make it more understandable for the casual viewer and dramatic for the confirmed viewer.

How is the narrative technique is developed?

The narrative will go through five stages.

1   **Posing the question** – The commentary team will pose the question of who will win the match. They will consider past form, who the main protagonists may be and what has happened in the past.

2   **A partial answer** – As the action unfolds, a partial answer is provided. This may be as the result of a goal, a service broken or a competitor breaking away from the pack.

3   **A reformulation of the question** – As the action unfolds, the question is posed in a different way. Can the team now losing, come back to draw level and eventually win? Can the tennis player break back and save the set? Can the runner maintain their lead, or will they be caught?

4   **Periodic reorganisation** – During time outs, breaks in play or half time, the question is reorganised and the past events are reviewed. Again, the question of who will win is posed.

5   **Answer revealed** – At the end of the action the answer to the question of who will win is answered. The discussion will turn to what the implications of the result may be to each team or competitor.

Sometimes this posing of the question will be spread over a period of hours. For example, if you watch the build up to the FA Cup final, it will start at around 12 o'clock while the teams are still at their hotels. Various stories as to how they got to the final are told, and the various characters introduced and built up. This is done to create a story which will give a human interest to those spectators who are less familiar with the sport. We can see similar narratives being built up around the Wimbledon final and the Six Nations rugby matches.

The effects of increasing television coverage of sport

1.   Money

Increased sums of money come into the sport from television companies who pay for the rights to broadcast the sports. Also, sponsors become more willing to spend more money on sponsoring sport as they know it will receive national attention. Hence, sports finances receive a boost on two fronts, and this enables them to spend more money on players, players' wages and stadiums. The development of football in the 1990s was based on increased income from television companies and firms offering sponsorship. This extra income enabled the owners of the clubs to spend money on players from overseas, who were superstars of the sport; in turn this makes the sport more attractive to the viewers who are willing to pay more to watch sport on television and at the grounds.

2.   Changes in the rules of the game

In order to make sports more attractive, the rules can be amended to make the action faster or to penalise negative play. For example, in Rugby Union the points for a try rose from four to five, bonus points are given to teams scoring four or more tries and losing by fewer than five points. One-day cricket has punished bowlers delivering no balls by offering batsmen a free hit on the next delivery to which they cannot be out. The golden goal rule in football was introduced to promote attacking play in extra time, rather than teams playing defensively and relying on the penalty shoot out to win the game.

3.   Changes in the presentation of the sport

For example, cricket authorities addressed the problem of low attendances by introducing day–night cricket matches, which start at around 4p.m. and run until around 10.30p.m. This caters for people who are at work during the day, but are keen to watch a match in the evening. The matches themselves have been organised as part of family entertainment, where the players are introduced by music, and there is additional entertainment such as firework displays, bouncy castles and barbecues on offer. To make the game look more spectacular, the players wear coloured clothing and use a white ball with black stumps.

4.   Changes in starting times

The start times of matches are regularly changed to suit the needs of the television audience. Football games may kick off from any time between 11a.m. and 10p.m., depending on where the game is played and when the audience is available. This is great for the television viewers, but comes at a high cost to the spectators at the game who become very inconvenienced.

Other forms of media coverage

Radio is an increasingly popular medium and, due to the wealth of radio stations on air, it is possible to devote stations entirely to sports coverage. BBC Radio Five Live is a current affairs and sports station that offers a viable option to television through its in-depth coverage. This is a good example of mediation in sport, because we cannot see the action, and so are completely dependent on the observations and interpretations of the commentators. A very skilled commentator is able to draw a vivid verbal picture of the action and the environment and develop the sense of drama for the listener.

Books are increasingly becoming an important source of media coverage, and they have the advantage of interpreting events we may not have fully understood at the time. They are often sources of new information which could not be revealed at the time. For example, we learnt that the Republic of Ireland international, Tony Cascarino, was never actually qualified to play for Ireland. Recently, there has been controversy over revelations in Roy Keane's book that have resulted in disrepute charges.

Books also include the writing of authors who help us understand the motivation and emotions of spectators. For example, Nick Hornby's *Fever Pitch* helped a lot of people understand their own obsession with their sport. **Films** and **videos** such as *Hoop Dreams*, *Chariots of Fire*, *True Blue* and *One Day in September* have benefited from the drama and excitement of sport.

The **internet** has also become a rich source of information for people following sports, and there is a vast number of websites dedicated to sport in general and to individual sports. The problem has been that much information has appeared in an unedited, unmediated format and often reflects the views of a minority.

REVISION *QUESTIONS*

1) Explain what is meant by the term 'media'.

2) How do the media affect sports events?

3) Give examples of forms of media.

4) Explain the differences between the three types of newspapers.

5) How is sport changed through its presentation on television?

6) Outline two positive and two negative effects of the increasing amount of sport shown on television.

CURRENT ISSUES IN SPORT

This section seeks to address some issues that are current in sport today, and to discuss why they have become issues. An issue can be seen as a topic about which people have strong views and about which there may be opposing views. Some issues evolve because people feel that steps should be taken to change what is happening in sport.

Sport and politics

Why is sport linked to politics?

1. Sport reflects the society in which we live, in terms of the inequalities, social issues and values. Politics plays a large role in influencing the standards, values and beliefs of a society. For example, Marx said that the economic system is the factor which influences society, and the economic system is put in place by the government (Coghlan, 1990).

2. Sport is part of the social superstructure and is strongly influenced by the economic system. Sport is not a structure on its own (Ponomaryov, 1981).

3. Sport forms part of the National Curriculum in schools. This is decided upon by the Department of Education and Employment, and must be implemented by schools.

4. Sport has been used as a tool of social policy to improve the standards of people's lives and give people worthwhile activities to engage in.

5. Sport is an economic tool as well. Investment in sport creates wealth through creation of jobs, spending by the public, manufacture of clothing and equipment.

6. Sport has a role to play in improving the physical and mental health of the nation, thus improving productivity and reducing spending on NHS treatment. However, there may be a cost in improving health and people living longer.

The government recognises the value of sporting success and failure as being an index of national wellbeing (Scott Fleming, 1995). The failure of the England football team to qualify for the World Cup in 1994 was compared to the failure of John Major to manage an increasingly divided and unpopular Tory Party.

As long as governments spend money on sport, then sport will always be used for political means. Countries do not spend millions of pounds to host major sporting events, such as the Olympic Games or the World Cup, without expecting political gains in return. Countries will host sports events to show the world what an excellent country they are, or to show the success of their political system. This elevates the country as a world power and attracts increased investment into the country.

The history of political involvement in sport in Britain

1960–65 – Woolfenden Reports recommend a body be set up to influence sport in the public sector, as the value of sport in maintaining social order and the desire for international success is recognised.

1965 – Advisory Sports Council set up to offer advice on sporting matters to the government.

1972 – Sports Council formed as an independent body to implement governmental policy 'at arms length'. Aim was to increase standards of sport and to increase participation rates. Start of 'Sport for All' campaigns.

1974 – Minister for Sport was established (David Howell) as part of the Department for the Environment.

1975 – White Paper on Sport and Recreation sought to limit the role of the government in sport. It stated, 'It is not for the Government to seek to control or direct the diverse activities of people's leisure time.' Thus, intervention was to be kept to a minimum.

1980 – Conservative Government persuaded athletes to boycott the 1980 Olympic Games in Moscow, as a protest at the Russian invasion of Afghanistan. Athletes felt they were being used as political pawns, and the majority ignored the boycott. The 1980s saw increasing government intervention due to issues of football hooliganism at home and abroad. In particular, Margaret Thatcher implemented a policy of membership cards in 1984 for football supporters, without which they would not be admitted into their home ground. A series of fatal disasters in football stadium (Heysel, Bradford's Valley Parade, Hillsborough) caused the government to commission Lord Justice Taylor to prepare a report into safety at football grounds. This led to the creation of all-seater stadium for the top clubs. Also, issues of drug use and violence in sport received attention from the government.

1980–88 – Sports Council downgraded the 'Sport for All' campaign to target groups with low activity levels and social problems. These included people in inner city areas and the unemployed.

1990 – The Conservative policy of privatisation was extended to the leisure industry through Compulsory Competitive Tendering (CCT) of leisure facilities.

1992 – John Major's own interest in sport gave a boost; he also formed a new department called the Department of National Heritage to represent the interests of sport, arts, tourism and heritage. This meant for the first time sport's interests were represented at the highest level, in the cabinet.

1995 – White Paper: Raising the Game tackled the issue of the demise of sport in schools, and attempted to re-establish the importance sport had in schools in the 1980s.

1997 – Conservatives lost power after 18 years, and Labour replaced the Department of National Heritage with the Department of Culture, Media and Sport. Chris Smith is its Secretary of State and Kate Hoey is the Minister for Sport.

The 1990s saw the Sports Council devoting their work to the development of excellence, rather than encouraging participation. They saw this as being the role of local authorities. Sports Council activities included gaining lottery funding for the United Kingdom Sports Institute, the World Class Performance Programme, Sportsmatch and funding for capital projects.

Sports Council became Sport England; other regional councils received new names.

Political involvement in sport

Government intervention in sport falls into three main categories.

1   Sport as a means of implementing social policy in order to improve people's lives. This involves the 'programmed welfare provision' of sport, such as running public sector facilities and promoting participation.

2   Government passing permissive and prohibitive laws. For example, the banning of cock fighting, but the refusal to ban fox hunting or hare coursing. There have been legal constraints placed on boxing.

3   Sport can be used as a means of diplomacy and to influence international relations.

Historically in Britain, the government has tried to be a provider and facilitator rather than a controller. Thus, the Sports Minister acts in an advisory capacity.

The Olympic Games and political involvement

The Olympic Games are the highest profile sports event in the world, and often they are used to make political statements because the perpetrators can be sure of receiving a world-wide audience. Some examples of political interference are shown below.

Berlin 1936

These games were used by Hitler to display the power of the German nation to the rest of the world, and the strength of his new breed of Aryan men, who were tall, muscular, blond haired and blue eyed. However, this display backfired when a black American athlete, Jesse Owens, won four gold medals. Hitler, who was overtly racist and had already started his persecution of the Jews, was so angry that he refused to acknowledge or talk to Jesse Owens.

Mexico City 1968

At the height of the civil rights movement of the 1960s, when black people in America were fighting for equal rights to white people, black athletes chose the winner's podium to give a black power salute. Tommie Smith and John Carlos, who were first and third in the 200 m final, received their medals wearing black socks and no shoes, to represent poverty. When the national anthem of America was played they each raised their right arm and, with a clenched fist wearing a black glove, they made their protest. This protest was repeated by the men's 4 × 400 m relay team. They were publicly reprimanded by the US Olympic Committee and their government for using a sports arena to make a public statement.

Moscow 1980

These games were held just after the Soviet army invaded Afghanistan in 1979, and the war was ongoing. The American Olympic Committee refused to send any athletes to the games as they condemned the invasion. Margaret Thatcher told the British athletes to boycott the games; however, a ban could not be enforced. Several British athletes did attend, but they did so under the Olympic Flag rather than the Union Flag, and despite winning five gold medals the national anthem was never played.

Los Angeles 1984

Rather predictably, these games were boycotted by the Soviet Union and thirteen other socialist countries as a political statement in protest at the Americans boycotting their games. The Soviet Union also thought that the Los Angeles Olympic Committee were violating the spirit of the Olympics by using the games for commercial gains.

Drugs in sport

Introduction

Drugs have probably been used in sport as long as sport has been played, in order for athletes to gain an advantage over their opponents (see also pages 347–54). Legend tells us that the Arthurian Knights drank magical potions from the cup of Merlin before their bouts, and the Ancient Olympics in Greece were discontinued amid allegations of doping and corruption. In the early 1900s cyclists used strychnine (a poison) to boost performance, and by the 1960s this had turned to amphetamines. In 1960, the Danish cyclist, Kurt Jensen, died after overdosing on amphetamines, as did the British cyclist, Tommy Simpson, during the 1967 Tour de France.

The most notorious drug cheat was probably Ben Johnson of Canada, who tested positive at the Seoul Olympics of 1988 for an anabolic steroid called stanozolol. Johnson had been beaten by his nearest rival, Carl Lewis, about a month before in an emphatic manner. However, when the Olympic 100 m final came around, Johnson led from gun to finish and won easily in a new world record time of 9.79 seconds. Two days later he tested positive for drugs and was stripped of his medal and world record. It was common knowledge that Johnson had been using illicit drugs for years, however, he maintains that the drug he was using was not stanozolol and that he had been set up.

More recently we have seen sprinters Mark Richardson and Dougie Walker test positive for nandrolone. Michelle de Bruin, who won three gold medals at the 1996 Olympics, tested positive due to a sample which had been tampered with by introducing whiskey. Alain Baxter of Scotland lost his bronze medal at the winter Olympics in 2002 after testing positive for a stimulant present in a nasal spray.

Classification of drugs used

Name of drug	Reason used	Side-effects	Sports associated
Anabolic steroids – artificial production of testosterone, e.g. nandrolone, stanozolol.	Development of muscle mass. Allow athlete to train longer by delaying fatigue.	Impotence, increased aggression, liver damage, heart problems Women: development of male features.	Athletics, particularly sprinting; football; tennis; weightlifting.

continues overleaf

continued

Name of drug	Reason used	Side-effects	Sports associated
Stimulants – Activate the nervous system, e.g. pseudo-ephedrine, cocaine.	Speed up reaction times; delay tiredness; increase alertness; increase aggression	Raised heart rate; raised blood pressure; rise in body temperature and overheating.	Cycling, football
Narcotic analgesics – act as pain killers, e.g. opiates such as heroin, codeine and morphine.	Tolerate pain from injuries or activity; used to mask injury.	Addiction; induces a state of stupor; risk of further injury.	All sports
Beta blockers – used in patients with high blood pressure, e.g. atenolol and metaprolol	Slows the heart rate; steadies shaking limbs; induces feeling of calm.	Reduces circulation; causes fatigue; can cause shortness of breath.	snooker, darts, shooting
Diuretics – remove fluid from the body, e.g. frumil and burinex.	Quick loss of weight; removal of other drugs quickly from the system.	Dehydration, cramps, overheating, muscle weakness, irregular heartbeat.	horse racing, boxing, rowing
Peptide hormones – 'naturally occurring' hormones, such as EPO and somatotropin (HGH).	Production of red blood cells increases oxygen-carrying capacity of the blood; speeds up repair time; muscle growth.	Excess blood clotting; increased risk of stroke.	long-distance running, cycling
Blood doping – an injection of blood to increase the red blood cell count.	Increased haemoglobin levels mean the body can carry more oxygen.	Blood clotting; kidney failure.	running, cycling

Nandrolone

This anabolic steroid has been the subject of some controversy, mainly because a spate of athletes tested positive for it and then strongly protested their innocence. These included athletes Merlene Ottey (the Jamaican sprinter), Mark Richardson and Dougie Walker, footballers Christophe Dugarry, Edgar Davids and Jaap Stam, and tennis player Petr Korda. The debate centred on the view that nandrolone could be produced naturally by the body, in particular if the athlete was supplementing their diet with legal substances such as vitamins and minerals. Attention has been alerted to problems in the process of drug testing and whether innocent athletes are being branded as 'cheats'. Unfortunately, because nandrolone is performance enhancing it cannot be legalised, as that would give potential users the chance to cheat. Eventually, Mark Richardson and Dougie Walker were cleared of any wrongdoing and were able to resume their athletic careers.

What happens in a drugs test?

1   Immediately after an event, athletes will be notified that they have been chosen for a drug test. Twenty-four hours' notice is given for out-of-competition testing.

2   The athlete is accompanied to the drug testing area by a chaperone; they may also be accompanied by a coach or manager.

3   The athlete must give a urine sample. Sealed drinks arc provided to help the athlete go to the toilet.

4   When the athlete is ready, the chaperone will take them to the toilet and must witness them filling the sample bottle.

5   The athlete will divide the sample into two bottles which are identified as sample A and sample B.

6   The A and B samples are packed into small cases and locked with seals. They are then sent to the laboratory for analysis.

7   Sample A is tested first, and if it is positive a second test will take place on sample B.

8   The samples are tested for banned drugs.

The facts of drug testing are fairly clear, in that certain drugs are banned and if they are found in a urine sample then the athlete is deemed to have cheated. However, the issues surrounding drug use are not so clear. To start to appreciate the issues surrounding drug use, complete the following activity on moral and ethical issues.

Think about the following questions and then decide whether you agree or disagree with the statement.

AGREE   DISAGREE

1   Drug use in sport gives users an unfair advantage.
2   Sports are natural and drug use is unnatural.
3   Morally the issue of drug use in sport is clear-cut – the use of drugs is always wrong.
4   Sport is a healthy activity and should not be polluted by products that will potentially damage health.
5   There are no good reasons why athletes should use drugs.
6   Drugs are taken by choice and users should be severely punished.
7   If athletes relied more on the advice of doctors there would be less drug taking in sport.
8   Sporting bodies like the IOC, Sports Council and national governing bodies are doing everything they can to eliminate drug use in sport.

Discussion of the activity on moral and ethical issues of drug use

Drug use in sport gives users an unfair advantage

This would appear to be true, as a chemical advantage is conferred on the user. However, it suggests that the competition was fair in the first place, and this is debatable. For example, where an athlete is born in terms of altitude and climate, what training facilities are available and financial support they receive will all give them an advantage or a disadvantage. In middle- and long-distance athletics, Kenyan athletes will immediately have an advantage because they can train at altitude and in the heat. Australian athletes receive an advantage due to the massive investment their government has put into sports facilities and financial support. Drugs are unfair, but sport is never played on an level playing field.

Sports are natural and drug use is unnatural

Drug use involves introducing chemicals into the body. However, some of these chemicals are hormones which occur naturally in the body, so it would be a mistake to call this unnatural. Blood doping refers to the practice of taking a natural substance, blood, out of the body and then replacing it at a later date.

To consider sport as a natural activity may be a mistake, as athletes seek many aids to boost their performance, such as spiked or studded footwear, the choice of certain types of clothing and the design of sports equipment. These technological advances do not make the athletes more skilled, but they do improve their performances.

Morally the issue of drug use in sport is clear-cut – the use of drugs is always wrong

At the Commonwealth Games of 2002 the 100 m champion, Kim Collins, failed a drugs test for an asthma medication which could be said to be performance enhancing. However, when he declared that he had forgotten to inform the authorities of his asthma he was reinstated. At the winter Olympics of 2002, Alain Baxter failed a drugs test by testing positive to a stimulant found in a Vick's nasal spray. He explained that he had a cold, but he was disqualified on appeal and lost his medal. Two similar situations with two different outcomes. Surely, either both are wrong or both are right? It shows that drug use is tolerated in certain situations where medical conditions are involved.

Athletes use pain killers to enable them to compete when, without their use, they would not be able to compete. Some of these drugs are legal and some are banned. However, ultimately any pain killer is performance enabling, if not exactly performance enhancing.

Sport is a healthy activity and should not be polluted by products that will potentially damage health

Drugs can have very dangerous, even fatal side-effects and should be banned for this reason alone. However, sport can itself be a dangerous activity and detrimental to health. Athletes can experience a whole range of debilitating injuries that can cause permanent damage. Also, overtraining can lead to risk of viruses, fatigue-related illnesses and damage to bodily structures.

There are no good reasons why athletes should use drugs

The reasons athletes take drugs are complex and varied. An athlete may be motivated to take drugs because they are fed-up with not getting into the medal positions and receiving the rewards this brings. Often we hear people moaning that our athletes do not win enough medals, and the athletes have to sneak back into the country in shame. The alternative is a glorious homecoming met by adoring fans and an appreciative media. The respect and recognition of the public seems to be a strong motivator for taking drugs. The financial gains of being a successful athlete are potentially massive, while little is to be gained by being an also-ran; again, this would seem to be a reason for taking drugs.

Drugs are taken by choice and users should be severely punished

It is fair to say that much drug taking is planned and carried out in a calculated and organised way. Athletes will seek the support of their coaches and doctors to ensure it is done properly and with minimum risk. However, there were instances in Eastern Europe during the 1970s where athletes were given pills and told they were vitamins; these pills were performance-enhancing anabolic steroids and were taken unwittingly by innocent athletes. Some athletes may feel that in the current climate they have little chance of success unless they use drugs. If everyone else is using drugs, are you really left with a choice?

If athletes relied more on the advice of doctors there would be less drug taking in sport

One would imagine that doctors would advise against the use of drugs and be wary of their negative effects. However, for doctors there may be money to be made in supplying drugs and ensuring they are used correctly. During the Dubin inquiry into the use of drugs by Ben Johnson, the role of his doctor, Jamie Astaphan, was shown to be central to the whole process of Johnson's use. Doctors should not be seen as a large group who all hold the view that drug use is wrong, because some doctors will be involved in the activity. Their expertise is also a commodity valuable to the athletes and coaches.

Sporting bodies like the IOC and national governing bodies are doing everything they can to eliminate drug use in sport

We would like to believe this is the case; however, it is not always in the interests of these bodies to reveal positive drugs tests. Drug use will taint a sport and can cause potential sponsors to be put off sponsoring that sport. There is evidence that several positive drugs tests at the 1984 Olympic games were 'lost' so as to avoid any scandal. Athletes themselves will find it difficult to attract sponsorship if they have been associated with drugs. It is often written in the contract between sponsor and sport or individual that any money will be withdrawn if drug use is made public. So the quandary is whether to publish the tests and accept the censure or to hush them up.

Commercialisation of sport

Commercialisation refers to the practice of applying business principles to sport. So, as well as having two teams competing to be the winner, you also have a variety of groups of people who are trying to make a profit out of the contest. This process involves sport becoming a 'commodity' – something which is bought and sold. The people who run sports and sports clubs can sell their commodity to television companies to show the action, or to sponsors to endorse the sponsor's product. However, this process of commercialisation has effects on the sports over and above bringing new sources of income into sports and clubs. It is fair to say that not all effects are positive for the competitors or spectators.

Sports have always had a commercial aspect because they are seen as being a means of entertaining the public. Throughout history, sports have attracted large audiences, even back in the days of the gladiatorial contests of the Romans, and the Ancient Olympic Games of the Greeks. In the late nineteenth and early twentieth centuries, the sports of football and cricket attracted vast audiences. The financial opportunities offered by sports were not truly exploited until the 1960s, and the major forces were the growth of television and the globalisation of sport. Television meant that sport could be watched beyond the confines of the stadium and, as a result, it became more commercially viable for television companies to pay for the rights to broadcast sports. Also, the sponsors now saw that television could spread the message of their products further afield. Globalisation of sport means the spread of sport to the different countries of the world, and thus the development of new audiences in new countries. For example, Britain now shows sports such as basketball and American football, football from Spain and Italy, and rugby union from Australia and South Africa.

However, commercialised sports do not work in all societies. They are predominantly found in developed societies where people have enough free time to be involved in watching sport, disposable income to spend on sport and means of private transport to travel to the venues.

For sports to work as a commercial success not only do they need certain characteristics, but so do the societies in which they are played.

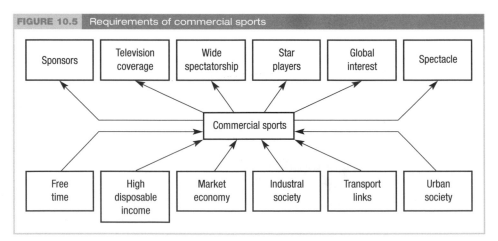

FIGURE 10.5   Requirements of commercial sports

Figure 10.5 shows that commercialised sports need sponsors and television coverage to bring extra revenue into the sport. However, they must also be global in their coverage and interest and have a strong support locally from which to draw spectators. Spectators add the key ingredient of 'atmosphere' to a contest, without which the spectacle would fall flat. Commercialised sports need to be a spectacle, in that they must attract and hold the audience's attention and be dramatic. This spectacle is helped by the development of star players, whom the audience know – some people may watch the contest purely to see their favourite player.

Societies where commercialised sports thrive will all have several characteristics in common.

✪   They are industrial societies which have high levels of output, thus making them wealthy and giving the people a high level of disposable income to spend on sports and high levels of free time during which they can watch these sports.

✪   Industrial societies tend to have high levels of urbanisation, meaning that most people live in towns and cities, which means that they can easily attend sports events that are urban based.

✪   Well developed transport links are needed to ensure that people can visit sports grounds.

Effects of commercialisation on sports

The introduction of new groups of people into sports

Prior to commercialisation, sports were run by governing bodies, and clubs by their owners and managers. However, the introduction of media professionals and companies offering sponsorship have led to new contracts being produced. As a result, these new groups of people have power over the clubs and the sport and can dictate certain aspects of the game. Thus, the television companies can dictate what time the action starts, in order for it to coincide with their peak audience figures, and sponsors can insist on logos being shown and having their brand name on clothing and equipment.

Increased merchandising

The development of merchandising has become one of the greatest successes in the commercialisation of sport. Rather than just supporting your team, you can now buy all types of merchandise to show that you support them. The most successful avenue has been in the form of replica clothing. Football shirts are the main target and they are now worn as fashion statements as much as to show allegiance to your team. Indeed, England's grey away strip was designed so that it would look good with jeans. The ECB, the governing body of cricket, introduced coloured clothing into the one-day league as a way of making it more of a spectacle; however, they also stated that it would become an additional source of revenue for the clubs who could sell the shirts. Most Premiership football clubs now have superstores attached to their grounds where supporters can buy merchandise. This has put a lot of pressure on parents whose children want the most up-to-date sports kits as a status symbol.

Rule changes

Commercialised sports need to be spectacles, and thus the governing bodies may make amendments to the rules to make them more exciting and dramatic. Changes are made to speed up play or prevent negative play, such as abolishing the back pass to the goalkeeper in football. Rugby union has been constantly tinkered with to speed up the game and stop static situations, such as rucks and mauls, from delaying the action. Cricket is currently experimenting with a form of cricket called 'power cricket', where the game consists of two innings of fifteen overs each, and runs are scored depending on how far into the stands the ball is hit. The aim is to maximise the entertainment value and thus the value of watching.

Commercialisation of the Olympic Games

Commercialisation in sport takes two main forms: the attraction of sponsorship and sale of broadcasting rights. These measures improve the chances of making profit from the sports event. However, to attract sponsorship you need an attractive product. The Olympics Games are attractive in themselves, but measures have been taken to make the Games more attractive, such as:

- ✪ glamorous opening ceremonies

- ✪ some events where professional athletes are able to compete

- ✪ attracting world sports stars

- ✪ setting world records

- ✪ adding new sports attractive to the audience.

The first Olympic Games to completely embrace the concept of commercialism was the 1984 Olympic Games in Los Angeles, which were funded by a combination of the sale of broadcasting rights and sponsorship. For example, Coca Cola paid £30 million, Mars paid £22 million and Eastman Kodak £21 million to ensure exclusive rights to sponsor the Olympic Games. The 1984 Olympic games made a profit $215m.

Where does the money for the Olympic Games come from?

Between 2001 and 2004, the International Olympic Committee (IOC) will receive $4531 million in revenue. The breakdown of where it comes from is as follows:

- ✪ $2236 million from broadcasting rights (50%)

- ✪ $1815 million from corporate sponsorship (40%)

- ✪ $380 million from ticket sales (8%)

- ✪ $100 million from merchandise (2%).

Sponsorship of the Olympic Games

In 1996, 32% of income to the Olympic Games in Atlanta came from sponsorship. This was brought about by TOP (The Olympic Programme), which restricts the number of sponsors. This enables companies to receive exclusive rights with regard to the type of product they are advertising. As a result, the sponsor will be willing to pay more in the knowledge that they will be the only one of that type of company providing sponsorship. So the sponsor pays for the publicity, but also to block their competitors from providing sponsorship.

At the 1976 Montreal Olympic Games there were 600 sponsors, which was seen as being too many, so it was decided to restrict the number of sponsors:

TOP 1 1985–1988: 70 sponsors paying $95m

TOP 2 1989–1992: 12 sponsors paying $175m

TOP 3 1993–1996: 10 sponsors paying $300m

TOP 4 1997–2000: 11 sponsors (no figures available)

TOP 5 2001–2004: 10 sponsors (no figures available)

TOP sponsors are guaranteed exclusive world-wide marketing opportunities, and this is protected by the creation of categories to ensure only one of each type. The sponsors for 2004 Athens Olympic Games are:

Coca-Cola	Panasonic
Kodak	MacDonalds
Visa	John Hancock
Time-Warner	Samsung
Xerox	SchlumbergerSema

At the Olympic Games there is no stadium advertising or advertising on competitor's clothing. The All England Tennis Championships at Wimbledon is the only other sports event which prohibits this type of advertising.

In 1996 Coca-Cola developed 88 advertisements for the Games and never showed the same advertisement twice in the 17 days of the Games. Their contract cost $41m.

Where does the money go?

✪ Ninety-three per cent goes to the 199 National Olympic Committees (NOCs), Organising Committees for the Olympic Games (OCOGs) and the International Federations (IFs).

✪ Seven per cent goes to the International Olympic Committee (IOC).

Amateurism and professionalism

Professionalism means accepting rewards, usually in the form of money, for playing sports. In the pre-industrialised forms of sport, rewards were commonly given to competitors and this was never seen as an issue. The players of sport in the Victorian era were the sons of the aristocracy and the middle class. As they came from families with money, it was not important that these players were paid because they already had the money to spend on sport or were in well-paid jobs.

Professionalism became an issue in the late nineteenth century as standards of play started to rise. In order to have better teams, the owners needed a commitment of time from their players. However, this resulted in their missing work and not receiving as much money as they could, so the owners started to pay players to compensate them for the time they had missed at work. The **amateurs** (unpaid sportspeople) did not believe that you should be paid for playing sport, and thus a conflict occurred. It was seen as being a class conflict because the amateurs tended to be from the upper classes while the professional tended to be working class. This conflict is one of the reasons that rugby split up into rugby union and rugby league; rugby union players did not agree with paying players, while rugby union players wanted to receive payments. In 1895 the two codes of rugby split, one to form the professional game and one to continue with the amateur game.

Nowadays, amateurism is seen as being outdated, and even in the Olympic Games the practice of professionalism is accepted. It is understood that to reach the standards of performance needed to be successful at an international level it is necessary to devote significant amounts of time to training and, indeed, to resting. This dedication does not leave enough time to work as well, so if we want the performances we must accept the professional status. There are still many sports which are predominantly amateur, mainly because there is not enough revenue from the sport to pay players. It is fair to say that the more commercialised a sport is, the more need for professional players to present the spectacle required.

The Olympic Games

The modern Olympics were reintroduced in 1896 as a result of the work of a French aristocrat, Baron Pierre de Coubertin. He was extremely interested in the work of Thomas Arnold at Rugby School, and he travelled to England to visit Arnold and discuss their views on the value of sport. He was also aware of games held from 1850 by the Much Wenlock Olympic Society in Shropshire, and he was later to meet their founder, Dr Penny Brooke. He was concerned about the lack of physical fitness and national pride among the youth of France, and saw the success Arnold had had in developing these qualities through sport. In 1894 he organised a conference involving 79 members from 12 countries and this resulted in the formation of the International Olympic Committee (IOC). Their aim was to use a sports festival to improve international relations and promote world peace. They presented four Olympic Ideals:

1   To unite the youth of the world every four years to play sport in a spirit of friendship. To meet each other and to get to know each other, as this leads to respect and respect leads to peace.

2   To develop the physical and mental self.

3   The importance of taking part and not the winning.

4   To use sport to develop peace and not prepare for war.

An interpretation of these ideals

1   Through international sports participation, international friendship, goodwill and peace will be created, which will lead to a happier and safer world.

STUDENT ACTIVITY

Consider the extent to which these ideals are still relevant to the modern Olympic movement.

2   To make the world aware of the benefits of sport/physical activity and the part it plays in developing the body and personality, thus producing better citizens through character building that follows participation in organised sport. Thus we get the motto: *Mens sana in corpore sano* (a healthy mind in a healthy body).

3   **a)**   Sport can 'demonstrate the principles of fair play and good sportsmanship'. These values will be transferred to everyday life.

   b)   To reinforce the values of amateurism and show that sport is fun and enjoyable. The reward of sport is in the playing. Sport is a supplement to make people's lives richer and should not become too important and certainly not a career.

   'The important thing in the Olympic Games is not winning but the taking part. The important thing in life is not conquering but fighting well.'

Symbols of the Olympic movement

FIGURE 10.6   The Olympic flag

✪   **The Olympic flag** contains a representation of the symbol of the IOC. This is the five interconnecting rings, each a different colour on a white background. The rings represent the five continents of the world (Europe, Africa, America, Asia and Oceania), which have been won over to Olympism.

✪   The **motto** of the IOC is *Citius, Altius, Fortius*, which means 'faster, higher, stronger'. This represents the toil of the competitors to run faster, jump higher and compete more strongly.

✪   The **Olympic flame** is a reference back to the era of the Ancient Olympic Games, which involved a torch being lit at the altar of Zeus. The tradition of the torch relay was not introduced until the Berlin Games of 1936.

✪   At each Games one of the competitors is chosen to read the **Olympic Oath** on behalf of the other competitors. The oath reads:

   In the name of all the competitors I promise that we shall take part in these Olympic Games respecting and abiding by the rules which govern them in the true spirit of sportsmanship.

✪   Doves are used as a symbol of **peace** at all the Olympic Games.

A brief history of the Olympic Games

I Athens 1896 – The first Olympic Games was held in Athens in tribute to the Ancient Olympics held in Greece up until 393 AD. The programme involved 43 events covering nine sports.

II Paris 1900 – In a tribute to de Coubertin, the second Games were held in Paris. The Games were poorly organised and involved a mix of recognised and unrecognised sports; the confusion made it difficult to work out who actually won medals. Some women were included among the 1319 competitors and played tennis and golf.

III St Louis 1904 – These games were held at the same time as the World Fair and were poorly attended, with only 617 athletes from 12 countries.

There were interim Games held in 1906 in Athens as a compromise to the Greeks who wanted to host all the Olympic Games! These are not officially recognised as an Olympiad.

IV London 1908 – These games were held in Shepherd's Bush and are notable because the British team had a massive medal haul of over 50 gold medals. These Games were also notable because the marathon distance was extended to 26 miles and 385 yards so that the race could be started outside Windsor Castle in the presence of the Royal Family, and finish at the Shepherd's Bush Stadium. This is still the recognised distance for a marathon race.

V Stockholm 1912 – This was a very successful Olympic Games and the number of competitors had now risen to 2035 from 22 countries.

VI Berlin 1916 – These Games were cancelled because of the First World War.

VII Antwerp 1920 – Despite being deeply affected by the war, de Coubertin worked hard to ensure that the Games continued, and many people who had been involved in the war competed.

VIII Paris 1924 – The number of competitors was still on the rise, with over 3000 competitors from 44 nations, although Germany had still not returned. Two British athletes, Eric Liddell and Harold Abrahams, were fierce competitors over 100 m; however, Eric Liddell was a devout Christian and when he discovered that the heats of the 100 m were on a Sunday he decided that he could not compete. As a result, he changed to the 400 m and won in a world record time of 47.6 seconds.

FIGURE 10.7 Harold Abrahams won the 1924 100 m in a new Olympic record

IX Amsterdam 1928 – By this time the Games had become well and truly established, with 2034 athletes from 46 countries. The involvement of women took a setback after several women collapsed after the 800 m race. The officials concluded that women were not physiologically suited to running long distances, and thus women's long-distance events disappeared until the 1964 Olympic Games.

X Los Angeles 1932 – The difficulty and cost of travel limited the number of competitors. However, the number of spectators attending was over one and a quarter million. These Games also saw the first Olympic village for the athletes.

XI Berlin 1936 – By this time Hitler's Nazi Party was in power and he used these Games as a political statement to demonstrate how mighty a world power Germany had become. However, Hitler's racist statements were undermined by the victories of black American athlete, Jesse Owens, who won gold medals at 100 m, 200 m, long jump and 4 × 100 m relay. Hitler was furious and chose to ignore the presence of Jesse Owens, who had disproved his ideals.

XII Tokyo/Helsinki and XIII London The Games were cancelled due to the Second World War.

XIV London 1948 – Despite being seriously damaged during the war, London agreed to host the Games. They were held at Wembley Stadium, where a track was hurriedly laid. There were over 4500 athletes from 59 countries.

XV Helsinki 1952 – things were getting back to normal after the disruption of the Second World War, although Germany was still not present. The Soviet Union returned after an absence of 40 years. The Czech athlete, Emil Zatopek, won the 5000 m, the 10 000 m and the marathon in what is seen as being as great a feat as the achievements of Jesse Owens.

XVI Melbourne 1956 – By 1956 the world was on the verge of war, as Hungary had been invaded by the Soviet Union, leading to the withdrawal from the Games of Spain and Hungary; Egypt and Lebanon withdrew due to the Suez Canal crisis. China withdrew over a row with Taiwan and did not return until 1984.

XVII Rome 1960 – These Games were the first to receive widespread television coverage, although mainly in black and white. There was little political disruption, except with regard to the South African team who had sent an all-white team despite around 89% of their population being black; South Africa was expelled from the Games and was not readmitted until 1992.

XVIII Tokyo 1964 – These Games were nicknamed the 'happy games', because all the athletes seemed to enjoy them so much and the Japanese spread a spirit of happiness.

XIX Mexico City 1968 – These games were surrounded by controversy and disaster. Mexico City was experiencing high levels of poverty and many citizens were unhappy at the amount of money being spent on the Games. Ten days before the Games were due to start, a demonstration turned into a battle between the protesters and the military, and resulted in 260 deaths and 1200 injured. This proved to be the end of the trouble, and the Games were marked with spectacular performances due to the thin air at the high altitude.

These Games also became notorious for the American 200 m athletes performing a black power salute during the medal ceremony, in protest at the treatment of black people in American Society.

XX Munich 1972 – Although these Games were well organised and brilliantly run, they were overshadowed by disaster. The simmering conflict in the Middle East between the Israelis and the Palestinians was brought to international attention. In the early hours of 5th September, a group of Palestinian terrorists broke through the lax security and reached the Israeli athletes. One was killed and another ten were held as hostages. The Palestinians demanded a helicopter to take them to the airport to catch a plane to the Middle East, and the release of Palestinian prisoners held in Israel. The German police decided to attack the Palestinians and, as the helicopter landed at the airport, they opened fire. This resulted in the Palestinians exploding hand grenades in the helicopter, killing all ten hostages. At the memorial service in the stadium the next day, it was declared that the Olympic movement would not be disrupted by terrorism and that the Games would go on. These Games saw the start of success for African athletes, and introduced the world to the Soviet gymnast, Olga Korbut. Mark Spitz achieved a record of seven gold medals, all with world-record performances in the swimming pool.

XXI Montreal 1976 – These Games were characterised by the massive financial cost that had to be borne by the taxpayers of Montreal, mainly due to the incompetence of the organisers, who lost control of the finances. Great athletes included Lasse Viren of Finland, who repeated his 5000 m and 10 000 m double of 1972, and Alberto Jauntorena of Cuba, who did the 400 m and 800 m double.

XXII Moscow 1980 – The boycott by Western countries, lead by USA as a protest over the Russian invasion of Afghanistan, undermined these well-organised Games. The British athletes were asked by Margaret Thatcher not to attend, but many did and competed under the Olympic flag. The British athletes were hugely successful, with gold medals for Daley Thompson, Allan Wells, Sebastian Coe and Steve Ovett.

XVIII Los Angeles 1984 – By this time, 140 different countries were competing in the Olympic Games. There would have been more had it not been for the revenge boycott of the Soviet Union and most of the Eastern European countries. The main achievement of these Games was the four gold medals won by the American sprinter, Carl Lewis. These Games were characterised by commercialisation, typified by a lavish opening ceremony and mass advertising.

XXIV Seoul 1988 – The big story of these Games was the disqualification of Canadian sprinter, Ben Johnson, who had failed a drug test for anabolic steroids after winning the 100 m final in a world record time. These Games had a massive 8465 athletes, mainly thanks to the lack of boycotts (except for North Korea) which had afflicted previous games.

XXV Barcelona 1992 – These Games were seen as being a great success because Barcelona had spent huge amounts on building facilities and developing a new road network. All countries with a National Olympic Committee were represented, including South Africa, who had recently dismantled their system of apartheid and released the ANC leader, Nelson Mandela. Germany took part as one nation once again. Among the highlights was Linford Christie winning the 100 m final, and the US 'Dream Team' in the men's basketball, which had been opened up to professional teams in a bid to make the Games more glamorous.

XXVI Atlanta 1996 – Despite traffic problems which made it difficult for the athletes to reach the stadium in time, and a bomb blast in Olympic Park, which killed one person and injured 110 people, these Games were successful due to the quality of performances. Michael Johnson completed the 200 m and 400 m double, and smashed the world record over 200 m; Carl Lewis became only the fourth person to win the same individual event four times when he won the long jump.

XXVII Sydney 2000 – These Games were declared to be the most successful ever by the IOC President, Juan Antonio Samaranch. This was due to the spirit in which the Games were competed and the quality of the performances. Great Britain had its most successful Olympic games for many years, including Steve Redgrave winning his fifth successive gold medal in rowing events.

XXVIII Athens in 2004 – The next Games will find the Olympics to be as relevant and exciting as ever, having grown from modest beginnings to become the greatest multi-sports event in the world.

REVISION *QUESTIONS*

1) Why is sport so often made into a political issue?

2) Give two recent examples of politics interfering with sport.

3) Explain four types of drugs that athletes may use and explain what effects they have.

4) Why might athletes choose to use drugs?

5) What activities are involved in the commercialisation of sport?

6) How can commercialisation negatively affect sports?

7) How has commercialisation been shown through the Olympic movement?

8) Why have sports had to embrace the concept of professionalism?

9) Why have the Olympic Games become so important to society today?

10) Choose two Olympic Games and research them thoroughly, finding out about their success, any problems encountered and who the main characters were due to their performances.

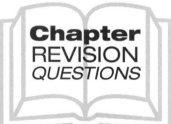

Chapter REVISION *QUESTIONS*

1) Choose a sport from the following list and trace its history from a folk sport to its modern day form: cricket, hockey, tennis or golf.

2) Take one of the sociological theories discussed and apply it to explain one of the influences on sports participation.

3) Choose a sports event covered by television and the media, and write a report on how the event has become 'mediated'.

4) Choose a current issue in sport to research and present your findings to the group. Your presentation should include an outline of the issue, an explanation of why it is an issue and the arguments involved in the issue.

BTEC NATIONAL IN SPORT AND EXERCISE SCIENCE

REFERENCES AND FURTHER READING

Beashel, P. and Taylor, J. (1996) *Advanced Studies in Physical Education and Sport.* Nelson.

Beashel, P., Sibson, A. and Taylor, J. (2001) *The World of Sport Examined.* Nelson Thornes.

Cashmore, Ellis (2000) *Making Sense of Sport.* London: Routledge.

Clarke, J. and Critcher, C. (1985) *The Devil makes work.* MacMillan.

Davis, R. J., Bull, C. R., Roscoe, J. V., Roscoe, D. A. (2000) *Physical Education and the Study of Sport.* London: Mosby.

Dunning, Eric, Figurational Sociology and the Sociology of Sport. University of Leicester, MSc in the Sociology of Sport, Module 5, Unit 8.

Dunning, Eric, *Notes on the Early Development of Soccer.* University of Leicester C.R.S.S.

Dunning, Eric, *The Civilizing Process.* University of Leicester. C.R.S.S.

Dunning, Eric and Sheard, Ken (1979) *Barbarians, Gentlemen and Players.* Oxford: Martin Robertson.

Haralambos, M. and Holborn, M. (1995) *Sociology: Themes and Perspectives.* London: Collins Educational.

Haywood, L. et al (1995) *Understanding Leisure.* Stanley Thornes.

Hodgson, D. *Anyone For Cocktails: Drugs, Sport and Morality.* University of Leicester. C.R.S.S.

Polley, M. (1998) *Moving the Goalposts – a history of sport and society since 1945.* London: Routledge.

Torkildsen,G. (1999) *Leisure and Recreation Management.* E&FN Spon.

Walvin, J. (1994) *The People's Game (the History of Football Revisited).* Mainstream Publishing.

Wesson, K., Wiggins, N. Thompson, G. Hartigan, S. (2000) *Sport and P.E.: A Complete Guide to Advanced Level Study.* London: Hodder and Stoughton.

Vamplew, Wray *Industrialisation and Popular Sport in the Nineteenth Century.* University of Leicester. C.R.S.S.

Websites

www.ausport.gov.au
www.bbc.co.uk/sport
www.olympics.org
www.sports-drugs.com
www.sportengland.org

FITNESS TESTING

Physical fitness can be split into two sections: health-related components and skill-related components. The health-related components of physical fitness include strength, aerobic endurance, muscular endurance, flexibility and body composition. Skill-related physical fitness includes balance, co-ordination, speed, agility, power and reaction time.

Health-related physical fitness is given this name as the components are involved in the prevention of a range of diseases, including cardiovascular diseases and all their associated problems. Skill-related fitness, however, is more relevant to sports people who wish to improve their performance in competitive environments.

By the end of this chapter students should:

- ✪ be aware of the importance of health-related fitness

- ✪ be aware of the importance of skill-related fitness for sports people

- ✪ be able to investigate the fitness requirements of a range of sports

- ✪ have a good understanding of the methods of health screening and fitness testing

- ✪ be able to prepare and conduct a range of fitness tests.

HEALTH-RELATED FITNESS

Components of health-related fitness

There are five main components of health-related fitness.

1   **Strength** is the ability of a muscle to exert force for a short period of time. The maximum force that can be generated is a result of the size and number of muscles involved, the types of muscle fibres that are activated, the physical condition of the muscle groups, the co-ordination of the muscle groups and the mechanics of the levers involved. Strength is most effectively developed when the muscle or muscle group is overloaded, which means the muscle is exercised against a resistance that it does not normally encounter. An overload can be achieved by lifting a weight that gives a resistance of at least 30% of maximal effort. Doing this stimulates the muscle to adapt, which leads to the size and therefore the strength of the muscle increasing.

FIGURE 11.1   Training to develop strength

2   **Aerobic endurance** is the ability to exercise continuously for prolonged periods without tiring. A person's aerobic endurance is determined by the amount of oxygen that can be transported by the body to the working muscles, and the efficiency of the muscles to use that oxygen. The heart is a muscle and, like skeletal muscles, will respond to exercise by getting stronger. The lungs also respond to training by becoming more efficient at exchanging the carbon dioxide that we produce for the oxygen that we need. At present, the best test to reliably measure aerobic fitness is the maximal oxygen uptake (VO_2max) test.

People with low levels of aerobic fitness tend to get tired more easily, and are not able to maintain activities for as long as people who do regular exercise. To improve aerobic endurance, it is necessary to perform aerobic-type exercises, such as walking, jogging, swimming and cycling.

3   **Muscular endurance** is the ability of a muscle, or a group of muscles, to sustain repeated contractions. In order to improve muscular endurance, it is necessary to exercise the specific muscle groups for periods of time. If a person wants to use resistance equipment to increase their muscular endurance, they would use low weights and high repetitions (12 or more).

4   **Flexibility** is defined as the range of motion around a joint. This movement, however, is restricted by the structure of the joint, and the muscles, ligaments and tendons around it. In order to improve flexibility a variety of stretching methods can be used. Flexibility is an important health-related fitness component as it helps to reduce the risk of injuries and increase performance by allowing muscles to work over a greater range of movement.

5   **Body composition** is the makeup of the body in terms of lean mass (muscle, bone, vital tissue and organs) and fat mass. It is normally expressed as percentage body fat, so if someone has an estimated 30% body fat, the other 70% is everything else in their body. Too much fat in the body will usually hinder athletic performance and has also been linked to conorary heart disease. A low-fat diet with restricted calorie intake, combined with aerobic exercise, is usually the best method of decreasing the percentage of body fat and increasing the lean body tissue.

Importance of health-related fitness

As our lifestyles have become much more sedentary over the years, the nation's fitness levels have dropped dramatically. As a result, we are experiencing higher levels of obesity, coronary heart disease (CHD), diabetes and a range of other diseases that can usually be prevented through taking part in health-related fitness. CHD is the main cause of death in the western world. However, many studies to date have evidence to strongly suggest that inactivity is the most significant cause of CHD. Therefore, taking part in a health-related fitness programme will reduce a persons risk of dying from a heart attack. Exercise is also an effective method of rehabilitation for people who have suffered from a heart attack.

It is important for people of all ages to have good levels of **aerobic fitness** in order to have a good quality of daily life. As children grow, they should take part in fitness activities in order to ensure their muscles, bones and cardiovascular systems develop well. As they get older, taking part in regular exercise will help to slow the aging process of the cardiorespiratory systems. Regular aerobic activity burns off quite a number of calories. The longer and harder a person exercises, the more calories they will burn. Therefore, regular aerobic exercise will also help to control a person's weight.

An area of fitness that people often neglect is **flexibility**. As we get older, our bodies become less flexible. If a person lacks flexibility they are more likely to injure themselves through over stretching and pulling a muscle. Even simple activities such as reaching up to a top cupboard shelf for a can of baked beans could leave a person in a great deal of pain.

It is important to maintain **muscular strength** for a variety of reasons. Again, as people get older, they are much more prone to back injuries, which can result in them spending days lying down, unable to move and in a great deal of pain. However, ensuring that the abdominal muscles are exercised regularly will help them to act as a girdle to support the back and prevent such injuries from occurring.

By taking part in resistance training exercises or weight-bearing activities, a person will be less likely to suffer from osteoporosis, a disease in which the bones become very fragile and much more likely to break after a fall.

Regular health-related exercise has a huge number of physical benefits which will help to improve the quality of a person's physical life. However, research to date also indicates that regular exercise has an impact on a person's mental health. People who are in stressful jobs or who are going through stressful periods in their lives, such as taking exams, will benefit from taking part in exercise in order to alleviate this stress. A range of hormones are released during and after exercise that act to relax the body, thus helping the person to relax.

Current fitness guidelines

Frequency of exercise

Frequency of exercise refers to the number of exercise sessions a person takes part in per week. In order to improve both aerobic fitness and to lose body fat or maintain body fat levels, you should take part in aerobic exercise at least three times a week. The American College of Sports Medicine (ACSM) recommends three to five days a week for most cardiovascular programmes. Physical activity should be spread out throughout the week, rather than done on consecutive days, in order to minimise the risk of sustaining injuries.

Duration of exercise

This refers to the length of time a person spends exercising. The exercise session should not include the time spent warming up and cooling down and should last at least 20 minutes in order to gain significant aerobic and fat-burning benefits. The longer the duration of the exercise session, the more kilocalories and fat will be burned and the greater the benefits to the cardiovascular system. It is important that the duration of the exercise increases gradually, not going from 20 minutes of exercise directly to 60 minutes or more.

Intensity

A person should exercise at a target heart rate of 60% to 90% of maximum. Target heart rate can be determined by carrying out the following calculations.

$$220 - \text{age} = \text{maximum heart rate}$$

$$\frac{(\text{maximum heart rate} \times 60)}{100} = \text{lowest heart rate for training effect}$$

$$\frac{(\text{maximum heart rate} \times 90)}{100} = \text{highest heart rate for training effect}$$

For example, a 50-year-old woman's maximum heart rate is:

$$220 - 50 = 170 \text{ bpm}$$

Her lowest heart rate for training effect would be

$$\frac{(170 \times 60)}{100} = 102$$

Therefore, 102 bpm is her lowest target heart rate regardless of the type of physical activity she decides to do.

SKILL-RELATED FITNESS

Components of skill-related fitness

These components of fitness are not essential to the maintenance of an individual's health. However, in order to be good at most sports, improvement in the skill-related components of fitness is crucial. There are six main components of skill-related fitness.

1   **Power** can be described as 'fast strength', in that it is a combination of strength and speed. An athlete needs to have power for sports that require explosive movements, such as sprinting, long jump, rugby and tennis. Resistance training and **plyometrics** training would help to train a person's power.

2   **Reaction time** is the time it takes for a person to respond to a signal. For example, sprinters need to have fast reaction times in response to the starter's pistol. If they are slow to respond they will have a bad start and are very unlikely to win the race.

3   **Agility** is the ability to change direction rapidly. It is used in situations where it is necessary to run around opposition team members or around a court. To train a person's agility, specific agility drills need to be carried out involving running sideways and forwards and backwards. Movement patterns should be chosen that are specific to the athlete's sport.

STUDENT ACTIVITY

Student Activity

Using a range of sources, including text books, journals and the internet, find a definition for each of the following:

✪ strength
✪ speed
✪ aerobic fitness
✪ muscular endurance
✪ flexibility
✪ body composition
✪ agility
✪ balance
✪ co-ordination
✪ reaction time
✪ power

Remember to reference each definition with the author's name, the date the reference was published, the title of the source and the publisher.

4 **Balance** is needed more in some sports than others. For example, gymnasts need good balance in order to carry out the majority of their exercises.

5 **Co-ordination** is the ability to perform complex motor skills. Running while throwing, passing, heading or catching a ball requires a lot of co-ordination, so a person must train in order to develop this skill.

6 **Speed** is the ability to perform a movement quickly. Speed of movement of either the total body or of a particular body part is an important component of performance-related fitness. Clearly it is important in all forms of racing, and also in games where it is necessary to dodge and get away from an opponent.

REVISION QUESTIONS

1) What is the difference between health-related fitness and skill-related fitness?

2) Regularly taking part in which component of fitness helps to prevent CHD? Explain your answer.

3) Which component of fitness is often neglected in sport and exercise training?

4) What are the current exercise guidelines, according to the ACSM?

5) In accordance with the ACSM guidelines, write a week's training programme that takes into consideration all of the health-related components of fitness for the following people:

a) an overweight 20-year-old male

b) a healthy 18-year-old

c) a 70-year-old female.

FITNESS REQUIRE-MENTS OF A RANGE OF SPORTS

In order to safely and effectively take part in sports it is necessary to have all the basic components of health-related fitness, however, depending on the sport, some components need to be trained more than others. For virtually every sport, it is necessary to have a low percentage of body fat, as excess fat acts to hinder performance. Different sports also have different skill-related component requirements, which also need to be trained in order for a player to excel in their sport.

There are a number of key aspects that need to be considered when planning a training program for a sports person:

✪ the length of the activity

✪ the strength required

✪   the flexibility required

✪   the skills required.

If the activity lasts for a period of less than 30 minutes, aerobic fitness and muscular endurance tend not to be major components that need to be trained. For example, weight lifting involves short bursts of intense activity for which the sports person does not need high levels of aerobic fitness or muscular endurance. However, a marathon runner needs to be able to run for continuous periods of two hours and over, so aerobic fitness and muscular endurance are key areas that need to be trained.

Some sports require the athlete to have high levels of strength, speed and power so that they are able to exert high levels of force against a resistance, as in the throwing events such as the shot put and javelin. Strength training is also necessary to build muscle mass in order to increase a person's sprinting speed.

Some flexibility is required by all sports people in order to avoid injury. However, some sports demand that the athlete has particularly high levels of flexibility in order to carry out the movements involved. Examples of these sports are gymnastics, martial arts and diving.

A number of sports involve a variety of the skill-related components of fitness. In order for athletes to improve in their sports they must take part in specific training practices to refine these skills. For example, a rugby player needs good hand/ball and foot/ball co-ordination, so they must take part in drills to practise these skills. Sprinters need good reaction times in order to get off to a good start in a race.

Football

Footballers need to train a variety of the health-related and skill-related components of fitness. A player's position also influences their training programme; for example, the goalkeeper needs quite a different training programme to that of a striker. However, the main components of fitness footballers need to train are:

✪   aerobic fitness and muscular endurance because a game of football lasts 90 minutes (or longer)

✪   strength, speed and power; their training should include some resistance work in order to allow them to jump high, kick the ball hard and sprint, to reach the ball quickly, dodge and mark opponents

✪   skill-related components, agility to dodge players and run after the ball, and foot/ball co-ordination.

Swimming

Swimming uses all of the major muscle groups of both the upper and the lower body; in this respect it is also known as a whole-body exercise. The type of fitness a swimmer needs depends on which stroke and what distance they compete in. However, both sprint and distance swimmers will need:

✪ muscular endurance in order to ensure that their muscles are able to continue to function and propel the body through the water for periods of time

✪ flexibility to allow them to complete the stroke effectively; the butterfly stroke especially requires the swimmer to have a good range of movement in the shoulder joint in order to perform the stroke efficiently and effectively

✪ aerobic endurance for the distance swimmer in order to complete long-distance swims

✪ muscular strength for the sprint swimmer in order to increase their speed through the water.

Cycling

For long-distance cycling, such as the Tour de France, an athlete needs extremely high levels of aerobic fitness and muscular endurance. However, for hill work and sprint finishes they will also need to train for muscular strength.

Racket sports

Tennis, squash and badminton involve bursts of intense activity for short periods. However, because these games usually last longer than 20 minutes, a player also needs to have high levels of aerobic fitness and muscular endurance. Some strength training should be carried out in order to hit the ball/shuttlecock with force. In tennis, some players may concentrate on improving their strength specifically in order to improve their serve. If the ball is hit with more strength it will travel faster, making it less likely to be reached by the opponent. There is quite a lot of skill required for these sports as the players need to have good racket/ball or racket/shuttlecock co-ordination. They also need to have high levels of agility in order to get to the ball/shuttlecock.

Rugby

Rugby players need a range of health- and skill-related components of fitness, but their specific training programme will be varied in accordance with their playing position. However, all rugby players will need to train the following components of fitness:

✪ aerobic fitness and muscular endurance because a game of rugby lasts at least 80 minutes

✪ strength and power in order to be able to tackle opponents, sprint and dodge opponents

✪ good hand/ball and foot/ball co-ordination and high levels of agility to get to the ball.

**STUDENT
ACTIVITY**

Different sports and their fitness requirements

Investigate the following sports and list the main components of fitness training required in order to excel in them. Explain why.
✪ gymnastics
✪ long-distance rowing
✪ martial arts
✪ archery
✪ triple jump

REVISION QUESTIONS

1) Explain why different sports require different types of fitness.

2) For the majority of sports, which component of fitness do you think is the most important and why?

3) Carry out a thorough investigation of the training programme of a sports person or sport of your choice. Include in your research a typical training programme for a week and explain which component of fitness is being trained at each training session.

4) Which sports do you think require the greatest amount of fitness training for all:

a) health-related components of fitness

b) skill-related components of fitness?

Explain your answers.

PRACTICE OF HEALTH SCREENING AND FITNESS TESTING

Exercise referral schemes

Exercise prescription is also known as exercise referral schemes. It came about in the 1990s in response to the need for greater exercise participation in order to help improve public health.

The scheme is based on the fact that doctors in surgeries see 70% of the population at least once a year, and 95% of the population once in three years. As a result, a doctor has the capacity to reach the majority of the population, giving them the opportunity to provide lifestyle advice and health promotion initiatives to the nation.

The doctor usually refers a person on to an exercise scheme if they meet at least one of a set of participation criteria:

- ✪ overweight/obese
- ✪ moderate hypertension (high blood pressure)
- ✪ smoke
- ✪ have osteoporosis
- ✪ have arthritis
- ✪ have mild depression.

Prior to participation the patient undergoes a basic medical examination, then they are directed to a leisure centre. Here they will take part in a fitness assessment to determine a suitable exercise programme prescription. Once the first series of exercises are completed, the patient will usually be given the option to continue their exercise scheme in order to maintain their fitness gains.

Health screening

Before taking part in an exercise programme all good health clubs will ensure a person completes a health screening process. The process usually involves completing a questionnaire called a Physical Activity Readiness Questionnaire (PAR-Q). It is designed to identify people for whom physical activity might be inappropriate. It should also highlight people who need to seek medical advice prior to taking part in activity in order to find out which type of activity is most suitable for them. The questionnaire is pretty standard, and an example is shown below.

Physical Activity Readiness		
Questionnaire	Yes	No
1 Has a doctor ever said you have a heart condition and recommended only medically supervised physical activity?	☐	☐
2 Do you have chest pain brought on by physical activity?	☐	☐
3 Have you developed chest pain in the past month?	☐	☐
4 Do you tend to lose consciousness or fall over as a result of dizziness?	☐	☐
5 Do you have a bone or joint problem that could be aggravated by the proposed physical activity?	☐	☐
6 Has a doctor ever recommended medication for your blood pressure or a heart condition?	☐	☐
7 Are you aware through your own experience, or a doctor's advice, of any other physical reason against your exercising without medical supervision?	☐	☐
8 Have you had any operations?	☐	☐
9 Have you suffered any injuries?	☐	☐
10 Do you or have you suffered from back pain?	☐	☐
11 Are you pregnant?	☐	☐
12 Have you recently given birth?	☐	☐

If you answered YES to one or more questions, talk with your doctor before beginning an exercise programme or taking part in fitness tests.

Once the PAR-Q has been completed, health clubs may well carry out a lifestyle analysis as another precautionary measure to ensure a person is ready to commence a fitness program. This analysis is usually in the form of a questionnaire, or can be carried out in a one-to-one interview. The areas covered include:

✪   profession

✪   alcohol consumption per week

✪   smoking per day

✪ medication

✪ diet

✪ previous exercise history.

Once these pre-activity tests have been carried out, the client will then take part in a series of health screening and fitness tests.

Fitness testing

Fitness testing is carried out for a number of reasons, the main one being to find out the fitness level of the client for all the different components of fitness. From this it is possible to determine which areas of fitness need to be improved upon. The client usually has an objective for taking part in a fitness programme, for example to lose body fat, increase upper body strength or train to run a marathon. Therefore, with these two main considerations in mind, a fitness programme can be devised.

Test procedures

Pre-test

Prior to taking part in any activity, most health clubs will carry out some health screening tests to determine a basic assessments of a person's cardiovascular and physical health. These tests include:

✪ resting heart rate

✪ resting blood pressure

✪ lung function

✪ height and weight and/or body fat percentage.

These tests are another safeguard to ensure a person is ready to embark on an exercise programme. If their resting heart rate was too high or too low, or their resting blood pressure was too high or too low, then they would be instructed to see a medical professional before taking part in the tests. If the lung function test showed that there was a problem with the person's lungs, again they would be instructed to seek medical help. A person's weight or body fat percentage is recorded to ensure the person is not obese. If a person is deemed obese then they will need to have their doctors consent to take part in fitness tests. Once the client obtains written consent from their doctor, they may then take part in the fitness testing procedures.

When a client arrives for their fitness tests, the tester should ensure that they are feeling fit, healthy and ready for exercise. This means that they are:

✪ feeling well

✪ have not eaten a heavy meal for three hours prior to the testing

✪ have not consumed alcohol the day before or on the actual day of testing

✪ are fully hydrated

✪ have not smoked for at least two hours prior to the testing.

If they have not adhered to these guidelines it may result in the client not performing as well as possible during the tests, which will lead to the test results being an inaccurate reflection of the person's true fitness levels.

The client will then need to be told exactly what the test involves. Often health clubs will ask the client to complete an '**informed consent**' form, which explains what the test involves, and any risks or discomfort the test may entail. The form includes a section stating that the client is volunteering to take part in the fitness test and is free to stop the test at any point. They then sign and date the form. This can then also act as a legal document should any problems arise during or after the test.

Fitness tests

There are a range of fitness tests available that test for the same components of fitness. However, the client's health and level of fitness should dictate which test is more appropriate. The majority of fitness tests for aerobic fitness, strength and muscular endurance can be placed into one of two categories:

1   sub-maximal

2   maximal.

In **sub-maximal** fitness tests the person does not have to exercise until they are exhausted. This kind of aerobic fitness testing is usually the preferred type for most health clubs because **maximal** fitness testing is usually uncomfortable and potentially distressing for their clients.

Some of the range of different tests used can be seen in the next section of this chapter. Usually, health clubs will test for the all the health-related components of fitness.

Throughout the testing period, the client should be supervised and asked how they are feeling. If the tester can see that the client is in distress, or heart rate readings are too high, then the test should be terminated for the client's own safety.

Test results

Once the fitness tests have been completed the results can be analysed. For each test there are reference tables of results that indicate whether the person has performed well for their age and sex, or has performed poorly and needs to pay particular attention to training that component of fitness.

From these results a training programme can be devised in conjunction with the client's long-term aims. In order to help to maintain a person's motivation, they will usually undergo further fitness tests so that they can see their progress and remain committed to the exercise programme.

REVISION QUESTIONS

1) Explain what 'exercise referral' is and give an example of a person who may take part in this scheme.

2) Why is it necessary to complete a physical activity readiness questionnaire (PAR-Q) prior to taking part in activity?

3) What types of illnesses is the PAR-Q trying to identify?

4) Why is it necessary to carry out a lifestyle analysis?

5) What condition should a person be in prior to taking part in fitness testing?

6) Give five possible reasons why a person may wish to take part in a fitness programme.

7) What is the difference between a maximal test and a sub-maximal test?

8) What is an 'informed consent form' and why is it necessary?

APPROPRIATE FITNESS TESTS

A number of tests are available to test both the health-related components of exercise and the skill-related components of fitness. In this section there are a variety of fitness tests with standard protocols and procedures that you should be familiar with and be able to administer.

Anthropometry

This is the measurement of the size and proportions of the human body and its different parts. Body size and structure measurements can be used for monitoring growth patterns and changes throughout training. They can also help the sports scientist to identify appropriate sports for individuals. For example, a tall lean person may be suited to sports such as the high jump, whereas a short stocky person may be more suited to throwing events. Therefore, anthropometry can identify, from body size and shape, which sports individuals should pursue. However, athletes who have physiques that do not match the prescribed body types can still be successful, as there are many other factors, that influence performance.

Tests

Standing height

This is a measure of the maximum distance from the floor to the highest point of a person's head.

STUDENT PRACTICAL

Equipment
stadiometer or marker
tape measure placed against a wall

Method

1   The person being measured should stand in bare or socked feet facing forwards, feet together and arms by the sides. Their heels, buttocks and upper back should all be in contact with the wall.

2   The tester records the height of the subject.

Results
Copy and complete the table below.

Name	Standing height (cm)

Body mass

Body mass is a measurement of the amount of particles a body contains. It is used in sports science rather than body weight, as body weight will vary according to gravity, but body mass remains the same. For example, if you went to the Moon where there is little gravity, your body weight would be much lower than here on Earth, but your body mass would remain unchanged.

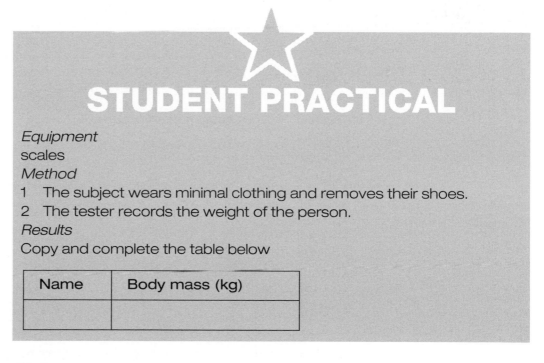

STUDENT PRACTICAL

Equipment
scales

Method

1   The subject wears minimal clothing and removes their shoes.
2   The tester records the weight of the person.

Results
Copy and complete the table below

Name	Body mass (kg)

Girths

Measuring a person's girth is usually performed before they take part in a diet and exercise programme that is designed to decrease the girths (weight loss), or to increase the girths (increasing muscle mass).

STUDENT PRACTICAL

Equipment
tape measure
Method
1 The circumference of standard anatomical sites around the body are measured. It is important to ensure the tape is horizontal and the tester does not hold the tape too tight or too loose against the person being measured.
2 Below is a table of common sites that are measured.
3 With a partner of the same sex, measure the girths listed in the table.

Waist	This measurement is taken at the narrowest waist level.
Hip	The hip measurement is taken at the level of the greatest protrusion of the gluteal muscles.
Chest	This measurement is taken at the end of a normal expiration and in the middle of the chest.
Arm (relaxed)	Ensure that the arm is relaxed and hanging by the side. The circumference is taken between the boney point of the shoulder and the boney point of the elbow
Arm (flexed)	Raise the arm to a horizontal position in front of the body with the elbow at a right angle. Contract the biceps muscle, then measure the largest circumference around the biceps.
Thigh	Stand with legs slightly apart and measure the circumference of the thigh, which is 2 cm below the buttock crease.

Results
Record your results in the table below.

Waist	
Hip	
Chest	
Arm (relaxed)	
Arm (flexed)	
Thigh	

From these measurements it is possible to determine if a fitness programme is achieving the desired aims of girth inch loss when losing weight, or girth inch gain when trying to increase muscle mass.

Body mass index (BMI)

BMI takes a person's weight in kilograms and divides it by their height in meters squared. It gives an indication of a person's body type and body composition. However, this test does not apply to elderly populations, pregnant women or very muscular athletes.

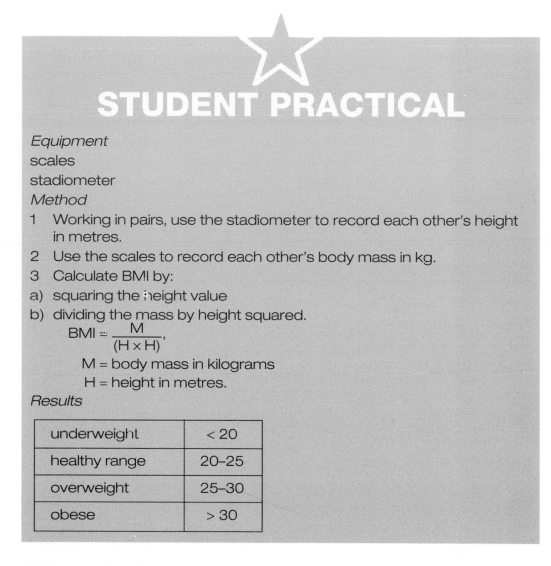

☆ STUDENT PRACTICAL

Equipment

scales

stadiometer

Method

1   Working in pairs, use the stadiometer to record each other's height in metres.
2   Use the scales to record each other's body mass in kg.
3   Calculate BMI by:
a) squaring the height value
b) dividing the mass by height squared.

$$BMI = \frac{M}{(H \times H)},$$

M = body mass in kilograms

H = height in metres.

Results

underweight	< 20
healthy range	20–25
overweight	25–30
obese	> 30

Waist to hip ratio

This is a very simple test to predict if a person is overweight and potentially at risk of suffering from CHD. This is based on the assumption that fat stored around the waist poses a greater CHD risk than fat stored elsewhere.

STUDENT PRACTICAL

Equipment
tape measure

Method

1 Using a tape measure, measure the girth of the person's waist in line with their navel and record the results.

2 Now measure around the widest region of the hips and record the measurement.

3 Divide the waist measurement by the hip measurement:

$$\frac{\text{Waist (cm)}}{\text{Hip (cm)}} = \text{waist to hip ratio}$$

Results

Sex	Acceptable		Unacceptable		
	excellent	good	average	high	extreme
male	< 0.85	0.85–0.90	0.90–0.95	0.95–1.00	> 1.00
female	< 0.75	0.75–0.80	0.80–0.85	0.85–0.90	> 0.90

Skinfold measurement

This is an estimation of a person's body fat. It can be made by measuring the thickness of skinfolds taken from a variety of sites.

STUDENT PRACTICAL

Equipment
skinfold calipers

Method

1 Ensure that the subject is wearing suitable clothing to allow you to reach all the necessary anatomical sites.

2 Work in same-sex pairs.

3 Pinch the skin at the appropriate site. This pinch should include a double layer of skin and the underlying fat tissue. Try to ensure that you do not have muscle tissue in your pinch.

4 Apply the callipers 1 cm below and at right angles to the pinch, then record the reading after two seconds.

5 Repeat the procedure, then record the mean of the two measurements.

The sites

The table on the next page shows the various sites at which the skinfold pinch is taken. The calliper is then applied 1 cm below and at right angles to the pinch.

continues overleaf

continued

Triceps	A vertical pinch half way between the middle of the tip of the shoulder and the elbow joint on the back of the arm.
Biceps	The pinch position is over the belly of the biceps muscle, 1 cm above the level of triceps on the front surface of the arm.
Subscapula	The pinch is made 2 cm below the bottom point of shoulder blade on a line running away from the centre of the body and downwards at about 45°.
Supra ilium	A fold is taken just above and at the same angle as the iliac crest (top of hip bone).

Results

Record your results in the table below.

Site	Value 1	Value 2	Mean
Triceps			
Biceps			
Subcapule			
Suprailium			
Total			

Males

Percentage body fat for the sum of the measurements at all four locations.

Sum of skinfold measurements (mm)	Age 16 to 29	Age 30 to 49
20	8.1	12.1
22	9.2	13.2
24	10.2	14.2
26	11.2	15.2
28	12.1	16.1
30	12.9	16.9
35	14.7	18.7
40	16.3	20.3
table continues next column		

Sum of skinfold measurements (mm)	Age 16 to 29	Age 30 to 49
table continued		
45	17.7	21.8
50	19.0	23.0
55	20.2	24.2
60	21.2	25.3
65	22.2	26.3
70	23.2	27.2
75	24.0	28.0
80	24.8	28.8
85	25.6	29.6
90	26.3	30.3
95	27.0	31.0
100	27.6	31.7
110	28.8	32.9
120	29.9	34.0
130	31.0	35.0
140	31.9	36.0
150	32.8	36.8
160	33.6	37.7
170	34.4	38.5
180	35.2	39.2
190	35.9	39.9
200	36.5	40.6

continues overleaf

continued

Rating	Age 16 to 29	Age 30 to 49
Very low fat	< 7	< 9
Slim	7 to 12	9 to 14
Acceptable	13 to 17	15 to 19
Over fat	18 to 28	20 to 30
Obese	> 28	> 30

Women

Sum of skinfolds	Age 16 to 29	Age 30 to 49
14	9.4	14.1
16	11.2	15.7
18	12.7	17.1
20	14.1	18.4
22	15.4	19.5
24	16.5	20.6
26	17.6	21.5
28	18.6	22.4
30	19.5	23.3
35	21.6	25.2
40	23.4	26.8
45	25.0	28.3
50	26.5	29.6
55	27.8	30.8
60	29.1	31.9
65	30.2	32.9

table continues next column

table continued

Sum of skinfolds	Age 16 to 29	Age 30 to 49
70	31.2	33.9
75	32.2	34.7
80	33.1	35.6
85	34.0	36.3
90	34.8	37.1
95	35.6	37.8
100	36.3	38.5
110	37.7	39.7
120	39.0	40.8
130	40.2	41.9
140	41.3	42.9
150	42.3	43.8
160	43.2	44.7
170	44.6	45.5
180	45.0	46.2
190	45.8	46.9
200	46.6	47.6

Rating	Age 16 to 29	Age 30 to 49
Very low fat	< 13	< 14
Slim	13 to 20	14 to 22
Acceptable	21 to 25	23 to 27
Over fat	26 to 32	28 to 34
Obese	> 32	> 34

Aerobic fitness tests

Maximal oxygen consumption test (VO$_2$max)

At present, the most reliable indicator of a person's aerobic fitness is the VO$_2$max test. However, as this test requires a great deal of equipment and

experienced testers, you will not be expected to carry it out, but it is useful to have an understanding of what this test entails. The person exercises on an appropriate ergometer (treadmill, cycle, rowing machine), and the exercise workloads are gradually increased from moderate to maximal intensity. Oxygen uptake is calculated from measures of oxygen and carbon dioxide in the expired air and minute ventilation, and the maximal level is determined at or near test completion. As this test requires the use of expensive equipment and takes quite some time to administer, other tests have been designed to predict a VO_2max score that are much simpler and cheaper to perform. Some of these tests require the subject to exercise to exhaustion (maximal tests), whereas others do not test the subject to their limit (sub-maximal tests).

Maximal tests

Multistage fitness test

The multistage fitness test, also known as the bleep test, is a very common test of aerobic fitness as it is easy to administer and requires little equipment. The test involves continuous running between two lines 20 m apart, in time to recorded beeps. The time between beeps decreases each minute. The initial running velocity is 8.5 km/hr, which increases by 0.5 km/hr each minute. The athlete's score is the level and number of shuttles reached before they are unable to keep up with the tape recording. There are published VO_2max score equivalents for each level reached.

STUDENT PRACTICAL

Equipment
marking cones
20 m measuring tape
Multi stage fitness test audio tape
tape recorder
recording sheets
Method
1   Mark out a 20 m distance with cones.
2   Put on the audio tape and follow the instructions.
3   Once you have exercised to exhaustion, note down which level you have attained.

4   Look at the scoring table in your multistage fitness test information and note down what your estimated VO_2max is.

Results

Name	Level	Estimated $\dot{V}O_2$max (l per minute)

Coopers 12-minute run

This test involves running for 12 minutes and then recording the distance covered during this time.

STUDENT PRACTICAL

Equipment
running track
marking cones
record sheet
stop watch
Method
1 Place cones at 50 m intervals around the running track.
2 Start a stopwatch and run for 12 minutes. Count each lap you complete.

3 After 12 minutes note down which cone you are up to if you do not complete a full lap.
Results
Work out how many miles you have covered (1 mile = 1600 metres). It is then possible to predict VO$_2$max by using the following equation:

$$\text{VO}_2\text{max (in ml per kg per min)} = (35.97 \times \text{miles}) - 11.29$$

Harvard step test

For this test, the athlete steps up and down on a bench at a rate of 30 steps per minute for five minutes or until exhausted. Once the subject has completed the test they record their recovery heart rate over a period of three and a half minutes.

STUDENT PRACTICAL

Equipment
step or platform 50.8 cm high
stopwatch
metronome
Method
1 Set the metronome to tick at a rate of 30 per minute.
2 Start the stopwatch and step in time to the metronome.
3 After five minutes sit down and find your heart rate.
4 Take your recovery heart rate for a 30-second period at 1 minute, 2 minutes and 3 minutes.
5 Record your results.

Results

Name	Heart rate at 1 min recovery	Heart rate at 2 mins recovery	Heart rate at 3 mins recovery	Heart rate at 5 mins recovery

Aerobic endurance can then be estimated by using the following equation:

$$\text{score} = \frac{100 \times \text{test duration in seconds}}{2 \times \text{total heartbeats in recovery period}}$$

Check your score on the table opposite

excellent	> 90
good	80–89
high average	65–79
low average	55–64
poor	< 55

Strength tests

These involve working against a resistance. A person's strength is a combination of the size and number of muscles involved, the types of muscle fibres that are activated, the physical condition of the muscle groups, the coordination of the muscle groups and the mechanics of the levers involved. There is no single test for strength as each test is specific to the action and muscle groups being tested.

1-RM tests (repetition maximum)

One repetition maximum tests (1-RM) are a measure of the maximal force a person can lift in one go.

STUDENT PRACTICAL

Equipment
free weights (barbells, dumbbells) or other gym equipment
Method
1   Depending on availability, attempt to carry out a 1-RM test on a range of muscle groups. Warm-up thoroughly, then select a weight you feel you can lift.
2   Choose subsequent weights until you can only repeat one full and correct lift at that weight.
3   Record your 1-RM for each exercise.

Results

Name of muscle group worked	1-RM (kg)

Work out your 1-RM in relation to your body weight for each exercise. This can be done by dividing the weight lifted by your body weight and multiplying this figure by 100:

$$\frac{\text{weight lifted (kg)}}{\text{body weight (kg)}} \times 100$$

Name of muscle group worked	1-RM (kg)	% of body weight

Handgrip strength test

In this test the subject squeezes a handgrip dynamometer as hard as possible in order to ascertain their strength. However, the validity of this test as a measure of general strength has been questioned, as it does not necessarily represent the strength of other muscle groups.

STUDENT PRACTICAL

Equipment
handgrip dynamometer

Method

1 Adjust the dynamometer so that it is appropriate for your hand size.
2 Hold the dynamometer in your dominant hand in line with the forearm and hanging by the thigh.
3 Squeeze the dynamometer without swinging the arm.
4 Record the results obtained at the end of the squeeze.
5 After a rest of around one minute, repeat the test. Take the best result from the two trials as your score.
6 Repeat the test with your other hand.

Results
Check your score with the rating table below

Rating	Males	Females
excellent	> 64	> 38
very good	56–64	34–38
above average	52–56	30–34
average	48–52	26–30
below average	44–48	22–26
poor	40–44	20–22
very poor	< 40	< 20

Abdominal strength test

This test involves performing complete sit-ups with varying degrees of intensity. There are eight levels in this test, which range from very poor to elite.

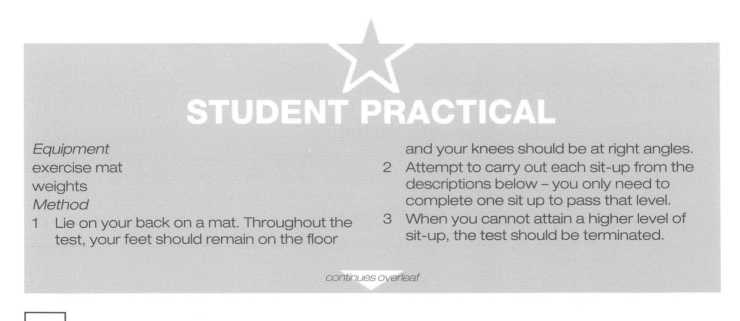

STUDENT PRACTICAL

Equipment
exercise mat
weights

Method

1 Lie on your back on a mat. Throughout the test, your feet should remain on the floor and your knees should be at right angles.
2 Attempt to carry out each sit-up from the descriptions below – you only need to complete one sit up to pass that level.
3 When you cannot attain a higher level of sit-up, the test should be terminated.

continues overleaf

continued

Level	Description
0	cannot perform level 1
1	wrist to thighs
2	elbows to thighs
3	hands together across abdominals, chest to thighs
4	hands across chest, forearms to thighs
5	hands behind head, chest to thighs
6	5 lb (2.5 kg) weight held behind head, chest to thighs
7	10 lb (5 kg) weight held behind head, chest to thighs

Level	Rating	Description
0	very poor	cannot perform level 1
1	poor	wrist to thighs
2	fair	elbows to thighs
3	average	hands together across abdominals, chest to thighs
4	good	hands across chest, forearms to thighs
5	very good	hands behind head, chest to thighs
6	excellent	5 lb (2.5 kg) weight held behind head, chest to thighs
7	elite	10 lb (5 kg) weight held behind head, chest to thighs

Results
The highest level of sit-up correctly completed is recorded and the appropriate rating level can be ascertained from the table opposite.

Muscular power

This is the ability to exert a maximal force in as short a time as possible, as in jumping and throwing implements.

Vertical jump test (Sargeant jump)

In this test the athlete jumps as high as possible.

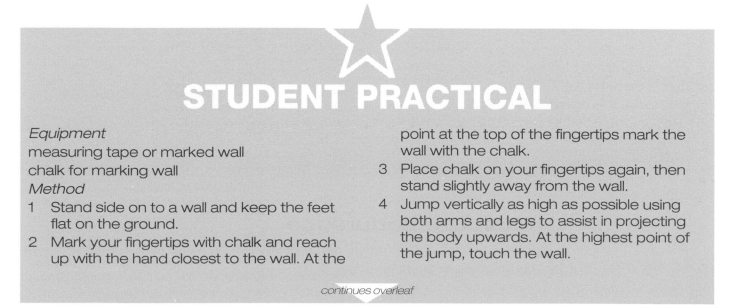

STUDENT PRACTICAL

Equipment
measuring tape or marked wall
chalk for marking wall
Method
1 Stand side on to a wall and keep the feet flat on the ground.
2 Mark your fingertips with chalk and reach up with the hand closest to the wall. At the point at the top of the fingertips mark the wall with the chalk.
3 Place chalk on your fingertips again, then stand slightly away from the wall.
4 Jump vertically as high as possible using both arms and legs to assist in projecting the body upwards. At the highest point of the jump, touch the wall.

continues overleaf

continued

5   Using a tape measure, record the difference in distance between the reach height and the jump height.
6   Repeat the test three times, with a brief rest period between each, and record the best attempt.

Results

Rating	Males (cm)	Females (cm)
excellent	> 70	> 60
very good	61–70	51–60
above average	51–60	41–50
average	41–50	31–40
below average	31–40	21–30
poor	21–30	11–20
very poor	< 21	< 11

Standing long-jump test (Broad jump)

In this test the athlete jumps as far forwards as possible.

STUDENT PRACTICAL

Equipment
measuring tape
non-slip floor or a long-jump landing pit
Method
1   Mark a line on the ground or use the take-off board on a long-jump runway.
2   Stand behind the marked line or take-off board with feet slightly apart.
3   Take off with bent knees from two feet, swinging arms to provide forward drive.
4   Land on two feet.
5   Measure the distance travelled.
6   Repeat the jump three times, with a brief rest period between each, and record the longest jump.

Results

Rating	Males (cm)	Females (cm)
excellent	> 250	> 200
very good	241–250	191–200
above average	231–240	181–190
average	221–230	171–180
below average	211–220	161–170
poor	191–210	141–160
very poor	< 191	< 141

Muscular endurance

This is the ability of a muscle to repeatedly carry out a series of muscle contractions without fatiguing.

Abdominal endurance test

This tests the abdominal muscles' endurance capability. It involves performing sit-ups at increasing rates, in time with an audio tape.

★ STUDENT PRACTICAL

Equipment
Abdominal endurance audio tape
tape recorder
floor mat

Method
1 Lie on your back with feet flat on the floor and knees bent at right angles. Place fingertips at the temples.
2 Curl upwards so the elbows touch the thighs.
3 Curl downwards so that shoulders return fully to the floor.
4 Curl upwards and downwards in time with the bleeps on the audio tape – one bleep signals the horizontal position, the next signals the vertical position.
5 The number of complete sit-ups is counted and the level the subject reaches is recorded.

Results
Check your score against the tables enclosed in the abdominal endurance test.

Speed

Sprint test

This test involves sprinting as fast as possible over a 35 m distance.

★ STUDENT PRACTICAL

Equipment
measuring tape or marked track
stopwatch
markers

Method
1 Mark out 35 m on a running track or suitable surface. Ensure that there is enough room at the end of the distance for the person to decelerate comfortably.
2 Time how long it takes for a person to run the 35 m distance.
3 Repeat this test three times, with a break between each. The best time to cover the set distance is then recorded.

Results

Rating	Men (seconds)	Women (seconds)
very good	< 4.80	< 5.30
good	4.80–5.09	5.30–5.59
average	5.10–5.29	5.60–5.89
fair	5.30–5.60	5.90–6.20
poor	> 5.60	> 6.20

Anaerobic endurance

30-second Wingate test

This test involves cycling on a cycle ergometer against a resistance.

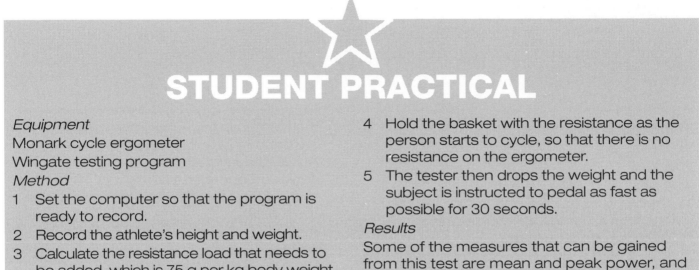

STUDENT PRACTICAL

Equipment
Monark cycle ergometer
Wingate testing program

Method
1. Set the computer so that the program is ready to record.
2. Record the athlete's height and weight.
3. Calculate the resistance load that needs to be added, which is 75 g per kg body weight.

   75 g × body weight kg = resistance

4. Hold the basket with the resistance as the person starts to cycle, so that there is no resistance on the ergometer.
5. The tester then drops the weight and the subject is instructed to pedal as fast as possible for 30 seconds.

Results
Some of the measures that can be gained from this test are mean and peak power, and a fatigue index determined from the decline in power.

Flexibility

Flexibility is the ability of a joint to move through its full range of motion. Each test is specific to a particular movement or joints, therefore there is no one set test to determine a person's flexibility.

Sit and reach test

This test measures the flexibility of the lower back and hamstrings.

STUDENT PRACTICAL

Equipment
sit and reach box

Method
1. Sit on the floor with legs out straight ahead.
2. Place socked or bare feet against the sit and reach box.
3. Both knees must be kept flat against the floor.

4. Lean forward slowly, as far as possible, and hold the greatest stretch for two seconds.
5. Repeat the test twice and record the best score.

Results
The score is recorded as the distance before (negative) or beyond (positive) the toes.

continues overleaf

continued

	Men (cm)	Women (cm)		Men (cm)	Women (cm)
elite	> +27	> +30	fair	−8 to −1	−7 to 0
excellent	+17 to +27	+21 to +30	poor	−19 to −9	−14 to −8
good	+6 to +16	+11 to +20	very poor	< −20	< −15
average	0 to +5	+1 to +10			

Shoulder flexibility test

This test measures the flexibility of the shoulder joints.

STUDENT PRACTICAL

Equipment
stick or towel
tape measure
Method
1   Hold a towel or a stick in front of the body
with both hands apart and palms facing
downwards.
2   Maintain this hand grip on the stick/towel,
then lift it over the head to behind the back.

3   Repeat the test, but after each test move
the hands closer together until the
movement cannot be completed.
Results
The minimum distance between the hands
while still being able to complete the test will
give the person's score.

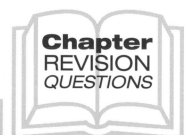

Chapter
REVISION
QUESTIONS

1) What is the difference between health-related
fitness and skill-related fitness?
2) Which sport do you think requires the greatest
amount of fitness? Explain your answer.
3) Give an example of three different people who
may benefit from exercise referral.
4) What are the ACSM guidelines for improving
fitness levels?
5) Choose which tests you would use to

measure the aerobic fitness, muscular
endurance, body composition and strength of
the following three people:
a) an elite marathon runner
b) a boxer
c) a slightly overweight middle-aged female
d) explain why you have chosen each test and
why it is appropriate for each person.
6) What are the benefits of being physically fit?

FURTHER READING

Hagerman, (2001) *Fitness Testing 101: A Guide for Trainers and Coaches.* University Press

Heyward, Vivian H. (1991) Advanced Fitness Assessment and Exercise Prescription. Champaign Il, *Human Kinetics*

Katch, F., Katch, V. and McArdle, (1996) *Exercise Physiology.* Williams and Wilkins

Maud, Peter J. and Foster, Carl. (1995) Physiological Assessment of Human Fitness. Champaign Il, *Human Kinetics*

Macdougal *et al.* (1991) Physiological Testing of the High-performance Athlete. Champaign Il, *Human Kinetics*

Nieman, (1998) *Exercise testing and Prescription: A Health Related Approach,* 4th edition. Mayfield Publishing Company

Rikli, Jones, (2000) *Senior Fitness Test Manual.* Human Kinetics

YMCA of the USA (2000) YMCA *Fitness Testing and Assessment Manual,* 4th edition. Human Kinetics

PHYSIOLOGICAL FACTORS OF SPORT AND EXERCISE

Sports men and women take part in competitions all over the world, from the hot and humid climate of Korea to the snowy and icy cold weather of the Canadian winter. Competing in these different countries places a range of stresses on the body. This chapter will examine how the environment impacts on performance and how training in different climates and at different altitudes results in physiological adaptation in order for athletes to cope better with these different environmental conditions.

Gender differences and sporting performance, and racial physiological differences between athletes will also be explored. Whether these differences can predispose athletes to be more likely to be successful will be discussed.

Lastly, illegal pharmacological aids (as decided by the IOC) will be examined; how they enhance performance and their side-effects, together with the ethical issues surrounding the use of these aids.

By the end of this chapter students should understand:

✪   the effects of environment on performance and training

✪   differences between the sexes and races and how these affect performance

✪   the effects of physiological aids on performance and health.

ENVIRON-MENT

High altitude

Anywhere more than 1500 m above sea level (5000 ft) is considered to be at high altitude. The further above sea level you travel the lower the **barometric pressure** becomes. This means that the higher up you go, the 'thinner' the air becomes as there are fewer air molecules in the atmosphere.

Therefore, although the percentage of oxygen, carbon dioxide and nitrogen within the air remains the same (20.93%, 0.03% and 79.04% respectively), every breath of air you take contains fewer and fewer molecules of oxygen (and carbon dioxide and nitrogen). As a result, a person must work harder to obtain the same quantities of oxygen compared with when they are at low altitudes. This means that an athlete who exercises or competes at high altitude will have to breathe much faster to take in enough oxygen for their energy systems to work normally than when they exercise at lower altitude.

In 1968 the Olympic Games were held in Mexico City, which stands at an elevation of 2300 m and is therefore classed as being at high altitude. In order to try to overcome the effects of 'thinner air', the athletes went through a period of **acclimatisation**, during which they trained at high altitude for a number of weeks. The body responds by physiologically by adapting to cope with the decreased levels of oxygen in the air.

Physiological adaptations to high altitude

The body undergoes a number of changes in order to increase oxygen delivery to cells and improve efficiency of oxygen use. These adaptations usually begin almost immediately and continue for several weeks. People vary in their ability to acclimatise – while some adjust quickly, others may take weeks to undergo physiological adaptation. Usually the body becomes approximately 80% acclimatised after 10 days at high altitude, and approximately 95% acclimatised after six weeks.

Initial adaptation response

The body's initial responses to being at high altitude are:

✪ an increase in respiratory rate (**hyperventilation**)

✪ an increase in heart rate (**tachycardia**).

When a person arrives at high altitude their respiratory rate and depth increase in response to the lower concentrations of oxygen in the blood. The increased breathing rate has the effect of causing more carbon dioxide to be expired and more oxygen to be delivered to the **alveoli**. The respiratory rate peaks after about one week of living at high altitude, and then slowly decreases over the next few months, although it tends to remain higher than its normal rate at sea level.

Heart rate also increases because the body's cells require a constant supply of oxygen. As there is less oxygen available in the blood, the heart beats more quickly to meet the cells' demands. However, heart rate will also start to decrease as more time is spent at high altitude.

Long-term adaptations

In the long term the body makes cardiovascular and metabolic changes.

Cardiovascular adaptations:

✪ decreased maximum cardiac output

✪ decreased maximum heart rate

✪ increase in the number of red blood cells

✪ increased **haemoglobin** concentration

✪ increased **haematocrit**

✪ increased capillarisation.

The bone marrow contributes to acclimatisation by increasing red blood cell production and, therefore, the blood's haemoglobin concentration. This increase is triggered by the kidneys' increased production of **erythropoeitin (EPO)**. New red blood cells become available in the blood within four to five days, and have the effect of increasing the blood's oxygen-carrying capacity. An acclimatised person may have 30% to 50% more red blood cells than a counterpart at sea level.

The cardiovascular system also develops more capillaries in response to altitude. This has the effect of improving the rate of diffusion of oxygen from the blood and into the muscles by shortening the distance between the cells and the capillary.

All these adaptations in the weeks following exposure are aimed at increasing oxygen transport to the body cells. This results in a reduction in the cardiac output required for oxygen delivery during rest and exercise compared with pre-acclimatisation.

Metabolic adaptations:

✪ increased excretion of bicarbonate via the kidneys

✪ an increase in 2,3-diphosphoglycerate (DPG) within the red blood cells

✪ an increase in the number of **mitochondria** and **oxidative enzymes**

✪ increased levels of lactic acid leading to reduced levels of lactic acid production.

The increased breathing rate means that more carbon dioxide than normal is breathed in, resulting in the body becoming more alkaline. To compensate for the body's increasing alkalinity, the kidneys excrete bicarbonate (an alkaline substance) in the urine. This adaptation occurs within 24 to 48 hours.

Within the blood cells, 2,3-diphosphoglycerate (DPG) increases. This is an organic phosphate that helps oxygen to dissociate (unload) from the haemoglobin to the body's cells much more easily. The increase in DPG helps to compensate for the blood's reduced oxygen level.

The increased number of mitochondria and oxidative enzymes appears to be due to the switch in the body's preferred fuel for energy production. At low altitude, carbohydrate is the usual energy source; however, at altitude fat is the preferred fuel. This change is not well understood, but may be due to the fact that a reduced oxygen supply causes a higher lactic acid level in the muscles and bloodstream. Carbohydrate metabolism also leads to increased production of lactic acid, but fat metabolism does not produce lactic acid as a by-product. Therefore, the change of the main metabolic fuel from carbohydrate to fat results in a reduced level of lactic acid production.

The body's adaptation to high altitude helps significantly, but does not fully compensate for the lack of oxygen in the air. There is a drop in VO_2max by 2% for every 300 m elevation above 1500 m, even after full acclimatisation.

Methods of acclimatisation

Athletes can acclimatise prior to competition at high altitude in a number of ways. The most common approach is for the athlete to spend a period of no less than two weeks training and living at the competition altitude prior to the event.

However, some problems do arise in this approach. Primarily, the athlete is not able to train to such a high intensity as when they are at sea level because of the reduction in oxygen molecules in the air. Therefore, their VO_2max is reduced. They may also suffer from slight insomnia that would have an impact on their recovery from training.

Some athletes acclimatise by training at a low altitude and then sleeping at a high altitude. The reasoning behind this is that the athlete can train at maximal levels if they are at low altitude, and then are exposed to **hypoxic stress** while sleeping, thus increasing the production of red blood cells and other physiological adaptations.

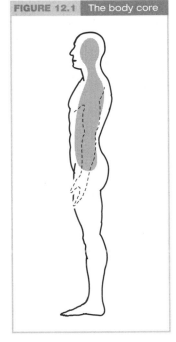

FIGURE 12.1 The body core

Thermoregulation

Thermoregulation is the process of maintaining a constant body core temperature. In humans this temperature is 37°C. The core of the body consists of the head, chest and abdomen (see Figure 12.1).

The skin temperature of the body can vary a great deal; however, if the core temperature is increased or decreased by 1°C or more, this will effect an athlete's physical and mental performance. Larger changes in core temperature will lead to **hypothermia** or **hyperthermia**, both of which can be fatal.

In order to assess the core temperature of a person, there are a number of places a specialised thermometer can be placed: the mouth, the ear, the rectum or under the arm. For sports scientists, the ear is the most common site for measuring core temperature, or, if the exercise allows, the rectal thermometer is used as this gives the most accurate readings of the true body core temperature.

STUDENT PRACTICAL

Taking core and skin temperature

Aim

The aim of this practical is to determine what the core temperature and the skin temperature of a person are.

Equipment

oral thermometer
sterilising fluid
skin thermometer
pen and paper

continues overleaf

continued

Method

1 Place a sterile thermometer under your tongue and leave it there for a few minutes.
2 Take the thermometer out of your mouth and record the temperature reading.
3 Place a skin thermometer on your hand and record the temperature reading.
4 Place the skin thermometer on your neck and record the temperature reading.
5 If you have time, take external readings from other parts of your body.
6 Disinfect/sterilise all thermometers before allowing another person to use them.

Results

Record your results in the table below.

Core temperature (°C)	
Hand temperature (°C)	
Neck temperature (°C)	

Conclusion

Try to answer these questions in your conclusion.

1 Is your core temperature the same as that of the person sitting next to you? If not, why do you think this is?
2 Why is your skin a different temperature to your core temperature?
3 Is there a difference between skin temperature readings taken from different sites of your body? Try to explain why this is.

Heat transfer

There are four different methods by which the body can lose and gain heat.

1 **Conduction** – Place your hand on the desk in front of you. How does it feel? If it feels cold then you are losing heat to it via conduction; if it feels hot then you are gaining heat by conduction. Conduction involves the direct transfer of heat from one object to another. Normally this method of heat loss is not significant unless a person is exercising in cold water. This is because water conducts heat away from the body approximately 25 times more quickly than air. At the same temperature, a person in water will lose heat from the body two to four times faster than in air.

2 **Convection** – Blow air over your hand. How does your hand feel? Your hand probably will have felt cooler after having air blown over it. This blowing of air molecules across your hand is the basis of convection. As air molecules are moved across the body, heat will be lost because convective air currents carry the heat away. Wind will increase the flow of air over the skin, thus increasing the amount of heat lost through convection. This is why a breeze feels good on a hot day, and why we use fans to help keep us cool.

3 **Radiation** – At rest, radiation is the main method of heat loss. It is the process by which heat is lost (via electromagnetic waves) to cooler objects in the environment, such as the floor, walls, trees, and so on. How much heat a person loses through radiation is determined by their size, mass and body composition. People with a high body fat percentage will loose less heat through radiation than a person with a low body fat percentage,

because body fat acts as an insulator to radiative heat loss. In contrast, a tall slim person will lose more heat through radiation than a short stocky person. In warm climates, the sun radiates heat to the body, which will increase its temperature. This makes getting rid of excess heat during exercise more difficult, because the sun's heat must also be dissipated.

4   **Evaporation** – In humans, evaporation of sweat from the body is the major method of heat dissipation, particularly during exercise. Heat is transferred continually to the environment as sweat evaporates from the skin surfaces and produces a cooling effect. However, if the environment is **humid**, evaporative heat loss is reduced. Heat is only lost when sweat evaporates, which it will not do in humid conditions. Therefore, on a hot, humid day, an athlete can be dripping with sweat, but because the sweat is not evaporating it does not cool them down.

STUDENT PRACTICAL

Investigating blood vessel dilatation and constriction

Aim
The aim of this practical is to see how blood vessel dilatation and constriction affect the colour of the skin.

Equipment
large beakers
hot water
ice cubes
thermometer
paper towels
skin thermometers (if available)

Method
1   Working in small groups, fill a large beaker with warm/hot water. Ensure the water is not too hot for you to place your hand in! Take the temperature of the water and write it down.
2   Look at your hand and make a note of its colour.
3   Place your hand in the water for about three minutes.
4   Remove your hand from the water, towel it dry, then record the skin temperature. Note down the colour of your hand.
5   Fill a large beaker with cold water and add a few ice cubes. After two minutes, take the temperature of the water and note it down. Ensure the water is not too cold for you to bear.
6   Place your hand in the water for about three minutes.
7   Remove your hand from the water, towel it dry, then record the skin temperature. Note down the colour of your hand.

Results
Record your results in the table below.

Temperature of water (°C)	Colour of hand
Hot	
Cold	

Conclusion
In your conclusion, try to answer the following questions.
a) Why did your hand turn the colour it did after having been placed in hot water?
b) Why did your hand turn the colour it did after having been placed in cold water?
c) By what process was your hand trying to loose heat when it was placed in the hot water?

Exercise in the heat

Exercise increases metabolic rate by 20 to 25 times, and could increase core temperature by 1°C every six minutes if thermoregulation did not take place. This would result in death from hyperthermia if exercise continued. Therefore, with the added stress of a hot environment, an exercising athlete has to maximise heat loss in order to perform optimally and to avoid hyperthermia.

There are three major forms of hyperthermia:

✪   heat cramps

✪   heat exhaustion

✪   heat stroke.

Heat cramps are muscle spasms caused by heavy sweating. Although heat cramps can be quite painful, they usually do not result in permanent damage.

Heat exhaustion is more serious than heat cramps. It occurs primarily because of dehydration and loss of important minerals. In order to lose body heat, the surface blood vessels and capillaries dilate to cool the blood. However, when the body is dehydrated during heat exhaustion, these dilated blood vessels constrict and significantly reduce heat loss. This can be observed by looking at the face of an athlete suffering from heat exhaustion – it will suddenly change from a red rosy appearance to a much paler colour or white.

If a person ignores the symptoms of heat exhaustion and continues to exercise, they will suffer from **heat stroke**, which is a life-threatening condition and has a high death rate. It occurs because the body has depleted its supply of water and salt, and results in the person's body temperature rising to deadly levels. If the core temperature of the body reaches 43°C or more, the proteins start to break down and change their structure permanently. Imagine cooking an egg, the egg white is mainly made up of protein; when the egg white reaches a certain temperature (around 43°C) it's structure changes from a runny viscous medium to a solid. The same principle applies to the body's proteins, such as the enzymes and hormones. Once heated to a certain temperature, the structure of the body's proteins will permanently change and will no longer be able to function. Therefore, it is vitally important that the core temperature is not elevated to this degree.

Heat loss in a hot environment

The **hypothalamus** acts as a thermostat and initiates the responses that protect the body from overheating. It receives information about the temperature of the body via two sources:

✪   indirectly from the thermal receptors in the skin

✪   directly by changes in blood temperature.

Heat loss through radiation is not possible if the environment is hotter than the person exercising. Therefore, there are only three forms of heat loss available to a person exercising in a hot environment.

Conductive heat loss occurs by the peripheral blood vessels dilating and bringing blood close to the skin's surface. This results in the rosy coloured skin associated with hot athletes. The heat from the blood warms the air molecules around the person and any cooler surfaces that come into contact with the skin. Conductive heat loss works in conjunction with convective heat loss.

Convective heat loss occurs much more rapidly if there is increased air flow around the body, e.g. if it is windy or a fan is being used. If there is little air movement, the air next to the skin is warmed and acts as a layer of insulation that minimises further convective heat loss. However, if the warmed air surrounding the body is frequently changed due to increased air currents, heat loss through convection will continue to remove excess body heat.

Evaporative heat loss provides the main source of heat dissipation. As the sweat evaporates, it cools down the skin surface. This has the effect of cooling the blood as it travels through the blood vessels that are close to the skin surface. In order for evaporative heat loss to occur maximally, the person must be hydrated and have normal levels of salt and electrolytes in their body.

The circulatory system is vitally important in ensuring that these three methods of heat loss can occur. Not only does the blood have to supply the muscles with oxygen and nutrients, it also plays a major part in thermoregulation. The blood is redirected to the periphery by dilatation of peripheral blood vessels. In extreme conditions, 15% to 25% of the cardiac output is directed to the skin. As a result of these two cardiovascular demands, the heart rate is higher when exercising in the heat than in normal conditions.

Heart rate is also elevated because of the slight to severe dehydration that often occurs while exercising in the heat. If the person is dehydrated, then plasma volume is decreased. A decreased plasma volume will lead to a decreased stroke volume. Therefore, as we know:

$$\text{cardiac output} = \text{heart rate} \times \text{stroke volume}$$
$$Q \text{(l per min)} = HR \text{ (bpm)} \times SV \text{ (ml)}$$

In order for cardiac output to remain the same, heart rate has to increase to make up for the decreased stroke volume.

$$Q = \uparrow HR \times SV \downarrow$$

STUDENT PRACTICAL

Heat stress

Aim

The aim of this practical is to see how the effect of exercising in hot conditions affects the cardiovascular system.

continues overleaf

continued

Equipment

bleep test

tape recorder

heart rate monitors

results table

sports kit – shorts and T-shirt for test 1; tracksuit bottoms, sweatshirt, woolly hat, gloves for test 2

weighing scales

sports hall

Method

Test 1 – normal conditions

1   Each person is weighed wearing shorts and T-shirt.

2   Working in pairs, place a heart rate monitor on the first person taking the test.

3   The first person takes part in the bleep test. At the end of each stage, the exercising person calls out their heart rate while their partner records this number and the appearance of the exercising person.

4   Once the exercising person has exercised to voluntary exhaustion, they towel down, put on a clean T-shirt and record their body weight.

5   The process is repeated for the second person.

Test 2 – hot conditions

This test should be carried out at least 48 hours after test 1. Ensure each person taking part is fully hydrated before taking part in this test.

1   Each person is weighed wearing shorts and T-shirt.

2   Working in pairs, place a heart rate monitor on the first person taking the test.

3   The person taking the test then puts on tracksuit bottoms, a sweatshirt, woolly hat and gloves.

4   The first person takes part in the bleep test. At the end of each stage, the exercising person calls out their heart rate while their partner records this number and the appearance of the exercising person.

5   Once the exercising person has exercised to voluntary exhaustion they remove their tracksuit bottoms, sweatshirt, hat and gloves, towel down and put on a fresh T-shirt and shorts. The person is then weighed.

Results

Record the results in the table below.

Stage	Heart rate		Appearance	
	Test 1	Test 2	Test 1	Test 2
1				
2				
3				
4				
5				
6				
7				
8				
9				
10				

Plot the heart rates for the normal and hot conditions on to a line graph.

Test 1

Weight before: _____

Weight after: _____

Weight difference: _____

Test 2

Weight before: _____

Weight after: _____

Weight difference: _____

Conclusion

Try to answer the following questions and explain the answers in your conclusion.

1   Was there a difference in the heart rates at each stage in the two tests?

2   Was there a difference in the person's appearance in the two tests at each stage of the bleep test? Was there any difference between the weight loss in test 1 and test 2?

3. Did the person manage to reach the same stage in the bleep test in both tests? Try to explain your results.

Heat acclimatisation

Athletes are able to cope much better with hot or humid conditions if they are acclimatised. Complete heat acclimatisation requires up to 14 days, but the systems of the body adapt to heat exposure at varying rates. The main effects of acclimatisation are:

- ✪ heart rate goes down
- ✪ **blood plasma** volume goes up
- ✪ skin blood flow goes up
- ✪ sweating occurs at a lower body core temperature
- ✪ sweat rate goes up
- ✪ sweat becomes more dilute.

In the first five days, plasma volume expands as a result of increased plasma proteins and increased sodium chloride retention. This increased plasma volume leads to a 15–25% reduction in heart rate at rest and during exercise from when first exposed to the hot environment.

The sweating mechanism is also adapted in three main ways:

- ✪ earlier onset of sweating
- ✪ increased amount of sweating
- ✪ increased dilution of sweat.

Once a person has started to acclimatise they will begin to sweat at a lower body core temperature. They will also produce more sweat in order to maximise evaporative cooling. The maximal non-adapted sweat rate for a male is one litre per hour, however, after acclimatisation, the sweat rate can double to two litres per hour. Sweat becomes more diluted due to conservation of salt (sodium chloride). The salt losses in sweat and urine decrease during days 3–9 of heat acclimatisation.

These changes result in increased heat loss for a given set of environmental conditions, and a smaller rise in body temperature.

In order to maximise an athlete's acclimatisation to a hot climate it is necessary to perform relatively intensive exercise in hot conditions. It is also necessary to consider the humidity of the environment. If a competition is being held in a hot and humid environment, the athlete must acclimatise for both heat and humidity. The athletes would also need to be exposed to environmental conditions for 24 hours a day, so it would not be advised for them to stay in accommodation with air conditioning.

Living in a hot environment

The main physiological response to living in a hot environment appears to be the evolution of a tall, slim body with little body fat. If you look at a typical person living in a hot climate such as Africa, they will usually be tall and slender. This will have the effect of increasing their surface-area-to-volume ratio, which will increase heat loss via conduction, evaporation and radiation.

Exercise in a cold environment

The effect of a cold environment on exercise performance depends largely on the severity of the cold and the type of exercise performed. Exposure to a moderately cold environment may actually have a positive effect on performance, as the cardiovascular system no longer has to divert blood to the periphery for heat loss in addition to supplying the exercising muscles with blood. This results in less stress being placed on the heart than when exercising in the heat. Therefore, it is not surprising that record performances during long-distance running and cycling are usually achieved in cool climatic conditions. However, exposure to extreme cold, such as in cross-country skiing, may cause an athlete's core body temperature to drop and maximal aerobic endurance (VO_2max) to be reduced, which will impair the athlete's performance.

If a person is exposed to a cold environment they may suffer from frostbite or hypothermia.

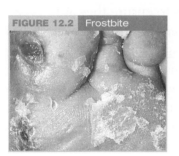

FIGURE 12.2 Frostbite

Frostbite usually occurs in a person's fingers or toes. It happens when a part of the body becomes extremely cold, significantly reducing blood supply to the area, which results in the body tissue freezing. The ice crystals that form will rupture and destroy the body's cells. The involved region turns a deep purple or red colour and has blisters, which are usually filled with blood. This tissue will then have to be amputated to prevent infection from spreading to other parts of the body.

Hypothermia is defined as a drop in the body's normal core temperature to 35°C or below. The condition usually comes on gradually and its severity varies in relation to how low the body core temperature drops – if it drops to 30°C or below this can lead to cardiac and respiratory failure that is soon followed by death.

Methods of gaining heat in the cold

When humans are exposed to a cold environment at rest, the body attempts to prevent heat loss as well as to increase heat production. It does this via three main physiological mechanisms:

✪ **constriction** of the peripheral blood circulation

✪ non-shivering **thermogenesis**

✪ shivering.

First of all, the body will decrease the blood supply to the peripheral circulation by constriction of the peripheral blood vessels (vasoconstriction). The purpose of this is to keep the blood close to the body core and redirect the blood away from the body's extremities and skin surface, where it would be cooled down by the environment. In humans, **vasoconstriction** can reduce heat loss by up to a third. The presence of **subcutaneous** fat also aids in maintaining the heat of the blood as fat is a very good insulator.

Secondly, a person will experience an increase in their metabolic rate, which is brought about by an increased release of the hormones thyroxin and adrenaline. An increased metabolic rate will generate body heat. This process is called **non-shivering thermogensis**. Lastly, a person will experience a rapid involuntary cycle of contraction and relaxation of skeletal muscles, which is called **shivering**. The process of shivering can actually increase metabolic rate to four to five times above resting levels.

A person can also conserve heat by adding clothing, which is a behavioural mechanism for minimising heat loss.

Cold acclimatisation

The main method by which an athlete can attempt to acclimatise to a cold environment is to increase their subcutaneous fat. This would have the effect of increasing the body's insulation to the cold, thereby reducing heat loss. However, in reality an athlete rarely wants to increase their body fat proportion, as excess fat will increase their body weight. Depending on the athlete's sport, this increase in body weight would usually decrease their performance. Therefore, the only real option for an athlete to attempt to conserve body heat is to ensure they are wearing appropriate clothing to protect them from the environment. Layered clothing has been found to provide the best insulation against the cold. In addition to this, the clothing should be 'breathable'. This is because during exercise, the athlete will sweat. This sweat must be allowed to evaporate – if it does not then the clothing may become wet. This then increases heat loss by conduction and evaporation. Therefore, clothing worn close to the body should be made of material that can transport moisture away from the body's surface to the next clothing layer for evaporation. Also, the head should always be covered because 30% to 40% of body heat can be lost through the head if it is left bare.

Time spent exercising in the cold before the competition would also be recommended, because the athlete would need to get used to breathing in cold air, as research has shown that extremely cold air can cause irritation to the mouth, **pharynx**, **trachea** and **bronchi**.

Living in a cold climate

The main human physiological response to living in the cold is the evolution of a shorter, rounder, more compact body. If you were to look at the average body dimensions of an Inuit you would notice that their bodies have evolved in this way. This shorter, more rounded body gives the person a relatively decreased surface-area-to-volume ratio compared with people living in hot environments. This will reduce heat loss by conduction, radiation and evaporation.

Exercising in water

When a person is submerged, their resting heart rate will decrease. This is attributed to the pressure of water on the body producing central pooling of the blood. This extra pressure acts to increase the rate of blood returning to the heart, which will result in an increased stroke volume. This in turn produces a lower heart rate.

However, when exercising in water an athlete must use more energy than when exercising on land in order to maintain buoyancy. When a person is swimming they must also maintain a horizontal position in the water and overcome **drag forces**, which are imposed on the swimmer by the water itself. As a result, swimming a given distance will use four times more energy than running the same distance.

Apart from swimmers, who train regularly in water, some athletes may undergo rehabilitation exercises in the water if they are recovering from a sports injury to the lower body. This is because the athlete can perform non-weight-bearing exercises and still carry out sport-specific exercises, such as the running action. As the water supports the athlete's body weight there will be much less stress placed on the injured body part than when exercising on land.

The main problem that a person may experience while exercising in water is the increased heat loss that can occur if the water is cold.

Cold water immersion

Water is deemed to be cold if it is less than 21°C. If a person swims in cold water, they will lose body heat quickly through conduction, and will try to increase their body heat by shivering. They will be using up energy trying to maintain their body heat, and the swimming action itself will also use up energy. If a person is exposed to cold water (less than 21°C) for long periods of time, they will eventually become exhausted or fall unconscious. If a person falls unconscious in the water, this may well result in death from drowning (see Table 12.1).

Table 12.1 Expected survival time in cold water

Water temperature	Exhaustion or unconsciousness in	Expected survival time
21–27°C	3–12 hours	3 hours – indefinitely
16–21°C	2–7 hours	2–40 hours
10–16°C	1–2 hours	1–6 hours
4–10°C	30–60 minutes	1–3 hours
0–4°C	15–30 minutes	30–90 minutes
0°C	Under 15 minutes	Under 15–45 minutes

Immersion in cold water can soon numb the extremities to the point of uselessness. Hypothermia quickly sets in, which will lead to unconsciousness and death. If a person is submerged in very cold water, the initial shock can place severe strain on the body and produce instant cardiac arrest.

The diving reflex – bradycardia

When diving most adults are able to hold their breath for up to a minute, and with training up to seven minutes. Most people can dive to a depth of 10 m, but there are free diving competitions in which athletes will dive down to depths of 100 m or more.

The diving reflex is the response to a cold water stimulus of the face. It triggers **bradycardia** and vasoconstriction of the blood flow from the periphery to the central nervous system (CNS) and vital organs. This results in the body 'shutting down', so the metabolic rate is significantly reduced and only the vital organs receive blood flow. This diving reflex is responsible for people surviving over thirty minutes of submersion in cold water without physical or mental damage. Trained human divers exhibit a bradycardia of up to 40–50%, so if their normal heart rate in the water was 80 bpm, during cold water diving it would be reduced to around 40 bpm. The greatest responses of the diving reflex appear to occur at a water temperature of 10°C.

STUDENT PRACTICAL

Cold water immersion

Aim

The aim of this practical is to see how the heart rate changes when the face is immersed in cold water.

Equipment

large bowl
ice
heart rate monitor
towels
thermometer

Method

1   Place a heart rate monitor on the subject.
2   Fill a large bowl with cold water and add ice cubes. Leave the water to stand for a few minutes, then take the temperature of the water and note this reading down.
3   Note down the heart rate of the person taking part in the practical. Take the heart rate at least three times over three minutes. Write down the average reading of these measurements.
4   Place a towel around the shoulders of your subject. They must then take a deep breath and plunge their face into the cold water for as long as they can bear (but no longer than one minute). Ensure that your tutor is present during this phase and able to monitor your subject's progress.
5   Take the heart rate every 10 seconds for the length of time your subject's face is submerged.
6   Always change the water before another subject takes part in the activity.

Results

Complete a table like the one below.

Time spent with face submerged (seconds)	Heart rate (bpm)
5	
10	
15	
20	

Plot a line graph with the subject's resting heart rate as the first point, then continue the graph with the heart rate plotted against length of time spent with the person's face submerged.

Conclusion

In your conclusion, try to answer the following questions.

1   Explain what happened to the heart rate in the first 20 seconds of immersion.
2   What happened to the heart rate after 20 seconds of immersion?
3   Did you get the results you expected? If not, can you explain why?

REVISION QUESTIONS

1) What is the main problem an athlete faces when exercising at high altitude?

2) List and then explain the physiological adaptations that aid an athlete to adapt to a high-altitude environment.

3) Research an athlete of your choice who has had to compete at high altitude. Find out how they acclimatised and how long they were exposed to the acclimatisation process.

4) What is the average body core temperature of a human?

5) List the four methods of heat transfer.

6) Which method of heat transfer produces the greatest heat loss in a hot environment?

7) If you were competing in a country such as Korea (where the football World Cup 2002 was held), other than the heat, what would you have to acclimatise for?

8) Why is heart rate higher in a hot climate, while working at the same intensity as in a cool environment?

9) What is the general body type of a person living in a hot environment? Explain your answer.

10) List the main methods of gaining heat in the cold.

11) Can a person acclimatise to a cold environment? Explain your answer.

12) What is and what triggers the 'diving reflex'?

13) What method of heat loss is the greatest while exercising in cold water?

SEX AND RACE

Body composition and sex

One of the main differences between the sexes that affects athletic performance is the difference in body composition. Males tend to have greater muscle mass and lower fat mass compared with females (see Table 12.2).

✿✿✿✿✿✿✿✿✿✿✿✿✿✿✿✿✿✿✿✿✿✿✿✿✿✿✿

Table 12.2 Differences in body composition between the sexes

Body tissue	Composition (%)	
	Male	Female
Muscle	45	36
Bone	15	12
Essential fat	3	12
Storage fat	12	15
Other tissue	25	25
Total	100	100

✿✿✿✿✿✿✿✿✿✿✿✿✿✿✿✿✿✿✿✿✿✿✿✿✿✿✿

A high percentage of body fat is not always a hindrance in sport. As females have a greater percentage of fat than males, they are more buoyant (body fat weighs much less than muscle mass), so they use up less energy than males staying afloat. Therefore, using the same amount of energy, females will be able to swim faster than males. This, together with their increased insulation from the cold, makes females more suited to open-water swimming, such as swimming the Channel. In 1978, a female set the world record for swimming the Channel, with a time of 7 hours 40 minutes. This record was unbroken for 16 years!

Maximal oxygen consumption and sex

An untrained male will have an average absolute VO_2max of 3.5 litres per minute, an untrained female will have an average absolute VO_2max of 2 litres per minute, which is 43% lower than the male's. The main reasons for this difference are that males are usually bigger than females, and there is a difference in body composition between the sexes. Females have approximately 10% more body fat than males, which will reduce their VO_2max because fat mass hinders performance.

Females also have have a lower blood haemoglobin content than males. This means that their blood has a lower oxygen-carrying capacity than males, which affects aerobic energy production. Research has shown that the female heart is slightly smaller relative to body size than the male heart. A relatively smaller heart would mean that a female's stroke volume is relatively lower than a male's. As cardiac output is the product of heart rate multiplied by stroke volume, in order for a female to maintain a certain cardiac output, her heart must beat faster than a male's.

$$Q = HR \times SV$$

Therefore, body size and fat percentage, the slightly lower oxygen-carrying capacity of the blood, plus a somewhat smaller heart might explain the gender differences in VO_2max.

Thermoregulation and sex

If you study males' and females' sweat rate per kilogram of body weight, women usually have lower sweat rates than men. Therefore, on average, males are able to lose more heat through evaporative heat loss than females. However, as females have a higher body surface-area-to-volume ratio than males, they are able to lose more heat through radiation. Research has shown that these variations in heat loss between the sexes evens out, so that there is no real difference in the ability to dissipate heat.

Muscle strength and power

If you were to extract exactly the same amount of healthy muscle from a male and from a female, then test the muscle tissue for the amount of force it could produce, there would be no difference between the two. Therefore, there is no difference in the strength of the muscle tissue between the sexes.

FIGURE 12.3   Male body builders

However, on average, males are stronger than females because of difference in body composition. The average female has less total muscle mass than the average male. The reason for this difference is largely due to the hormone **testosterone**. Testosterone acts on the body in a number of ways, including increasing muscle growth. Studies have shown females taking testosterone injections for a period of time, increased their muscle mass and decreased their body fat percentage. The females undergoing this study also began to develop secondary male characteristics, such as growth of facial hair, deepened voices and increased aggression.

Studies have also shown that the number of slow-twitch and fast-twitch fibres is no different in the male and female populations. Therefore, it is not the muscle quality that differs between the sexes, but the muscle quantity.

Some research has suggested that females are able to out-perform males at ultra-distance events. However, other investigations into events lasting from 50 km to six days have shown that males attain better performances than females in these events. Nevertheless, as ultra-distance competitions are fairly new, more research needs to be carried out in this area in order to gain a better understanding of male and female performance.

Training differences between males and females

Research suggests that males and females should not take on the same volume of training. It would appear that elite female athletes perform optimally at a training volume that is around 10% to 15% lower than that observed in elite male athletes. If the volume of training is increased for a female it often does not improve performance and can lead to over-training. This is again due to the hormone **testosterone**. As previously discussed, testosterone is responsible for aiding muscle growth. However, it is also critical for tissue repair. As training results in the breakdown of tissues, males are able to recover much more quickly from training than females because of this hormone.

It is important to note that all these differences are based on the average results taken from males and females. However, in reality there are many individual women with significantly higher VO_2max values, strength, endurance and training ability than individual men.

STUDENT PRACTICAL

Differences in strength between the sexes

Aim

The aim of this practical is to determine if there is a difference in strength between the males and females in your class. Differences in upper body and lower body will also be compared.

Equipment

multigym or free weights

pen and paper

weighing scales

Method

1 The whole class should warm up thoroughly before taking part in any strength tests.

2 Working in pairs, go around the multigym or use the free weights. Lift an amount you feel comfortable with, then continue adding weights until you have reached your 1 rep max. Ensure that you have short breaks between lifts. Write this weight down.

3 Record your body weight.

continues overleaf

continued

4   Work out what weight you lifted (kg) in relation to your body weight (kg). This can be calculated by:

$$\frac{\text{weight lifted (kg)}}{\text{body weight (kg)}} \times 100$$

5   Complete a table that takes into account the whole class's results, then work out the average weight lifted in each exercise for males and for females. Repeat this, but use weight lifted in relation to body weight.

Results

Complete a table like the one below.

Exercise	Weight lifted	Percentage of body weight

Conclusion

In your conclusion, try to answer the following questions.

1   Was there a difference in the average weight lifted by each sex? Can you explain why there is this difference?

2   Which exercise produced the greatest difference between the sexes? Why do you think this is?

3   Why is body weight sometimes taken into account when comparing the amount of weight a person can lift?

Eating disorders

Eating disorders lead to a negative energy balance, which means that more energy is being exerted than being consumed. This could lead to under-nutrition or an imbalance of nutrient intake. A person who has disordered eating might display the following symptoms:

✪   intense fear of gaining weight
✪   distorted body image
✪   chaotic eating patterns/strict dieting.

Disordered eating can leave the person with low energy levels and increased susceptibility to infection, slower recovery from injury and depression. Disordered eating can take on two forms, annorexia nervosa or bulemia nervosa.

Anorexia nervosa

People who have anorexia nervosa often have low self-esteem and an immense need to control their surroundings and emotions. It is often a reaction to anxiety, stress and or unhappiness. A doctor would diagnose a person as having anorexia nervosa if their body weight was 15% less than normal.

There are two main types of anorexia nervosa.

✪   **Restricting type** is when the person maintains their low body weight purely by restricting food intake and increased activity (i.e. compulsive exercise).

✪   **Binge-eating/purging type** is when the person restricts their food intake but also regularly engages in binge eating and/or purging behaviours. Purging is the process of removing food and fluids from the body before they can be properly digested and includes self-induced vomiting, and using **laxatives**, **diuretics** or **enemas**.

Together with lowered body weight, a person with anorexia nervosa may also display a variety of other physiological symptoms that a doctor would look for before making a diagnosis. In a female who has already started her menstrual periods, an absence of at least three consecutive menstrual cycles may indicate anorexia nervosa. This is due to a reduction in oestrogen production (**hypooestrogenemia**). A person with anorexia nervosa may also have an irregular or low heart rate (bradycardia) and frequently feel weak and dizzy. Lanugo (fine facial hair) may appear. They may have an orange appearance due to hypercarotenaemia, which is an excess of carotene, the precursor to vitamin A.

Bulimia nervosa

A person with bulimia nervosa is usually of average or above-average weight and it is therefore often harder to tell visually if a person is suffering from this condition. The condition involves recurrent episodes of binge eating. An episode of binge eating is characterised by both of the following:

✪ within a two-hour period, eating an amount of food that is definitely larger than most people would eat during a similar period of time and under similar circumstances

✪ a sense of lack of control over eating during the episode – the person cannot stop eating nor control what they eat or the amount they eat.

The person would then try to prevent weight gain by purging, fasting or performing excessive exercise. If a person purges after excessive eating they have an increased risk of mortality due to excessive loss of electrolytes during the purging of the food. This loss of electrolytes can lead to abnormal nervous impulse transmission that can effect the normal function of the heart. Repeated self-induced vomiting can also lead to death as the person risks choking on the purged food.

If the person carries out this binge eating and inappropriate compensatory behaviour at least twice a week for three months they would be described as having bulimia nervosa. An individual may simultaneously meet the criteria for both anorexia nervosa and bulimia nervosa. If this occurs, then only the diagnosis of anorexia nervosa, binge-eating/purging type is given.

In the UK it is estimated that there are 125 000 people with bulimia and 70 000 people with anorexia nervosa. Only one in ten cases are male, but research suggests that eating disorders amongst males is on the increase.

Eating disorders are very common in sports people and are more prevalent among sportswomen than men. Studies from America suggest that up to 62% of professional sportswomen have some form of eating disorder.

But why are sports people more prone to eating disorders? This could be due to the fact that some sports emphasise body weight and smallness (e.g. gymnasts, jockeys).

Therefore, the athlete has to maintain a certain body weight that may be below their healthy body weight. Also, certain personality characteristics of individuals at risk of developing an eating disorder are the same as those required for top-level sports performance. Professional sports people are often obsessive, competitive, perfectionist and have a high degree of self-motivation, which are traits frequently seen in people with an eating disorder.

Female health problems

Ammenorrhea

The IOC classifies ammenorrhea as one menstrual period or less per year. There are two type of ammenorrhea.

1   **Primary**: this means that the female has not had a menstrual period by the age of 16.

2   **Secondary**: this is when the female has begun menstruation, but her periods then stop.

Amenorrhoea occurs more often in athletes than in the general population – it is reported that 34% to 66% of female athletes are amenorrhoeic as compared with 2% to 5% of the general population. There is no specific body-fat percentage below which regular menstruation ceases. A high training regime can result in amenorrhoea as it has been shown that rest can restore menstruation with no increase in body weight.

Osteoporosis

Osteoporosis is the name for decreased bone mineral density. The bones of the skeleton are continually being renewed. This process involves the bones being broken down by **osteoclasts** and then re-formed by **osetoblasts**. The re-formation of the bones requires the laying down of minerals in order to maintain the density of the bone. However, if a person has osteoporosis, their bones are reformed with fewer minerals than before, which makes them weak and brittle and more prone to fracture. Peak bone mass is achieved between the ages of 18 and 25. After that, bone mass is lost at rate of 0.3% to 0.5% per year. However, menopausal women lose 3% of bone mass per year for an average of 10 years, after which it returns back to a loss of 0.3% per year.

Research has shown that weight-bearing exercise, such as running and resistance training, increases bone mass.

Female athletic triad

This is the name for a syndrome of three interrelated components:

- disordered eating
- ammenorrhea
- osteoporosis.

A female athlete may feel pressured to maintain an unrealistically low body weight, which results in an eating disorder. This, in combination with a high training load, often leads to ammenorrhea. Ammenorrhea can then result in the athlete suffering from osteoporosis. Research has shown that if the female is able to return to eating healthily and attains a normal body weight then she will recommence regular menstruation. However, the effects of the reduced bone mineral density are not reversible. The health of the skeleton is determined by the length and severity of menstrual disturbance – the longer it continues, the greater the risk of osteoporosis.

Race

Take a look at the Sydney 2000 Olympic 100 m sprint final. What do you notice about the line up? Now examine the endurance races. Where were the winners from? What about the swimming competition? What do you notice about the race of the swimmers?

FIGURE 12.4 The 2000 Olympic 100 m sprint final line up

From this olympics it seems clear that athletes of certain races are better suited to certain sports. This section will examine a few different races and their sporting prowess in the world today. At present, the top athletes for both short- and long-distance running events tend to come from Africa and, as a result, this section pays special attention to athletes from this country

West African athletes

At present, every men's world record from 100 m to 1 mile belongs to a runner of African descent. In sprinting, the last time a white athlete held the world record for the 100 m was in 1960. The 10-second time barrier for sprinting 100 m has been broken 200 times, but always by black athletes. This would lead one to believe that athletes of African origin have a natural athletic advantage over competitors whose ethnic origin lies elsewhere.

Research suggests that this theory does hold true, and that the physique of athletes from this region is better suited to sprinting. These athletes generally have lower body fat, longer legs in comparison with the rest of their bodies, and narrow hips. They also tend to have greater muscle mass, higher bone mineral density, higher levels of testosterone, a higher percentage of fast-twitch muscle fibres and more anaerobic enzymes.

Research strongly suggests that no amount of training can break through the percentage of genetically inherited fast-twitch muscle fibres. The greater the number of fast-twitch fibres an athlete has, generally the better they will be suited to speed events. Therefore, if an athlete does not have a certain proportion of fast-twitch muscles, he or she cannot hope to be a champion sprinter or jumper. This would suggest that sprinters are born and cannot be made.

East African (Kenyan) athletes

With regard to the middle- to long-distance running events, the East Africans, particularly the Kenyans, are dominant. The top 60 times for the 3000 m steeplechase are all held by Kenyan athletes. Kenyan athletes also hold more than half of the top times for the 5000 and 10000 meters.

The vast majority of top Kenyan runners come from one area of the country, the Kalenjin region. Athletes coming from this part of Kenya have won more than 70% of Kenya's Olympic medals in world running. The fact that the Kalenjin region is at high altitude has made many scientists believe that their adaptation to living at high altitude has given them an increased athletic prowess at endurance events. These athletes have been shown to have a greater number of red blood cells, a larger lung capacity, a high proportion of slow-twitch muscle fibres and more energy-producing enzymes in their muscles, which are better able to utilise oxygen than those of athletes living at normal altitudes. These adaptations would increase the athlete's oxygen-carrying capacity and would certainly aid the athlete in endurance running events.

Caucasian athletes

White people (Caucasians) tend to have more natural upper-body strength, and tend to have evolved with a **mesomorphic** body type and relatively short arms and legs. As a result they dominate weightlifting and wrestling. They also excel at the field events and hold 46 out of the top 50 throws for shot put and hammer.

Caucasian people also tend to dominate the swimming events – very few African athletes reach any swimming final. This could be due to the fact that African athletes tend to have heavier skeletons and smaller chest cavities, which would leave them at a disadvantage when competing in water.

Indian athletes

For the second consecutive Olympic Games, India, with a population of 1 billion people, brought home only a single bronze medal from Sydney. With this number of people, statistics would suggest that they should have taken home many more medals. However, athletes of Indian origin do excel at some sports, in particular cricket. This is probably due to social and cultural influences rather than a physiological predisposition to the sport.

Research clearly shows that genetic evolution has strongly influenced the physiological make-up of people living in different environments, which may well determine if a person has the chance to be an elite athlete. However, dedication, commitment and good fortune are also factors that play a major role in determining if the athlete will win or lose.

As well as the physiological traits of athletes coming from different ethnic origins, it is also necessary to take into account the social, cultural and economical factors of the country the person grew up in, as these have a huge affect on determining whether a person will take up certain sports. This may help to explain why some races excel in some sports but not in others.

REVISION QUESTIONS

1) What are the main differences between the body composition of males and females?

2) Does having a greater percentage of body fat always decrease sporting performance?

3) Why do males usually have a greater muscle mass than females?

4) Are males' muscles stronger than females' muscles? Explain your answer.

5) Explain what the female athletic triad is and why it is dangerous to a female's long-term health.

6) Explain the difference between anorexia nervosa and bulimia nervosa.

7) Why are eating disorders a potentially life-threatening illness?

8) If you were coaching a group of male and female sprinters, would you give them exactly the same training program? Explain your answer.

9) What is the world record for the 100 m sprint, and who holds it?

10) From what ethnic origin is the person who holds the 100 m world record, and is it what you would expect? Explain your answer.

11) Why are some athletes from Kenya better suited to endurance running?

12) How could living at altitude affect a person's endurance performance?

13) Why do Caucasian athletes tend to dominate swimming events?

PHYSIO-LOGICAL AIDS IN SPORTS AND EXERCISE

Instances of athletes using performance-enhancing substances date back over 2000 years. As far back as 668BC, the winner of the 200 m sprint in the Olympic Games prepared for the event with a special diet of dried figs. In sport today, virtually all athletes will take substances to improve their performance. This is because athletes face enormous pressure to excel in competition, as winning a race not only gives them a gold medal, they can also earn a lot of money and a lot of fame from a win. The competition life of an athlete is relatively brief, which means that athletes only have a short time to do their best work. Although athletes must know that training is the best path to victory, they are also aware that some drugs can boost their efforts and give them a greater chance of victory even at the expense of their health and their athletic careers. Some of the substances athletes take are illegal, as defined by the IOC, whereas others are perfectly legitimate ways of naturally improving one's performance, such as consuming a sports drink during a game, or eating a special diet of dried figs!

In this section, we will only be exploring pharmacological aids used by athletes, all of which are banned by the IOC, but are still frequently used by athletes today.

The practice of using artificial substances or methods to enhance athletic performance is called **doping**. The first drug tests on athletes were conducted at the Olympic Games in Mexico in 1968. Since then, drug testing has become a major part of sporting competition and new methods of detecting drugs are always being sought (see also pages 281–85).

Drug testing procedures

Athletes can be tested after an event or 'out of competition'. For an event test, the chosen athletes are told at the end of the competition that they are to be tested. For out-of-competition testing, athletes are contacted and must then take a drug test within 24 hours of receiving the testing notice.

For the test, the athlete is accompanied into the toilet by a chaperone who watches the athlete pass their urine into a small plastic container. The urine is then poured into two containers, A and B. If sample A tests positive for drugs, then sample B is tested for confirmation.

If the urine sample contains a banned drug, this can lead to the athlete being disqualified from their sport. Occasionally, the athlete may have inadvertently taken a banned substance, as some drugs are present in cough and cold remedies. This will usually result in a less serious ban. If an athlete refuses to take a drug test, then they are considered to have been taking drugs and this may result in them being banned from competing in their sport.

Types of drugs

The majority of pharmacological aids used by athletes today were initially designed by the medical profession in order to treat patients with various illnesses or disorders. Many types of drugs are available to the athlete, and what they take is determined by the sport in which they compete. The main effects of the different groups of drugs are to:

- build muscle mass
- increase the delivery of oxygen to exercising tissues
- provide pain relief
- stimulate the body
- relax
- reduce weight.

Building muscle mass

Athletes competing in sports that require a high muscle mass, such as weightlifting, throwing events, sprinting, or boxing, may take muscle building drugs. There are a variety of drugs available that will increase the muscle mass of an athlete, including anabolic steroids, human growth hormone (hGH) and insulin.

Anabolic steroids

Anabolic steroids are man-made substances. They were developed in the late 1930s primarily to treat hypogonadism, which is a condition in which the testes do not produce enough testosterone. This reduction in testosterone production resulted in impaired growth, development and sexual functioning. It was later discovered that anabolic steroids could not only treat males with hypogonadism, but could also increase the growth of skeletal muscle in humans. Today, athletes and others abuse anabolic steroids to enhance performance and improve physical appearance. However, just taking anabolic steroids will not increase muscle bulk; the athlete must still train hard in order to achieve an increase in muscle mass. The main advantage in taking these drugs is that the muscles recover more quickly from training. This will allow the athlete to train at a higher level and for longer than if they were not taking these drugs.

Anabolic steroids can be taken orally, in tablet form, or injected directly into muscle tissue.

The main **side-effects** of taking anabolic steroids are:

- liver and kidney tumours
- jaundice
- high blood pressure
- severe acne
- trembling.

There are also some sex-specific side-effects.

Males:

- shrinking of the testicles
- reduced sperm count
- infertility, baldness
- development of breasts
- increased risk for prostate cancer.

Females:

- growth of facial hair
- male-pattern baldness
- changes in or cessation of the menstrual cycle
- enlargement of the clitoris
- deepened voice.

Scientific research also shows that aggression and other psychiatric side-effects may result from abuse of anabolic steroids. Depression can be experienced when the person stops taking the drugs and may contribute to them becoming dependent on anabolic steroids.

Human growth hormone

Human growth hormone (also know as human chorionic gonadotropin, hCG) is a naturally occurring protein hormone produced by the pituitary gland and is important for normal human growth and development, especially in children and teenagers. Low hGH levels in children and teenagers result in dwarfism. Growth hormone stimulates the development of natural male and female sex hormones. In males, growth hormone acts to increase testosterone levels and results in increased muscle development, as with anabolic steroids. Excessive hGH levels increase muscle mass by stimulating protein synthesis, strengthen bones by stimulating bone growth and reduce body fat by stimulating the breakdown of fat cells.

When the effects of growth hormone were first learnt, the hormone could not be produced artificially. This meant that athletes could only obtain growth hormone in its natural form, either from dead bodies or dead animals. Research suggests that athletes or athletes' coaches would rob graves for the sole purpose of extracting growth hormone from the brains of people who had recently died. Clearly this was a highly unethical and illegal process, so athletes would also extract growth hormone from dead animals. However, if the athletes took the hormone from dead animals they ran the risk of contracting animal diseases such as Creutzfeldt-Jakob disease (CJD). Nowadays, growth hormone can be produced in labs and is widely available. The use of hGH has become increasingly popular because it is difficult to detect.

Growth hormone is not banned for female athletes because it would not lead to muscle development and might naturally occur in high levels if the athlete is pregnant. The side-effects of growth hormone in males are the same as those of anabolic steroids together with enlarged internal organs. The athlete taking the drug may also develop **acromegaly**, which results in the person's hands, feet and lower jaw growing much larger than normal. If a person's lower jaw grows faster than the rest of the bones of the face, their teeth will become misaligned and they will need to wear braces.

Insulin

Insulin is produced naturally in the body by the pancreas. Its main function is to help to control the concentration of sugar within the bloodstream. If there is too much sugar, insulin acts to remove this sugar by stimulating the synthesis of glycogen or fat. People with diabetes Type 1 need to inject insulin into their body regularly, as their pancreas no longer produces adequate amounts of insulin to maintain blood sugar levels. Athletes may take insulin in combination with anabolic steroids or growth hormone as it also helps to increase muscle mass by stimulating protein synthesis. The main side-effects of abusing insulin are **hypoglycaemic** responses such as shaking, nausea and weakness. If too much insulin is taken this may lead to severe hypoglycaemia, which could lead to coma and death.

Increasing oxygen in tissues

Athletes competing in endurance sports are the principal abusers of drugs that increase the oxygen supply to their muscle tissues. There are two main methods of increasing the oxgyen supply to the tissue, these are by taking erythropoietin (EPO) or by blood doping.

Erythropoietin

EPO is a naturally occurring protein hormone that is secreted by the kidneys. After being released into the bloodstream it acts on the bone marrow, where it stimulates the production of red blood cells (erythrocytes). Medically, EPO is used to treat certain forms of **anaemia**. Since EPO increases a person's red blood cell count, it will result in increased blood haemoglobin concentrations. Therefore, after taking EPO, a person's blood will have an increased oxygen-carrying capacity which potentially has the effect of increasing an athlete's performance. Endurance athletes, such as those who compete in marathons, the Tour de France, cross-country skiing, and so on can use EPO to increase their oxygen supply by as much as 10%.

EPO is difficult to detect because it is identical to the naturally occurring form produced by the body. As there is no established normal concentration range of EPO it is very difficult to determine if an athlete has been using EPO.

The main side-effect of taking EPO is an increase in the 'thickness' of the blood. This thickened blood will not flow through the blood vessels very well because it has a greater resistance. As a result, the heart must work harder to pump blood around the body, which will increase the chances of the athlete suffering from a heart attack.

Blood doping

Blood doping is the practice of artificially increasing the amount of red blood cells in the body in order to increase oxygen delivery to the tissues in an attempt to improve athletic performance. Records show that blood doping research was initially conducted in the Second World War in order to try to increase the endurance of pilots. As the pilots who were dropping bombs had to avoid antiaircraft guns, they needed to fly higher. However, flying at higher altitudes disturbed the normal functioning of the central nervous system, which resulted in errors being made. In 1944–45 the US navy infused 1300 ml of blood into two subjects and tested their physiological reactions at simulated high altitude. They found that these subjects were able to tolerate lower oxygen levels and have normal functioning of the central nervous system. Research also showed that the subjects exhibited a lower heart rate response during exercise following the transfusion.

The effects of blood doping were then realised by the sporting world, and blood doping became an illegal method of increasing the athlete's oxygen-carrying capacity of blood. There are two main methods of blood doping. First, athletes may undergo a **homologous transfusion**, in which they receive blood from an individual of the same blood type. The red blood cell count is then increased by the amount that is transferred. The second method is via **autologous transfusion**. This means the athlete's own blood is used. An amount of blood is removed from the athlete and frozen for six to eight weeks. Over this period, the athlete's body makes new red blood cells to replace those that have been removed. The removed blood is then transfused back into the athlete which results in the athlete, having an increased number of red blood cells compared with pre-transfusion.

Blood doping was not banned until 1985; however, at present there are no tests available to determine with certainty if an athlete has been cheating by blood doping.

The side-effects of blood doping are the same as taking EPO, but there is the increased risk of contracting diseases such as HIV or of receiving the wrong blood type if the athlete undergoes homologous transfusion. Reports have also been made in the past of athletes receiving blood from a person who was taking performance-enhancing drugs. Once the blood was transfused, the receiver would have traces of the drug in their bloodstream and would test positive for these drugs.

Pain relief

At some point in their career, most athletes will probably suffer from a sport injury. If this injury occurs during competition, athletes may try to mask their injury pain with drugs, such as narcotics, cortisone and local anaesthetics.

Narcotics are taken in order to reduce the amount of pain felt from injury or can be used as recreational drugs. The main narcotics used are morphine, methadone and heroin. They act to give the person a 'high', which helps to mask the pain of the injury; however, they will also affect mental abilities, such as balance and co-ordination, which may have a detrimental effect on performance. In addition, athletes who continue to compete with a sport injury run the risk of further damage or complications to the injured area.

Stimulants

The main stimulants used by athletes are amphetamines. Caffeine (in high doses) and ephedrine are also stimulants that have been used by athletes. Stimulants act to mimic the action of the sympathetic nervous system by constricting the blood vessels supplying blood to skin, dilating the blood vessels supplying the heart and skeletal muscles, dilating the bronchioles to increase ventilation and increasing the release of glucose from the liver. They have the effect of increasing a person's mental alertness and also help to conceal feelings of exhaustion. As a result, athletes competing in endurance events, contact sports, or those demanding fast reactions may take stimulants in order to enhance their performance.

As stimulants hide feelings of fatigue, it is possible for athletes to over-exert themselves to the point where they can suffer heat stroke and cardiac failure. Other side-effects include increased blood pressure and body temperature, increased and irregular heartbeat, aggression, anxiety and loss of appetite. If an athlete requires medication to treat asthma or other common respiratory disorders they are at risk of inadvertently taking stimulants as these commonly prescribed substances often contain powerful stimulants.

Relaxation

Beta blockers are medically used to treat heart disease, to lower heart rate and blood pressure and reduce anxiety. These drugs act to interfere with actions of the sympathetic nervous system, which controls involuntary muscle movement. They slow the heart rate, relax muscle in blood vessel walls, and decrease the force of heart contractions. Athletes may use these drugs in sport in order to reduce anxiety levels and to prevent their body from shaking. As a result, athletes who take part in sports that require steady nerves and hands (e.g. snooker, archery, shooting and darts) may abuse this type of drug.

The side-effects of taking this drug include lowered blood pressure, slow heart rate and tiredness. In extreme cases, the heart may actually stop because it has been slowed down too much.

Weight reduction

Diuretics act to help increase the excretion of fluids from body tissues and to help reduce high blood pressure. The main reason diuretics are misused by competitors in sport is to reduce their body weight quickly in sports where weight categories are involved. Hence, boxers, weightlifters or judo competitors may take this drug in order to remain in their weight category. If their body weight is only slightly above the category lower limit, they will be competing against athletes who are larger than them and, therefore, also presumably have a greater muscle mass, which would leave the athlete at a disadvantage. Athletes may also take diuretics in order to reduce the concentration of other banned substances by diluting the urine, or to attempt to eliminate the banned substance from their body in order to escape detection of the drug through testing.

Possible side-effects of taking diuretics include dehydration, which could then lead to dizziness and fainting, vomiting and muscle cramps. If the athlete becomes severely dehydrated through taking the diuretics, the effect on the kidneys and the heart could lead to death.

Ethics

There are many arguments as to whether drug taking in sport is **ethical** or not. The majority of people think that the use of doping substances or doping methods to enhance performance is cheating. By taking drugs, the athlete gains an unfair advantage over the other athletes taking part in the competition. Not only is it cheating, but also drug misuse is often harmful to an athlete's health.

The debate as to whether drug taking in sport should be allowed has been ongoing for many years. Many drugs are not detectable, such as growth hormone, EPO and blood doping, so it is very likely that some athletes are getting away with cheating. Some believe that a number of athletes are taking some form of pharmacological aid but are not tested positive because they use masking drugs or simply stop taking the drug for a certain period prior to competition. Some scientists predict that in the future, it may well be impossible to detect whether an athlete has had some pharmacological intervention in order to enhance performance. The main reason for this thinking is the new

development of **genetic doping**. At present, as far as we know, this practice is only being performed for medicinal purposes, but it cannot be ruled out as a potential performance enhancing practice for the future.

? REVISION QUESTIONS

1) Why do you think some athletes take pharmacological aids to try improve their performance?

2) Name the main six different groups of drugs and, in each case, give an example of an athlete who might take them to improve their performance.

3) Give the potential side-effects of one of each group of drugs.

4) Discuss the concept of two Olympics, one where athletes have not taken any pharmacological aids and one where athletes are allowed to have taken pharmacological aids.

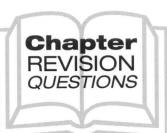

Chapter REVISION QUESTIONS

1) What climatic stresses did the England football team face when playing in the 2002 World Cup, and how did they try to prepare for these?

2) If you were coaching a group of male and female athletes to high altitude, how would you train them and would you give them exactly the same training regime? Explain your answer.

3) Research the 1968 Olympic Games held in Mexico City. Name three events in which world records were broken and three events where the results were lower than expected. Try to explain these findings.

4) Explain why you think the Kenyan athletes are dominating the long distance-running events.

5) Research an athlete of your choice who has been banned from taking part in sports because they have been found to have taken a pharmacological aid. Name:

a) the aid

b) how it may have enhanced their performance

c) possible side-effects from taking this aid.

SPORTS MASSAGE

Massage can be used to alleviate problems and to enhance an athlete's performance. It can also be used to treat injuries of people who are engaged in physical activities, such as gardening and walking, who do not consider themselves athletes. Everyone can benefit from massage therapy as it promotes relaxation, improves circulation and produces a feeling of wellbeing.

By the end of this chapter students should be able to:

✪ understand what sports massage is and when it should be used

✪ assess and identify the massage requirements of sports performers

✪ identify and undertake a treatment strategy for the provision of sports massage for a sports person

✪ identify a rehabilitation strategy and performance improvement programme for a selected sports person

✪ understand the role of the sports therapist and their influence on sports performance.

WHAT IS SPORTS MASSAGE?

Massage has been used by the Chinese, Greeks and Indians for around 3000 years. It was used at the ancient Olympic Games by the Greeks, who reserved massage for the athletes rather than the 'common man' who lacked athletic grace. Greeks regarded athletes as representative of all the best characteristics of being a man, as they had to push themselves to the limits of their endurance and suffer extreme pain in achieving their goals.

Today, athletes still push themselves to the extreme limits of their physical capabilities and place massive amounts of strain on their bodies. These strains and stresses result in muscular and connective tissue problems, of varying severity, which can be alleviated through massage. The foundations of today's massage techniques were developed by a Swede, Per Henrik Ling (1776–1839). His techniques, known as Swedish massage, spread throughout Europe and eventually the world. Sports massage developed in the UK through the 1990s to the point where it is commonplace for teams and athletes to employ a massage therapist. It has been established for longer in America, Australia and Canada.

Sports massage

Sport massage is scientific manipulation of soft tissue to aid an individual who partakes in physical activity. Soft tissue comprises structures such as muscle, tendon, ligament and skin. Manipulation of soft tissue is designed to restore normal functional activity to tissue that is experiencing problems or imbalances. Thus, sports massage is aimed at preventing injury, treating injury and enhancing performance.

The benefits of sports massage

Massage should be an integral part of every athlete's preparation for competition and post-event routine. It is as important as warming up and cooling down. There are many benefits, some of which are listed below:

- reduced muscle tension and resulting pain

- aiding recovery from training by reducing delayed onset muscle soreness (DOMS) and removing waste products

- improved flexibility through stretching, breaking down scar tissue and promoting circulation

- improving posture

- reducing anxiety.

When is sports massage contra-indicated?

Under certain circumstances, conditions may be present that sports massage may make worse and hence should not be carried out. These conditions are called **contra-indications**, and the massage therapist needs to know what they are and how to deal with them.

When the client is unwell or has a temperature over 100°F

These symptoms suggest that the client is entering a period of illness which may be made worse by massage. Massage will improve circulation of the toxins and make the condition more serious.

Skin diseases and disorders

Skin may become inflamed due to allergies or medical conditions such as eczema and psoriasis. Infections can be recognised by swelling, redness and pain. Massaging these areas can cause further irritation and the infection may be spread or passed on to the therapist.

Vein diseases

Phlebitis is the inflammation of the veins. Thrombosis is a blood clot and is often accompanied by phlebitis. Massage may disturb the blood clot, which will then travel round the body and may block a blood vessel in the heart, lungs or brain with serious consequences.

Varicose veins occur when the non-return valves in the veins become slack. This can result in pooling of blood in the veins. The veins become enlarged and painful to the touch. Attempts to massage an area where varicose veins are present could cause further damage and intense pain.

Recently injured areas

The site of an injury will be swollen, bruised and painful to the touch. There may also be a reduction in function of the muscle or joint. Massage will act to disturb the process of healing and may make the condition worse through increasing blood flow and thus swelling.

Pregnancy

Massage is not advised for a pregnant woman who is experiencing nausea and vomiting, as it may make their symptoms worse. Massage of the back and abdomen must be avoided during the first sixteen weeks as the friction could promote miscarriage. However, in the later stages of pregnancy massage of the lower limbs may be beneficial in promoting venous return.

CLIENT ASSESS-MENT

The initial consultation with your client is as vital as the treatment itself. The consultation will involve recording the client's history and keeping a record of these details and the details of the physical assessment.

The information required about a client's history is as follows:

- ✪ what physical activities they are involved in
- ✪ at what level they are competing
- ✪ what their training schedule is
- ✪ what injuries they have previously suffered
- ✪ what treatment they have previously received
- ✪ details of any medication they are taking.

This information helps to build up a picture of your client and you may get some clues to their current injury. The next set of questions will establish the cause and nature of their current problem.

- ✪ Where is the pain felt?
- ✪ How did the injury occur?
- ✪ Did the pain come on immediately or gradually?
- ✪ Is the pain a sharp ache or a dull throb?
- ✪ How did they feel after the injury occurred?
- ✪ Could they observe any swelling or redness?
- ✪ What treatment have they subsequently received?
- ✪ How are they currently restricted; which movements cause them pain?

At this point you may have identified a contra-indication or cause for concern beyond your expertise, and you may choose to refer your client to their general practitioner before continuing with treatment.

The information you are given needs to be recorded on a record form similar to the one shown below.

Confidential medical history

Name: .... Occupation: ....

Age: .... D.O.B: ....

Address: ....

....

Tel: Day .... Eve .... Mob ....

Sex: .... Height: .... Weight: ....

Sport played: .... Frequency/intensity: ....

GP name/address: ....

Medical history: ....

....

....

Present complaint: ....

History of injury: ....

....

....

I confirm that the information I have given is accurate to the best of my knowledge and I have not withheld any details. I accept that I will receive sports massage therapy at my own risk.

Signed: .... Date: ....

Print name: .... Therapist signature: ....

Notes – physical assessment:

STUDENT ACTIVITY

Practice a consultation with a partner. Each partner should take the role the client and therapist in turn and complete a consultation as if it were a real situation. The client should pretend that they have a particular injury and convey their symptoms to the therapist. However, if they have a real injury then they should use this situation.

Proposed treatment

Once the consultation and physical examination have been completed, it is useful to discuss your diagnosis of the problem and how you intend to treat it. You will suggest how many treatments your client may need and what this treatment will involve. It is also a good time to make any suggestions as to what they can do to help their recovery. For example, you may suggest that they stretch the surrounding muscles twice a day, or use ice treatments.

If you have not discussed your prices, now is the time to do so, and always make a record of whether a client has paid. A form such as the example below should be kept with their medical notes.

Date	Treatments given and progress	Fee	Date

Environment

The sports massage therapist needs to be versatile with regard to where they work. The environment where you are working may be beyond your control, particularly if you are working at a sports event. However, if possible you need to take care to prepare your environment for the treatment session.

The ideal environment is a warm, quiet room that is smartly decorated and has adequate ventilation. The temperature is particularly important as a warm room will promote muscular relaxation and be more comfortable for the client, as they may have to remove clothing.

Hygiene must be maintained to the highest standards. This involves the therapist and their room.

- ✪ The room must be kept clean and tidy.

- ✪ The therapist must keep their hands clean.

- ✪ A basin should be available for this purpose.

- ✪ Clean towels should be supplied.

- ✪ There should be adequate arrangements for waste disposal.

The therapist must ensure that they have the relevant equipment available. The equipment they need will include:

- a massage couch
- massage oil, cream or talcum powder
- cologne to wipe off excess massage oil
- wet wipes to clean areas such as the feet
- tissue or cotton wool
- privacy screens.

If the therapist is working in the field they must ensure that they are equipped with the items listed above. It is essential that they have a portable couch and portable screens in case there is no private area at the venue.

Other issues to consider

Confidentiality

The therapist must be aware that information provided by their client and information regarding their medical details are subject to the strictest confidentiality. It is a breach of professionalism to discuss a client and their condition with anyone else.

There may be occasions when you wish to seek the advice of a fellow professional regarding a client. This is acceptable if you have previously asked your client for permission and explained the situation to them.

Comfort

The comfort of your client is of paramount importance. This is why it is important to have an adjustable couch with a face hole, and to supply pillows for their head or to rest flexed limbs. Towels are important to keep a client covered while they are being massaged and to avoid undue embarrassment; towels will also keep the client at a comfortable temperature.

The couch you use should be adjustable in height to suit your needs. The comfort of the therapist is also important as they have to work for long periods of time and do not want to become injured themselves. The recommended height for a couch is to mid-thigh of the working therapist.

Moral and legal considerations

Massage can be a fairly invasive and personal experience for both the therapist and the client. It is important that the therapist maintains their professionalism at all times and does not behave in an inappropriate manner, or enter into a relationship with a client that is other than professional.

The therapist also needs to have a understanding of health, safety and hygiene regulations in order to implement safe practices. The relevant legislation is the Health and Safety at Work Act 1974, Fire Precautions Act 1971 and COSSH regulations 1999. They should also be aware of the Consumer Protection Act 1987 in case a client is unhappy with the treatment they received and is seeking compensation.

TREATMENT STRATEGY

Once the problems have been diagnosed and a course of treatment identified the therapist is ready to start work.

Preparation of the client for a sports massage

Once the therapist has completed their consultation and initial assessment, it is time for the treatment to start. You will explain what treatments you will conduct and what clothing you need them to remove. It is essential to give clear instructions and be confident about giving them, so the client does not feel embarrassed. It is important to have a private changing area and to respect client's privacy.

The client may have to undress down to their underwear and the areas not being massaged need to be covered by towels. This is to keep the client warm while that area is not being massaged, and to help them remain relaxed throughout the treatment.

The therapist must also prepare their room and ensure they have all the materials they require. Preparation of the environment is covered earlier in the chapter, as is the relevant health and safety legislation which must be adhered to by the therapist.

Establishing rapport

The success of the course of treatment you are offering will depend on your physical skills, but also your personal skills. It is essential that you establish a rapport or professional relationship with your client. You need your client to have trust in your ability and your professionalism. The preparation of your client for treatment will involve the following:

- relaxing the client and putting them at ease
- showing a caring attitude
- being professional at all times
- maintaining client confidentiality
- explaining the course of treatment and the effect it will produce
- being tactful and respecting their privacy.

Massage treatment

By this point the environment has been prepared: the room is well presented, the temperature is appropriate and all the relevant equipment is available. The client has been prepared for the treatment and is positioned correctly on the couch. Now the treatment commences and will last for the duration agreed between therapist and client. The treatment provides a further opportunity for the therapist to establish a rapport with their client. This may involve the therapist explaining each of their treatments as they progress. However, the client may prefer not to converse with the therapist and this silence should be respected. The treatment should be relaxing and conversation may be disturbing. The therapist may choose to play some relaxing music during the treatment.

Massage oils

There are a range of oils available to the therapist to prevent friction and promote smooth movement over the client's body. The most commonly used oils are vegetable oils as they have little fragrance, are easily absorbed into the skin and provide a source of nutrition. These oils include olive oil, sunflower oil and grapeseed oil. They are all liquid at room temperature. Palm oil, which is solid at room temperature, becomes liquid on contact with the skin and can also be used. Essential oils such as lavender and rosemary may be used, but the therapist must be qualified as an aromatherapist.

Baby oil is not recommended as it forms a barrier over the skin and will not be absorbed. The therapist should also use a sports cologne at the end of the massage to remove any excess oil that has not been absorbed.

Talcum powder can be used for massage and is the traditional lubricant for Swedish massage. However, it should not be used on dry skin as the extra friction it produces can make it uncomfortable. There is some evidence that it could be cancer forming if inhaled by the therapist over a period of time. Some clients may prefer the use of talcum powder, particularly if they are involved in a form of competition where they cannot appear with oil on their skin.

Massage techniques

There are three main techniques which can be used:

- ✪ effleurage

- ✪ petrissage

- ✪ frictions.

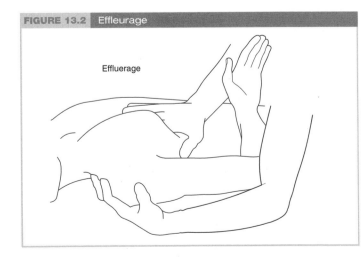

FIGURE 13.2 Effleurage

Effluerage

Effleurage

This technique involves stroking movements and is used at the beginning and end of a massage. It can be performed with varying degrees of pressure and is broken into light and deep stroking. Light stroking is performed with the whole hand, keeping the fingers together. The hand should be kept relaxed and the speed and pressure should vary according to stage of the massage. Light stroking is used to spread the massage oil, identify the tense areas and start to relax the muscles.

As more pressure is applied the technique becomes deep stroking, with the aim of increasing blood flow in deeper blood vessels and through the lymphatic system. The pressure can be increased by placing one hand on the top of the other, by using the heel of the hand, the outside of the hand, the pads of the fingers and the pad of the thumb.

Pressure is consistent throughout the stroke, except when passing over a bony prominence as this will cause discomfort. The strokes should be performed in the direction of the heart as they are aiming to promote venous return.

Effleurage can be used to:

- ✪ introduce the client to the touch of the therapist
- ✪ start to relax the client
- ✪ warm the muscles
- ✪ spread the massage oil
- ✪ promote blood circulation
- ✪ stimulate lymphatic drainage
- ✪ link between techniques
- ✪ end the massage.

Petrissage

Petrissage involves applying pressure, with the basic movement being to compress and then to release tissues. This is done by applying direct pressure or picking up and squeezing the muscles fibres.

Applying pressure to compress muscle tissue on to underlying structures is known as 'kneading'. This movement is performed in a circular manner using the palm of the hand, although additional pressure can be applied using the fingertips, the ulnar border of the forearm, or even the elbow.

'Picking up' involves grasping and lifting up the muscle and then squeezing the fibres with the forefinger and thumb. Once the muscle is released the blood will return, bringing oxygen and nutrients. This technique is carried out by moving steadily away from the heart.

The aims of petrissage are to:

- ✪ reduce stiffness by improving mobility of tissues
- ✪ stretch muscle tissue
- ✪ stimulate blood circulation and promote venous return
- ✪ promote lymphatic drainage
- ✪ relax tense muscles
- ✪ promote mental relaxation.

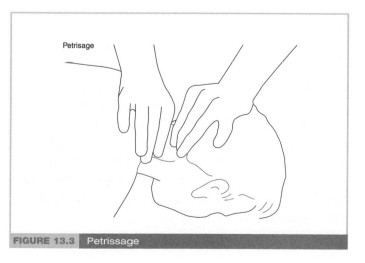

Petrisage

FIGURE 13.3 Petrissage

FIGURE 13.4 Frictions

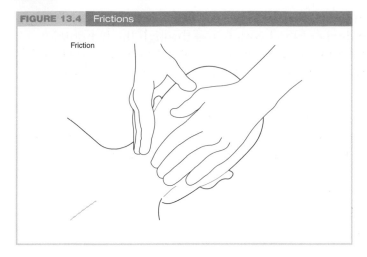

Friction

Frictions

Frictions are small movements over a specific, localised area using the pads of the fingers or thumbs. This technique involves applying considerably more pressure than is used during petrissage.

The fingers are moved in a circular or transverse direction across a small area of tissue. The fingers do not move across the skin, however, they do move the skin across tissue. Greater pressure can be applied to stimulate deep muscle tissue or to break down recently formed scar tissue. It is unproven whether friction does break down scar tissue, but it can separate adhesions between repaired muscle fibres.

The client needs to be warned that the treatment may be fairly painful, although only for a short period of time. The therapist should only perform the technique if they are confident it will be beneficial to the client.

The aims of friction are to:

- ✪ stimulate blood flow
- ✪ separate adhesions between fibres
- ✪ minimise the effects of scar tissue
- ✪ promote flexibility
- ✪ promote the healing process.

Other sports massage techniques

Other techniques available include tapotement, vibrations and trigger points. **Tapotement** describes a range of techniques that involve striking the skin in a percussive manner. Tapotement includes **hacking**, which is where a muscle is struck using the outside of the hands with palms facing each other. This will stimulate the blood flow to the skin and superficial muscle tissue. Hacking tends to have an opposite effect to many other techniques, which promote blood flow to deep muscle tissue, and it may be counterproductive.

Cupping involves the therapist making a cup shape with their hands and then, with their hands palm down, they strike the skin. The hands are moved rapidly up and down a muscle, making a noise like the sound of horses hooves. This has the effect of compressing air between the therapist's hands and the skin of the client and will again promote blood flow to the surface.

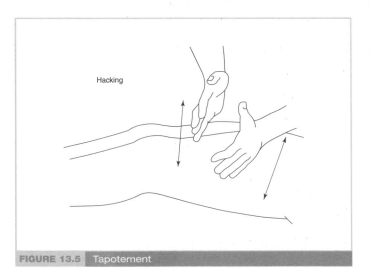

Hacking

FIGURE 13.5 Tapotement

Vibration can be used to finish off a massage. The technique involves the therapist supporting a muscle with one hand and vibrating the other hand from side to side as they move up and down the muscle. This produces a feeling of stimulation in the muscle and promotes blood flow and increased mobility in the muscle tissue.

Trigger pointing is a technique involving the therapist applying sustained pressure in one specific place. They may apply pressure with a finger or thumb, but if this is not enough they may need to use their elbow. A trigger point is an area of high tension where muscle fibres have failed to relax after a contraction and are held in spasm. It can cause pain at that point or referred pain which is felt at a distance away from the trigger point. The therapist will apply pressure to the point to create pain which will start to subside after seven to ten seconds. As pain subsides, more pressure is applied and this procedure continues for around one minute. The pressure has the effect of inducing a relaxation response in the tissue and returning a blood supply to tissue starved of oxygen.

REHABIL-ITATION STRATEGY

The massage therapist's responsibility does not end at the massage stage. They will need to evaluate the success of their treatment using the following methods:

✪ asking for immediate client feedback

✪ stretching and loading affected muscles

✪ performing specific tests

✪ client feedback once they return to sporting action.

Based on the results of the treatments, the therapist may prescribe more treatments using the same techniques, or a change of massage techniques. Failure of the client to recover from their injury may lead to the therapist referring the client to other medical personnel, such as doctors, physiotherapists, osteopaths or chiropractors.

Treatment strategies

The sooner an injury is treated then the greater the chances of a complete recovery and the faster the rehabilitation. The immediate treatment can be summarised by the acronym SALTAPS.

S   **See** the injury occur and the mechanism of injury.

A   **Ask** the casualty what is wrong and where they have pain.

L   **Look** for signs of bleeding, deformity of limbs, inflammation, swelling and redness.

T   **Touch** the injury or close to the injury (gently **palpate**) for signs of heat, tenderness, loss or change of sensation and pain.

A   **Active** movement – Ask casualty to move the injured area. If they are able to, ask them to move it through is full range of movements.

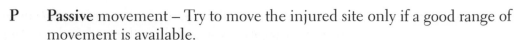

P   **Passive** movement – Try to move the injured site only if a good range of movement is available.

S   **Strength** – If the casualty has been taken through the steps above with no pain, use resisted movements to assess loss of function. For example, with an injured ankle you would assist the casualty to their feet, then ask them to stand unaided, then progress the test to walking and running.

This process will determine the extent and severity of the injury, although it may be obvious. Treatment at this stage should consist of rest, ice, compression and elevation (RICE).

R   **Rest** – As soon as a person has injured themselves they should be told to discontinue their activity. Further activity could cause further injury, delay healing, increase pain, and stimulate bleeding.

I   **Ice** – An ice pack or cold compress should be applied to the injured area. This will help to reduce the swelling and pain of the injury (see **cryotherapy** on page 418 for more details).

C   **Compression** – Gentle pressure should be applied to the injury site by surrounding the area with padding, a compressive bandage or a cloth. Compressing the injured area will reduce blood flowing to the injury site and also help to control swelling by decreasing fluid seeping into the injured area from adjacent tissue. After applying a compression bandage, the casualty's circulation should be checked by squeezing the nail beds of the injured limb. If blood is seen to return to the nail bed on release, the compression bandage is not too tight. The compression bandage should be reapplied after 24 hours in order to maintain compression over the injury site.

E   **Elevation** – The injured area should be supported in a raised position above the level of the heart in order to reduce the blood flow to the injury, which will further help to minimise swelling and bruising at the injury site.

The healing process

The length of the healing process depends upon a number of factors, such as the severity of the injury, the fitness level of the athlete, the age of the athlete and the treatment they receive. Healing can be split into three phases: acute, repair and remodelling.

Acute phase

The aim during the acute phase is to reduce the flow of blood to the affected area. This will minimise the amount of swelling in the area. This treatment is represented by the acronym RICE as outlined above.

The repair phase

This phase would begin on the third day after injury, when the swelling has been reduced. By this stage the blood vessels that were damaged will have been restored, enabling them to deliver oxygen and nutrients to the damaged tissue. Muscle cannot produce new tissue, so it produces scar tissue. This scar tissue is mainly collagen, which is fibrous and inelastic; it is not as strong or flexible as muscle tissue and as a result the muscle's function is reduced. The repair phase must attempt to make this new tissue as strong and as supple as muscle tissue. The following treatments can be used at this stage.

1   **Ice** – Ice will initially constrict blood flow into an area. Once it is removed it will cause blood vessels to dilate and increase the blood flow into the area. This increased blood flow will promote healing and the ice will also have a pain relieving, anaesthetic effect.

2   **Massage** – Effleurage would be the most appropriate technique at this stage. Techniques involving more pressure may cause further damage.

3   **Stretching** – Gentle stretching of the damaged muscle will promote the elasticity of the new tissue. This will produce a stronger and more resilient muscle once rehabilitation is complete.

4   **Gentle resistance exercises** – This will improve the strength of the muscle and should involve very light weights or isometric work, where muscles contract but do not produce movement.

The remodelling phase

The final phase of rehabilitation takes place from around four weeks to up to a year after the injury. The scar tissue is becoming stronger and more pliable as the resistance placed on it increases. This scar tissue needs to be massaged to stretch it, using deeper, firmer massage techniques. Strength training will start to be stepped up with the aim of returning muscles to their original strength. Developmental stretches should be used to improve the range of motion available at a joint. The recovering athlete should also be given proprioception or balance exercises to retrain the nervous system that has been damaged along with the muscle fibres and blood vessels.

Part of the process of recovery is that your client must be educated to minimise the risk of further injury. They should understand the importance of warming up properly and cooling down afterwards. They should be aware of the factors that can increase the chances of injury, such as poor flexibility, poor technique, inadequate equipment, clothing and footwear, fatigue and traumas or collisions.

THE ROLE OF THE SPORTS THERAPIST

To be an effective sports therapist you need a range of personal skills and a sound base of knowledge. Most therapists are sports people themselves or have a strong interest in sport. To practice as a sports therapist you will need to have a relevant qualification. These can be obtained by studying full-time for a year at a College of Further Education where they offer courses that are certified by the VTCT. There are several private training providers, such as Premier Training International or The Society of Sports Therapists, who offer an excellent range of courses and career opportunities.

A massage therapist must have at least the following knowledge:

- anatomy and physiology
- exercise physiology
- massage techniques
- the physical effects of massage techniques
- the effects of stretching techniques
- the effects of sports massage.

The physical skills they will need are:

- at least six massage techniques
- strapping techniques
- relaxation skills
- stretching techniques
- resistance training techniques
- electrotherapy treatments such as ultrasound and electric shock
- possibly manipulation of joints
- first aid.

They will also need personal skills such as:

- honesty
- reliability
- empathy
- professionalism
- good listening skills
- good communication skills.

A sports massage therapist can set up their own business wherever they see fit. Usually therapists are located at sports clubs (professional and amateur), sports centres, health and fitness clubs and medical clinics. There are more and more travelling therapists who will visit clients at home or offer pre-competition and post-competition massage at sports events such as the London marathon. There are also fitness professionals who offer other services, such as personal trainers offering their clients personalised training sessions, who can also offer massage therapy. It is useful for a massage therapist to have a sound knowledge of training techniques so they can understand their client's conditions and give them specific training advice.

A sports massage therapist needs to know their limits and when to seek advice or refer a client to a medical practitioner or a physiotherapist. The diagnosis of certain conditions and traumatic injury may require more extensive training and expertise; however, once a diagnosis has been made the sports massage therapist may be able to provide treatment. For this reason, many sports massage therapists work alongside other sports injury specialists, such as physiotherapists. This relationship is often mutually beneficial. The golden rule is, if in doubt refer the client, as inappropriate treatment can make a condition worse, which will damage your reputation.

In summary, sports massage therapy has a huge role to play in the treatment of sports injury. If used appropriately it can speed up the recovery process and return a client to a state of full functionality. All types of people will benefit from sports massage therapy and it offers a rewarding and satisfying choice of career.

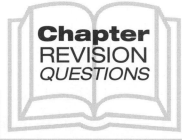

Chapter REVISION QUESTIONS

1) What benefits does sports massage provide?

2) Give three situations when sports massage should not be used.

3) What equipment does a sports massage therapist require?

4) Describe the procedures that need to be undertaken before a client can be treated.

5) Explain the difference between the techniques of effleurage, petrissage and frictions.

6) What benefits does oil have over talcum powder?

7) When is SALTAPS used and what does it stand for?

8) Explain the three stages of the healing process.

9) What advice would you offer a client after you have treated them?

FURTHER READING

Cash, Mel (1998) *Sports and Remedial Massage*. London: Mosby

Paine, Tim (2000) *The Complete Guide to Sports Massage*. London: A&C Black (Publishers) Ltd.

Watt, Joan (1999) *Massage for Sport*. The Crowood Press

CHAPTER 14

EXERCISE, HEALTH AND LIFESTYLE

A person's lifestyle can have a huge impact on their long-term health. This chapter will explore how today's lifestyle affects health and how exercise plays a significant part in improving a person's physical health and mental wellbeing. Modern day health issues will be examined, together with government schemes to try to increase the nation's health.

By the end of this chapter students should be able to:

- ✪ demonstrate an understanding of the terms, health, lifestyle and exercise
- ✪ understand how exercise plays a part in the maintenance of health
- ✪ evaluate the role of exercise in contemporary life
- ✪ realise the negative effects of exercise.

HEALTH, LIFESTYLE AND EXERCISE

Health

Health describes a person's state of being and is therefore somewhat subjective. To most people, being healthy is when they are free of disease or disability. However, people suffering with a disease or disability may also feel that they are in good health if they are able to manage their condition so that it does not impact greatly on their quality of life.

 **Definitions**

Health

The World Health Organisation (WHO) defines health as '*a state of complete physical, mental and social wellbeing and not merely the absence of disease or infirmity*'.

Mental health relates to people's emotions, thoughts and behaviours. A person with good mental health is able to handle everyday events. The full definition of health by WHO also includes the need for an individual to have social connections and support networks, as these can radically influence their mental and, eventually, their physical health. Therefore, the optimal functioning of a person's physical body is only one aspect of their health – their state of mind also needs to be sound in order for a person to be regarded as being healthy.

Lifestyle

Our lifestyle has become much more sedentary over the years. We now have methods of transport that require little physical exertion; cars and buses have replaced walking and cycling. There are now relatively few manual occupations, and the majority of people's careers are spent in an office-based environment. Everyday tasks such as laundry, cleaning and cooking require little effort as they are all aided by labour-saving devices. It is now even possible to go shopping by sitting in front of a computer and logging on to the internet. For entertainment, the average person spends less time participating in active leisure pursuits and prefers to sit in front of the TV. The average adult watches over 26 hours of television each week, which is a virtually totally sedentary activity.

Children also spend much less time pursing activity-based play and choose computer games, videos or the TV to occupy their free time. All these factors have lead to the modern person taking part in very low levels of physical activity.

Our diets have also changed significantly over the years – today we have the largest range of foods available to us, but we are choosing to eat foods that are high in saturated fats and simple carbohydrates. Fast-food restaurants are flourishing because they are used so regularly by our society. As a result of the sedentary lifestyle and diet choices there is now a huge rise in obesity and other forms of ill health.

STUDENT ACTIVITY

Activity diary

This activity is designed to try to determine how much time you spend each day taking part in physical activity and how much time is spent pursuing sedentary activities.

1 Keep an activity diary for at least one full day.

2 Copy and complete the table below.

3 Write down the time of day in column 1, what the activity is in column 2 and write an S next to it if it is sedentary or an A it if it requires physical activity.

4 Total up the time spent on S activities and then total up the time spend on A activities.

Time	Activity	Time spent on activity

5 From your activity diary, do you think you are spending enough time pursing physically active tasks, or too long on sedentary tasks? Explain your answer.

6 Search on the internet and in text books to find out how people lived 50 years ago compared with how we live today. Find out the following:

a) how they travelled

b) how they carried out everyday cleaning chores

c) how and what they ate

d) what kind of leisure activities they took part in.

Exercise

Fitness

If a person is physically fit, their body is able to function with energy and alertness and without undue fatigue. They should have ample energy to engage in leisure activities and be able to meet the physical stresses of everyday life. Muscular strength, endurance and aerobic fitness are the main aspects of a person's physical fitness. The level of a person's physical fitness can be influenced by regular, systematic exercise. Proper nutrition is also important to a person's physical fitness, because energy expenditure depends on consuming adequate nutrition. If a person's kilocalorie intake is inadequate then fitness levels will drop.

Physical activity

Physical activity is defined as the state of being active. It can increase a person's basal metabolic rate by around 10%. This elevated basal metabolic rate can last for up to 48 hours after the completion of the activity. By taking part in physical activity kilocalories will be expended; the number of kilocalories used depends on the type and intensity of the activity. The more muscles that are used in the activity and the harder you work, the more kilocalories will be used up to perform the activity. For example, swimming the front crawl uses both the arms and the legs and will therefore use more calories to perform than walking, which only really uses the leg muscles.

The body weight of the person will also have an impact on the number of kilocalories burnt while taking part in a physical activity. The heavier the person, the more kilocalories are required to move the heavier weight, so a heavier person will burn more calories than a lighter person when performing the same activity at the same intensity.

REVISION QUESTIONS

1) What factors are important when assessing if someone is healthy?

2) What does WHO stand for?

3) What is the definition of health as stated by the WHO?

4) How does having a good social network aid in making a person healthy?

5) Why are people today living a much more sedentary lifestyle than 30 years ago?

6) What are the health concerns associated with living a sedentary lifestyle?

7) What does the term 'physical fitness' mean?

8) What is physical activity?

9) What is the main benefit of taking part in physical activity?

Taking part in physical activity often reduces a person's appetite, so they are less likely to over-eat at their next meal. All these factors mean that if a person takes part in physical activity they are more likely to lose or control their body weight.

MAINTEN-ANCE OF HEALTH

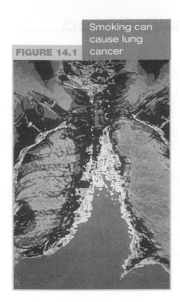

FIGURE 14.1 Smoking can cause lung cancer

Many factors that determine a person's health are controllable to some degree, especially lifestyle behaviours such as smoking, diet, physical activity and alcohol consumption. Other factors are uncontrollable; these include a person's sex, genetics and age. However, the uncontrollable factors can interact with the controllable factors, for example, smoking may interact with genetic factors to increase the likelihood of a person developing lung cancer.

The government commissions scientists to carry out research in order to examine what the major contributors to premature death are in the population, and also what causes the greatest amount of ill health and disability. Health risk factors are also assessed in terms of their contribution to disease for the population. For example, smoking is associated with causing many diseases and premature death.

Taking part in regular exercise has consistently been shown to have many benefits to a person's physical and mental health. Many types of disease can be alleviated or prevented by taking part in regular exercise. Discussed below are the main types of ill health that can be eased or prevented by taking part in regular exercise.

Coronary heart disease (CHD) and exercise

CHD is the leading cause of death in the western world, mainly because of a combination of poor diet and inactivity. Coronary heart disease is a narrowing of the coronary arteries, which are the blood vessels that pass over the surface of the heart and supply it with blood. CHD is usually a result of a build-up of fatty material and **plaques** within the coronary blood vessels, this is known as athersclerosis. When a person with CHD takes part in a physically demanding task, the coronary arteries may not be able to supply heart muscle with enough blood to keep up with the demand for oxygen and this will be felt as a pain in the chest (**angina**). If a coronary artery becomes completely blocked, the area of the heart muscle served by the artery will die, resulting in a heart attack.

Taking part in regular exercise appears to reduce the risk of heart disease directly and indirectly. Research has shown that exercise:

✪ increases levels of HDL cholesterol; HDL cholesterol is the 'good' cholesterol and acts to clean the artery walls, which in turn reduces athersclerosis

✪ decreases the amount of triglycerides in the bloodstream; triglycerides are another type of fat and high levels in the bloodstream have been linked with increased risk of heart disease.

The American College of Sports Medicine (ACSM), recommends the following amounts of exercise for people suffering from or at risk of CHD:

- moderate activity for at least 30 minutes every day of the week

- to expend at least 1400 calories per week to reduce the risk of CHD

- to expend at least 1500 calories per week to stop the increase of fatty plaques in arteries

- to expend at least 2200 calories per week to reverse the effects of athersclerosis.

Exercise and hypertension (high blood pressure)

A person is deemed to have hypertension if their blood pressure consistently reads at $\frac{140}{90}$ or higher. Hypertension is a very common complaint and around 15% to 25% of adults in most western countries have high blood pressure. If a person with hypertension does not reduce their blood pressure they are more at risk of suffering from a stroke or a heart attack.

Studies have shown that people with hypertension who take part in regular aerobic exercise usually experience a reduction in resting blood pressure. In order to reduce high blood pressure, people should exercise three to five times a week, at an intensity of at least 50% of maximum heart rate, for at least 30 minutes of continuous activity. At least one weights session a week should also be included in order to maintain muscle strength.

Exercise and diabetes

Today more and more people are suffering from diabetes, a disease which places people at higher than average risk for heart disease. Diabetes is a disease in which the body does not produce or properly use insulin. Insulin is produced in the pancreas and is a hormone that controls the level of blood sugar. The cause of diabetes is unknown, however, genetics, obesity and a lack of exercise are thought to play a significant role.

There are two types of diabetes, one is insulin dependent (type 1) and the other is non-insulin dependent (type 2). Type 1 diabetes means the person's pancreas is no longer producing insulin, so it is necessary to inject insulin in to the body every day to stay alive. It occurs most often in children and young adults. However, adults may become type 1 diabetic later on in life, for example Steve Redgrave, the British rower, became type 1 diabetic prior to taking part in the Sydney 2000 olympics. Type 1 diabetes accounts for around 5% to 10% of diabetes.

Type 2 diabetes means that a person's body is either unable to make enough insulin or it has become less sensitive to insulin, which results in elevated levels of glucose in the bloodstream. It is the most common form of the disease and accounts for 90% to 95% of diabetes. Diet and exercise can often control type 2 diabetes, although insulin medication may also be necessary. Today, type 2 diabetes is nearing epidemic proportions, due to an increase in obesity and a decrease in activity levels. Type 2 diabetes usually effects people later on in life; however, because of inadequate activity and poor diet, children today are developing type 2 diabetes.

There is good evidence to suggest that physical activity has a role in the prevention, and also in the treatment, of type 2 diabetes. Studies have shown that the risks of developing diabetes are lower in people who are physically active than in those who are sedentary. Exercise can also help to treat people with type 2 diabetes, as it improves a person's sensitivity to insulin.

People with uncontrolled diabetes should be referred to their doctor. They should not take part in strength training or high-impact exercises as they can strain weakened blood vessels in the eyes or injure blood vessels in the feet.

People who are taking insulin should take special precautions before embarking on a workout programme because glucose levels vary dramatically during exercise. Type 1 diabetics may need to decrease insulin doses or take in more carbohydrates prior to exercise to help to maintain blood glucose levels during exercise.

Obesity and exercise

A person is classified as being obese if they are 20% or more, heavier than the correct weight for their height. The number of people who are obese is rising rapidly throughout the world, making obesity one of the fastest developing public health problems.

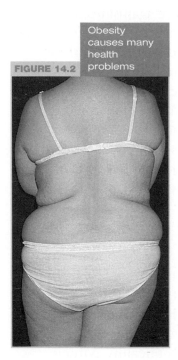

FIGURE 14.2 Obesity causes many health problems

The World Health Organisation has described the problem of obesity as a 'worldwide epidemic' and has estimated that around 250 million people worldwide are obese, which is about 7% of the adult population. Obesity takes years to develop and results from the amount of energy being consumed exceeding the amount of energy expended. This excess energy is then stored mainly as fat. Research to date suggests that in England, over 50% of the adult population are overweight and 17% of men and 21% of women are obese.

Obese people are at risk of developing a number of medical conditions, which can cause poor health and premature death. These include:

- ✪ osteoarthritis
- ✪ rheumatoid arthritis
- ✪ some forms of cancer
- ✪ coronary heart disease (CHO)
- ✪ deep vein thrombosis (DVT)
- ✪ diabetes (type 2)
- ✪ gallbladder disease
- ✪ gout
- ✪ hypertension
- ✪ stroke.

When a person takes part in exercise they burn up kilocalories, which results in the person being in a state of negative energy balance. This means that they will start to burn kilocalories from their fat stores and so lose weight.

The best forms of exercise to combat obesity are fat-burning exercises of low intensity and of long duration; walking is a very good type of exercise for obese individuals. This is because walking is a low-impact exercise and will therefore place less stress on the joints than a high-impact exercise. The person should aim to walk at a pace that increases their breathing rate and heart rate but still allows them to talk.

Arthritis and exercise

Arthritis is a condition in which the synovial membrane of one or more joints has become inflamed. There are a number of forms of arthritis. Rheumatoid arthritis is a long-term inflammation of the synovial membrane lining the joints. Osteoarthritis is a condition in which the cartilage in the joints become diseased or damaged (see Figure 14.3). Cartilage serves as a shock absorber, or cushion, between the bones and provides a smooth surface that allows the bones to move against each other with less friction. When this cartilage is damaged, the joint will become inflamed as the cartilage becomes rougher and thinner, and the joint may swell up as there is an increased production of synovial fluid in the joint. As the cartilage continues to wear away, growths of bone called bone spurs may form around the edges of the joint. Eventually, the bones that meet at the joint rub against each other, which can be extremely painful and can severely reduce movement in the joint.

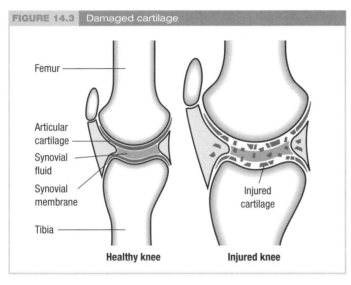

FIGURE 14.3 Damaged cartilage

Femur

Articular cartilage

Synovial fluid

Synovial membrane

Tibia

Injured cartilage

Healthy knee　　**Injured knee**

Exercise plays a key role in treating almost all forms of arthritis. Exercises that help to alleviate arthritis are mobilising exercises and exercises to strengthen muscles. Mobilising exercise will help to keep the joints moving and help to prevent them becoming stiff. When a person takes part in mobilising exercises, they increase the production of synovial fluid into the joint, which helps to lubricate the joint. Mobilising exercises will also increase blood flow to the tissues around the joint, which will help to keep the joint healthy. Muscle strengthening exercises will help to build up the muscles around the joint and so help to protect the joints. Swimming and hydrotherapy are good examples of effective ways of strengthening muscles as well as mobilising joints. A person suffering with arthritis will usually have good days when they feel less pain, and bad days when they feel more pain. It is better to exercise on good days, although taking part in exercise every day may well help to prevent joints becoming stiff and painful, and keep muscles strong.

Osteoporosis and exercise

Osteoporosis is a disease in which the mineral density of bones is decreased, which results in bones becoming fragile and more likely to break. Women are four times more likely than men to develop the disease. Osteoporosis is largely preventable for most people and requires a healthy diet with the RDA of calcium and vitamin D, together with appropriate exercise. Prevention of this disease is very important because, while there are treatments for osteoporosis, there is currently no cure. If a person has exercised regularly in childhood and adolescence, they are more likely to build strong, dense bones, which will stand them in good stead for later on in life. The best exercise to build bone density is weight-bearing exercise such as walking, jogging, aerobics, racket sports and hiking.

Depression and exercise

A number of studies have attempted to explore the effects of exercise on depression and found that exercise increases self-esteem, improves mood, reduces anxiety levels, increases the ability to handle stress and makes generally makes people happier than those who do not exercise.

There are a number of theories that try to explain why exercise has this effect. Some people believe that depression results from people having low self-esteem and bottling up their emotions. For these people exercise is seen as a **catharsis**, which enables them to get rid of negative emotions such as anger, sadness and frustration. While taking part in exercise, it is possible to discharge these emotions in a healthy, safe and acceptable manner.

Another explanation is that depressed people may well view themselves, their future and their surrounding environment in a negative manner. Exercise has the effect of altering this negative thinking style; for example, people who take part in regular fitness classes may develop a more positive view of themselves as they start to attain their desired weight and body shape. By doing this they have achieved a goal which may well give them a sense of success and accomplishment.

People who experience depression may spend a great deal of time dwelling on past failures and continually blaming themselves for having acted in a certain way. However, taking part in exercise provides them with a temporary distraction and takes their mind off their worries.

Lastly, some people believe depression occurs as a result of a decreased production of certain chemicals in the brain, specifically adrenaline, dopamine and serotonin. Exercise has been shown to increase the levels of these substances, which may have the effect of improving a person's mood after having taken part in exercise.

You may have experienced a positive mood change from exercise, but are unable to determine which mechanism exercise has made you happier. A great deal more research is being carried out to try to determine why and if exercise really does alleviate depression and, if so, by which mechanisms. However, for the last decade or so, exercise has been prescribed as a method of combating depression.

Government-backed campaigns

In order to prevent many diseases and to try to keep the nation as healthy as possible, the government has backed a number of campaigns. A large proportion of these campaigns involve increasing the nation's physical fitness levels. By spending money on these campaigns it is thought that people will be less susceptible to a range of diseases later on in life, which will result in them requiring less medical care.

Obesity has been targeted as being a huge issue for British people, and The Association for the Study of Obesity has been formed. This aims to raise awareness of obesity as a public health issue within the UK and to encourage research to try to combat the problem.

The government has also established the Nutrition Task Force, which aims to reduce the amount of energy derived from saturated fat in the diet by at least 35%, and from total fat by at least 12% by 2005.

The Physical Activity Task Force has also been set up to explore ways of encouraging people to increase their activity levels. The Health Education Authority also launched an 'Active for Life' initiative to encourage people to include regular physical activity in their lives in order to help to improve their physical and mental health.

REVISION QUESTIONS

1) Explain how taking part in exercise helps to prevent coronary heart disease.

2) When is blood pressure deemed to be high?

3) What are the two types of diabetes? Explain how they differ.

4) Why is obesity a potentially life-threatening condition?

5) What is arthritis and how does exercise help to alleviate the problem?

6) What is osteoporosis? Give examples of five types of exercise that would help to prevent this condition.

7) Explain the different theories that suggest that exercise acts as an antidepressant.

8) Why does the government back exercise campaigns for the nation?

STUDENT ACTIVITY

Government-backed exercise campaigns

Use either textbooks, journals, the internet or visit a health club or leisure centre in your area to carry out the following activity.

1 Try to find out what campaigns have been launched over the last 10 years to try to increase exercise participation by the nation.

2 Find out if particular groups of people have been targeted and, if so, why.

3 How have people been encouraged to take part in exercise?

4 Give an example of a campaign you could introduce into your health club or leisure centre to try to increase participation of a group of people of your choice.

**CONTEMP-
ORARY
LIFESTYLE**

Ageing

Ageing affects the body in many ways; the overall effects, however, result in the decrease of a person's physical fitness levels. This is obvious when you look at the ages of the majority of competitive world-class athletes – very few are over 30 years of age.

After the age of 30, muscle mass decreases, joints become less mobile, hormone levels are lowered and the immune system becomes less effective. Brain mass also decreases as a person gets older because once the cells of the central nervous system die, they do not get replaced. The function of the cardiovascular system becomes impaired as the artery walls become thicker and less elastic. As a result, coronary heart disease accounts for 70% of deaths in those over the age of 65. As muscle mass decreases with age, a person's energy requirements will also decrease. Frequently, as people get older their activity levels are also reduced, which will cause increased loss of muscle tissue. As a result, scientists do not know how much of the muscle lost during ageing is a result of the ageing process itself or just due to reduced activity levels.

However, taking part in regular exercise as people get older has been shown to have a number of benefits in offsetting the ageing process. Older people who have taken part in regular exercise have been shown to have increased muscle strength, balance, joint suppleness and overall physical co-ordination. Physical activity also reduces blood pressure and body weight, and therefore reduces the risk of heart disease. Taking part in regular exercise benefits a number of other conditions and diseases, including osteoporosis, certain cancers and diabetes. Older people may suffer from loneliness as the years go by. Exercise participation often entails contact with other people, so by taking part in exercise, older people will benefit from social contact by increasing their mental health as well as their physical health.

In order for a person to remain fit and healthy as they get older, they should undertake a balanced programme of moderate physical activity for 30 minutes a day. The 30 minutes can be broken up into shorter periods such as 10 minutes of brisk walking in the morning and 20 minutes of swimming in the afternoon. Most forms of regular, moderate physical exercise are suitable for anyone at any age. Walking is the easiest and most natural form of exercise as it does not require any special skills or equipment. The health gains from walking however, are particularly valuable for older people, as they improve muscle strength, balance and posture. Resistance training should also be undertaken in older adults as it helps to reduce or prevent the decline in muscle mass that usually occurs as a result of ageing.

STUDENT ACTIVITY

Age and sporting performance

Consider the following:

- ✪ a football team in the premiership
- ✪ a rugby union or league team in the premiership or super league
- ✪ a county cricket team
- ✪ the European golfing team for the Ryder cup.

1 Find out the average age of the players and the age of the oldest and youngest players.

2 From this data, try to determine which sports have older players and why they are still able to excel in this sport despite or because of their age.

3 In each sport, examine the position (where appropriate) of the oldest player and explain if this has a bearing on their age and ability.

Diet

Today, with new methods of food production, preservation, transport and marketing, there is a huge range of foods available to us. However, despite these increases in food technology, modern meals are less nutritious than in the 1950s. Despite the food shortages of the post-war period, people ate more bread and milk, had higher levels of fibre and calcium intake, drank few sugary soft drinks, obtained most of their vitamin C from vegetables rather than juices and drinks, and ate more red meat which gave them more iron. This diet was very close to the current recommendations on healthy eating. Today, the nation's diet tends to be lacking in a number of important nutrients, including fibre, calcium, vitamins and iron. This is because a high proportion of the population relies on snacks and fast foods as their main source of nutritional intake. As a result, the Western diet is generally high in fat and sugars, resulting in a huge increase in obesity. Estimates in 1990 suggested that 1 in 20 children aged 9 to 11 could be classified as clinically obese. If a person is obese they are much more likely to suffer from coronrary heart disease, which is currently the lead killer in Britain. As we are continuing to rely on foods that do not give us the right balance of vital nutrients, a number of people are suffering from poor nutrition. This can not only impair physical and mental functioning, but can also increase the risk of suffering from a range of diseases including anaemia, diabetes and osteoporosis. A number of nutrition experts have also linked poor nutrition to emotional and behavioural problems, such as hyperactivity and attention deficit, that are seen to occur much more frequently among children today.

Exercise

During the 1960s, 70s and 80s, participation in regular physical activity gradually increased, with more women and older people taking part. However, from the 1990s to the present, participation in sport appears to have levelled off. Although there has been a huge increase in spending on sporting clothes, far more money is spent on sportswear than on actual participation. We also spend much more money on spectating sports rather than taking part. So it seems that today it is fashionable to 'look the part' and wear sporty clothes, but when it comes to actually taking part in sport, as a nation we prefer to remain on the couch or in the stands and watch the professionals.

STUDENT ACTIVITY

1 Keep a financial and sport spectating/taking part diary for two weeks. In this diary, make a note of any money spent on sporting clothing, equipment or activity. Also make a note of how much time you spend watching sport and taking part in sport.

2 Find out the total for each column and then write down your results. Do you spend more time watching sports than taking part? Do you spend more money on sporting clothes and equipment than taking part in sports?

3 Discuss your results with the rest of the class and find out what the general class trend is.

Day	Clothing/ equipment (£)	Taking part in exercise/ sport (£)	Watching (hour)	Taking part (hour)

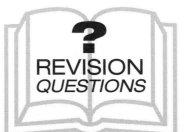

REVISION QUESTIONS

1) Why should people take part in exercise in order to offset the effects of ageing?

2) Give five different types of exercise that an elderly person would be able to carry out.

3) How does our diet compare with the diet in the 1950s?

4) What are the problems associated with today's diet?

5) What is poor nutrition?

NEGATIVE EFFECTS OF EXERCISE

Overuse injuries

Overuse injuries develop over a long period of time from repeated stress. They occur as a result of anatomical variations, such as flat feet or leg length differences, which can create biomechanical problems, or from training errors. If a person trains daily at a high intensity and does not allow the body adequate time to adjust and recover they are likely to sustain overuse injuries.

Shin splints

Shin splints is a common runners complaint and is the name given to inflammation of the periostium (the tissue covering the bone) of the tibia. Running on hard surfaces, wearing incorrect trainers, suddenly increasing training duration and/or frequency, and participating in sports where a lot of jumping is involved can leave an athlete more susceptible to this injury. A person suffering with shin splints will usually feel pain at the front of their shin and some tenderness over the inside of the shin. The area may also be swollen and red.

The only cure for this injury is rest. Applying ice in the early stages will also help to decrease the pain. A sports therapist or doctor may give the person anti-inflammatory medication to decrease the swelling.

Chondromalacia patellae

If a person is suffering from chondromalacia patellae, there is damage to the surface of the underside of the kneecap. It usually occurs as a result of gradual persistent rubbing on the bone underneath.

The person will experience pain in the knee joint, which is at its worst when walking up or down hills or stairs. RICE (rest, ice, compression and elevation) will help to reduce the pain by reducing the swelling. A person suffering from this condition must rest in order to try to allow the body to recover from this condition.

Bursitis

Bursae are sacks of fluid that can be found around synovial joints.

The purpose of a bursa is to help lubricate the movement at the joint. However, repeated impact on the joints can lead to inflamation of the bursa. If a person is suffering from bursitis then they will feel the injured bursae at rest and during exercise, and limited mobility at the site of the bursae.

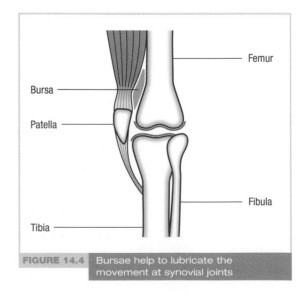

FIGURE 14.4 Bursae help to lubricate the movement at synovial joints

Rotator cuff injury

The rotator cuff muscles control rotation of the shoulder. A person who trains for throwing events or plays racket sports will place the rotator cuff muscles under a great deal of stress. If the person experiences a sudden sharp pain in the shoulder it is likely to be because they have ruptured a tendon in one of the rotator cuff muscles. However, repeated bouts of overarm activity can result in a gradual onset of pain as a result inflammation of the tendons of the rotator cuff muscles. Rest and ice are the only methods of initial treatment, followed by heat treatment and possible rehabilitation with a sports therapist or physiotherapist.

The cost of sports injuries

If you have been in any hospital Accident and Emergency department on a Saturday afternoon, you will no doubt have seen a range of people in various sporting kits suffering from some injury that has been sustained while taking part in sport. According to the Sports Council there are thousands of sports injuries in England and Wales. It costs millions of pounds to treat these injuries. Sports injuries can also prevent people from working – thousands of working days are lost each year due to people suffering from sports injuries. A study took place to estimate the health benefits of exercise against the costs of treatment of exercise-related injuries. The results suggested that while there were clear economic benefits associated with exercise for adults aged 45 and over, for younger adults (15–44 years old), there is a net cost to the British taxpayer of £25 per year in treating their sports injuries. Therefore, with regard to the economy of the National Health Service, it would seem that exercise for adults aged 45 and over should be encouraged, but younger adults should be discouraged from taking part in exercise. It must be noted that this is a purely financial point of view.

Exercise addiction

Repeatedly exercising beyond the requirements for good health is an indicator of exercise addiction. Exercise addiction is also known as compulsive exercise, obligatory exercise and athletica anorexia. A person with this condition no longer chooses to exercise, but feels compelled to do so and feels guilty and anxious if they do not exercise. Nothing will deter this person from exercise, be it injury, illness, a social event or bad weather, as exercise takes over their life. In fact, a compulsive exerciser plans their life around their exercise regime.

Many compulsive exercisers do so to feel more in control of their lives, and the majority of them are female. Exercise addiction often accompanies an eating disorder (see pages 342–44 for more information on eating disorders). The excessive duration and frequency of workouts usually begin as a means to control a person's weight and are eventually taken to an extreme.

Although exercise is an important part of physical health, compulsive exercise can cause physical and psychological harm. Excessive exercise can damage soft tissue, bones and joints. If a person does not allow time for their body to recover after exercise, then minor injuries cannot heal and can result in long-term damage. Excessive exercise will also destroy muscle tissue if it is not given time to recover, especially if diet is restricted.

The menstrual cycles of females who are addicted to exercise are often affected; sometimes they may skip a period or, in extreme cases, periods may stop altogether (a condition called amenorrhoea). This condition can lead to a decrease in the bone mineral density and result in the person suffering from osteoporosis later in life.

A person's mental health is also affected if they are addicted to exercise. They are often anxious and depressed, with a negative image of themselves. As taking part in exercise dominates their life, they have little time for a social life. Work or school work may also suffer, because working out always comes first, so they end up skipping homework or missing out on time spent with friends.

Over-training may also be a consequence of exercise addiction. It happens when a muscle is worked too often to allow it to recover. All muscles need time to repair themselves and to build up their depleted energy reserves. Training when the muscle is not fully recovered means that the muscle will be damaged further. If this process continues it will eventually result in over-training, which can then result in tendon and muscle damage and a decrease in the ability of a person's immune system to cope with infection. A person suffering from over-training may exhibit tiredness, lack of training desire, loss of appetite, loss in strength and/or size and frequent injuries or illness.

Ergogenic aids

Athletes of any age will frequently try to gain an advantage over their opponents. While most athletes rely on training programmes to increase their endurance, skill, speed and power, some athletes will resort to an ergogenic aid to improve their performance. An ergogenic aid is something that is taken by the athlete in order to try to improve their performance. While some ergogenic aids are allowed in competitive sports, such as glycogen loading or vitamin supplementation, a number of other ergogenic aids are not permitted.

Steroids are a very popular drug in the athletics arena and evidence shows that steroids are used by a number of male and female athletes. The sports that are enhanced by taking anabolic steroids are ones that rely on strength and size, like sprinting, rugby, body building and weightlifting.

This is because anabolic steroids help build muscle tissue and increase body mass by acting like the body's natural male hormone, testosterone. In the past, steroids were only really used by athletes competing at a high standard, however, today non-athletes are also using steroids.

Steroids can cause serious health problems. Many changes take place inside the body and may not be noticed until it is too late. Some of the effects will go away when steroid use stops, but some may not.

Possible side-effects for males and females include the following:

✪   high blood pressure and heart disease

✪   liver damage and cancers

✪   stroke and blood clots

✪   nausea and vomiting

✪   increased risk of ligament and tendon injuries

✪   severe acne, especially on face and back.

In males, as the body starts to produce less of its own testosterone, the testicles may begin to shrink. Females, on the other hand, may start to take on some secondary male characteristics (e.g. a reduction in breast size, increased facial and body hair and a deepened voice) as steroids act as the male hormone testosterone.

Steroids can also affect a person's state of mind. A person taking steroids may experience severe mood swings, anxiety and panic attacks, depression and aggression. Information on more ergogenic drugs and their effect on a person's health and performance can be found on pages 347–53.

Success in sports takes commitment, a lot of hard work, talent and skill. If a person uses drugs to try to increase their performance then it is a form of cheating and interferes with fair competition. Abusing drugs is also very dangerous to one's health.

Ergolytic agents

Ergolytic agents are substances that impair physical and/or mental performance. If a person uses these substances they will undo the benefits gained through training. Below are some ergolytic agents that have been used by sports people.

✪   **Alcohol** – This can increase a person's self-confidence and alter their perception of fatigue. However, drinking alcohol can cause severe dehydration and decrease performance.

✪   **Amphetamines** – Athletes may take these socially or in the belief that they will increase their performance by increasing central nervous system arousal. They do increase heart rate, but also increase blood pressure and may cause dizziness, stomach upset, irritability, insomnia and, in extreme cases, death.

✪   **Tobacco** – Tobacco products increase a person's heart rate and blood pressure, which will ultimately decrease a person's performance and seriously affect their health.

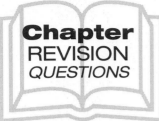

Chapter REVISION *QUESTIONS*

1) Explain why you think the nation should try to improve its participation in physical activity.

2) Give examples of how people can be encouraged to take part in more exercise.

3) How has our lifestyle lead to CHD becoming the leading cause of death in Britain?

4) Why is too much exercise not a recipe for good health?

? REVISION *QUESTIONS*

1) How do athletes sustain overuse injuries?

2) Give examples of overuse injuries that the following athletes may suffer from:
a) marathon runner
b) javelin thrower
c) football player
d) swimmer.

3) What effect are sports injuries having on the nation's economy?

4) What is exercise addiction?

5) What are the problems associated with exercise addiction?

6) What is:
a) an ergogenic aid
b) an ergolytic agent?
Give three examples of each.

7) Carry out research to find out how a sports person of your choice has taken some form of banned (as stated by the IOC) ergogenic aid and how it was supposed to enhance their performance.

8) Explain how you think high-profile sports people who take drugs have an effect on society.

FURTHER READING

Bouchard, C., Shephard, R. and Stephens, M. (1994) *Physical Activity, Fitness and Health*. Human Kinetics

Sharkey, (1996) *Fitness and Health*. Human Kinetics

Shephard, R. L. (2001) *Aerobic Fitness and Health*. Human Kinetics

Weinberg, R. S. and Gould, D. (1999) *Foundations of Sport and Exercise Psychology*, 2nd Study Guide Edition. Human Kinetics

BIOMECHANICS

Biomechanics involves anatomy, physics and mathematics. Therefore, some of the information in this chapter will recap on topics covered in Chapters 1 and 7. Biomechanics is concerned with internal and external forces acting on the human body, and on implements used by humans (bats, balls, etc.) during sport, and the effects produced by these forces. Biomechanics can be used to analyse techniques, which allows athletes or coaches to improve performance or avoid injury.

By the end of this chapter students should be able to:

✪ describe the initiation and development of movement

✪ explain the mechanical principles that underpin movement

✪ apply the mechanical principles that underpin movement

✪ apply a qualitative model of analysis to a specified movement pattern.

INITIATION AND DEVELOP-MENT OF MOVEMENT

Actions and movement

Movement in sport and exercise is a result of muscle contractions. Bones, joints and tendons are an essential part of the movement, but the contracting muscle provides the energy. The strength of a muscle contraction is determined by how many muscle fibres are involved, and by the cross-sectional size of a muscle. There are a number of different types of muscle contraction. (See also page 180)

✪ A **concentric** muscle contraction occurs when a load is placed upon a muscle and the muscle shortens. This type of contraction is evident when performing the up part of an arm curl exercise (Figure 15.1). This is where you contract the bicep muscle and lift the weight towards your body. During this movement the biceps' length is decreased.

✪ An **eccentric** muscle contraction is the opposite of this, i.e. when a load is placed upon a muscle and the muscle lengthens. This would be the case in the down part of an arm curl exercise. In this exercise you would contract the bicep muscle (although it still gets longer) in order to slowly return the weight to the original starting position. Exercises can be performed to improve the eccentric strength of a muscle. With the aid of a partner an athlete could perform just the down phase of a bench press (their partner would help return the bar to the starting position). Such an exercise is often referred to as a negative.

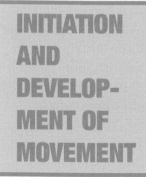

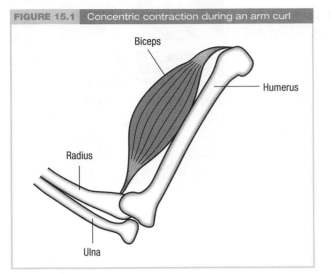

FIGURE 15.1 Concentric contraction during an arm curl

Biceps

Humerus

Radius

Ulna

✪ There is a third type of muscle contraction, called an **isometric** muscle contraction. This is where the muscle contracts but there is no change in length of the muscle and no motion at the joints. An example of this would be pushing against a wall or holding a static position (e.g. hand stand) in gymnastics.

The amount a muscle contracts depends on a number of factors. A muscle does not have to be big in order to develop force. The isometric tension or force generated in a muscle is a function of the amount of overlap between actin (thin filaments) and myosin (thick filaments) within the muscle fibres. When a muscle fibre is at, or close to, its resting length, maximal **cross bridge formation** (actin–myosin bond) occurs. If the fibre is not at its resting length, cross bridge formation will be reduced, resulting in less tension. The force generated by a muscle is also dependant on the velocity of the contraction. During an isometric contraction, the contraction velocity of the muscle is zero – it is not moving. The actin and myosin filaments will have an infinite period of time to affect cross bridges, resulting in maximal tension production. As the velocity of the muscle contraction increases, the time available to form cross bridges is decreased, resulting in less tension production. Consequently, velocity of muscle contraction and force production are **inversely** related.

Muscles are attached to bones via tendons. When these muscles contract (except in an isometric contraction) bones move (i.e. they are pulled together or allowed to move apart). This movement will occur about a fixed point, that is, a joint. It is the muscles that cause movement – the bones are the things that move and the joints allow this movement to take place. All movements can be described by the action that occurs at a joint. Take the bicep curl mentioned previously, in the up phase of this movement the forearm is moving towards the upper arm. The angle at the elbow between the forearm and upper arm is decreasing. This movement is termed **flexion** or, in this case, more correctly, flexion at the elbow. The majority of movements have an opposite movement. For example, the opposite of flexion at the elbow is **extension** at the elbow (where the angle at the elbow joint is increasing). Flexion and extension occur in a forwards or backwards direction (not to the side). Since not only the type of movement (increasing or decreasing the joint angle), but also the direction of the movement is important, all movements are described relative to a reference position. This position is termed the anatomical reference position (see Figure 15.2). This position is important when referring to extension – extension is the widening of a joint angle, but once the anatomical reference position has been reached, to go beyond this would be **hyperextension**.

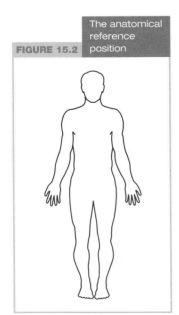

FIGURE 15.2 The anatomical reference position

A movement of a body part (e.g. arm) away from the midline of the body is termed **abduction**. The opposite movement, towards the midline of the body (back to the anatomical position). is known as **adduction**. Moving the whole arm away from the body sideways would be abduction, returning it would be adduction.

Circumduction is a combination movement involving all of the actions of flexion, abduction, extension and adduction.

Rotation is a movement that occurs about an axis passing through a bone that moves at a certain joint. Imagine the hip joint with the femur (bone in the upper leg) coming out of it. The femur could rotate within the hip joint – not move forward or back, which would be flexion and extension, or side to side which would be abduction and adduction. Lateral rotation is outward rotation (outward with reference to the front of the femur, so knees going outwards). Medial rotation involves inward rotation (in the case of the hip joint, this would be knees in).

Flexion, extension (hyperextension), abduction, adduction and rotation are the major movements involved with most joints (see pages xx to xx). However, there are some movements that are either specific to a particular type of joint or are given a different name when occurring at certain joints (see also pages xx to xx).

✪　Moving the hand forward so the palm faces upward is flexion at the wrist. This action is similar to moving the top of the foot (instep) towards the front of the leg; however, this movement is not termed flexion at the ankle but **dorsi flexion**. The opposite action moving the foot, so the angle increases at the ankle, is not extension but **plantar flexion**.

✪　Eversion and inversion are actions that are exclusive to the foot. **Inversion** is the action of turning the sole of the foot inward, towards the opposite foot. **Eversion** is the movement of turning the sole of the foot outward, away from the midline.

✪　Pronation and supination are another set of specific actions, which occur in the forearm. The radius and ulna (the two bones in the forearm) are arranged so that the **distal** end of the radius (the end near the hand) can cross over the ulna. This is called the radioulnar joint. **Pronation** is the movement of crossing the radius over the ulna, which results in the palm of the hand turning inward. **Supination** is the opposite action, where the radius is moved back across the ulna. The palm of the hand is turned outward.

✪　Moving a bone upwards (e.g. the scapula, as in shrugging the shoulders) is termed **elevation**. The opposite action is called **depression** and involves movement to a more inferior position.

✪　**Protraction** and **retraction** are similar movements, but refer to forward (protraction) and backward (retraction) movements.

During any of the above movements there are four main functions associated with muscles, and the active muscles can be divided into the following: agonists (prime movers), antagonists, stabilisers and assistors.

✪　The **agonist** is generally the muscle being exercised.

✪　The **antagonist** is the opposing muscle and acts in contrast to the agonist.

✪　The **stabiliser** muscles are those that hold a joint in place so that the exercise can be performed. The stabiliser muscles are not necessarily moving during exercise, but provide stationary support.

✪　The assistors help the agonist muscle doing the work.

FIGURE 15.3 The frontal plane divides the body from front to back

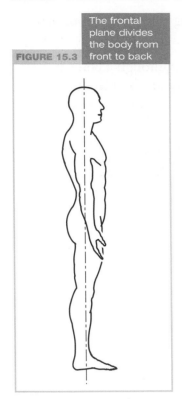

For example, when doing biceps curls, the biceps is the agonist, the triceps is the antagonist, the brachialis acts as an assistor and various muscles, including the deltoids, are the stabiliser muscles. However, when doing a triceps push down, now the triceps are the agonists and the biceps are the antagonists. Again the deltoid muscles are the stabiliser muscles. (See also page x.)

For convenience when describing movements, the body can be divided up into various segments. This is essential for two reasons: first, everybody will be referring to the same thing, and secondly we can look at particular sections of the body separately. Generally the body is divided into the upper extremities, the lower extremities and the trunk, head and neck. The upper extremities are further split into upper arm, forearm and hand. Similarly, the lower extremities consist of the thigh, lower leg and the foot. Sometimes the trunk is separated into the thorax (chest area) and the abdomen (lower trunk area).

The human body is also divided into three anatomical planes: the frontal, sagittal and horizontal.

✪   The frontal plane divides the body from front to back, and is sometimes referred to as the lateral plane since it bisects the body laterally from side to side, dividing it into front and back halves (see Figure 15.3). Abduction and adduction movements, such a star jumps and side bends, occur in this plane.

✪   The **sagittal** or **anteroposterior** plane bisects the body from front to back, dividing it into right and left halves (see Figure 15.4). Flexion and extension movements such a biceps curls, knee extensions and sit-ups occur in this plane.

✪   The horizontal (or transverse) plane divides the body into an upper and lower half (see Figure 15.5). Rotational movements such as pronation, supination and rotation occur in this plane.

Each plane of motion has an associated axis of rotation.

✪   Flexion occurs in the sagittal plane; the axis of rotation for flexion would be through the body from side to side. This axis is called the **frontal axis** (see Figure 15.6).

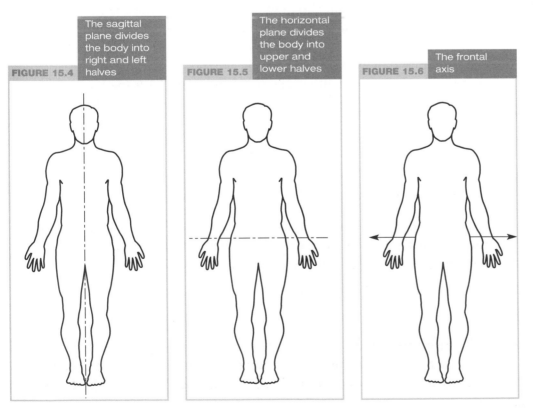

FIGURE 15.4 The sagittal plane divides the body into right and left halves

FIGURE 15.5 The horizontal plane divides the body into upper and lower halves

FIGURE 15.6 The frontal axis

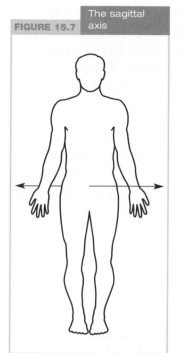

FIGURE 15.7 The sagittal axis

✪ The **sagittal axis** has the same direction as the sagittal plane of motion and runs from front to back at a right angle to the frontal plane of motion (see Figure 15.7).

✪ The **vertical axis** runs straight down through the top of the head and is at a right angle to the transverse (horizontal) plane of motion (see Figure 15.8).

Each joint in the body is surrounded by ligaments, tendons, muscles and a joint capsule. All these things affect the amount of movement that can occur at each joint. The extent of the movement at each joint is called the **range of motion** (ROM). Joints can allow movement in different planes – some produce movement in one plane only, while others can cause movement in two or three planes. Hence, the range of motion at a joint would refer to a particular direction.

STUDENT ACTIVITY

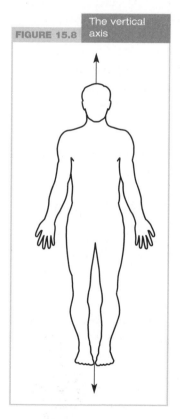

FIGURE 15.8 The vertical axis

Movements

The following tasks are based on the practical activities in Luttgens, Deutsch & Hamilton (1992) (see suggested reading). These specific tasks relate to the leg; similar examples can be used for other regions of the body. They are best performed in small groups.

1 a) Lie face down and flex your leg at the knee by raising the foot.
   b) Oppose the movement by pushing against the ankle.
   c) Find the muscles used for this movement and name them.
2 a) Sit on a table with your legs hanging over the edge. Extend one leg at the knee.
   b) Oppose the movement by pushing against the ankle.
   c) Find the muscles that are causing this movement and name them.
3 a) Stand and rise on your toes.
   b) Which is the main muscle in the lower leg that contracts?
4 a) Sit on a table with your legs hanging over the edge. Raise the thigh of one leg.
   b) Oppose the movement by pushing down on the knee.
   c) Which thigh muscles are contracting?
5 a) Lying face down on a table, raise one leg with your knee straight.
   b) Oppose the movement by pushing down at the knee.
   c) What are the muscles causing this movement?

Lever systems

A lever is a system that magnifies force. Levers consist of a lever arm, a pivot point (which is called a fulcrum), a load force and an effort force. (See also page xx.)

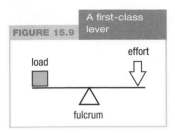

FIGURE 15.9 — A first-class lever

The effort force creates a turning effect around the fulcrum. The size of this turning effect is dependent on the amount of the force and its distance from the fulcrum. Changing the distance from the fulcrum to the load force changes the amount of force magnification. There are three types of levers: first class, second class and third class. A first-class lever has the fulcrum located between the effort force and the load force on the lever arm (see Figure 15.9). An example of this type of lever is the neck.

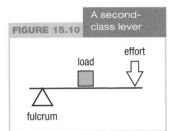

FIGURE 15.10 — A second-class lever

A second-class lever has the load force located between the effort force and the fulcrum on the lever arm (see Figure 15.10). An example of a second-class lever is the ankle.

A third-class lever has the effort force located between the fulcrum and the load force on the lever arm (see Figure 15.11). An example of this type of lever is the elbow.

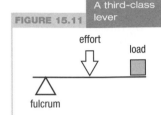

FIGURE 15.11 — A third-class lever

STUDENT PRACTICAL

Force generated by muscle

Aim

The aim of this practical is to measure the maximal force generated by the quadriceps and hamstrings and to understand the implications for sport.

Equipment

tape measure

multigym

Method

1 Warm up thoroughly.
2 Measure each person's one repetition maximum (the most they can lift in one go) performing a leg curl. Do this for each leg separately (i.e. the left leg and then the right leg).
3 Repeat this one repetition maximum performing a leg extension.
4 Record the one repetition maximums (1-RMs) four values for each person.
5 For each exercise, measure the distance between the joint centre (knee) and the point of contact of the weights. This is recorded as j for the leg curls and k for the leg extensions and is measured in centimetres.

Results

The force generated by each leg is calculated from the following equations. The equations have been over-simplified to enable easy calculations, so the values are only approximate. Remember, you will have two hamstrings values, right and left leg, and two quadriceps values (you will perform each calculation twice).

$$\text{Hamstrings force} = \left(\frac{j \times 1\text{-RM (leg curl)}}{3}\right) \times 9.81$$

where j = distance between knee and point of contact of the weights

$$\text{Quadriceps force} = \left(\frac{k \times 1\text{-RM (leg ext.)}}{5}\right) \times 9.81$$

where k = distance between knee and point of contact of the weights

Conclusion

Discuss the following points.

- Which muscle group generates the greater force?
- What implications does this have?
- What other muscles are involved in the leg curl?
- What other muscles are involved in the leg extension?

continues overleaf

continued

✪ Could you work out the force generated by the biceps in an arm curl?
The values 3 and 5 in the equations are an estimate of the distance between the joint centre and the insertion of the particular muscles, and 9.81 is the acceleration due to gravity.

REVISION QUESTIONS

1) Explain the three planes of motion and their associated axes.
2) Give examples of sporting movements that occur in:
a) the sagittal plane
b) the frontal plane
c) the horizontal plane.
3) Give examples of sporting movements that occur around the:

a) sagittal axis
b) frontal axis
c) vertical axis.
4) Describe the different types of levers and give examples both in the body and in sporting equipment.

EXPLAINING MECHANICAL PRINCIPLES

Forces

A force is something that can start or stop a movement, or speed up or slow down a movement, or even change the direction of a movement. There are a number of ways to categorise force.

✪ Forces can be considered as contact forces or non-contact forces. A **contact force** exists when two things come into contact; a **non-contact** force exists when the objects are not physically touching. The force of gravity, electrical forces and magnetic forces are classic examples of forces that exist between two objects even when they are not physically touching.

✪ Forces can also be categorised as internal forces or external forces. **External forces** are forces that act on an object from the surrounding environment, e.g. one player contacting another in rugby. An **internal force** is a force that acts within a system, e.g. forces produced by contracting muscles.

The significance of whether a force is internal or external is related to the ability of that force to change an object's total mechanical energy. When work is done upon an object by an external force, the total mechanical energy of that object is changed. The object could either gain energy or lose energy. When work is done upon an object by an internal force, the total mechanical energy of that object remains constant.

Scalars are quantities described solely by size or magnitude – a distance of 10 m is a scalar measurement.

Vectors are quantities described by both magnitude and direction – a displacement of 10 m in a northerly direction is a vector.

Linear motion

The motion of objects can be described by such measures as distance, displacement, speed, velocity and acceleration. These mathematical quantities, which are used to describe the motion of objects, can be divided into two categories: vector and scalar. These two categories can be distinguished from one another by their distinct definitions.

Distance and displacement are two quantities that seem to mean the same thing, yet have different definitions. **Distance** is a scalar quantity that refers to the length of the path a body follows during its motion. **Displacement** is a vector quantity that refers to how far from its initial position an object has moved, or its change in position. If an athlete ran 2 km north, then 2 km south, they would have run a distance of 4 km but a displacement of 0 km. Displacement, being a vector quantity, the 2 km north is cancelled by the 2 km south. The equations for distance and displacement, as for other measures (speed, velocity, etc.) are given in Chapter 1 (see pages xx to xx).

Just as distance and displacement have different meanings, so do speed and velocity. **Speed** is a scalar quantity that refers to how fast an object is moving. A fast-moving object has a high speed. An object with no movement at all has zero speed. **Velocity** is a vector quantity that refers to the rate at which an object changes its position. Imagine a person moving rapidly (jumping form side to side) always returning to their original starting position. While this might result in a lot of activity, it would result in a zero velocity. Because the person always returns to the original position, the motion would never result in a change in position. Since velocity is defined as the rate at which the position changes, this motion results in zero velocity. You must describe an object's velocity as being 10 mph south. Since a moving object often changes its speed during its motion, it is common to distinguish between the average speed and the instantaneous speed. Instantaneous speed is speed at any given instant in time. Average speed is the speed for the entire duration of the movement and is found by dividing total distance by total time. The same applies to velocity.

Acceleration is a vector quantity that is defined as the rate at which an object changes its velocity. Therefore, an object is accelerating (or decelerating, which is negative acceleration) if it is changing its velocity. People often refer to a person accelerating if they are moving fast, however, an athlete can be moving very fast and still not be accelerating. If an object is not changing its velocity, then it is not accelerating. Therefore, an object with a constant acceleration is not the same as an object with a constant velocity. If an object is changing its velocity, be it by a constant amount, or a varying amount, it is accelerating.

Acceleration is caused by a force acting on a body. If this force is gravitational, the acceleration is called the acceleration due to gravity. The value of this acceleration is 9.8 metres per second squared (ms^{-2}), the direction is toward the centre of the Earth or downward. The acceleration due to gravity is denoted by the symbol g. To simplify calculations g is approximated to the value of 10 ms^{-2}.

Mass and gravity

Mass is the amount of matter in a body. The unit of measurement is the kilogram (kg). It is a measure of inertia or the reluctance of a body to move. The greater the mass of an object, the harder it is to move. For example, a fly-half might be easier to tackle to the ground than a prop forward if they are both standing still. Weight (sometimes confused with mass) is due to the force of gravity acting on an object. It depends on mass, since weight is equal to mass multiplied by the acceleration due to gravity. The more mass in a body, the more force of gravity is acting on it. Weight is a force, so it is measured in newtons (N)(see page xx). The force of gravity is the attraction of a body to the Earth. Throw a stone in the air and it will come down. Jump up in the air and you will come back to Earth. Gravity is a non-contact force; you do not have to have contact with the floor for gravity to have an effect. The point at which gravity is said to act on the body is called the centre of gravity (CG). This is the point about which a body's weight is evenly distributed or balanced. The human body is not a rigid object, so the centre of gravity does not remain in one place. Lifting your arms in the air will raise your centre of gravity.

Momentum

A further concept in describing motion is momentum. The momentum of an object is the amount of motion it has. Consider the fly-half and the prop forward mentioned above. If both were running towards you at 5 metres per second (ms^{-1}), which would you prefer to tackle? Given that the prop may weigh 110 kg (over 17 stone) and the fly-half may be close to 85 kg (around 13 stone), the prop would be harder to stop. It would seem, therefore, that the amount of motion is a combination of the mass of a body and its speed. This is how momentum is determined: mass multiplied by speed (or, more accurately, mass multiplied by velocity).

> momentum = mass × velocity

Note that since velocity is a vector, momentum must also be a vector. In any collision between two objects the total momentum before the collision is the same as the total momentum after the collision. This is known as the conservation of momentum.

Angular motion

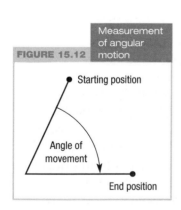

FIGURE 15.12 Measurement of angular motion

Starting position

Angle of movement

End position

In sport, movement or motion is quite often not linear (in a straight line), for example a golf swing, or the action of the leg in running. However, the same concepts and principles used to describe linear motion can be used to explain angular motion or motion in a circle. The major difference in measuring angular motion is the basic unit of measurement. With linear motion metres (m) are used to measure distance and displacement, and all subsequent units are derived from that (e.g. ms^{-1}, ms^{-2}). With angular motion, changes in position are measured by angles in units of degrees (°).

The position of a particular object (e.g. a golf club) at any moment in time is its angular position. This measured with reference to something else, for example, the ground, a vertical line or another object. If angular position changes, as would be the case in a golf swing, the difference between the starting position and the final position is called the angular displacement. It is symbolised by the Greek letter theta (θ). The rate of change of angular displacement is termed **angular velocity**. It is calculated in the same way as linear velocity, but instead of displacement divided by time it is angular displacement divided by time. Therefore, the average angular velocity of a rotating object is defined as the angular displacement divided by the time taken to turn through this angle. Hence:

$$\omega = \frac{\theta}{t}$$

where ω = average angular velocity
θ = angular displacement
t = time taken

The symbol for angular velocity is the Greek letter omega (ω) and is measured in degrees per second ($°s^{-1}$) or radians per second ($rads^{-1}$). One **radian** is equal to $57.3°$, since $360°$ is equivalent to 2π (Greek letter pi) radians. When examining linear motion, there is an important difference between average and instantaneous velocity. This distinction also exists in angular motion. Angular acceleration can be calculated from angular velocity and is defined as the rate of change of angular velocity:

$$a = \frac{(\omega_f - \omega_i)}{t}$$

where a = average angular acceleration
ω_f = final angular velocity
ω_i = initial angular velocity
t = time taken

When examining linear motion, an object's inertia (or resistance to movement) is determined by its mass. With angular motion, this resistance to movement is not only due to the object's mass, but also the distribution of its mass. For example, a golf club has a large proportion of its mass at the club head, while a tennis racket has its mass more evenly distributed. The golf club would have greater angular inertia. **Angular inertia** is more commonly called moment of inertia and is calculated as:

$$I = \Sigma m_i r_i^2$$

where I = moment of inertia
m_i = mass of any particle within the object
r_i = distance from particle to axis of rotation

The units for moment of inertia are kgm^2. From the equation for average angular velocity, it is evident that the distance the majority of the mass is from the axis of rotation has more effect on angular inertia than the object's overall mass. If you increase an object's mass you increase its moment of inertia by the same magnitude (so a heavy cricket bat is harder to swing than a light cricket bat). However, if you increase the distance between the majority of the mass and the axis of rotation (i.e. you make the object longer) the effect on inertia is the square of the increase in distance (double the distance results in quadrupling the effect on inertia). Thus, swinging a driver (a long club) in golf is a lot harder than swinging an iron (a shorter club). Golf club designers are trying to overcome this problem by designing drivers that are relatively light, using materials such as carbon fibre and titanium.

Given that moment of inertia exists (i.e. objects are reluctant to move angularly) a force is needed to produce angular motion. Imagine a tennis player putting topspin on a ball – to spin the ball they must produce a force towards the top of the ball. This force allows the ball to spin in an angular motion. The turning effect produced by a force is called a torque. A **torque** is equal to the product of the force and the distance between this force and the axis of rotation. This distance is referred to as a **moment arm** because a torque is sometimes termed a moment of force (see page 19). The units of measurement for torque are Nm. Torques are vector quantities, that is, they are direction specific. In the case of the player who has just hit the topspin, if you are sitting near the umpire's chair and the tennis player hitting the topspin is on the right-hand side of the court, the direction of the force will be anticlockwise. If the same player put a clockwise force on the ball, this would be backspin.

STUDENT PRACTICAL

Centre of gravity
Aim
When we describe the velocity of something, we normally describe the velocity of its centre of gravity. The aim of this practical is to measure the location of the centre of gravity of the human body and to understand the implications for sport.
Equipment
weighing scales
large board (an old door is ideal)
tape measure
two pivot points (thin blocks of wood will do)
Method
1. Record the subject's mass (kg) and height (cm).
2. Place the board on the floor with a block of wood underneath each end.
3. Underneath one piece of wood place the weighing scales and record the reading)
4. Measure the distance between the two pivots in cm.

5. Ask each subject to lay on the board (anatomical position) with their heels directly above the block of wood not on the scales. The scales will be at the head end.
6. Take a new mass reading (r) of the subject in this position (remember to subtract the mass of the board and block). For example, if the reading with somebody on the board is 40 kg, and is 10 kg with nobody on the board, the mass should be recorded as 30 kg.
7. You should now have four values: the mass of the person (m), their height (h), the distance between the pivots (y) and the mass of the person lying on the board (r).
Results
Work out the location of the centre of gravity by:
Height of centre of gravity = $\frac{r \times y}{m}$
where r = mass on the board
m = mass standing up
y = distance between pivots

continues overleaf

continued

Conclusion

In your conclusion, answer the following questions based on your results.

1   How could you calculate percentage height of centre of gravity?

2   Calculate the average height of your group, comparing males with females.

3   In which sports might the position of the centre of gravity play an important part?

REVISION QUESTIONS

1) What is the centre of gravity of an object?

2) What is the displacement of an athlete competing on a running track if they cover:

a) 100 m

b) 200 m

c) 800 m

3) Give definitions of angular displacement, velocity and acceleration.

4) What is the speed and velocity of a runner if they cover:

a) 100 m in 10 seconds

b) 400 m in 56 seconds

c) 500 m in 3 minutes 57 seconds.

5) Explain mass and the effect it has on motion?

6) From your answer to number 5, explain why rugby players tend to be larger than the average male.

7) Why do Sumo wrestlers need to be big in order to be good at their sport?

APPLYING MECHANICAL PRINCIPLES

Newton's laws of motion

Newton's first law of motion (sometimes called the law of inertia) states that *every body continues in its state of rest or motion in a straight line unless compelled to change that state by external forces acting upon it* (e.g. an ice hockey puck when hit continues in straight line until hit by another player). Strictly speaking, there are always external forces acting on an object, for example gravity, friction and wind resistance.

Newton's second law of motion (known as the law of acceleration) states that *the rate of change of momentum of a body is proportional to the force causing it and the change takes place in the direction in which the force acts* (e.g. when the ice hockey puck is struck by another player it will change direction).

Newton's third law of motion (referred to as the law of reaction) states that *for every force exerted by one body on another, there is an equal and opposite force*

exerted by the second body on the first (e.g. when the ice hockey player leans against the side of the rink, the wall pushes back on him, stopping him falling over). According to Newton, when a runner exerts a force on the ground, the ground pushes back. This force is called ground reaction force. A force can be defined as a push or a pull. When running or walking we use the energy in our leg muscles to push backwards on the ground with one foot while the other foot is moving forward. When we push backwards on the ground, the ground also pushes forward on us.

Shock absorption and impact

Materials undergo **mechanical stress**, such as tension and compression. **Tensile stress** (tension) is when an object is being pulled from both ends, for example, if you are hanging from a chining bar your arms will be being stretched from both ends. The bones in your arms will be under quite a high tension. **Compression** is the opposite of tension. The body undergoes compressive loads frequently in sport, for example, the body can experience two-and-a-half times its own body weight during running. This can increase to five times body weight during landing from a volleyball smash or a basketball lay up.

The spine also endures high compression loads in some sports. Consider the forces involved in the spine during the delivery stride of a fast bowler in cricket. Another type of load that the body can be subjected to is **torsion** – a twisting action. An example would be the forces in the tibia (shin bone) if you tried to pivot on one foot. The movement of your body would cause a twisting action in the lower leg.

Extreme tension, compression and torsion forces can lead to injuries, but repeated moderate forces over a prolonged period can also be a problem. Injuries caused by repetitive actions are called overuse injuries. The injuries caused by these forces (either from a one-off incident or over time) range from soft tissue injuries (e.g. tears and bruising) to fractured bones. Compression fractures are a common type of fracture. An injury of this type can be caused by a significant **trauma**, which could result in other problems, such as ligament or tendon damage. In some instances fractures may occur as a product of osteoporosis, a condition which leads to the loss of bone density. With overuse injuries, overtraining is one of the major contributing factors. Inappropriate trainers or running shoes (with a lack of shock absorption) and running on the wrong type of surface (e.g. concrete or tarmac) are also causes. As mentioned, considerable forces are experienced by the ankles and knees in running. This force needs to be reduced in some way. Soft surfaces can absorb some of the force, as can running shoes that have good shock absorption. Grass is soft to run on and will produce fewer injuries than harder surfaces such as concrete or tarmac.

STUDENT PRACTICAL

Restitution

Aim

The coefficient of restitution is a measure of an object's elasticity upon striking a surface. It determines how high an object will rebound. The aim of this experiment is to measure the coefficient of restitution of various sports balls and understand the implications for sport.

Equipment

tape measure

various balls (e.g. football, netball, basketball, tennis ball, hockey, volleyball)

various surfaces (e.g. wood floor, grass, a gym mat, concrete)

Method

In turn, perform the following for each ball on each surface.

1 Drop the ball from a height of two metres on to the surface. The ball must be dropped (not thrown) vertically on to the surface.

2 Measure the two-metre height from the centre of the bottom of the ball.

3 Record the rebound height. This may require a few practice drops in order that one of the experimenters can place their head at the approximate rebound height to enable a more accurate reading.

4 Repeat the whole process twice, so you have three readings for each ball on each type of surface.

5 Record the results in a table, and use the mean value of the three scores.

Results

It is possible to calculate the coefficient of restitution using the following equation:

$$\text{coefficient of restitution} = \sqrt{\frac{r}{d}}$$

where $\sqrt{}$ = square root of

r = rebound height

d = drop height

Conclusion

1 Which ball/surface has the highest coefficient of restitution and why?

2 Which ball/surface has the lowest coefficient of restitution and why?

3 Is it possible to alter the coefficient of restitution of a ball? If so how? (Hint: think of pressure)

4 Do any sports require a certain coefficient of restitution? If so which? The rules may specify a rebound height.

Projectiles

Many sports involve projectiles (balls, javelins, shuttlecocks, even humans in the long jump, high jump etc.). A projectile is considered to be any object which has no external forces acting on it other than gravity. An object is only said to be a projectile if it experiences no (or negligible) air resistance, as this would be an external force. However, for convenience we will look at all objects as projectiles. The shape of the flight path of a projectile would be symmetrical if we discount air resistance and lift. In practice, however, air resistance (which causes a drag force) and aerodynamic factors (that cause lift) will act to shorten or lengthen the flight path of a projectile. Any object moving through a medium (be it air or water) will experience a drag force, which resists the motion of the object. The greater the velocity of the moving object, the greater the drag force; for example, a cyclist experiences far greater drag forces than a runner. That is why slip streaming plays such a vital part in cycling. A cyclist can save as much as 30% of his energy by cycling close behind a competitor or team-mate.

The drag force also depends upon the size and shape of the object. A downhill skier in a tuck position wearing a racing suit will generate less drag force than a recreational skier standing more upright and wearing salopettes and a ski jacket. The final factor that affects drag is the density of the medium of transport. Water creates more drag than air.

The flow of air (or water) around a projectile depends upon the shape of the projectile. A smooth symmetrical shape will have a symmetrical flow around it. However, in sport many objects are not symmetrical. Consider an **aerofoil**, which has an asymmetric profile. Air travels faster over the top of an aerofoil than underneath it. This means that the air pressure is lower above the aerofoil than below it. This is called **Bernoulli's principle**. The difference in pressure creates an upward force that causes the aerofoil to lift. Various sporting projectiles exhibit lift, for example the javelin and discus. In some cases, an aerofoil is inverted and used to create a downwards force. **Spoilers** on racing cars force the cars on to the ground, which makes them less likely to skid (lose traction), especially when cornering.

Spin also influences the **trajectory** of a projectile. If an object is spinning, its surface interacts with the passing air molecules to a greater extent than if it was not spinning. This can cause the air to slow down or speed up, depending on the direction of spin. The spinning object will cause unequal pressure and hence a force to act on the object, similar to the force on an aerofoil. This force may cause lift, as in the case of a golf ball, which is normally hit with backspin. However, it could be used for swerve (bending a football round a wall) or topspin (causing a volley ball to dip). The surface material of the object also plays an important part in its trajectory. Two good examples are the golf ball and the cricket ball. A golf ball is covered in dimples, which means the interaction between the surface of the ball and the surrounding air is increased. If a golf ball is hit with backspin, the dimples increase the amount of lift force on the ball. This in turn means the ball will travel further, hence it will get closer to the hole. The down side is that the dimples not only increase the amount of lift on the ball, but they will also accentuate any sideways movement. This is why golf balls can be hooked or sliced quite dramatically.

With a cricket ball, the seam has a major effect on its flight characteristics. The airflow around the ball interacts with the ball's surface. The airflow near the surface of the ball is called the boundary layer, and this starts to form at the front of the ball, becoming thicker as it goes round the ball, until about half-way round when it separates from the ball. However, the seam on the cricket ball makes the airflow around the ball asymmetrical, which creates uneven air pressure, which causes the ball to move sideways. The aim of the swing bowler in cricket is to bowl the ball with the seam at the correct angle to produce this sideways movement. It is important that the ball is bowled so the seam stays in one position. This is difficult and requires a lot of skill. The amount of movement is also affected by the condition of the surface of the

ball, which is why the swing movement produced by the bowlers might vary throughout an innings.

Friction

The force of friction applies when you move any two surfaces against each other. Friction acts in the direction opposite to the direction of motion. The magnitude of the frictional force depends on the contact force (the force pushing the surfaces together) and the nature of the contacting surfaces. The larger the contact force the larger the friction force. It would be more difficult to push a heavy person on a set of skis on a flat area of snow than it would be to push a lighter person. The reason racing cars create large down forces with the use of a spoiler is to stop them sliding off the track. Different surfaces have different **coefficients of friction**. For example, rubber has a high coefficient of friction when interacting with most materials. This means it will not slide very well. Car and cycle tyres are made of rubber to stop them slipping. The outer sole of running shoes are also made of rubber to give them a better grip. However, too much friction between surfaces and shoes can lead to ankle and knee injuries. In contrast, skis on snow have a very low coefficient of friction; this enables them to slide easily over the snow. Synovial joints have an extremely low coefficient of friction, which reduces wear and tear on joints.

REVISION *QUESTIONS*

1) Explain the law of inertia.
2) What effect does drag have in sport?
3) What effect does friction have in sport?

MODELS OF MOVEMENT ANALYSIS

Teaching skills requires not only knowing what to teach (i.e. being aware of the correct technique), but also knowing how to eliminate errors and avoid actions that limit performance or cause injury. Developing a model of a skill allows a coach to observe, analyse and then correct the technique of their athletes, comparing their performance with a gold standard. The first part of developing a model of performance is to determine the aim of the skill in question. In the volleyball serve, the objective is to strike the ball so the opposition either cannot return the ball or find it difficult to do so. It is also important that the serve is legal (no foot fault, time fault, ball travels within playing area, etc.). To achieve this objective, accuracy is important, as is timing and power. If the ball is miss hit, hit too softly or inaccurately it will be easier for the opposition to return the ball.

The next step is to devise a theoretical model of the skill. This could be done with the help of a video of an elite performer. The skill can be divided into phases and the biomechanical features of each phase identified. It is common to divide skills into three phases. It is important to identify where one phase ends and the next phase begins. Most striking, kicking, hitting and catching skills are divided into a preparation phase, a force production phase and a recovery phase. Examining the volleyball serve, it has a preparation phase that consists of holding the ball in the non-striking hand and drawing the hitting hand back. The force production phase involves bringing the hitting hand into contact with the ball. The recovery phase is to stop the movement of the body and be ready for the next action. Even repetitive skills, like running, swimming or cycling, can be divided into three similar phases. Take running as an example. The preparation phase could be the foot landing on the floor (the heel strike in normal running).

STUDENT ACTIVITY

Biomechanical analysis of skill

1 Select a skill to analyse (e.g. golf swing, serve, sprint start).
2 Obtain film footage of the skill (you could film this yourself or use available footage from the internet, for example).
3 Divide the skill into phases and discuss the purpose of each phase.
4 Analyse each phase anatomically (what happens at each joint).
5 Examine the mechanical aspects of the movement (speed production, force generation, angular motion).

Driving off from the front of the foot is the force production phase. Recovery will be bringing the foot through ready for another heel strike. If the skill is more complex (e.g. the triple jump) the skill can be broken into major phases that are then subdivided into further sections. With the skill divided into parts, it is then possible to examine the anatomical and mechanical aspects of each phase. For the volleyball serve, what position is the hitting hand in? What position are the hitting arm and shoulder in? What about the trunk and the legs? How is power generated? Where is the ball struck? How is topspin created, or does the ball float? Look at stability and timing.

With a model in place, it is now possible to observe your own athlete and evaluate their performance in relation to that of the model. Highlight the areas that need improving or contain errors. If you are teaching the volleyball serve, one of your players might consistently serve to the left-hand side of the court. You have worked out that this is caused by them bringing their arm across their body in the recovery phase. You now need to decide how to correct the error. You might wish to break the movement down into its phases and concentrate on one phase, or you could run through the action in slow motion. A video of the correct technique could be shown. Whatever you decide, it is important that after a period of coaching you repeat the observation to see if your player has improved. The goal of the coach is to identify faults in performance and make corrections to prevent injury and improve performance.

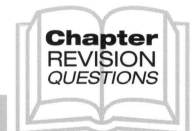

Chapter REVISION QUESTIONS

1) Describe the movements that can occur about joints and give sporting examples of each.
2) What are agonist and antagonist actions?
3) Examine a sit-up. For the upwards phase, explain which muscle is the:
a) agonist
b) antagonist
c) stabiliser
d) assistor.
4) Explain Newton's laws of motion and give sporting examples to illustrate each.
5) What effect does compression have on the human body?

SUGGESTED FURTHER READING

Carr, G. (1997) *Mechanics of Sport: A Practitioners Guide*. Champaign, Ill: Human Kinetics

Luttgens, K., Deutsch, H. and Hamilton, N. (1992) *Kinesiology: Scientific Basis of Human Motion*, 8th edition. Madison, Wisconsin: WCB Brown & Benchmark

Wirhed, R. (1997) *Athletic Ability and the Anatomy of Motion*. London: Mosby

SPORTS INJURIES

Any injury that is sustained while taking part in sport is deemed a sports injury. People who take parts in sports regularly will usually have suffered from at least one type of sports injury. This chapter will explore the different types of sports injuries and how they can occur. Methods to identify, prevent and treat the injuries will be explored, together with rehabilitation procedures. By the end of this chapter students should be able to:

✪ identify the risk factors that can result in sports injuries and ways to prevent these injuries from happening

✪ be aware of how connective tissues respond to injury

✪ have an understanding of the different treatments used to deal with sports injuries

✪ understand the principles of rehabilitation and devise a basic rehabilitation programme.

RISK FACTORS AND PREVENTION OF SPORTS INJURIES

Taking part in sports can result in injury to any part of the body. These injuries can be caused by a variety of factors, which can basically be grouped into two categories: extrinsic risk factors and intrinsic risk factors.

Extrinsic risk factors

An **extrinsic** risk factor is something outside of the body that can cause an injury. These include:

✪ inadequate warm up

✪ environmental conditions

✪ footwear

✪ other sports people.

Inadequate warm up

This is a very common cause of sports injury. The warm up prepares both the body and the mind for the exercise that is to come by gradually taking the body from its non-active state to being ready for the exercise. How long it takes to warm up will vary from person to person, and will depend on their level of fitness. The

Warm Up
Devise a warm up for a sport of your choice that consists of the following components:
✪ a pulse raiser
✪ a mobiliser
✪ a stretch.

environment will also affect the length of the warm up; in cold surroundings it will be necessary to carry out a longer warm up than in hot surroundings.

A warm up should consist of three components: a pulse raiser, to get the blood flowing more quickly around the body and so help to warm up the muscle tissues and make them more pliable; a mobiliser in which the joints are taken through their range of movement, such as arm circles to mobilise the shoulder joint; then the main muscles that are going to be used in the sport should be stretched.

Environmental conditions

The environment in which we perform sports can have a big impact on the likelihood of sustaining an injury. The environment encompasses the area in which a sport is played, so if you were playing basketball the environment would consist of the sports hall, and include the playing surface, the lighting and the temperature. If the lighting was poor, a player may be more likely to misjudge tackles and injure themselves or another player. If the surface was wet, then a player would be more likely to slip over because the surface becomes much more slippery when it is wet.

Footwear

Although a sportsperson may be wearing the correct footwear, certain types of footwear make a person more susceptible to injury. For instance, the studs on a footballer's or rugby player's boot can make the wearer more susceptible to leg injuries because the studs plant the foot in the ground, so if the person is turning on a planted foot they are more likely to twist their knee.

Incorrect footwear can also be a factor in causing a person to injure themselves while playing sport. For example, a marathon runner needs a lot of cushioning in their trainers to absorb the repeated impact or running; if they were to wear trainers with little padding they would be much more likely to sustain an overuse sport injury.

Other sports players

In contact sports, players are more likely to sustain a sports injury from a collision with another player. For instance, after a rugby game players will often come away with at least a few bruises from tackling or being tackled by other players. In non-contact games, players can also sustain sports injuries from other players from foul tackles or collisions with them.

Intrinsic risk factors

An **intrinsic** risk factor is a physical aspect of the athlete's body that can cause an injury. These include:

✪ muscle imbalance	✪ poor technique
✪ poor preparation	✪ overuse
✪ postural defects	✪ age.

Muscle imbalance

A muscle imbalance means that one muscle in an antagonistic pair (see pages xx) is stronger than the other muscle. This is often seen in footballers, who have strong quadriceps muscles from extending their knee to kick the ball, but their hamstring muscles are not as strong. This can result in knee injuries because the hamstring muscles are not strong enough to put a brake on the kicking action of the knee. As a result, when a striker goes to score a goal they can over-kick, so that their knee hyperextends and gets injured.

Poor preparation

This includes a player's fitness levels. If a person is not fit to take part in a sport then they are more likely to injure themselves because they are so tired that they develop a poor sports technique. A sports person must also acclimatise to the environment in which they are going to play. For example, if a marathon runner living in England takes part in a race in Australia in the summer time, then they have to train in hot conditions to get their body used to coping with the heat.

Postural defects

Most people are born with a slight postural defect, such as having one leg slightly longer than the other. However, if there is a large difference between the two legs, this can affect the person's running technique, which may then place more strain on one side of the body, which would then make the person more likely to sustain injuries after long periods of exercising.

Poor technique

If a person is not using the correct methods for exercising, they are more likely to sustain a sports injury. For example, if a swimmer continues to perform the front crawl stroke incorrectly with their arms, they may be prone to shoulder or elbow injuries.

Overuse

An overuse injury is caused because a sports person does not take time to recover after exercise. Every time we exercise we place our body under strain, which means the body has to repair itself afterwards. If a person does not allow their body to repair itself it will become weaker, until eventually parts of the body become injured.

Age

As a person gets older, their body eventually starts to become weaker and more prone to injuries. Therefore, the older you become, generally the more prone to injuries you are.

Preventative strategies

Besides maintaining fitness and doing a warm up, an important way to prevent sports injuries is to wear protective clothing. Suitable clothing minimises the risk of sustaining an injury in any sport. At the very least, people should wear are loose fitting or stretchy clothing and appropriate trainers. Jewellery should be removed.

Types of injury

Injuries can be categorised into soft tissue and hard tissue injuries. Soft tissue is the muscles, tendons, ligaments and skin, whereas hard tissue is the skeleton, including joints, bones and cartilage.

Soft tissue injuries

Sprain

A **sprain** is a stretch and/or tear to a ligament and is often caused by a trauma that knocks a joint out of position, and over-stretches or **ruptures** the supporting ligaments. Sprains often affect the ankles, knees or wrists. There are three degrees of ligament sprain.

First degree sprains commonly exhibit the following symptoms:

✪ some stretching or tearing of the ligament

✪ little or no joint instability

✪ mild pain

✪ little swelling

✪ some joint stiffness.

Second degree sprains commonly exhibit the following symptoms:

✪ some tearing of the ligament fibres

✪ moderate instability of the joint

✪ moderate to severe pain

✪ swelling and stiffness.

Third degree sprains commonly exhibit the following symptoms:

✪ total rupture of a ligament

✪ gross instability of the joint

✪ severe pain initially, followed by no pain

✪ severe swelling.

Strain

A **strain** is a twist, pull and/or tear to a muscle or tendon, and is often caused by overuse, force or over-stretching. If a tear in the muscle occurs, surgical repair may be necessary. Muscle strains can also be classified into three categories.

First degree strains commonly exhibit the following symptoms:

✪ few muscle fibres are torn

✪ mild pain

✪ little swelling

✪ some muscle stiffness.

Second degree strains commonly exhibit the following symptoms:

- ✪ minimal to moderate tearing of the muscle fibres

- ✪ moderate to severe pain

- ✪ swelling and stiffness.

Third degree strains commonly exhibit the following symptoms:

- ✪ total rupture of the muscle

- ✪ severe pain

- ✪ severe swelling.

Haematomas

A **haematoma** is bleeding either into or around a muscle. If the bleeding is within the muscle it is called an intramuscular haematoma. This type of haematoma will lead to a pressure build-up within the muscle tissue as the blood is trapped within the muscle sheath (Figure16.1). This will result in a marked decrease in strength of the injured muscle, a significant decrease in muscle strech and a long recovery period.

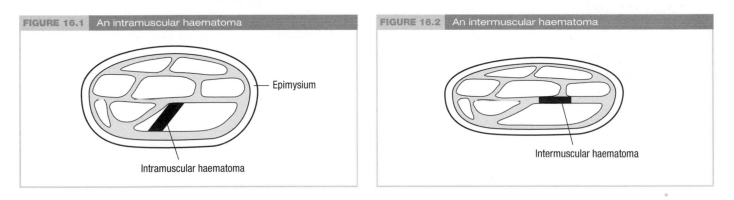

FIGURE 16.1   An intramuscular haematoma

Epimysium

Intramuscular haematoma

FIGURE 16.2   An intermuscular haematoma

Intermuscular haematoma

Bleeding around the muscle tissue is called an intermuscular haematoma. This type of haemotoma is much less severe than an intramuscular haemotoma because the blood can escape from the damaged muscle and into the surrounding tissues, so there is less pressure in the area and the injury recovers much more quickly.

Oedema

This is swelling in the tissue due to trauma. The swelling may be a combination of tissue fluid and blood. The blood comes from local damage to capillaries at the injury site.

Bursitis

Bursitis is inflammation or irritation of a bursa (see page 38). Bursae are small sacs of fluid that are located between bone and other moving structures such as muscles, skin or tendons. The bursa allows smooth gliding between these structures. If the bursa becomes inflamed it will feel painful and restrict movement within that area. Bursitis is an injury that usually results from overuse.

Tendinitis

Tendinitis is inflammation or irritation of a tendon. It causes pain and stiffness around the inflamed tendon, which is made worse by movement. Almost any tendon can be affected with tendonitis, but those located around a joint tend to be more prone to inflammation. Tendinitis usually results from overuse.

Contusion

A contusion is the technical term for a bruise. Contusions are often produced by a blunt force such as a kick, fall or blow. The result will be pain, swelling and discoloration.

Abrasion

An abrasian is when the surface of the skin is grazed so that the top layer is scraped off, leaving a raw tender area. This type of injury often occurs as a result of a sliding fall.

Hard tissue injury

Dislocation

This is the displacement of a joint from its normal location. It occurs when a joint is over-stressed, which makes the bones that meet at that joint disconnect. This usually causes the joint capsule to tear, together with the ligaments holding the joint in place. Most dislocations are caused by a blow or a fall. If a person has dislocated a joint then it will usually look out-of-place, discoloured and/or misshapen. Movement is limited, and there is usually swelling and intense pain.

Subluxation

A subluxation is when one or more of the bones of the spine moves out of position and creates pressure on, or irritates, spinal nerves (see Figure 16.3). This interferes with the signals travelling along these spinal nerves, which means some parts of the body will not be working properly.

Cartilage damage

Normal synovial joint function requires a smooth-gliding cartilage surface on the ends of the bones. This cartilage also acts to distribute force during repetitive pounding movements, such as running or jumping. Cartilage injury (see page 376) can result in locking, localised pain and swelling around the affected area. It appears as a hole in the cartilage surface. As cartilage has minimal ability to repair itself, it needs treatment in order to minimise the deterioration to the joint surface.

Haemarthrosis

Haemathrosis is where there is bleeding into the joint (see Figure 16.4). It is a serious injury and swelling of the injury site occurs very rapidly. The

FIGURE 16.3 A subluxation

FIGURE 16.4 A haemarthrosis

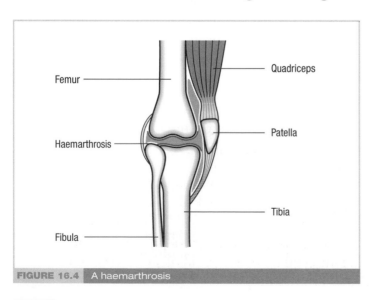

Femur
Quadriceps
Haemarthrosis
Patella
Tibia
Fibula

swelling works to protect the joint structures by limiting or preventing movement of the injured joint.

Fractures

A fracture is the technical term for a broken bone.

Fractures result whenever a bone is hit by enough force to make it break, creating either a small crack or, in a serious fracture, a complete break. There are five main types of fracture.

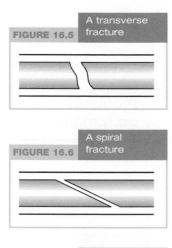
FIGURE 16.5   A transverse fracture

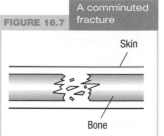
FIGURE 16.6   A spiral fracture

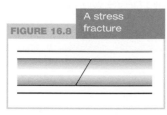
FIGURE 16.7   A comminuted fracture

Skin

Bone

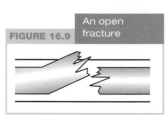
FIGURE 16.8   A stress fracture

FIGURE 16.9   An open fracture

1   **Transverse fractures** are usually the result of a direct blow or force being applied at a sideways angle to the bone (see Figure 16.5). The resultant shape of the bone ends helps transverse fractures stay in alignment more easily than those of other fractures, where the resultant ends do not line up so readily.

2   **Spiral fractures** are also known as oblique fractures (see Figure 16.6). They usually occur as a result of a twisting moment being applied about the long axis of the bone, for example, the foot being held trapped by football boot studs while the leg twists around it.

3   A **comminuted fracture** is where there is splintering of the bone so that the bone is broken into a number of pieces (see Figure 16.7). This type of fracture can take longer than others to heal, and is usually caused by direct trauma.

4   A **stress fracture** is an overuse injury. It occurs when muscles become fatigued and are unable to absorb added shock. Eventually, the fatigued muscle transfers the overload of stress to the bone, causing a tiny crack called a stress fracture (see Figure 16.8). Stress fractures usually occur because of a rapid increase in the amount or intensity of training. The impact of an unfamiliar surface or incorrect trainers can also cause stress fractures.

5   An **open fracture** is also called a **compound fracture**. It is generally a more serious type of injury because the bone breaks through the skin (see Figure 16.9). The break causes considerable damage to surrounding tissue and can cause serious bleeding if a large artery is ruptured. It also exposes the broken bone to the possibility of infection, which can interfere with healing.

Spinal injuries

Any injury to the spinal cord has serious effects on a person's ability to function normally. A **lesion** (damage) to the spinal cord may cause **quadriplegia**, **paraplegia**, or chronic painful conditions, depending on the location of the injury. A lesion high in the cervical spine is usually fatal. Damage to the spinal cord at the level of the two upper thoracic vertebrae usually results in quadriplegia, whereas lesions to the lower thoracic vertebrae may give rise to paraplegia. Spinal injuries can be caused by a variety of physical incidents; collapsed rugby scrums and falling off a horse in a riding event tend to be the most common causes of spinal injuries in sport.

STUDENT ACTIVITY

Sports Injuries

Draw up a table like the one below.

Sport	Type of injury	Extrinsic	Intrinsic	Protective equipment
Football	Transverse fracture to the 5th metatarsal	Yes, tackle from another player	No	Football boots

Complete the table by listing the types of injury you or your colleagues have sustained while playing different sports. State whether it was from an extrinsic or intrinsic source and describe how it occurred. In the 'protective equipment' box, if appropriate, write what you could have worn to prevent the injury.

REVISION QUESTIONS

1) What is an extrinsic risk factor?

2) Why is a warm up necessary in order to avoid sustaining a sports injury?

3) What is an intrinsic risk factor? Give three examples.

4) What are the main methods of preventing sports injuries?

5) Give examples of five different sports people who have sustained different soft tissue sports injuries.

6) Give examples of five different sports people who have sustained different hard tissue sports injuries.

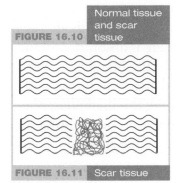

FIGURE 16.10 Normal tissue and scar tissue

FIGURE 16.11 Scar tissue

TISSUE INFLAM-MATORY RESPONSE

Muscular system

For a detailed discussion of skeletal muscular structure and function read Chapter 7.

When a muscle tissue is damaged it undergoes a repair process, which begins on the third day after injury once the swelling has been reduced. By this stage the damaged blood vessels will have been restored, enabling them to deliver oxygen and nutrients to the damaged tissue. Muscle cannot produce new tissue, so it produces scar tissue. This is mainly collagen, which is fibrous and inelastic; it is not as strong or as flexible as muscle tissue and as a result the muscle's function is reduced.

Ligaments and tendons

Ligaments and tendons are soft tissues that are primarily made out of collagen. Ligaments connect bone to bone and tendons connect muscles to bone. Ligaments and tendons can adapt to changes in their mechanical environment due to injury, disease or exercise. A ligament or tendon is made up of **fascicles**. Each fascicle contains the basic fibril of the ligament or tendon, and the fibroblasts, which are the cells that make the ligament or tendon.

Unlike normal ligaments, healed ligaments are partly made up of a different type of collagen, which has fibrils with a smaller diameter and is therefore a mechanically inferior structure. As a result, the healed ligament often fails to provide adequate joint stability, which can then lead to re-injury or a chronically lax (permanently slightly unstable) joint.

Scar tissue

When a person is injured scar tissue is formed which acts as a glue to hold torn fibres together. Scar tissue forms primarily in muscles, tendons, ligaments and joints. It has 'plastic' properties, which means it can be influenced by stretching and moulding. It is laid down in a disordered 'kinked' formation (see Figure 16.10).

Scar tissue will shorten if not stretched regularly. Therefore, the initial stages of repair leave the tissue with a region of short, tight scar tissue. If the athlete takes part in a rehabilitation program of stretching it will help to ensure that the scar tissue forms in parallel lines in order to give the repaired tissue greater strength. However, if the athlete performs movements that stress the injured area it can cause re-tearing of tissue, which stimulates the formation of more scar tissue to take its place.

Stages of injury

There are three stages of injury:

1   acute stage (48 to 72 hours after injury)

2   sub-acute stage (72 hours to 21 day after injury)

3   chronic continuum (21 days after injury).

REVISION QUESTIONS

1) Why are sports people more likely to injure an area that has previously been injured?

2) Name three sports people who have had recurrent sports injuries.

3) What is the purpose of scar tissue?

4) What are the stages of injury and what happens at each stage?

During **stage 1** (acute stage) the injured body part will usually undergo a period of swelling, which is also known as inflammation. When the injured area starts to swell it will feel painful because the swelling creates pressure on the nerves surrounding the damaged tissue. The swelling occurs because the surrounding blood vessels are ruptured allowing blood to bleed into the area and tissue fluid to gather around the injury site. The injured area will usually look red because the blood vessels surrounding the injury site **dilate**, which also has the effect of making the injured area feel hot. The injured area will show a reduced function or a total inability to function because of the pain and swelling. The level of the above signs and symptoms will be directly related to the degree of the injury – the greater the degree of damage, the greater the effects of inflammation will be.

At **stage 2**, the sub acute stage, the body is starting to try to repair the injury. The ends of the torn blood vessels are sealed by blood clots, then the body follows a four-step approach to healing the injury site: there is absorption of the swelling, followed by the removal of any injury debris and the blood clot, then new blood capillaries grow in order to supply the injured area with blood, and finally the damaged tissue is repaired by scar tissue. During the final phase the patient should ensure that they perform correct stretching exercises in order to ensure that the scar tissue lines up along the line of stress of the injured tissue.

Stage 3 (chronic continuum) is the stage of remodelling. This is where the body transforms the repaired tissue to become more like normal body tissue.

RANGE OF TREATMENTS

SALTAPS

SALTAPS is a set procedure for examining an injured person and attempting to diagnose the type and the degree of injury. It stands for: see, ask, look, touch, active movement, passive movement, strength testing. See pages 365–66 for a full explanation of each stage.

In minor injuries, all stages of SALTAPS can usually be completed; however, if a person sustains a serious sports injury, such as a fracture or dislocation, the assessment should not be completed because further injury may occur.

STUDENT ACTIVITY

Assessing a sports person's injury

Imagine you are the physiotherapist for a sports player/team of your choice. One of the players sustains an injury (again of your choice). Run through the series of steps you would follow in order to assess where the injury had occurred and the extent of the damage. Remember to stop the process of SALTAPS in the appropriate section if your player has a serious injury.

First aid

First aid is the immediate treatment given to an injured person. When a suitably qualified person arrives on the scene they then take over the care of the person. Anyone with some knowledge of first aid can have a huge impact on the health of an injured person, so it is always useful to know some basics. By completing a recognised first aid qualification you will gain a very good basic knowledge of what to do in an emergency situation. It is not in the scope of this book to cover all aspects of first aid because practical work is required to compliment the theoretical principles of first aid. Therefore, this section will only cover some very basic aspects of first aid.

Immediate treatments

It is necessary to establish what is wrong with the person. If they are lying on the ground you should follow the guidelines below.

1   Assess the situation – identify any risks to yourself and to the casualty.

2   Make the area safe, such as turning off an electric switch.

3   Give first aid if appropriate. Establish if the person is conscious and then check their ABC; this would be thoroughly covered in a First Aid Course:

   airway – they have an open airway

   breathing – they are breathing

   circulation – check their circulation by assessing if they have a pulse.

4   Try to get help as soon as possible.

If you follow a first aid course you will be taught how to:

✪   check the ABC

✪   open a person's airway

✪   deal with them if they are not breathing by giving them artificial resuscitation

✪   check if a person has a pulse and how to administer cardiac compressions if they do not.

Calling for an ambulance

If a person is injured and you believe the injury requires professional attention, you must ensure that someone calls for an ambulance. If you are dealing with a casualty by yourself, minimise the risk to them by taking any vital action first (check their airway, breathing and circulation), then make a short but accurate call.

1   Dial 999 and ask for an ambulance.

2   Give your exact location.

3   Give clear details of the accident and the severity of the injuries your casualty has sustained.

4   Give the number, sex and approximate age of the casualty.

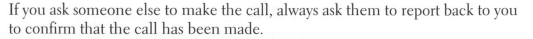

If you ask someone else to make the call, always ask them to report back to you to confirm that the call has been made.

When the paramedics arrive, tell them as much as possible about how the casualty has behaved, such as if they went unconscious, if they needed artificial resuscitation, and so on.

Contents of a first aid box

A first aid box should contain a number of items in order for a person to effectively administer first aid. The contents of a first aid box for a workplace or leisure centre must conform to legal requirements and must also be clearly marked and readily accessible. Below is a list of materials that most first aid kits contain.

- ✪ **Sterile adhesive dressings** (plasters) – There should be a range of sizes for dressing minor wounds.

- ✪ **Sterile eye pads** – A sterile pad with a bandage attached to it to cover the eye following eye injuries.

- ✪ **Triangular bandages** – These can be used as a pad to stop bleeding, or to make slings, or used as a sterile covering for large injuries such as burns.

- ✪ **Safety pins** – These may be necessary to secure bandages.

- ✪ **Large and medium wound dressings** – A sterile, non-medicated dressing pad with a bandage attached to it.

- ✪ **Disposable gloves** – These should be worn at all times when dealing with blood or body fluids.

- ✪ **Face shield for resuscitation** – This may be used to prevent contamination by the casualty's vomit, blood or other body fluids.

Bleeding

A person may suffer from external bleeding, which is usually obvious to the first aider as blood flows out from the site of injury. Internal bleeding, however, is not so obvious – it is not visible as the blood is flowing out of the injury site into the body. The first aider should ensure they are adequately protected when dealing with a casualty who is bleeding, in order to ensure they do not expose themselves to any blood-borne viruses such as HIV.

External bleeding should be treated in the following manner:

- ✪ lay casualty down

- ✪ apply direct pressure with a gloved hand or finger to the site of bleeding; as soon as possible, place a clean dressing over the wound

- ✪ elevate and rest the injured part when possible

- ✪ seek medical assistance.

Internal bleeding is difficult to diagnose, but some of the potential signs and symptoms are:

- coughing up red frothy blood
- vomiting blood
- faintness or dizziness
- weak, rapid pulse
- cold, clammy skin
- rapid, gasping breathing.

The treatment for a person you suspect has internal bleeding is as follows:

1 lay the casualty down
2 raise the legs or bend the knees
3 loosen tight clothing
4 urgently seek medical assistance
5 give nothing by mouth
6 reassure the casualty.

Shock

When a person is suffering from shock, there is not enough blood going to the major organs of the body. Shock can be caused by number of things, including burns, electric shock, allergic shock or severe injuries. A person suffering from shock will usually have cool, moist skin, a weak, rapid pulse and shallow breathing. Other symptoms may include nausea, vomiting, or trembling. The treatment for a conscious casualty suffering from shock is to reassure them, then try to find and treat the cause of shock, e.g. control any bleeding. Keep the casualty lying down and check for neck, spine, head or abdomen injuries. If there are none of these injuries then the feet should be raised so that they are higher than the casualty's head.

FIGURE 16.12 The recovery position

Unconscious adult casualty

If you see a person lying on the ground, talk to them first to see if they respond – they may just be asleep! If they do not respond, speak to them with a louder voice, asking them if they are all right. If you still receive no response, gently shake them. If the person is not injured but is unconscious, then they should be placed into the recovery position (see Figure 6.12). This position helps a semiconscious or unconscious person breathe and allows fluids to drain from the nose and throat so that they do not choke. The casualty should not be moved into the recovery position if you suspect that they have a major injury, such as a back or neck injury.

Fractures

As stated previously, there are five different types of fracture. All the closed fractures can be treated in a similar manner, but an open fracture needs special attention. A person can be diagnosed as having a fracture if the injured area looks deformed or is tender, if there is swelling in the area, if the casualty cannot move the injured part, if there is a protruding bone, bleeding or discoloured skin at the injury site. A sharp pain when the individual attempts to move the injured body part is also a sign of a fracture. The casualty should be told firmly not to move the injured part, since such movement could cause further damage to surrounding tissues and make the casualty go into shock.

A fracture should be immobilised in order to prevent the sharp edges of the bone from moving and cutting tissue, muscle, blood vessels and nerves. The injured body part can be immobilised using splints or slings. If a casualty has an open fracture, the first aider should never attempt to push the bones back under the skin. A dressing should be applied to the injury site to protect the area and pressure should be applied in order to try to limit the external bleeding. A splint can be applied, but should not be placed over the protruding bone.

Cold application

When a person sustains a soft tissue injury, blood vessels are torn and blood cells and fluid escape into the spaces among the muscle fibres. The application of something that is cold to the injured area has the effect of decreasing the flow of this fluid into the tissues and slows the release of chemicals that cause pain and inflammation. Cold also decreases the feeling of pain by reducing the ability of the nerve endings to conduct impulses.

Because cold reduces bleeding and swelling within injured tissue, it is best used in the acute stage of injury, i.e. within the first 48 hours after an injury.

RICE

If a person has suffered from a soft tissue injury such as a strain or a sprain, then ensuring that they follow the RICE (rest, ice, compression, elevation) regime will help to limit the severity of their injury. See page 366 for details of this regime.

Cryotherapy

Cryotherapy is cooling an injured body part to minimise the swelling and bruising of an injured area and to reduce pain. By cooling the injury site, the local blood vessels are constricted, so blood flow to the area is reduced.

Ice bags (plastic bags with ice cubes in, a bag of frozen vegetables or chemical cold packs) can be used. The injured area should be covered with a cloth towel in order to prevent direct contact of the ice with the skin, which could cause a blister or 'ice burn'. The cold application should be applied to the injured area for no more than 20 minutes. During these 20 minutes the person's skin will pass through four stages of sensation, which are

1   cold

2   burning

3   aching

4   numbness – as soon as the skin feels numb the cold therapy should be stopped.

The cooling procedure should be repeated every two waking hours.

There are a number of methods of cryotherapy on the market, including ice and gel packs, ice bath immersion and cans of spray.

Other treatments

Heat treatments

The application of heat to an injury site will act to dilate the local blood vessels, thus increasing the blood flow to the area. This type of treatment should only be given in the sub-acute stage in order to aid in the healing process. The increased blood supply will have the effect of absorbing the swelling and removing the dead cells from the injury site. It will also help to increase the growth of new blood vessels in the area and help scar tissue to form. The application of heat to muscles allows them to relax and aid in pain relief.

Heat treatment would not be suitable during the acute stage of injury, on an open wound or where tissues are very sensitive, such as the genital region.

Contrast bathing

Contrast bathing is the process by which alternating treatments of both hot and cold therapy are applied to the injury site and should be applied during the sub-acute phase. The application of a hot treatment will increase the blood flow to the area then, when this if followed by a cold treatment, the blood flow to the area will decrease and take with it the debris from the injury site. The injured site should be immersed in alternating hot and cold water for periods ranging from one to four minutes, with increased time initially in the cold water.

Bandaging and taping

This is carried out in order to prevent injury, or to treat or rehabilitate an injured joint. Both are performed in order to increase the stability of a joint when there has been an injury to the ligaments that normally support the joint. They limit unwanted joint movement, support the injury site during strengthening exercises and protect the injury site from further damage.

Taping involves the use of adhesive tape, whereas bandaging uses strips of cotton and/or specialised pressure bandages. Their purpose is to restrict the joint movement to within safe limits. Taping should not be carried out if the joint is swollen or painful, or if there are any lesions around the taping area. The person who applies the taping/bandaging should be careful to ensure that they do not bind the injury site too tightly so that circulation is affected.

Bandaging can be used to create pressure around the injury site in order to restrict swelling.

REVISION QUESTIONS

1) Explain what SALTAPS is and when you would use it.

2) What is the purpose of first aid?

3) What does ABC stand for in relation to first aid?

4) What is shock?

5) Name six things that a first aid box should contain.

6) What does RICE stand for and when would you use it?

7) What is cryotherapy and what is its purpose?

8) Why and when would you use heat treatment on an injury?

9) Why would you use taping on a sports injury?

TREATMENT AND REHABILITATION

Rehabilitation is the restoration of the ability to function in a normal or near-normal manner following an injury. It usually involves reducing pain and swelling, restoring range of motion and increasing strength with the use of manual therapy (massage and manipulation), theraputic methods such as ultrasound and an exercise programme.

If a sports person does not rehabilitate their injury effectively, they are much more likely to sustain another injury to the same area.

The stepladder approach to rehabilitation

The stepladder approach to rehabilitation involves putting the injured body part through a graduated series of execises. As the injury heals, the exercises should become more and more demanding until the injured body part is back to its pre-injured state.

The levels are increased when the person is able to complete all the exercises with no pain. If the pain is felt for 20 seconds or less, the person can continue to carry out the same level of rehabilitation exercises. However, if the pain or ache lasts for longer than 20 seconds, the person must stop the exercises and wait 24 hours before regressing to the previous step or even the first step if the pain was severe.

1   During the acute stage of injury, the person should rest in order to minimise the initial swelling and protect the injury from further damage. However, prolonged immobilisation can have deleterious consequences on a person's recovery. For every week of immobilisation, a person may lose up to 20% of their muscle strength. Prolonged immobilisation will lead to stiffness of the joints in the injury area and a decrease in ligament strength. However, if the injured area is mobilised early on in the

rehabilitation process, re-growth of the damaged tissues is encouraged and sports ability and skills are maintained. When a therapist introduces early mobilisation into the rehabilitation it is termed 'aggressive rehabilitation'.

2   During the sub-acute phase, the person may start to exercise the injured body part. The joint should be moved through its pain-free range in order to increase the range of movement of the joint, help to strengthen and lengthen the muscles around the injury and also to help the scar tissue to form in alignment. Throughout these exercise the person should feel no pain.

3   During the active rehabilitation stage the person should commence progressive strength training exercises, together with mobilising exercises, to strengthen the injured body part.

4   Lastly, the person follows a functional rehabilitation training stage in which they take part in a graduated return to the usual training regime to improve the player's balance and movement co-ordination, restore specific skills and movement patterns and to give the player some psychological reassurance that they have returned to full fitness.

Examples of exercises in the stepladder approach

Acute stage
Very little exercise should be performed during this stage as the aim of the treatment is to control the bleeding and swelling and protect the injured body part from further damage. RICE is recommended at this stage for 24 to 48 hours.

Sub-acute stage
Stretching the injured body part is very important during this stage in order to help ensure that the new tissue is laid down in the correct orientation. If there are any signs that the injured body part is not ready to commence this stage, such as heat or swelling around the injury, then stretching should not be started. When stretching, the person should have their injured body part made as warm as possible. This can be done through use of a thermal heat pack or a soaking in a hot bath. Stretches should be held (static stretches) to the onsest of discomfort for 15 to 20 seconds. However, a person should never stretch to the extent that they are in pain.

Stretching should be performed for short periods of time and frequently throughout the day.

Active rehabilitation
The strengthening exercises that can be used during this stage start with **isometric** exercises. This is where the muscle contracts but no joint movement occurs. Once these have been carried out and no pain has been felt, **concentric** muscle contractions can be carried out. This is where the muscle shortens, for example the biceps shortening in a biceps curl (see Figure 16.12).

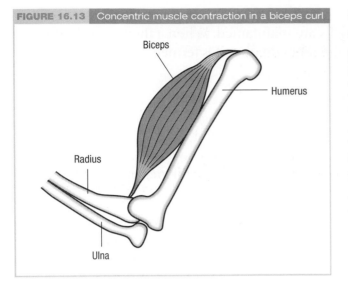

FIGURE 16.13 Concentric muscle contraction in a biceps curl

- Biceps
- Humerus
- Radius
- Ulna

Once this type of muscle contraction can be carried out with no pain, **eccentric** muscle contractions can be performed. This involves the muscle lengthening under tension. An example of this is the quadriceps muscle lengthening as the knee flexes into the sitting position (see Figure 16.13).

If the person has injured their leg(s), initially all the strength-training exercises should be carried out in a non-weight-bearing position, so the injured body part should not take the weight of the body. Instead, the person should be sitting down, lying down or standing on their good leg. The next stage is partial weight bearing, where the arms are used to help support the body weight. Lastly, the exercises can be carried out with the full body weight on the injured body part.

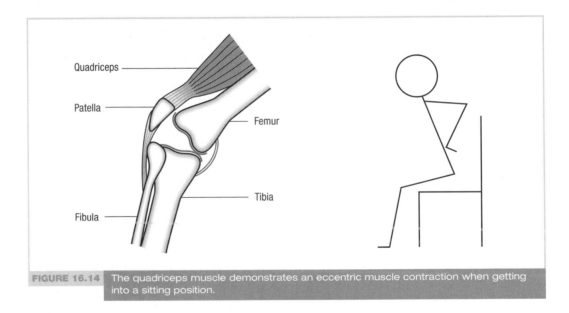

- Quadriceps
- Patella
- Femur
- Tibia
- Fibula

FIGURE 16.14 The quadriceps muscle demonstrates an eccentric muscle contraction when getting into a sitting position.

Functional rehabilitation

Initially this stage should involve the very basic elements of the sports person's usual sport. For example, a footballer would start with running on the spot or in a straight line. Then they would progress to running up and down hills, then on a diagonal and changing direction. This would then progress on to skill training and involve training the various ball skills required. Once they are able to complete these exercises with no problems, they can commence full training and eventually be ready for competitive play.

REVISION QUESTIONS

1) What is the 'stepladder' approach to rehabilitation?

2) What is the purpose of each of the four stages of this approach?

3) Give examples of exercises you would give:
a) a badminton player
b) a basketball player
c) a gymnast during the functional rehabiliation stage.

Chapter REVISION QUESTIONS

1) Give an example of a sports person of your choice who has sustained a sports injury. Explain what you would have done if you were their sports therapist. Include in your analysis:
- ✪ SALTAPS
- ✪ RICE
- ✪ methods of rehabilitation.

2) Which type of sports injury do you think is the hardest to treat? Explain your answer.

3) Explain why you think footballers tend to be susceptible to sports injuries around the knee.

4) Which type of sport do you think produces the greatest amount of sports injuries? Explain your answer.

5) How would you rehabilitate a racket game sports player who had strained their shoulder muscles?

FURTHER READING

Alter, M. (1996) *Science of Stretching*. Champaign, Ill: Human Kinetics
Bird, S., Black, N. and Newton, P. (1997) *Sports Injuries*. Stanley Thornes
Blakey, P. (1996) *Stretching without Pain*. Bibliotek Books
Guten, G. (1991) *Play Healthy Stay Healthy*. Champaign, Ill: Human Kinetics
Grisogono, V. (1989) *Sport Injury A Self-Help Guide*. John Murray
Hudson, M. (1998) *Sports Therapy A Practical Approach*. Stanley Thornes
McAtee, R. (1999) *Facilitated Stretching*. Campaign, Ill: Human Kinetics
Milroy, Dr P. (1994) *Sports Injuries family Health Guide*. Ward Lock
Read, M. (1997) *Sports Injuries*. Butterworth Heinmann

CHAPTER 17

PRACTICAL SPORTS PERFORMANCE

Practical sports performance is concerned with developing an individual's ability in certain sports. This chapter aims to examine practical performance, both as a player and an official. It looks at improving knowledge and understanding of technical aspects, rules and regulations of sports. This chapter will also look at how to evaluate performance with the aim of suggesting improvements. This is a very practically based topic, so much of the work will be done in the gym or on the training field. Rather than attempt to cover all sports, this chapter will address the above issues in relation to selected examples (which could be applied to other sports).

By the end of this chapter students should be able to:

✪ apply knowledge, skill, proficiency and techniques in at least one team and one individual sport

✪ understand and apply the rules, regulations and scoring systems in the identified sports

✪ demonstrate the ability to officiate in the identified sports

✪ evaluate personal performance and officiating skills in the identified sports.

KNOWLEDGE, SKILL, PROFICIENCY AND TECHNIQUE

Classification

When undertaking to analyse and improve performance in a selected sport, the sport chosen will depend on the resources, facilities, equipment and expertise available. If you are doing it as part of a group, it may be necessary to pick sports in which you have less experience. A good general introduction would be to take part in a number of sessions related to different sports.

Sports can be categorized into team or individual sports. **Team sports** include basketball, cricket, football, hockey, netball, rugby and volleyball. **Individual sports** include athletics, badminton, cycling, golf, gymnastics, rowing, squash, swimming, table tennis and tennis. This is not the only method for categorising sport. For example, sports can be classified as **invasive sports**, in which it is necessary to invade the opponent's half with the aim of scoring points, goals or trys. Basketball, football, hockey, netball and rugby are all invasive sports. Such sports can be analysed in terms of attacking and defending. If you are trying to score, you are attacking, and if you are attempting to stop your opponents scoring, you are defending. Moving from attack to defence, or vice versa, is referred to as the transition period. In these types of sport, a player will come into direct contact with their opponents.

FIGURE 17.1 Volleyball is a non-invasive team sport

Not all team sports are invasive sports. For example, cricket is one of a small group of sports (softball, baseball and rounders) that involve striking and fielding. The aim is to accumulate as many points or runs as possible when it is your turn to bat. Volleyball is another team game that is not invasive. It is a central-net sport; the net divides you from the opposition. The aim is to stop your opponents from returning the ball over the net. The same principles apply to badminton (except the object is a shuttlecock), table tennis and tennis. The main difference between these sports and volleyball is the number of players (six as opposed to one or two) and the use of a racket. Squash is also a racket sport, but it is different in that players occupy the same area of the court.

Some sports (e.g. gymnastics) require the competitors to reproduce a movement or series of movements as accurately as possible. Competitors are then judged on the quality and difficulty of their performance. Diving, figure skating and trampolining fall into this category. In some sports the competition is quite simply a race. In cycling, swimming and some athletic events the athletes race against each other or the clock and the fastest one is the winner. Certain sports may include obstacles to avoid (e.g. skiing and canoeing). In other sports, rather than the fastest being the winner, it could be the person who goes the furthest or the highest (e.g. the long jump or the high jump). Target sports provide another group; archery, golf and rifle shooting are all examples.

Even with such an extensive list of different types of sport, it is still possible to think of sports that do not fall into any of these categories (e.g. boxing and snooker).

Component parts

When trying to improve performance in any sport it is necessary to break the sport up into its component parts. All sports can be divided up into a range of skills. It is important, when examining skills, to look at the purpose of the skill in addition to the way it is produced. The sport of volleyball, for example, can be divided into five basic or core techniques.

1   The volley is the most common method of passing the ball in volleyball (hence the name). It consists of passing the ball overhead using both hands. It is used to control the ball when received from the opposition, other than from a smash, (e.g. from a service or when the ball has been volleyed back over the net). It is used to set up an attack and it can be used to place the ball back over the net (e.g. when the opposition players are out of position).

STUDENT ACTIVITY

Classification

Classify different sports into the following categories:

✪ power production (involving generating speed and power)

✪ movement replication (producing a desired movement, as in gymnastics)

✪ coincidence anticipation (requiring co-ordinated movements).

2   The dig or forearm pass is an underarm action (both arms) that is used to recover the ball from a serve or smash, or when the ball has been played close to the ground. Occasionally it can be used to return the ball over the net when in difficulty.

3   The smash or spike is an attacking shot, hit one-handed and above the height of the net. The aim is to prevent the opposition from returning the ball.

4   The serve is the method of introducing the ball into the game. For skilled performers this would be considered as an attacking shot, with the aim of making it difficult for the opposition to return the ball.

5   The final skill is the block, which is a defensive action that attempts to rebound or reduce the speed of the ball when smashed by an opponent.

Having determined the core techniques, you then need to outline the technical qualities of each action (i.e. the coaching points or how to perform the skill). Take the volley as an example. The first key point would be the body position or stance. This would apply in the vast majority of sports (e.g. shooting in basketball, passing in hockey, batting in cricket, hitting a golf ball and riding position in cycling). Where should your feet be? What about the hands and fingers? Should the knees be straight? Where is bodyweight distributed? Will you be front on or side on? These are the questions that need addressing when coaching the skill.

Next, there is the execution of the skill. When and where should the ball be struck? Where should you aim for? After this is the follow through. This can include preparation for the next action, so it is important to consider in what position you will end up after executing the skill.

With all this information it is possible to build up a model of the skill, what it should look like and how you should perform it. This is essential for coaching somebody how to perform the skill and when trying to correct errors in performance. The same method of breaking a skill down can be done in individual sports. For example, sprinting can be divided into the start, the pick up phase, maintaining top speed and dipping at the line. Each section could be analysed in detail to look at its purpose and how it should be carried out effectively.

Tactical awareness

In addition to the technical skills, tactical awareness is important. For example, using volleyball as an example again, players not only have to know how to perform a skill, but also when to perform it. They need to know where abouts on court they should be, where their team-mates are and where the opposition players are. Tactical skills in this situation are as important as technical skills. Setting the ball to be hit if a hitter is not in position will be of no benefit. Equally, setting the ball to be hit against the opponent's best blocker may be ill advised. If the person volleying the ball is setting up an attack (as is the job of the setter), they are aiming to get the ball in the best position possible for an attacking shot while trying to disguise their intentions from the opposition.

It may be that the sport you are analysing is an individual sport (e.g. sprinting). There would be fewer tactical considerations in this example, but there are always some tactics that apply. In sprinting these might include being first out of the blocks, which puts pressure on the opposition, or if a series of races is involved, conserving energy for later rounds.

STUDENT ACTIVITY

Skills
Select one team and one individual sport and discus the main skills within that sport. Explain coaching points, reasons why the skill would be performed and expected outcomes.

Assessment
From a sport of your choice, devise a method of assessing performance in the skills mentioned above. It could be based on accuracy, time or body position for example.

Assessment

When coaching and analysing skill, it is essential to have some means of assessing ability. The method used most often is just to observe the performer performing the skill. An experienced coach or assessor can look at an athlete/player and determine their ability level and highlight errors in technique. If a more formal method of assessment is required, video footage of the skill can be taken or an observation checklist can be devised. Alternatively, rather than concentrating on the performance of the skill, the end result could be assessed. This means looking at the outcome as opposed to the method of achieving it. It could be that a target is introduced, so if coaching serving, having a score for each area of the target would give an indication of how accurate the server was. Another method is to count the number of times the performer successfully completes the skill.

STUDENT ACTIVITY

Skills test
Devise a skills test that could be used by groups of people in particular sports. For example, a basketball skills test involving passing, dribbling, shooting and agility could be designed.

FIGURE 17.2   A volleyball smash

An interesting way to build enjoyment into the assessment is to devise a skills test. For example, a skills test to assess the skill of smashing in volleyball could involve using targets (e.g. smashing towards a certain area), timed elements (e.g. the number of successful hits in a certain time) and some competition (e.g. introducing blockers).

RULES, REGULATIONS AND SCORING SYSTEMS

Objects and timing

The rules and regulations of a sport govern the way it is played. The first consideration in any sport is how to win. How can one team or competitor win the match, game, race or competition? The simplest method is first over the line, and includes cycling, swimming, running and motor racing.

Some sports are time dependant. A game of rugby lasts for 80 minutes, consisting of two halves of 40 minutes. The team with the most points at the end of the game wins; if the scores are tied the game is declared a draw. Rugby is played with a running clock, i.e. time is continuous. Time is only stopped for injuries and other such stoppages, so the end of the game contains a short period of injury (or added) time. Not all time-dependant sports use a running clock. In basketball, the clock is stopped every time the ball goes out of play. Although the official time of the game is 40 minutes, the game will last much longer. If the scores are level at the end of a basketball game, the game is not a draw; a five-minute extra period is played to determine the winner. If additional extra periods are needed they are used. There are some time-dependant sports that can be decided before the total time has elapsed. In test cricket, there are five days in which to complete the match, but the team with the highest score after two innings is the winner. If after this time neither team has won, the game is a draw (unless the scores are level, in which case it is a tie).

In a number of sports the first team or player to reach a certain score or number of sets is the winner. Tennis and volleyball are examples. In some sports it is not a set score but the highest score that wins. This would be the case in gymnastics.

Although there are undoubtedly exceptions and we have only examined a few sports, it would seem that the objective of most sports is to get the highest, fastest or furthest score, whether it is measured in sets, goals, baskets, points, seconds, metres, tries, holes, games, matches or runs.

Even though some sports are not time dependant (e.g. tennis), time can still have an impact on the game. The longer a game lasts, the more tired players become and the more fitness comes into play. The amount of time an average game, match or race lasts will determine the type of training that an athlete does.

Scoring

There are many different scoring systems in sport. One method of scoring is to have a goal into which a ball must be thrown, hit, struck or kicked (e.g. football, hockey and handball). Each goal advances the score by one. In certain sports a goal may count for more; for example, a goal from open play in basketball (referred to as a basket) can count for two or three points depending on where the shot was taken from. Rather than having a goal, some sports require the players to advance the ball to a certain area. In rugby union, the object is to ground the ball on or behind the try line, which results in five points being scored. In rugby league, a try is worth four points. There are also other methods of scoring in rugby: points are awarded for conversions, penalties and drop goals.

Several sports require that the player is serving in order to score any points (e.g. badminton and squash).

As can be seen in the examples, the number of points scored for a particular action varies from sport to sport. In cricket, it is possible to score anywhere between one and six runs from a single shot. In American football, six points are awarded for a touchdown, three for a field goal and one for an extra point. It is also possible to gain two points via a safety (tackling a player with the ball in his own end zone). In golf, the scoring (for stoke play) is simple – the player who takes the least number of total shots is the winner. In match play golf, each hole is won or lost (or halved if neither player wins). Therefore, the player who wins most holes is the winner.

Team numbers and substitutions

Beside the timing and scoring of games, another important factor in the nature of play is the number of players allowed and the timing and number of any substitutions. A number of sports require 11 players (e.g. football, cricket and hockey). Basketball only has five players, while volleyball has six and netball seven. A rugby league team consists of 13 players and a rugby union team 15.

The players in a team can be changed through substitutions. In many sports there are limits on the number of substitutes that can be used in a game. However, some sports allow unlimited substitutions, that is, players can be replaced and then re-enter the game (e.g. basketball). In other sports, once substituted a player must remain off the field (e.g. football). Some sports permit blood replacements for the duration of an injured player's treatment (e.g. rugby). Not all sports allow substitutions, or do so only in exceptional circumstances. In cricket, a substitute is only sanctioned for an injured player, and the substitute cannot bat, bowl or field in specialist positions.

Sports not only have different rules regarding the number of players and substitutes, they also require different player numbers or letters on display.

Conditions of play

The rules and regulations of sport also cover the facilities that are necessary in order to play or take part in a particular sport. A number of sports can be played on different surfaces. Tennis is played on grass courts, clay courts and hard courts. Volleyball can be played indoors or outdoors. Outdoor volleyball is beach volleyball, a game played with only two players on each side as opposed to six in the indoor game.

Beside specialist facilities, certain sports require specific equipment. This equipment is used to protect the players. A hockey goalkeeper wears padding and a helmet for this purpose. Football players wear shin pads to protect their legs. Other rules exist that are aimed at an individual's safety. In the triathlon

there are rules concerning the temperature of the water that the competitors are expected to swim in. If the water is too cold the race must be stopped.

All of the rules and regulations concerning different sports can be found via the sport's national governing body. These provide an invaluable source of information about all aspects of the sport (results, coaching, rules, clubs and links to other organisations). In a number of cases, national governing bodies change the rules as laid down by the international federation or associations. These are normally only minor changes.

STUDENT ACTIVITY

Governing bodies

Investigate the regulations set out at least three sports governing bodies. http://www.sportengland.org is a good place to start it lists many governing bodies of sport.

OFFICIATING

The job of an official is to enforce the rules of a sport and keep it under control. In addition, officials may take on the role of starter, timer and scorer. Officials need a detailed knowledge of the rules of the sport, plus the ability to apply the rules in a competitive situation. Officials also have to ensure that the game or competition is safe. Equipment and facilities are checked prior to a match, game or race.

Different sports have different roles and responsibilities and even different names for their officials. The senior officials are usually referred to as umpires, referees or judges. Each will have a designated role. They may have to concentrate on particular players or a certain area of the court or field of play. If a disagreement occurs one official will have the final say. In the case of uncertainty, in some sports it is possible to seek the advice of another official who has the use of video footage of the game. In cricket, this official is called the third umpire, while in rugby league they are referred to as the video referee. The specific events that they can adjudicate on are laid out by the sport's governing body, and the main official on the field of play will ask for assistance from this official. They cannot just pass on information as they see fit.

A lot of sports also have other officials, such as assistants, line judges, scorers and timekeepers. The number and duties of these officials depend on the sport and on the level of competition. The rules will state the officials that are required, but in reality, especially at a local level, the senior officials may take on the duties of the assistants if none are available.

Assessing the performance of an official involves examining their control of a game or match. It should include looking at their knowledge of the rules and how they communicate with fellow officials and players. Assessing a match official is quite a common occurrence. If officials wish to progress to a higher level they must undergo assessment to see if they are suitable to move to the next level. It is not only their officiating that will be assessed, but also their fitness. Competitive sport is physically demanding. The speed of play is often fast, yet matches can be quite long in duration. In order to keep up with what is going on, it is essential that officials have a good level of fitness. The higher the standard of the competition, the more demanding the level of player performance, so the fitter the officials need to be.

STUDENT ACTIVITY

Fitness
Assess what you think the basic fitness requirements are for five officials from a variety of sports.
Officiate
Officiate at least two different sports (individual and one team).

Consider things like:
✪ player control
✪ timing
✪ specific rules
✪ playing advantage.
Write a short report on the match, game, race or competition.

EVALUATING PERFORMANCE

With a thorough knowledge of a sport and the skills involved in that sport it is possible to carry out a systematic observation of a performer in order to gather information about their performance. This will usually be done by a coach or teacher, based on a visual observation. The observation could be an overall impression of a whole movement, or it could have a more narrow focus by just examining part of a skill. A good strategy for observation is to divide the movement into phases. It could be that the whole skill is observed initially and then certain parts are selected for further analysis. This would be a good way to observe weaknesses in performance. Watch the whole skill to locate the weakness, then observe that aspect of the skill further.

It is important when evaluating a performer that the performance is also assessed in a competitive situation. Evaluating skills without the pressure of match conditions may produce different results. A player might serve 9 out of 10 balls in court during practice, but only 5 out of 10 in a match. This would show that their technical ability is good, but that during a game they cannot reproduce this ability. The level of the performer will affect the number of observations that are required. Players with little experience are highly inconsistent in performance, so more observations are needed. With more skilled performers there is greater consistency, so evaluating a few performances may be sufficient. Video offers the opportunity to record the movement and analyse it in more detail. It is also possible to play back the skill to the performer so they can evaluate their own performance, or they can have aspects of the movement highlighted to them. Other benefits include the ability to slow down or freeze the action to emphasise specific points.

Evaluation of performance includes identifying both strengths and weaknesses in the performance. However, observation and evaluation are only the first steps in the process of analysing performance. After evaluating the performance it is necessary to identify the underlying causes of the strengths and weaknesses. That is, based on an optimum model of performance, what are they doing right and wrong and why? For example, as a golf coach you may observe that your player is consistently slicing the ball (that is the weakness). You need to work out what is causing this. The final stage is to implement strategies to improve performance. What can the player or athlete do to improve? This is where the coach will feed back to a player on what they are doing wrong, what is causing it and what they can do to correct the problem. The last part is very important. It is no use simply identifying the problem; the solution is what the player is after. Equally, too much information is difficult to take in, so it should be concentrated on a few key points. The amount, timing and type of feedback given to a performer are important considerations in effectiveness. Visual feedback is very effective, for example, when coaching batting in cricket, chalk can be used to draw the correct footwork positions on the floor.

STUDENT ACTIVITY

Analysis
This could be done as a small group project, with the group presenting their analysis and recommendations.

1   Obtain film footage of a subject performing a skill in a sport of your choice. Compare this performance with a model of correct performance (film footage of an elite performer, for example).
2   Identify strengths and weakness in performance and suggest remedial action to correct technique.

TECHNOLOGICAL DEVELOPMENTS IN SPORT

Technology has long been a part of sport. With the development of new materials and the large amount of money that is now involved in sport, scientists are creating sports equipment and technologies that are dramatically changing performance. They are changing the nature of the game, the skills necessary to succeed in the sport, the injuries associated with the sport and the cost of participation. This chapter examines the impact technology has had on sport. It looks at how technology has shaped the development of certain sports and how current technologies are being use to improve performance. The ethical considerations of technological development are also discussed. The cases used are not an extensive list of all the technology within sport, but offer selected examples.

By the end of this chapter students should be able to:

✪   investigate the evolutionary development of technology in sport, its applications and implications

✪   describe the current application of technology to enhance sports training and performance, and examine the potential implications of technological development for the future of sport

✪   describe the potential positive and negative effects of technological developments in sport.

THE DEVELOPMENT, APPLICATIONS AND IMPLICATIONS OF TECHNOLOGY

Materials and equipment

Pole vault

Technology has had a major effect on some sports. The pole vault is a good example. In the 1896 Olympics, competitors used a bamboo pole in the pole vault event, the winning height was just over 3 m and the competition took place on grass. As the height vaulted started to increase, mats were used for landing. The world record increased steadily from this time until the 1960s when, suddenly, with the introduction of new materials, the record height increased dramatically. Initially aluminium was used for the pole, and more recently fibreglass and carbon fibre. Carbon fibre and fibreglass are composite materials, which waste little energy when bending and have a good strength-to-weight ratio. Currently the world record is around double what it was back in

FIGURE 18.1 The pole vault has developed greatly over the years

1896. Carbon fibre is the main material used in pole vaults, because it is light, durable, has a high stiffness and is resistant to twisting.

Bats and rackets

The use of advanced material in sport is not always welcomed. Aluminium has been used in the design of baseball and cricket bats, but both sports' governing bodies decided to ban them because they made the ball travel too far and they damaged the ball. Despite this, softball bats are made from aluminium as well as titanium. These softball bats have bigger **sweet spots** and lead to greater ball velocity off the bat.

In tennis, rather than ban certain materials, the International Tennis Federation introduced restrictions on the size and design of tennis rackets. Early tennis rackets were made of wood, then steel and aluminium. Up until 1978, a tennis racket was defined as the implement used to hit the ball, which meant a player could use anything as a racket. Manufactures were increasing the size of the racket and altering its design. One designer came up with the 'spaghetti stringing system', which allowed players to impart greater topspin on the ball. It created a big talking point in the tennis world.

The current target in designing tennis rackets is to minimise the vibration of the racket, which equates to less risk of injury but also maximises power and accuracy. The high stiffness of carbon fibre makes it ideal for imparting high forces to the ball and reducing vibration of the racket upon impact with the ball. Kevlar is also used due to its additional strength, durability and ability to dampen vibrations.

Volleyball

In some sports, technology is used solely to prevent injury or to stop equipment becoming damaged. Volleyball is a good example. Beach volleyballs are made from nylon and plastic because these materials have better durability and maintain the shape of the ball more easily. The environment (heat, salt water and sand) of a beach will ruin a leather ball, which will split and can become waterlogged and heavy.

Even the nets are made from nylon and plastic, which protects them from the ultraviolet (UV) rays of the sun. In indoor volleyball, kneepads are made from plastic foams, like ethylene vinyl acetate (EVA), covered with a softer elastic material. These protect athletes from bruising, fractures and friction burns associated with contacting the floor.

Cycling

Aerodynamics and material science play a big part in cycling performance. Cycling is a constant battle against air resistance – the faster a cyclist travels the more air resistance they encounter. There are two problems: drag and direct friction (also known as surface friction). An object moving through the air disturbs the air flowing around it, which forces the air to separate from the object's surface. A region of low pressure builds up behind the object, resulting in drag. Aerodynamic designs help the air move more smoothly around a body and reduce drag. Direct friction occurs when moving air comes into contact with the outer surface of the rider and the bicycle. Direct friction is less of a factor than drag.

Many different materials have been used in the design of racing bikes. Two important properties of materials used in bike design are yield strength and ultimate strength. When you bend some objects and then let go they will return to their original form. The point at which you bend an object and it will not return to its original form is a measure of its **yield strength**. There is also a point where it will break, and this is the material's **ultimate strength**. Road bikes used to be made of steel, which has an excellent ultimate strength, with lower yield strength. This means that a steel frame will bend well before it breaks, decreasing the chance of a catastrophic break down. Steel is also the most affordable of the materials used to make bikes. The major drawback of steel is its relatively high weight. Aluminium is also used to build road bikes. However, aluminium has yield strength very close to its ultimate strength and is therefore prone to breaking. Aluminium frames have oversized tubing and thick welds to lessen the chance of the frame breaking. Even with oversized tubing, an aluminium frame is lighter than a steel frame. Recently, titanium has been used to build frames for road bikes. It has a great strength-to-weight ratio, being strong yet light. Titanium alloys are considerably stronger than aluminium, carbon fibre or steel frames. Titanium is, however, an expensive metal. Like titanium, carbon fibre is a relatively new choice of material for performance road bikes. It has similar properties to titanium in that it is light, with a high ultimate strength and relatively low yield strength. This means that frames made of these materials are extremely light and resilient. However, as with titanium, carbon fibre is expensive.

Frame builders and designers have been working on creating more aerodynamically efficient designs. Recent designs have concentrated on changing from round tubes to oval or tear-shaped tubes. There is a fine line between maintaining a good strength-to-weight ratio while improving aerodynamic efficiency. Improvements to wheels have also made a big impact on the sport. A standard spoked wheel creates a lot of drag as it rotates. In disc wheels, discs made of aluminium alloys or carbon fibre composites replace the spokes in conventional wheels. While heavier than spoked wheels, they produce less drag and turbulence when they spin.

While improvements to frames and components have improved aerodynamic performance, the cyclist is the largest obstacle to improvement. The human body is not very aerodynamic. Body positioning is important; road cyclists use drop bars to reduce the area they present to the oncoming air, which helps reduce the amount of resistance they must overcome. Reducing the frontal area helps riders increase their speed and efficiency. In addition to positioning, small details like clothing can also make a big difference in reducing friction. Tight-fitting synthetic clothing is worn by riders to reduce direct friction. Tactics can also play a part. In road racing, cyclists group together in a pack known as the **peloton**. Cyclists who are in the peloton can save over 30% more energy than a cyclist who is not in the pelotan.

Canoeing and rowing

Kayaks and canoes are made almost exclusively from plastics. They used to be made of wood, but wood is heavy, breakable and easily distorted, while plastics withstand even the most extreme conditions. Now boats are constructed from a number of reinforced plastic composites, including carbon fibre, fibreglass and Kevlar.

Rowing boats also used to be made of wood. Again, they are now made from a wide range of plastic or plastic-based materials, including fibreglass and carbon fibre. Paddles and oars need to be strong, yet light and manoeuvrable, so they are also made from plastic and fibre-reinforced materials. Helmets, although not required by the rules in kayaking, are worn by many paddlers. Helmets are most often made from carbon fibre composites, which are light and allow kayakers to move their heads quickly.

Golf

Golf clubs have evolved enormously over the years. Modern drivers have shafts constructed from carbon fibre and club heads made from oversized hollow titanium. The overall weight of the club has decreased, while the length of the club has increased. The bigger club head has the mass concentrated around the outside of the hitting face. The result is a club that can hit the ball a greater distance due to the ability to generate more speed, but also a club than can hit the ball more accurately due to a bigger sweet spot.

Javelin

In 1984, the International Amateur Athletic Federation (IAAF) adopted new rules to ensure javelins would land point first, so the landing position would be known exactly. When a javelin is thrown, air travels around it. The airflow is inclined to separate on the upper surface. Flow separation, as with the cyclist, increases the drag force. With a javelin, the direction of the force is opposite to that of the gravitational force, that is, it provides lift. Therefore, the separation of the flow around the javelin actually increases the flight time. New javelins have been designed to stop them travelling too far and endangering athletes at the other end of the track. This design, with a new weight distribution, prevents the javelin from floating and shortens flight time and distance.

Facilities and surfaces

Sometimes it is not equipment that uses technology, but the playing surface of a sporting environment. Synthetic pitches are used in hockey and football (especially five-a-side football). However, these pitches are no longer allowed in top-flight football. The advantages of a synthetic surface include consistency of bounce, ability to be used in all weather conditions, good grip and low maintenance costs. Some sports use technology in less obvious ways, for example swimming pools are designed to minimise wave interference, allowing swimmers to go faster.

Technology is also used in the design of sports stadiums. Many stadiums around the world have retractable roofs, i.e. that can open and shut. The Skydome in Toronto is an example; it is used mainly for baseball.

STUDENT ACTIVITY

Materials
Describe the benefits of certain materials in a variety of sports. This could be done in groups, with each group given a particular material to investigate. Each group could then present their findings to the rest of the groups.

Roofs create a particular problem to stadium designers. They are needed to keep spectators dry, but they should not detract from the atmosphere inside the stadium. Consider the Olympic Stadium in Sydney, which was built to house over 100 000 people. Placing a traditional roof on this stadium would have meant building a massive structure that would block out natural light. Therefore, the roof was constructed of polycarbonate, which weighs less and allows light to pass through it. A similar roof can be found on the San Siro stadium in Milan.

Clothing

The development of new fibres and new processes can be used to benefit performance. The development of elastic materials has had an enormous impact on sportswear. Many sports require competitors to wear skin-tight clothing for aerodynamic benefits.

FIGURE 18.2 Clothing can make an athlete more aerodynamic

Elastic materials are also useful in treating injuries (e.g. compression bandages). Materials have been designed with **wicking properties** that draw moisture away from the skin. It is important to draw moisture away from the skin so that it does not become damp and cold. Wicking properties are brought into play either by the fibre or the finish that is put on fabric. Breathable outer layers are also important. All clothing should be breathable to allow sweat to pass out of clothing, keeping the body warm and dry. Materials such as Pertex and Goretex allow this to happen. Goretex also stops rain entering the clothing. Pertex does this to an extent, but is more shower proof than rain proof. However, Pertex is more breathable than Goretex, so is better in high-intensity activities were the body generates lots of heat. Many manufactures have developed similar materials to Goretex. These fabrics allow sweat to be released so people stay dry in wet conditions. This sweat transfer helps prevent heat loss via **conduction** in cold conditions by keeping the body and clothing layers drier. In adventurous sports (climbing, walking, skiing) clothing is normally made up of a series of layers to keep the body warm and dry. The base layer next to the skin is made from synthetic fibres rather than natural fibres such as cotton. These materials are designed to wick moisture away from the skin. In addition, they wash easily and will dry relatively quickly. The mid layer is usually a thin fleece top or jacket. Most people use a waterproof as their outer layer.

Swimming

Technology has had a major influence on competitive swimwear in recent years. Full-length suits are now commonplace in high-level competition. These suits have been designed to reduce drag and friction when moving through the water. The design of the material used in these suits is based on the V-shaped ridges on a shark's skin, called dermal denticles, which decrease drag and turbulence around the shark's body. These allow the surrounding water to pass over the shark more effectively. The material is also very elastic to improve fit and range of movement.

One of the concerns in using such a suit is the possibility of a swimmer becoming too hot, although research has shown that even after two hours of training there is no increase in a swimmer's core temperature compared with wearing ordinary swimwear. The suits have been approved for competition by the Fédération International de Natation Amateur (FINA).

Technology is also used in other areas of swimming. Goggles for swimmers are made from polycarbonate, a shatter-resistant plastic. Polycarbonate lenses are scratch resistant, durable and have **high optical** clarity. Before the introduction of polycarbonate, goggles were made from glass. The lenses were not as durable and posed serious danger to the eye and face if shattered. Manufacturers use a PVC plastic strap and neoprene seals to keep the goggles comfortably on the face and make them watertight.

TRAINING AND PER-FORMANCE ENHANCE-MENT

Altitude

It is well established that exercising at high altitude affects performance, especially at a physiological level. The ability to perform intense exercise when at high altitude is impaired. The reduced oxygen availability at high altitude will lead to maximum oxygen uptake being reduced compared with that at sea level. Also, heart rate and breathing rate and will be higher for the same intensity of exercise at high altitude. During recovery, heart rate also takes longer to return to normal. Athletes competing at high altitude should have an acclimatisation period of around three weeks. This period will see improvements in the body's physiological response to exercise. These improvements are due in part to an increased haemoglobin concentration, pulmonary ventilation and more blood in the capillaries. The end result is more oxygen reaching the working muscles. This improvement in performance has been used by athletes to try and benefit their performance when at sea level. This is known as altitude training. Hypobaric (low pressure) chambers can also be used, although this type of equipment may be expensive. Evidence shows that living at high altitude and training at sea level could be more beneficial. In general, training at high altitude improves exercise performance at high altitude but not at sea level.

Fitness and performance assessment

The advent of sports scientists, fitness coaches and specific training facilities has had a big influence on sport. Specialist equipment is used in training and testing the performance capacity of players. Treadmills and cycle ergometers are used for the physiological analysis of performance. Spirometers, body fat measures, heart monitors, sphygmomanometers and blood analysis equipment are used to examine physical condition. Isokinetic machines are regularly used to examine muscle function and strength. These machines can also be useful in increasing muscle strength, particularly when recovering from injury. Force plates can be used to provide information on force characteristics of an activity. Video analysis is used to examine skills with the intention of improving performance and reducing injury risk.

Although injury prevention has become more successful due to knowledge of biomechanics, injuries will always be common in sport. However, players are recovering more quickly due to advances in technology. Technologies such as ultrasound can stimulate the repair of soft tissue injuries by producing vibration. Laser therapy decreases pain and inflammation and increases blood supply to the injured area.

Heart rate monitors

Heart rate monitors are a vital part of training in some sports. They can be used to evaluate the intensity of exercise and set targets for training and competition. Heart rate monitors are light and do not interfere with performance in certain sports (e.g. cyclists, triathletes). They can be used to ensure players are working at or above target intensity. Heart rate monitors can also be used to measure the performance of an athlete during a race and to feed back information to a computer to provide a detailed analysis of the event.

Match analysis

Match analysis involves looking at the ability of players during a game. Various match analysis systems exist, offering various levels of data and information, such as the number of passes, headers, shots, trys, assists and tackles in a match. Specific match events can be input in real time (during the game) or after the match. Modern systems use cameras that can be linked directly to a computer and the film analysed straightaway. Computerised systems that automatically calculate the positions and track the movements of players using camera, video and computer technology are becoming more commonplace.

The Australian Institute for Sport has an audiovisual services section. It provides video analysis equipment that players can use during competition. The audiovisual team can send in specially shot sports footage of different competitors to any location. This footage can be analysed and used by a coach to make changes during a competition.

Video referee or umpire

In recent years many sports authorities have come under pressure to use video technology where official's decisions are in doubt. Rugby league uses a video referee to decide whether, for instance, a try should be allowed. The third umpire is common in test cricket and one-day internationals, where video replays have been used for decisions on run outs. A number of sports have been reluctant to use video technology even though it would be relatively easy to use. It would take less than a minute for a football referee to be advised if an incident was a penalty or not, but FIFA (Fédération Internationale de Football Association) believes that the constant referrals of decisions to a video official would disrupt the flow of the game. Football flows more than any of the other sports where video replays are used. In cricket, the ball is already dead by the time a decision is required, while in football the game may still be going on.

POSITIVE AND NEGATIVE EFFECTS OF TECHNOLOGY

The use of technology in sport has been demonstrated. Large improvements in performance have been made in some sports. However, the use of technology in sport equipment presents some ethical questions. Performance can be improved by using technology, but should there be any limits on the use of such technology? What about the cost of this technology? If performance is due solely to technology, the competitors with the most money will have an advantage. Is it the idea of sport to find the most accomplished athlete or the best scientist?

Sport needs to protect the essential elements of competition – the idea of a challenge. For example, cycling is a test of speed, power and endurance. This always needs to be the case. It is a difficult dilemma. We all want technology to benefit sport by making performance better, faster, more powerful and reducing the risk of injury. We want improved training facilities and equipment, however, most of all we want competition. Consider the dullness of 2002 Formula One motor racing season. Improved technology may have made for superior performance, but if this technology is not available to all competitors, the outcome becomes predictable. Motor racing spectators do not just want to see fast cars, they want to see a competitive race.

STUDENT ACTIVITY

Sports technology

Discuss the positive and negative effects of technology in sport. Consider safety factors, new training methods, cost of equipment and risk of injury. Again, this could take the form of a debate or presentation with one group presenting positive aspects and another group presenting negative aspects.

REVISION QUESTIONS

1) To what uses has carbon fibre been put in sport?
2) Which sports use titanium? For what do they use it?
3) What are the benefits of using aluminium in sport?
4) Outline the recent developments in swimming clothing.
5) Which sports have benefited from the use of video technology?

FURTHER READING

Shrier, E. W. and Allman, W. F. (1987) *Newton at the Bat*. Englewood Cliffs, N.J: Prentice Hall

SPORTS INDUSTRY EXPERIENCE

Ultimately, the aim of an education is to prepare a student for a career in their chosen field. In this case, you are studying for a career in a sports-related field. Luckily, the sports industry as a whole is expanding rapidly and becoming more diverse. During the years that you study your subject it is advisable that you seek as much hands-on experience as you can. This takes several forms: first, actually playing sport and experiencing the different types of facilities and services; secondly, seeking part-time employment in a relevant sport or leisure facility and thirdly, undertaking periods of work placement in sporting environments.

This chapter is designed to give students an understanding of the sports industry and the types of occupation available. By the end of the chapter students should be able to:

- ✪ understand the difference between private, public and voluntary sector facilities

- ✪ differentiate between the types of occupation available

- ✪ prepare materials for job applications

- ✪ evaluate their experiences in the workplace.

SECTORS OF PROVISION

The provision of sport in Britain has happened in a fairly haphazard manner. Historically, it has been the responsibility of groups of individuals to form and manage their own clubs and teams for other like-minded people. There are still many clubs and teams operating that were formed in the nineteenth century. Occasionally the government has become involved. For example, the Baths and Wash-Houses Act of 1846 saw the development of swimming pools, the aim being to raise the standards of hygiene among the general public.

The provision of sports facilities and opportunities in Britain is the result of the interaction between the public, private and voluntary sectors. Each of these sectors will be examined in turn.

BTEC NATIONAL IN SPORT AND EXERCISE SCIENCE

Definitions

The public sector

The public sector is defined as institutions funded by money collected from the public in the form of direct and indirect taxes.

The public sector

The public sector collects money through income tax, community charges, business taxes, valued added taxes on spending and national insurance. It then makes decisions on how to spend this money. These decisions are based on priorities and are seen as political decisions. For example, the current Labour Government sees the National Health Service and education system as the priorities for spending. This position is the basis for their decisions on spending. This government does not see sport as being important and allocates only a relatively small amount of its budget to sports facilities, organisations and performers.

The public sector is made up of national government and local government (or local authorities), each of which have different responsibilities in sports provision.

FIGURE 19.1 National government's responsibilities in sports provision

National government is funded by taxes (income tax, VAT, business taxes) and receives money from the national lottery (lotto). Its role in sport is indirect, as it does not fund buildings or the running of facilities, but provides money to other organisations to spend on sport (see Figure 19.1). It has a role as an 'enabler' and the main recipient is Sport England. National government provides grants and loans to local authorities, as well as offering technical assistance. Sport is the responsibility of the Department of Culture, Media and Sport, formerly the Department of National Heritage, and in particular the Minister for Sport. This Department has the following roles in sport:

✪ represents interests of sport, arts, tourism and heritage

✪ promotes sporting success at the highest levels

✪ helps develop government sporting strategy

✪ funds the Sports Councils in Britain and Northern Ireland

✪ funds other agencies involved in sports provision

✪ distributes money raised by the national lottery.

Sport England

Sport England was formed by Royal Charter in January 1997 to replace the GB Sports Council. The restructuring of the Sports Council was announced in 1995 after extensive consultations dating back to 1987. This consultation period resulted in the government policy paper *Sport: Raising the Game*. The GB Sports Council was replaced by Sport England, responsible for the development of sport in England. The Sports Councils for Scotland, Northern Ireland and Wales were virtually unchanged, while a new organisation, the UK Sports Council (now UK Sport) took responsibility for issues at UK level.

Sport England is accountable to the government via the Secretary of State for Culture, Media and Sport. Its work is assessed by the House of Commons through the Culture, Media and Sport Select Committee and the Public Accounts Committee.

The members of the council of Sport England are appointed by the Secretary of State for Culture, Media and Sport. For example, Trevor Brooking is the Chair of Sport England. The head office of Sport England is based on Euston Road in London, and there are ten regional offices across England.

The work of Sport England can be seen as being threefold. In summary it is:

✪   getting more people involved in sport

✪   providing more places to play sport

✪   winning more medals through higher standards of performance.

Involving more people in sport

Sport England currently has three programmes working to involve more people in sport. They are Active Schools, to get schoolchildren off to the right start; Active Sports, to support sports people and help them get more from their sport; and Active Communities, to provide sport for all.

The GB Sports Council had previously run successful campaigns such as Sport for All (1972–1977), 50+ and All to Play For (1983–1984) and Ever Thought of Sport (1985–1986).

More places to play sport

Sport England aims to ensure that the right facilities are provided in the right places and managed to high standards. It is involved in planning, design, development and management stages, but mainly in an advisory role rather than owning and managing facilities.

More medals through high standards of performance

Sport England supports the development of excellence by running initiatives such as the World Class Performance programme.

Sport England is also responsible for running the administration of five national sports centres. It must be noted that the centres are actually managed by a private company, Leisure Connection, having been put out to private tender. The centres and the sports they provide are:

✪   Bisham Abbey – tennis, weightlifting, soccer, hockey and squash

✪   Crystal Palace – athletics, swimming, martial arts and basketball

✪   Lilleshall – soccer, hockey, cricket, gymnastics, table tennis and archery

✪   Holme Pierrepont – water-based activities

✪   Plas y Brenin – mountain and outdoor activities.

STUDENT ACTIVITY

Find out the following information regarding the government's role in sport.

1   Who is the Secretary of State for Department of Culture, Media and Sport?

2   Who is the Minister for Sport?

3   Where is your local office of Sport England or Sports Council for Scotland, Northern Ireland and Wales?

4   What is the address of your local office?

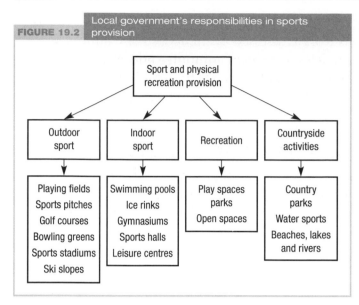

FIGURE 19.2 Local government's responsibilities in sports provision

Local government

Local government or local authorities are responsible for providing facilities for sport and physical recreations. Provision is usually divided into the areas shown in Figure 19.2.

Facilities in the public sector are usually named after the town or city they are in, for example, we have Colchester Leisure Centre, Watford Baths and Wimbledon Recreation Centre.

The organisation of local authorities

Local government is broken down into two tiers:

1 County Councils, e.g. Hertfordshire

2 District Councils, e.g. Watford or Dacorum.

London is an exception and has unitary authorities, such as the London boroughs of Havering and Hillingdon. Other exceptions are in areas of large population such as Manchester, Birmingham, Leeds and Newcastle.

County and district councils have different responsibilities. County councils are concerned with 'broad', county-wide issues such as education, the police, the fire service, highways and traffic and the social services. District councils are concerned with local issues such as sport and recreation facilities, housing, refuse collection and food, safety and hygiene.

Some areas have parish councils as part of the second tier. These are involved in planning matters and very local issues. They may be involved in providing for sport through the use of parish halls and village halls.

STUDENT ACTIVITY

The government (national and local) spends around £1000m a year on sport. There are many courses to study sport in Britain and there is a huge amount of media coverage of sport. Thus, we can assume that sport is significant in British society. But why? What are the benefits of playing, watching and talking about sport? Answer the following questions to understand the importance of sport in our society.

1 List the ways you can think of that sport contributes to the British economy.

2 What benefits does sport have for participants and spectators? Consider why you participate in or watch sport.

3 What are the social benefits of sports participation and watching sport? How does it improve the world we live in?

4 What are the international benefits of sports participation?

5 What are the educational benefits of sports participation?

How are local authorities funded?

The majority of funding will come from the council tax and will go to the county council, with the rest going to the local authority and some to the county police force. Other sources include receipts from trading, such as leisure centre entry fees and rents from council housing, loans from banks and grants from national government.

Private sector provision for sport

Private sector sport is provided by individuals or groups of individuals (companies) who invest their own money in facilities. As a result these facilities are usually named after people, such as David Lloyd clubs, although some have a brand name, such as Virgin Active or Cannons.

The private sector provides sports facilities for two main reasons:

1   to make a return on their investment for themselves and their shareholders

2   to make a profit out of sport.

Claims are sometimes made that it is for other altruistic reasons, such as improving the standards of a sport or improving the community the facilities are in, but they would not exist unless they could make a profit.

What types of facilities does the private sector provide?

The private sector provides for sports increasing in demand. It is able to respond quickly to new trends or to instigate new trends. Government-owned facilities find it takes them a lot longer to respond to trends because their budgets are tighter and they have a long process to go through to secure funds. The private sector provides facilities where they can attract large numbers of customers, or more exclusive facilities where they can attract fewer customers but charge them more. The areas the private sector is involved are:

❂   **active sports** – tennis, golf, health and fitness suites, snooker and pool, water sports and ten pin bowling

❂   **spectator sport** – stadiums for football, rugby, cricket, tennis, golf; football is by far the most popular spectator sport

❂   **sponsorship** – this has risen from £129m in 1985 to £285m in 1995.

CASE STUDY

The area of largest growth in the private sector in the 1990s was the health and fitness industry. In 2002 the Fitness Industry Association published the 2001 State of the Industry Report into the public and private sectors. The main findings regarding the health and fitness industry were as follows:

- there are over 4000 public sector facilities and 2800 private sector facilities
- total membership of clubs had increased by 21% since 2000
- the number of clubs had increased by 6%
- there are 720 private sector sites and 386 public sector sites at the planning stage
- 8.9% of the population are members of health and fitness clubs compared with 13.2 in the USA
- there are 33 520 full-time and part-time staff employed in the industry.

The industry is still expanding and looking very healthy, offering excellent career opportunities. The major players in the industry are listed below.

- **David Lloyd Leisure**, www.davidlloydleisure.co.uk – David Lloyd Leisure is the UK's number one health and fitness club operator, with 49 clubs (38 which offer rackets facilities) and over 240 000 members. They are part of Whitbread plc, that also owns Curzons and Marriott Hotel Leisure Clubs. Their facilities are usually very large with several thousand members and they are fairly luxurious.

- **Fitness First**, www.fitnessfirst.com – Fitness First had 112 clubs by the end of 2001, with another 82 being opened up in 2002. They currently cater for 266 000 members and employ 2200 staff. They have chosen to position their clubs close to city centres to make themselves easily accessible to workers, and they advertise fitness at an affordable price to people of all shapes, sizes and fitness levels.

- **Cannons Group Ltd**, www.cannons.co.uk – Cannons have 62 UK clubs catering for 170 000 members; these consist of 45 Cannons Health Clubs, the Harbour Club in London and 16 Cannons Leisure Management clubs, 11 of which are local authority clubs.

- **Esporta Clubs**, www.esporta.co.uk – Esporta has 41 clubs with 180 000 members in the UK, and plans to reach 48 by the end of 2002. They see themselves as being at the premium end of the market by offering high quality facilities within luxurious clubs.

- **Holmes Place Health Clubs**, www.holmesplace.co.uk – Holmes Place was founded in 1979 and was floated on the London Stock Exchange in 1997. They run 42 clubs (including six for local authorities) and have a round 132 000 members. They have also successfully moved into Europe.

There are many other health and fitness operators in the UK, such as:

Livingwell Health Clubs – www.livingwell.co.uk

LA Fitness – www.lafitness.co.uk

Greens Health and Fitness – www.greensonline.co.uk

Total Fitness – www.toalfitness.org

Crown Sports – www.crownsportsplc.com

Invicta Leisure – www.invictaleisure.co.uk

Bannatyne Fitness LTD – www.bannatyneleisure.com

Virgin Active – www.virginactive.co.uk

Spirit Health and Fitness – www.spirit-fit.com

Topnotch Health Clubs – www.topnotchhealthclubs.com

Next Generation – www.nextgeneration.co.uk

Fitness Exchange group – www.fitness-exchange.net

JJB Sports Health Clubs – www.jjb.co.uk

Spring Health Leisure Clubs – www.springhealthleisure.com

Clubhaus – www.clubhaus.com

Seb Coe Health Clubs – www.sebcoehealthclubs.com

Moat House Hotels – www.moathousehotels.com

Odyssey – www.odyssey-group.co.uk

HilifeGroupPLC – www.hilife.accessweb.co.uk

The Sportz Academy – www.sportzacademy.co.uk

The role of the private sector can be well summarised by this quote from George Torkildsen (1991):

The major difference between the commercial operator and the public or voluntary operator is the raison d'être *of the business, the primary objective of the commercial operator being that of financial profit or adequate return on investment.*

Voluntary sector

The largest sector for participation in sport in Britain is the voluntary sector, particularly in the form of competitive sport. The voluntary sector accounts for:

- ✪ 500 000 officials
- ✪ 150 000 clubs
- ✪ 6.5 million members.

Most amateur clubs are run on a voluntary basis. Some voluntary clubs own facilities, but the majority hire facilities, usually provided by the public sector. The voluntary sector offers opportunities for people to fulfil new roles in their leisure time within the management of a club.

Most clubs, such as football and athletics clubs, that people join to enable them to participate in competitive sport are in the voluntary sector. Voluntary sector clubs often work in partnership with the private or public sector, for example they use public sector facilities or gain sponsorship from the private sector (e.g. in the evening you may find the swimming pool at your leisure centre being used for club training sessions).

Funding of voluntary clubs

The voluntary sector is funded primarily by its members in the form of subscriptions. Every club will have an annual subscription fee and match fees. This is to cover the costs of playing, travel and equipment. The club may try to raise some money in the form of sponsorship; this is often by a local company or by one of the players. Some clubs have local benefactors who put money into a club as a gesture of goodwill. Clubs will also run fund-raising events such as discos, race nights or jumble sales, particularly if they are trying to raise money for a tour or special event.

Clubs can apply for other sources of funding such as:

- ✪ national lottery grants
- ✪ grants from national governing bodies
- ✪ grants from government
- ✪ grants from the local authority.

These types of grants are usually to enable clubs to build or improve their facilities.

Definitions

The voluntary sector

The voluntary sector is defined as inclusive and exclusive clubs that operate as non-profit making organisations and which are essentially managed by and for amateur sportsmen and women.

(Butson, 1983)

STUDENT ACTIVITY

Go to your college library and find out the names of voluntary clubs in your area for the following sports:
- ✪ athletics
- ✪ ice skating
- ✪ rugby union
- ✪ rugby league
- ✪ hockey.

Partnerships

Partnerships occur when two or more of the sectors come together to provide opportunities for sport. We have already seen how the public sector rents out its facilities to the voluntary sector to give them an opportunity to play sports. Sponsorship, which is primarily provided by the private sector, is given to the public and voluntary sectors.

Sports facilities are also built as partnerships. For example, the new English National Stadium at Wembley is a private sector initiative by Wembley plc, however, they have received a national lottery grant from the public sector. They will also go into partnership with other private sector organisations to raise finance and gain sponsorship.

Compulsory competitive tendering (CCT), which was introduced into the leisure industry in 1990, was aimed at developing partnerships between the public and private sectors. The aim was to hand the management of sports centres to private sector organisations while the ownership of the centres remained with the public sector (local authorities). The theory behind this arrangement was that the private sector companies would aim to run the centres for profit and thus they would be run more efficiently. Today we can still see the benefits of this arrangement in our local sports facilities.

STUDENT ACTIVITY

Visit your local sports centre and try to find examples of partnerships between the three sectors.

REVISION QUESTIONS

1) Explain the two parts to the private sector and summarise what each part does to promote participation in sport.

2) Why does the public sector provide facilities for sport?

3) What types of sports does the private sector provide for?

4) How does the private sector differ from the public sector in terms of its aims?

5) What is the role of the voluntary sector in sports provision?

6) How does the voluntary sector raise money to enable people to participate in sport?

7) What is a partnership and why are they needed in sport?

EMPLOY-MENT OPPORT-UNITIES

During your time studying for your National Diploma you should be thinking about what type of job you would like when you are qualified. You may have a clear idea about the type of job you would like and where you would like to work, but not what type of work you would like to do. Ultimately you have to ask two questions:

1 What am I going to do for employment?

2 What skills and qualifications do I need?

You may find that you have to go on to study at a higher level or complete a part-time course to gain the additional skills you need. Sport science courses lead people to a wide range of career opportunities, where they can apply all their knowledge or specialise in certain areas. They include:

- ✪ fitness instructor
- ✪ leisure attendant
- ✪ sports centre manager
- ✪ sports coach
- ✪ sports development officer
- ✪ sports teacher
- ✪ professional sports performer
- ✪ sports massage therapist
- ✪ sport scientist
- ✪ sports nutritionist
- ✪ sport psychologist
- ✪ sports groundsman
- ✪ sports retailer.

FIGURE 19.3 A fitness instructor

Fitness instructor

Description of work

Involves assessing people's fitness levels, designing their exercise programmes and instructing these programmes in the gym. Fitness instructors may also teach aerobics classes, circuit classes and supervise people in the gym.

Qualifications needed

Instructors need sound anatomy and physiology knowledge gained from a sport science course and also a recognised fitness instructor's award from a training organisation such as Premier Training International, YMCA or Focus. To teach specific skills such as aerobics, circuits or stability ball work extra qualifications are required. First aid and CPR qualifications are also essential.

Fitness instructors can take further qualifications to become a personal trainer. The difference between a fitness instructor and a personal trainer is that a personal trainer will have their own group of clients and will supervise every session their clients spend in the gym. They provide personal care and help to vary the clients' workouts and provide motivation. Fitness instructors are collectively responsible for the members of a gym.

Personal skills

Instructors must be able to communicate with the range of people they will encounter in their gyms. A friendly, outgoing personality type is important, as is remaining calm under pressure.

Progression and career prospects

The greater number of skills an instructor acquires, the more opportunities they can create for themselves to open up new sources of income. They can become senior instructors and then be in a position to train and develop fitness instructors. Some instructors will start to take on personal training clients and may eventually become self-employed.

Salary

Fitness instructors start on between £11 000 and £14 000 a year, depending on their qualifications and where they work. A senior fitness instructor can expect to earn around £16 000. Personal trainers earn on average £20 000 to £25 000 a year, depending on where they work and how much they charge.

Leisure attendant

Description of work

Leisure attendants are responsible for preparing and supervising facilities in a leisure facility. This will include the sports hall, swimming pool and changing facilities. Most leisure attendants will also be involved in coaching or supervising sports sessions in their sports hall.

Qualifications needed

An NVQ or GNVQ in Leisure or Recreation is needed as a basis to gain skills and knowledge. The National Pool Lifeguard Qualification is also needed to work poolside and this includes first aid and CPR, although a First Aid at Work qualification is also recommended. In order to coach sports, leisure attendants need specific national governing body coaching awards.

Personal skills

Leisure attendants need to be outgoing and people oriented. Communication skills are important as you may have to deal with a range of people.

Progression and career prospects

Leisure attendant is usually the starting point of a career that can lead on to supervisory and then management levels.

Salary

Starting salaries are around £10 000 to £12 000.

Sports centre manager

Description of work

Managing a sports centre is a multidimensional job and involves some of the following activities: managing and motivating staff; programming facilities and organising activities; establishing systems and procedures; preparing and managing budgets; monitoring sales and usage; marketing and promoting the centre; dealing with members and any complaints or incidents.

Qualifications needed

Managers may have been promoted into this position having qualified with a BTEC National Diploma or GNVQ. Most managers will hold higher-level qualifications such as a degree or HND in Leisure Management or Business Studies.

Personal skills

To be an effective manager you need the following personal qualities: confidence; enthusiasm; assertiveness; communication skills; self-motivation; presence and professionalism.

Progression and career prospects

These depend upon the company you work for; however, centre managers can be promoted into regional managers or other senior management positions.

Salary

Centre managers can expect to earn between £25 000 and £35 000, depending upon the size of the centre and their own performance.

Sports coach

FIGURE 19.4 A sports coach

Description of work

Sports coaches are responsible for developing the physical fitness and skills of their athletes. They need to be able to evaluate their athletes' performances and offer feedback to improve their performances. As a result they will require knowledge of many aspects of sport science, such as anatomy and physiology, biomechanics, nutrition, psychology and sports injury.

Sports coaches are usually former or current competitors in their sport. Some people get the opportunity to coach in sports centres as part of their job.

Qualifications needed

Every sport will have their own system for awarding coaching qualifications, and coaches must hold the relevant award. Many coaches also hold qualifications in sport science and awards from the National Coaching Foundation (NCF).

Personal skills

Coaches need to be able to motivate athletes and have their trust. They need to be good communicators and listeners and be able to show patience and empathy towards their athletes.

Progression and career prospects

There are still relatively few full-time coaches in Britain as most work on a voluntary basis. However, with more lottery money being spent on sport, the opportunities are increasing.

Salary

The salary will depend upon the sport, whether it is professional or amateur and where the coaching is carried. In a sports centre, a coach can expect to earn between £10 and £15 an hour.

Sports development officer

Description of work

A sports development officer works to increase participation rates in sport and provide opportunities for people to play sport in a local area. They will work for local authorities and may have responsibility for specific groups of people, such as ethnic minorities, women or disabled people. They are also involved in strategic planning for sport and work in partnership with providers of facilities, such as local authority facilities and schools.

Qualifications needed

Competition is very tough for these desirable positions and candidates will have a degree or HND in Sport Science or Leisure Management, along with a range of coaching qualifications. However, a person with a BTEC ND in Sport Science who also has experience of coaching and working for a local authority may also be successful.

Personal skills

You need an interest and knowledge in a range of sports and the needs of a community. You have to be able to communicate with people from different backgrounds and be sensitive to their needs. Good leadership, motivational skills and an organised approach to work are also necessary.

Progression and career prospects

There was a rapid growth of sports development officers in the 1980s and this is still an expanding field; there are also more development officers working to increase participation levels in certain sports such as football and rugby. There is a career structure in sports development, although opportunities for promotion are fairly limited. Promotion can be within a local authority to another area of leisure.

Salary

A sports development officer can expect to earn around £17 000 to £22 000, with senior sports development officers earning up to £30 000.

Sports teacher or lecturer

Description of work

Teaching sport traditionally involved becoming qualified as a PE teacher; however, opportunities now exist to teach on sport science courses as well. Many teachers will specialise in one subject or area, such as exercise physiology or sport psychology, while other teachers will be happy to deliver a range of subjects. Sports teachers now work in all education facilities, with expanding opportunities in colleges of further education and universities. PE teachers used to have to teach a second subject, such as geography or maths, but today sport and PE are seen as being academic subjects where you can study for a GCSE or 'A' level, and the demands of teaching have increased.

Qualifications needed

A teacher needs to be educated to degree level and to be qualified as a teacher. There are two ways to do this: first, to take a four-year teaching degree such as a Bachelor of Education (BEd) or a Batchelor of Arts with Qualified Teaching Status (BA (QTS)); or to take a three-year degree in Sport Science or Sport Studies and then to complete a one-year Postgraduate Certificate in Education (PGCE). It is important to note that in order to be a teacher you must have passed English, maths and a science at GCSE grade C or above and have passed at least two 'A' levels.

Personal skills

Teaching is a very demanding profession and you need to be patient and able to deal with young people and their various needs. Teachers need to be organised, maintain discipline and be able to adapt their communication skills to the group they are teaching. You should also have a good level of personal fitness and enjoy working with young people.

Progression and career prospects

Teaching is a career that always offers progression. There are always opportunities to take on extra responsibilities, such as head of year and head of department.

Salary

Pay will depend upon experience and the type of establishment, whether a state or independently funded organisation. Starting salaries are around £16 000, with senior teachers earning around £25 000.

Professional sports performer

Description of work

Ultimately the goal of every sports performer would be to play their sport full-time at a professional level. However, it is only the most talented who get this opportunity and there are only a limited number of sports where you can play professionally. Football, cricket, rugby league, rugby union and golf have the largest number professional players. However, we find that most professional players have to have a second job to ensure their income. Playing sport on a semi-professional basis can be a better alternative, as the demands of training and playing will be less and it can be fairly lucrative.

Qualifications needed

No formal qualifications are needed, although you need to investigate the best route into a sport as every sport will be slightly different in how it recruits young players.

Personal skills

Technical efficiency at the chosen sport, along with physical fitness are the most important assets; however, self-motivation, commitment and determination will also be needed.

Progression and career prospects

Professional sports people can progress into coaching, management and administration in their sports.

Salary

Salary depends upon the sport and the level at which you compete. Young professionals may earn just a couple of thousand a year, while the top performers can earn millions of pounds.

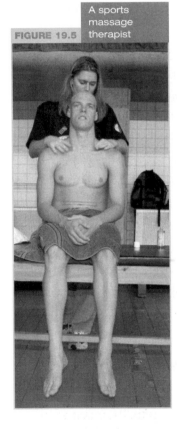

FIGURE 19.5 A sports massage therapist

Sports massage therapist

Description of work

A sports massage therapist has a varied job, using their massage skills to prepare athletes for competition, help them to warm down after competition and then deal with any injuries or soreness they may suffer. They can also treat people who do not consider themselves as athletes but whose activities, such as gardening or work, are causing them discomfort and pain. A sports massage therapist may be based at a client or work in the field at training grounds or accompanying athletes to competitions.

Qualifications needed

A sports massage therapist needs to hold a sports therapy diploma. These courses are accredited by the Vocational Training and Charitable Trust (VTCT) and can be studied at most colleges of further education. Private training organisations, such as Premier Training International, also offer these courses in an intensive twelve-week format. It is possible to do a degree in sports therapy or sports rehabilitation at a limited number of universities.

Personal skills

A sports massage therapist always needs to adopt a professional approach, as their job involves physical contact with people. They should be patient, caring and sensitive to an individual's needs; a high standard of personal hygiene and good communication skills will be important to be successful.

Progression and career prospects

Sports massage therapists are usually self-employed and, as a result, there is no clear career ladder. They should be willing to set up and expand their own business and develop their careers by learning new skills and techniques.

Salary

A sports massage therapist should earn between £20000 and £30000 a year, depending on how many treatments they perform a week.

Sport scientist

Description of work

The aim of the sport scientist is to maximise the performance of an individual in their care. This will involve applying their knowledge and skills in the subjects of physiology, biomechanics and psychology to give the performers any possible advantage. Physiology will involve fitness testing and monitoring physical condition; biomechanics will involve examining the performer's technique and equipment to analyse where improvements can be made; psychology will be applied to ensure the performer is correctly prepared mentally.

Qualifications needed

A sport scientist will hold a degree in sport science and possibly a master's degree in their chosen field of expertise.

Personal skills

An in-depth knowledge of sport science and sports performance are essential, as is the ability to communicate with athletes, treat them with respect and be tactful. Sensitivity, patience and enthusiasm are also valuable traits to possess.

Progression and career prospects

These types of jobs are hard to come by, but nowadays the British Olympic Association and professional sports teams often employ a sport scientist. Professional football teams employ sport scientists to advise their coaches and to perform physiological tests.

Salary

There is no set scale for sport scientists and their salary will depend upon their qualifications and who employs them. Salaries range from £15 000 to £25 000.

Sports nutritionist

Description of work

A sports nutritionist gives an athlete advice about how to organise their diet to ensure they maximise the effects of their training and reach competition in the best possible shape. This will involve advising athletes on kilocalorie intake and what percentage of kilocalories should come from carbohydrates, fats and protein; how to re-fuel and re-hydrate in the post-training period; and how to organise their pre-training meal. A nutritionist may also provide advice on the use of supplements.

Qualifications needed

A sports nutritionist needs to be qualified as a dietician first. This will involve completing a three-year degree to become recognised as a State Registered Dietician. To specialise in sports nutrition you need at least one year's experience before completing a Sports Dietetics course run by the Sports Nutrition Foundation.

Personal skills
A nutritionist needs to be well organised and empathetic towards people and their individual needs and lifestyle. Well-developed communication and interviewing skills are essential, as is being a good listener.

Progression and career prospects
Most nutrition work has to be done on a freelance basis, as the NHS does not employ sports nutritionists. However, opportunities exist within professional clubs as many embrace the holistic approach to training for sport. In particular, rugby union clubs will pay meticulous attention to the nutritional needs of their players. Many sports nutritionists also work with Olympic squads across a range of sports.

Salary
A sports nutritionist can expect to earn £20 000 to £25 000 a year, depending on their clients and how they are employed.

Sport psychologist

Description of work
A sport psychologist is involved in mentally preparing athletes for competition. It is a varied job which will differ depending on the individual needs of performers. A psychologist will be involved in helping teams and individuals set goals for the short and long term, learn strategies to control arousal levels and stay relaxed in stressful situations. They can offer intervention strategies when an athlete has psychological difficulties, such as loss of confidence or a loss of form, and they can help an athlete through difficult periods, such as periods of injury or coming to terms with failure or defeat.

Sport psychologists are often involved in lecturing and conducting research, as well as actually practising their skills.

Qualifications needed
A sport psychologist would usually be a graduate or sport scientist who had then completed post-graduate training. This would involve a master's degree or a PhD in sport psychology. There are also various training organisations who offer diplomas in sport psychology to people who wish to understand more about psychological preparation.

Personal skills
Psychologists need to have good listening and interviewing skills in order to assess the needs of their athletes and to develop strategies to help them. A psychologist should be able to build up a relationship of trust and be seen as someone who the athlete can talk to confidentially.

Progression and career prospects
Most sport psychologists are self-employed and work with teams and individuals on a freelance basis. Many sport psychologists will be based in universities and they combine lecturing with their consultation work, and are often heavily involved in research.

Salary

This depends upon how the psychologist operates and how much work they undertake. A sport psychologist could expect to earn £25 to £30 an hour for their consultation work.

Sports groundsman

Description of work

A groundsman is responsible for preparing and maintaining the condition of outdoor facilities, such as golf courses, cricket pitches, football pitches and tennis courts.

Qualifications needed

Entrance qualifications are not essential, however, you can study for an NVQ in turf management, or go on to HND or degree level. These courses need to recognised by the Institute of Groundsmanship (IOG).

Personal skills

Candidates need work to high standards and have pride in their job. They also need to be willing to work in all types of weather and not be afraid of getting their hands dirty.

Progression and career prospects

Usually groundsmen will work their way up from the bottom and learn on the job; it is reckoned that it takes around five years to develop the knowledge needed. It is possible to gain promotion to senior groundsman and then more senior positions within a facility.

Salary

This depends vastly on your responsibilities. A groundsman may start on around £9000, with a senior groundsman earning upwards of £20 000.

FIGURE 19.6 A sports groundsman

Sports retailer

Description of work

Sports retail involves working in a sports shop, selling sports goods. This can involve using your knowledge of sport and matching a client's needs to specific products. For example, different types of runners will require different types of running shoes and you will need to be able to identify which shoes they need.

Qualifications needed

A knowledge of sport is needed, but many people working in retail will need business skills and customer care skills. A GNVQ in business studies or leisure studies would be appropriate. If you have aspirations of running a sports shop, it may be necessary to hold an HND or degree in a management-based subject.

Personal skills

An ability to deal with members of the public and be willing to meet their needs as necessary. You must be good at communicating and be able to stay calm under pressure.

Progression and career prospects

Progression is good in the retail industry and you can progress up to supervisory and management positions. Many large organisations will have training schemes and graduate training schemes to help you to develop your career.

Salary

A retail assistant would earn around £10 000 a year, however, they may benefit from receiving commission on sales. A shop manager would earn over £20 000.

STUDENT ACTIVITY

Choose three people who work in sport in different capacities and arrange to interview them. Before you go, prepare a list of questions you might ask regarding the job they do, how they became qualified and how their career has developed.

PREPARING FOR A PERIOD OF INDUSTRY EXPERIENCE

Before you go on a period of industrial experience you will need to prepare materials. You may be expected to submit a CV or fill out an application form. This is what will do when you are preparing to find a job for yourself, so you should have these dual aims in mind.

Applying for a job

To apply for work you need to use a suitable method to approach a prospective most employer. Most job advertisements will specify which method you should use. There are three main methods that you may be asked to use.

- ❂ **Curriculum vitae** (CV) – A concise written document that summarises your skills, qualifications and experience to date for a prospective employer. It needs to be accompanied by a covering letter.

- ❂ **Application form** – Some jobs will not accept a CV and will ask you to complete a pre-designed application form asking you to show why you are suitable for the job. This also needs to be accompanied by a covering letter.

- ❂ **Letter of application** – Some jobs will require you to apply in writing. The information will be similar to that of a CV, but presented in a different format.

Curriculum vitae

A CV is used for a range of reasons:

- ❂ to demonstrate your value to the employer
- ❂ as a marketing tool to get an interview
- ❂ to sell yourself to the employer.

There are three main styles of a CV.

1   **Chronological** – This is the most common format and involves you presenting your experiences of education and work in date order.

2   **Functional** – This type highlights your skills and is directed towards a certain career. For example, you may be qualified in more than one subject, but you would only highlight the skills that are relevant for the type of work you are trying to gain.

3   **Targeted** – This type of CV emphasises skills and abilities relevant to a specific job or company. It is tailor-made for one job. You would examine the job specification and then adapt your CV to show how you meet the job specification.

Preparing a CV

A CV needs to be prepared meticulously and you should spend time deciding what your main selling features are. If you are still a student, you may not have been involved in full-time work, but you will still have important features to highlight. You must include any work experiences, part-time work or voluntary work you have undertaken. You will need to start by compiling a biography of your life with dates and events. You will also need to consider what skills you have at present, and which skills are transferable to the type of work you are seeking.

Content of a CV

1   Personal details – Full name and address, home telephone number and mobile number, e-mail address and date of birth.

2   Current position and current employment – If you are employed you will state your position and your main responsibilities.

3   Key personal skills – Highlight your main personal skills, attributes and abilities.

4   Education and qualifications – State the names and dates of all academic qualifications received, with the most recent first.

5   Training or work-related courses – Include any additional vocational or on-the-job training you have received.

6   Previous employment – State all the past employment you have had with the following information: name of employer, job title and a brief summary of responsibilities. Also include any periods of work placement.

7   Leisure interests – Here is an opportunity to show the interests you have outside of the academic environment. State the sports you play and at what level (it may be appropriate to list some of your achievements in sport), and other hobbies and activities in which you are involved. It is particularly good to state any positions of responsibility you have held, such as club captain, scout leader or cadet force rank.

8   Other relevant information – Anything else you feel may be of value to the employer, such as an ability to drive.

9 References – Give the name, addresses and phone numbers of two people who can vouch for you. If you have a current employer, they should be the first; if not, a past employer or someone else in a position of responsibility, such as a teacher, would be appropriate. It is important that you ask them before using them as a reference in case they are not willing to write you a reference.

Example of a CV

Curriculum Vitae

Name: Rebecca Sewell

Date of Birth: 17th October 1978

Address: 125 Mill Crescent, Reading, Berks. RG6 3JS

Nationality: British

Tel: 01345 245131 (home); 01345 684877 (work); 07754 759868 (mob)

Email: racsewell@aol.com

Current employment
Fitness instructor at the Premier Gym in Reading (2000–2002)
A graduate in Sport Science (BSc Hons) with specialist skills in fitness instruction, teaching circuits and aerobics and core conditioning training.

Main responsibilities:
- teaching aerobics and circuits
- conducting fitness assessments, designing exercise programmes and instructing workouts
- selling memberships and sports clothing.

Key skills include:
- fitness testing, programme design and instructional skills
- ability to teach exercise to music
- good communication skills
- good motivator of people
- financial management skills of budgeting and monitoring budgets
- computer and internet literate
- first aid and CPR competent
- selling and marketing skills.

Education and qualifications
1996–1999 Thames University. BSc (Hons) Sport and Exercise Science (2:1 gained).
1994–1996 Reading College of Sport. BTEC ND Sport Science
8 distinctions, 8 merits, 2 passes.
1991–1994 Campbell School, Reading. 10 GCSEs: PE (A), English Lang (A), English Lit (A), French (A), Biology (B) Maths (B), Chemistry (B), German (B), Geography (B), Physics (D).

Work-related courses
Fitness Trainers Award (1999)
NVQ RSA Exercise to Music (1998)
NPLQ (2000)
First Aid at Work (2001)
Stability Ball Training (2002)

Previous employment
1999–2000 Leisure Attendant at Springfield Baths. Main duties included pool supervision and lifeguarding, laying out equipment in the sports hall, coaching and teaching children's sport at weekends and during holidays.

Previous work experience
1995 Three-week placement at Hills Spa Health and Fitness Centre. This involved shadowing the fitness trainers and duty manager, serving the members and advising them in the gym.

Hobbies and interests
I am involved in local athletics and am captain of the ladies team. I run the 800 m and 1500 m and am currently the Berkshire county champion at 800 m.
I enjoy travelling overseas, particularly to Australia and New Zealand.
My hobbies are reading and going to the cinema.

Other relevant information
Full driving license and own car.

References

Mr W. Samways
Fitness Manager
Premier Gym
Garfield Road
Reading
Berks RG16 4LP
01345 874098

Miss J. Gatehouse
Head of Sport Science
Thames University
Stratton Way
Easthampton
Bucks BK34 7BJ
0152 854339

Filling in an application form

Many employers will produce their own application form, which you need to fill in when applying for a position. They will use this form to select the candidates they wish to interview. It is important, therefore, to give yourself plenty of time to complete the form. Forms that are completed incorrectly or untidily will probably be discarded without being read. If you complete the form properly, you will already have an advantage over your rivals. Remember, you only get one chance to make a first impression. Here are some useful tips on completing the form.

✪ Photocopy the form first and use the copy to practice on. Check it over and, when you are satisfied, copy it on to the original.

✪ Read the instructions on the form carefully and follow them exactly. For example, it may ask you to use black ink or block capitals. This is important because the form may need to be photocopied and will only copy well in black ink.

✪ Even if some of the information on the form is given in the covering letter, you must still include it on the from. Never write 'refer to CV', as the reader may not bother.

✪ Think about answers very carefully and plan your responses. For example, questions such as 'Why do you want to work for this company?' need to be researched and responded to appropriately.

✪ Check that your references are willing to provide a reference for you before put in their details.

✪ Take a photocopy of your form so that you can remind yourself what you wrote before an interview.

✪ Make sure you do not miss the closing date and post the form well in advance.

✪ Include a covering letter with your application form.

Letter of application

A letter of application relates your experience to a specific company or job vacancy; it should always be sent with a CV and perhaps an application form. It should be businesslike and complement the information in your CV. If you are writing in response to an advertisement, make reference to the job title and where you saw the vacancy advertised, and ensure the letter is addressed to the correct person. Indicate why you are attracted to the position advertised, and highlight why you think you are suitable and what key personal skills and experiences you have that are relevant to the vacancy. Finish the letter by stating that you look forward to hearing from them soon and would be delighted to attend an interview at their convenience.

(Your name) _____

(Your address) _____

_____

_____

_____ (Name of person applying to)

_____ (Address of company writing to)   Date _____

_____

_____

Dear _____ (person's name)

(Explain why you are writing, i.e. for which job and where you saw the vacancy)

_____

_____

(Explain what you are currently doing, i.e. employment or education)

_____

_____

(Discuss why you are applying for the job and what you like about it.)

_____

_____

(Justify why you are suitable for the position – relevant experience or skills.)

_____

_____

(End your letter by saying that you can attend an interview and hope to hear from them soon.)

_____

_____

Yours sincerely,*

_____ (Sign your name)

_____ (Type your name)

* If you do not have a person's name and addressed the letter to 'Dear Sir or Madam', you should end with 'Yours faithfully'.

Where to find job advertisements

The following are good sources of job advertisements:

- local newspapers
- regional newspapers
- national newspapers
- job and careers centres
- trade publications

- recruitment agencies
- direct contact with employers
- word of mouth
- the internet.

The internet is an excellent source of jobs in sport and the websites are regularly updated. Try the following websites to source jobs:

www.leisure opportunities.co.uk

www.leisurejobs.com

www.thefitnessjobs.com

www.leisurenadhospitalitybusiness.co.uk

Trade publications are also an excellent source and they should be available in your college library. The following are particularly worth looking at:

Leisure Management and Leisure Opportunities

Leisurenews and Jobs

All Sport and Leisure Monthly

Health and Fitness

STUDENT ACTIVITY

Go to your library or learning centre and, using some of the sources listed above, find three jobs which you would be interested in applying for.

THE WORK PLACEMENT

Audit of personal skills

The work placement is an opportunity to try out a job and start to understand what knowledge and skills are needed for that position. Before you start your placement ask yourself the following questions.

1   **What skills have I at present?** Look at practical skills of coaching and teaching, key skills such as written and verbal communication skills, problem solving and application of number, IT skills, skills gained from previous work experiences such as clerical and administrative skills.

2   **What skills would I like to acquire?** This is difficult because there may be skills you have not gained because you haven't been in a situation to gain them. As a result you may not be aware that you need them. However, try to be realistic and think what skills you may need in a job, such as communicating with the general public.

3   **What qualifications have I gained?** This is just a list of all the qualifications you currently hold. Also list here any qualifications you are hoping to gain.

4   **What personal qualities have I got?** Think about personal qualities in the following areas:

a) Working with other people: Are there particular people you would not like to work with? Do you prefer to work in large or small groups? How do you feel about working as part of a team? Are you happy dealing with the public?

b) Leadership: How good are you at leading groups? Do you prefer to lead large or small groups? How do you feel about selling to people?

c) Responsibility: How do you feel about responsibility in the following areas – cash, equipment, other people's work, meeting deadlines, other people's safety and welfare.

d) Any other personal qualities you think you possess.

5 **What do you want from a job?** Split this up into things you would want and things you would not want. Consider the following areas:

a) Pay: Do you want enough to get by on or is getting a high wage important to you? Would you like to be paid by results? Would you like to be paid extra for extra work you have done?

b) Hours: Do you want to work fixed hours (9–5), or do you not mind doing shift work? How do you feel about overtime?

c) Prospects: How important are the opportunities for promotion and the presence of a career structure?

d) Location: Do you have a fixed idea of where you want to work, or are you willing to relocate to find the right job? How important is an easy journey to work to you?

e) Working with others: Is it important for you to work as a part of a group, or would you rather work alone? How do you feel about managers and supervisors, and are you looking for a certain style of leadership?

f) What the job entails: Are you looking for job satisfaction or a job that pays well? Are you keen to utilise certain skills and abilities? Do you want to help other people?

Answering these questions will start to give you an idea of what your next step should be. You can discuss this audit with your tutor or work placement officer when you have a meeting with them to arrange your industrial placement. This will help you to gain a placement which is fulfilling, worthwhile and develops your skills and personal qualities.

Once a decision has been made about your future career it is an appropriate time to think about setting goals. Remember, you may not be able to walk into your dream job immediately and while this remains your long-term goal it is important to set realistic short-term goals to lay the pathway to achieving your dream job. To recap on goal setting, it would be appropriate to read the section on goal setting in Chapter 3.

The work placement diary

During your placement you will be required to carry out a piece of academic work to fulfil the criteria of this unit. Your tutor will give you full details of this work, however, the following information will give you an idea of the types of task you will be required to complete.

1   Interview a member of staff and find out what the roles and responsibilities of their job are, and how they have come to be in their position. Also find out what qualifications they have and what skills they need to do their job effectively.

2   Find out the organisation's operating procedures for a range of tasks. An operating procedure is how a company completes certain tasks. This will depend upon the type of organisation you work for, but try to find out how they deal with new customers, how they manage the work they do in the gym, how they deal with cash and cashing up, how they manage the pool, and so on.

3   It is of utmost importance that you are inducted in health and safety procedures on the first day. Take a note of the following: what the evacuation procedure is; where the fire exits are; where the assembly point is; where the first aid kit is; who is a trained first aider; where the phone for emergencies is; where the fire extinguishers are; what safety equipment is available and when you need to use it.

4   Make a record of what you did each day in the workplace and any new skills you gained. At the end of the placement, evaluate what qualifications and skills you need before you are prepared to start work.

Work-based project

During your two-week placement you need to complete a work-based project that will develop your knowledge and also be useful to your employer. On the first day, discuss this with your employer because they may have a project with which they need help, and this may be beneficial to both of you. Here are some ideas.

✪   Conduct a study into gym or club usage – When is it heaviest and why?

✪   Conduct a study into the local competitors in the area.

✪   Take an area of the club that is underachieving and develop a proposal for how to improve its performance.

✪   Survey members' attitudes to certain parts of the club, such as the equipment in the gym.

✪   Help to organise a social event or a competition in the gym.

✪   Prepare materials to educate the centre's users on a topic such as pre- and post-exercise nutrition, weight training for maximal fat loss or using interval training to improve aerobic fitness.

Your findings should be reported using an appropriate method of communication.

Assessment of performance

Your performance should be evaluated by three people:

1   yourself

2   your placement supervisor

3   the tutor who visits you on industrial placement.

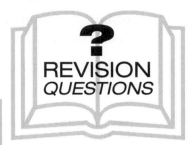

REVISION QUESTIONS

1) Briefly describe the three sectors of provision for sport.

2) Explain the changing role of the Sports Council/Sport England.

3) Choose three occupations in the sports industry and compare the types of activities each job entails.

4) Describe three ways of finding out about job vacancies.

REFERENCES AND FURTHER READING

For further information on the sports industry look at the following texts:

Beashel, P., Sibson, A. and Taylor, J. (1997) *The World of Sport Examined.* Nelson Thornes

Colquhoun, M. (1993) *The Leisure Environment.* Pitman Publishing

Torkildsen, G. (1999) *Leisure and Recreation Management.* E&FN Spon

Wesson, H. K., Wiggins, N., Thompson, G. and Hartigan, S. (2000) *Sport and P.E.: A Complete Guide to Advanced Level Study.* London: Hodder & Stoughton

For further information careers in sport look at the following texts:

Department of Further Education and Employment (1999) *Working in Sport and Fitness*

Fyfe, Louise (1998) *Careers in Sport.* London: Kogan Page

Edwards, Lois (1997) *Great careers for people interested in Sports and Fitness.* London: Kogan Page

Marks, Steve (1998) *Working in the Leisure Industry.* How to books LTD

Sports Council (1996) *Careers in Sport Compendium.* Published by The Sports Council

acclimatisation physiological adaptation to a change in climate or atmosphere

aerofoil an airfoil is a specific shape that is curved on top and almost flat on the bottom

aesthetic pleasing to the eye

affinity attraction for a substance

alveoli air sacs in the lungs in which gaseous exchange takes place

anabolic steroids drugs that act in conjunction with resistance training to increase a person's muscle mass (*anabolic* = protein building)

anaemia low concentrations of red blood cells

angina chest pain plus a feeling of suffocation

atom the smallest unit of a chemical element; can combine to form molecules

barometric pressure the pressure of the atomsophere

baroreceptors receptors that detect a change in pressure

Bernoulli's principle the concept that as the speed of a moving fluid (e.g. air or water) increases, the pressure within the fluid decreases.

bradycardia a decrease in resting heart rate

buffering the ability to mop up hydrogen ions or hydroxide ions to maintain the pH of an environment

capillary action the tendency of certain liquids to travel or climb through small vessels

catharsis release of negative emotions: evacuation of the bowels

cervical relating to the neck

chemoreceptors receptors that detect a chemical change

coefficient of friction a measure of the opposing force and the load during a sliding process; higher values mean more resistance.

concave curving inwards

conduction the transfer of heat via direct contact

constrict to become narrower or smaller

convex curving outwards

cross bridge formation the connection between myosin (thick filaments) and actin (thin filaments) within the muscle that allows muscle contraction.

crystalline a crystalline material is one in which the molecules are arranged in a regular pattern

density how much matter there is in a certain amount of space

derivative the derivative of a function represents the gradient of the function when graphed

diffuse the movement of particles from a high concentration to a low concentration

disaccharide two carbohydrates joined together

diuretic a substance that increases urine production

doping the practice of using artificial substances to enhance athletic performance

dwarfism an inherited characteristic that results in extremely short stature

element a substance that cannot be broken down into simpler substances (e.g. oxygen, sodium, iron)

enema a liquid solution administered into the rectum to clear out the bowels

enzyme a protein that speeds up reactions

erythropoeitin a hormone that stimulates the production of red blood cells

ethical in accordance with certain moral standards

fatigue tiredness from physical exertion

field setting a natural environment, as opposed to a laboratory setting

fuse to join together

genetic doping using genes to change the genetic make up of a person to enhance their athletic performance

glass transition temperature the temperature at which a polymer changes from a hard and brittle condition to a rubbery condition

haematocrit a measure of the amount of fluid in the blood. 42–45 is an average value

haemoglobin a pigment in the blood which transports oxygen from the lungs to the rest of the body (*haem* = blood)

hallucination an illusion of the mind causing a person to see something that is not there

helix a simple spiral or coil with a constant diameter

hexose a carbohydrate that has six carbon atoms

humid a high concentration of water in the air

hydrolysis a chemical reaction in which a compound reacts with water

hyperthermia an increased core body temperature (*hyper* = high, *therm* = temperature)

hypertonic describes a solution with a higher concentration of dissolved particles than blood

hypertrophy an increase in the size or mass of muscle cells

hyperventilation an excessive increase in breathing rate

hypoglycaemic low levels of blood glucose

hypooestrogenaemia low levels of oestrogen

hypothermia a decreased core body temperature (*hypo* = low)

hypothesis theory used as a basis for investigation

hypotonic describes a solution with a lower concentration of dissolved particles than blood

hypoxic stress low oxygen levels in the air

informed consent agreement subject to full information (e.g. about the tests or procedures about to be performed)

intra-subject variation the difference in a value when measuring the same thing for the same person (e.g. if you measure blood pressure three times in a row you will get three different values)

inverse the opposite or reverse of something, when referring to measurements: as one value goes up, the other goes down.

isometric contraction of the muscle where there is no change in its length. (*iso* = the same, *metric* = length)

laxative a substance that increases the production of faeces

lever a rigid structure that exerts pressure or sustains force via a muscular force with a pivot point

macronutrient a nutrient required in large amounts

mandible the lower jaw bone

mass is the quantity of matter, it is a measure of inertia

mesomorph a body with a muscular build

micronutrients a nutrient required in small amounts

modulus a high modulus material is more difficult to bend than a low modulus material

molecular weight the molecular weight of a substance is the number of grams required to make up exactly one mole, a mole being a specific number of atoms

molecule smallest part of a chemical compound, made up of atoms (e.g. a water molecule is made up of two hydrogen atoms and an oxygen atom)

monosaccharide a single sugar

net a net value is the resulting value after all values have been added together

neuromuscular junction junction between a neurone and a muscle

offal the edible internal parts of animals

optical clarity the ability of something to transmit visible light

organic made up of a group of compounds containing rings of carbon atoms linked to other atoms

osteoporosis a disease that results in low levels of bone mineral density, which leaves the person more likely to sustain fractures

palatability the tastiness of something – the more palatable something is, the tastier it is

partial pressure the amount of pressure exerted by a gas proportional to the concentration of the gas

piezoelectricity the electric current produced by ceramic materials when they are subjected to mechanical pressure

pilot study a trial run when data is collected from a limited number of subjects

plaques fatty deposits on artery walls

plasma the clear fluid in which blood cells are suspended

polysaccharide many carbohydrates molecules joined together

pulmonary refers to anything to do with the lungs

raw data unprocessed data collected during the investigation

research design the specific method of investigation in a research project (e.g. a comparison of fitness between two groups)

silicate minerals that contain a silicon substance in a crystal structure

statistic a value calculated from the sample of people you are investigating (e.g. average height)

statistical tests mathematical procedures used to analyse data

stool also known as faeces, semi-solid waste matter consisting of undigested food and other secretions evacuated from the bowels

subcutaneous below the skin surface (*sub* = below, *cutaneous* = skin)

superconductors a substance that will conduct electricity, without resistance, below a certain temperature

suture a connection between bones

sweet spot the place on a bat, club or racket where contact with a ball results in the best hit (greatest ball speed and minimum vibration)

synthesis the production of a substance

tachycardia an increase in heart rate

thermogenesis the generation of heat

thermoregulation the maintenance of a constant body temperature (*therm* = temperature)

tidal volume the amount of air breathed in and out in one breath

trauma damage or wound to the body caused by an impact.

treatment something you impose on somebody, e.g. a training programme

vital capacity the maximum volume of air that can be breathed out in one breath